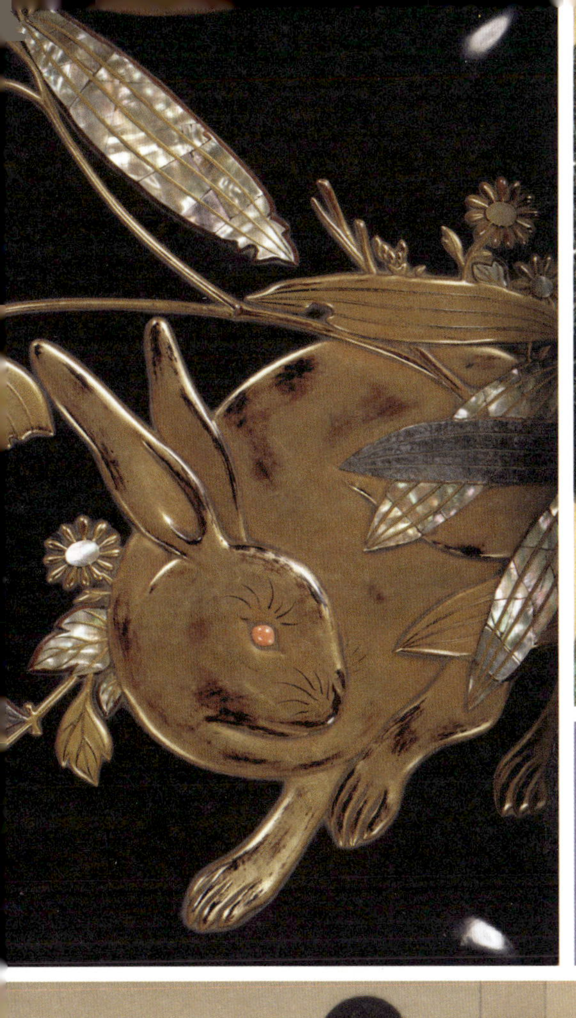

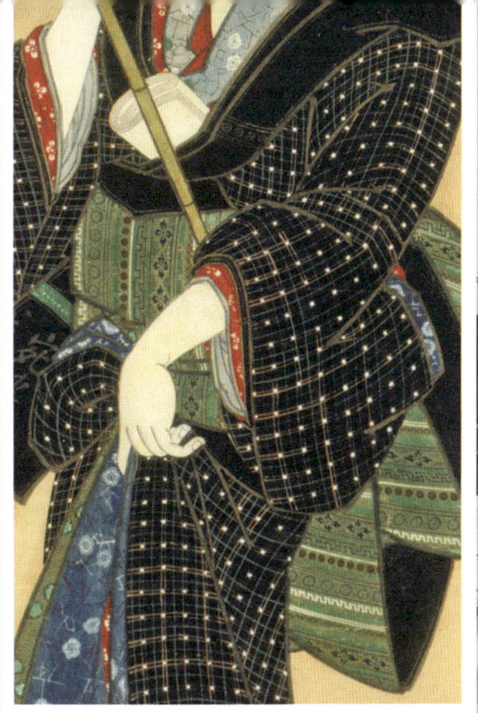

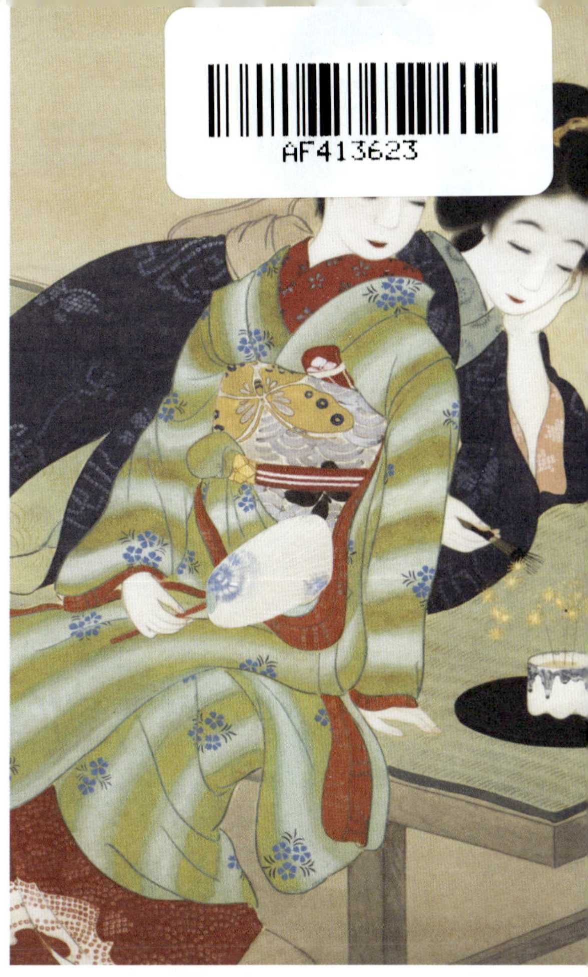

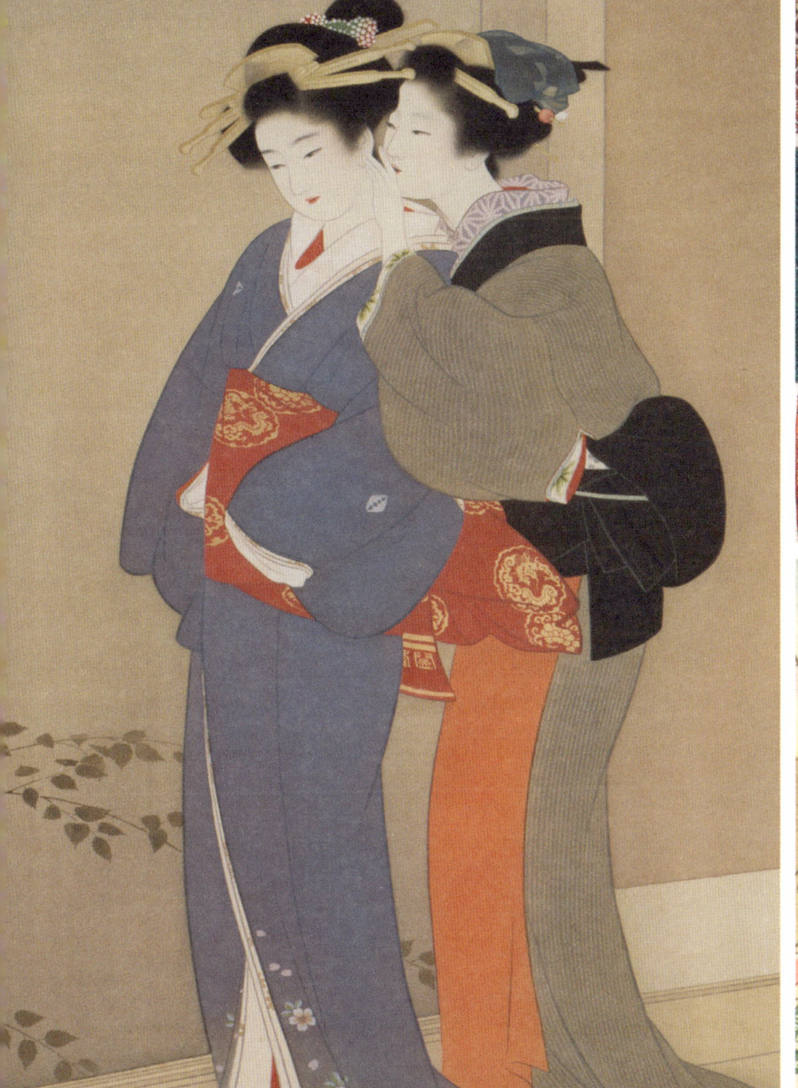

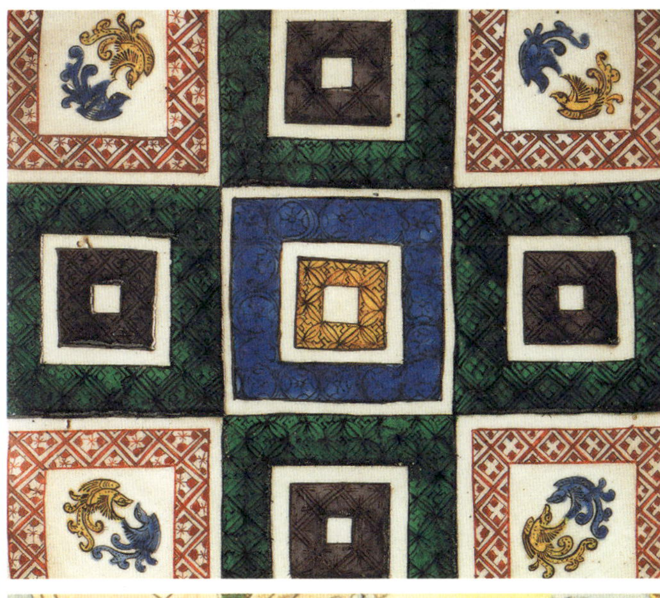

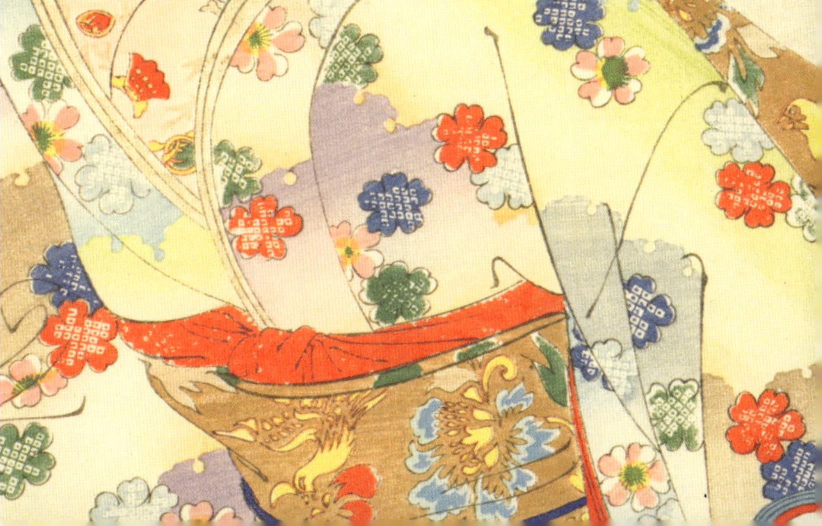

Colors in Japanese Art

Nobuyoshi Hamada

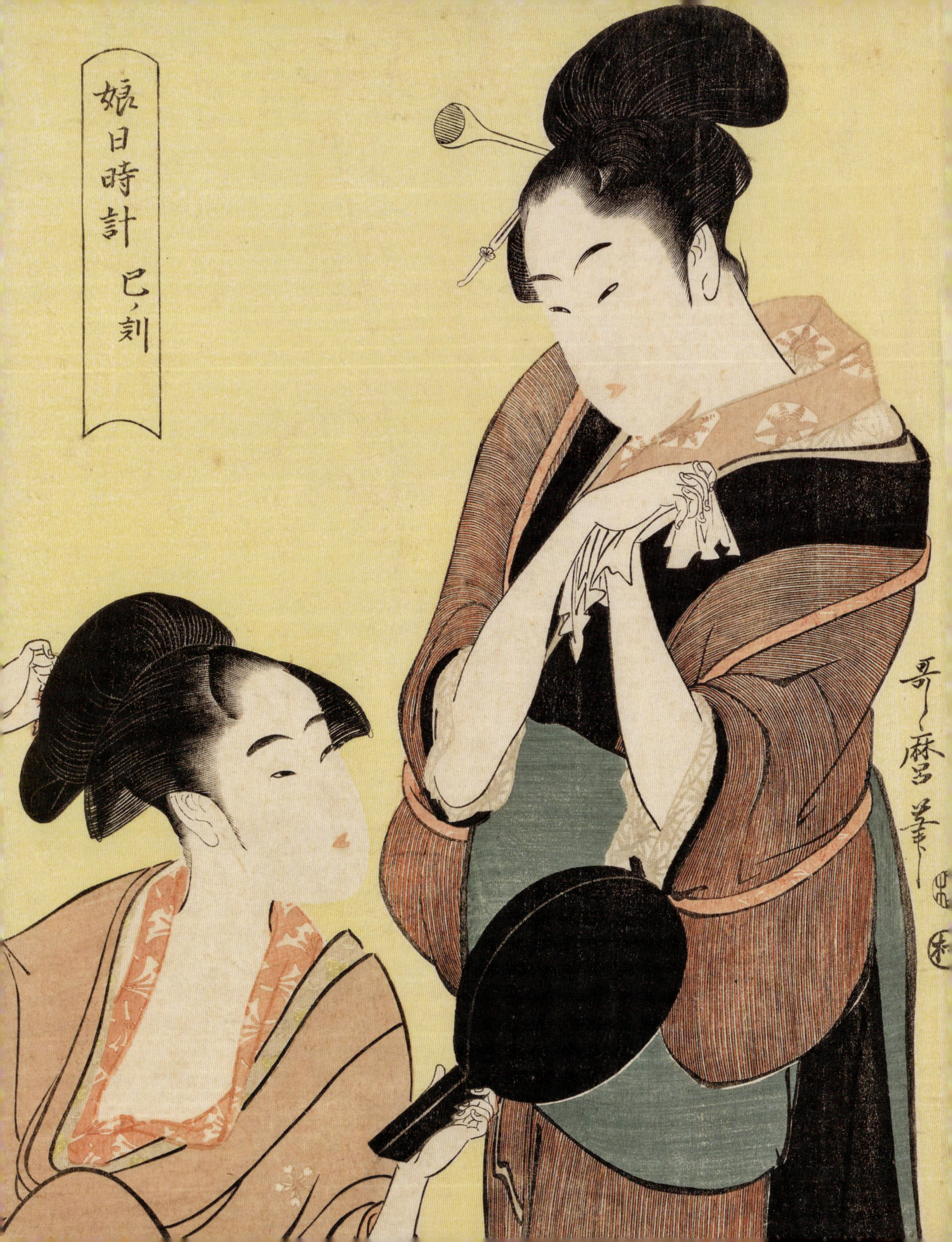

娘日時計　巳ノ刻
哥麿筆

Colors in Japanese Art

THE USE OF COLOR IN JAPAN'S FINE AND DECORATIVE ARTS

Nobuyoshi Hamada

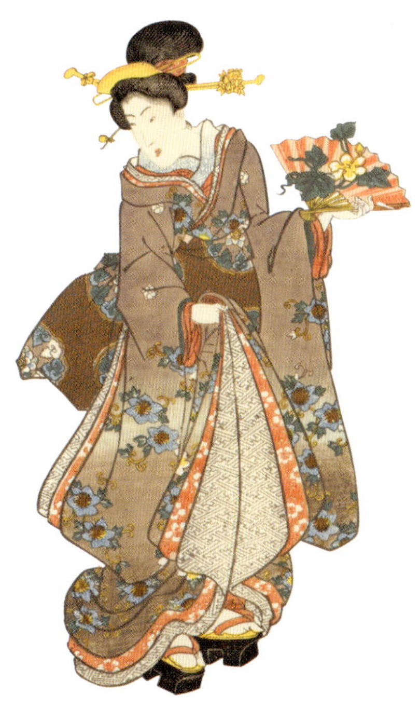

TUTTLE Publishing

Tokyo | Rutland, Vermont | Singapore

Contents

This book selects 283 main colors from Japanese traditional colors, categorized in the order of red, purple, blue, green, yellow, brown, black and white, and gold and silver, with color samples and explanations of their names. Special topics in the world of color are also featured including layered color schemes (25 pieces), plant color names (11 colors), bird color names (11 colors), and Kabuki actor color names (7 colors).

Why I Wrote This Book

Color coordination is the act of combining two or more colors to create a new visual effect. Beautiful colors come to life when combined with the right color partners. When we find the balance of colors in a palette pleasing, it means those colors are in harmony. Conversely, when a color combination feels unpleasant, it is described as clashing or discordant. This feeling of pleasure or displeasure doesn't arise from an objective standard, but rather from our inherent subjective sensations and preferences.

When we look at colors, we don't perceive them in isolation but always consider their balance with surrounding colors. The harmony or disharmony of colors can make them appear beautiful or difficult to perceive.

Nevertheless, pleasing color coordination must be appreciated by a large number of people, and this requires judgments that could serve as objective criteria for color aesthetics. There are no fixed rules for color harmony; instead, it seems that the key lies in achieving a balanced blend of unity and variation in color coordination within the context of the times and trends.

In Japan, the fundamental concept of color coordination revolves around the sensation of colors based on white, which absorbs all colors, and black, which reflects them. It wouldn't be an exaggeration to say that color coordination in Japan begins with these achromatic colors of white and black. Additionally, Japanese aesthetics emphasize the beauty of "white space," which extends beyond the realm of spatial composition and pattern shapes to apply to the world of color coordination as well.

In Japan, contrasting color combinations have been prevalent since ancient times. This can be observed in various aspects of life, from red and white *manju* used for celebrations to the black and white attire worn during weddings and funerals. It

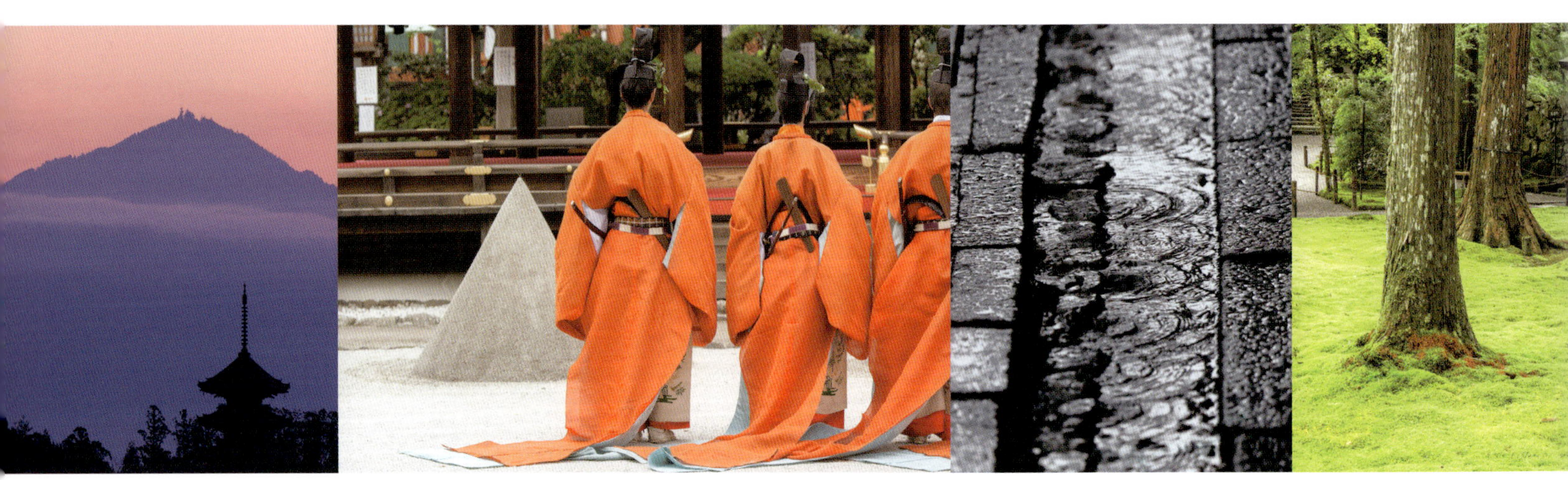

becomes evident that color coordination based on saturation contrast and brightness contrast is derived from everyday life.

Additionally, Japanese people are sensitive to the seasons, admiring the contrast of the cherry blossoms blooming deep in the mountains in spring and sighing in appreciation of the contrast provided by the vibrant autumn foliage coloring the mountainsides in the autumn. It seems that this sensitivity to nature is the basis of their admiration of the subtleties of color contrast and coordination.

Japanese colors often have a subdued and elegant aspect, appreciating the gradation of low-saturation colors. Traditional Japanese ink painting, known as *sumi-e*, is an art form that uses only the contrast of ink density to create expressions. While it has its origins in China, it continues to receive high praise as a Japanese art form that resonates with the most refined sensibilities.

In the Rinpa school, pioneered by Tawaraya Sōtatsu and Hon'ami Kōetsu and later developed by Ogata Kōrin, there was a blossoming of brilliant color balances skillfully utilizing vibrant colors, gold, and silver mud. They pursued rich decorative and design beauty with a modern sense. Centered around painting, it hinted at inclusivity encompassing calligraphy and various crafts.

In this book, we introduce the flow of traditional Japanese color coordination by identifying it within artworks, crafts, and textiles, accompanied by the names of traditional colors.

—Nobuyoshi Hamada

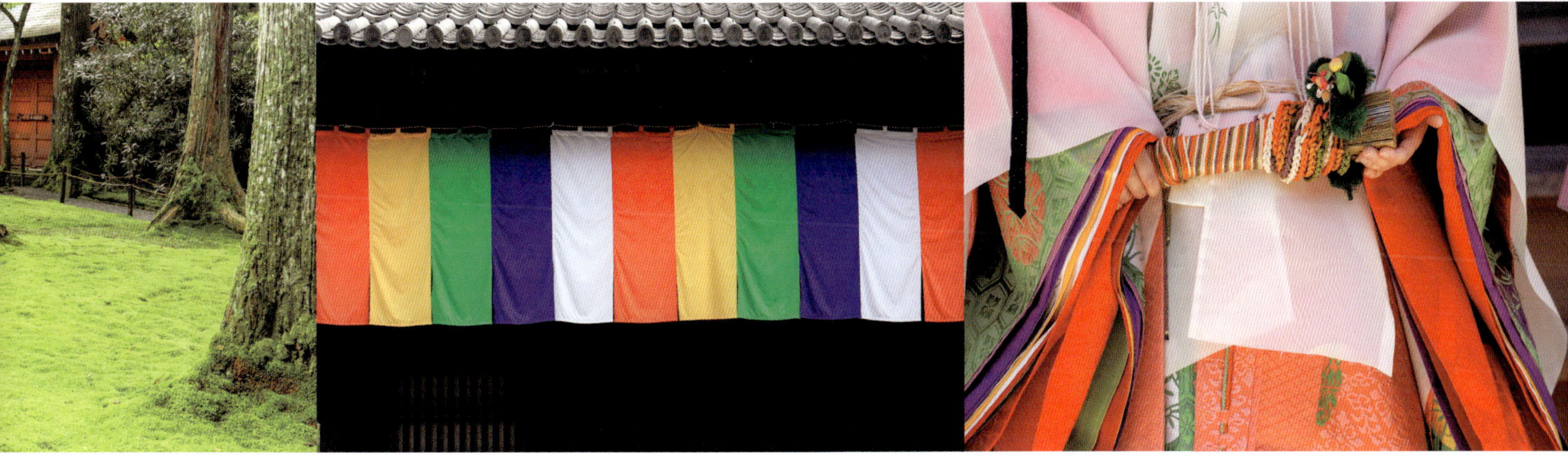

The Color Red in Japanese Culture

Red is the color of the sun's brilliance, the color of flames, and the color of blood. From ancient times, it has been perceived as a color that evokes vitality and energy. It has been used in religious rituals and symbols and as a talisman against evil. Moreover, because this vermilion color has antiseptic properties, it has been used in the murals of ancient burial mounds. Even now, it is used as a symbol of passion, vigor, and flamboyance.

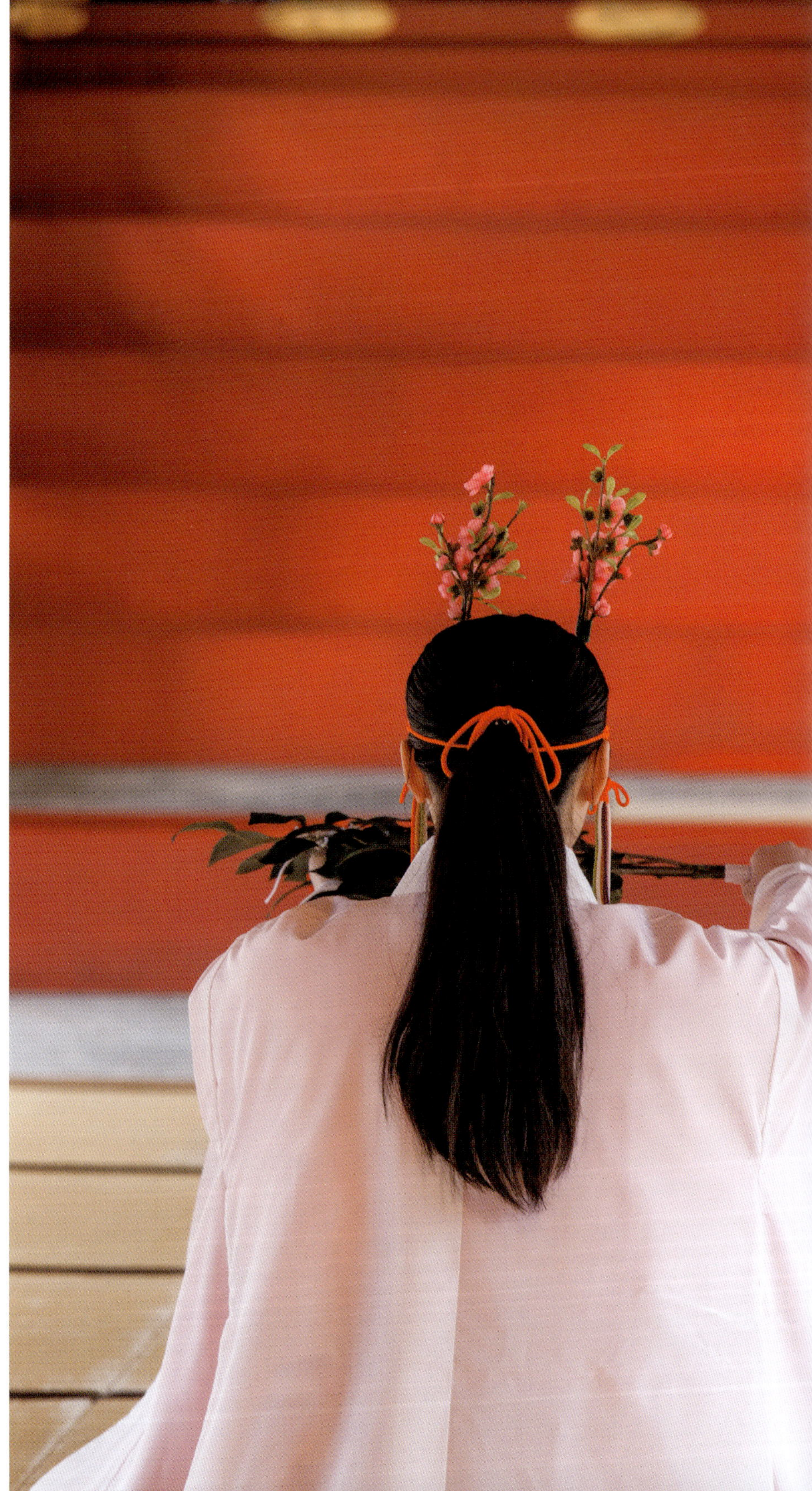

Right Peach Blossom Festival, Iwashimizu Hachimangu Shrine, Kyoto
Top far right Kurama Fire Festival, Yuki Shrine, Kyoto
Bottom far right Thousand Torii Gates, Fushimi Inari Taisha, Kyoto

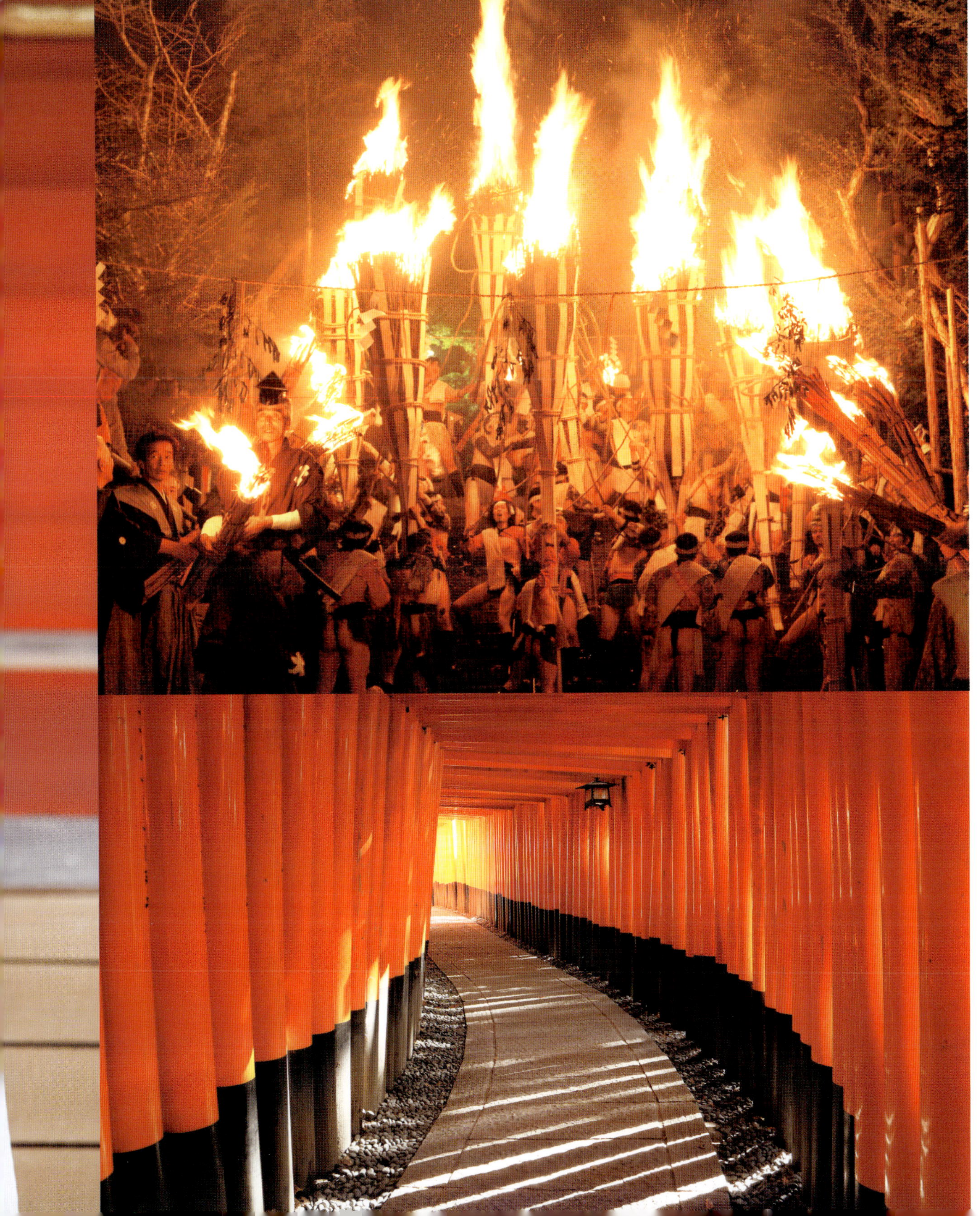

Japanese Color Schemes Based on Red

The image of red is often associated with the symbol of life—the sun—by many people. It also evokes passion, excitement, love, danger, and people who favor this color are often considered proactive and assertive. The the color red evokes feelings of self-assurance, warmth, passion, strength, dynamism, cheer and excitement. The color red seems to emit energy outward, representing affection, benevolence, courage, and vitality, but it can also symbolize war, revolution, and violence. Although its shades range from warm to cool, it is classified as a warm color. When colors are shown in the same position, red appears slightly forward compared to blue, so it is also referred to as an advancing color.

In color coordination, combinations like red with white, red with black, and red with gold have been frequently used in traditional patterns and decorations. Colors such as silver or light and dark gray enhance the brilliance of red. Combining red with its complementary color, cyan-green, or with green and blue, creates very intense color combinations.

In Japan, pillars of shrines and temples are often colored vermilion, and the red *hakama* worn by shrine maidens symbolize protection from evil spirits. Fushimi Inari Taisha in Kyoto, the main shrine dedicated to the god of agriculture and abundant harvests, has a vermilion torii gate as a symbol of the sun deity for the autumn harvest.

During the Heian period, the color of court robes (*hō*) was specified, and with advancements in dyeing techniques using madder (*akane*), *suō* fragrance (*suōhō*), and red flowers (*benibana*), red played a role in enriching the culture of the aristocracy. It wasn't until the late Middle Ages that red became more accessible to the common people, as textile industries developed in various regions of Japan, including Nishijin in Kyoto.

Color Pattern Based on Light Colors

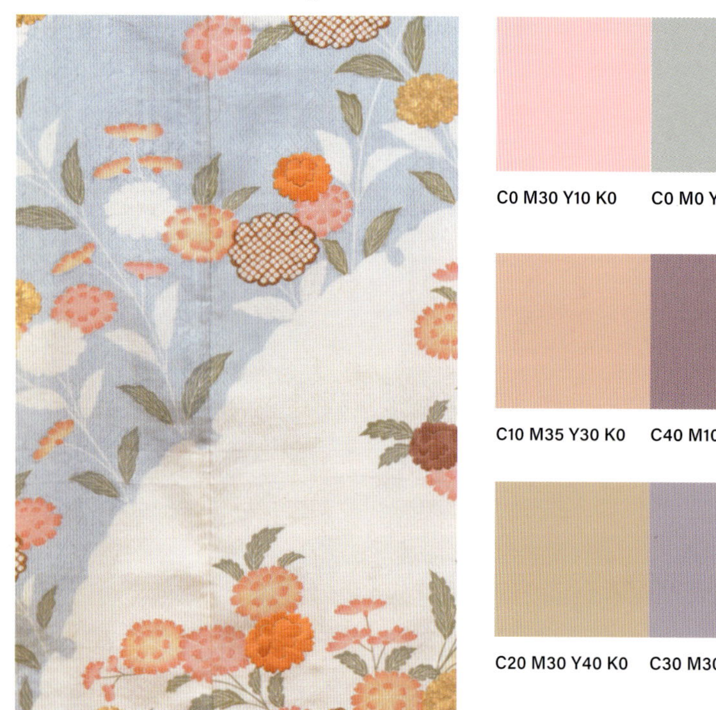

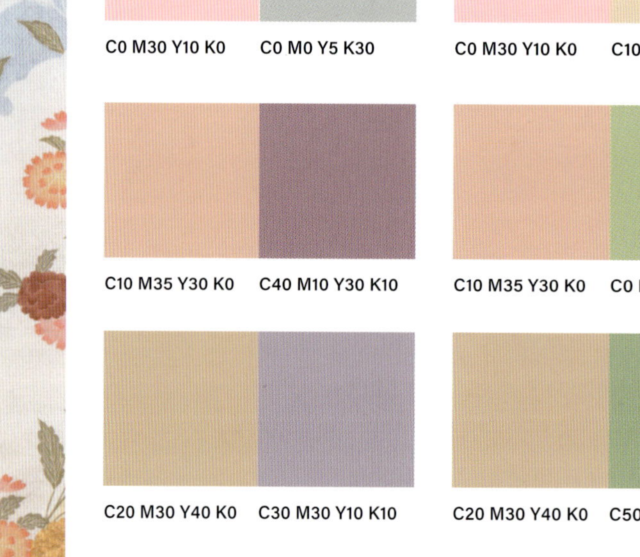

C0 M30 Y10 K0	C0 M0 Y5 K30	C0 M30 Y10 K0	C10 M20 Y30 K0
C10 M35 Y30 K0	C40 M10 Y30 K10	C10 M35 Y30 K0	C0 M20 Y30 K0
C20 M30 Y40 K0	C30 M30 Y10 K10	C20 M30 Y40 K0	C50 M10 Y50 K10

Detail from "Dyed Asa Aya Kosode with Snow Circle and Kerria Pattern." Edo period, 18th century.
Tokyo National Museum. Source: ColBase at https://colbase.nich.go.jp

Color Scheme Based on Vivid Colors

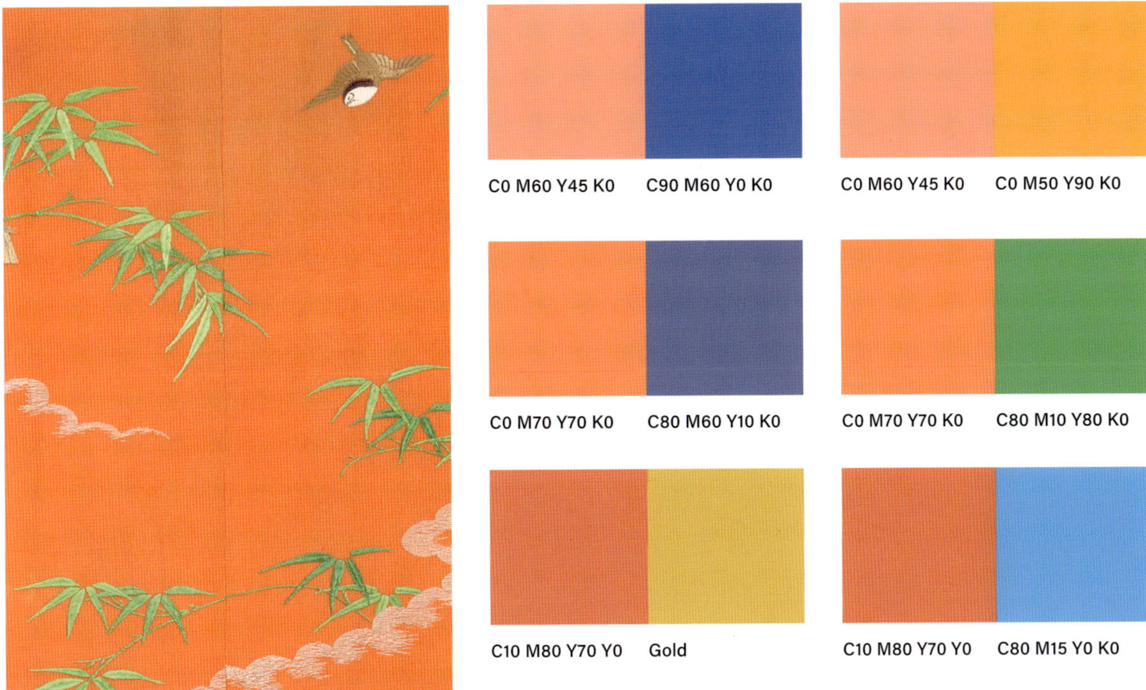

| C0 M60 Y45 K0 | C90 M60 Y0 K0 | | C0 M60 Y45 K0 | C0 M50 Y90 K0 |

| C0 M70 Y70 K0 | C80 M60 Y10 K0 | | C0 M70 Y70 K0 | C80 M10 Y80 K0 |

| C10 M80 Y70 Y0 | Gold | | C10 M80 Y70 Y0 | C80 M15 Y0 K0 |

Detail from "Red Crepe Kosode with Bamboo Sparrow and Chrysanthemum Pattern." Edo period, 19th century
Tokyo National Museum Source: ColBase at https://colbase.nich.go.jp

Color Scheme Based on Dark Colors

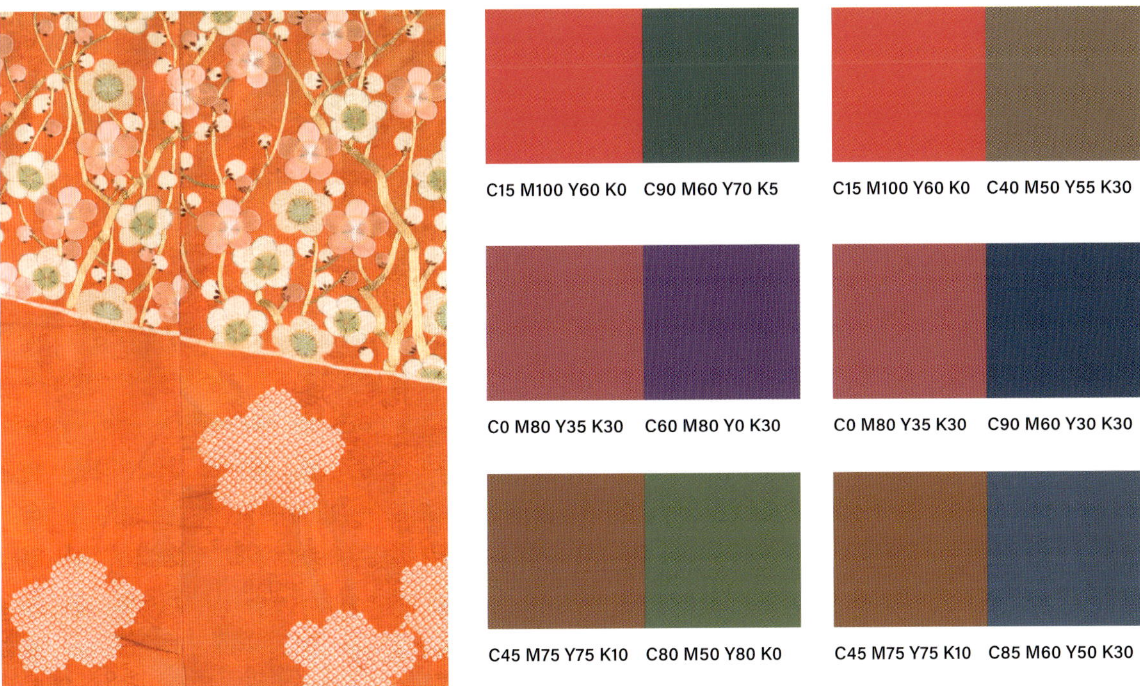

| C15 M100 Y60 K0 | C90 M60 Y70 K5 | | C15 M100 Y60 K0 | C40 M50 Y55 K30 |

| C0 M80 Y35 K30 | C60 M80 Y0 K30 | | C0 M80 Y35 K30 | C90 M60 Y30 K30 |

| C45 M75 Y75 K10 | C80 M50 Y80 K0 | | C45 M75 Y75 K10 | C85 M60 Y50 K30 |

Detail from "Red Damask Kosode with Plum Grove Pattern in Yuzen Dyeing and Shibori Stitching" Edo period, 19th century.
Tokyo National Museum. Source: ColBase at https://colbase.nich.go.jp

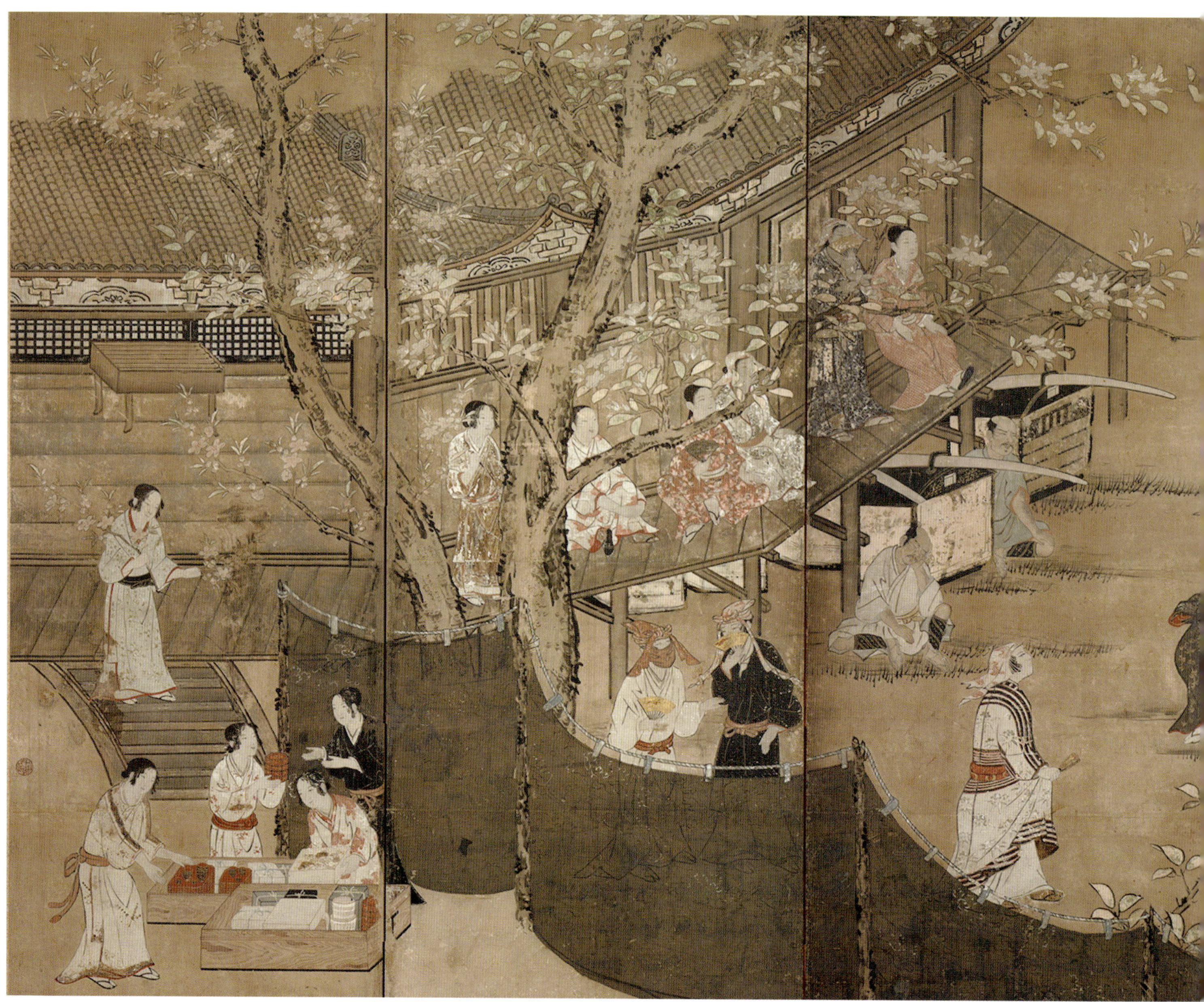

"Screen Depicting Leisure Under the Blossoms" National Treasure, by Kano Nagamitsu. Edo period, 17th century.
Tokyo National Museum. Source: ColBase at https://colbase.nich.go.jp

Depicted on this six-fold folding screen is a cherry blossom viewing scene dating from sometime near end of the Azuchi-Momoyama period to the beginning of the Edo period. Under the white Hawthorn blossoms, where curtains are draped all around, children in red kimonos—the protagonists of this banquet—watch the dancing women on the veranda of an octagonal hall. The attire of the women joyfully dancing in the center appears to be the latest fashion trend. Their makeup is also meticulously done, with expressive eyebrows and subtle ink added to the corners of the eyes to give them a three-dimensional look. Beside them, women dressed as men with swords at their waists dance to the then-popular "Okuni Kabuki." This artwork, which beautifully captures the scene of people celebrating spring, represents the Japanese appreciation of the seasons.

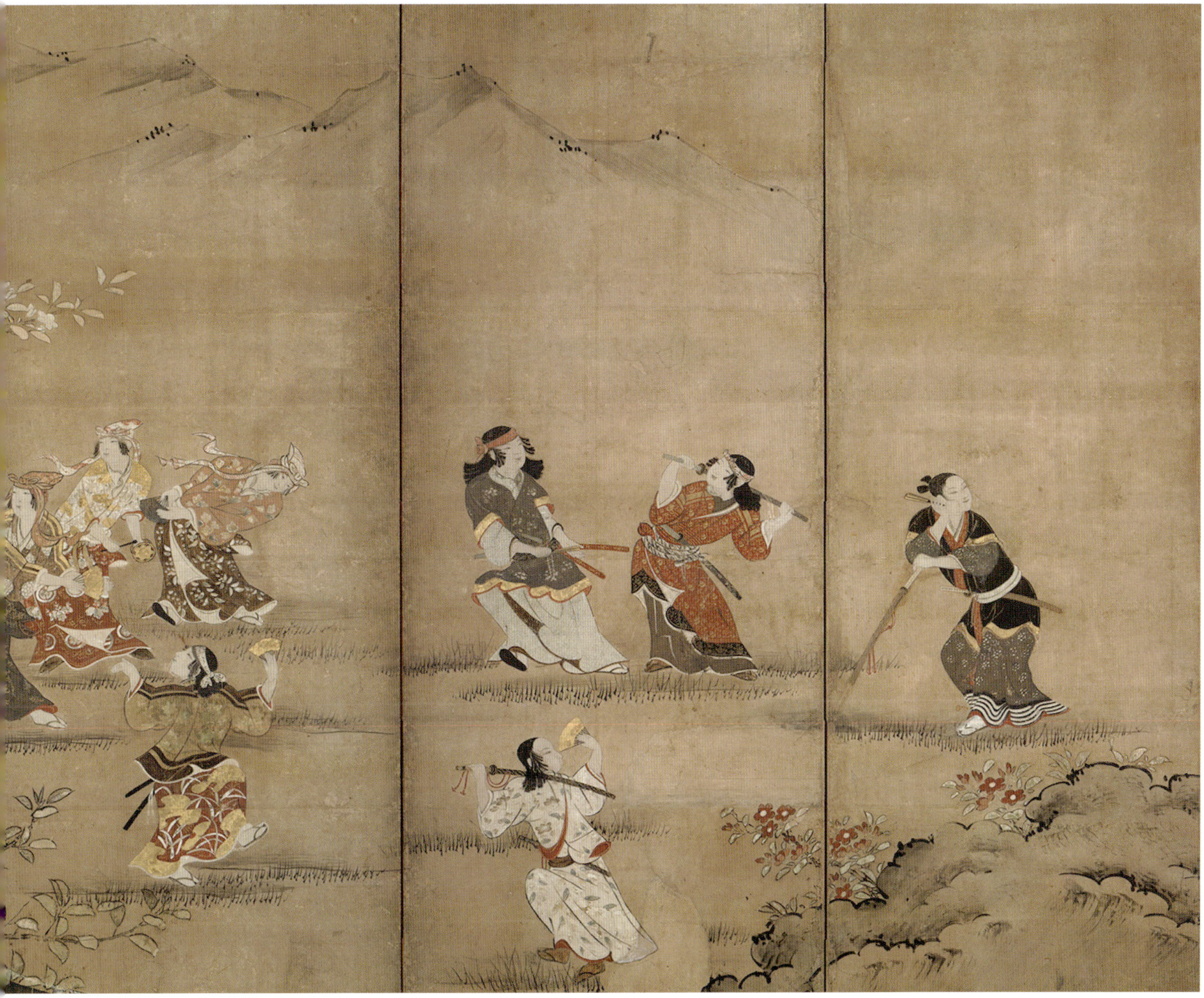

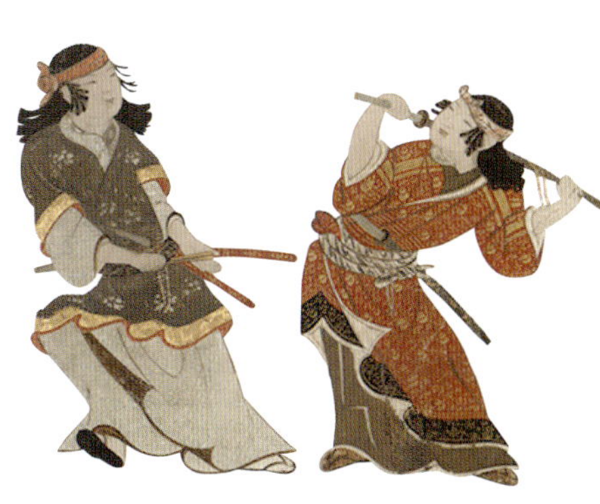

58 Beni-tobi   62 Kokiake/Kuroake   63 Suōko   252 Gofun

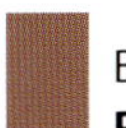

Beni-tobi
Pompeian Red

This is a deep reddish-brown color, a tint of red reminiscent of a bird kite's color. "Beni-tobi" (red kite) initially featured a yellowish hue but gradually shifted to a redder tint. By the middle of the Edo period, specifically around the Tenmei period (1781–1789), color variations were introduced, like "Kontobi" (navy kite), "Murasakitobi" (purple kite), "Aitobi" (indigo kite), and "Kurotobi" (black kite), all based on this fundamental kite color.

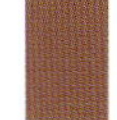

Kokiake/Kuroake
Deep Scarlet/Black Scarlet

A deep crimson color made by adding purple roots to madder red dye. According to the Nara-era *Engishiki* (a book of laws and customs), for one bolt of deep crimson damask, forty kin (a traditional unit of weight, approximately 600 grams) of madder, thirty kin of purple grass, three stones of ash, and 840 kin of firewood were used. This recipe indicates a color of significant darkness, likely a deep blackish red. Until the Heian period, the order of colors for individuals in the imperial court, aside from the crown prince's ocher, was deep purple for the first rank, light purple for the second and third ranks, deep crimson for the fourth rank, and light crimson for the fifth rank, with the darker colors considered to be higher in status.

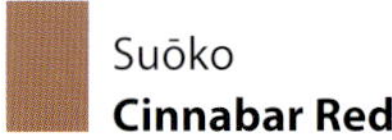

Suōko
Cinnabar Red

This is a reddish-brown color created by adding a hint of yellow to the red of sappanwood. Cloves were often used to produce the yellow hue added to the deep red color. Because this fragrant spice was particularly costly, it was often substituted with safflower. The vibrancy of the resulting color depended on the substance used to add yellow.

Gofun
Powdered Shell

A white pigment used in Japanese paintings, made by exposing crushed plankton shell to weather conditions for several years, followed by grinding, rinsing, and drying. It is used as the ground color in paintings and for coloring architectural elements. During the Momoyama period, it was used to create raised depictions of cherry blossoms and chrysanthemum petals in murals.

Koubai
Light Plum Blossom

This is a faint red color with a hint of purple. The color name typically describes the color of plum blossoms that bloom in early spring. It is a type of dye made from safflower, and depending on the depth of the dye, it can be categorized as dark red, medium red, and light red. When people used the term "red plum" they generally refer to the medium shade. In terms of kimono colors—red plum on the lighter end of the scale and cinnabar on the darker end. The gradation of red in this color scheme is exceptionally elegant. The plum tree belongs to the rose family. Originally from China, it was introduced to Japan around the Nara period as a medicinal plant. In the *Manyoshu,* the earliest anthology of Japanese poetry, when people mentioned flowers, they often meant plum blossoms.

Kokutan
Ebony

Kokutanis an old name for oak, and it refers to a deep navy black color achieved by crushing its fruits, brewing them, and using iron mordant for dyeing. When using alkaline solution mordants, it results in a yellow-brown color known as "Kikurage" (yellow oak). Kokutan, like black dye, was used for mourning attire.

Hiwamoegi
Yellowish Green

An intense yellowish green color that falls between "Hiwa" (a bright green bird) and "Moegi" (sprout green). In the *Tekagami Moyō Setsuyō* (a compendium of patterns and designs), it is described as "Hiwamoegi," which is an old name for a lighter shade. While green dyes have historically used *kariyasu* (Chinese grass) to add yellow to blue, this color is made with a high concentration of *kariyasu* with a lower concentration of indigo to achieve a strongly yellowish green.

Kiniro
Gold

Kiniro is a deep yellow color with a slight hint of red, characterized by its shiny and beautiful appearance similar to gold. During the Edo period, it was also referred to as "Yamabukiiro" because it resembled the color of yamabuki (*Kerria japonica*) flowers found on large and small gold koban coins.

(Page 15) Wearing an *eboshi* hat, with a sword at her waist and a golden fan in her hand, a dancer strikes a pose. Her black garment is adorned with Genji wheel motifs in red, creating an elegant, luxurious color combination that catches the eye. She appears to be carrying a large hemp bundle on her back, suggesting that this is a ceremonial dance of purification.

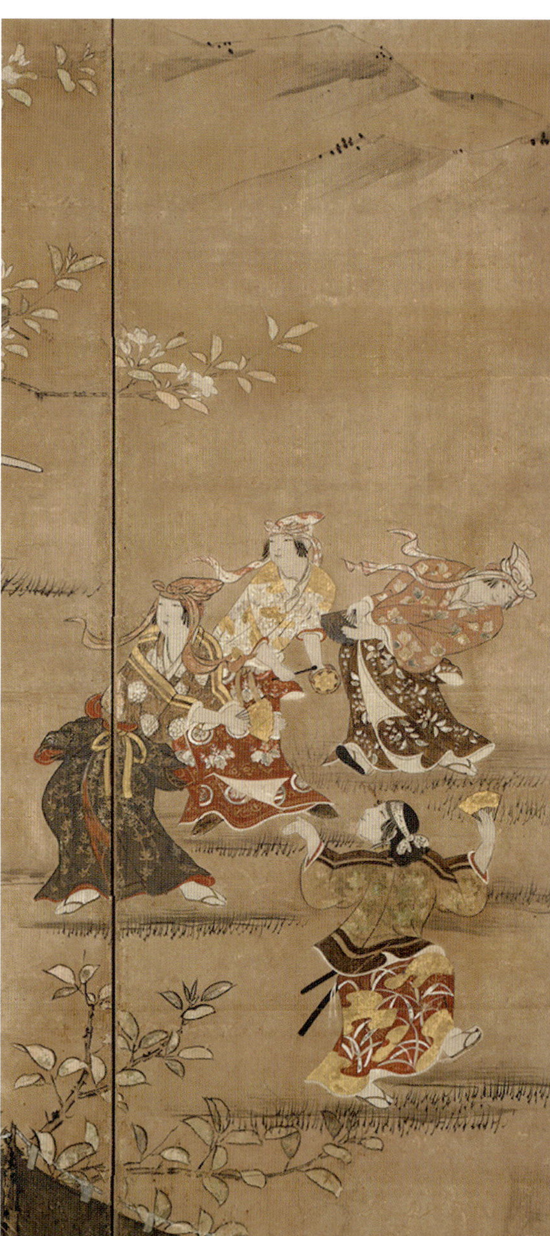

Detail from "Screen Depicting Leisure Under the Blossoms"
Tokyo National Museum.
Source: ColBase at https://colbase.nich.go.jp

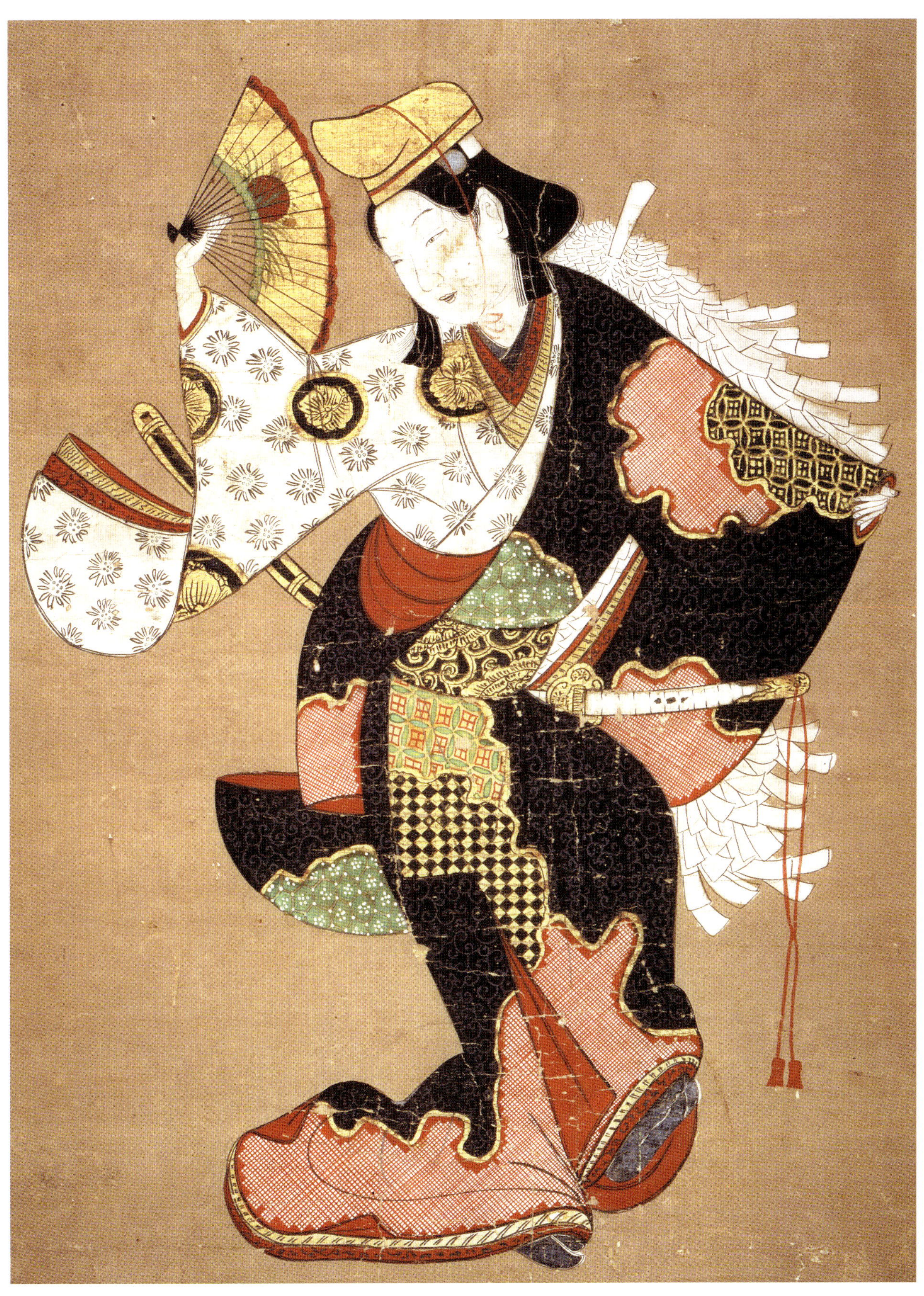

14 Koubai	278 Kokutan	142 Hiwamoegi	281 Kiniro

"Various Dance Forms" Artist Unknown.
Edo period, 17th century.
Itabashi Ward Art Museum.

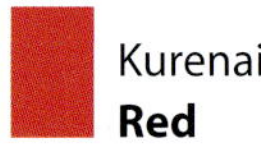

Kurenai
Red

Kurenai refers to a vivid red color achieved by dyeing with only the red pigments from safflower, excluding the yellow pigments. Safflower-based red dye tends to fade easily, so the fabric is often dyed with it only after being pre-dyed with other dyes such as turmeric or gardenia. One famous production area is the Mogami region in Yamagata Prefecture, where a coarse safflower dye known as "Kurenai mochi" was produced and transported to Kyoto and Edo (now Tokyo) for refinement into the final "Hon-Kurenai" dye. Its production was limited, and it was highly valuable, comparable even to gold.

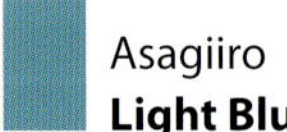

Asagiiro
Light Blue

Asagiiro is a light blue color made with Japanese indigo, resembling the pale color of scallions, which is why it's called "asagi." It is a representative name for light shades of blue in traditional Japanese dyeing. During the Edo period, rural samurai in Edo Kinban (Edo Watch) would wear *haori* (a type of outerwear) with light blue cotton linings made from asagi-dyed fabric. Consequently, in Yoshiwara, a famous pleasure quarter in Edo, they teased these samurai as unsophisticated, calling them "Asagi-ura" (referring to the light blue lining).

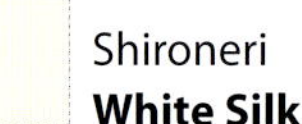

Shironeri
White Silk

Shironeri is a refining technique used to remove the yellowish tint from raw silk, resulting in a pure white, lustrous silk. In ancient times, many silk fabrics retained some natural color, so pure white silk achieved through shironeri was considered special and received special handling.

A lady stands by a fence woven from bamboo. She is dressed in a combination of red undergarments and a white kimono, creating an elegant contrast. This artwork is by Nishikawa Sukenobu (1671–1750), an artist active in Kyoto during the early Edo period. Sukenobu excelled in portraying beautiful women with delicate features, like the lady in this piece. His works introduced a new style to the depiction of women, combining richness with dignity.

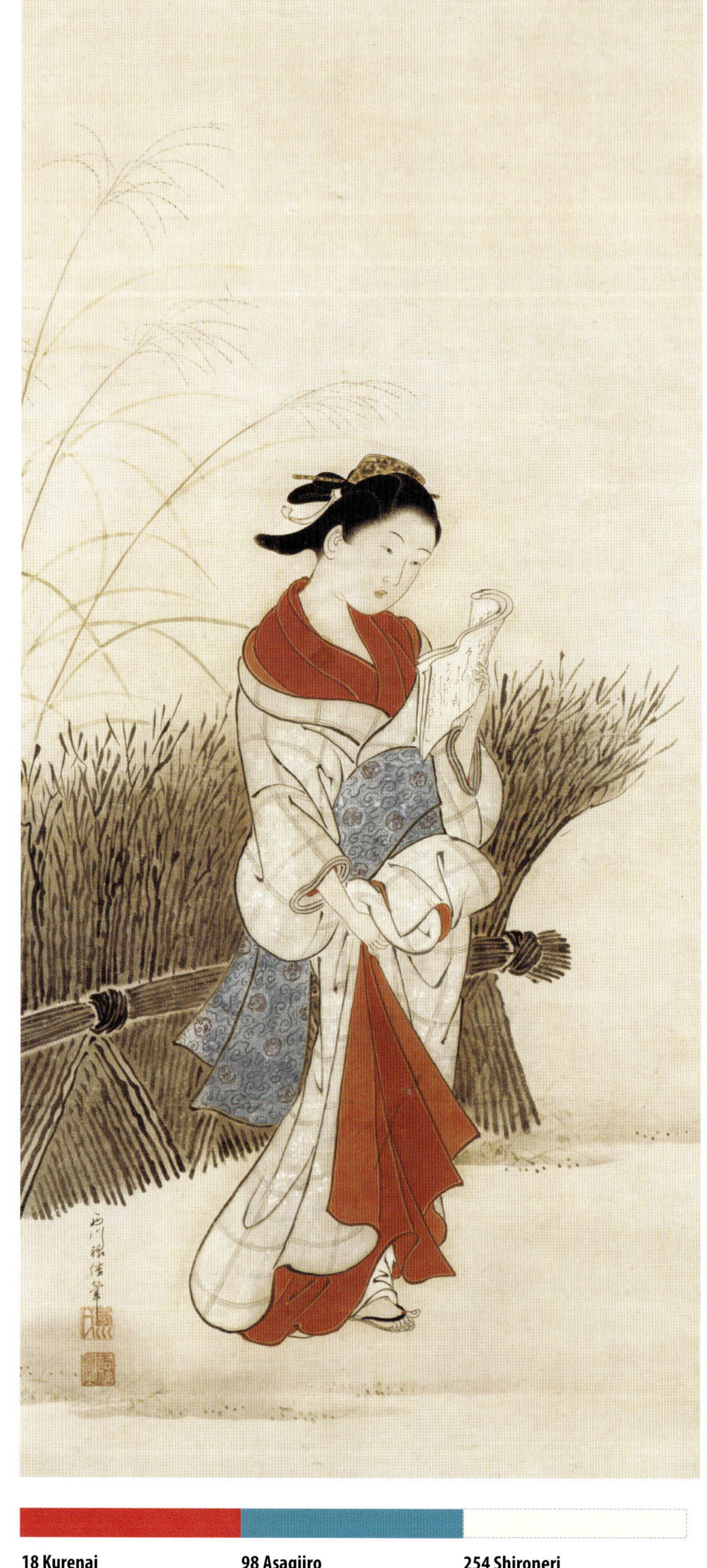

**"Beauty by Autumn Hedge" by Nishikawa Sukenobu.
Edo period, early 18th century**
Aichi Prefectural Museum (Kimura Teizo Collection)

18 Kurenai	98 Asagiiro	254 Shironeri

Medium Yellowish Red

Jinzamomi is a moderately intense red color with a faint yellowish tint. It is often used as an alternative to safflower-based red dye because safflower dye was expensive. During the Edo period, use of safflower dye was frequently restricted. However, during the Jōō era (1652–1655), a merchant named Jinzaburō from Nagachō in Kyoto managed to create a color similar to red plum blossoms without using safflower, and this imitation red was called "Jinzamomi."

Taiko
Light Pinkish-red

Taiko is a pale pink color obtained by dyeing with safflower. It falls between cherry blossom pink and crimson. The book *Teijō Zakki* (authored by Ise Teijō), which explains the customs and practices of samurai during the Edo period, gives this description: "Taiko is the clothing of people with peculiar tastes. Taiko is a hunting robe dyed in peach color." By this, we take it that it was considered a color for lower-ranking officials and was used in hunting attire.

Kurobeni/Kurokoubai
Dark Reddish-black/Dark Purplish-red

Kurobeni refers to a deep purplish-red color or a dark reddish-black color. It involves dyeing with safflower as a base and then applying black color with the betel nut. It can be described as a red with black undertones or the reverse—a black with red undertones. This dyeing technique was commonly used for luxurious kosode (a type of kimono) fabric during the early Edo period. Kurobeni was also referred to as "Kurokoubai" or simply "kuro" (black).

A woman dressed in a red kimono sits gracefully, gently smiling. Her serene expression and gentle black eyes are charming. The combination of a black background with a colorful design on the obi and kimono was quite modern for the time. The beauty paintings by Takehisa Yumeji (1884–1934) are known as "Yumeji-style" and were highly popular from the late Meiji era to the Taisho era.

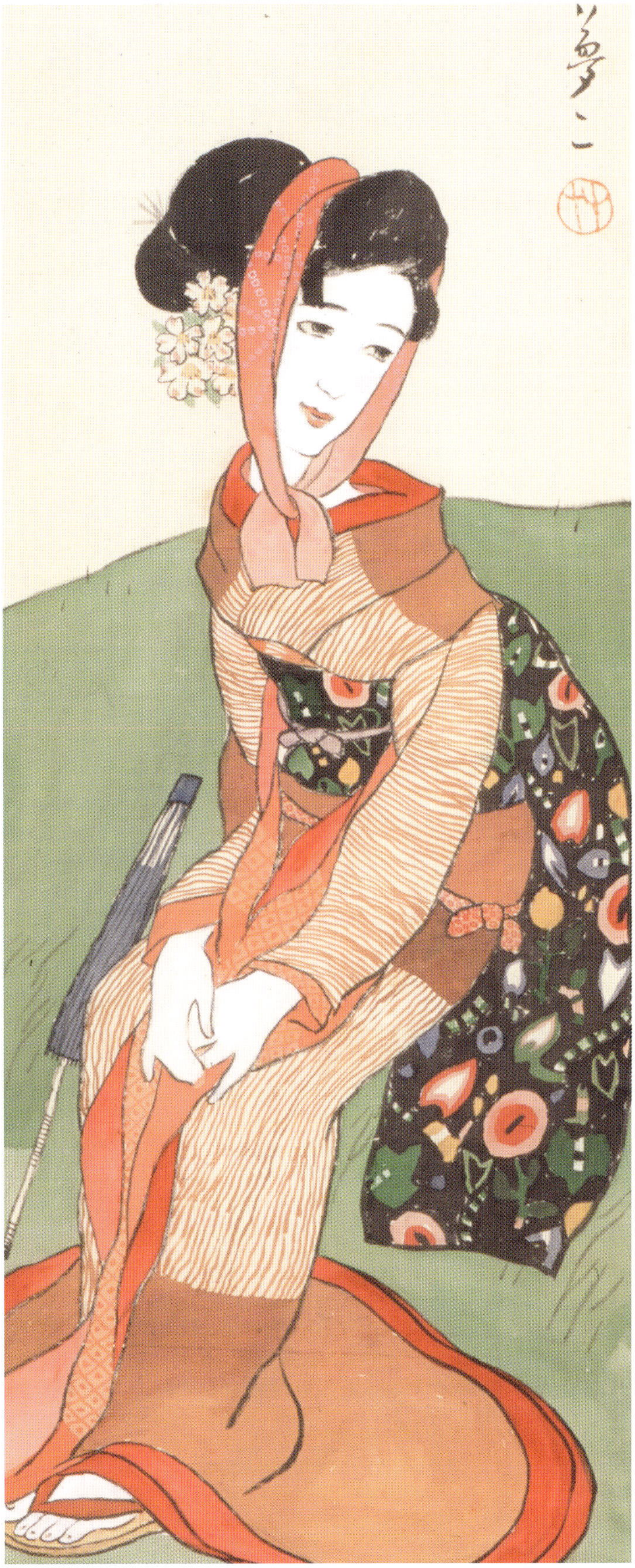

**"A Woman Resting in the Grass" by Takehisa Yumeji.
Early Taisho Era, 20th century.**
Shizuoka City Museum of Art.

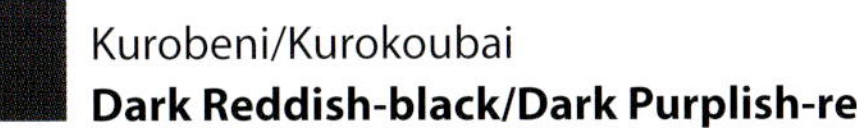

| 21 Jinzamomi | 4 Taiko | 222 Kurobeni/Kurokoubai |

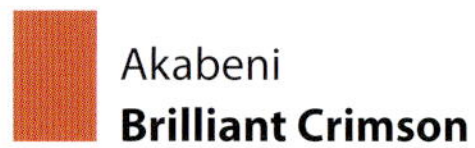

Akabeni
Brilliant Crimson

Akabeni is a vivid crimson color that has been used in various dyeing applications since the early Edo period. It's been mentioned in pattern books and dyeing literature, and was even used for the base fabric of kimono in *Gohiinakata,* a work written during the Kanbun era. At this time, red and crimson shades were in particular demand, and besides akabeni, scarlet shades and mottled crimson were also favored for kimono. Especially during the Tenna to Jōkyō eras (1681–1688), mottled crimson fabrics were a major trend. Red-crimson dyeing involved using substitutes like *akane,* (a dyer's madder) and *myōban* (potassium alum) due to the high cost of safflower dyeing.

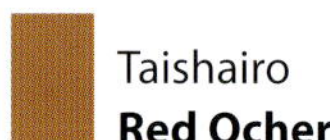

Taishairo
Red Ocher

A yellowish-red-brown color obtained from red earth. Similar to "Bengarairo" (a red obtained from safflower) and "Ōdoiro" (yellow ocher), it is composed of iron oxide. In the *Kojiki,* pigments obtained from red earth were referred to as *aka* and were prized, particularly those from Shanxi Province Daixian, which became famous and were known as *daiza.* High-quality *daizairo* is characterized by its yellowish-red-brown hue. When red earth is fired, it transforms into a deeper red shade characteristic of daizairo, and with further maturation, it turns into a purple-red soil known as *shido.*

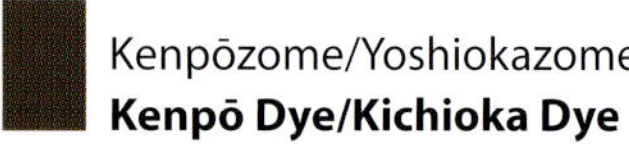

Kenpōzome/Yoshiokazome
Kenpō Dye/Kichioka Dye

This refers to a dyeing technique developed by Kichioka Kenpō during the early Edo period. It refers to a black color with a brownish tint. It is achieved by repeatedly dyeing the fabric with darkened *yōbai* (Chinese bayberry/*Myrica rubra*) and decocted iron, resulting in a very deep brown/faded black.

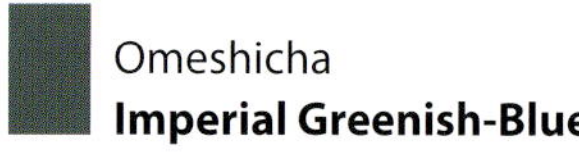

Omeshicha
Imperial Greenish-Blue

It refers to a muted greenish-blue color used to dye "Omeshicha chirimen," a respectful term for clothing. This term originated from the high-quality silk crepe favored by the 11th Shogun Tokugawa Ienari, called *omeshiiro,* later shortened to *omeshi.* It is likely that the brownish tint used to achieve omeshi was called "Omeshicha."

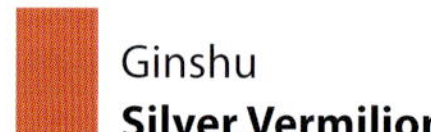

Ginshu
Silver Vermilion

Unlike naturally sourced vermilion and cinnabar, *ginshui* is a synthetic vermilion pigment made by mixing mercury with sulfur and then heating it to produce a strong yellowish-red color. From the Yayoi period to the Kofun period, the practice of applying vermilion to the inner walls of burial mounds and to the remains of the deceased as an offering for repose and rebirth was performed. Vermilion represented the shedding of blood, symbolizing the hope for rebirth, and the inclusion of mercury served as a preservative.

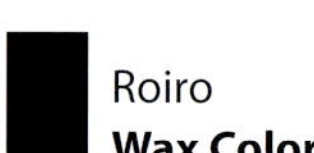

Roiro
Wax Color

Roiro-nuri is a lacquer technique that achieves a deep black color. In roiro-nuri, refined lacquer without the addition of oils is used for coating, resulting in a color that is close to black. After the topcoat sets, it is polished to bring out a glossy finish using ingredients like rapeseed oil and fine pumice powder. "Rashoku" refers to a very slightly yellowish-gray, similar to the color of candle wax, that's used in this process.

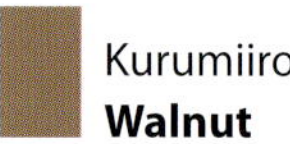

Kurumiiro
Walnut

Refers to a yellowish-brown color obtained from the bark, husks, and roots of walnut trees. Dyeing with walnut was practiced as early as the Nara period, as mentioned in the Shōsōin documents, which described the dyeing of paper.

This piece features a design of a swallowtail butterfly with its wings spread out as a decorative element on a collar pin (*eri-dome*). The deep crimson color and the green in the center to create balance result in a very timeless piece. Rokudai Kutsutani Taki Jirō was born into a family of bag makers that had been in business since the Edo period. In the Meiji era, the family began supervising and selling Western clothing and accessories, contributing to the development of Meiji-era craftsmanship using traditional techniques.

The sides of this box are tinted with vermilion lacquer, and the entire surface is covered with intricate patterns, boldly designed with detailed lines depicting melon leaves and petals. This design primarily employs techniques such as *hiramaki-e* (flat lacquer) and *enashiji* (pear-skin texture). The color scheme and style of the artwork show the influence of the vibrant and colorful characteristics of Momoyama-era lacquerware. *Kōdai-ji makie* refers to the lacquerware decoration inside Kōdai-ji Temple in Kyoto, which was used to adorn the mausoleum of Toyotomi Hideyoshi and his wife Kōdai-ji no Tsubone. The techniques and designs from Kōdai-ji makie were also applied to the furnishings and other belongings cherished by Hideyoshi and Kōdai-ji no Tsubone, which are held by the temple.

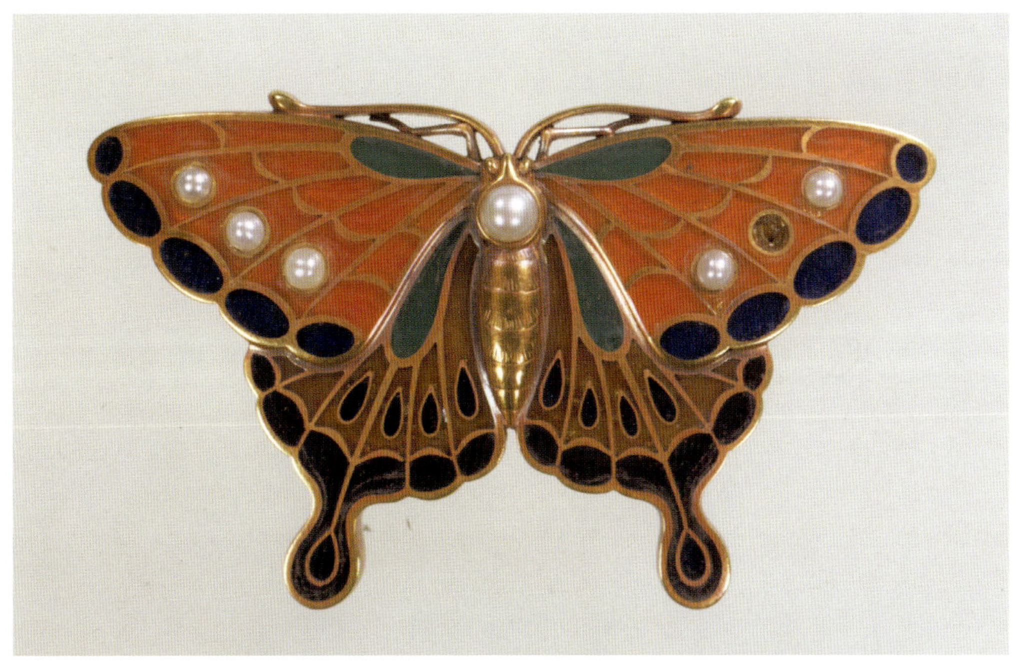

"Brooch" by Katsutani Takijirō, 1892.
Tokyo National Museum
Source: ColBase at https://colbase.nich.go.jp

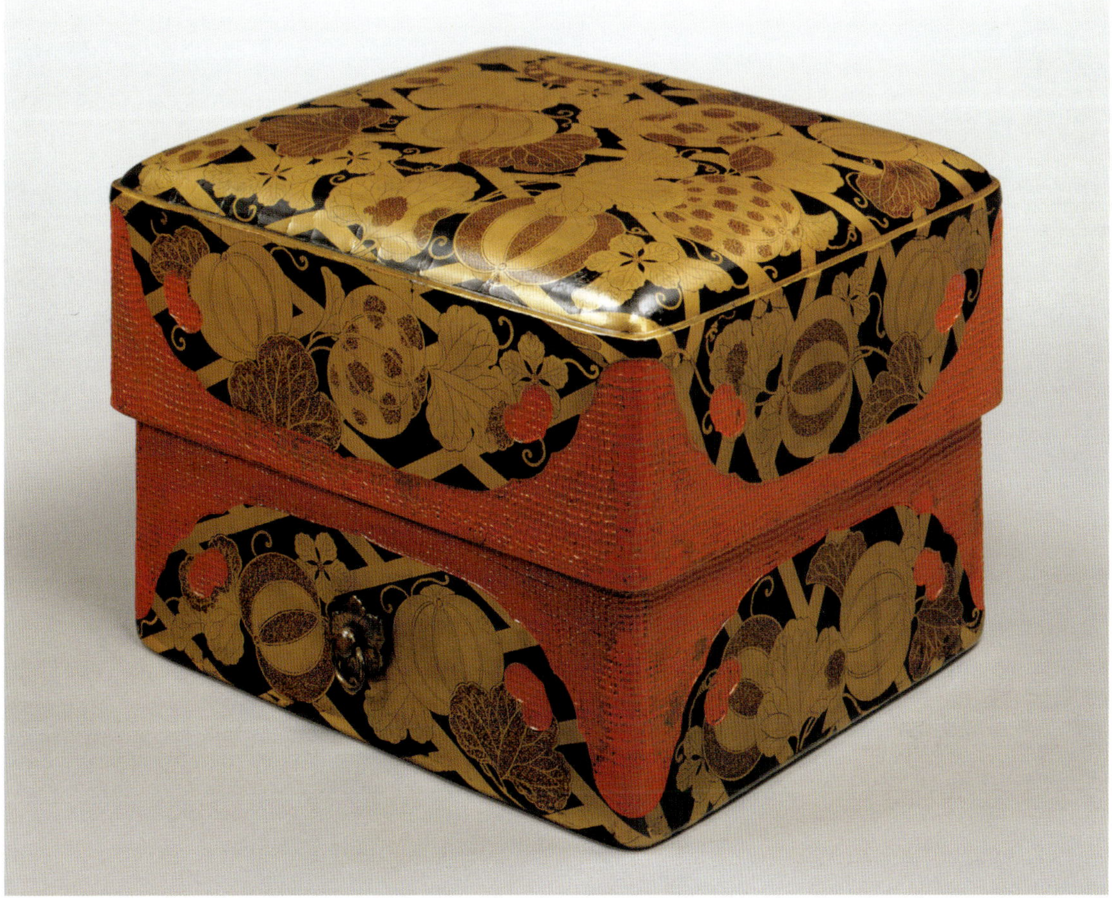

"Melon Design Maki-e Square Red Box".
Edo period, 17th century.
Tokyo National Museum.
Source: ColBase at https://colbase.nich.go.jp

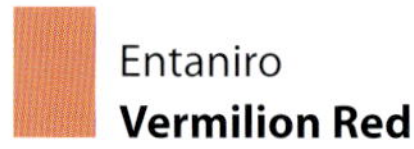

Entaniro
Vermilion Red

Entaniro refers to a bright orange color produced by mixing lead with sulfur and saltpeter and then firing it. It was traditionally used as an undercoat for various structures, including temples and shrines, for preservation and rust prevention. However, when exposed to the air for an extended period, it can change to a purplish-brown color. It is less durable in sunlight compared to vermilion but is still used as an affordable alternative for undercoating before painting.

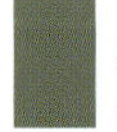

Aoni
Cactus

Aoni is a dark, dusky yellowish-green color resembling blue earth, originally used as a

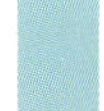

pigment. To achieve this color, *ai* (indigo) and *ōhagaki* (yellow balsam) dyes were used.

Byakugun
Pale Green

Byakugun is as light ultramarine blue. It is created by finely grinding azurite, a blue pigment derived from the mineral lapis lazuli. This color is indispensable in Japanese painting, often used in paintings from the Momoyama period and screen paintings of the Rinpa school during the Edo period.

Ake
Scarlet

Ake is a deep red color with a yellowish tint, achieved by dyeing with a mixture of madder and ash lye. It is one of the oldest dye colors, and it is made with the aim of resembling the colors of the sun or fire, symbolizing strong vitality. During the 7th and 8th centuries, it was high in the hierarchy of colors, second only to purple. This color is known for its richness and ability to stand out even from a distance. It is also known for its durability. As a result, it was commonly used in various contexts, including the ornamentation of medieval samurai armor, the attire of feudal warlords, and garments worn during the Sengoku period.

Ukoniro
Turmeric Yellow

Ukoniro is a vibrant yellow color obtained by dyeing with the roots of the *ukigusa* plant. Adding vinegar during the dyeing process results in a bright yellow with less red undertones, while using lye intensifies the red hues. During the early Edo period when bold colors were favored, this color was popular alongside scarlet. Cotton dyed with ukoniro was used for newborn baby clothes and undergarments, as well as for wrapping antique artworks and ceramics.

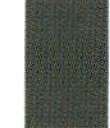

Onandocha
Dark Teal

Onandocha is a dark bluish-green color created by adding brown to *onandoiro*. It is described in the essay "Guzatsubo" by Tagami Nakamasa (1825) as follows: "After storing blue-green fabric dyed with ai [indigo] and akamatsucha [brown tea] for a long time, it changed color into a very deep shade. We named this color 'Onandocha' because it gained such a deep and appealing hue."

**"Polychrome Porcelain Teapot" Collaborative work by Ninnami Dohachi and Sahē.
Edo period, 19th century.** Tokyo National Museum. Source: ColBase at https://colbase.nich.go.jp

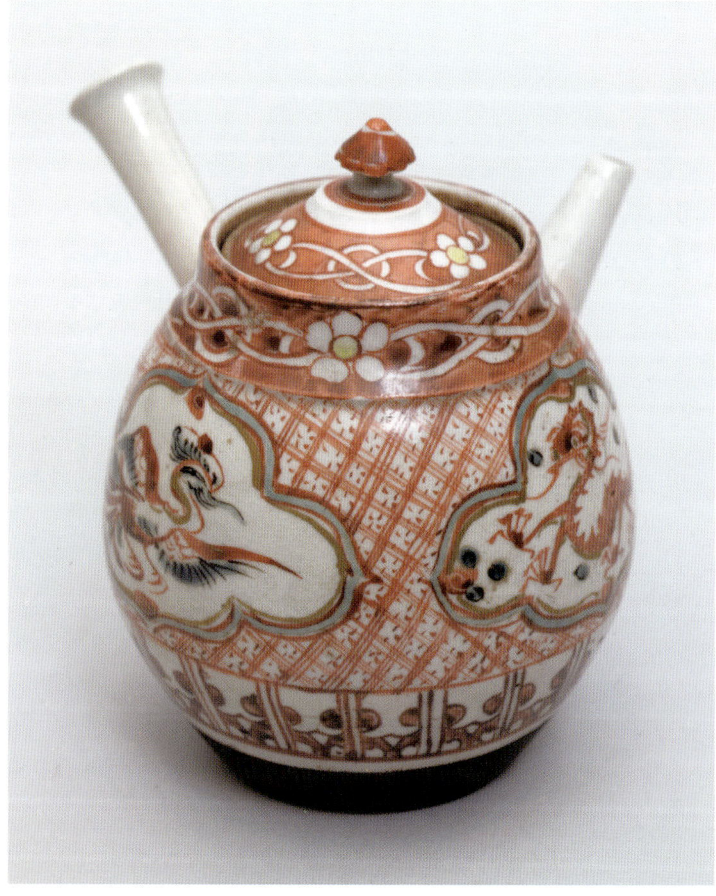

A teapot decorated with a dragon, a phoenix, and the sun in red, green, and yellow colors in the style of Wu Zhou red ware—a collaborative work by Ni-Ami Dohachi and Sapei. Dohachi (1783–1855) was the second son of the first generation Takahashi Dohachi. He excelled in reproducing traditional Japanese-style ceramics such as Nisei and Kansan. Sapei is Aoki Mokubei, also a late-Edo ceramic artist. He studied pottery under Okuda Ei in Edo and created excellent celadon pieces and tea utensils.

32 Entaniro   **157 Aoni**   **101 Byakugun**

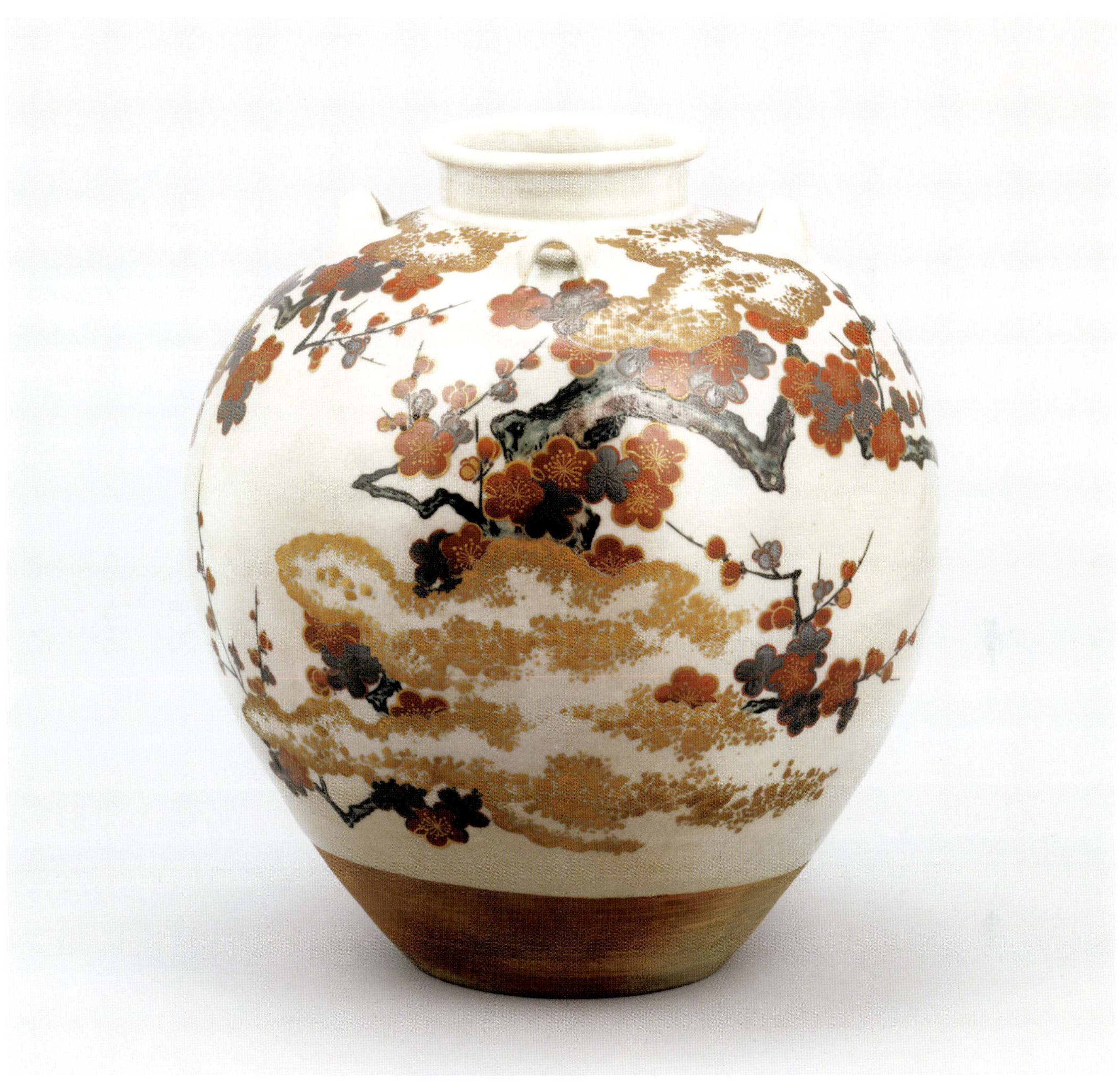

"Jar for Tea Leaves with the Moon and Plum Blossoms" by Jūbun. Nonomura Ninsēi Important Cultural Property. Edo period, 17th century.
Tokyo National Museum.
Source: ColBase at https://colbase.nich.go.jp

On a white background, lushly blooming plum blossoms and the moon are vividly depicted in red, green, gold, and silver. Nonomura Ninsē's distinctive feature was his use of gold and silver in overglaze enamels. The overall arrangement of gold clouds adds movement to the plum blossoms and the silvery moon, creating an enticing visual effect. Ninsē was a master ceramic artist from the early Edo period who achieved great success in Kyoto ceramics through his vibrant colors and painterly touch. Numerous polychrome teapots produced by the Ninsē workshop have been passed down through the ages.

Zakuroiro replicates the color of the pomegranate fruit, a slightly purplish red. However, it can often refer to the bright orange color of the pomegranate petals. In the present day, this hue is often associated with a crimson-red color similar to garnet, but in Japan, the fascination with the vibrant orange of pomegranate flowers may suggest that Zakuroiro was originally orange. It's uncertain when pomegranates were first introduced to Japan, but they were already cultivated in the early Heian period, as recorded in the *Honzo Wamyo*.

"Enamel Peony Design Covered Jar".
Imari Ware (Kakiemon Style).
Edo period, 17th century.
Tokyo National Museum.
Source: ColBase at https://colbase.nich.go.jp

Ruriiro refers to a brilliant shade of blue with a hint of purple, often considered the finest shade of blue, and it has been highly regarded as one of the Seven Treasures of Buddhism. This deep blue color comes from the mineral lapis lazuli, mined primarily in Persia.

Kamenozoki is an extremely pale blue, the lightest shade of indigo dye. Indigo dye comes in various shades, including white indigo, light indigo, medium indigo, and deep indigo, each with its own name. Kamenozoki is the result of briefly dipping thread or fabric into a vat of indigo during the dyeing process. The name was taken from the color one would see when peering inside a pot of water.

Sabiseiji is a color resembling the rusted, bright bluish-green color of celadon. Rust occurs when metals are exposed to the air and develop surface oxidation. For iron, this results in a reddish-brown or black color, while for copper, it turns green or black. Colors with rust often have lower saturation and a muted or subdued appearance.

Shu is a red pigment naturally produced from cinnabar, and it is used for deep red colors. It is said that the more high-quality natural cinnabar is, the more red it appears. However, compared to vermilion or red lead, natural cinnabar tends to be a lighter shade of red with a slight yellowish tint. The product from Chenzhou, Hunan Province, China, is partic-

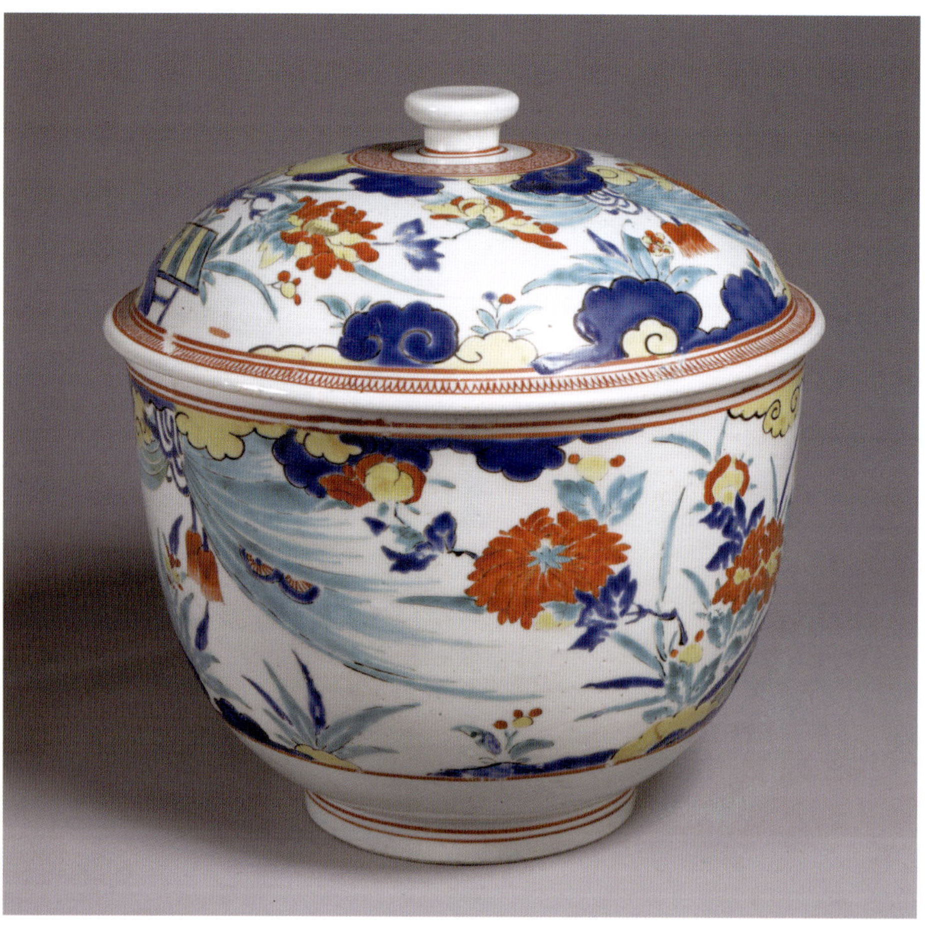

The brilliant red of peonies stands out against the white porcelain, and the graceful leaves are depicted in a refreshing and rhythmic manner. The design is based on Chinese landscapes and motifs from Jingdezhen, and the central theme is the Chinese national flower, the peony. However, it has been adapted into a Japanese design that doesn't necessarily evoke the feeling of Jingdezhen. Its rich colors resemble the early Kakiemon style.

23 Zakuroiro   **111 Ruriiro**   **96 Kamenozoki /Nozokiiro**   **152 Sabiseiji**

ularly well-known for its exceptional quality. As a result, the term "Chen Sha" is commonly used to refer to natural cinnabar. The word "true" in "true cinnabar" implies that it is natural cinnabar, in contrast to artificial red lead.

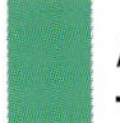

Aomidori
Turquoise

Aomidori is a color that cannot be precisely categorized as either blue or green but is a greenish shade of blue. It's mentioned in the *Engishiki*, an ancient Japanese text, and is achieved by adding a small amount of yellow ocher to indigo dye, resulting in a shade of greenish-blue similar to azure.

"Color Enamel Flower and Bird Design Large Deep Bowl" (Important Cultural Property). Imari Ware (Kakiemon Style). Edo period, 17th century.
Tokyo National Museum.
Source: ColBase at https://colbase.nich.go.jp

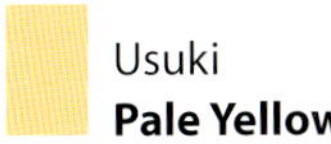

Usuki
Pale Yellow

Usuki is a pale yellow obtained by dyeing with *kiyoshi,* a plant extract, mixed with ash. The tint is determined by the amount of ash used. During the Edo period, pale yellow was often referred to as "Tamago" (egg).

On a slightly bluish-white porcelain base, vibrant and translucent colors such as red, green, yellow, ultramarine, and black are applied. These colorful hues are arranged rhythmically, surrounding two birds resting on rocks with outspread feathers, and large chrysanthemum and peony flowers. The vessel has a deep bowl shape and is believed to have originally come with a lid. This style of overglaze enamel design takes inspiration from colored porcelain produced in Jingdezhen, China. However, this bowl has a graceful finish with ample white space, distinguishing it as a Japanese-style overglaze enamel porcelain that deviates from the Chinese style. The Kakiemon style is one of the styles of Arita ware, established by the first Kakiemon, characterized by colored enamel applied to a milky-white base. The white space enhances its artistic quality.

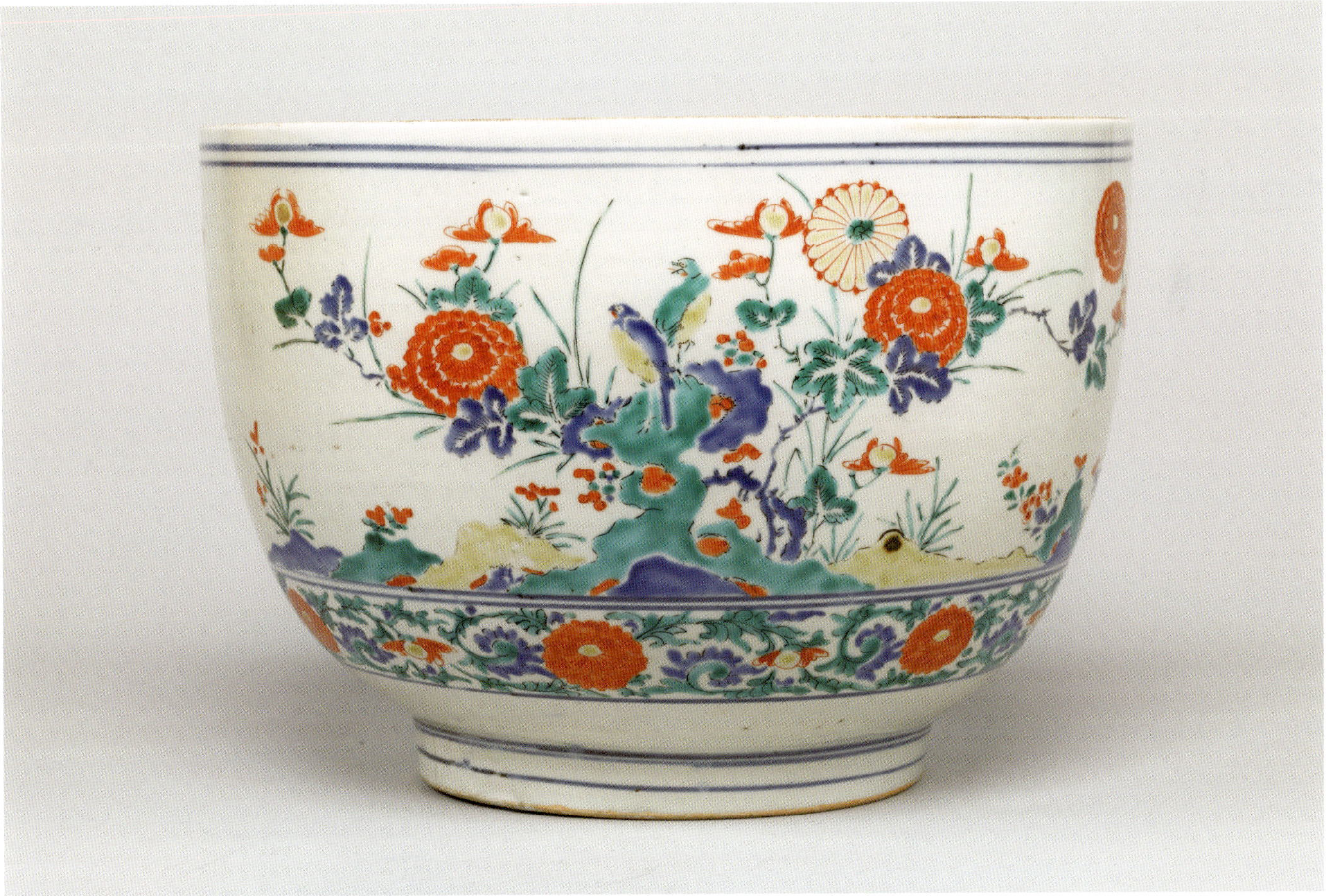

27 Shinshu/Mahoso   **150 Aomidori**   **176 Usuki**

Nakabeni is a medium shade of red created from safflower petals. Petals are rubbed to extract the color. Due to the tendency of safflower-based red dye to fade easily, it is often pre-mordanted with yellow dyes such as turmeric or yellow oak leaves before dyeing. In the lighter shades of beni dyeing, you can find colors like peach, light pink, and others. Medium shades are also available.

"Polychrome Chicken and Textile Patterned Flat Dish". Imari Ware. Edo period, 18th century.
Tokyo National Museum.
Source: ColBase at https://colbase.nich.go.jp

In the center of a flat bowl, a pair of chickens are encircled by fish leaping over waves of red. This exquisite style is created using underglaze blue, with multicolored overglaze enamels such as red, yellow, and green, and then further embellished with gold accents. It is known as "Kokin-ran," "Tenjiku," or "Kinrande" when done by hand, or "Sometsuke" when done by dyeing. This shape, with a rim that spreads like a guard of a helmet, is commonly referred to as "Kabuto-bachi" because it resembles a wide and deep helmet when turned upside down.

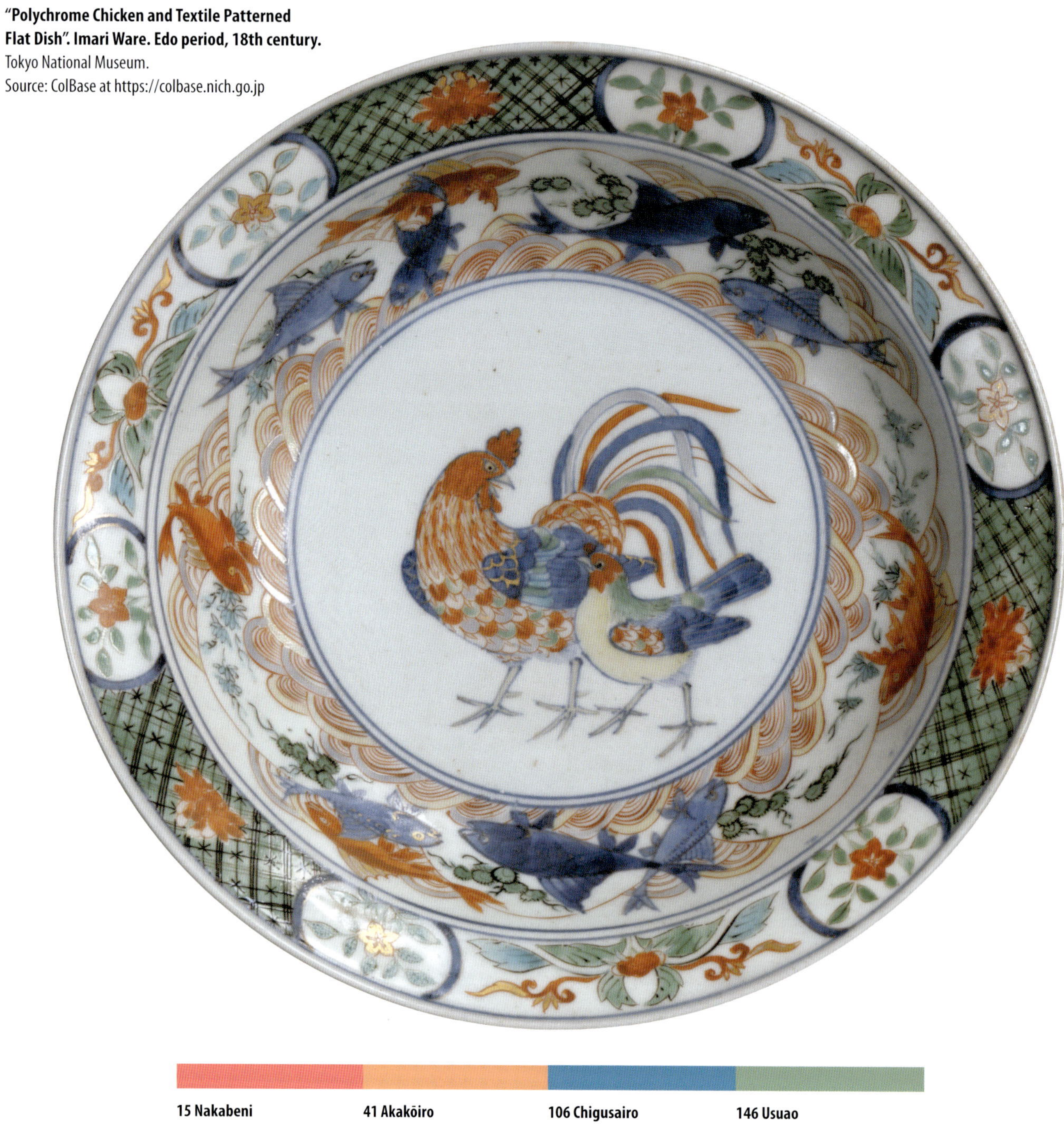

| 15 Nakabeni | 41 Akakōiro | 106 Chigusairo | 146 Usuao |

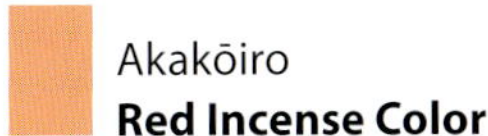

Akakōiro
Red Incense Color

This is a pale reddish color that gets its name from the lingering fragrance of incense on dyed fabrics or paper. It was highly valued by the nobility. Fragrant materials like agarwood and kyara were boiled to create the dye, and depending on the dyeing method, various shades and hues of "kouiro" can be achieved. Among them, the darker shades with a reddish tone are referred to as "akakou" (red incense).

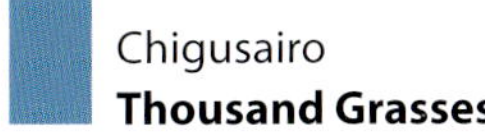

Chigusairo
Thousand Grasses

This is a bright, slightly purplish blue, resembling the color of the delicate blue flowers of the *tsukigusa,* or dew grass, which blooms in early summer. It was commonly used for the everyday attire of commoners during the Edo period.

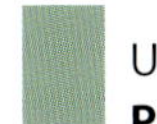

Usuao
Pale Green

Green is now commonly referred to as "ao" as a general term for the color of mature plant leaves, and officially called "midori." However, the practice of colloquially referring to green hues as "ao" has persisted into later generations.

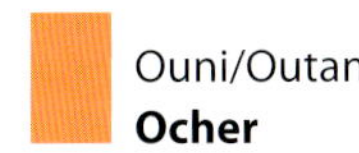

Ouni/Outan
Ocher

Ouni is an alternative name for lead vermilion pigment. It is described as a reddish-orange color dyed with safflower and *zhishi* in the *Engishiki*, an ancient Japanese book of regulations and customs. It was used as the color of ceremonial attire for the crown prince. Due to its placement above purple in the color hierarchy, it was considered one of the prohibited colors.

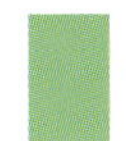

Naeiro
Seedling Color

This color name comes from the appearance of rice field full of seedlings. It is a somewhat muted, pale greenish-yellow color. *Moyou* is a dye created by combining indigo and yellow pomegranate, while *naeiro* dye is created by combining blue-white oak and cut straw to achieve a color resembling young rice seedlings.

This is a pear-shaped water dropper made for the European market during the early 1680s. The design features grapes and a chipmunk painted with delicate brushwork. The grapes are symbolically associated with *budo,* which can be read as "the martial way," and the chipmunk is associated with *ritsusu,* which can be read as "to regulate" or "to govern." When combined, they form the phrase "budo o ritsusu," which signifies the concept of regulating or governing the martial arts, making it a favorable design for the samurai class.

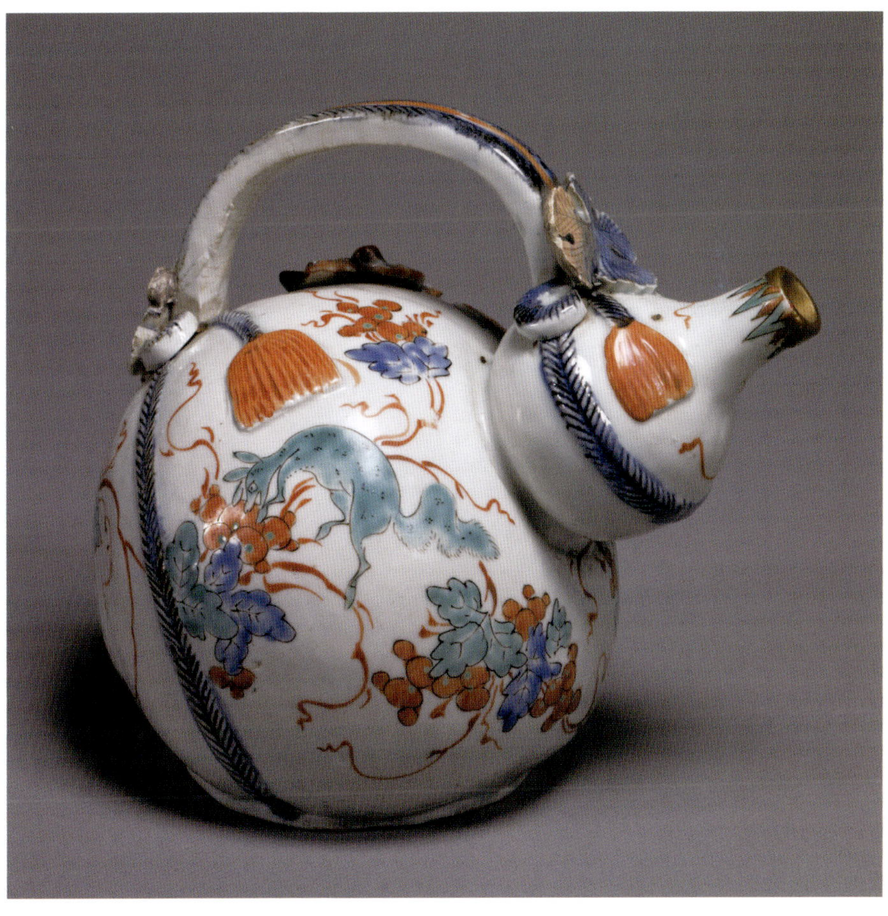

"Polychrome Porcelain Gourd-shaped Water Pourer with Grape and Squirrel Pattern". Imari Ware (Kakiemon Style), Edo period, 17th century.
Tokyo National Museum.
Source: ColBase at https://colbase.nich.go.jp

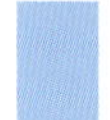 Ikkonzome
One Kin

Ikkonzome is an ancient dyeing technique and it is used to describe a light color dyed with safflower. It got its name because a single unit of dye called a *kin* would produce this color on a piece of silk fabric (equivalent to two bolts). During the Heian period, dark safflower dye was quite expensive and restricted to the wealthy and high-ranking individuals. Regulations pertaining to the level color in commoners' attire were in force at the time. Ikkonzome was a "tazayaroiro," meaning "acceptable color," requiring an acceptable amount of safflower dye.

Wasurenagusairo
Forget-me-not Blue

Forget-me-not is a perennial herb in the violet family that produces small pale blue flowers from spring to summer. The message it conveys in clothing, porcelains and other objects is, of course, "Please do not forget me."

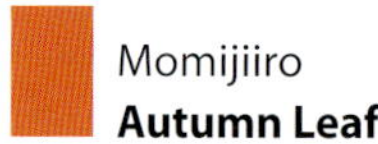 Momijiiro
Autumn Leaf

This is a deep red shade, reminiscent of the colors that leaves turn in autumn. "Momiji" is a term that refers to autumn colors in general and the red and yellow of maple trees in particular. The word comes from the ancient verb "momidzu," plant life's act of changing its colors from green to red and yellow colors. Later, this verb became a noun and was used to denote the red worn by Heian period courtiers.

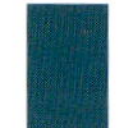 Hanada
Pale Blue or Azure Blue

A traditional color name for light blue dye, known since ancient times. It is lighter than indigo but darker than light blue. It is a pure blue color obtained from single indigo dyeing. The term "hanada" means a field of flowers, specifically referring to the blossoms of the Asiatic dayflower. This plant was known as "hanadairo" during the Heian period and later as "hanairo" during the Edo period. Today, the typical sequence for indigo dye shades, from lightest to darkest, is *asagi*, *hanada*, *ai*, and *kon*.

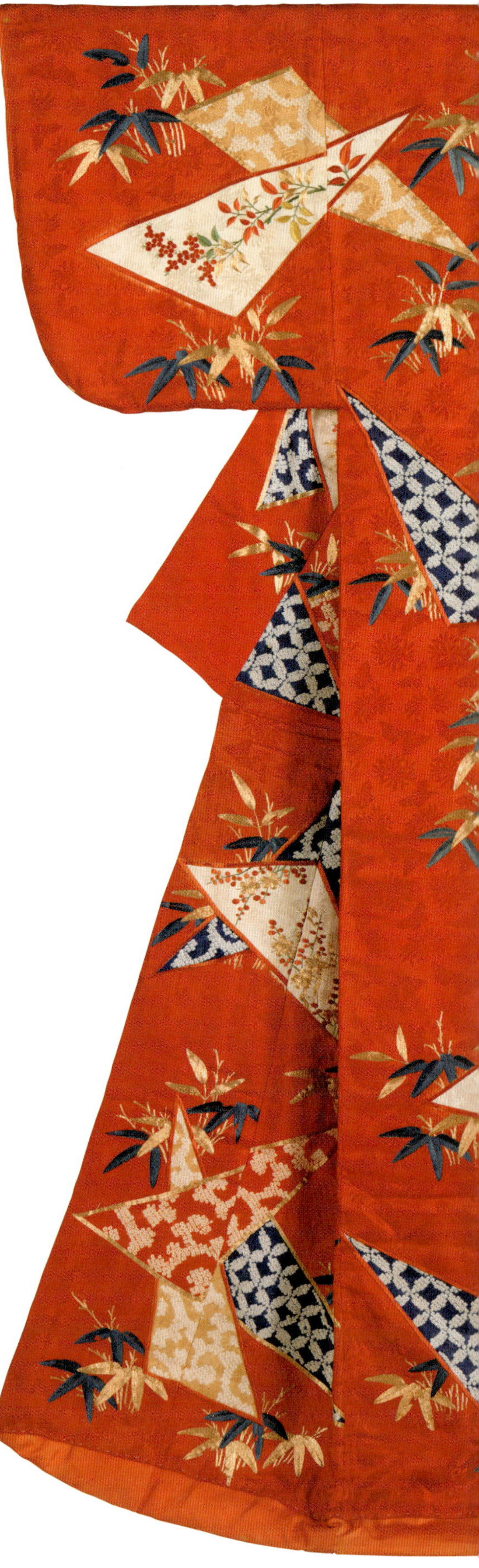

"Red Silk Kosode with Triangular and Bamboo Design Shibori and Embroidery."
Late Edo period, 19th century.
Stored in the National Museum of Japanese History.

6 Ikkonzome   **102 Wasurenagusairo**

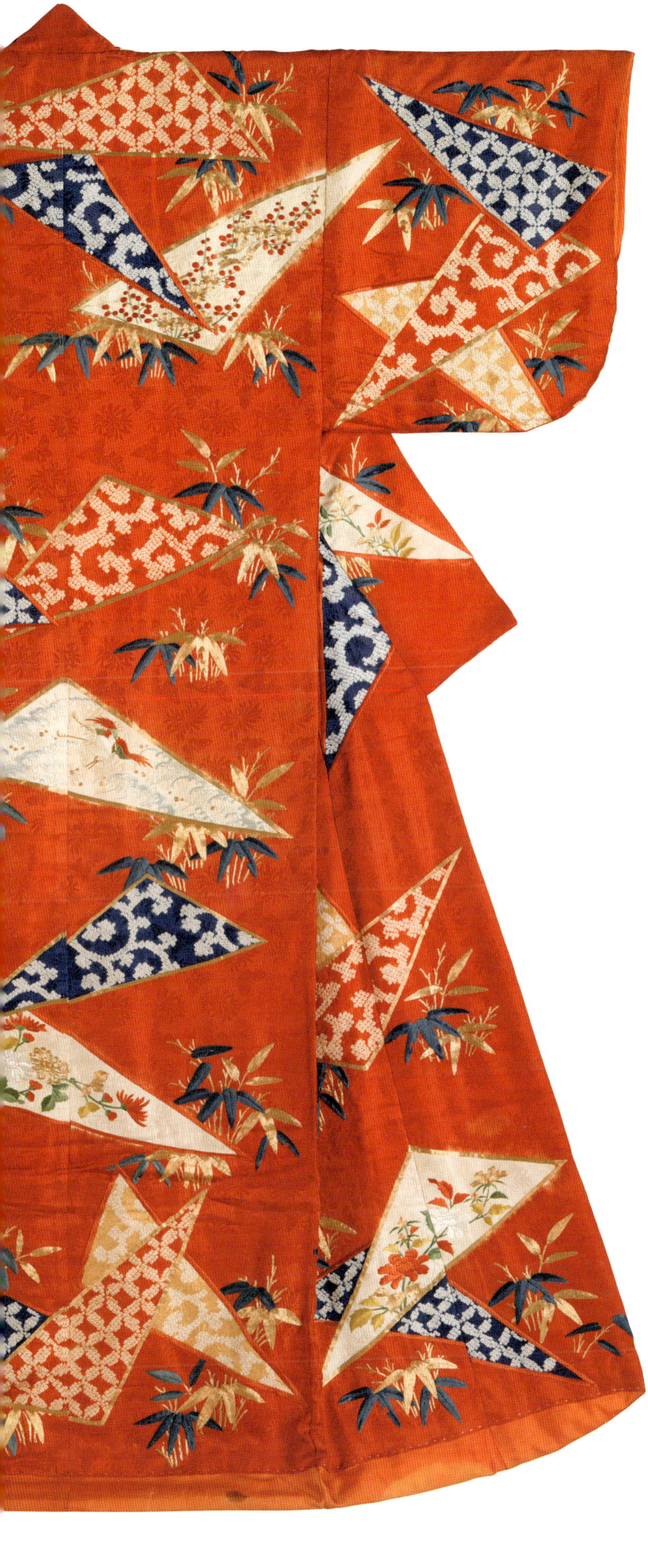

A kimono adorned with a scattered pattern of triangles and bamboo leaves. It's not entirely clear what it represents, but it appears to involve scattering several triangles and incorporating small patterns within them, which is now referred to as "minato-tori." This design combines the techniques of *kanoko shibori* (a type of tie-dye) and embroidery. The shibori is applied to the fabric and processed into triangles, followed by intricate appliqué work.

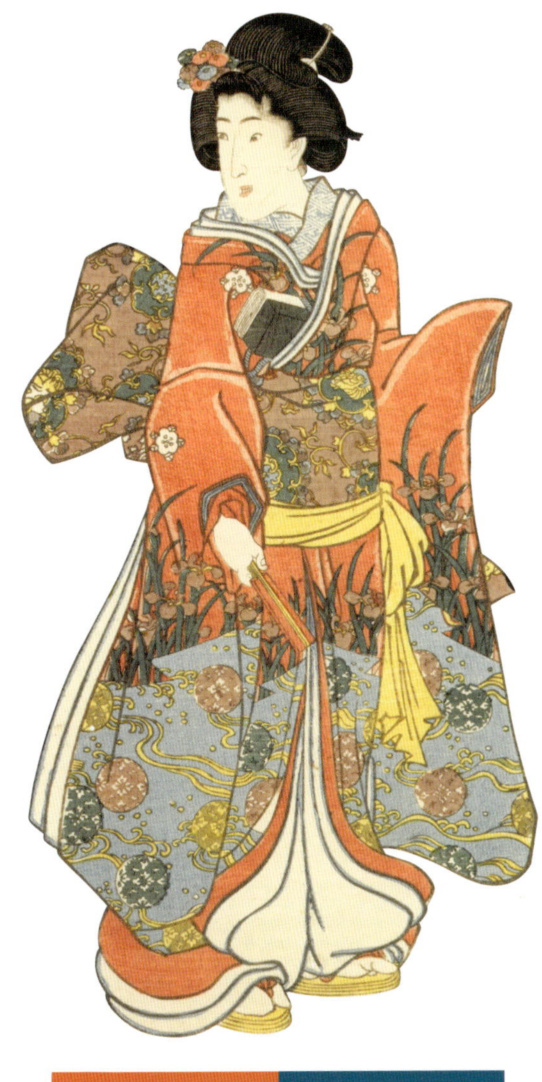

Detail from "Dawn Pilgrimage in Spring" by Utagawa Toyokuni.
National Diet Library Digital Collection.

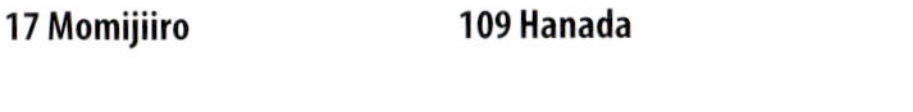

17 Momijiiro   109 Hanada

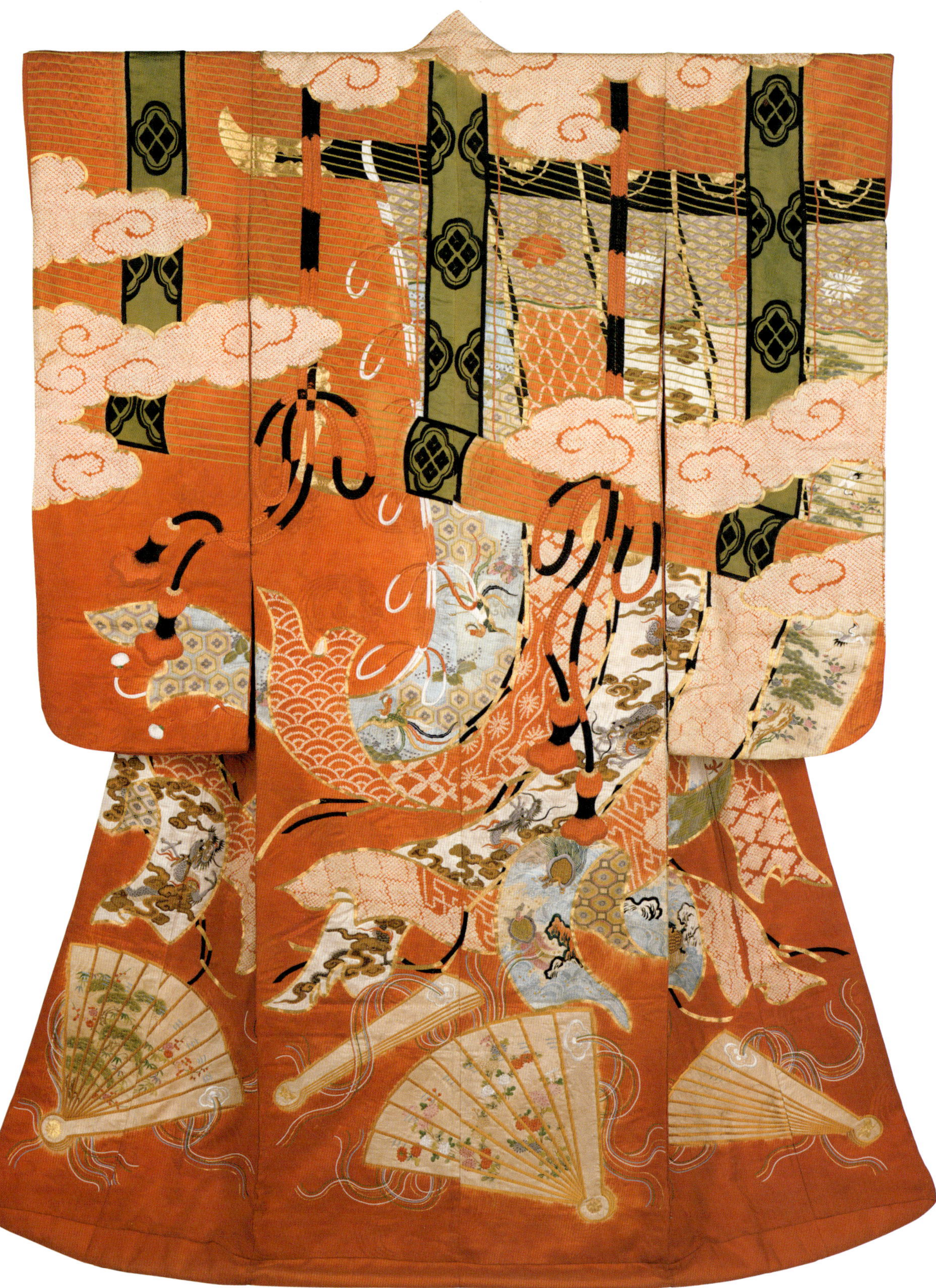

"Red Crepe Furisode with Curtain and Cypreses Fan Pattern in Shibori Stitching". Edo period, 19th century.
National Museum of Japanese History Collection.

An opulent furisode kimono features yuzen-dyed cypress fans near the hem, while above the waist, auspicious clouds, seven treasures, and blue waves float on a trailing curtain motif. Other lucky symbols like cranes, turtles, pine, bamboo, plum, and chrysanthemum are worked into the motif. The intricate embroidery in gold and colored threads throughout enhances the outlines and details, making this an exquisite piece of craftsmanship.

28 Imayouiro	3 Haizakurairo	118 Sabiasagiiro

Imayouiro
Elegant Deep Red

The name "Imayoiro" refers to the colors fashionable at the present time, with "Ima" referring to the Heian period. It was used as a color name for the deep shade of red plum blossoms. It is evident from Heian period images that the red made from the blossoms was favored by women of the imperial court. However, in the *Genji Monogatari* (*Tale of Genji*), the color is described as a pale and diluted shade of red rather than a deep red. During that time, deep red dye was considered inappropriate, so imayoiro denoted a "pale red color," a color lighter than that achieved by a single dyeing process.

Haizakurairo
Ashen Cherry Blossom Pink

Haizakurairo refers to a pale pink color with a hint of gray, similar to the color of cherry blossom petals. It is a subdued and modest color, making it a preferred color among upper-class young women. The term "Sakurairo" refers to a similar shade used in the same context. The origin of the term suggests that "Haizakurairo" is a cherry blossom color with a touch of gray, while "Sakuranezumi" refers to a mouse-gray color with a touch of cherry blossom pink. Since these color names are still used today, they are likely relatively recent additions to the color palette.

Sabiasagiiro
Rusty Light Blue

This is a slightly muted, pale greenish-blue color. The term "asagi" in the color name refers to a light shade of blue derived from indigo dye, and the addition of "sabi" suggests that rust has dulled the original color, resulting in a more subdued, muted hue. There is no documentation of the dyeing method for *sabiasagiiro* in Edo-period literature. Given that the underlying color, asagi, became popular in the mid-Edo period, it is believed that sabiasagiiro also gained popularity during this time.

Hanezu
Scarlet Flower

Hanezu is a slightly yellowish, strong red-orange color. It is also known as "Toudai" or "Tangtai." It is said to be an old name for "ukon" (turmeric) and is also associated with the alternate name for the lotus flower. In the *Engishiki*, the regulations for this include "one roll of yellow-red damask, ten kan and eight ryō of benibana [safflower], and one tou and two shō of ukon [turmeric]." In the *Okumi-no-In Shiki*, a set of regulations established during the reign of Emperor Monmu in the year 701, the color name changed from "Hanezu" to "Ouni" (yellow-red).

Sakurairo
Cherry Blossom Pink

Sakurairo is a faintly colored, pale pink shade reminiscent of fully-bloomed cherry blossoms. It is lighter than the *taiko* color mentioned in the *Engishiki*. This color name is used not only to describe the color of cherry blossoms but also to denote the slightly flushed complexion of a tipsy woman. A favorite of women, it was also used in the clothing of noblemen and warriors.

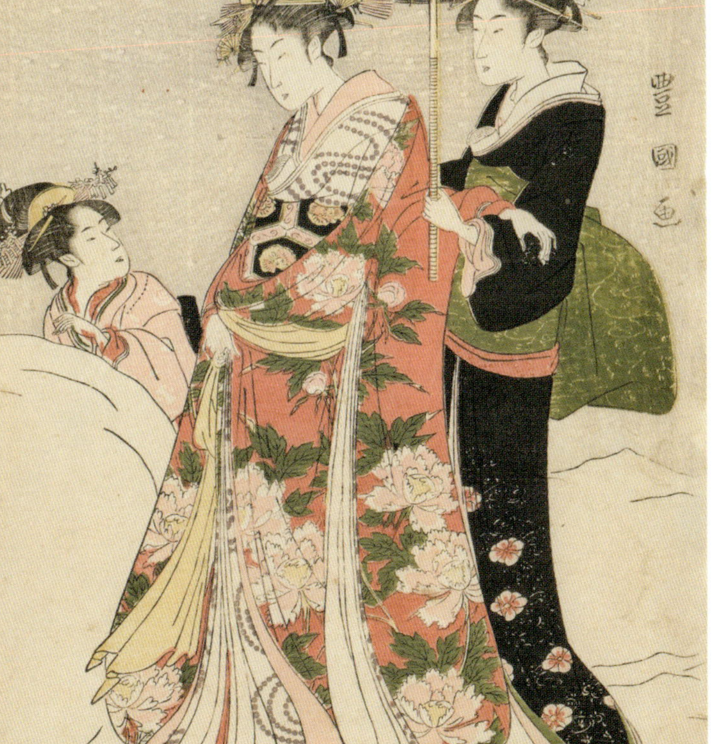

"Snow Viewing" by Utagawa Tokoyuni.
Edo period, 18th century.
Tokyo National Museum.
ColBase at https://colbase.nich.go.jp

53 Hanezu   **1 Sakurairo**

Akebonoiro
Dawn Color

This is a light reddish hue with a hint of yellow that resembles the sky at dawn. It is similar to "Shinonomeiro," a light pink orange. Another color in the same range called "sakeiro," named for the color of salmon flesh, is a similar yellowish pink.

Rikyū Shiracha
Rikyū White Tea

A pale yellow-brown color with a touch of gray. Although the name includes "cha," which means "tea," the color tone is more in the gray range. The name seems to be a trendy one borrowed from Rikyū, whose name is practically synonymous with the tea ceremony, to lend it a sense of style and sophistication.

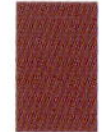

Fujinezumi
Wisteria Gray

A grayish-purple color with a soft, bluish tint. It was an especially popular color in women's clothing during the Edo period and beyond. It was introduced in a fashion magazine called *Shinkomairo* around 1894, during the Meiji era. It also became popular for the collars and fabrics of traditional Japanese clothing during the Taisho era (1918).

Suō
Raspberry Red

A deep reddish-purple created by extracting the pigment from the core of the sappanwood tree, using alum and lye. This dyeing technique was introduced to Japan from China during the Nara period, and it was used to produce various shades of red and purple. Depending on the mordant used, it can create a range from red to purple. Textiles dyed with *suō* were often referred to as "imitation red" or "imitation purple."

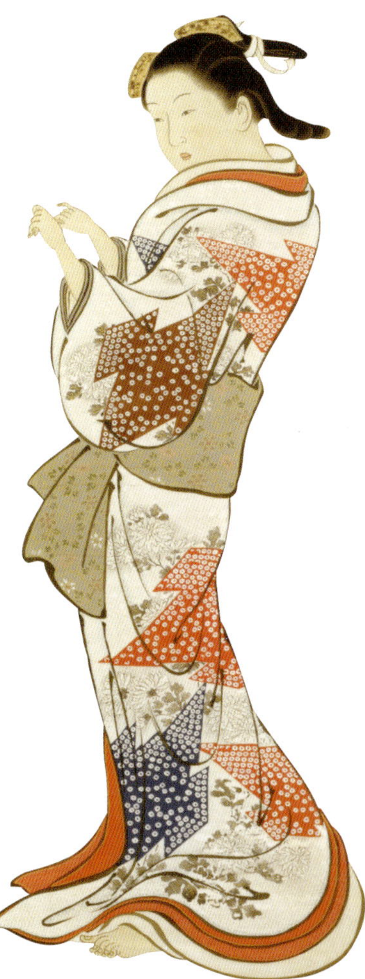

The intricate patterns, artfully painted on a white kimono, together with the graceful manner in which it is worn, exude an aura of sophistication and elegance. The viewer can sense the poignant emotions of the young woman, who appears to carry a profound sentiment within her attire. Her gestures, as she draws the lantern's light nearer and attempts to silence the tolling bell, hint at the presence of a man with whom she must inevitably part when the time arrives.

Detail from "Beauty with Pillar Clock"
by Nishikawa Yusin.
Edo period, 18th century.
Tokyo National Museum.
Source: ColBase at https://colbase.nich.go.jp

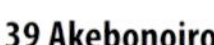

39 Akebonoiro   **189 Rikyū Shiracha**   **76 Fujinezumi**

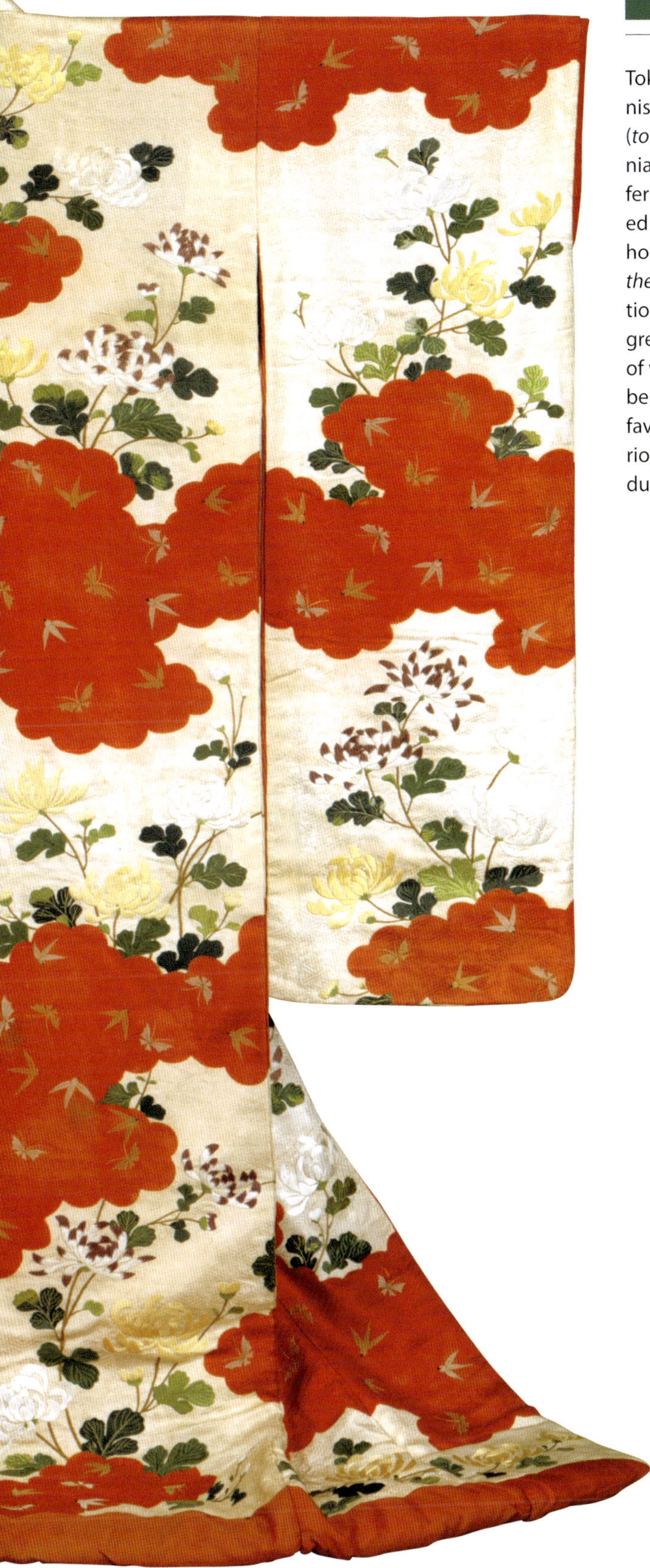

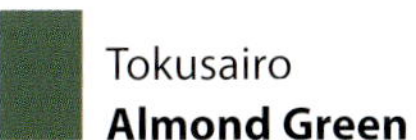

Tokusairo
Almond Green

Tokusairo is a deep green color reminiscent the stems of the horsetail plant (*tokusa*). Tokusa is an evergreen perennial herbaceous plant belonging to the fern family, and it was commonly planted in the corners of gardens in older homes. In *Heike Monogatari* (*The Tale of the Heike*), there is a passage that mentions wearing hunting clothes in this green color, and a *moegi-jime* (a type of waistband) in a mellow yellow color beneath, indicating that this color was favored for clothing by medieval warriors. It is said that it was a popular color during the Genbun era (1736–1741).

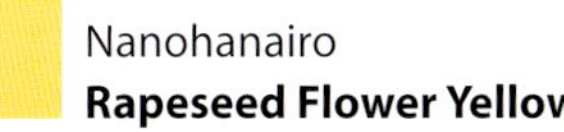

Nanohanairo
Rapeseed Flower Yellow

Nanohanairo is a bright yellow color with a greenish tint that is both bright and cool. Along with "Yamabukiiro" it is one of the few colors in the yellow spectrum inspired by flower colors. Rapeseed, or *aburana*, is an annual or biennial plant belonging to the *Brassicaceae* family, and it has been cultivated for its seeds, from which oil has been extracted since ancient times.

The entire surface of this glossy, satin-finished *furisode* is adorned with a vibrant red *Genji-gumo* (Genji clouds) pattern, creating a bold and delightful color scheme. Within the clouds, small birds and butterflies, as well as blooming chrysanthemum flowers in raised embroidery reveal the refined preferences of the court. It is possible that this garment was worn by young noblewomen in the late Edo period and early Meiji era.

"White Damask Furisode with Chrysanthemum, Cloud, Bird, and Butterfly Patterns".
Meiji period, 19th century.
Tokyo National Museum.
Source: ColBase at https://colbase.nich.go.jp

60 Suō   **155 Tokusairo**   **180 Nanohanairo**

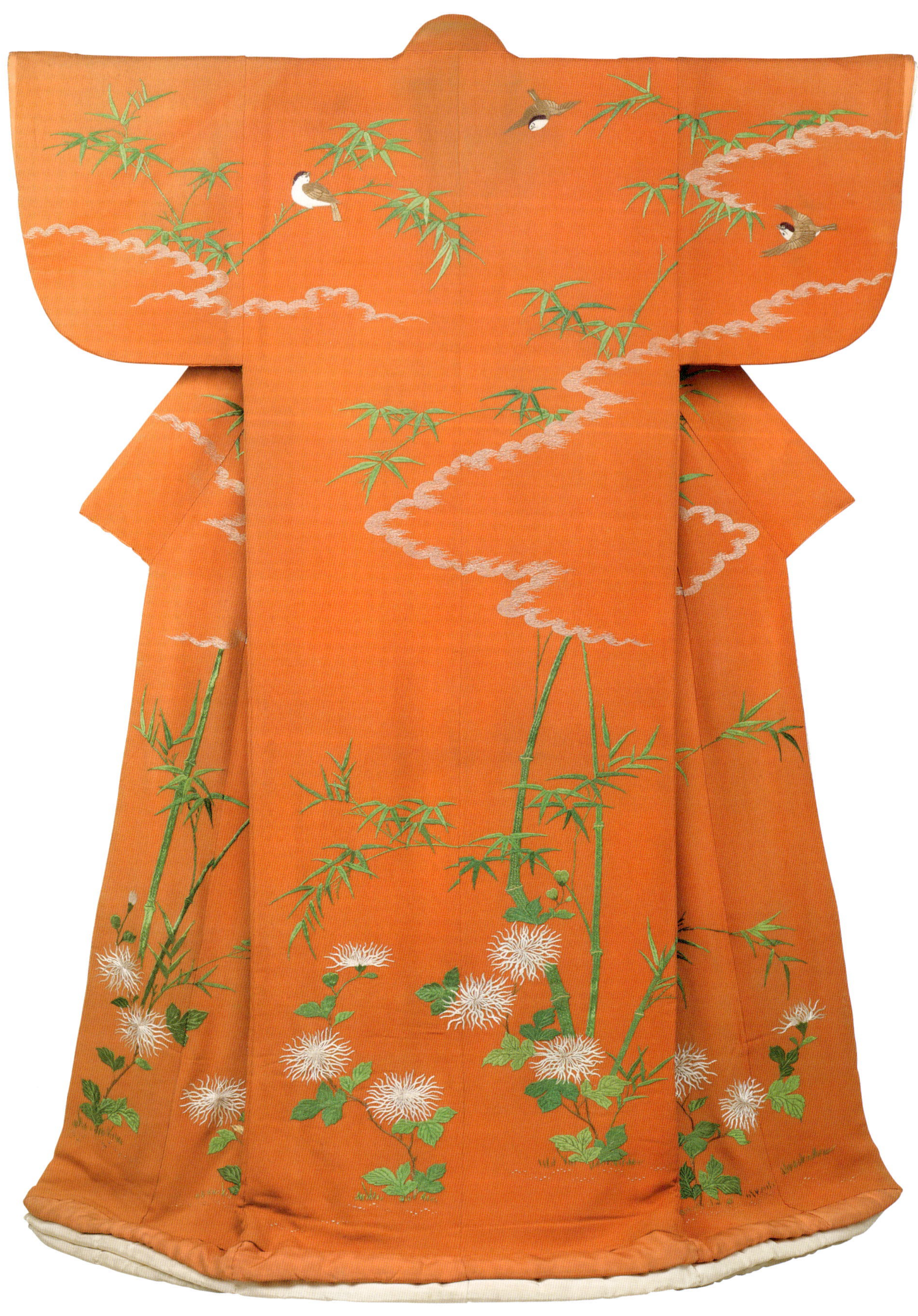

"Red Crepe Kosode with Bamboo, Sparrow, and Chrysanthemum Pattern".
Edo period, 19th century.
Tokyo National Museum. Source: ColBase at https://colbase.nich.go.jp

This is a *furisode* dyed entirely in a luxurious shade of red, with a traditional pattern featuring bamboo and sparrows. Additionally, there is embroidery of white chrysanthemums on the hem. This kimono was commonly worn as everyday attire by court women. The patterns such as *Genji-gumo* (Genji clouds) and distinctive chrysanthemums were typically used in the kimono of aristocratic women during the later years of the Edo period.

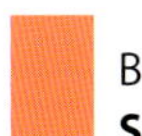

Benihi
Scarlet Red

A brilliant reddish color with a hint of yellow obtained from dyeing with red safflower and yellow dyes such as turmeric and Japanese barberry. The term "hi" originally referred to the red color produced by dyeing with safflower but later came to be used for colors achieved by layering red from safflower mordanted with alum and the red from the alum-mordanted *suō* dye. The color was historically used for the *hakama* (culotte-style pants) worn by female court attendants.

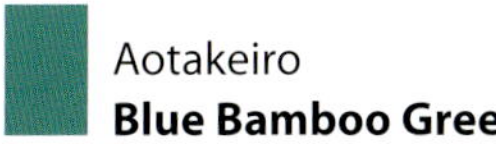

Aotakeiro
Blue Bamboo Green

A color derived from the green of blue bamboo, a bright and rich green color with a slightly emphasized bluish tone. This is the name associated with the typical color of bamboo. Other colors associated with bamboo shades include "Wakatake" (young bamboo), "Rochiku" (old bamboo), and "Susudake" (soot bamboo).

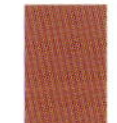

Benikaba
Red Birch

Benikaba is a reddish-brown, somewhat orange color, similar to a shade of brownish-orange. Originally, the name likely referred to the deep red hue with a tinge of brown found in birch bark, which is similar in color to the spikes of a *kaba* plant, and it can also be counted among the shades in the brown color spectrum. It has been described as a brown shade in sample books from the Edo period, such as the *Shikisomeisho*.

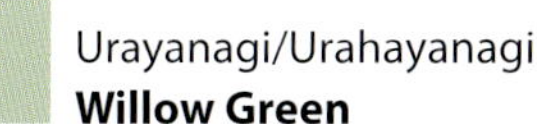

Urayanagi/Urahayanagi
Willow Green

A pale yellow-green shade, derived from leaves with a whitish underside, such as willow leaves, mugwort, and kudzu leaves. The color name is also used to describe a green that is even lighter and has more of a whitish tinge than "Yanagiha" (willow leaf green) It is mentioned in color sample books from the late Edo period, but specific dyeing methods or fashion trends associated with this color are not readily available in historical records.

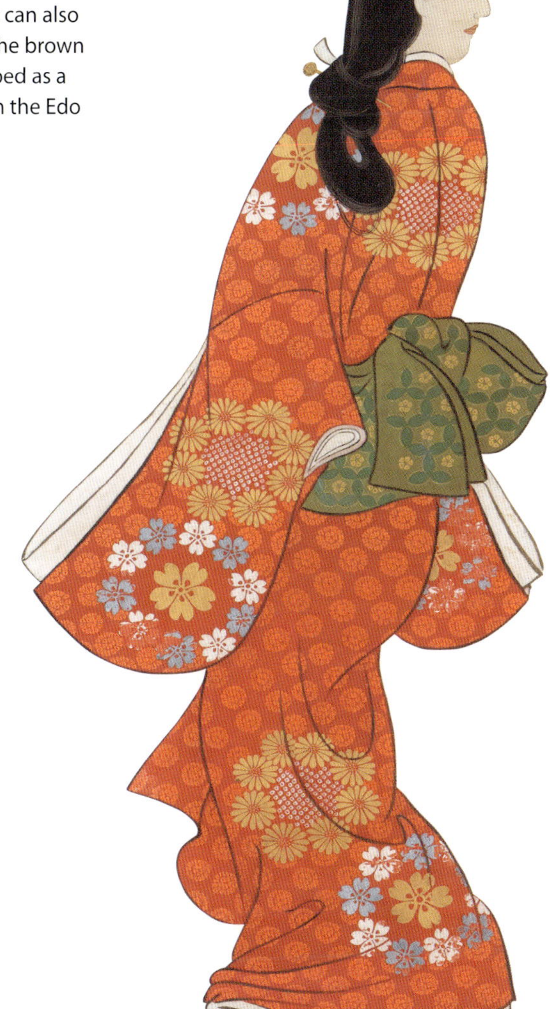

A woman dressed in vivid scarlet attire has halted to look over her shoulder. She is wearing a kimono with chrysanthemum and cherry blossom embroidery on a crimson background. Her obi, with long ends hanging on both sides, features the popular *yoshiya musubi* knot style, which was popularized by the famous actor Yoshikichi Uemura. Her hairstyle, known as *tamamusubi*, elegantly ties the ends of her hair into a loop, capturing the fashion trends of that era.

Detail from "Portrait of a Courtesan Looking Over Her Shoulder" by Hishikawa Moronobu. Edo period, 17th century.
Tokyo National Museum.
Source: ColBase at https://colbase.nich.go.jp

24 Benikaba	144 Urayanagi/Urahayanagi

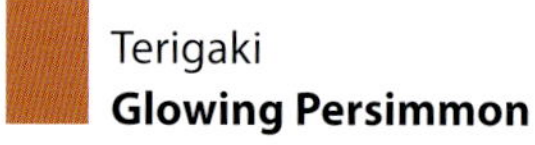

Terigaki
Glowing Persimmon

Terigaki refers to the deep reddish-orange color of ripe persimmons' skin. In the color chart of *Te Kagami Moyou Setsuyou* (*A Guide to Patterns for Hand Mirrors*), it is described as "Terigaki. Old name: Kubairo, also called a color resembling this one with a touch of pale blue or Kakinokishi (persimmon) color." There are various color names associated with persimmons, such as "Senkaki," "Saru-gaki," "Sarashi," and "Konoe-gaki." These names are based on the color of the persimmon fruit and the color of persimmon tannin dye, creating two distinct color variations.

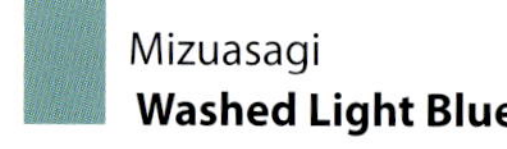

Mizuasagi
Washed Light Blue

Mizuasagi refers to a light shade of *asagi* (light blue) that looks like it has been washed and exposed to water. It is lighter than asagi color and even paler than *mizuiro* (another light blue shade). It is slightly darker than "Mizome," as mentioned in *Te Kagami Moyou Setsuyou* as "commonly called 'Nozokiiro' or 'Kamenozoki' by the public."

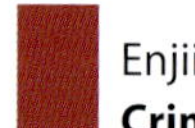

Enjiiro
Crimson Red

Enjiiro is a deep crimson color with a touch of black. This color name has been around for a long time and is said to have originated from the Yan Kingdom, which was in the northern region of ancient China, referring to the red fat found in that region. There are two types of enjiiro dye: plant-based genuine enji (natural red) made from safflower dye and animal-based synthetic enji made from cochineal insects that infest tropical plants. The vibrant red color obtained from cochineal is what in English is called crimson or carmine.

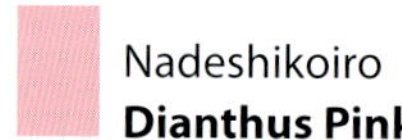

Nadeshikoiro
Dianthus Pink

Nadeshikoiro refers to a soft, slightly purplish, light pink color reminiscent of the flowers of the *nadeshiko* (Dianthus) plant. Like other pale pink shades, it is a light pink hue with a hint of purple, residing within the peach color range. In terms of kimono colors, it was considered a color for young people. For men's kimono, it was described as having a "light purple on the surface and blue or red plum on the back," while for women's kimono, it was described as having "red plum on the surface and red or blue on the back." It is believed to have been made using safflower, which was popular during that time. The name comes from the practice of calling beloved children "Nadeshiko" as an endearment, and it is associated with this delicate and charming flower.

From the vivid red hem of the figured silk fabric, plum trees rise up towards the shoulder mountains, depicting a scene where plum blossoms bloom in competition. Along the way, there are two levels of space with a unique design that scatters the petals of deer-hide tied plums. Upon closer inspection, there has been a significant alteration around the sleeves, with both sleeves swapped, and the sleeve length has been considerably shortened. Initially, it appears to have been an elegant furisode (a type of formal kimono for young, unmarried women).

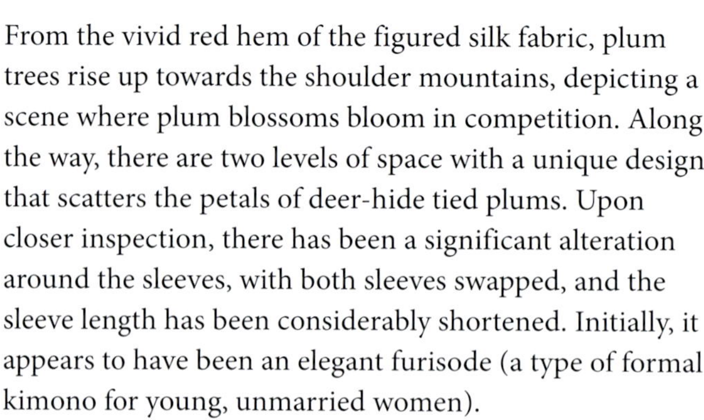

Detail from the "Mist, Spring Plum Viewing" by Utagawa Toyokuni, 1858.
National Diet Library Digital Collection.

55 Terigaki   **100 Mizuasagi**

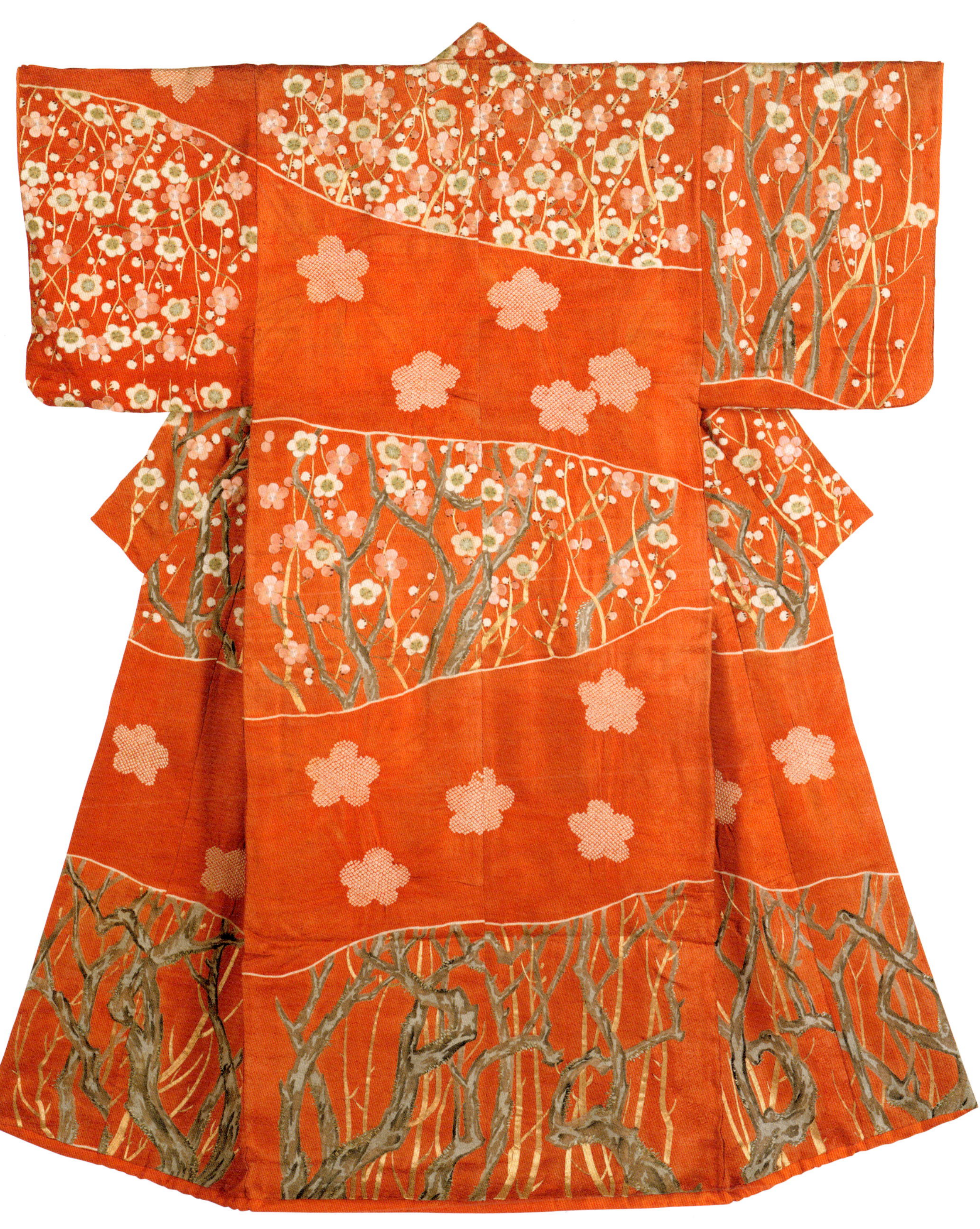

"Red Damask Kosode with Plum Grove Pattern in Yuzen Dyeing and Shibori Stitching". Edo period, 19th century.
National Museum of Japanese History.

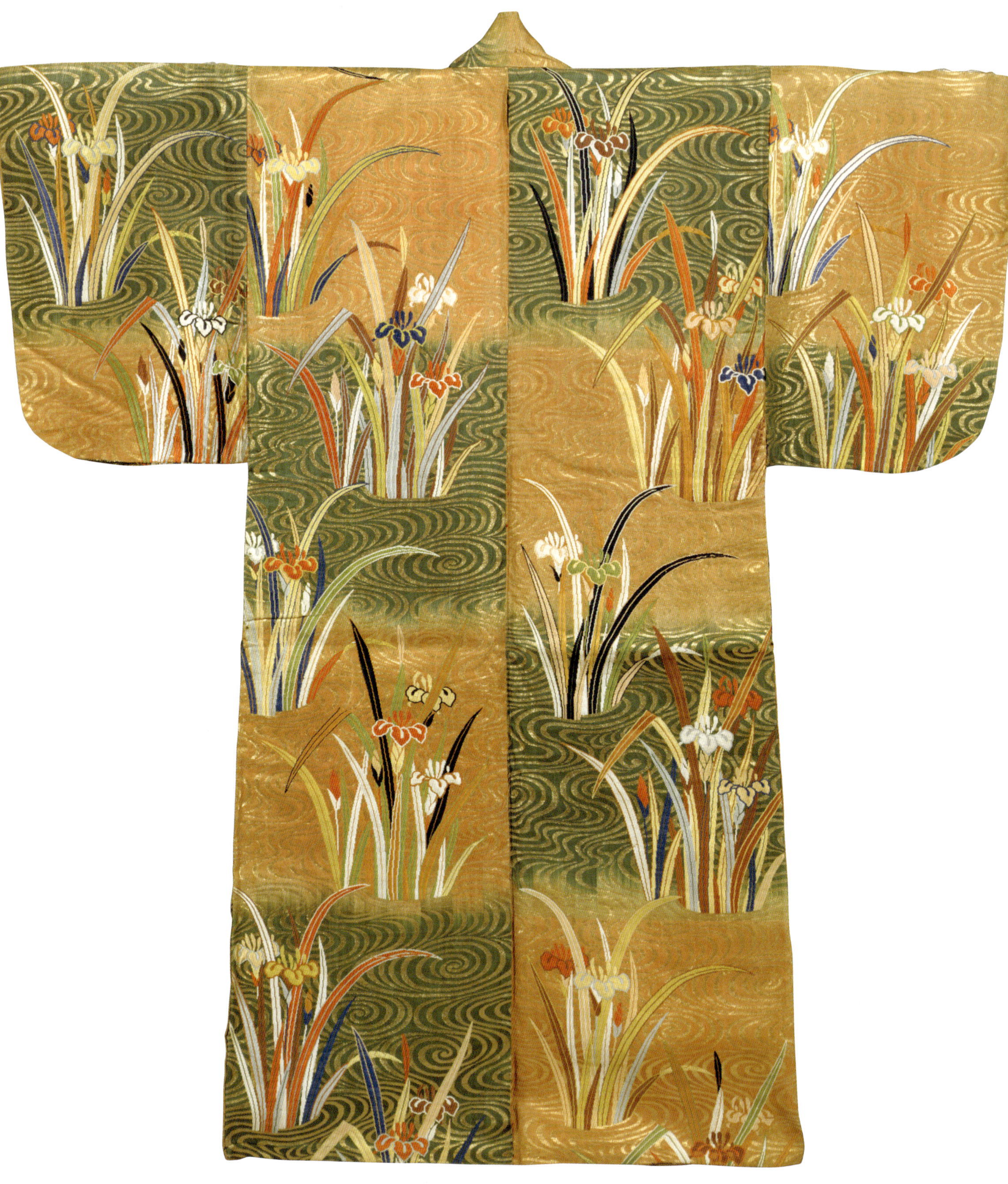

44 Kanzouiro/Kōjiiro	116 Kachiiro/Kachin-iro	148 Tokiwairo

"Crimson and Fresh Green Segment with Japanese Iris Pattern Tang Weave". Edo period, 18th century.
Tokyo National Museum.
Source: ColBase at https://colbase.nich.go.jp

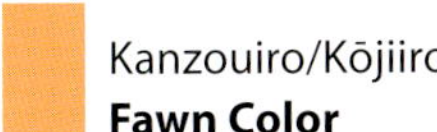

Kanzouiro/Kōjiiro
Fawn Color

Kanzouiro/Kōjiiro is a perennial plant in the lily family, and the color name is inspired by its petals. The flowers bloom sequentially from the bottom and wither in a day, which led to the nickname "forget-me-not" because wearing them was believed to help people forget their worries and heartaches. During the Heian period, people wore garments dyed with this color when in mourning. This yellowish hue was created through the mordant dyeing process using *akane* (madder) and *shikon* (purple gromwell) or *beni-bana* (safflower) and *shikon* during the early Heian period.

Kachiiro/Kachin-iro
Coarse Wool

A deep blue, darker than navy, with a reddish hue that appears black, it was made by pounding indigo leaves to create dye. The name also applies to heavily saturating the fabric with the dye. *Kachi* has an auspicious meaning, as it associated with victory, and samurai favored this color, using it to dye their fabrics and leather armor.

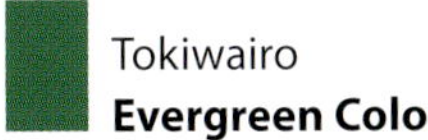

Tokiwairo
Evergreen Color

A deep green color with a strong blue undertone. "Tokiwa" refers to something that remains constant, and it's used to describe evergreen trees like pine and cedar that retain their green leaves throughout the year. A poem from the *Shinsen Rokujoudai* (circa 1244, by Fujiwara no Nobumitsu) references the use of the Tokiwa pine as dye since ancient times.

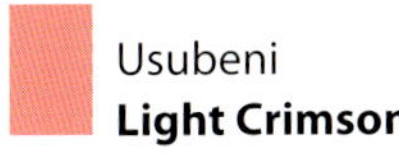

Usubeni
Light Crimson

A color name used to describe a light shade of red dye. It is lighter than "Chukurenai" (medium red) and slightly paler than "Beni-umeiro" (light plum red). It is created by adding a similar amount of turmeric dye (*ukon-zome*) to the underdye, resulting in a warm color with a slight yellowish tone. Usubeni is commonly used as a descriptive term for colors with a pinkish hue, ranging from a light, peach-like shade to a deeper, reddish tone. It is still used today in various contexts like lipstick.

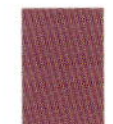

Ume Murasaki
Plum Purple

Ume refers to the red color of red plums, and it is used to describe a slightly subdued purple color with a hint of red. While there is no documented historical source for red-purple dye in the Edo period, the color name "Ume murasaki" matches the color "Umeguro" associated with plum blossoms, which began appearing in dye sample books and other sources from the late Edo period to the early Meiji period. Its tone is a redder version of "Benifujiiro" (crimson wisteria color), and the dyeing method is believed to be relatively light.

The brocades of China's Tang dynasty have long be treasured for their workmanship, the innovative method of their weaving, their floral, geometric and other patterns. In the Noh costume, it is used primarily in *kosode* (a short-sleeved kimono) and is worn mainly by female characters. The use of red color is for young female roles, while the absence of red is used for middle-aged and elderly roles. In the Noh play *Mugen-Nosaka*, the female character wears a Tang brocade as a flowing robe.

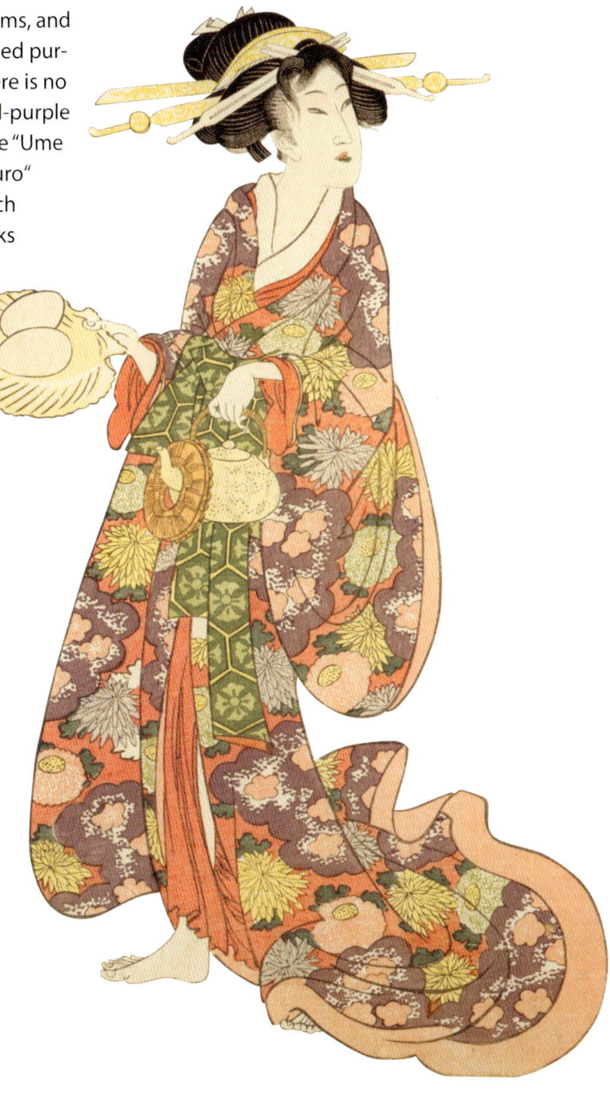

Detail from "Collection of Beautiful Women" by Utagawa Toyokuni, 1858.
National Diet Library Digital Collection.

13 Usubeni 86 Ume Murasaki

The Colors in Japanese Kabuki Costumes

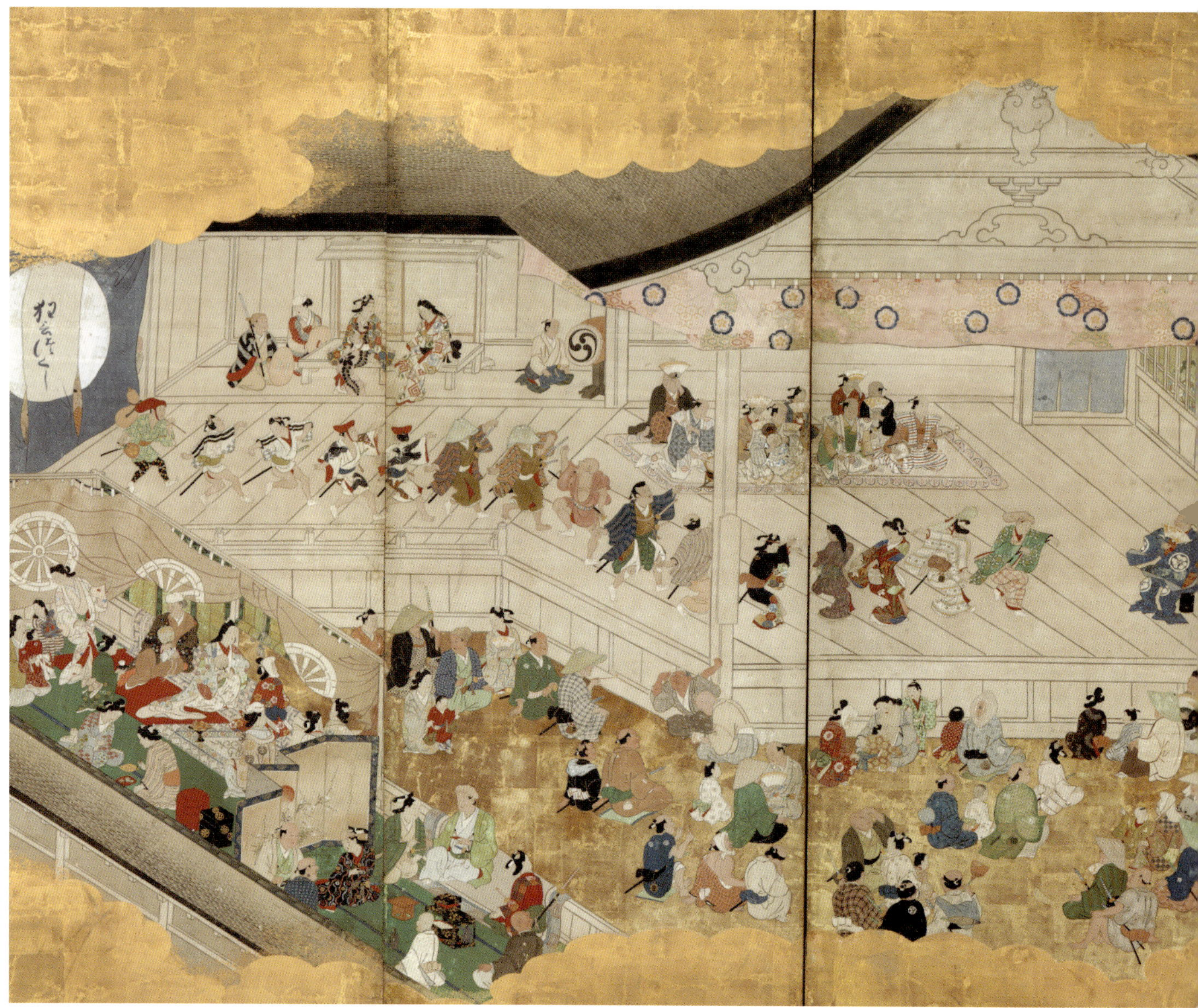

Red is the life of Kabuki, Red is also the origin of Kabuki. Originally, the word "Kabuki" was a popular term in the Tensho era, derived from the verb "kabuku," which means to dress flamboyantly. In essence, it was to stand out in front of people, and the color red, which is also the color of vitality, appeared as a color for rough scenes. However, when this intense red color is used for *onnagata* (female roles played by men), it is transformed into a sensuous and quite erotic symbolism. Kabuki's color palette seems to avoid complicated intermediate colors, and in scenes where a large number of actors appear as part of the background, apart from *jidaimono* (historical plays), which have their own set of rules, they tend to wear matching costumes. In the final scene of *Dōjōji*, for example, a large number of catchers appear, and in *Uroko Shiten*, the costumes are red with golden scale patterns, symbolizing the body and tail of the snake that the *shite* (leading actor) is transformed into.

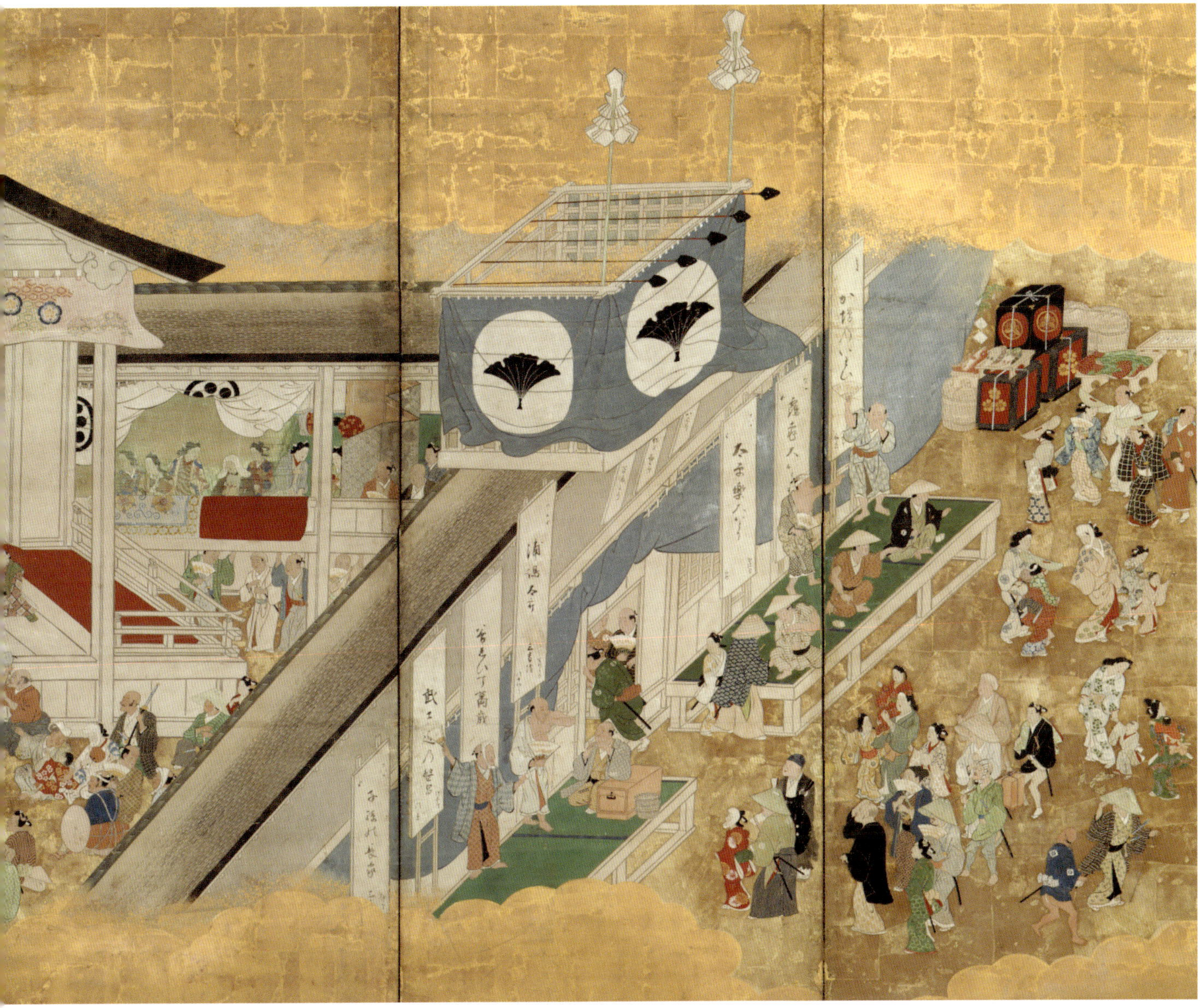

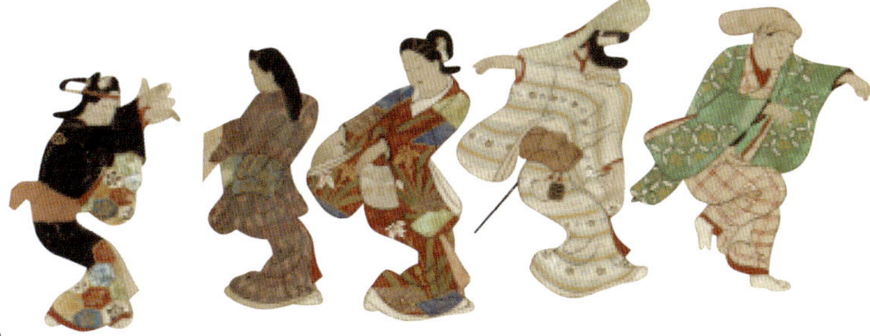

"Kabuki Theater Folding Screen" by Hishikawa Moronobu. Edo period, 17th century. Tokyo National Museum. Source: Colbase at https://colbase.nich.go.jp

This artwork by Hishikawa Moronobu depicts a Kabuki theater, with the entrance to Nakamura-za, a playhouse, on the right. A signboard with the name of the play is hung at the entrance, and men are calling in spectators. As you move inside, you see a lively scene of actors performing a glamorous dance with a full cast. The audience sits on the ground and looks up at the stage, each watcher enjoying the performance. From the expressions and gestures of the audience—each member enjoying the play in their own fashion—we see that both the performers and the audience are portrayed with great attention to detail, bringing them to life.

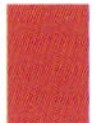

Karakurenai/Kokikurenai
Foreign Crimson/Deep Red

This refers to a vivid crimson color achieved through intense dyeing with safflower. In the Nara period, it was referred to as "Kurenai no yashio," which meant dyeing eight times to achieve a deep and intense color. The word "kurenai" is said to have referred to imported dyes from the country of Wu (China). "Han" (唐) represents imported red, and to emphasize its beauty, it began to be called "Foreign Red" or "Tang Red."

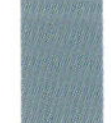

Sabiasagiiro
Rusty Light Blue

This is a slightly muted greenish-blue color with a hint of rust. "Rust" (*sabi*) refers to a color with lower saturation and a muted or subdued appearance, while "light blue" (*asagi*) refers to a light shade of indigo dye. There are no records of the dyeing method or popularity of this color in Edo-period literature. As the base color, light blue, was popular in the mid-Edo period, it is commonly believed that this variation would have also been popular during that time.

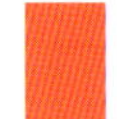

Shōjōhi
Scarlet Vermilion

This refers to a particularly intense shade of vermilion with a yellowish undertone. "Shōjō" can refer to a creature resembling an orangutan or a sacred beast resembling a monkey in Chinese mythology. There are various theories about the origin of the name, including stories of dyeing with the blood of such creatures or the influence of costumes worn by the character Shōjō in Noh theater, which features red hair, a flushed face and red garments. In the late Muromachi period, fabrics dyed in this color were brought on Nanban ships (ships from Southern barbarian countries), and warlords of the Warring States period eagerly acquired these vibrant and stimulating fabrics, using them for garments such as *jinbaori* (warrior surcoats).

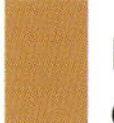

Kincha
Golden Brown

In the early Edo period, it seems to have referred to a reddish-white tea color, but generally, it denotes a yellowish-brown color with a golden tinge. Because of the association with gold, kincha is sometimes confused with the color yamabukiiro. However, yamabukiiro is lighter and has more of a yellowish tone. Dyeing in this color began in the early Edo period, and *Tōsei Somemono Kan* (1696) describes a method of dyeing with the bark of the Chinese bayberry tree and applying alum to darken the color.

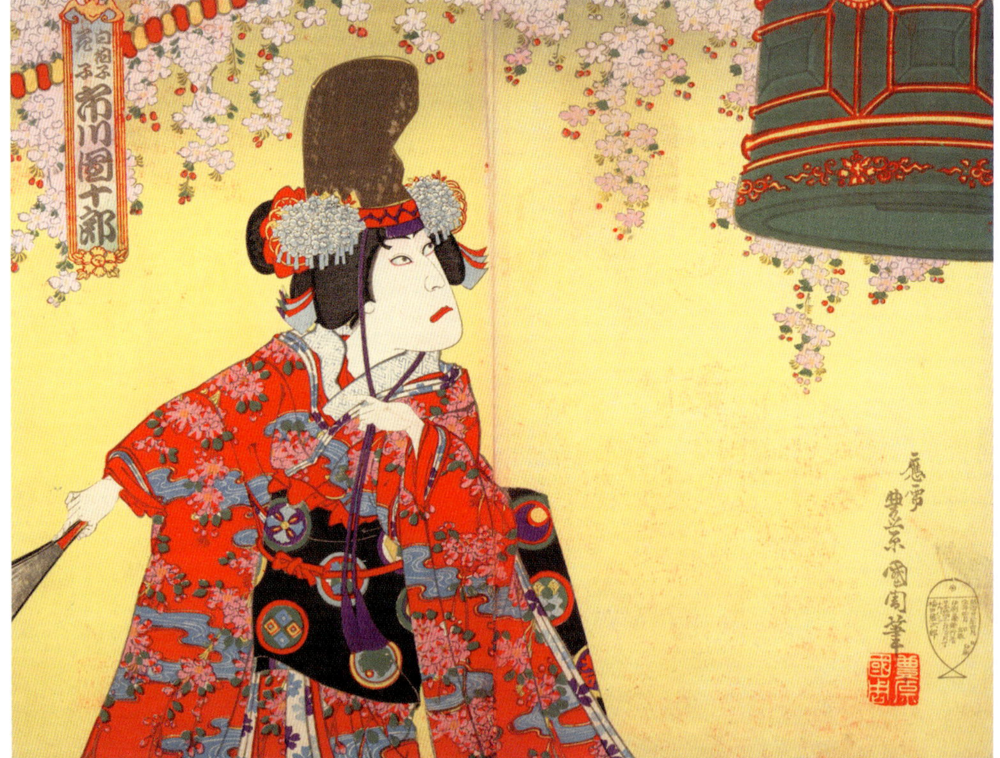

20 Karakurenai/Kokikurenai   118 Sabiasagiiro

**"Shirabyoshi Hanako, Ichikawa Danjuro"
by Toyohara Kunichika, 1890.**
National Diet Library Digital Collection.

In the image of Ichikawa Danjūrō as the protagonist, Shirabyōshi Hanako, in *Kyō Shōko Musume Dōjōji*, the costume's most striking feature is the vibrant vermilion-colored hanging sleeves (furisode) adorned with cherry blossoms. The costumes change one after another through techniques like *hikinuki*, and the vividness of the red garment is eye-catching. When the scarlet kimono is removed, a light blue kimono representing a young girl's attire is revealed, and the dance transitions into a graceful performance.

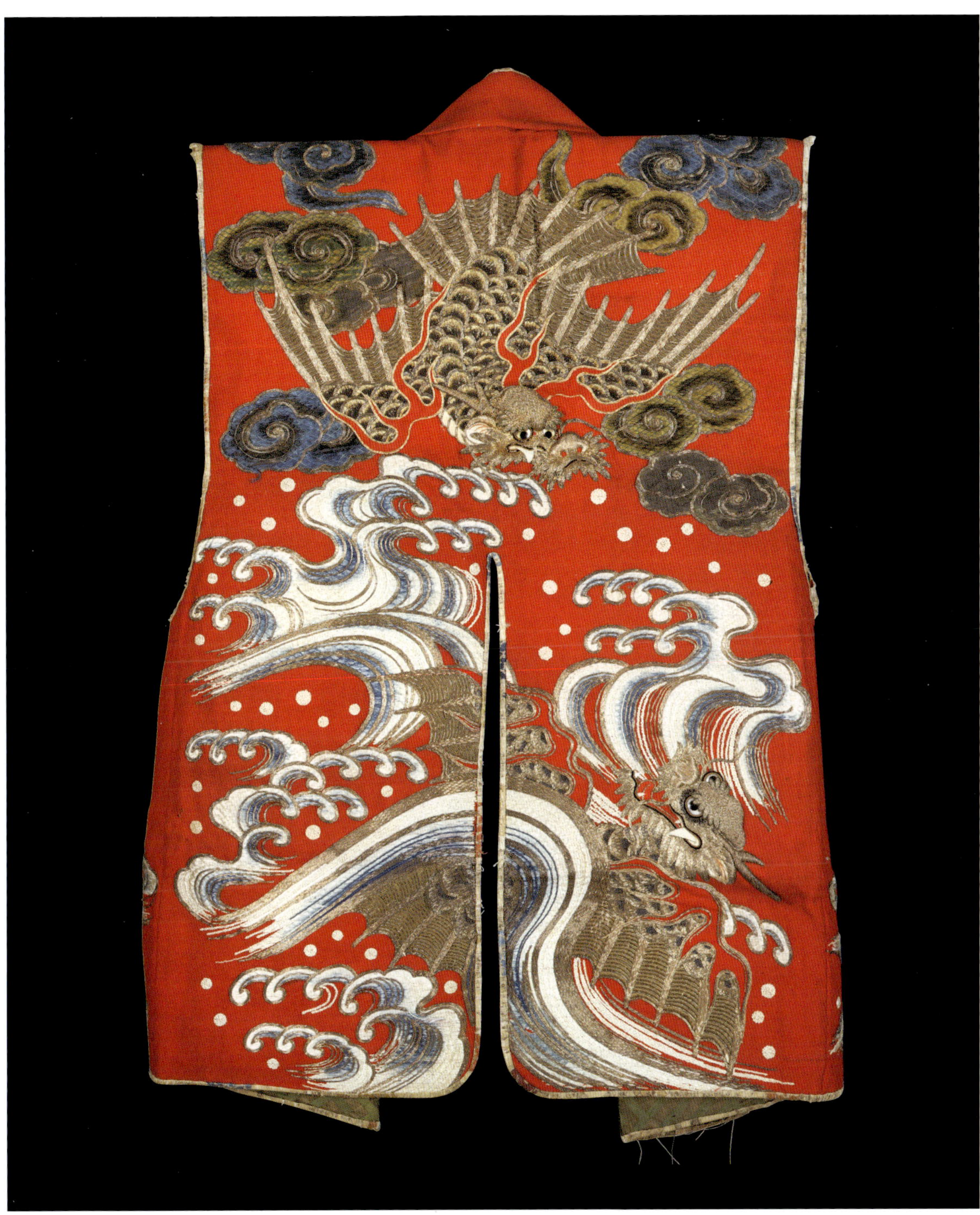

16 Shōjōhi   206 Kincha

"Scarlet Vermilion Jinbaori with Embroidered Dragon, Phoenix, and Wave Patterns". Edo period, 19th century.
Tokyo National Museum.
Source: ColBase at (https://colbase.nich.go.jp)

This striking garment features a symbolic depiction of a dragon with wings and clouds on a vivid red background, with wave patterns embroidered, creating a strong visual impression. Designed with the expectation of standing out on the stage, it is flamboyant and glamorous even from a distance. A *jinbaori* is a sleeveless outer garment worn over armor, and this one in vibrant Scarlet Vermilion is quite remarkable. It is said that this garment was used by the female Kyōgen performer, Bandō Mitsue, for her role as Minamoto no Yoshitsune in the play *Ichitani Wakan Kumogiri*.

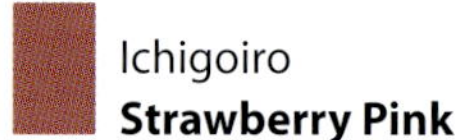 Ichigoiro
Strawberry Pink

This color is used to describe a bright, slightly purplish red color resembling ripe strawberries. The term "strawberry" here refers to the Dutch strawberries brought to Nagasaki in the 10th year of Tenpō (1839) from the Netherlands. Prior to that time, the term "strawberries" referred to the wild variety. The color name "Ichigoiro" is thought to be a translation of "strawberry," but the actual fruit is slightly redder and more vibrant, whereas "strawberry color" has a subdued, purplish undertone.

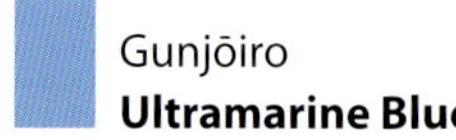 Gunjōiro
Ultramarine Blue

This color is achieved using the mineral pigment ultramarine, resulting in a deep blue color. Originally, this name referred to the color of lapis lazuli, a mineral gemstone, but it was replaced with rock ultramarine, made from azurite, as lapis lazuli was extremely expensive, comparable to precious gemstones. It is an essential color in Japanese painting and has been used in works like the wall paintings from the Momoyama period and folding screens of the Rinpa school during the Edo period.

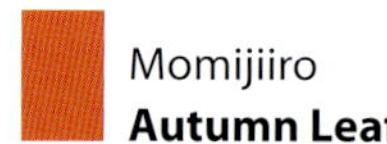 Momijiiro
Autumn Leaf

"Momiji" refers to the vivid color of maple leaves when they turn red in autumn. In the Heian period, there was a color called "momiji" in the color palette, the outer hue being red and the inner being "Souhō" (a deep crimson color). Along with "momiji," there are various terms used to describe different shades of red leaves, such as "Koumomiji" (yellowish-red leaves), "Aomomiji" (bluish-red leaves), "Hajimomiji" (light red leaves), and "Momijimomiji" (maple red leaves), each representing various nuances of color in the autumn foliage.

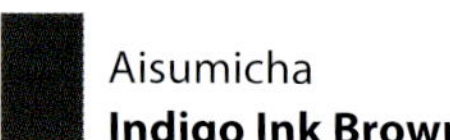 Aisumicha
Indigo Ink Brown

This color refers to a dark ink-like color with a hint of indigo. According to *Tekagami Moyō Setsuyō* (a compendium of patterns and designs), this color name comes from the tradition of men in Asakusa, Tokyo, who, during a reconciliation after a quarrel that occurred during the festival of Negaya Gongen, celebrated their reconciliation by dyeing and wearing matching garments of the same color. This practice marked the resolution of the dispute, leading to the name "aisumicha."

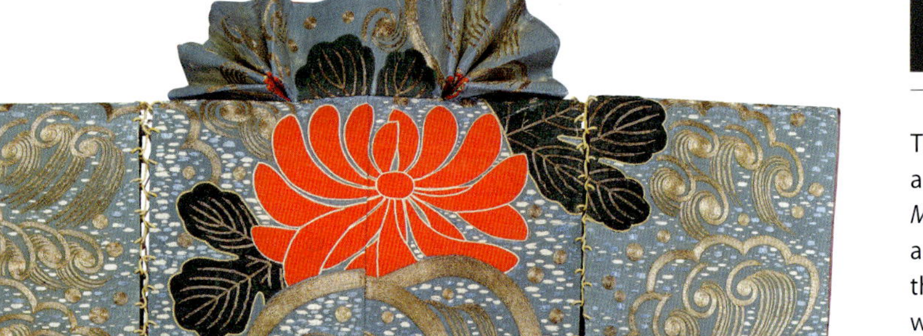

"Light Blue Velvet Child's Kosode with Chrysanthemum and Water Pattern". Edo period, 19th century.
Tokyo National Museum.
Source: ColBase at https://colbase.nich.go.jp

29 Ichigoiro   **104 Gunjōiro**

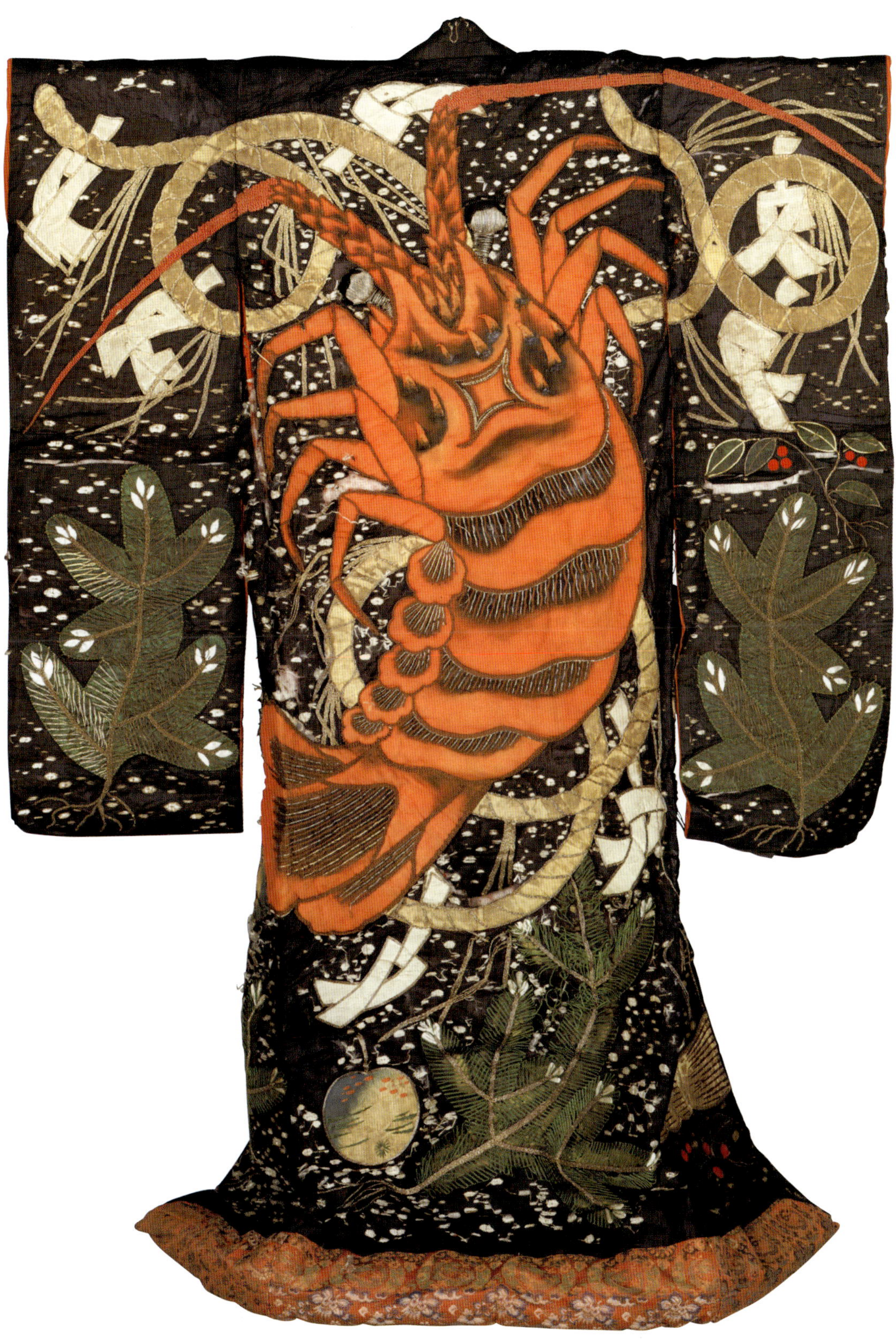

"Lobster and Shimenawa with Young Pine Design Hakama".
Late Edo period, 19th century.
Tokyo National Museum.
Source: ColBase at https://colbase.nich.go.jp

The Color Purple in Japanese Culture

Purple has been considered a noble color in both the Eastern and Western worlds, often reserved for aristocrats, clergy, and other privileged individuals. In Japan, deep purple was assigned as the clothing color for the highest rank in the "Jūnikai Kan'i" (Twelve-Level Cap and Rank System), and was regarded as the king of colors. Additionally, in the ancient Phoenician civilization, which was a maritime nation on the eastern coast of the Mediterranean, people dyed fabrics with a purple dye extracted from shellfish around the 13th century BC. This color became known as "Royal Purple" or "Imperial Purple" and was highly cherished as a symbol of clothing.

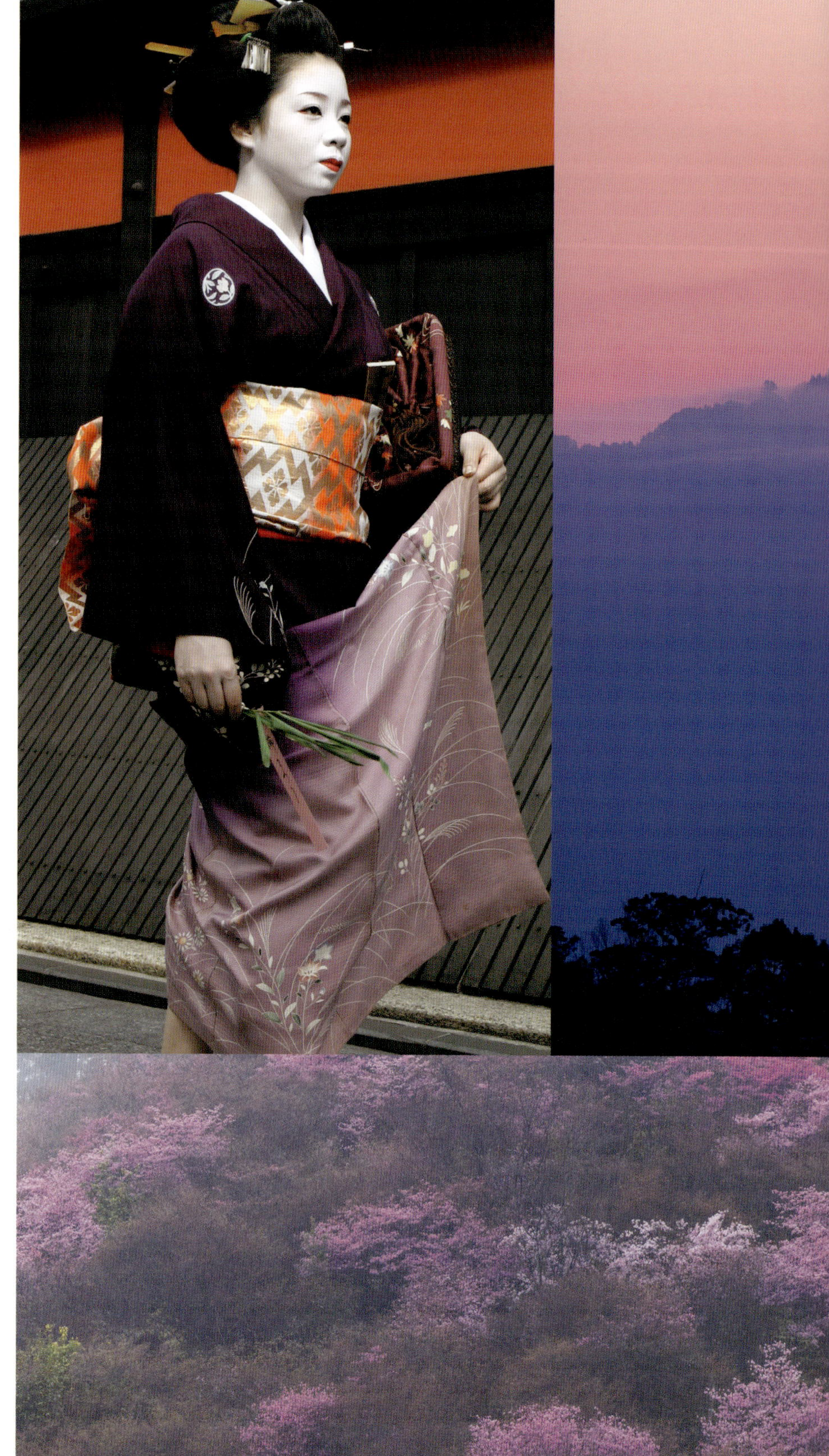

Top right Kushi Matsuri (Comb Festival), Yasaka Jinja Shrine, Kyoto.
Top far right Dawn at Mount Hiei, Kyoto.
Bottom right Rhododendron at Makio, Kyoto.
Bottom far right Kagura Dance, Jōnangū Shrine, Kyoto.

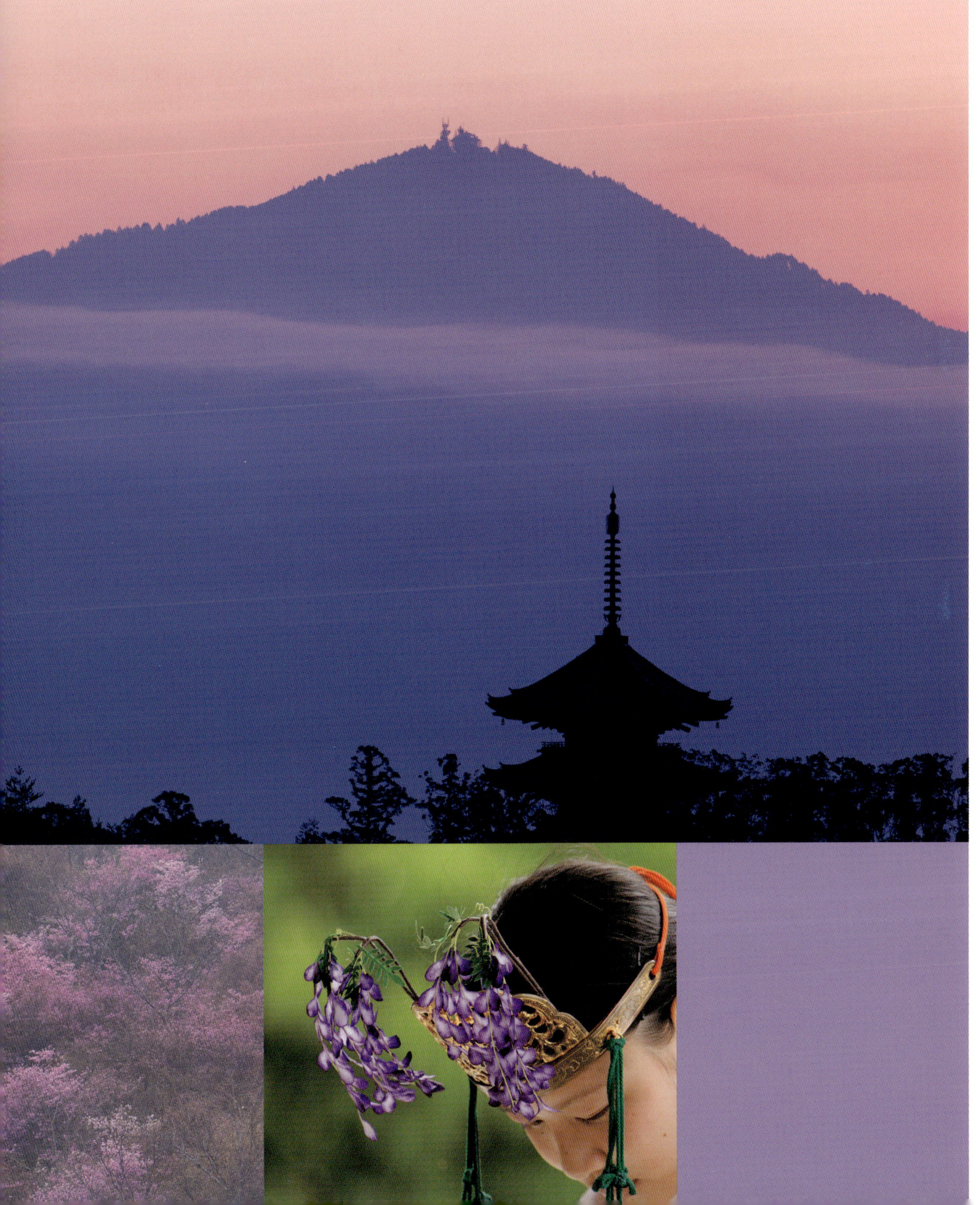

Japanese Color Schemes Based on Purple

Purple has symbolized nobility since ancient times, and its association with high status can be traced back to the introduction of Chinese Sui and Tang dynasty clothing traditions alongside the spread of Buddhism. In the system that indicated the seating arrangement at the imperial court based on the type of headwear, purple was considered a high-ranking color. The dyeing of purple was challenging due to the scarcity of the dye and the complex dyeing process. Moreover, the deeper the purple, the more expensive it became. As a result, it was prohibited for commoners to wear purple, and it was referred to as a "forbidden color."

In Japanese culture, purple is highly regarded, as seen in *The Tale of Genji*, where Lady Murasaki represents an idealized woman. Aristocrats in the imperial court attached special significance to this color, calling it "Yukariiro", and they used the term "murasaki no yukari" to describe relationships that developed through a fateful connection, often involving romantic love. The transition from purple being exclusively associated with the upper class to becoming a color that anyone could wear occurred during the Meiji era.

Purple, created by combining blue and red, is neither purely blue nor purely red. Its appearance varies depending on the balance of blue and red. It's a subtle color that combines the characteristics of both colors, blending the warmth of red and the coolness of blue. This juxtaposition of contrasting colors creates a mysterious color that can simultaneously convey joy and sadness. Purple, which melds seemingly incompatible contrasting colors, is well-suited to suggest emotional states marked by poignant affection.

When it comes to color schemes involving purple, it often consists of predominantly purple, sometimes combined with white or black. While complementary colors like yellow and orange can also work well, they may give off a dramatic impression, suitable for ceremonies and festivals. From a psychological perspective, purple enhances sensitivity, evokes emotional richness, and expresses intuitive and emotional aspects of the mind. It is a color with artistic and mystical qualities, attracting individuals with heightened sensibilities.

Color Scheme Based on Light Colors

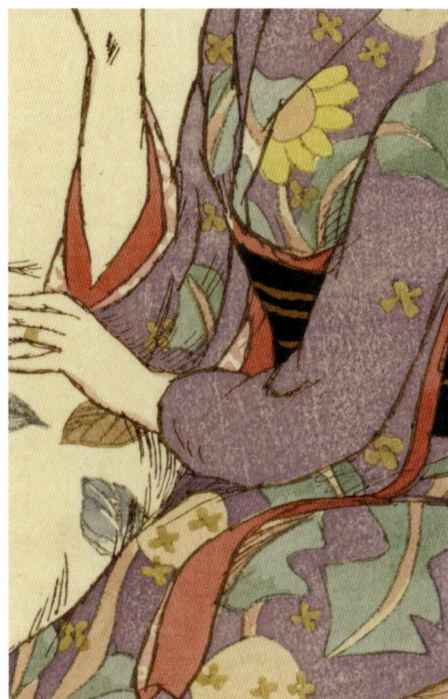

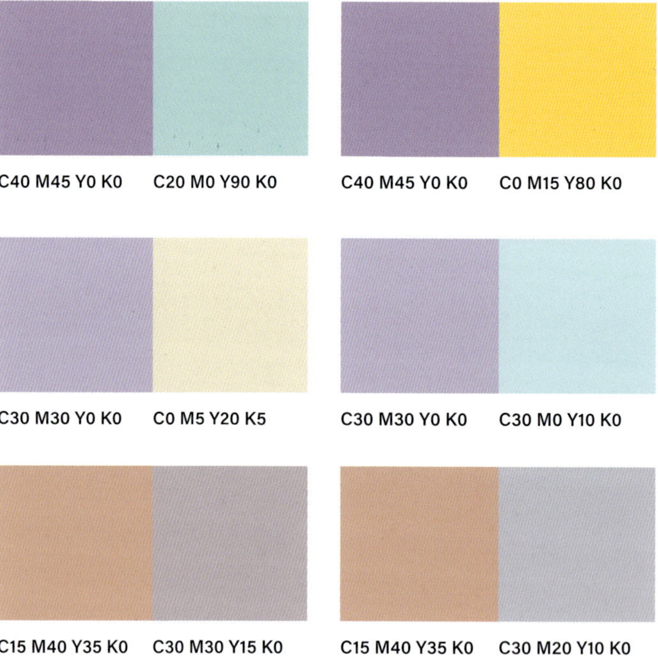

C40 M45 Y0 K0	C20 M0 Y90 K0	C40 M45 Y0 K0	C0 M15 Y80 K0
C30 M30 Y0 K0	C0 M5 Y20 K5	C30 M30 Y0 K0	C30 M0 Y10 K0
C15 M40 Y35 K0	C30 M30 Y15 K0	C15 M40 Y35 K0	C30 M20 Y10 K0

Detail from "Six Views of Nagasaki"
by Takehisa Yumeji, 1941.
National Diet Library Digital Collection.

Color Scheme Based on Vivid Colors

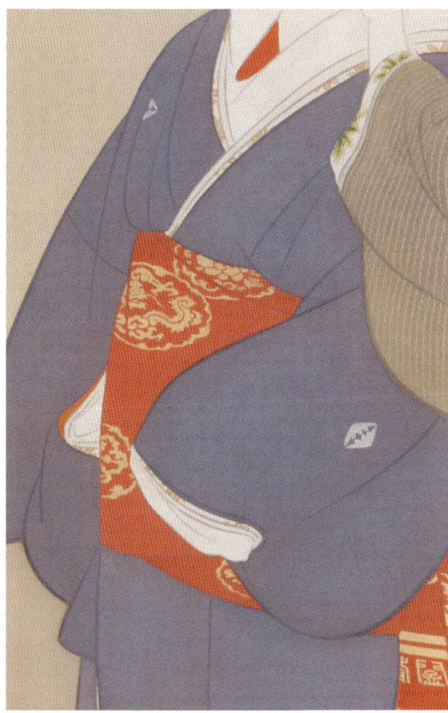

C55 M60 Y0 K0	C100 M55 Y0 K0
C30 M80 Y0 K0	C65 M10 Y30 K0
C35 M80 Y30 K0	C60 M0 Y0 K0

C55 M60 Y0 K0	C0 M55 Y100 K0
C30 M80 Y0 K0	C50 M0 Y90 K0
C35 M80 Y30 K0	C40 M10 Y100 K20

Detail from "Spring Evening" by Uemura Shoen, 1936.
Nara Prefectural Museum of Art.

Color Scheme Based on Dark Colors

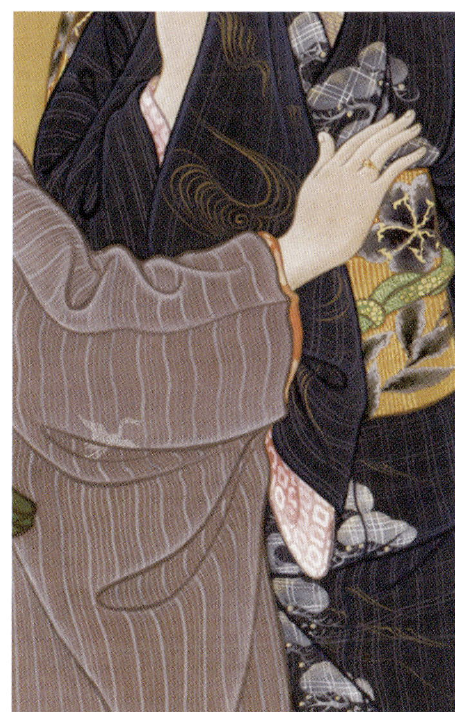

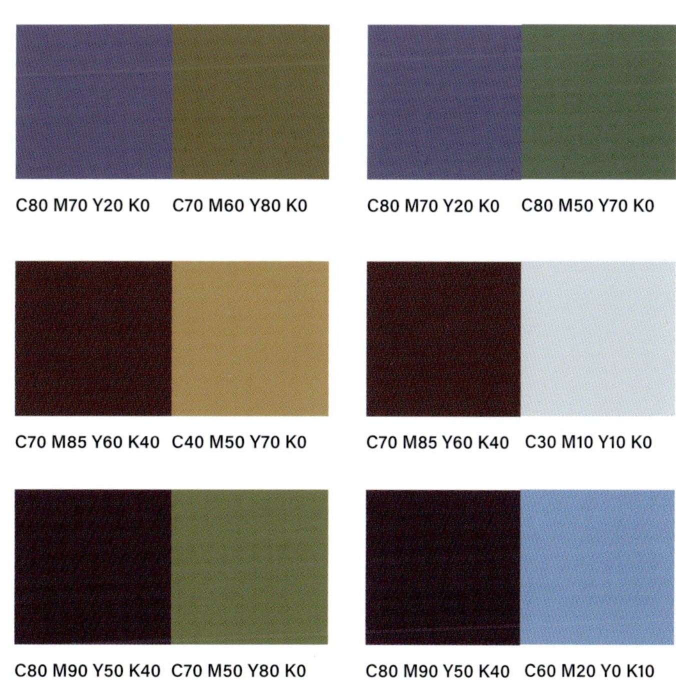

C80 M70 Y20 K0	C70 M60 Y80 K0
C70 M85 Y60 K40	C40 M50 Y70 K0
C80 M90 Y50 K40	C70 M50 Y80 K0

C80 M70 Y20 K0	C80 M50 Y70 K0
C70 M85 Y60 K40	C30 M10 Y10 K0
C80 M90 Y50 K40	C60 M20 Y0 K10

Detail from "Onaidoshi" by Shimazaki Ryuu, 1908.
Tokyo National Museum.
Source: ColBase at https://colbase.nich.go.jp

The picture scroll depicting the seasons' flora and fauna is painted with brilliant ultramarine blue layers. White and pink chrysanthemum petals are heightened using *gofun* (white lead-based paint). The screen teems with a variety of colors and creatures, evoking the emotions of the seasons. In this scroll, a total of sixty types of plants and birds make appearances. Sakai Hōitsu, the founder of the Edo Rinpa school, learned various painting styles, including Kano, from a young age. However, he later became deeply enamored with Ogata Kōrin's work, producing delicate, graceful, and emotionally rich works of art.

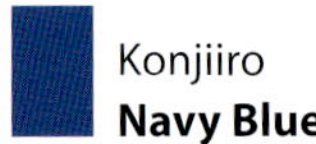

Konjiiro
Navy Blue

This is a dark and elegant shade of blue with a hint of purple. Like Prussian blue ("gunjō"), it is made from azurite (lapis lazuli), but high-quality azurite pigment was expensive, and it was mostly imported from the continent since the Nara period (729–749). Konjiiro is a specific shade of deep blue with a vivid purplish hue. It's worth noting that there was a distinction between natural lapis lazuli-based konjiiro (*ishi konjiiro*) and synthetic Prussian blue-based konjiiro.

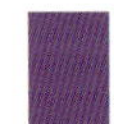

Ayameiro
Iris

This is a deep purple with a reddish undertone. The Japanese name can also be translated as "shobu," though *ayame* (iris) and *shoubu* (sweet flag) belong to different plant families). The colors became synonymous around the Genroku period (late 17th century). The overlapping colors of ayameiro include a blue overtone and a red or red plum undertone, plus other various shades of color, and it was used in the summer season.

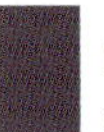

Budōnezumi/Ebinezumi
Grape Gray

This is a grayish color with a reddish tint, similar to the color of grape skins. "Budou" was an old term for grapes, which is why this color is sometimes referred to as "Ebinezumi." The use of color names like budōnezumi began during the middle to late Edo period. While this color is closer to grape skin color, "Budouiro" today typically refers to a bluish purple, reflecting the introduction of new grape varieties with a darker purple hue. Budōnezumi was a popular color during the Heian period and is frequently mentioned in court literature.

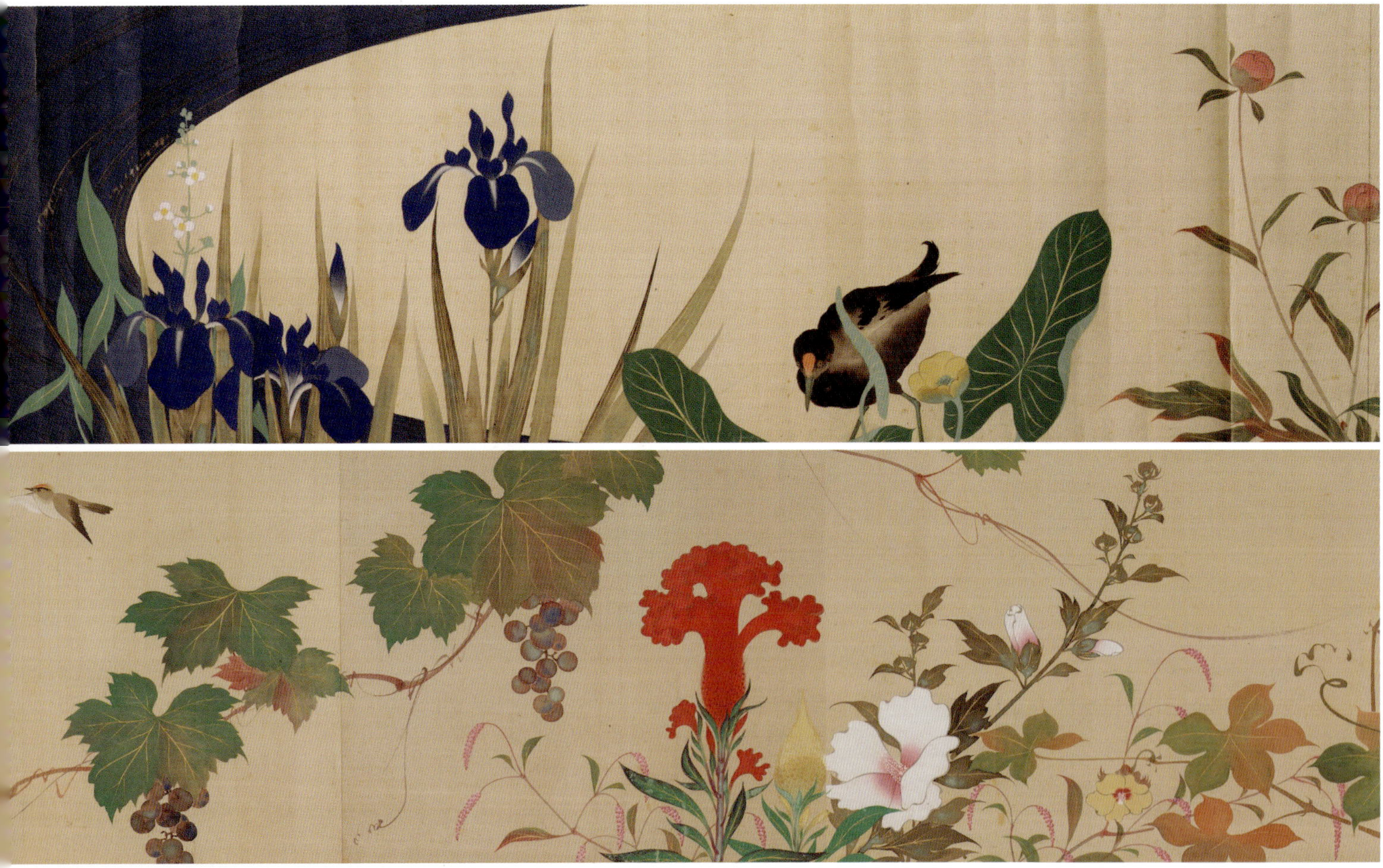

Detail from "Four Seasons of Flowers and Birds Scroll" by Sakai Hōitsu, 1818. Tokyo National Museum. Source: ColBase at https://colbase.nich.go.jp,

82 Konjiiro   70 Ayameiro   92 Budōnezumi/Ebinezumi

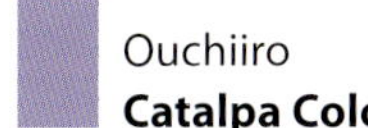
Fujiiro
Wisteria Color

Fujiiro is a representative pale purple color, inspired by the color of wisteria flowers. A softer version of the purple worn by nobility, was a popular color for women's clothing throughout different eras. Due to its association with the Fujiwara clan's flower emblem (wisteria), it was undoubtedly a popular color for warriors as well. During the Edo period, it was often created using a combination of madder and safflower to achieve a clear shade, while a substitute dye using suou (sappanwood) and iron oxide was also commonly employed.

Ouchiiro
Catalpa Color

Ouchiiro is a pale bluish-purple color inspired by the flowers of the *toono* (Japanese pagoda tree) tree. "Ouchi" is an old name for the sandalwood tree, which has been cherished for its pleasant fragrance. However, the term "ouchi" is distinct from "sandalwood," and it was applied to a deciduous tree in the Mahogany family that blooms with light purple flowers in May and June. "Ouchi," the tree's name, comes from the fragrant wood it produces when burned. This color was worn often in late spring and early summer. It's overtone is light purple with an undertone of blue.

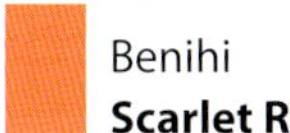
Benihi
Scarlet Red

Benihi is another vivid scarlet color, often used alongside *shoujouhi* with a vivid vermilion hue. It is created by layering yellow-based dyes to achieve a slightly yellowish, vivid red. Compared to the original vermilion dye (*honhi*), which was made from madder using an alum mordant, benihi has a stronger reddish tone. In the medieval period and beyond, due to the complexity of the madder dyeing process, benihi was favored over honhi.

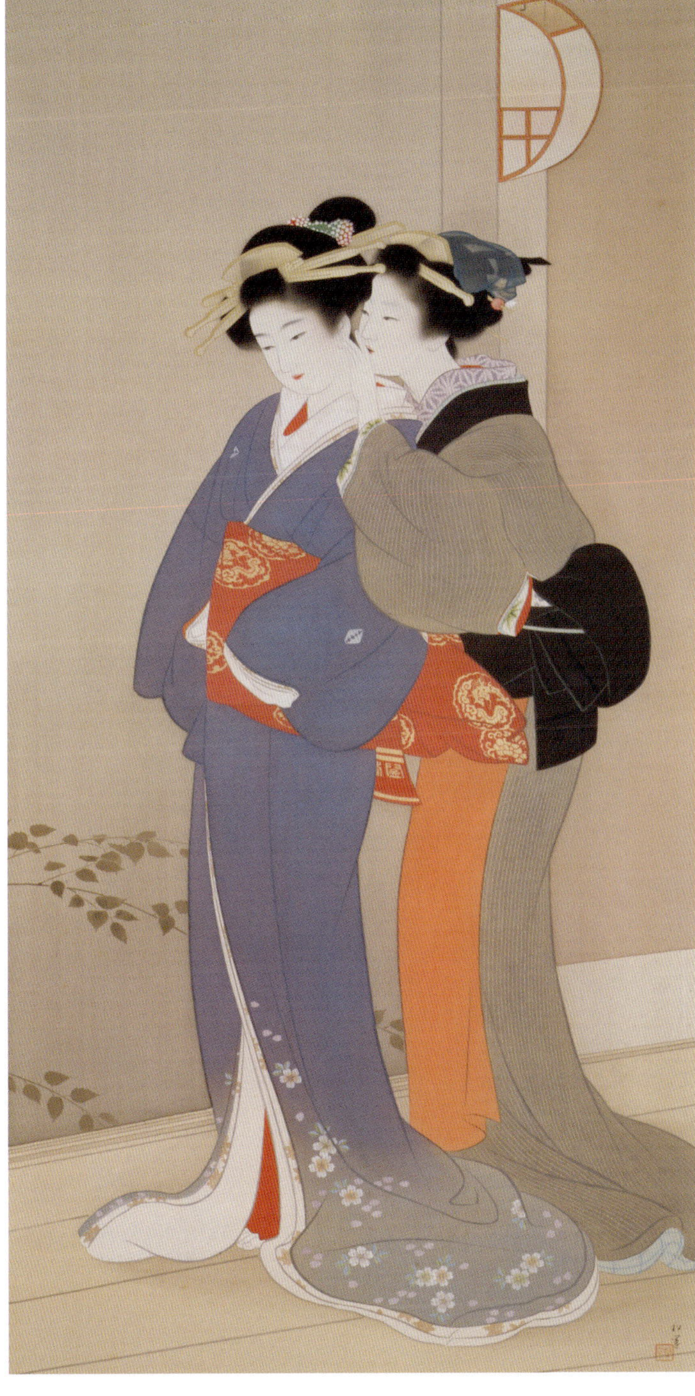

In this picture, a lady wearing a subdued wisteria-colored kimono listens closely as another woman whispers into her ear. The listener's gaze is serene. Graceful evening cherry blossoms adorn the hem of her kimono, depicting a beautiful spring evening moment where the branches of yellow roses settle gently in the dim garden. This expression of feminine beauty through art embodies the unique spirit of the Rinpa School and serves as the basis of its artistic sensibility.

73 Fujiiro   **72 Ouchiiro**   **33 Benihi**

"Spring Evening" by Uemura Shoen, 1936.
Stored in Nara Prefectural Museum of Art.

Hashitairo
Half-color or Intermediate Purple

A light purple color dyed with madder root, used to represent an intermediate or incomplete shade of purple. The term "han" means "between" or "intermediate" but can also mean "end" or "edge." Additionally, it refers to colors that fall between the light and dark shades of purple and crimson, which cannot be expressed by their respective names. It encompasses colors that fall between restricted and permitted colors. In weaving, when the warp threads are thin and the weft threads are also light purple, it is considered "Hanshoku" or an intermediate shade of purple.

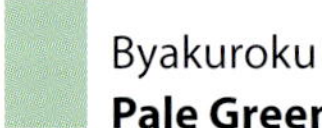

Byakuroku
Pale Green

A light green color with a hint of white. This color is created from the powdered mineral malachite known as *ganryokusei,* which is further ground with water to produce the delicate green color used in Japanese paintings. It has been used for coloring Buddhist statues and paintings since the Nara period.

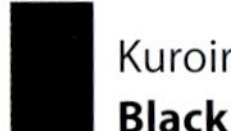

Kuroiro
Black

This, like *shiro* (white) is one of the oldest color names in Japan. During the Heian period, it was made using iron mordant made from white oak charcoal, and later it was made with iron mordant made from gallnuts. Black gradually replaced colors like purple and scarlet for courtiers of the fourth rank or higher. It was also used alongside white for the clothing of monks and priests during festivals and ceremonies.

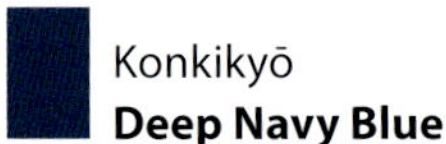

Konkikyō
Deep Navy Blue

A rich, dark blue-purple color created by mixing *kon* (deep blue) with *kikyō* (bellflower). The color name has been used since the Heian period. During the Meiwa period (1764–1772), this color became popular for kimono.

"Six Views of Nagasaki" by Takehisa Yumeji, 1941. National Diet Library Digital Collection.

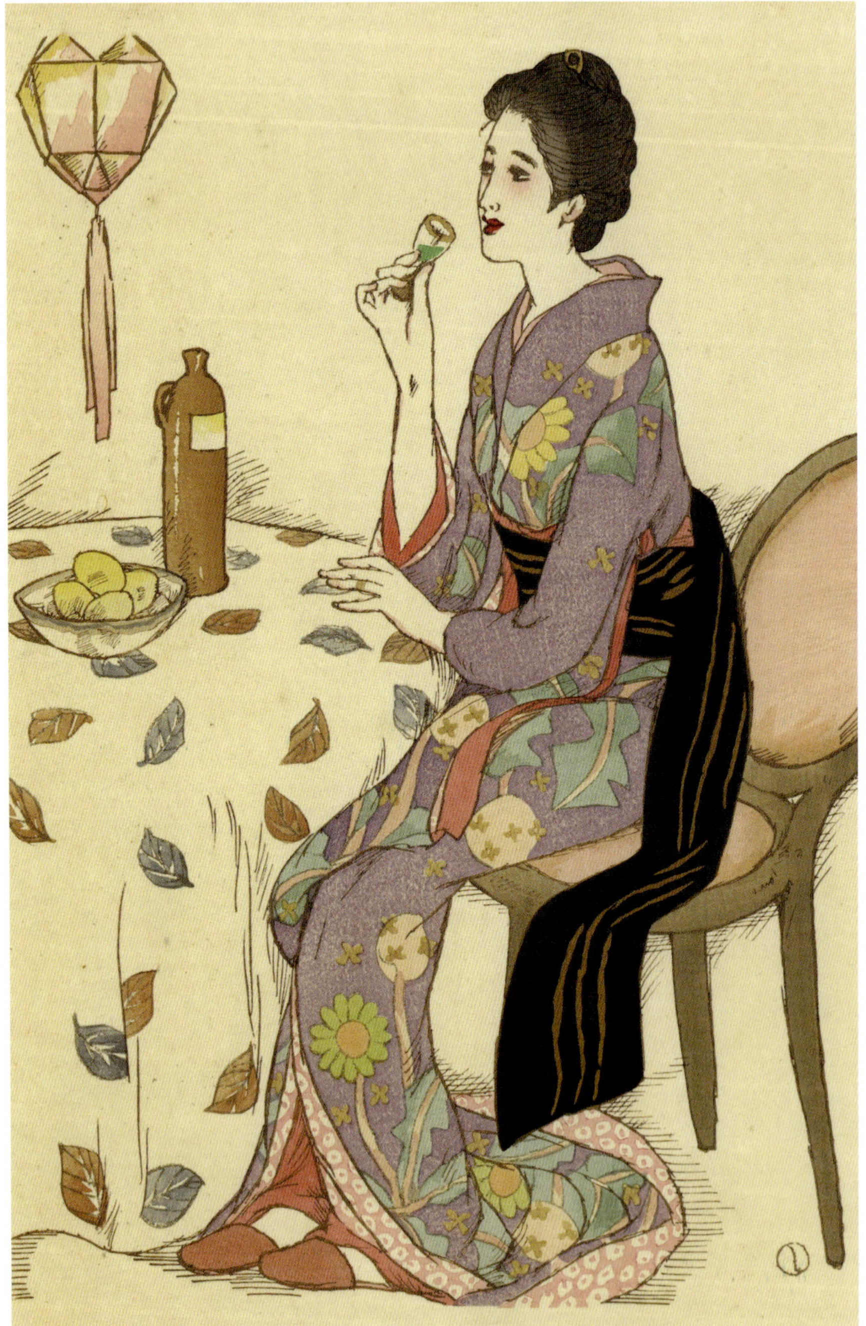

A wine bottle and appetizers sit atop a dainty tablecloth, and an elegant woman is tilting her glass. She wears a deep purple kimono with bold dandelion patterns, and a tightened black obi seems to enhance the scene. Even the casual lantern and the slippers at her feet reveal glimpses of Yumeji's dreamy world.

68 Hashitairo   145 Byakuroku   280 Kuroiro

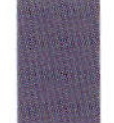

Benifūji
Crimson Wisteria

A pale purple color with a hint of red, resembling the color of wisteria. The dyeing process involves overlaying indigo with *benibana* (safflower) dye. Colors in this elegant wisteria category were popular in the late Edo period, and there are also mentions of "Aifūji" as a color name. While "Fujiiro" was considered suitable for mature women, this soft purple was considered more appropriate for younger women's wardrobes.

Futaai
Dull Bluish-purple

This color is produced by dyeing with two different shades of indigo and safflower (*benibana*) dye. It results in a dull bluish-purple color. This dyeing technique dates back to the Heian period and was characterized by color depth variations that were achieved by adjusting the ratio of indigo to safflower according to the wearer's age. Over time, this technique led to various intermediate and subdued shades.

Yanagizome
Willow Dye

A faintly grayish yellow-green color, reminiscent of willow leaves. Willow trees were admired by aristocrats during the Heian period, and there are references to yanagi colors in literature. However, the specific dyeing technique known as *yanagi-zome* may not have been introduced during that era.

Detail from "Onaidoshi"
by Shimazaki Ryuu, 1908.
Tokyo National Museum.
Source: ColBase at https://colbase.nich.go.jp

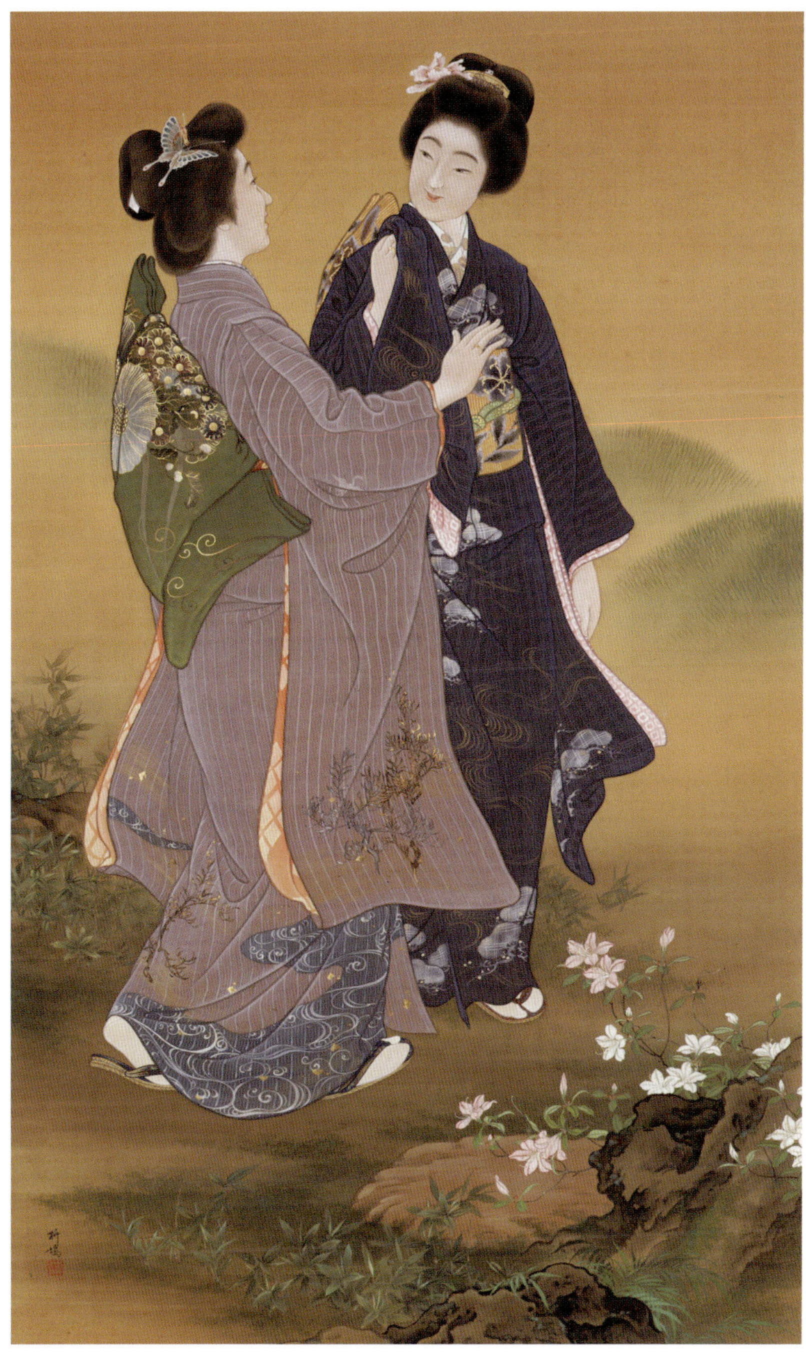

One lady is wearing a light purple furisode with a dark green obi, while the other is dressed in a deep blue kimono. Their relaxed gestures indicate that they are close friends who know each other well. Shimazaki Ryūji (1865–1937) was a Japanese painter during the Meiji to early Showa periods. He initially studied Western-style painting under Kenkichi Sakurai but later switched to traditional Japanese painting. He excelled in *bijinga* (paintings of beautiful women) under the guidance of artists like Matsumoto Fūko and Kawabata Gyokusho.

83 Konkikyō　　66 Benifūji　　74 Futaai　　140 Yanagizome

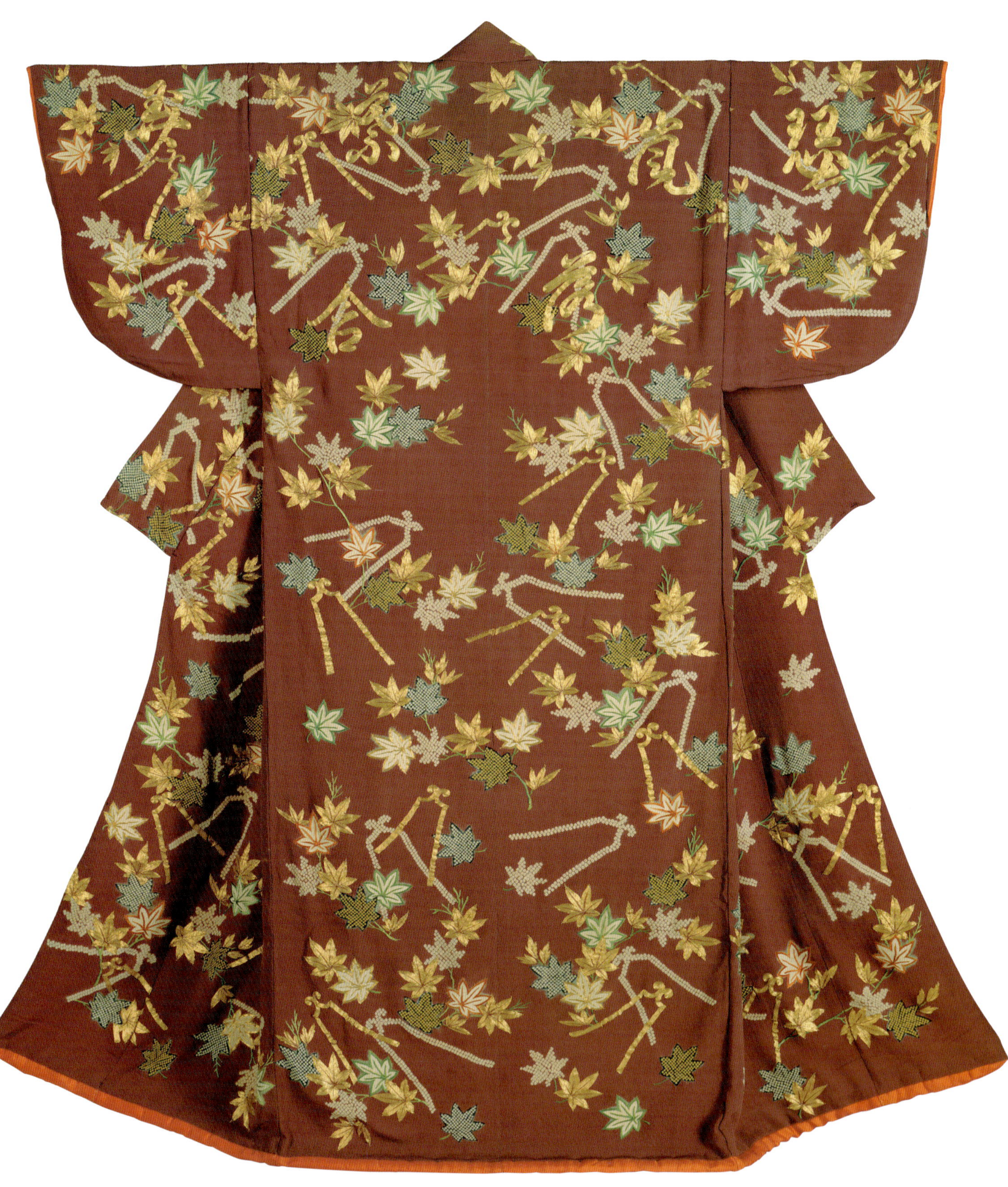

69 Edo Murasaki	**171 Kikuchiba**	**140 Yanagizome**

"Purple Crepe with Koto Pillar, Maple, and Letter Patterns Tie-dyed Sewn Kosode". Edo period, 18th century.
National Museum of Japanese History and Folklore.

The entire surface this shrunken silk fabric features a scattered design of koto (a traditional Japanese string instrument) strings and maple leaves. The gold thread stands out vividly against the rich background color, and contrasts sharply with the *shika* (stencil) pattern. From the sleeves to the main body of the garment, kanji characters from Chinese poems, such as 嵐 (storm), 落 (autumn), and 葉 (leaf), and, are incorporated into the design, blending seamlessly. These are based on the regulated verses from the third year of the Tendoku era (959) recited during the poetry contest in the imperial court by Minamoto no Jun, a poet from the mid-Heian period. The rhyme goes, "Following the storm, leaves contain melancholy; Water splashes on rocks, spring water plays the elegant koto" (from *Waka Rōeishū*, Autumn section).

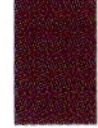

Edo Murasaki
Edo Purple

Meaning "purple dyed in Edo," it refers to a bluish-purple color. In contrast to the traditional purple dyed with the *shikon* root in Kyoto, there's another a version called "Edo Murasaki" dyed with the then-commonly used *suou* plant. The color of the headband worn by Sukeroku in Kabuki's *Sukeroku Yukari no Edozakura* is representative of this hue.

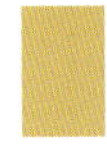

Kikuchiba
Yellowed Autumn Leaves

A color name derived from the hue of decaying fallen leaves, describing a brownish-yellow-orange. In the Heian period's *Rakkōbun* (*A Story of Decay*), references to "kikuchiba-colored Tang clothing" and "a wrapping of light kikuchiba material" suggest it was a favored clothing color back then. Moreover, during this period if was also used for textiles and for weaving, where warp threads were dyed red, and weft threads dyed yellow.

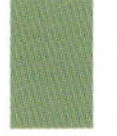

Yanagizome
Willow Dye

This name refers to a color resembling willow leaves, a faintly grayish yellow-green. In the Heian period, the color of willow was included in the color schemes for textiles and weaving, but there is no record of dyeing. The color scheme for textiles was described as "surface: white, reverse: blue" (from *Gan'isho*) and for weaving, it was "warp thread: bright yellow-green, weft thread: white." Willow was beloved by the nobility of the time, and willow-colored attire frequently appears in literature.

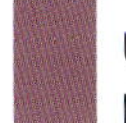

Ume Murasaki
Plum Purple

This refers to the reddish color of red plum blossoms, used for a dull red-purple. "Ume" can refer to both the red color of red plum blossoms and the red color of plum-dyed fabric, and is also used as a modifier to express redness. "Ume nezumi" (plum-gray) can be seen in dye sample books from the late Edo period, so "ume murasaki" (plum-purple) is also considered a relatively new dye color name.

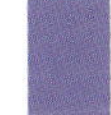

Fuji Murasaki
Wisteria Purple

A slightly deeper color reminiscent of wisteria flowers, with a bluish tint. This color was widely used from the end of the Meiji era to the Taisho era. With the import of chemical dyes, vibrant colors with high chroma were produced and became popular as a sign of Westernized sophistication. This shade was frequently used in kimonos worn by heroines in Meiji literature, from Higuchi Ichiyō to Natsume Sōseki, and in paintings of beautiful women, starting with artists like Kaburaki Kiyokata. Variations of wisteria such as "light wisteria," "red wisteria," "young wisteria," "Komachi wisteria," and "blue wisteria," were created and became widely popular.

Akakōiro
Red Incense Color

This is the color of incense tinged with red. The dye consists of core materials from woods such as agarwood and aloeswood. Incense holds deep ties with Buddhism and holds a position just below purple in terms of prestige. Incense dye comes in various shades depending on the dyeing method; lighter shades are called "usukō" (light incense), while those with a reddish hue are called "akakō" (red incense). Since incense woods were very expensive, alternatives like safflower and knotweed were widely utilized.

This purple kimono is adorned with an arrow-feather pattern created by bundling the warp threads at regular intervals to form a kasuri thread, which is then shifted to produce an arrow-feather-like kasuri pattern. Kasuri patterns are widely used in fabrics like cotton, tsumugi silk, and omeshi silk. Especially during the Meiji to early Showa periods, fine arrow-feather patterns were especially popular with young women.

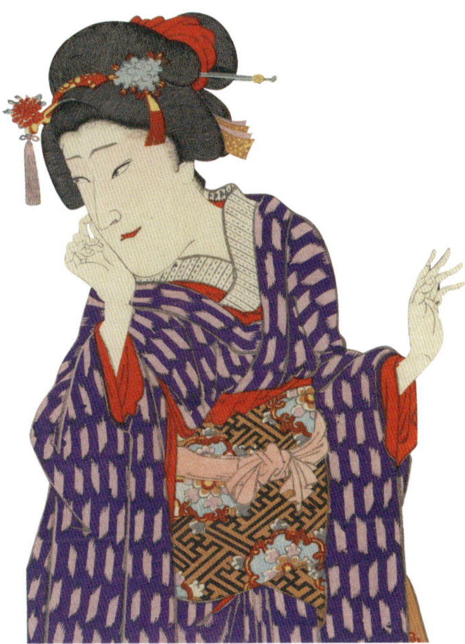

Detail from "Fragrance of Plum Blossom at Shunkai's Haruna" by Kunichika Toyohara, 1893. Yamaguchi Prefectural Hagi Art Museum and Uragami Memorial Museum.

86 Ume Murasaki	**80 Fuji Murasaki**	**41 Akakōiro**

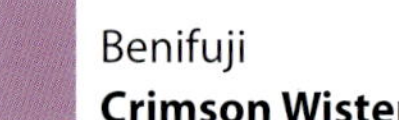

Benifuji
Crimson Wisteria

A wisteria color with a reddish hue, a light shade of purple. The wisteria color created by the intermixing of indigo and red or purple and *suō-ō* (a dye derived from the Rubia cordifolia plant) was popular in the late Edo period. Even today, conventionally, reddish wisteria colors are referred to as "enifujiiro," and bluish wisteria colors are called "aofujiiro."

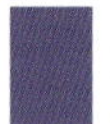

Benikakehanairo
Gentian

It refers to a vibrant bluish-purple color achieved by dyeing over a base dyed with red in floral patterns. During the Edo period, craftsmen sometimes invented new colors, and these color names directly reflected the dyeing process. The book *Tegakami Moyō Setsuyō* states, "Benikake Hanairo. Old, light, then dyed twice with indigo, using both red and blue flowers for dyeing," indicating a color tone that falls within the spectrum of two shades of indigo. Among the color names with a hint of red, there are "Benikake sorairo" (a sky blue with a hint of red) and "Benikake nando" (a deep blue with a hint of red), signifying a sophisticated and cool tone within the bluish-purple range.

Wakatakeiro
Young Bamboo Color

Waka is green color resembling the color of young bamboo, lighter than "Aotake." Bamboo is often depicted in a brighter green to emphasize its youthful appearance. While the color "Aotakeiro" has been known since the Edo period, "Wakatakeiro" as a distinct color name emerged during the Meiji era.

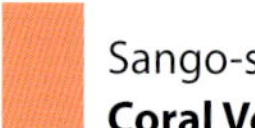

Sango-shuiro
Coral Vermilion

A bright and vivid red-orange color resembling the hue of red coral gemstones. The term "benisango" refers to deeper red corals, while lighter shades are called "tokisango." The powdered red coral was used as a stable pigment in Chinese painting due to its resistance to discoloration and was eventually introduced to Japan. This color is known as "Coral Pink" in English, derived from an ancient Greek term, and it remains in common use today.

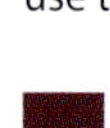

Shikon
Dark Purple Blue

A color created when indigo dye, which inherently contains some redness when dyed deeply, results in a surface with a reddish tinge. This effect is similar to the phenomenon seen in the interaction of colors in a purple shade, thanks to the unique reflection properties of madder dye (red). Similar colors include "nasu-kon," named after the color of eggplant, and "tetsu-kon," a purple-tinged dark blue.

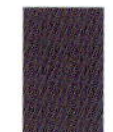

Messhi/Keshimurasaki
Dull Purple

A subdued purple color with a hint of gray. This name can also be read as "Keshi," meaning to suppress or tone down the coloration. It suggests that the color has lost the vibrancy of red or purple hues, resulting in a muted and somewhat dusky shade. During the Heian period, it was considered a high-ranking color after purple, and *Engishiki*, a historical Japanese text, describes three levels of *messhi* dyeing techniques: deep, medium, and light. In the Heian period, purple was the representative color.

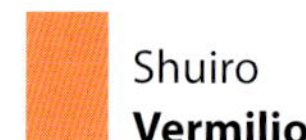

Shuiro
Vermilion

A prominent red color with a slight yellowish hue. Natural vermilion was called *shusa*. High-quality vermilion was obtained from the Chunzhou region in Hunan Province, China. It was often referred to as *shinsha* in reference to its place of origin. On the other hand, artificially produced vermilion using mercury is known as *ginshu*. This color is well-known color among red pigments.

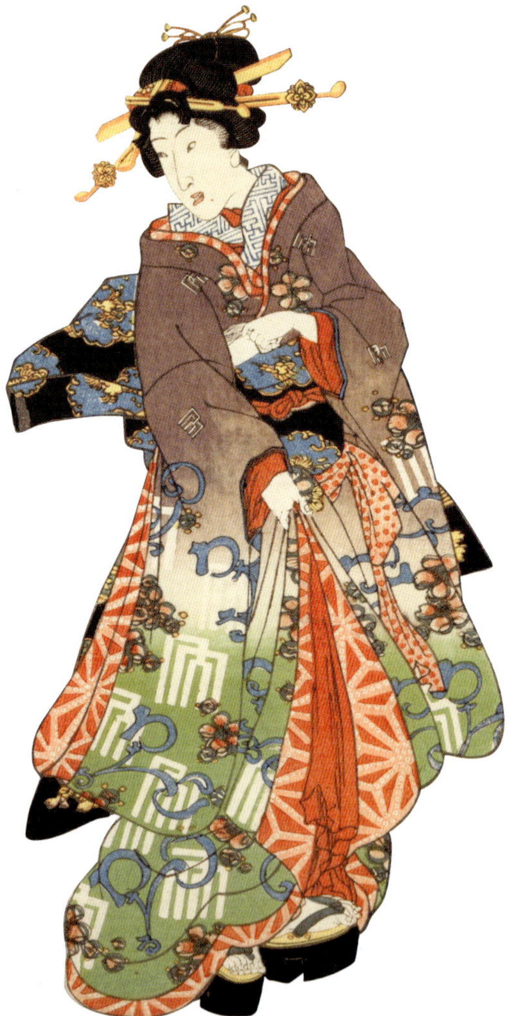

Detail from "Flower Comparison in the Mountains of Asakusa" by Utagawa Kunisada 1857.
National Diet Library Digital Collection.

| 66 Benifuji | 81 Benikakehanairo | 147 Wakatakeiro | 37 Sango-shuiro |

A kosode with a pattern of bamboo arranged in concentric circles on a purple satin ground, combined with plum trees in semicircular snow patterns. It mainly employs a deer pattern *shibori* technique with a purple base. Compared to early Edo period examples, the shibori technique is notably more refined with evenly spaced motifs, representing the typical Genroku style. The distinct boundary between the indigo and purple colors in the shibori indicates a high level of skill and precision in the dyeing process. Although there's no pine tree in the pattern, the plum tree, when rounded and covered with snow, can be interpreted as a pine, resulting in the auspicious "Shōchikubai" motif (pine, bamboo, and plum).

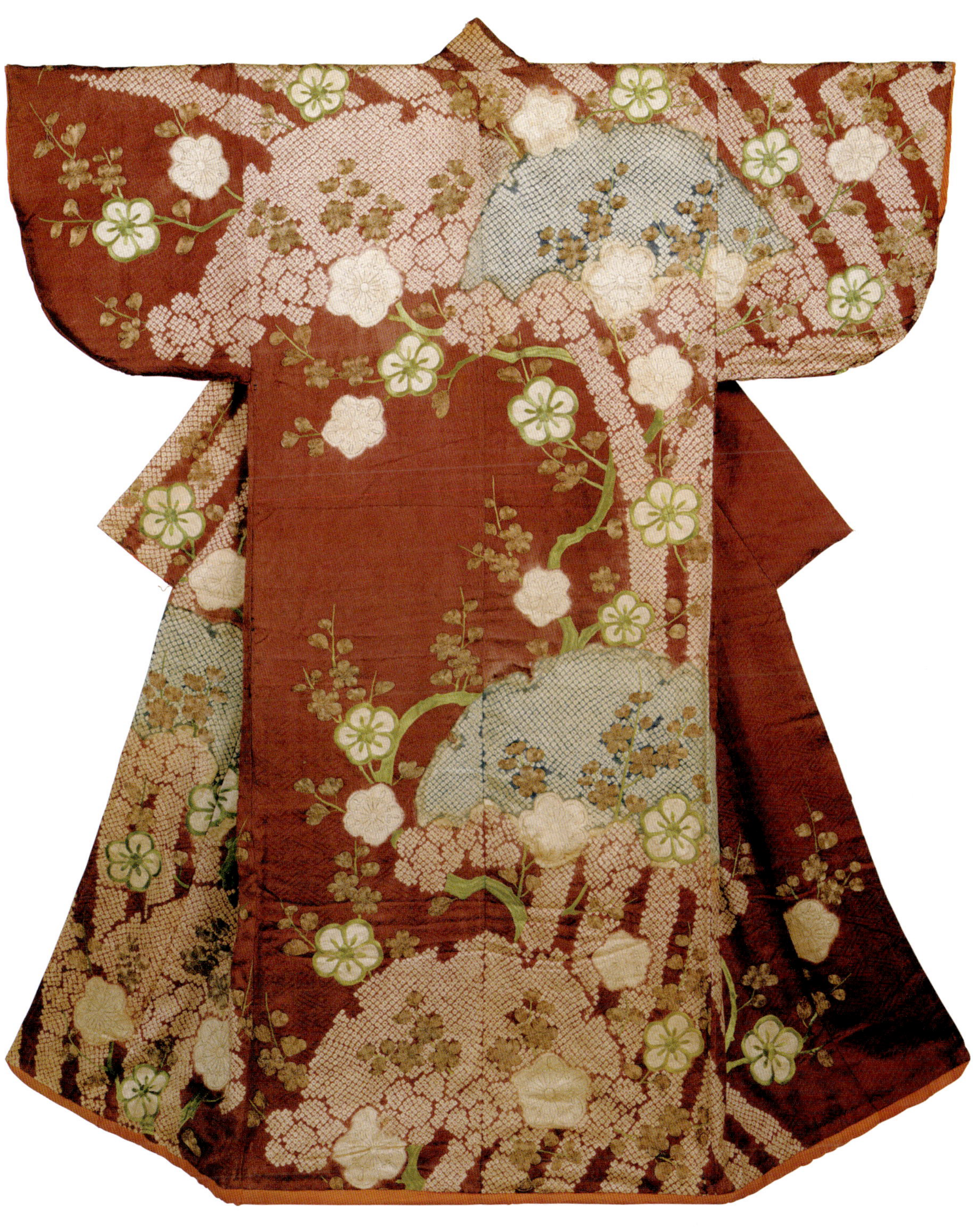

87 Shikon **93 Messhi/Keshimurasaki** **35 Shuiro**

"Purple Lustrous Satin with Plum Tree Pattern Shibori-sewn Kosode". Edo period, 17th-18th century.
National Museum of Japanese History Collection.

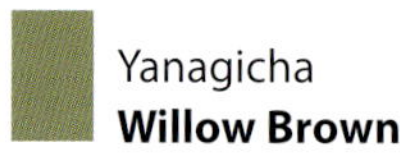

Usuiro
Pale Purple

In common usage, this name generally refers to pale colors. However, in the context of traditional color names, it specifically refers to a light shade of purple made with purple gromwell root and camellia ash or alum. In the context of the highest-ranking color, purple, it is used to distinguish the lighter shades from the darker purples. The dyeing technique is mentioned in the *Engishiki*, where it describes dyeing one *aya* (a type of silk fabric) with about five kilograms of purple root. This amount is only one-sixth of what is needed to achieve a deep purple.

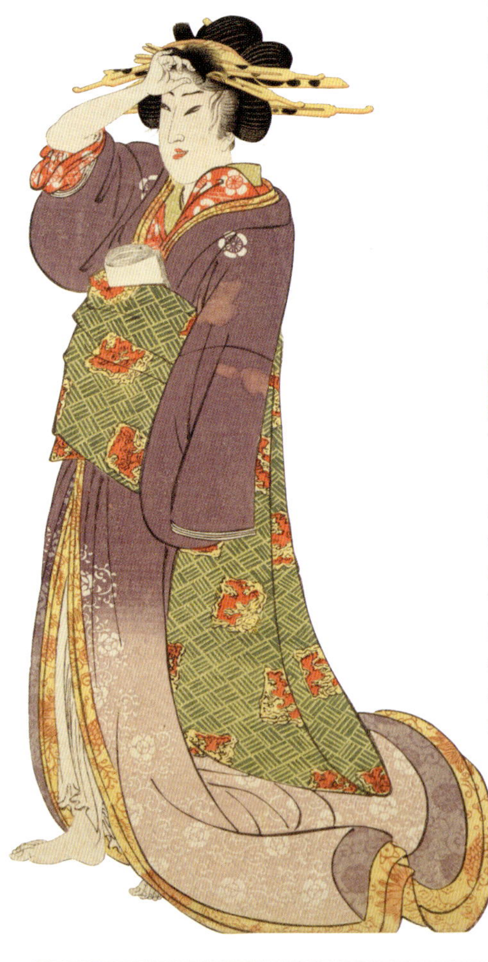

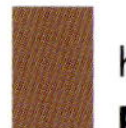

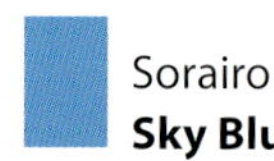

Yanagicha
Willow Brown

This name refers to a color resembling tea with a hint of yellowish-green, roughly the color of dull greenish-yellow reminiscent of willow leaves. In the color chart in the *Tekagami Moyō Setsuyō* (a compendium of patterns and designs), it is also referred to as "Ikokucha," and may be derived from the preference of Tokugawa Yorifusa (son of Tokugawa Ieyasu,) also known as Ikō, for this particular color. Yorifusa favored this color, hence its alternate name being created in his honor.

Murasaki
Purple

This name refers to a rich and glossy purple color achieved through low-temperature processing of purple gromwell root and camellia ash. Purple, along with crimson and blue, has been used since ancient times. When referring to the depth of purple, it is categorized as either dark or light. Purple carried symbolic meanings of nobility and elegance. Although it was officially recognized as a court color in Japan from the "Kanmuryou" system during the reign of Emperor Kotoku in 647, it is believed that even before that, during the reign of Empress Suiko in 603, the color for the highest rank, "Daitoku," was likely purple.

Kakishibuiro/Kakiiro
Persimmon Tannin Color

This is a dull yellowish-red color obtained by crushing unripe persimmons and extracting the liquid, or by dyeing with persimmon tannin or *benibara* (a type of madder root). This color name has been used since the Heian period, derived from the ripe red color of persimmon fruit, and it encompasses a wide range of shades in the orange spectrum. Paper layered with persimmon tannin is called "shibugami" and has been used for raincoats (*amagappa*) and in creating patterns. In Kabuki theater, it's a color associated with the Ichikawa family and is called "Danjurocha."

Detail from "A Collection of Beautiful Women" by Utagawa Toyokuni.
National Diet Library Digital Collection.

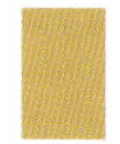

Sorairo
Sky Blue

This is a bright blue color resembling a clear sky on a sunny day. It has been used as a color for undergarments and linings since the early Edo period. It is considered a medium shade, as it is lighter than "hanairo" (flower colors) but darker than "asagi" (light blue). This color name has been in use since the Edo period and was favored during the Genroku era. It was used for samurai's ceremonial cords, linings of men's garments, workwear, and undergarments. During the Meiji and Taisho periods, even cobalt blue was sometimes referred to as sky blue. Today, it typically denotes a pale blue with a hint of purple is considered sky blue, while a lighter version is considered aqua.

Kikuchiba
Yellowed Autumn Leaves

A color resembling the brownish-yellow hue of fallen leaves as they decay. In *The Tale of Genji* a passage reads, "The very fine, delicate hues of decayed leaves, scattered and pounded into a fine powder, filled the air." Yellow decayed leaves are also mentioned in Heian literature, often associated with the end of autumn and the beginning of winter attire. Some theories equate "tan decayed leaves" with "yellow decayed leaves."

In the deep mountains, snow-capped flowering trees grow in clusters. Beautifully arranged cranes, pheasants, or hawks perch on pine branches, resting their wings, against the backdrop of the cascading waterfall. At the hem are illustrations such as bows and arrows, falcon hoods, quivers, hats, and hunting dogs, suggesting a scene of a day's hunting. The flowering trees, waterfalls, and plants are resist-dyed, and after dyeing the background in purple and applying a white underlayer, blue brushwork is added to the waterfalls. Various embroidery techniques are employed to create rich and intricate decorations.

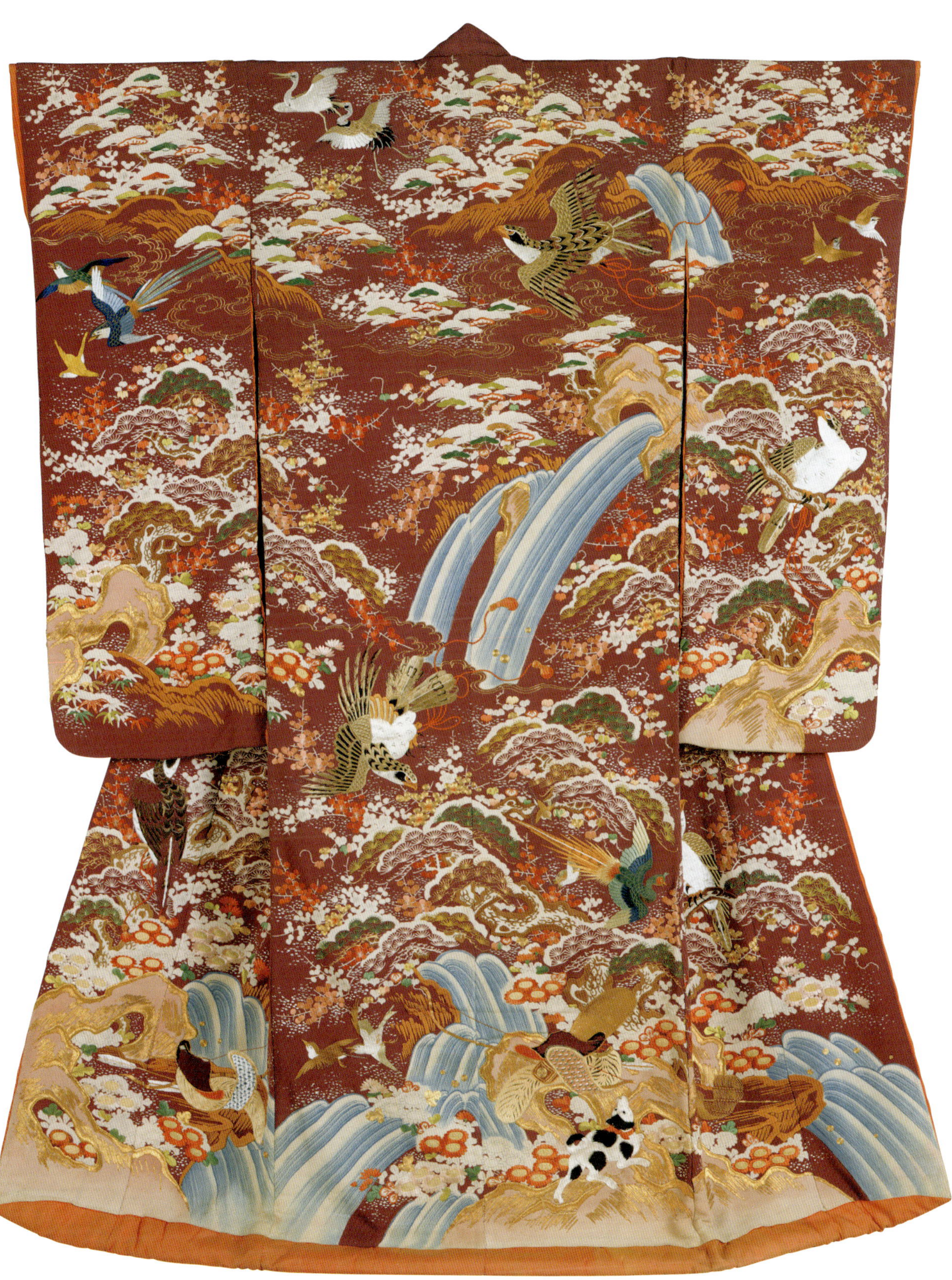

84 Murasaki   56 Kakishibuiro/Kakiiro   103 Sorairo   171 Kikuchiba

"Purple Shusu Silk Furisode with Falconry Pattern Dyed and Embroidered".
Edo period, 19th century.
National Museum of Japanese History Collection.

Layered Color Palettes in the Tale of Genji

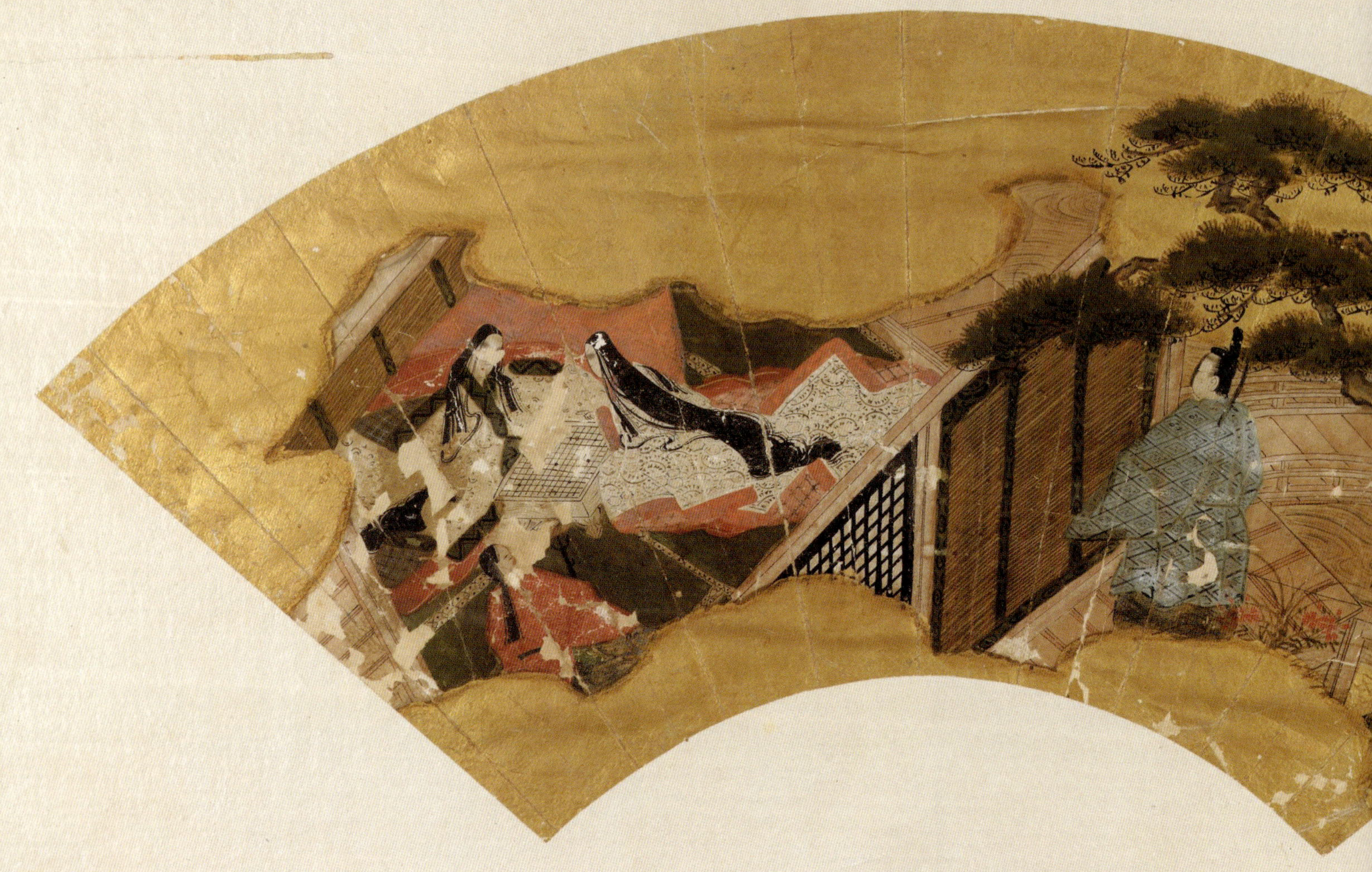

"Illustration of The Tale of Genji on a Folding Fan (Utsusemi)" Muromachi Period, 16th century.
Tokyo National Museum. Source: ColBase at https://colbase.nich.go.jp

"Kasane no irome" refers to the layered colors visible when wearing a kimono with both its outer fabric and lining showing, or when layers of kimono overlap, revealing hues at the sleeves, collar, and hem. Even if the same color is worn in a set season, it may be referred to by different names according to the season. Furthermore, the color combinations can vary depending on the type of kimono garment or according to family traditions. In the Heian period, men wore *nou* (directly-dyed garment), *karigi* (hunting garment), and *shitagasane* (undergarment), while women wore combinations of outer and inner fabrics such as *kara-koromo* (Tang Chinese garment), *uchigi* (lined garment), and *hosonaga* (narrow garment), or layered colors such as *itsutsuginu* (five-layer garment) and *hitoe* (single-layer garment), with specific colors determined by season and age for both genders. Women would refine their sense of color coordination and enjoy competing with each other in layering and color choices, enhancing the beauty of their outfits day by day. Reflecting their love for the changing seasons, the names of colors were often based on seasonal flowers, resulting in over 180 variations of color combinations for kasane. This appreciation for layered colors continued into the Edo period, influencing the designs of kosode (short-sleeved kimono), which often featured two or three layers.

SPRING COLORS

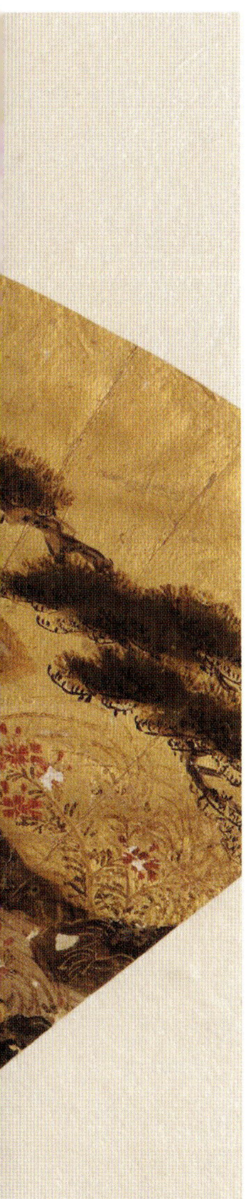

Crimson Plum
(Koubai)

**Outer: Crimson Plum/
Inner: Safflower**

**Wearing Period: Winter
to spring, especially on
festive occasions. Young
people wear it until
January 15th.**

This design imitates the color of red plum blossoms. While white plum blossoms are enjoyed for their fragrance, red plum blossoms are appreciated for the vividness of their petals' color. Color names associated with red plum blossoms include "Beni-ume-nioi" (scent of red plum blossoms), "Tsubomi-beni-ume" (bud of red plum blossom), "Uramasari-beni-ume" (inner sohō red plum blossom), and "Setsushita-beni-ume" (snow below red plum blossom).

Birch Cherry
(Kabazakura)

**Outer: Safflower/
Inner: Red Flower**

Wearing Period: Spring.

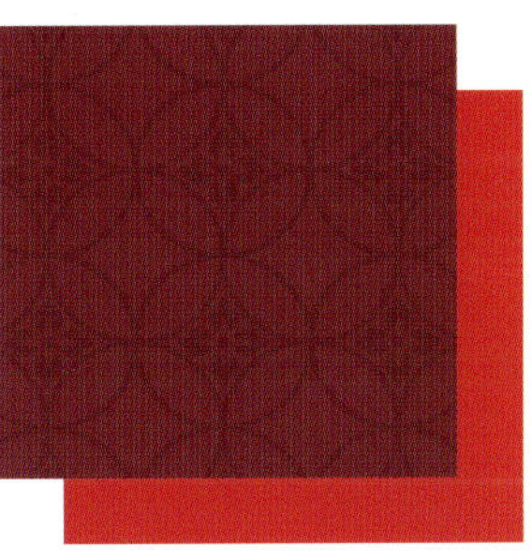

Kabazakura, or "Birch Cherry," is an old name for the Uwamizuzakura, which is a type of cherry tree resembling the birch tree's bark. There are two theories about this color: one that it's inspired by the tree's flowers and another that it's named after the color of cherry bark used by woodworking craftsmen to bind bentwood pieces together.

White Wisteria
(Shirafuji)

**Outer: Light Purple/
Inner: Deep Purple**

Wearing Period: Spring.

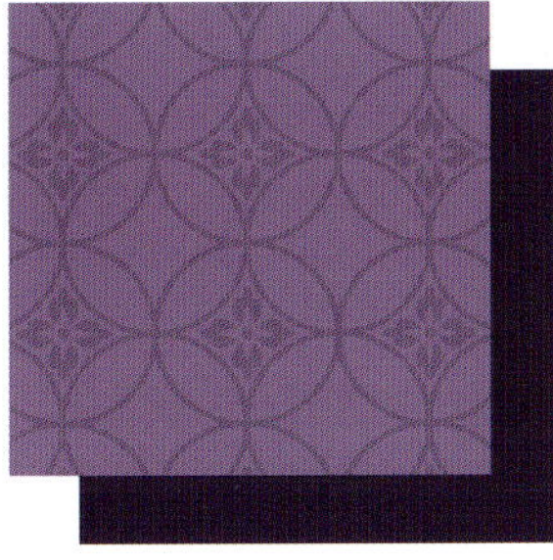

The name indicates the variation of wisteria called "Shirobanafuji," (white wisteria) but the color on the surface is not white; instead, it's a pale purple similar to the color of regular purple wisteria. There are no mentions of garments of this color in Heian literature, suggesting it might be a color from later periods.

Plum (Ume)

**Outer: White/
Inner: Safflower**

**Wearing Period: From
November to February
of the following year.**

In the still-chilly air of early spring, when the skin is still tinged by the cold, this design captures the color of blooming white plum blossoms. The white of the outer fabric represents the color of the blossoms, while the inner lining of "Sohō" (vermilion) represents the color of the tree's trunk and branches. Color names associated with plum blossoms include "Ichijōbai" (single-layer plum), "Baibai" (plum overlay), "Urame" (inner plum), and "Shiraume" (white plum).

Willow (Yanagi)

**Outer: White/
Inner: Light Blue**

**Wearing Period: From
winter to spring.**

This design represents the new buds of catkin willow, displaying white downy growth at the tips of its branches. The color of willow is also referred to as "Usuyanagi" (pale willow), derived from its light green hue. Color names associated with willow include "Omoyanagi" (facial willow), "Kiganagi" (yellow willow), "Aoyanagi" (green willow), "Hana-yanagi" (flowering willow), and "Yanagi-cho" (willow overlay).

Cherry Bud Green
(Sakuramoegi)

**Outer: Bud Green/
Inner: Red Flower**

Wearing Period: Spring.

This color suggests mountain cherry trees viewed through branches with budding green leaves. The red beneath suggests the hint of red in the newly-sprouted young leaves. Depending on the type of attire, one theory suggests the inner lining may be purple or indigo, while the outer fabric may be blue or indigo as well.

SUMMER COLORS

Mugwort (Yomogi)
Outer: Light Pale Green/
Inner: Deep Pale Green
Season: Summer
This color represents the color of mugwort leaves that grow during the summer. This plant grows in the mountains and has a distinctive scent. It has been traditionally used to ward off evil spirits. It is often placed at the eaves of houses along with irises during the Children's Day festival, and it is also common to put it in bathwater.

Iris Laevigata
(Kakitsubata)
Outer: Light Pale Green/
Inner: Light Pink Plum
Season: Summer, April, May
This color represents the reddish-plum color of the irises that bloom in wetlands in early summer. While the color of irises is generally a deep purple, in this case, it is depicted as light pink plum or *futai* (pale purplish-blue) in layered color combinations.

Wild Orange
(Tachibana)
Outer: Deep Decayed Leaf/
Inner: Yellow
Season: Summer
This color represents the hue of ripe tachibana oranges, known in ancient times as "Kishu mikan" or "Kouji mikan." The tachibana tree, also called "Ukonn," stands on the western side of the lower terrace of the southern part of the Shishinden Hall in the Kyoto Imperial Palace. There are numerous ancient poems dedicated to tachibana, but attire inspired by them is not found in Heian literature.

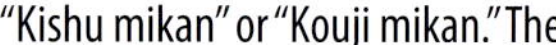

Lily (Yuri)
Outer: Red/
Inner: Decayed Leaf
Season: Summer
This color represents the flowers of the princess lily that grow in the early summer in mountainous areas. While these flowers come in yellow and red varieties, this color mainly depicts the dark red ones rather than the white ones. Lilies are perennial plants found primarily in temperate regions, and many varieties are cultivated for horticultural purposes.

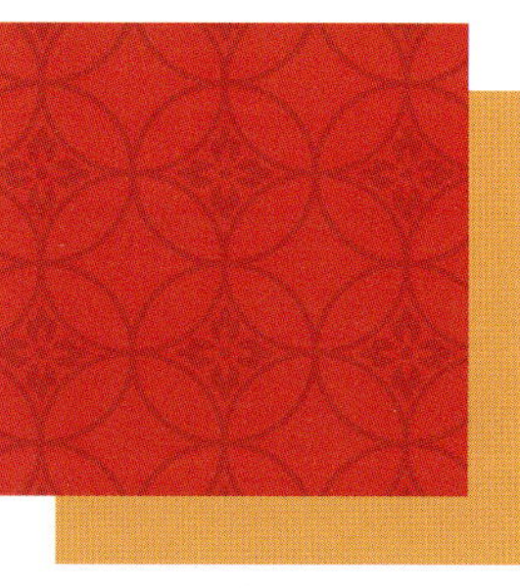

Summer Bush Clover
(Natsu Hagi)
Outer: Blue/
Inner: Deep Purple
Season: Summer
This color represents the summer-blooming bush clover, which blooms with purple-red flowers amidst lush green foliage. Bush clover is typically associated with autumn flowers, so the summer-blooming variety would have been considered unusual. There are many poems dedicated to autumn bush clover, but few to the summer-blooming variety.

Dianthus (Nadeshiko)
Outer: Red/
Inner: Light Purple
Season: April, May, and sometimes June
This represents a color inspired by the delicate flowers of the dianthus plant that grows wild in the mountains and fields from summer to autumn. Color names associated with dianthus include "Hiro nadeshiko" (white dianthus), "Hana nadeshiko" (flower dianthus), "Kara nadeshiko" (Korean dianthus), and "Nadeshiko no wakabairo" (dianthus young leaf color).

AUTUMN COLORS

Patrinia Scabiosifolia
(Ominaeshi)
**Outer: Pale Green (Length-
wise) and Yellow (Crosswise)/
Inner: Blue**
Season: July and August
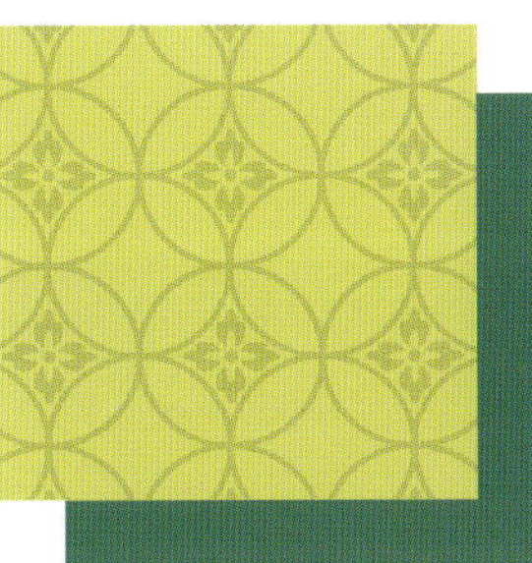
This color represents the shade
of *ominaeshi* flowers, which
bloom with numerous small yellow
florets from late summer to autumn. It reflects the slightly
greenish color of the flower. Ominaeshi, a member of the
honeysuckle family, is one of the "Seven Flowers of Autumn." It
is also known as Maiden flower or Damsel flower.

Gentiana Scabra
(Rindō)
**Outer: Pale Susuki (Japanese
pampas grass)/Inner: Blue**
**Season: Autumn, from Sep-
tember to the 5th lunar term**
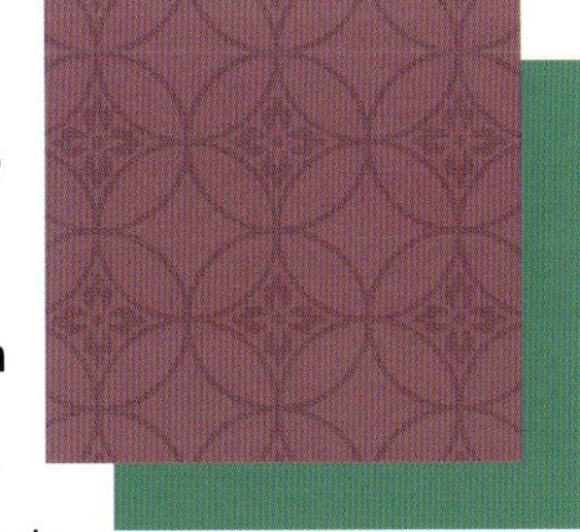
This color represents the bell-
shaped, blue-purple flowers of
the gentian (*rindō*) that grow in the
wild and bloom in the autumn. By using a light madder on the
surface, the color appears more vibrant than the actual flower.
It has medicinal properties in its roots and has been used since
ancient times as an antiseptic and tonic.

Autumn Leaf
(Momiji)
Outer: Red/Inner: Deep Red
Season: Autumn

This color represents the
appearance of maple leaves
turning red or yellow due to
frost in late autumn. Among the
various trees, the red maple leaves
are particularly beautiful. The term "momiji" originally referred
to the action of extracting colors, not a specific tree's leaves.

Bush Clover (Hagi)
Outer: Purple/Inner: White
Season: June and July

This color represents the
purplish-red color of the bush
clover (*hagi*) flowers that bloom
in the mountains during late
summer. Hagi is a plant that
evokes a strong sense of autumn for
Japanese people. From the Heian period onwards, hagi was depicted in various forms, including lacquerware, cloisonné, and
yuzen dyeing, and it became popular as a high-end art form.

Decayed Leaf
(Kuchiba)
**Outer: Deep Red/
Inner: Deep Yellow**
Season: Autumn

This represents the color of
withered and decaying fallen
leaves, and there are three main
color systems within this palette:
red, yellow, and blue. The color described here is a standard yel-
low-orange. Both the hunting garment (*kariginu*) and the inner
lining of the trousers (*akome*) are dyed yellow, while the outer
withered leaves may have shades of yellow, red, or blue, resulting in layered colors referred to as "Kikuchiba" (yellow-brown),
"Akakuchiba" (red-brown), and "Aokuchiba" (blue-brown).

Aster Tataricus
(Shion)
**Outer: Purple/Inner: Susuki
(Japanese pampas grass)**
Season: Autumn
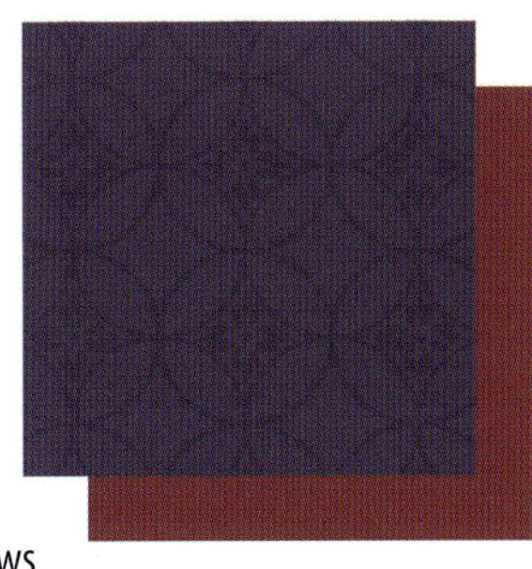
This color represents the pale
purple flowers of the *aster
tataricus* (*shion*), a perennial
herb in the daisy family that grows
in mountainous grasslands and blooms with numerous light
purple flowers in the autumn. Shion was cultivated in gardens
for its beautiful color. It is believed to have been introduced
from China or Korea as a medicinal plant in ancient times.

WINTER COLORS

Ice (Kōri)
Outer: White/Inner: Blue
Season: Winter

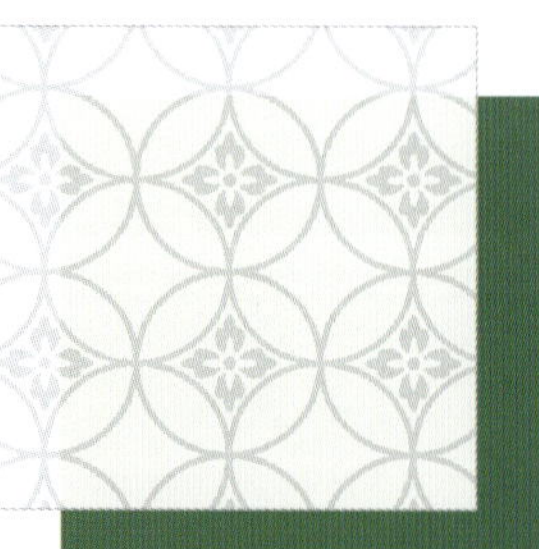

This color represents the whiteness of ice. While the outer and inner colors appear monotonous at first glance, they can be enhanced by polishing with clam shells, striking with a kizuchi (a type of wooden mallet) to add gloss, or applying sizing to create variations.

Under the Snow
(Yuki no Shita)
Outer: White/Inner: Light Pink Plum
Season: From Winter to Spring

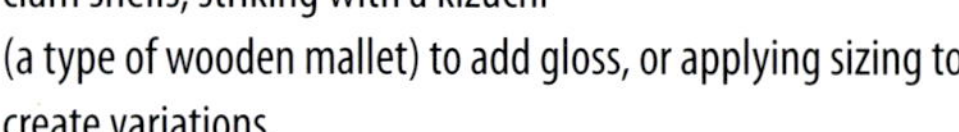
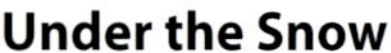

This represents the color of red plum blossoms lightly covered with snow, also known as "Snow Under Red Plum Blossoms." There is no mention of garment of this color in Heian literature, but it appears in *Otogi-zōshi* from the Muromachi period: "The boy, happily thinking about it <omitted> many things kept under the snow."

Withered Grass Color
(Kareiro)
Outer: Light Brown/
Inner: Blue
Season: Winter

This represents the color of grass and flowers in a winter-browned field, appearing a pale brown hue. When used in winter, it evokes the lingering essence of autumn, reminiscent of warm winter days spent wandering through dried-up meadows.

Heavy Ice (Kōri-kasane)
Outer: Torinokoiro (A pale yellow-gray)/Inner: White
Season: Winter

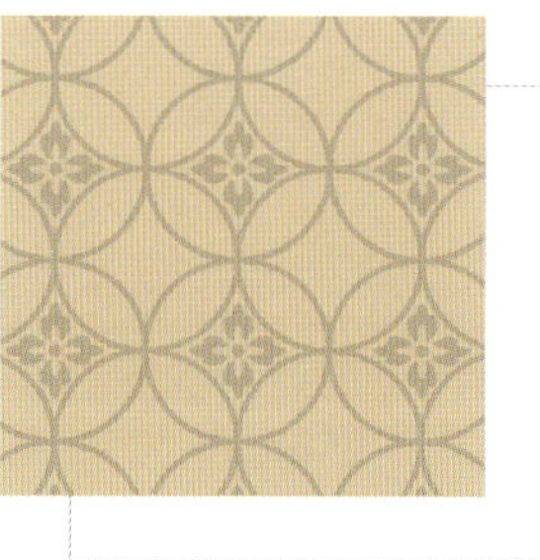

This color represents the appearance of ice. While it is similar to kōri, the outer color is "Torinokoiro," which is a pale grayish-yellow color introducing a variation in the white color scheme.

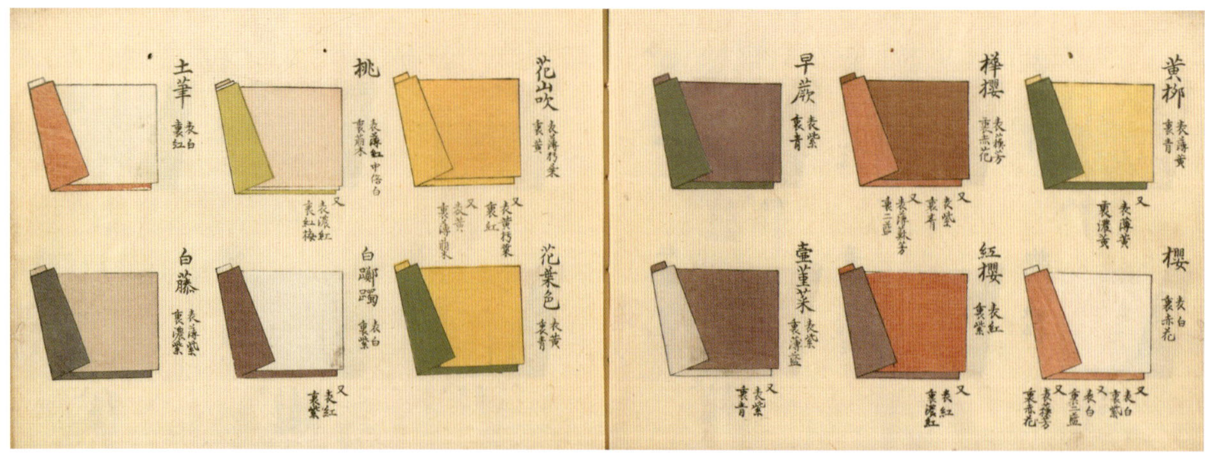

Pages from the *Jūshoku-mokuroku* by *Inokai Masataka*, published 1817.
National Diet Library Digital Collection.

VERSATILE COLORS FOR ANY SEASON

Pine (Matsukasane)
Outer: Blue/Inner: Purple
Season: All Seasons

This represents the pine tree, known for maintaining its greenery throughout the four seasons, making it a timeless color. The blue on the front represents the color of the leaves, while the purple on the back represents the trunk. Pine trees, due to their evergreen nature, have been revered in literature and art as auspicious trees.

Grape (Ebizome)
Outer: Sōhō (A reddish-purple)/Inner: Hachijō (A pale blue)
Season: All Seasons

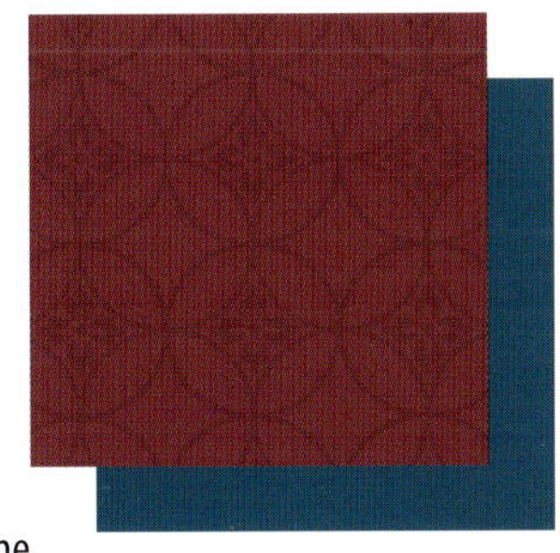

This represents the color of the fruit of the mountain grapevine, known as "Ebizome." It seems to have been a favored color since the Heian period. In dyeing, it refers to a light purple with a reddish tint due to shikon (purple root), but in weaving, there may be slight differences, with the warp being dyed in red or crimson and the weft being dyed in purple.

Cinnabar Fragrance (Suōkō)
Outer: Sōhō (a reddish-purple)/Inner: Yellow
Season: All Seasons

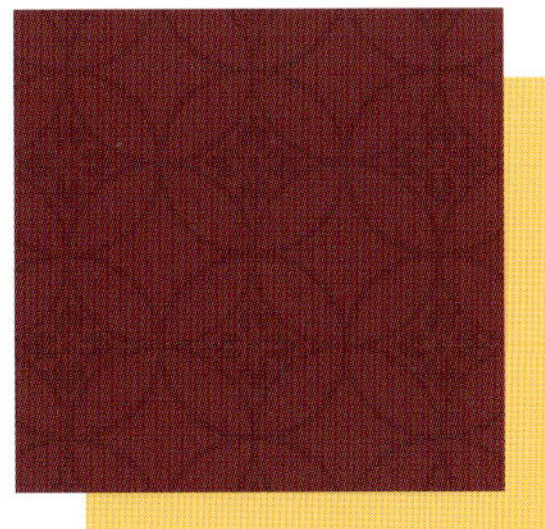

The term refers to a color reminiscent of the dye of the Suōkō tree. Suōkō (literally "aromatic Suō") is a reddish-brown color obtained by adding yellow to Suō's red. However, the layered color of Suōkō also incorporates yellow on the reverse side, resembling the dyed color. While Suōkō dyeing traditionally involves the use of Suō and cloves, commonly, yellow dye is used in place of cloves.

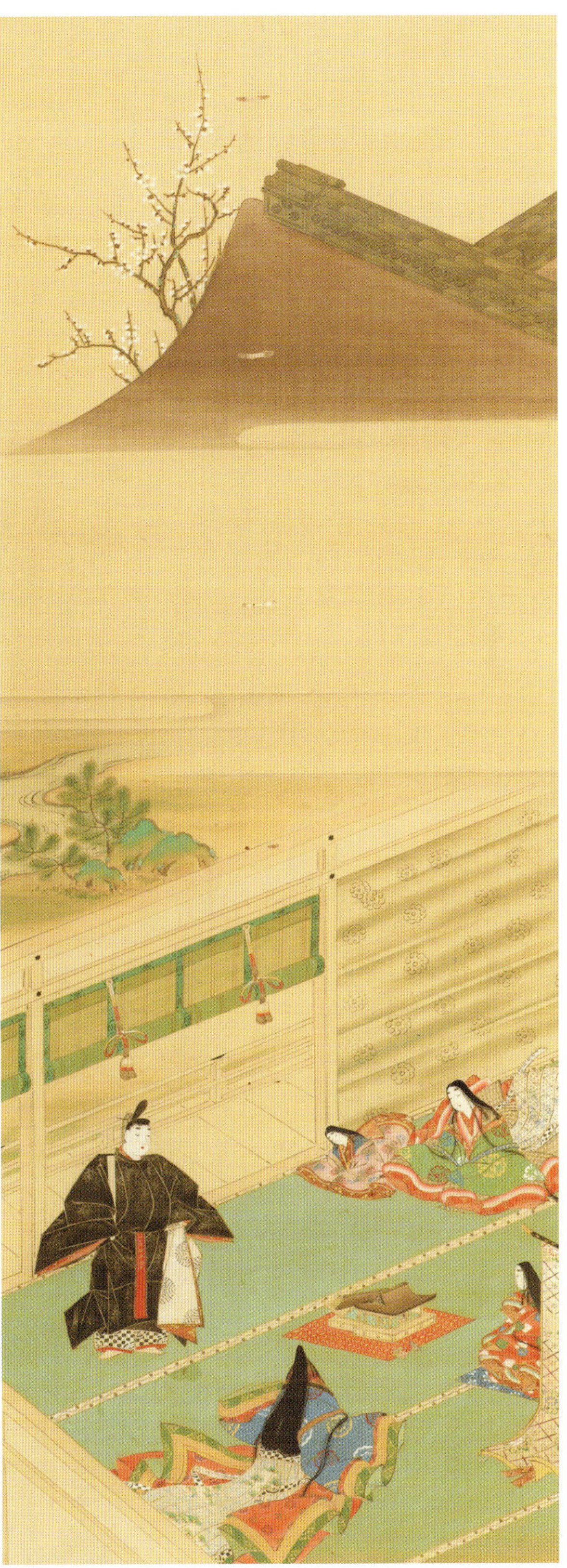

Detail from "The Tale of Genji Illustration: 'Momiji no Ga'"
by Sumiyoshi Hironao. Edo period, 19th century
Tokyo National Museum. Source: ColBase at https://colbase.nich.go.jp

The Color Blue in Japanese Culture

All of us here on Earth coexist with the color blue, born from the blue sky and deep blue sea. Blue has been a symbol of mystery and eternity transcending time and space. The first things we associate with this color sky and water, evoking sensations of coldness and coolness. Blue has always been a sacred color, carrying spiritual significance alongside religious emotions in Western culture, and it is humanity's most beloved color.

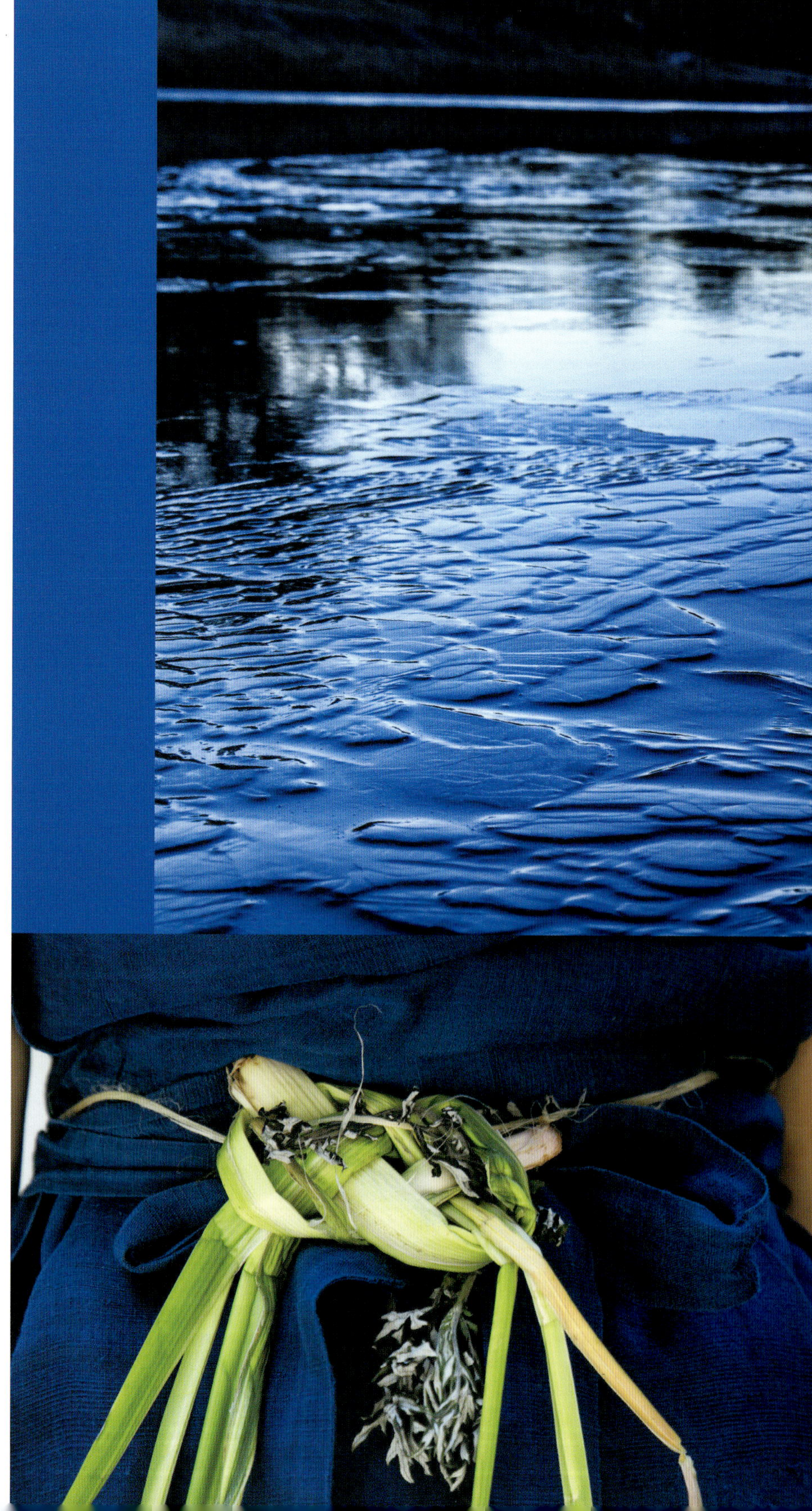

Top Ice—Kamogawa River, Kyoto.
Bottom right Misogi (Purification) Ritual—Kamigamo Shrine, Kyoto.
Middle bottom Hydrangeas—Zenrinji Temple, Kyoto.
Bottom far right Horse Racing Ritual—Kamigamo Shrine, Kyoto.

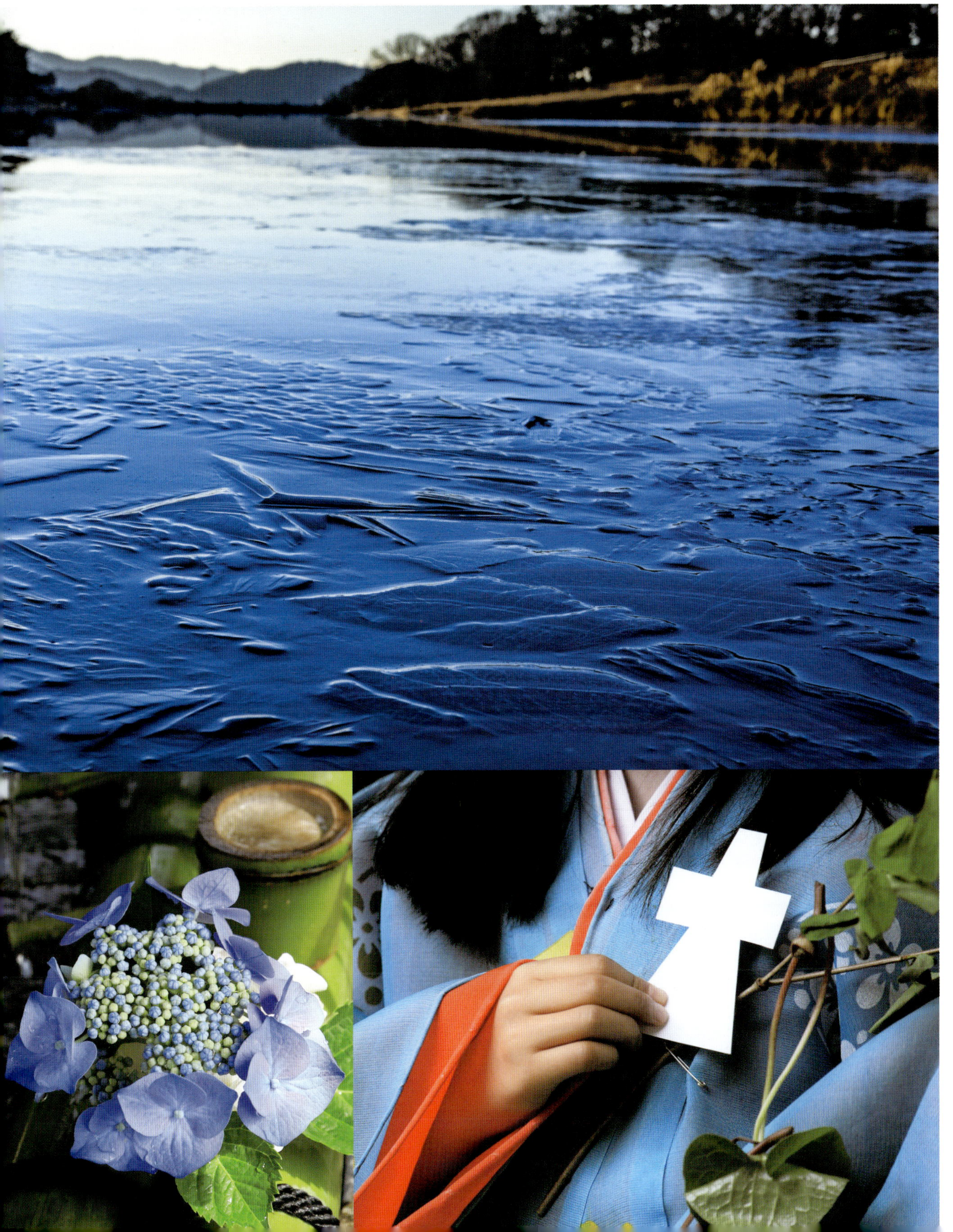

Japanese Color Schemes Based on Blue

Blue encompasses a wide range of hues spanning between blue and green, as seen in expressions like "blue sky," "blue sea," "green leaves," and "green grass." Nowadays, words like "red," "blue," "white," and "black" are used as adjectives to describe colors, but originally they indicated brightness and intensity. "Bright," "vague," "evident," and "dark" corresponded to these four colors, with red representing brightness, white indicating conspicuousness, black signifying darkness, and blue conveying an intermediate shade, encompassing gray and green as well.

In ancient Chinese Yin-Yang theory, there were five elements: wood (blue), fire (red), earth (yellow), metal (white), and water (black). Blue was associated with wood and listed as the first primary color.

The perception of blue is not unrelated to association or symbolism. It can evoke feelings of clarity, coldness, strength, and a somewhat masculine aura. Additionally, attributes like silence, coolness, depth, and loneliness are often associated with blue, resembling sharp nuances.

Compared to colors like red, blue appears slightly receded when placed in the same position, hence referred to as a "receding color." Falling into the cool color spectrum, blue can be considered a representative color of the cool spectrum in a sense.

Combining colors within the same color range may result in a too cold impression, so it's advisable to pair blue with colors slightly further away. Similar hues like purple or violet, which share a bluish tone, can create a sense of warmth. Blue is often paired with complementary colors like red, orange, and yellow, producing a clear and vivid effect. Among blue tones, azure and navy blue are commonly used in art and decoration, while triadic color schemes involving golden and red hues represent traditional basic forms.

Color Scheme Based on Light Tones

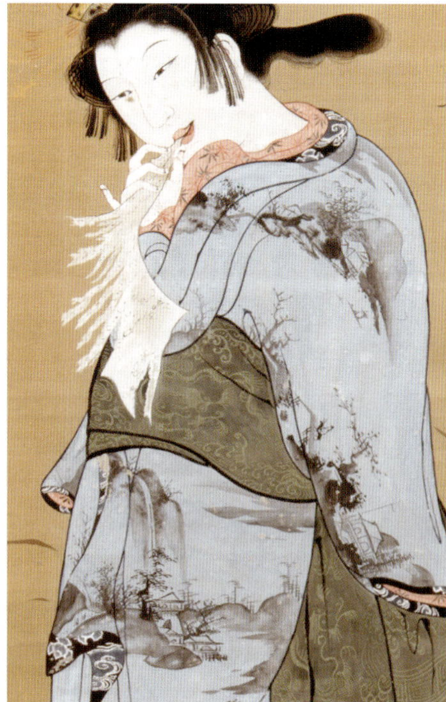

Detail from "Portrait of a Beauty" by Soga Shōhaku.
Edo period, 18th century.
Nara Prefectural Museum of Art.

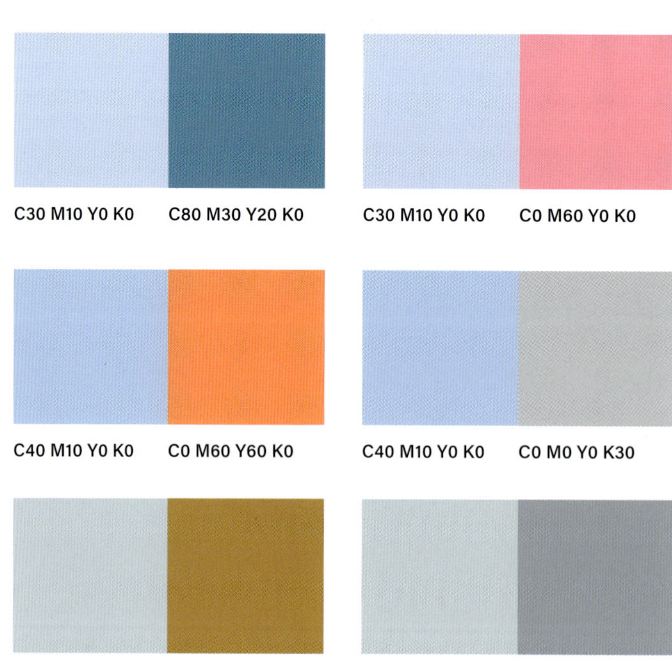

C30 M10 Y0 K0	C80 M30 Y20 K0	C30 M10 Y0 K0	C0 M60 Y0 K0
C40 M10 Y0 K0	C0 M60 Y60 K0	C40 M10 Y0 K0	C0 M0 Y0 K30
C30 M10 Y10 K0	C35 M50 Y80 K0	C30 M10 Y10 K0	C50 M30 Y20 K0

Color Scheme Based on Vivid Colors

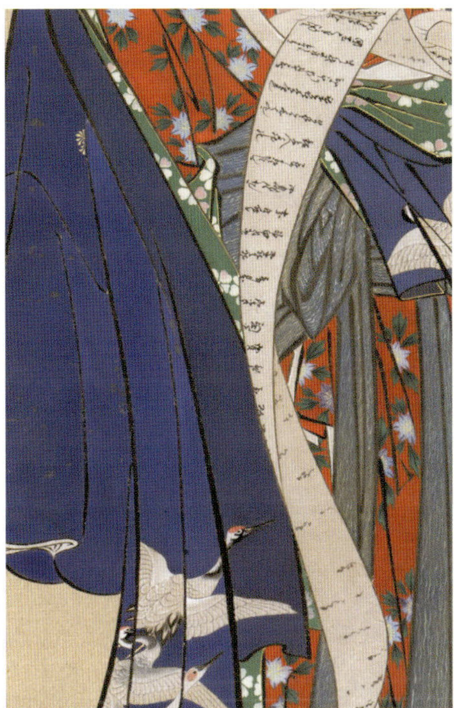

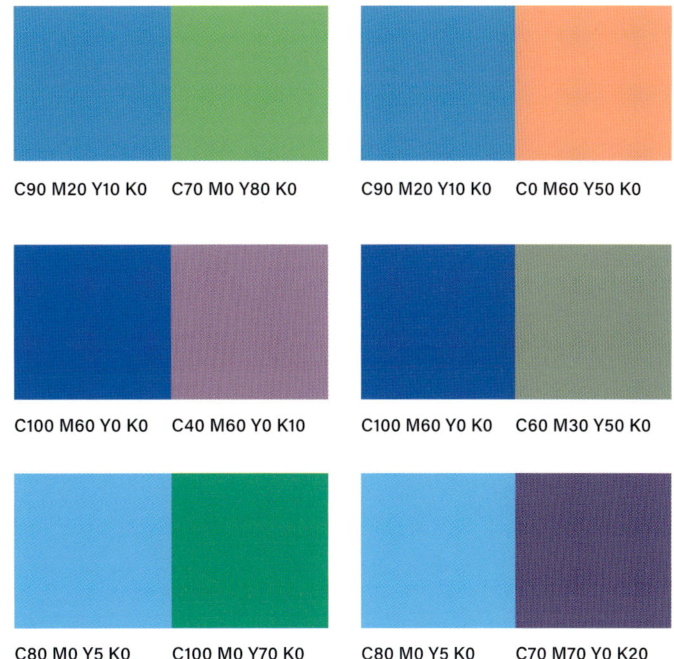

C90 M20 Y10 K0   C70 M0 Y80 K0   C90 M20 Y10 K0   C0 M60 Y50 K0

C100 M60 Y0 K0   C40 M60 Y0 K10   C100 M60 Y0 K0   C60 M30 Y50 K0

C80 M0 Y5 K0   C100 M0 Y70 K0   C80 M0 Y5 K0   C70 M70 Y0 K20

Detail from "Courtesan Reading a Letter" by Katsukawa Shunshō. Copied by Yamagishi Gyokai.
Tokyo National Museum.
Source: ColBase at https://colbase.nich.go.jp

Color Scheme Based on Deep Colors

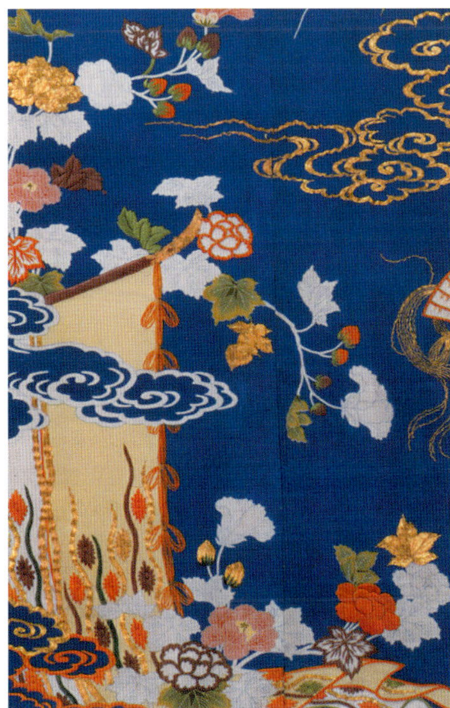

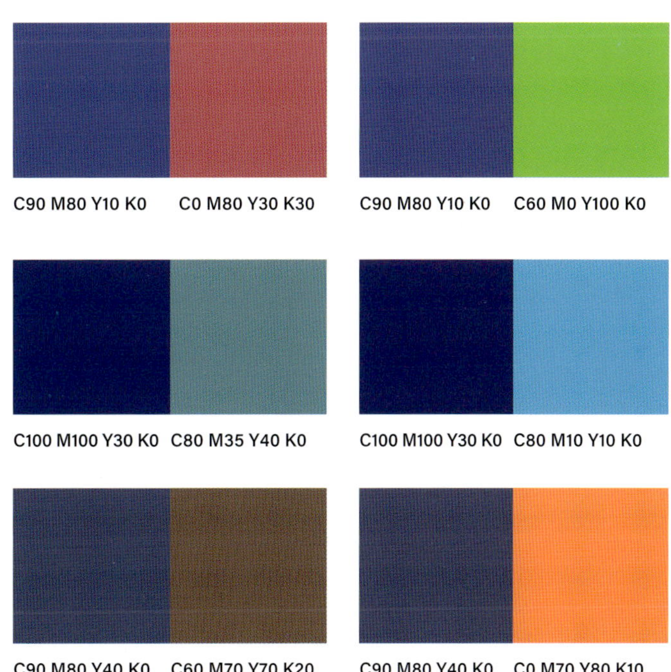

C90 M80 Y10 K0   C0 M80 Y30 K30   C90 M80 Y10 K0   C60 M0 Y100 K0

C100 M100 Y30 K0   C80 M35 Y40 K0   C100 M100 Y30 K0   C80 M10 Y10 K0

C90 M80 Y40 K0   C60 M70 Y70 K20   C90 M80 Y40 K0   C0 M70 Y80 K10

Detail from "Crepe Kimono with Autumn Grass Pattern". Edo period, 18th century.
Tokyo National Museum.
Source: ColBase at https://colbase.nich.go.jp

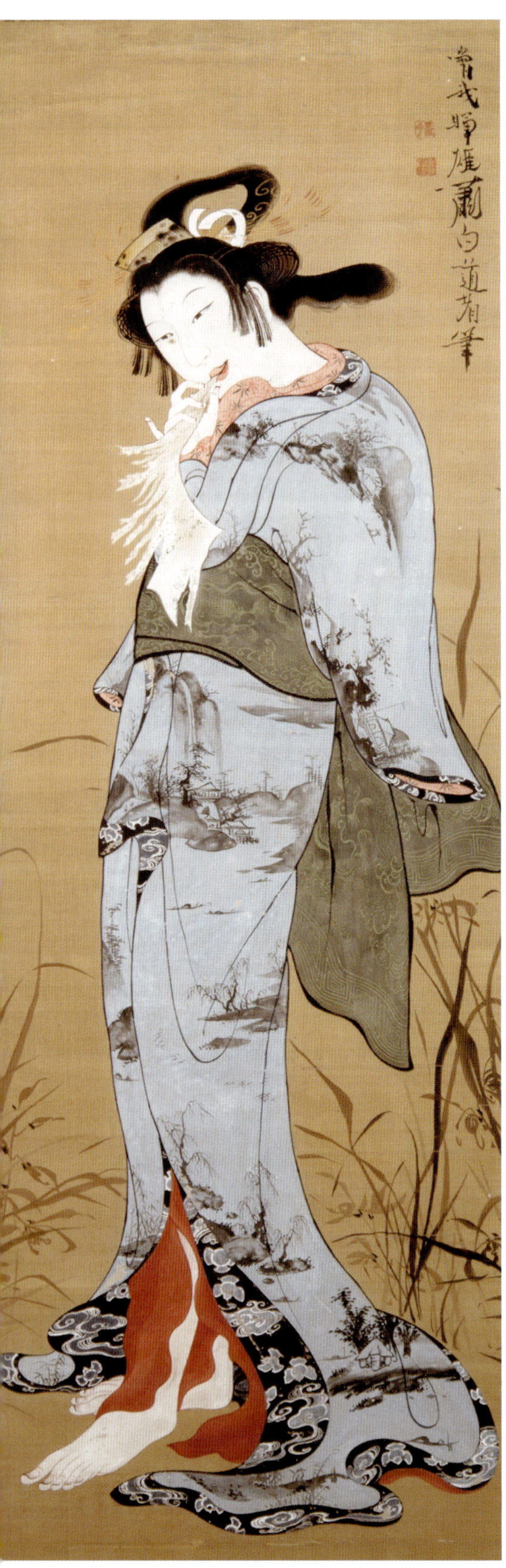

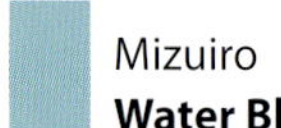
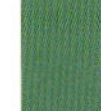

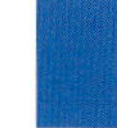
Mizuiro
Water Blue

This refers to a color name representing the clear hue of water, used in dyeing that infuses a slightly lighter shade of green onions and a hint of indigo. In Ihara Saikaku's *The Life of an Amorous Man* in a passage: "Sew the water-colored silk lining with light stitching of water chestnuts." This indicates the popularity of this color in both garments and lining fabric during that period—a favorite in summer clothing.

Rokushō
Verdigris

This color refers to the slightly bluish green patina that forms on the surface of copper or copper alloys. It is a natural green pigment introduced from China during the Asuka and Nara periods. There are both natural and artificially produced Rokushō, both of which consist of a mixture of copper carbonate, which forms the patina/ green rust on copper, and cupric hydroxide.

Sohi
Bright Red-Orange

Sohi is a bright red-orange color made with madder and a solution of wood ashes. It is similar in hue to *hi* (scarlet) but lighter. Unlike hi, it was not considered a color of high rank, and people of the fifth rank or higher were allowed to wear it. In ancient China,

the names of colors varied based on the number of times the dyeing process was repeated, with *ichi* (one-time dyeing) being called *moegari*, *ni* (two-time dyeing) as *akane*, *san* (three-time dyeing) as *sohi*, and *shi* (four-time dyeing) as *shu*.

Ao
Blue

Ao represents the color of a clear sky or the sea. It is also used as a general term to describe colors ranging from indigo shades to greenish shades with added yellow. In pigments, it is divided into *konjō* (navy blue), *gunjō* (ultramarine blue), and *ryokusei* (malachite green). In dyes, ao is commonly used to refer to colors centered around *ai* (indigo) with the addition of yellow-returning agents such as *kariyasu* and *kihada*. Specifically, fabric dyed only with ai is called *hitoe*, while fabric dyed with the addition of yellow is called *ao*.

Sumiiro/Sumizome
Ink Black

Sumiiro refers to a calm deep color that is close to black but has a faint brightness remaining. It is a gray-black color close to sumi's *gosai*, which includes five shades of sumi: dark, medium, scorched, heavy, light, and pure. While it was traditionally associated with mourning attire and the robes of hermit monks, in modern times, black and gray colors became fashionable, and this deep shade was considered an elegant color.

A disheveled woman tearing a letter with her teeth stands with hollow eyes. Mud-caked bare feet peek out from her disheveled hem, giving off an unsettling atmosphere. The light indigo kimono adorned with landscapes and the obi with cloud dragons suggest that this artwork represents either the ill-fated life of the Chinese literati Qu Yuan or the Noh play *Aizomegawa* in which a woman throws herself into a river after receiving a forged letter.

"Portrait of a Beauty" by Soga Shōhaku. Edo period, 18th century.
Nara Prefectural Museum Collection.

97 Mizuiro   **153 Rokushō**   **36 Sohi**

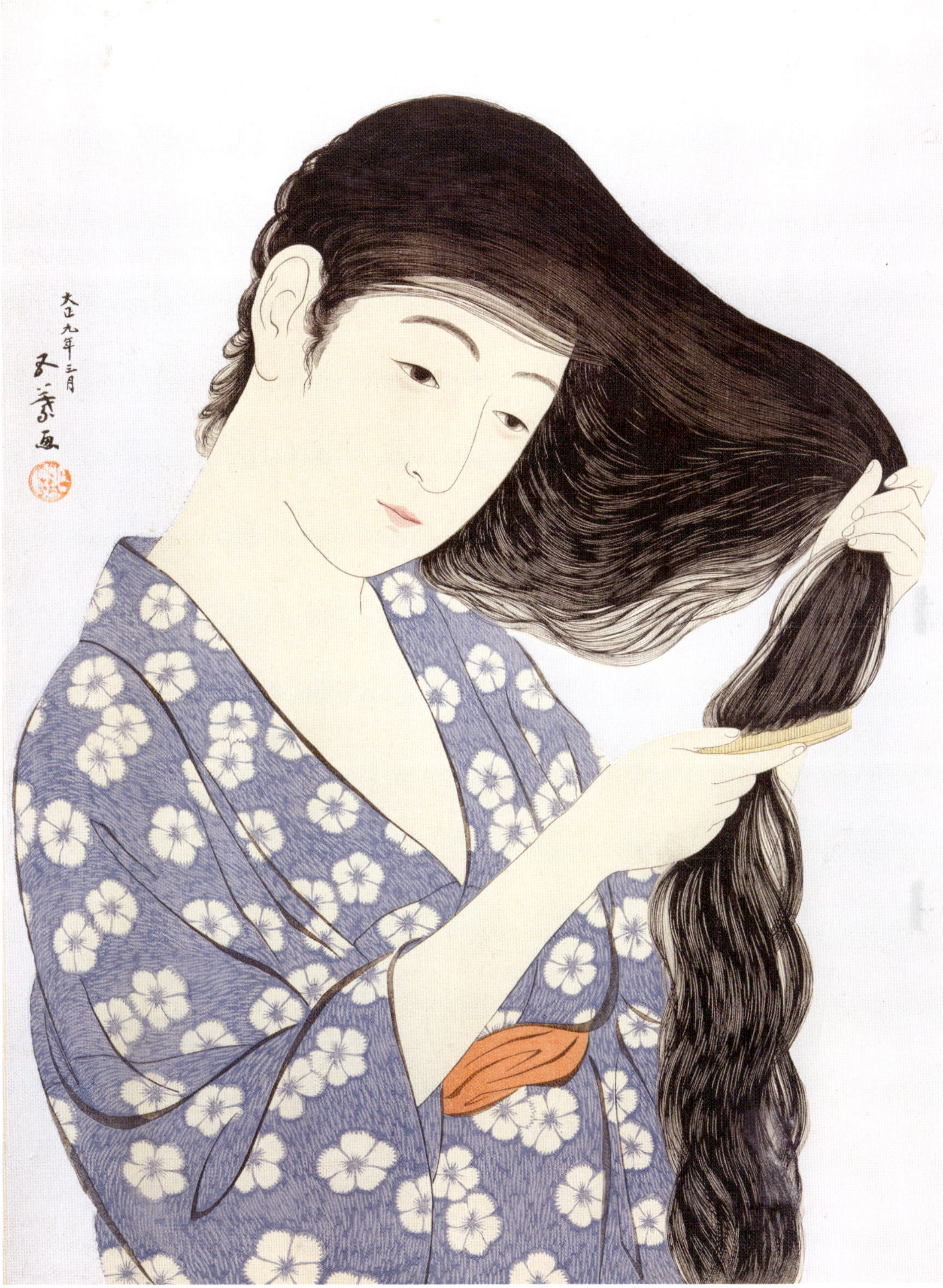

A woman in a light and breezy yukata, adorned with scattered *nadeshiko* (dianthus) patterns on a pale blue base, is carefully combing her damp black hair with a zelkova comb. The background, with its cloud-like brushwork, exudes an atmosphere reminiscent of the steam from the bath. Drawn with graceful lines, the depiction of her neck, nape, and extending to the shoulders radiates an elegant aura. It's a representative masterpiece of the "Goyō" beauty portraits.

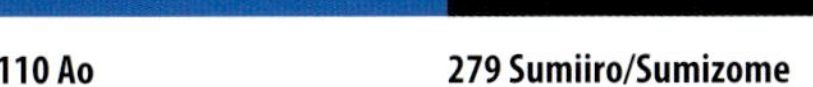

110 Ao   **279 Sumiiro/Sumizome**

"Woman Combing Her Hair" (partial)
by Hashiguchi Goyō, 1920.
Shimane Prefectural Museum of Art.

Graceful waves are depicted in navy and green; beyond the crest of the waves, a slender waxing crescent moon is boldly designed in dark brown. The form of the vessel, with its steeply angled sides and a notch, resembles a type of tea bowl reminiscent of those fired in the Korean Peninsula, but with a slightly intentional distortion added to the rim, giving it charm and character. This is believed to be an early work of Nonomura Jinsei, who established a pottery workshop near the gate of Jinnan Temple in Kyoto in the mid-17th century of the Edo period. It is known to have been fired under the guidance of Kanamori Munewa, as indicated by the inscription on the box: "Made in Jinnanji Ware, Shunryo, from the teachings of Soowa Ro at the temple."

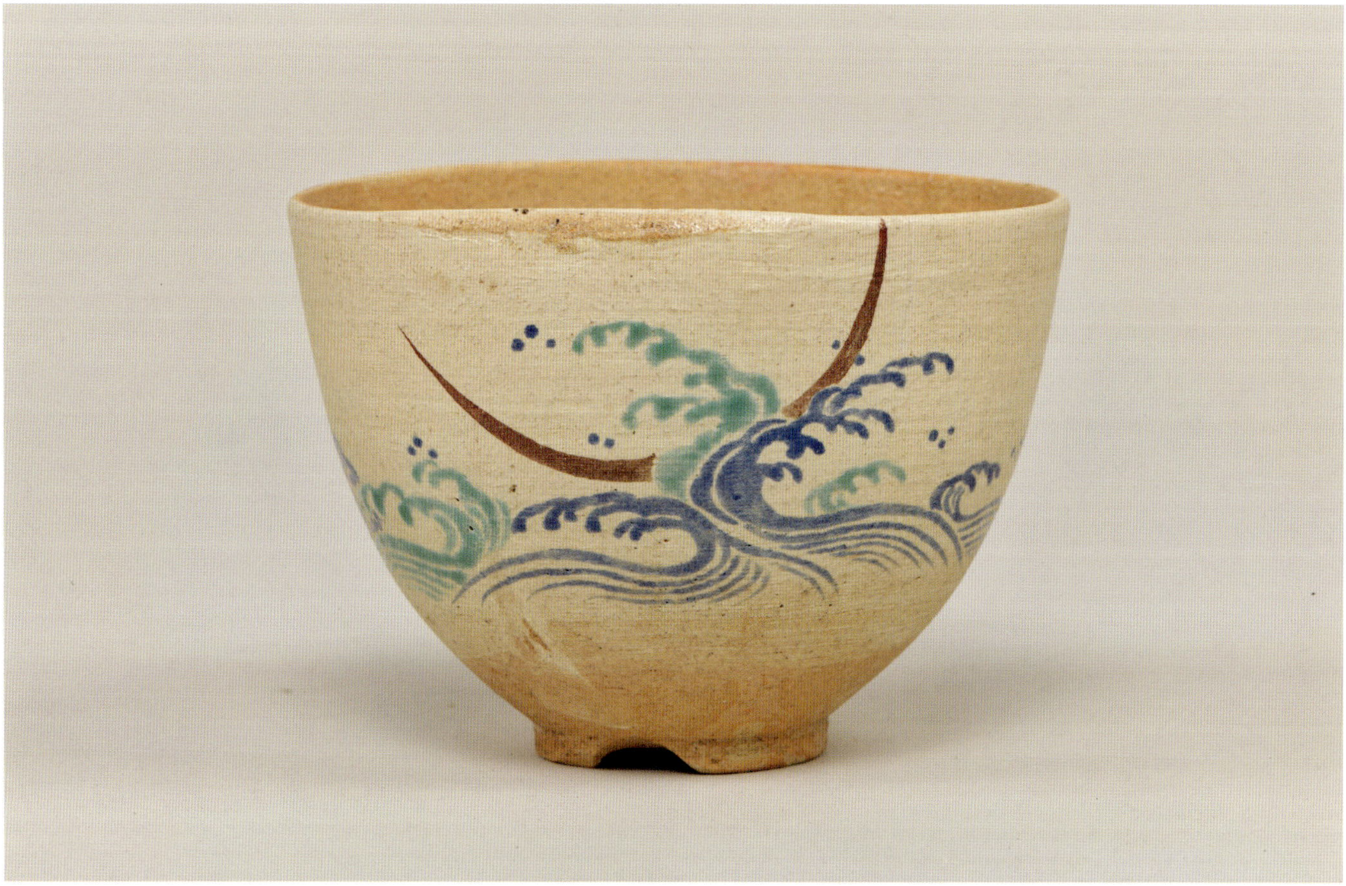

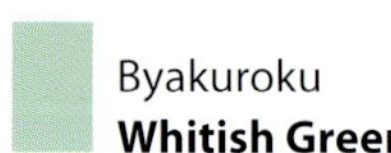

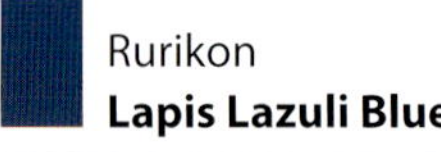

112 Rurikon   145 Byakuroku   192 Tonokoiro

"Colored Porcelain Teacup with Wave and Crescent Design" by Nonomura Ninsei. Edo period, 17th century.
Tokyo National Museum. Source: ColBase at https://colbase.nich.go.jp

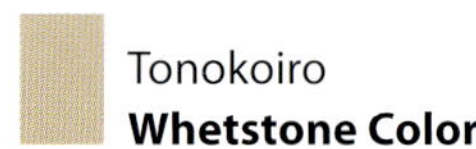

Rurikon
Lapis Lazuli Blue

This is a deep purplish-blue color with a touch of lapis lazuli, slightly brighter and more vivid than navy blue. It's also known as "konruri." In the magazine *Shoshokan Mankou* (published between 1837 and 1853) it states, "Indigo-dyed items are unchanging. There are navy blues, pale blues, and others. A new method called 'steam navy,' applies steam to previously dyed navy, to imitate lapis lazuli navy." The steaming resulted in a slightly brighter and more vivid dye, resembling lapis lazuli navy.

Byakuroku
Whitish Green

Byakuroku refers to a light green color created by grinding malachite (a mineral) into powder, mixed with water.

Tonokoiro
Whetstone Color

Tonoko is the powder produced when sharpening whetstones. This color describes a dull yellow with a hint of reddishness, similar to the color of pumice, Tonokoiro is used for various purposes, including coloring the undercoat of lacquerware and creating wooden patterns on boards and pillars. It can also be obtained by roasting yellow ocher.

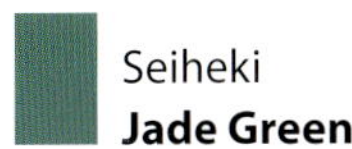

Seiheki
Jade Green

It refers to a dull bluish-green color. "Seiheki" was the name of a jade stone in ancient China, and it is believed that the bluish-green color of clothing in Japan originated from the hue of this jade stone. Both *ao* and *heki* refer to the bluish-green spectrum, so it is thought that this term was used to describe the bluish-green color. Considering its use as the color of Buddhist monks' robes, it seems to have been a subdued and modest shade of bluish-green.

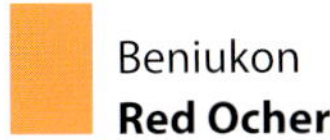

Beniukon
Red Ocher

This is a vibrant orange color created by applying safflower red dye (*beni*) on a yellow ocher (*ukon*) undercoat. It's a lustrous and vivid color. In the book *Koshoku Ichidai Otoko*, written by Ihara Saikaku in 1682, there is a passage that reads, "As the evening approaches, a woman prepares to go out with a garment dyed in beniukon." This color was favored during the late Edo period, especially for striped and checkered kimono linings, providing a lively contrast to the plain outer fabric.

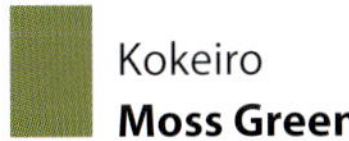

Kokeiro
Moss Green

This is a deep and vivid moss green color, often used as a general term for various green shades. During the Edo period, colors similar to Kokeiro included Yanagicha (willow tea) which was brighter and Mirucha (seaweed tea) which was darker. Although references to moss and moss clothing can be found in Heian literature, it was not yet used as a specific clothing color. The subtle beauty of moss has been appreciated in Japan for a long time and is considered essential in Japanese gardens.

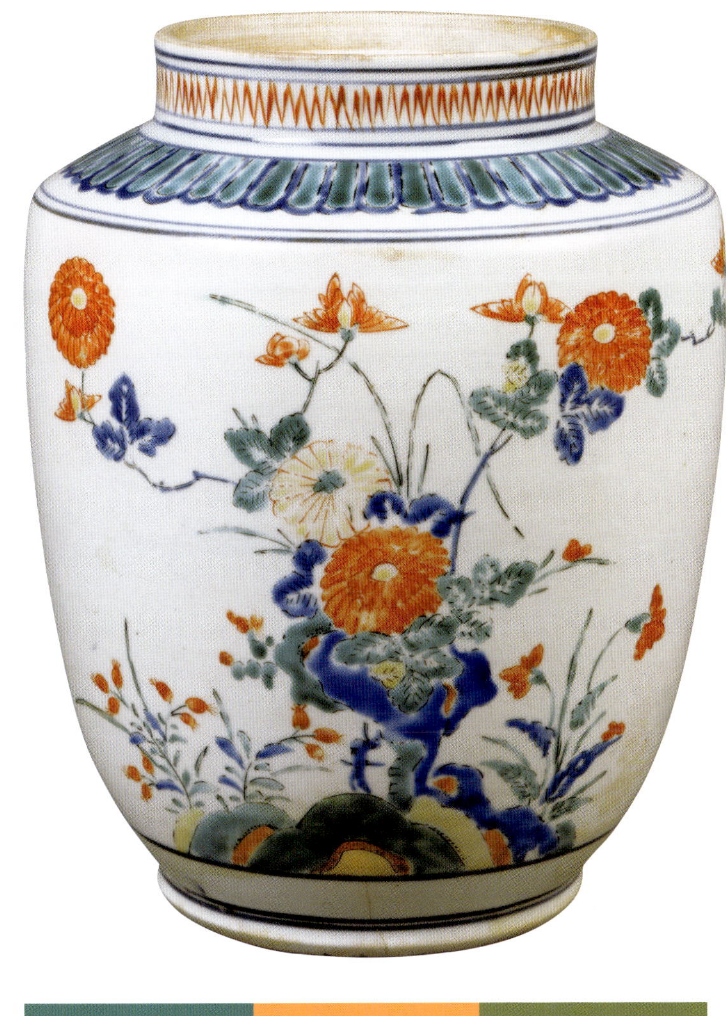

| 119 Seiheki | 45 Beniukon | 139 Kokeiro |

"Colorful Porcelain Vase with Chrysanthemum Design".
Arita Ware, in the style of Kakiemon. Edo period, 18th century.
Aichi Prefectural Ceramic Art Museum Collection.

Characteristic of the Uemon style is the vivid depiction of crimson chrysanthemums and navy foliage against a milky-white base. This milky-white base is referred to as *nigorigote*. In Arita, the technique of firing white porcelain was transmitted by potters who came from the Korean Peninsula, and the first porcelain in Japan was produced in the early 1610s. These porcelain pieces were called Imari ware, named after the port of Imari from which they were shipped. The vividness of polychrome enamels, centered around the red decoration of the Kakiemon style, gained popularity overseas, and it is said that large quantities were exported to various parts of Europe.

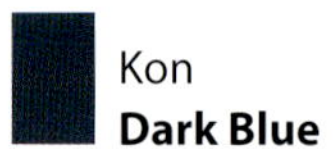

Kon
Dark Blue

Kon refers to a deeply saturated, almost blackish blue color, slightly leaning towards red. It's the darkest and deepest shade of ai-zome (indigo dye). Kon has become widely established as a popular everyday color. In the late Muromachi period, businesses specializing in kon were known as "Konkaki," and in the Edo period, they were referred to as "Konya." The more saturated ai-zome becomes, the more it tends to lean towards a purplish hue. A rich, purplish kon is called "Shikon" or "Nasu-kon," while a kon with a greenish undertone is known as "Tetsu-kon."

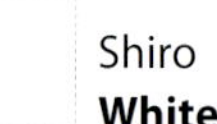

Shiro
White

Shiro simply means white. It is the brightest color and is often associated with purity, cleanliness, and sacredness in ancient Japanese culture. White has been revered and used in religious contexts and rituals to symbolize purity and innocence.

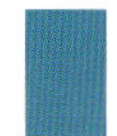

Hana Asagi
Light Flower Blue

This is a bright shade of light blue with a slight greenish tint. "Hana" refers to the flower color, indicating a shade of blue obtained by applying the blue juice extracted from the flowers of the duckweed plant (*Lobelia chinensis*) during the dyeing process. "Asagi" generally refers to a light blue color achieved through *ai-zome* (indigo dye). The specific dyeing technique may have evolved over time, making it challenging to define the exact shade.

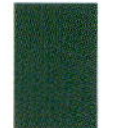

Biroudo
Velvet

This is a dark bluish-green color. It derives its name from its resemblance to the glossy wings of a swan, written as *tengajuu* which also means "velvet." Velvet was introduced to Japan via Portuguese Nanban ships during the Tenbun era (1532–1554) and weaving commenced in Kyoto during the Keicho era (1596–1614).

This is a large dish with a diameter exceeding 45 centimeters. The entire white and round surface is gracefully adorned with blue underglaze depicting a tiger and a pheasant within a bamboo grove. The wide rim is embellished with small incised markings. The brushwork of the blue underglaze painting may appear inexperienced, with uneven shades of blue, but it is filled with a rugged and powerful quality. The lively dynamism of the tiger's tail, which seems to undulate, conveys a vivid sense of movement.

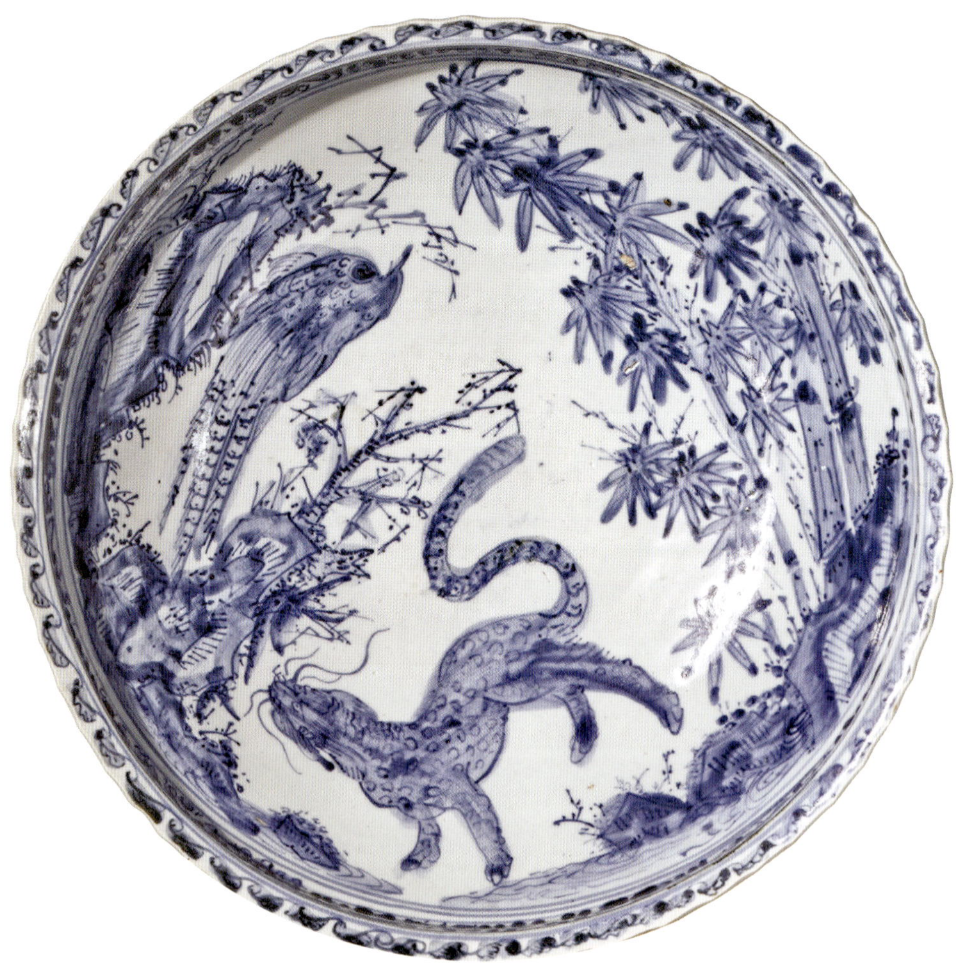

114 Kon   251 Shiro

"Blue-and-White Large Bowl with Bamboo and Tiger Design". Imari Ware. Edo period, 17th century.
Tokyo National Museum.
Source: ColBase at https://colbase.nich.go.jp

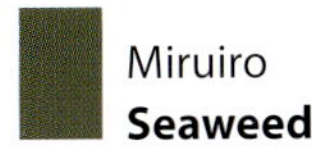

Miruiro
Seaweed

Miruiro is a color resembling olive green, inspired by the color of seaweed (*miru*) that grows on rocks in shallow sea waters. The olive green hue, not having a traditional Japanese name, adopted the term "miruiro." This dusky and cool-toned color was believed to be used by Kamakura samurai and Muromachi cultural figures during the medieval period. It remained in use until the early Meiji period, when Western-style, vibrant colors became fashionable.

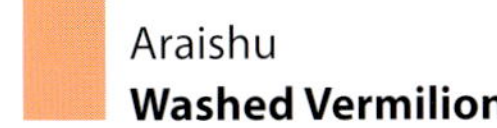

Araishu
Washed Vermilion

Araishu is a pale, washed-out red-orange color that resembles a diluted or faded shade of traditional vermilion. The term "arai" suggests the washing or diluting of colors, and it signifies colors that have been washed or faded. During the Meiji period, the widespread adoption of chemical dyes led to the popularity of vibrant Western-style colors. In response, traditional Japanese colors like araishu emerged as a new trend.

With vigorous brushwork covering the entire white background, two energetic birds crested myna birds, are depicted alongside bamboo and various flowers and grasses scattered around. The myna is considered a domestic bird, and was favored as a symbol of good luck in Chinese art. On the outer edge of the reverse side, there is a picture of pine, bamboo, and plum depicted in colored enamel. Although there is an inscription in the center of the bottom, it is difficult to read due to the green overglaze paint covering it.

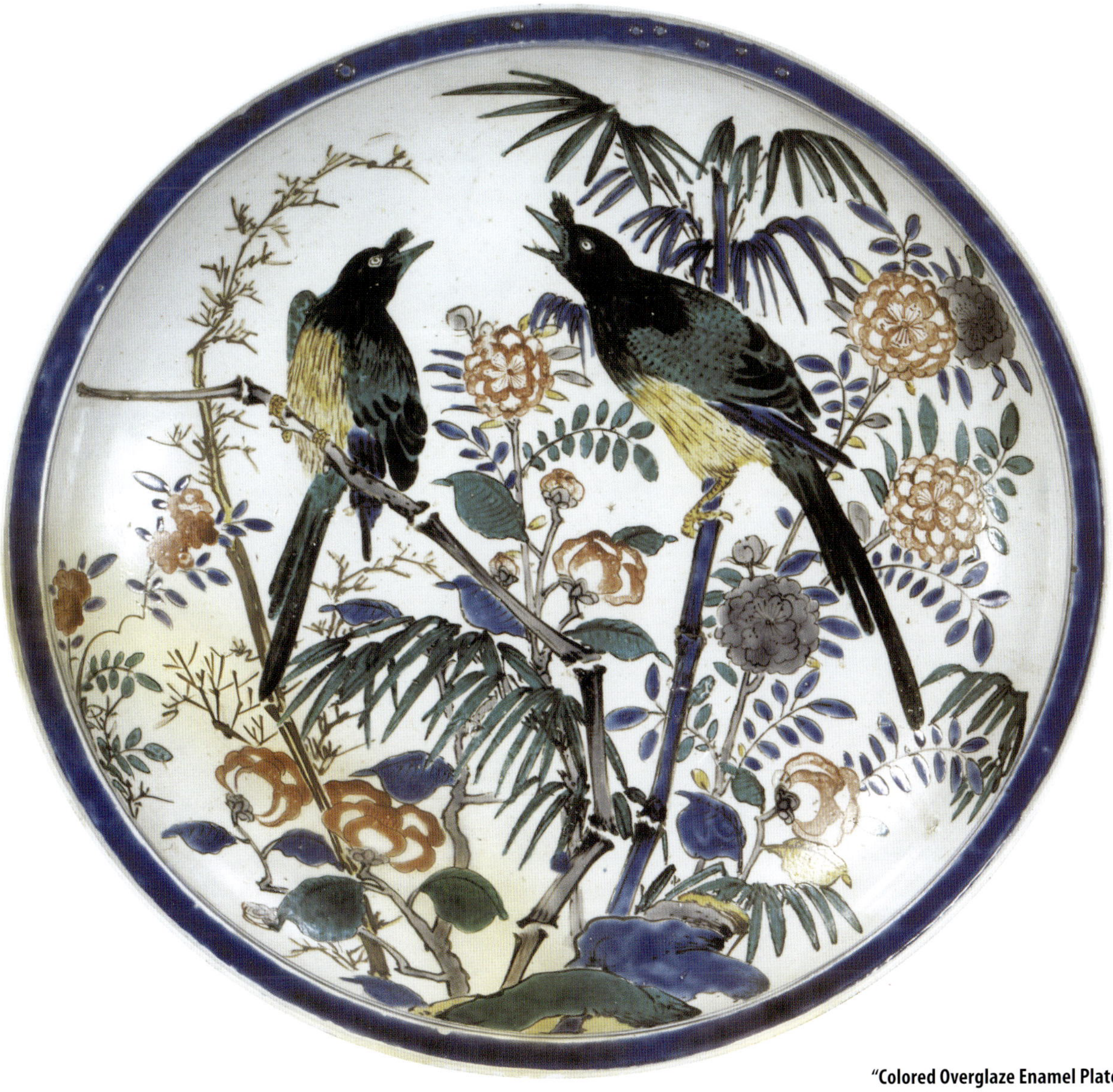

"Colored Overglaze Enamel Plate with a Motif of Crested Myna Birds" (Important Cultural Property).
Tokyo National Museum.
Source: ColBase at https://colbase.nich.go.jp

| 108 Hana Asagi | 164 Biroudo | 158 Miruiro | 40 Araishu |

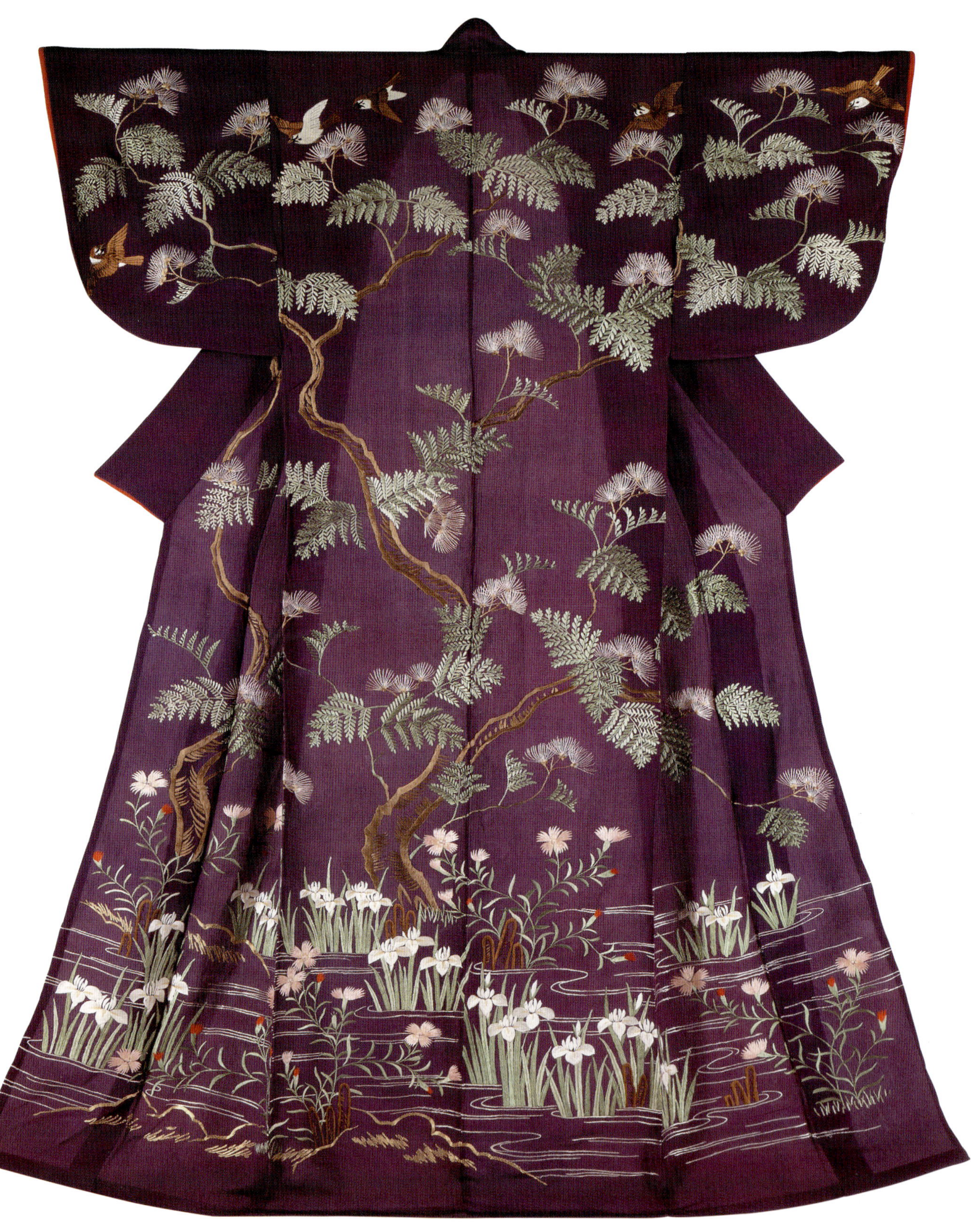

"Blue Silk Crepe Kimono with Embroidery of Sparrows, Lotus, Iris, and Peonies". **Meiji Period, 19th century.**
Held at the Nara Prefectural Museum of Art.

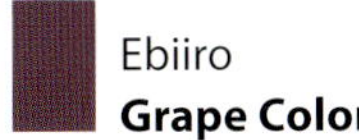

Ebiiro
Grape Color

A reddish-purple color inspired by the ripe fruit and juice of the wild grape (*budou*). In the *Engishiki*, the dyeing material and quantities are listed as "one piece of grapevine twill fabric, three kin of purple grass, one go of vinegar, four sho of ash, and one kin of firewood," indicating that the dye was made by boiling purple grass and adding vinegar to bring out the reddish-purple color.

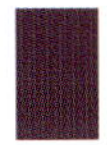

Kakitsubata
Iris

A purplish-red shade inspired by the color of the iris flower. The name "Kakitsubata" is derived from the practice of rubbing the juice of these flowers on fabric for dyeing, meaning "flower used for dyeing."

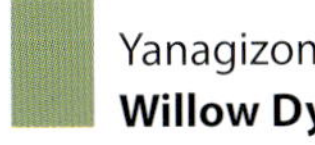

Yanagizome
Willow Dye

A slightly grayish yellow-green color resembling willow leaves. Although willow (*yanagi*) was appreciated by the nobility in ancient times, this specific dyeing technique using willow as a colorant likely became popular during the Edo period.

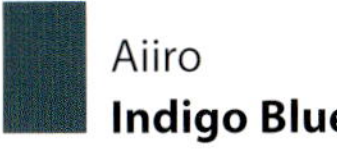

Aiiro
Indigo Blue

Unlike pure indigo dye, this shade is achieved by combining indigo with yellow dye (*kiinugasa*), resulting in a deep bluish-green color. In the Heian period, it referred to a greenish shade achieved by combining yellow and green dye, not pure indigo.

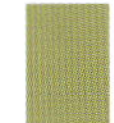

Hiwacha
Dull Yellow Green

Dull yellow-green color resembling the feathers of a warbler bird (*hiwa*). It is created by layering yellow (*kariyasu*) over a pale blue base (*asagiiro*).

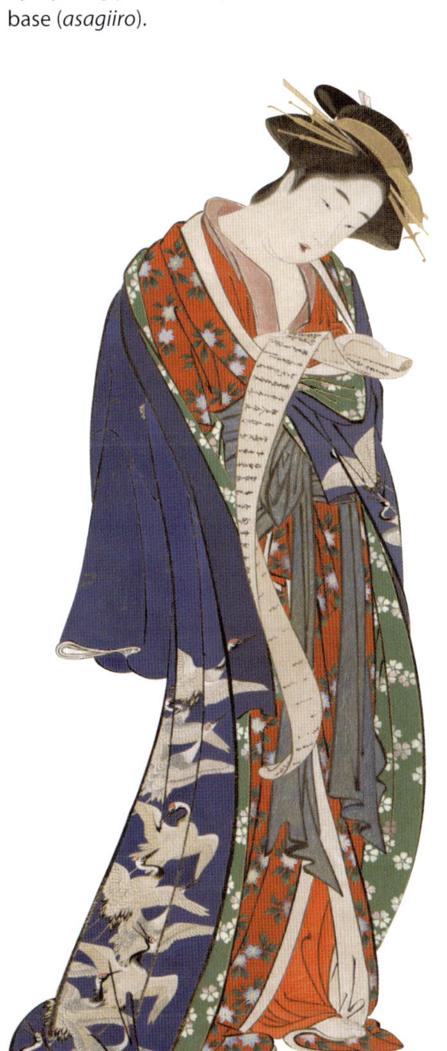

From the hem stretching up to the shoulders, trees intertwine and spread their leaves across the navy background of this kimono, blooming soft pink flowers along the way. Beneath the blossoms, sparrows flutter about, their lively chirping filling the air. Along the hem, irises bearing flowers stand in orderly rows, their blooms swaying rhythmically in the breeze. The silk fabric, woven with strong twisted threads and subsequently processed, reveals vertical wrinkles, making it preferred for summer kimono as it remains comfortable against the skin even in humid weather.

**Detail from "Courtesan Reading a Letter"
by Katsukawa Shunshō, copied by Yamagishi Gyokai.**
Tokyo National Museum.
Source: ColBase at https://colbase.nich.go.jp

Kabairo
Reed Color

Inspired by the color of cattails, this color is also very like the color of the bark of the Japanese cherry birch (*uwamizuzakura*). Both are deep brownish-orange colors with a hint of red.

123 Aiiro   **207 Hiwacha**   **54 Kabairo**

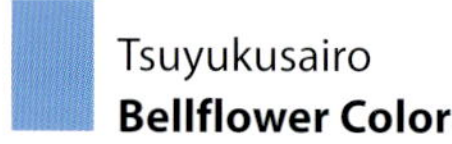

Tsuyukusairo
Bellflower Color

Used to describe the vivid blue color of bellflowers that bloom in early summer mornings. The name "Tsuyukusa" means "morning dew grass." In ancient times, its juice was used for dyeing fabric. It is still used in yuzen and stencil dyeing due to its ability to be easily removed by bleach.

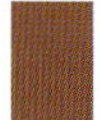

Azukiiro
Azuki Bean Color

A muted purplish-red color resembling the color of azuki beans. Although this color name dates back to the Edo period, the specific dyeing technique used is unknown. The color red has been associated with prayers, protection against evil, and warding off mis-

fortune since ancient times, which is why azuki beans were used to make red rice for celebratory occasions.

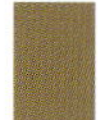

Shibazome/Fushizome
Drab

Obtained by dyeing with extracts from various types of deciduous trees like oak, chestnut, and oak, which contain tannin.

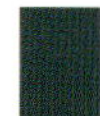

Onandoiro
Tapestry Blue

A shade of indigo dye, characteristic of the Edo period. It refers to a dark blue color with a greenish undertone. Shades of this color include iron, rust, and wisteria variations, all of which are popular as kimono colors. The dyeing techniques for this color are akin to closely guarded secrets of each dye house and have not been widely disseminated. However, it appears that in addition to the base dyeing, thin pink, yellow ink, yellow ocher (*gobai-ko*), and brown were also used.

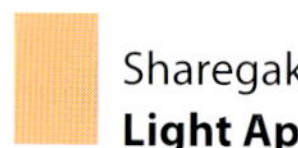

Sharegaki
Light Apricot

This color resembles the shade of washed and sun-dried persimmons. It is lighter than "Araigaki" (washed-out persimmon) and slightly darker than "Usugaki "(pale persimmon). The name was coined during the Genroku era. Like all the persimmon shades, it is associated with various shades of orange.

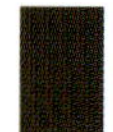

Binroujizome
African Brown

This is an elegant black-brown color made using betel nut as a dye. Fabrics such as silk or hemp, which have been dyed with indigo or red as an underlayer, are dyed using a mixture of boiled betel nut and materials such as willow, poplar, or plum bark. During the Edo period, it was used in garments like black-patterned textiles, and its deep and rich hue was highly favored.

From the right shoulder to the hem, a flowing indigo blue pattern created with shibori technique forms zigzag motifs in vibrant colors. Embroidery and stenciling create the image of wisteria flowers beginning to bloom on a pine tree. The lively inclusion of large blossoms represents the Tang pine, with spreading pine needles radiating outward, and the central circular element likely representing the male stamen. The design of wisteria flowers on pine trees is a motif found in works such as *The Tale of Genji* and *The Pillow Book,* evoking the early summer scene deeply ingrained in the Japanese psyche since ancient times.

Detail from "Princess Komatsu Playing with Thread by the Seashore" by Utagawa Toyokuni.
National Diet Library Digital Collection.

105 Tsuyukusairo   **59 Azukiiro**   **226 Shibazome/Fushizome**

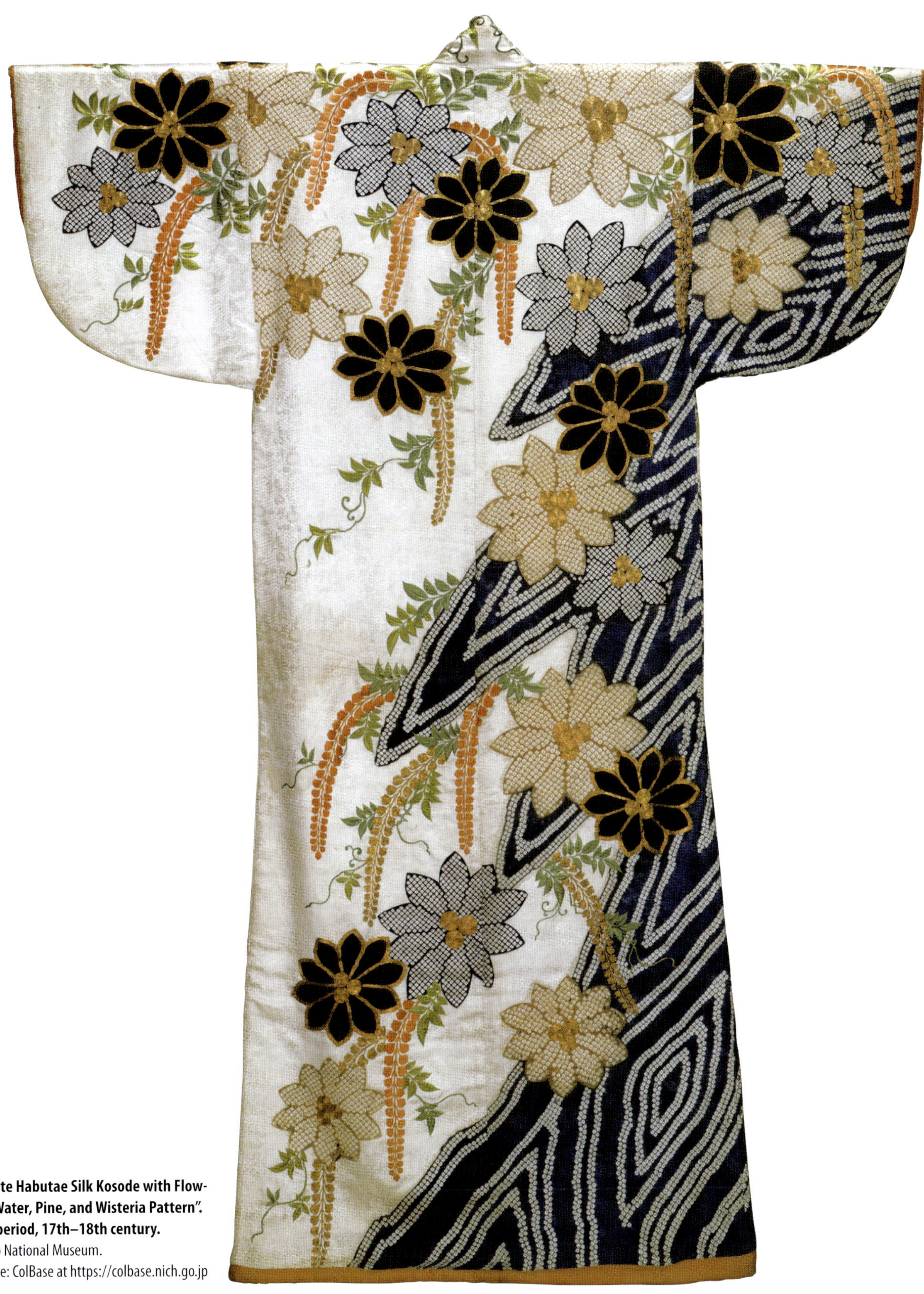

**"White Habutae Silk Kosode with Flow-
ing Water, Pine, and Wisteria Pattern".
Edo period, 17th–18th century.**
Tokyo National Museum.
Source: ColBase at https://colbase.nich.go.jp

This is a kosode (short-sleeved kimono) featuring auspicious patterns such as a folding screen, cypress fans, peonies, and cloud motifs combined with autumn wildflowers on dyed rinzu silk fabric. The subdued color, dyed with indigo, was commonly seen in the late Edo period, and this overall-patterned formal kimono is intended for married women.

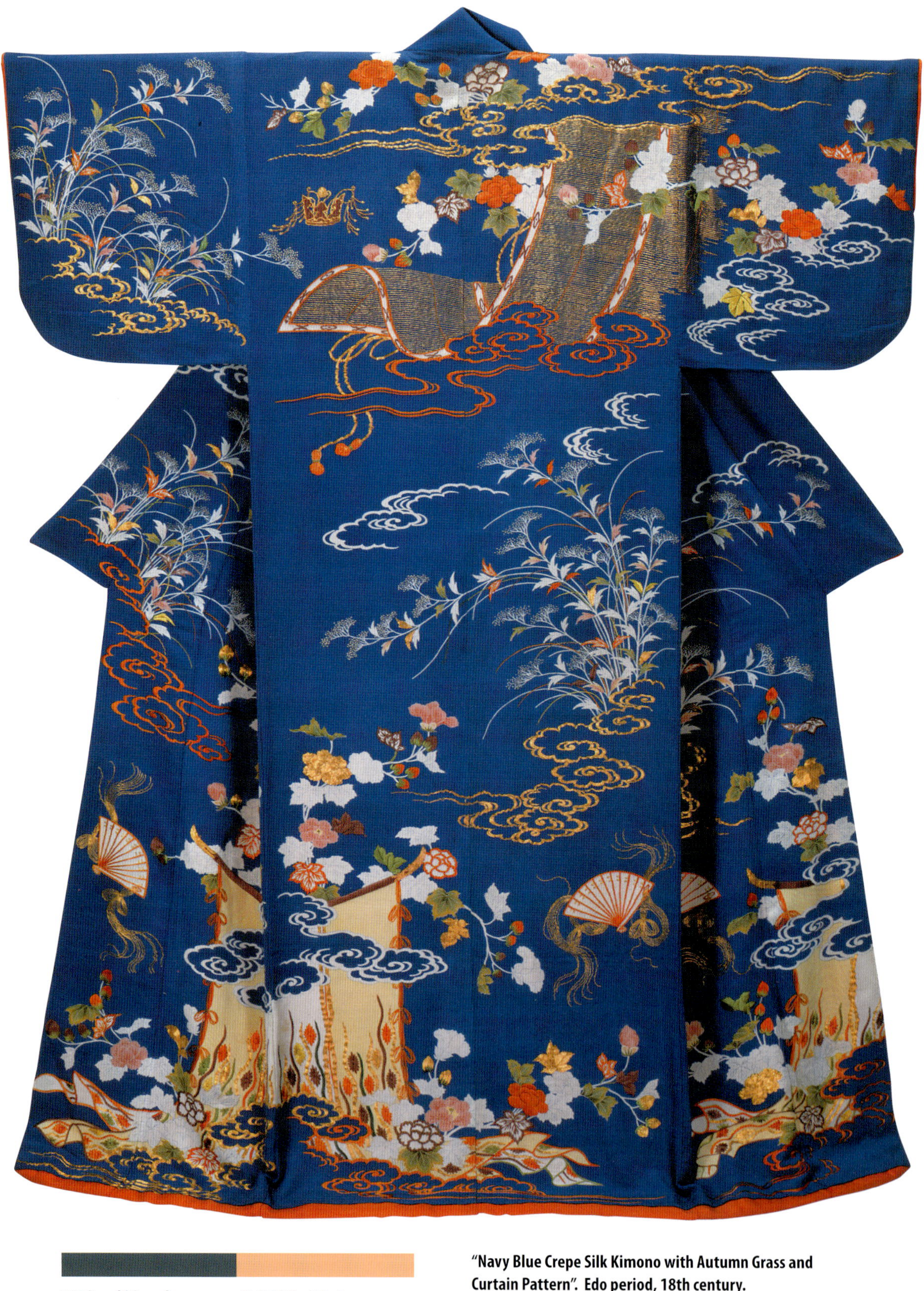

130 Omeshi Onando **46 Shishiiro/Nikuiro**

"Navy Blue Crepe Silk Kimono with Autumn Grass and Curtain Pattern". Edo period, 18th century.
Tokyo National Museum. Source: ColBase at https://colbase.nich.go.jp

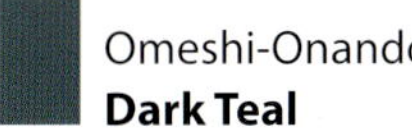

Omeshi-Onando
Dark Teal

This name is used for a subdued blue color with a tinge of gray. "Omeshi-shrink Momen" is a high-quality fabric woven with two differently colored warp threads arranged in pairs to create narrow vertical stripes, known as "Goryu-tome-jima". "Omeshi" is an honorific term for wearing clothes, and it gained its name from the fact that the 11th Shogun Ienari Tokugawa favored high-quality shrink momen. The name "Omeshi-Onando" is believed to have appeared around the Kansei era. Other color names associated with Omeshi include "Omeshi Cha" (Omeshi tea) and "Omeshi Nezumi" (Omeshi mouse gray).

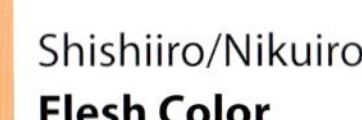

Shishiiro/Nikuiro
Flesh Color

A pale reddish color with a slight yellowish tone, reminiscent of the color of skin. "Shishi" is an archaic term for meat, referring to the color of meat from animals such as wild boar or deer. Although it has been used since the Nara period, it later came to be used interchangeably with "Nikuiro" (flesh color) or "Hadairo" (skin color). Also, during the Heian period, it was used to describe the healthy complexion of young maidens as "akara otome" (rosy-cheeked maiden) or "kurenai niou shoujo" (girl with the scent of rouge). This color was also applied to Buddhist statues and dolls.

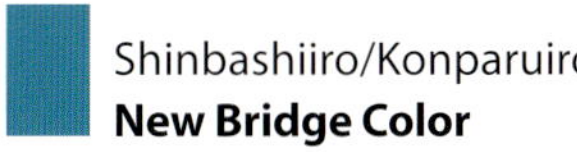

Shinbashiiro/Konparuiro
New Bridge Color

A bright bluish-green color with a greenish tint, similar to pale blue. The name originates from the geisha in the entertainment district of Shinbashi in Tokyo, who favored this color. This light bluish-green shade, introduced during the mid-Meiji period through imported chemical dyes, became popular for its fashionable and vivid appearance. In the Taisho era, it was widely in vogue. Today, it is referred to as Turquoise Blue in Western color terminology. Artists like Kaburaki Kiyokata and Uemura Shōen used this color in their paintings of beautiful women.

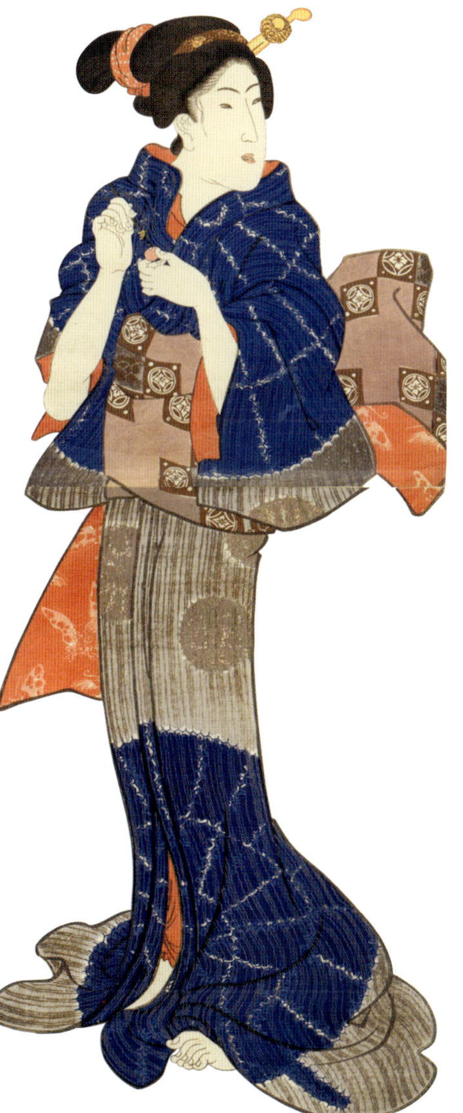

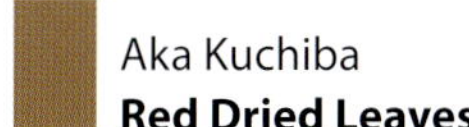

Aka Kuchiba
Red Dried Leaves

A reddish-brown color resembling the hue of withered autumn leaves. This color name has been used since the Heian period, and there are various shades of "Kuchiba" or withered leaf colors, such as "Ki Kuchiba" (yellowish withered leaf), "Ao Kuchiba" (blue withered leaf), "Nure Kuchiba" (wet withered leaf), and more. According to *Nihon Sōhō* (Japanese Dyeing Methods) written in 1909, achieving this color involved repeated dyeing with a concentrated solution of catechu (tannin) and fixing the color with iron mordants.

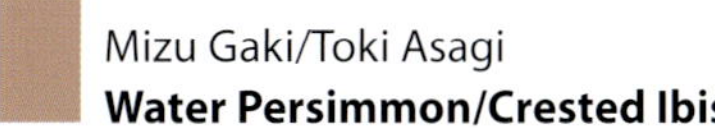

Mizu Gaki/Toki Asagi
Water Persimmon/Crested Ibis

"Mizu Gaki" refers to a color that resembles persimmon with a watery hue, while "Toki Asagi" suggests a light blue with a pinkish tint, similar to the color of a flamingo. As mentioned in *Tekagami Moyō Setsuyō*, "Mizu Gaki, commonly known as Toki Asagi," is a reddish color similar to the hue of *toki* (Japanese crested ibis).

Kurikawacha/Kurikawairo
Chestnut Shell Brown/Chestnut Shell Color

A deep reddish-brown color inspired by the hue of chestnut shells. "Kurikawa" refers to chestnut shells and husks, which contain tannin substances that were traditionally used in leather tanning and dyeing. "Kurikawacha" became a fashionable shade of brown during the Edo period, and it was popular for obi sashes among women. Additionally, in medieval warrior tales, horses with reddish-brown coats were called "Kurige" (chestnut horses).

Detail from "Portrait of a Beautiful Woman" by Utagawa Toyokuni.
National Diet Library Digital Collection.

107 Shinbashiiro/Konparuiro   51 Aka Kuchiba   64 Mizu Gaki/Toki Asagi   243 Kurikawacha/Kurikawairo

This is a refined komon (small pattern) kimono featuring a subdued color scheme of black, brown, and vermilion stripes, expressing both calmness and strength. The design of "Rikan-shima" is said to have been favored by the second generation of kabuki actor Arashi Kichisaburo, also known as Rikan. During the mid-Edo period, kabuki became the ultimate entertainment for commoners, and not only the patterns but also the colors of costumes worn by kabuki actors became fashionable in the townspeople's fashion.

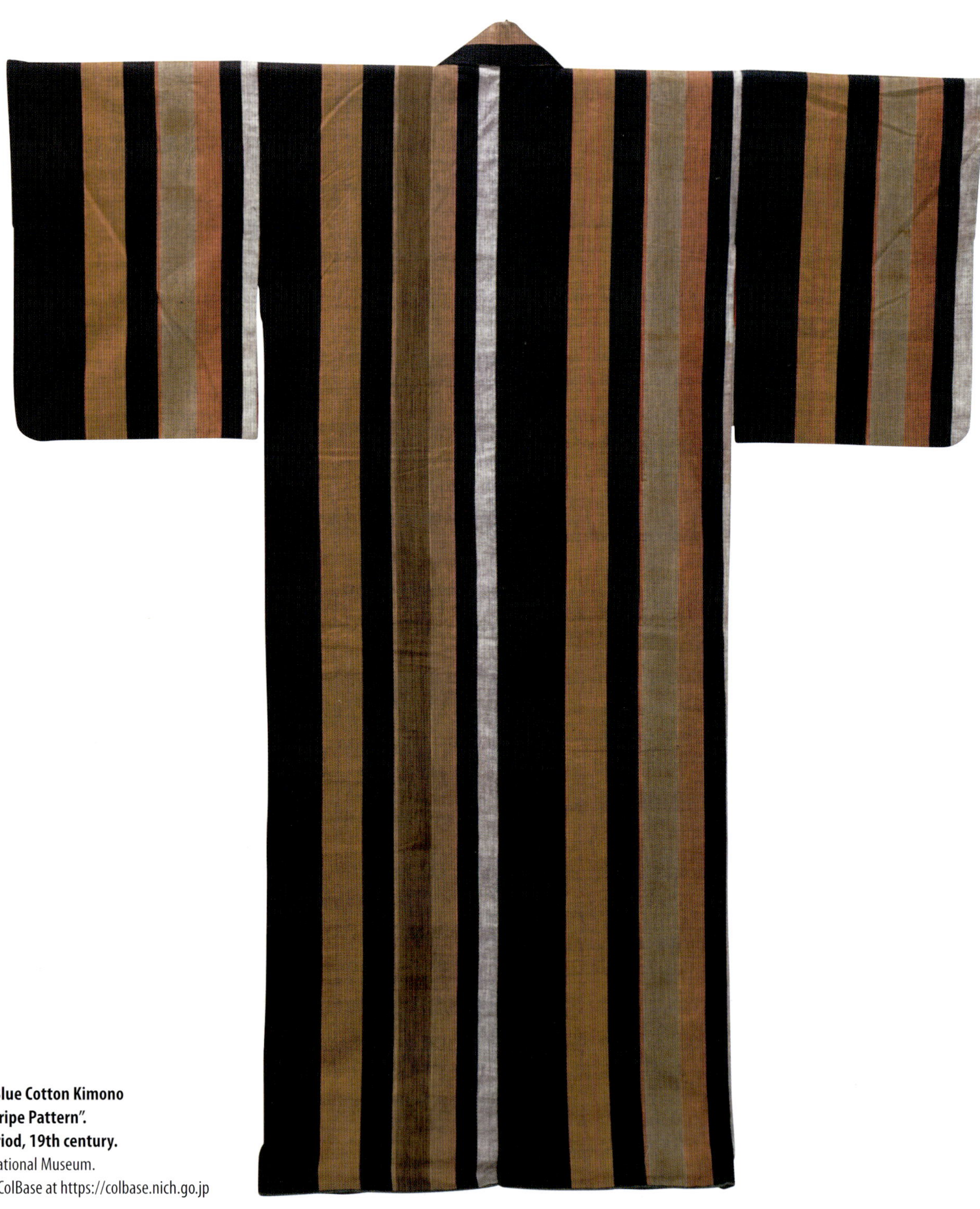

**"Dark Blue Cotton Kimono
with Stripe Pattern".
Edo period, 19th century.**
Tokyo National Museum.
Source: ColBase at https://colbase.nich.go.jp

129 Sabionando   4 Sakuranezumi   230 Tonocha   210 Uguisucha

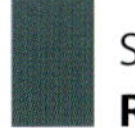

Sabionando
Rusty Teal

A subdued blue color with a hint of gray, giving it a mature and calm appearance. *Sohi* (rust) encompasses the meanings of "wabi" and "sabi," connoting a color that is aged and subdued. In traditional colors, "rust" implies colors that are muted with a grayish tone compared to the original color, while "iron" is indicates colors with a greenish tint

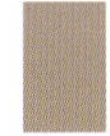

Sakuranezumi
Cherry Blossom Gray

A pale cherry blossom color with hints of gray or light ink gray. During the Edo period, shades of brown and gray, known as *cha* and *nezu*, were popular, but having nezu in the name doesn't necessarily mean it's a gray color. Sakuranezumi is one of the lighter colors with a slight reddish undertone, resembling the color of cherry blossoms. Other color names with nezu in them include "Umenezu" and "Fujinezumi."

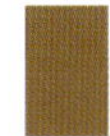

Tonocha
Whetstone Brown

A brown color with a hint of red, also known as "Togicha." "Togi" refers to rough stones or abrasive materials used for sharpening metal tools, often called "Togi-to." This dye color has been around since the early Edo period and can be frequently seen in publications such as those published in 1666 and subsequent editions of kimono design books.

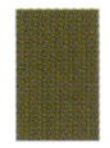

Uguisucha
Japanese Bush Warbler Brown

It is used for olive-colored hues with a tinge of brown. During the Edo period, all colors within the olive spectrum were referred to by this color name associated with brown and treated as shades of brown. It was a preferred color for women's kimono sleeves. This color name can be found in popular novels and *joruri* (traditional Japanese puppet theater), and it is also used in the clothing colors depicted in Ukiyo-e prints of beautiful women and actors.

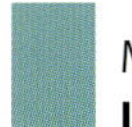

Mizuasagi
Light Blue

A lighter and paler shade of blue-green compared to asagi. It is slightly darker than "Mizunozoki" and is close to the color of water or light aqua. The *mizu* in this color name refers to dilution rather than the color of water itself. When using this light shade of blue, especially on undyed white fabric, it tends to show a slightly greenish tone due to the lack of adequate bleaching. To prevent this yellowing, a light shade of *asagi* was often applied as an underlayer.

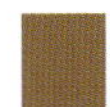

Sodenkaracha
Traditional Chinese Tea Brown

A deep brown with a slight blackish tone, used for this specific shade. It is named after Tsuruya So-den, a Kyoto-based dyer who is said to have originated this color. According to *Tekagami Moyō Setsuyō* this was a popular around the Tenwa era (1681–1684).

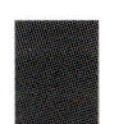

Keshisumiiro
Charcoal Gray

It is a color resembling the ash produced by extinguishing fires such as firewood and charcoal, not as deep black as ink. The name does not appear in old dyeing records, so it is believed to be a color name from the Meiji period onwards. In Natsume Sōseki's *Eiichi Shōhin* from the year 1909, a description reads: "In the middle of the body, only one leaf, green left behind in the color of extinguished charcoal."

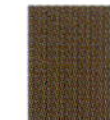

Momoshiocha/Yōkaniro
Soy Sauce Brown

This is a reddish-brown color with a resemblance to chocolate. The *momo* indicates the extensive dyeing process involving numerous repetitions, while *shio* refers to the method of dipping or soaking during dyeing. It's also called "Yōkaniro" because of its resemblance to the dark purple-brown color of *yōkan*, a traditional Japanese sweet. However, this color is not commonly used to describe the actual color of yōkan but is often associated with the faded appearance of a monk's black robe, which takes on a brownish hue due to wear and fading.

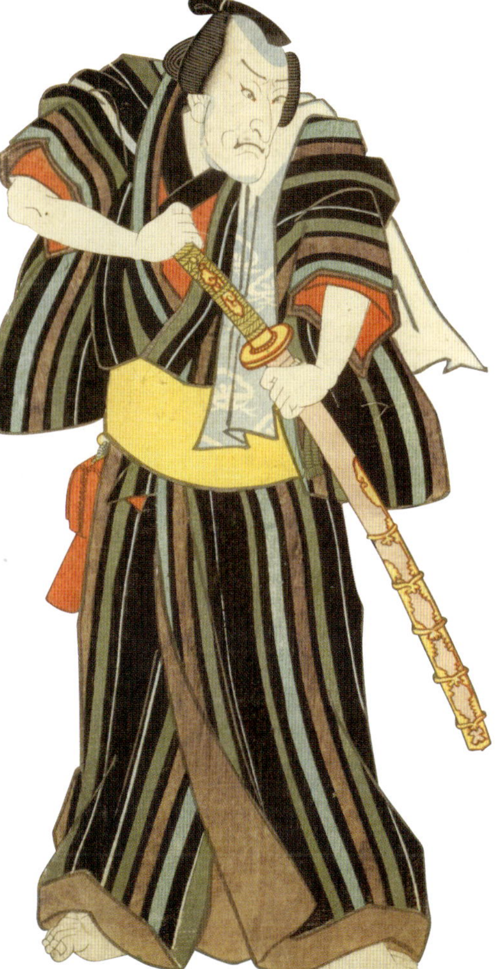

Detail from "Redgate Gensaiemon, Izu-ya Yosaburō, Otomé, the Beloved Mistress of Akama" by Utagawa Toyokuni, 1853.
National Diet Library Digital Collection.

100 Mizuasagi   231 Sodenkaracha   276 Keshisumiiro   248 Momoshiocha/Yōkaniro

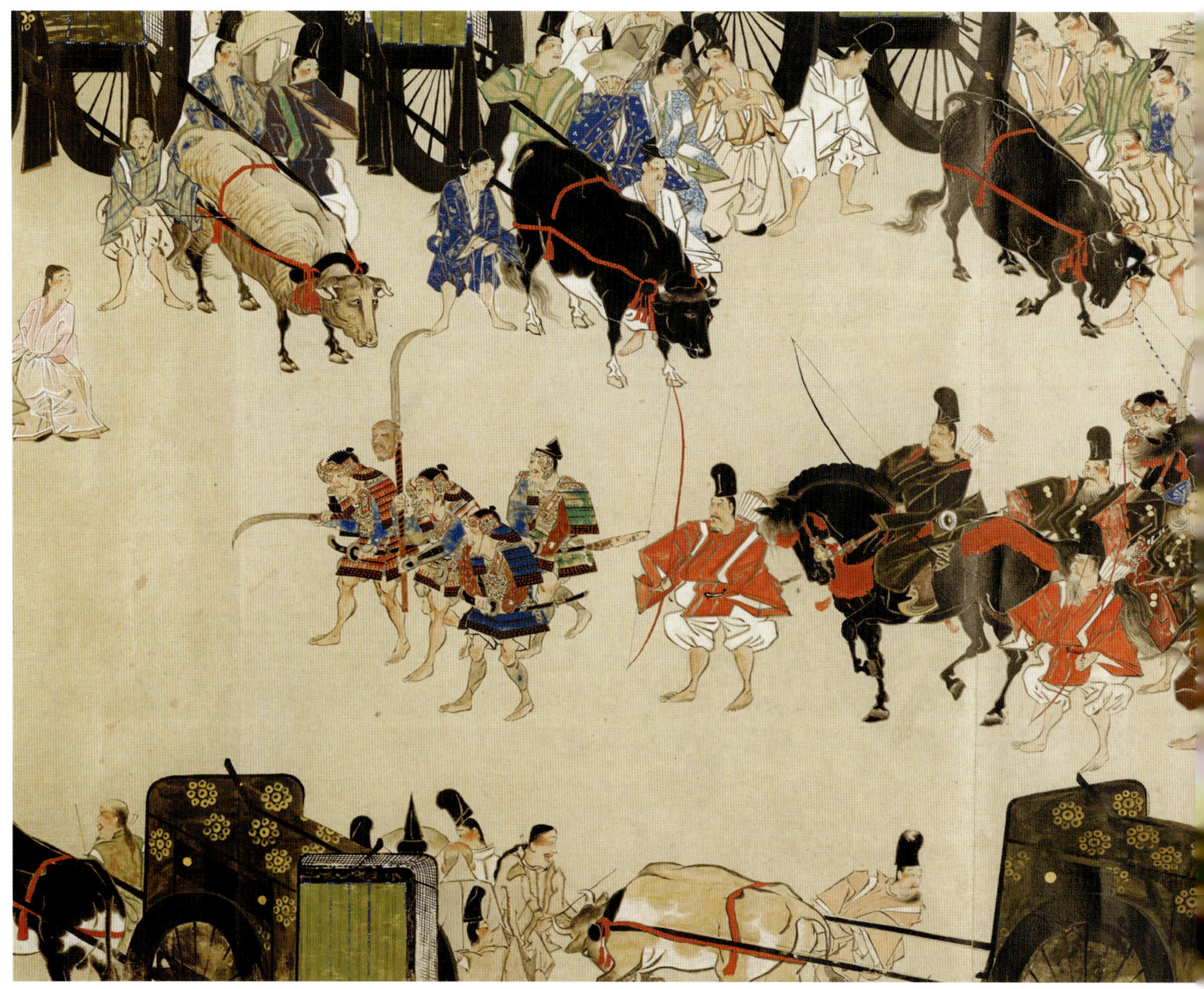

Battle Costumes Showcasing Power and Might

The *Heiji Monogatari Emaki* is an illustrated scroll based on the war chronicle "Heiji Monogatari," which depicts the events of the Heiji Rebellion in 1159. Currently, there are three scrolls: "Sanjo Palace Night Attack" (Boston Museum of Fine Arts), "Shinsei no Maki" (Tokyo, Seikado), and "Rokuhara-no-hama Gyoko no Maki" (Tokyo National Museum, a national treasure), along with fragments of the "Rokuhara Battle" scroll, which are preserved in various collections. The scene depicted here is from the "Shinsei no Maki," showing the capture of the severed head of Shinsei (Fujiwara Michinori), who had committed suicide while fleeing towards Nara, and the procession of warriors parading it through the streets of the capital.

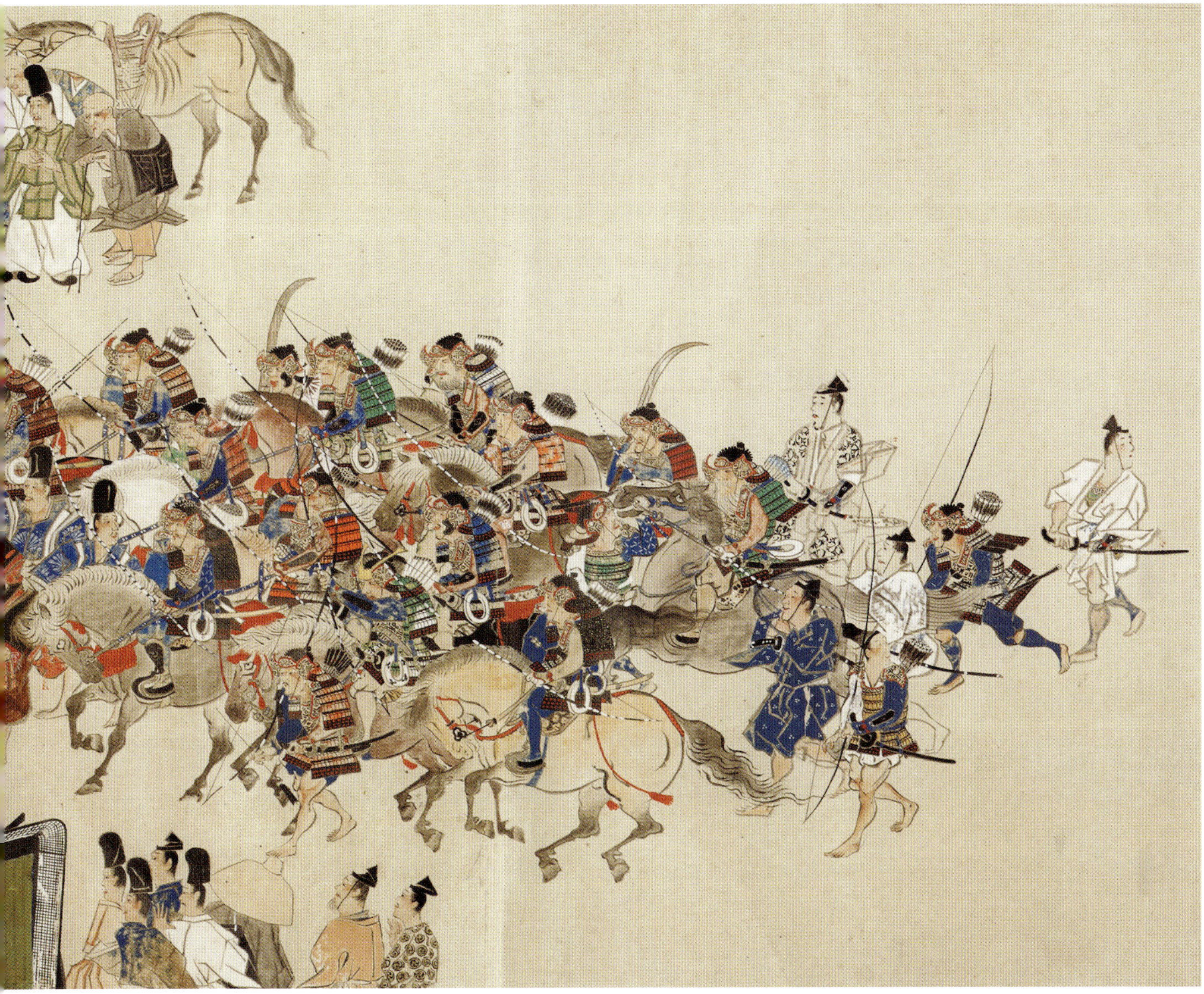

A bull cart has stopped by the roadside, clearing a wide path along the main road for a procession of armored warriors riding horses, advancing silently. At the forefront is Shinsei's head, firmly bound to a large sword, and the onlookers cannot conceal their astonishment. The composition of the painting is powerful and dynamic, especially in the portrayal of the crowd and the agile movements of the warriors. Even the smallest details of armor and weaponry are depicted with chilling precision. The orderly composition and vibrant colors used in the artwork make it arguably one of the greatest masterpieces among battle scrolls. The illustrated scroll featured here is a reproduction created by Kano Harukawa-in Yonobu, among others, in the fourteenth year of Tenpo (1843).

Detail from "The Tale of the Heiji Rebellion Illustrated Scroll: Shinsei Volume" (Reproduction) Text: Sumiyoshi Hirochika (Reproduction) Art: Kano Harukawa-in Yonobu et al (Reproduction), 1843.
Tokyo National Museum. Source: ColBase: https://colbase.nich.go.jp

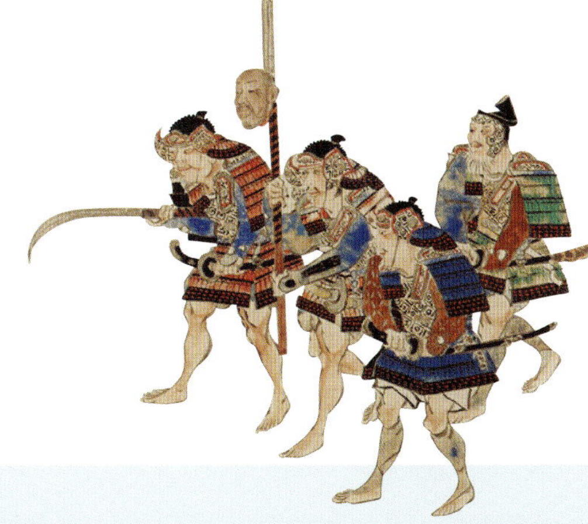

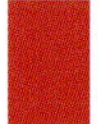

Karakurenai/Kokikurenai
Carmine/Deep Red

This is a vivid red color achieved through intense dyeing with red safflower, which gives a deep, rich red with a beautiful purple hue. The *Engishiki* (a book of regulations and customs) specifies the quantity of safflower and its raw materials required to dye the fabrics used for the noble's garments. At that time, safflower was as expensive as gold of the same weight.

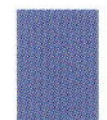

Benimidori/Benikakesorairo
Aqua/Red-tinged Sky Blue

Refers to a pale blue-violet shade that has a hint of red. "Aqua" can also mean blue, as in "Aqua gem" (green-blue gem) and "Aqua sky" (blue sky). The color name "Benikake sorairo" comes from a dyeing technique where red is overlaid on top of sky blue. When combining these two dyes, you get various shades such as "Futaa ai" (indigo) or "Benikake hanairo" (pinkish-purple).

Detail from "The Tale of the Heiji Rebellion Illustrated Scroll: Shinsei Volume" (Reproduction). Text: Sumiyoshi Hirochika (Reproduction). Art: Kano Harukawa-in Yonobu et al (Reproduction), 1843. Tokyo National Museum.
Source: ColBase at https://colbase.nich.go.jp

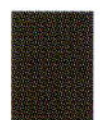

Benikeshinezumi
Poppy Gray

Benikeshinezumi is a dark purplish-red with gray undertones, as if overlaying red with ink. According to the *Tekagami Moyou Setsuyou* it was also referred to as "Kuroga-ki" (black persimmon) but it is actually a distinctly different color. Post-Genroku era, fashionable colors included chic patterns in tea or black, like stripes, lattices, and small patterns on kimonos.

Aikobicha
Indigo-tinged Tea

A dark green-brown color, resembling indigo-tinted tea. The dye was made from the bark of willow or plum trees boiled in alum after underdyeing with light yellow. This results in a shade favored by common folk, known as "midori" (green) or "kohakucha" (brown).

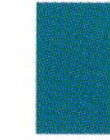

Kujakuao
Peacock Blue

Kujakuao is a relatively new color name, introduced during the Meiji era from the West as a translation of "Peacock blue." It refers to the deep blue of male Indian Peacock feathers. There's also a "Kujaku midori" derived from the green of peacock feathers, which translates as "Peacock green."

Ainezumi
Indigo Gray

A somber blue color with gray undertones. There is also a darker shade with a stronger blue tint called "Konnezumi." Ancient equivalents to the gray color included were dull purplish-gray, oak-tree bark color, light black, and so on. In the Edo period, Ainezumi was embraced as one of the "hundred shades of gray."

The two leading figures stand tall, wearing black robes and cormorant-feather hats. Following them are warriors in vermilion and green attire. The distinct complementary color scheme of red and green, yellow and purple, which stands out even from afar, is a characteristic feature of their attire. In this era, amidst the bloody battlefields, emerged magnificent armor influenced by the imperial color culture. Armor and helmets adorned with colorful threads and given beautiful names can be seen in scrolls and other documents. In the early Kamakura period when the *Heiji Monogatari* was written, armor displayed various color schemes and patterns, expressing the imposing presence of the warriors who wore them. The colors are also related to the "kasane no irome" (layers of colors) of the Heian period, and the warriors' attire seems to have incorporated the color culture of the elegant the courtiers.

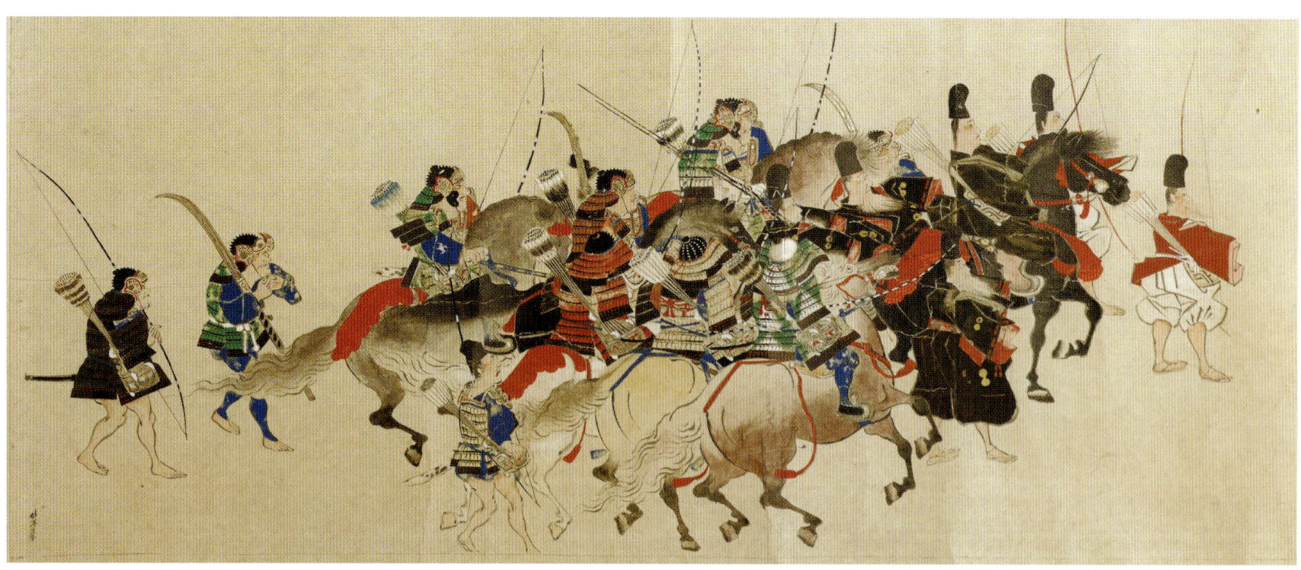

20 Karakurenai/Kokikurenai　75 Benimidori/Benikakesorairo　269 Benikeshinezumi　214 Aikobicha

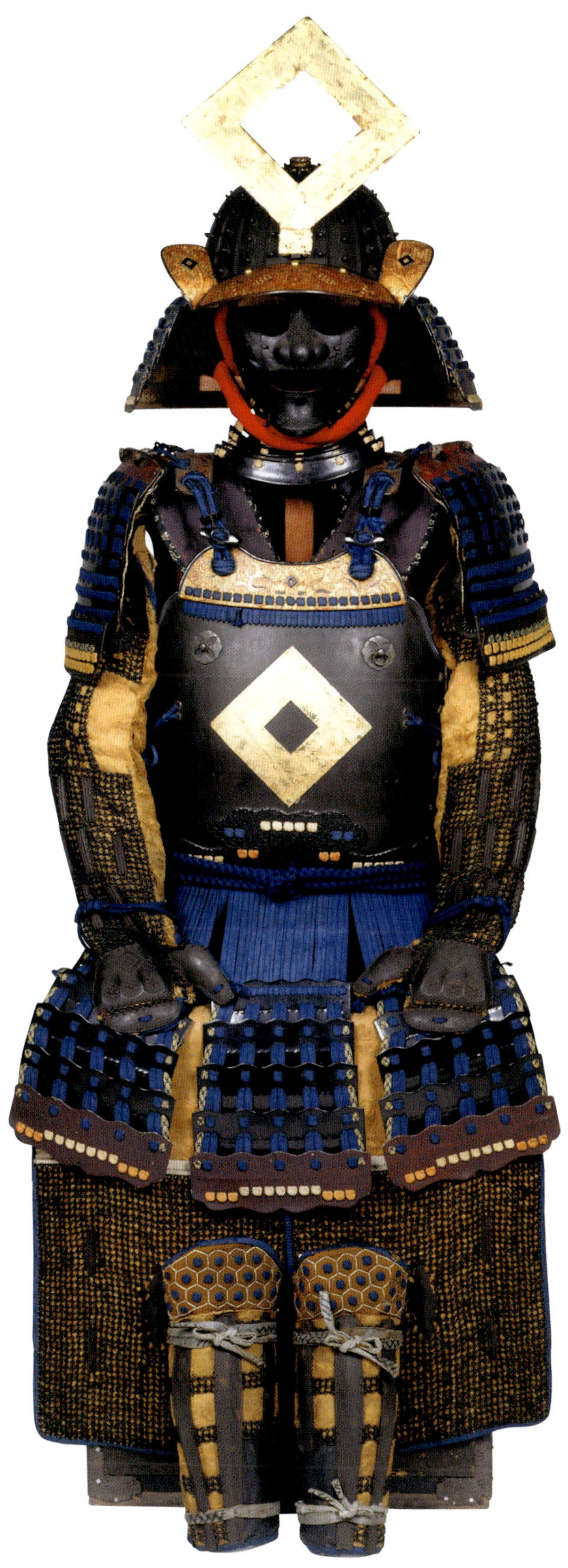

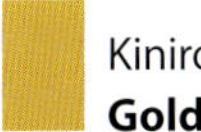

Kiniro
Gold

Golden yellow with the strong shine that metal gold possesses. It is also referred to as "Koganeiro" (golden color). Gold has symbolized eternity and immutability in Buddhism since ancient times, and it has also been a symbol of the highest spiritual realm.

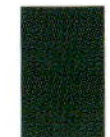

Aimirucha
Brown-tinged Dark Blue

A dark blue tinged with brown. The name combines two trendy color names, "Aimirucha" and "Cha." "Aimirucha" refers to a type of seaweed with a deep greenish-yellow color, while "Cha" represents a blackish tone. It is said that during the Genbun era (1736–1741), this color was fashionable for boys' kimono sleeves, and during the Horeki era (1751–1764), it was popular for hemp jackets.

The "Kon-ito-i" is a braided cord made from silk dyed with indigo, with tags attached to it. The helmet (*kabuto*) is a sixteen-panel iron helmet with a rust-colored finish, with a single nail-pierced family crest (*mon*) on the front panel. The eyebrows (*maebisashi*) and cheek guards (*fukikaeshi*) are decorated with decorative leather coated with gold leaf, known as *kin-karakawagane* leather, with family crests applied to the cheek guards. Hanging on the left and right sides and the back of the helmet to protect the neck from the collar is the "Sode-koro," consisting of five sections, with shoulder guards covered in wrinkled leather. The body (*dou*) is finished with a rust-colored lacquer over six panels of Buddhist armor plates, with chest plates, back plates, and shoulder guards covered in kin-karakawagane leather. A family crest in gold leaf is applied to the center of the front body armor. This helmet belongs to the Okajima family, a branch of the Okayama Bicchu family, and has been passed down to the Okajima family, retainers of the Kaga domain.

"Kon-ito-i Six-Plate Dou Gusoku".
Helmet Inscription: Made by Katsushika Tsunesada, a resident of Kasaizu. Edo period, 18th to 19th century.
Ishikawa Prefectural History Museum.

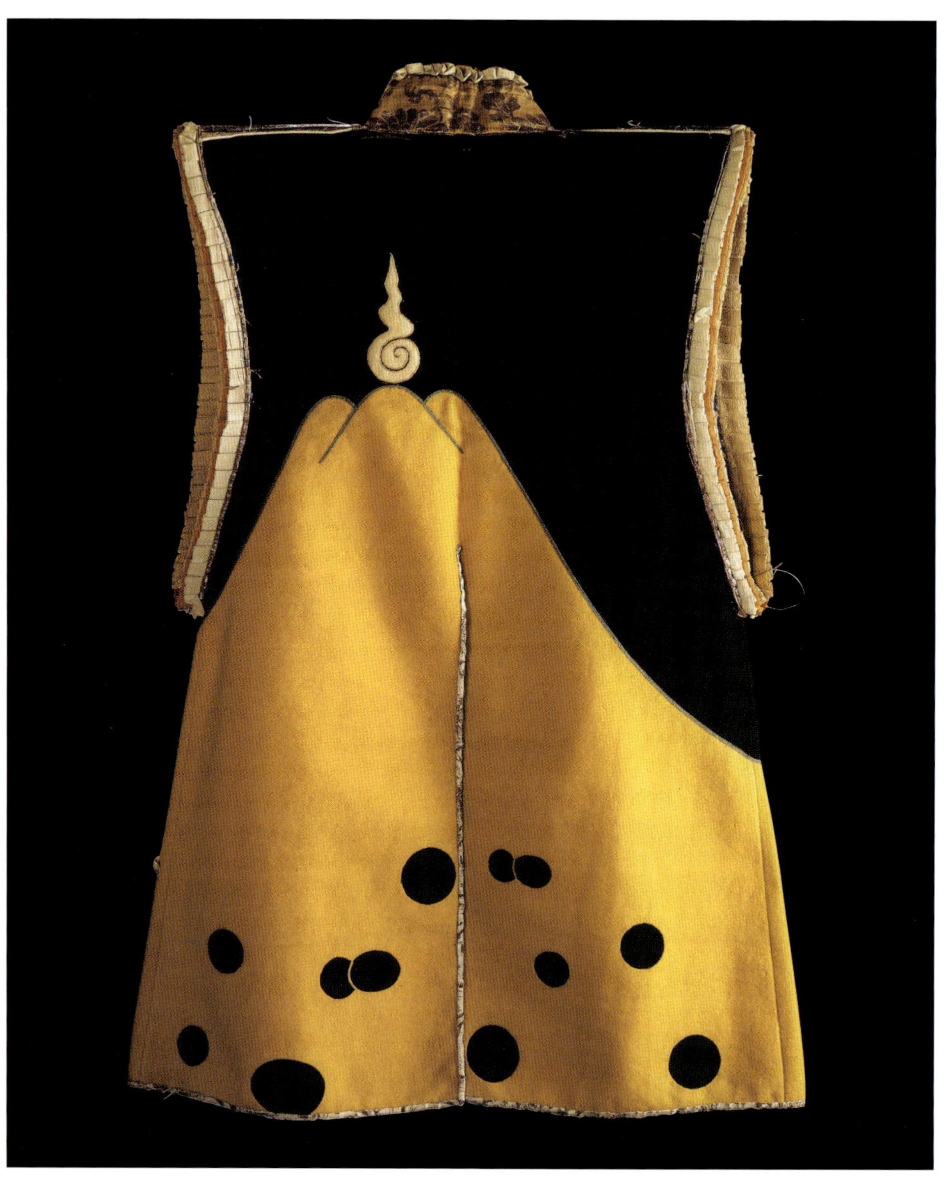

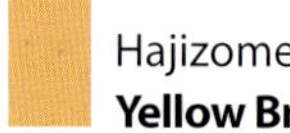
167 Hajizome   **280 Kuroiro**

"Mount Fuji Divine Flame Pattern Black and
Yellow Gauze Jinbaori".
Edo period, early 17th century.
Stored in the Osaka Castle Tenshukaku.

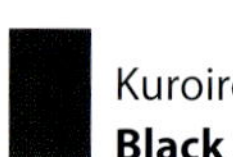
Hajizome
Yellow Brown

A deep, warm yellow. When dyed with the extract from *yamabuki* (*Kerria japonica*), and using the ash extract from camellia, it produces a warm yellow hue. Yamabuki grows wild in the mountains and produces wax from its fruits, which was traditionally used for dyeing paper. Due to its beautiful autumn foliage, yamabuki is also known for its overlapping color called "Hijimomiji," derived from the Japanese words for "yellow" and "maple leaves."

Kuroiro
Black

Kuroiro is used as a general term for the darkest color, or a color close to black, but true black is pure black. Since the Edo period, meticulous dyeing techniques have been used with materials such as gallnuts, pomegranate rinds, bark of willow or plum trees, goby berries, and iron filings to create what is known as "uwaguro," or "top black," which became the official color for formal kimono sleeves.

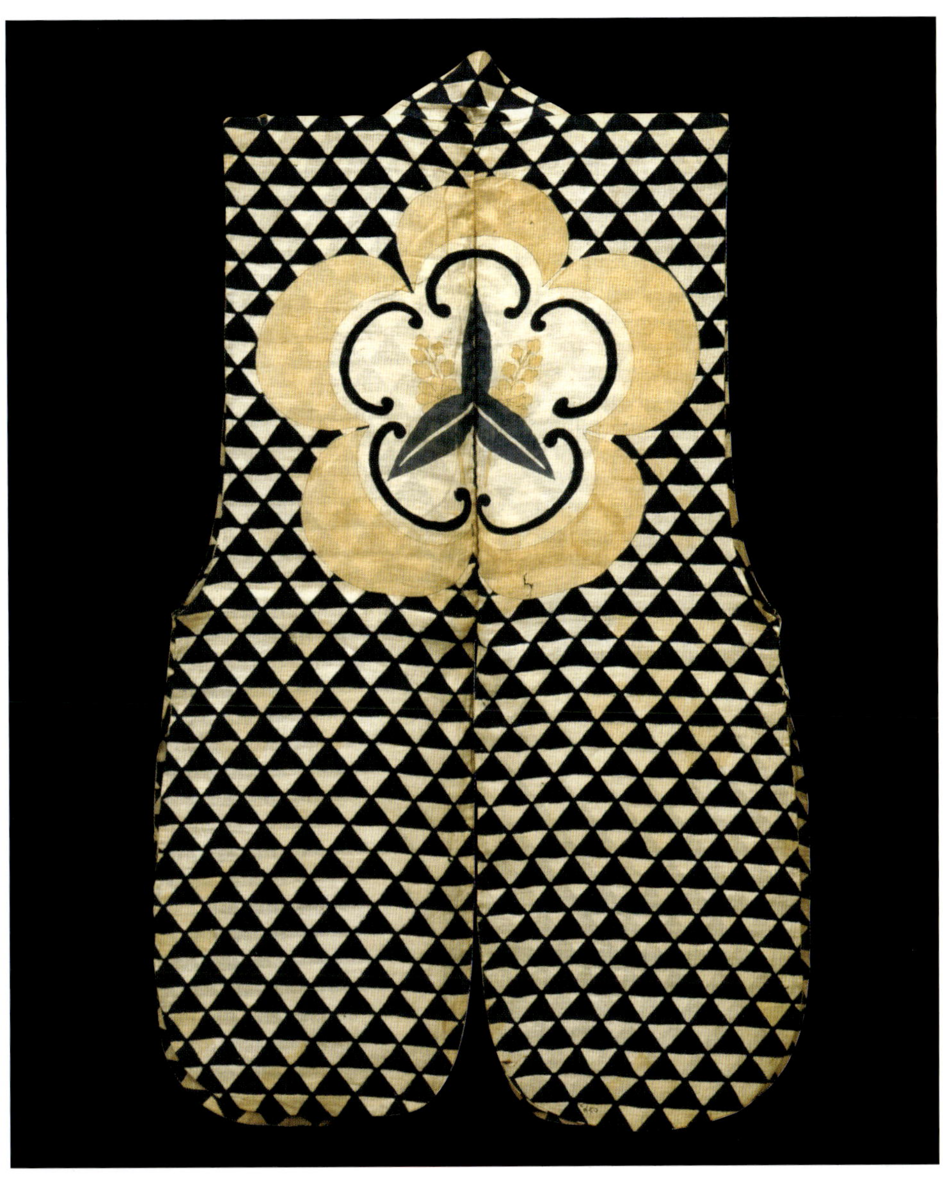

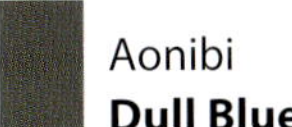

266 Aonibi

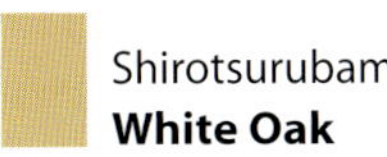

194 Shirotsurubami

**"White Hemp Jinbaori with Scaled Saw Pattern and Five Gourd Stand Saw Crest".
Edo period, 19th century.**
Tokyo National Museum.
Source: ColBase at https://colbase.nich.go.jp

Aonibi
Dull Blue

A light blue with a tinge of black. It is a color achieved by combining blue with ink-based dyes like sumi and then mordanting with iron. During the Heian period, wearing clothing in dull colors like Aonibi indicated mourning for close relatives who had passed away. In classical court literature, "Nezuiro" (dull color) was a term used to represent achromatic or unsaturated colors, along with "sumizome" (ink-dyed) and "usumizome" (light ink-dyed). It seems to have been a general term for colors that couldn't be easily categorized.

Shirotsurubami
White Oak

A slightly yellowish off-white. While oak is commonly associated with black dye, when using mordants such as camellia ash or alum, it dyes into a yellowish earthy color. This light brown is called "Shirotsuru" or "white oak," and it is considered to be in the range of what is now called beige. "Tsuru" is an old name for acorns, the fruit of deciduous trees in the beech family. It has been used for dyeing since the Heian period and was used for the clothing of lower-class individuals, as well as for mourning attire.

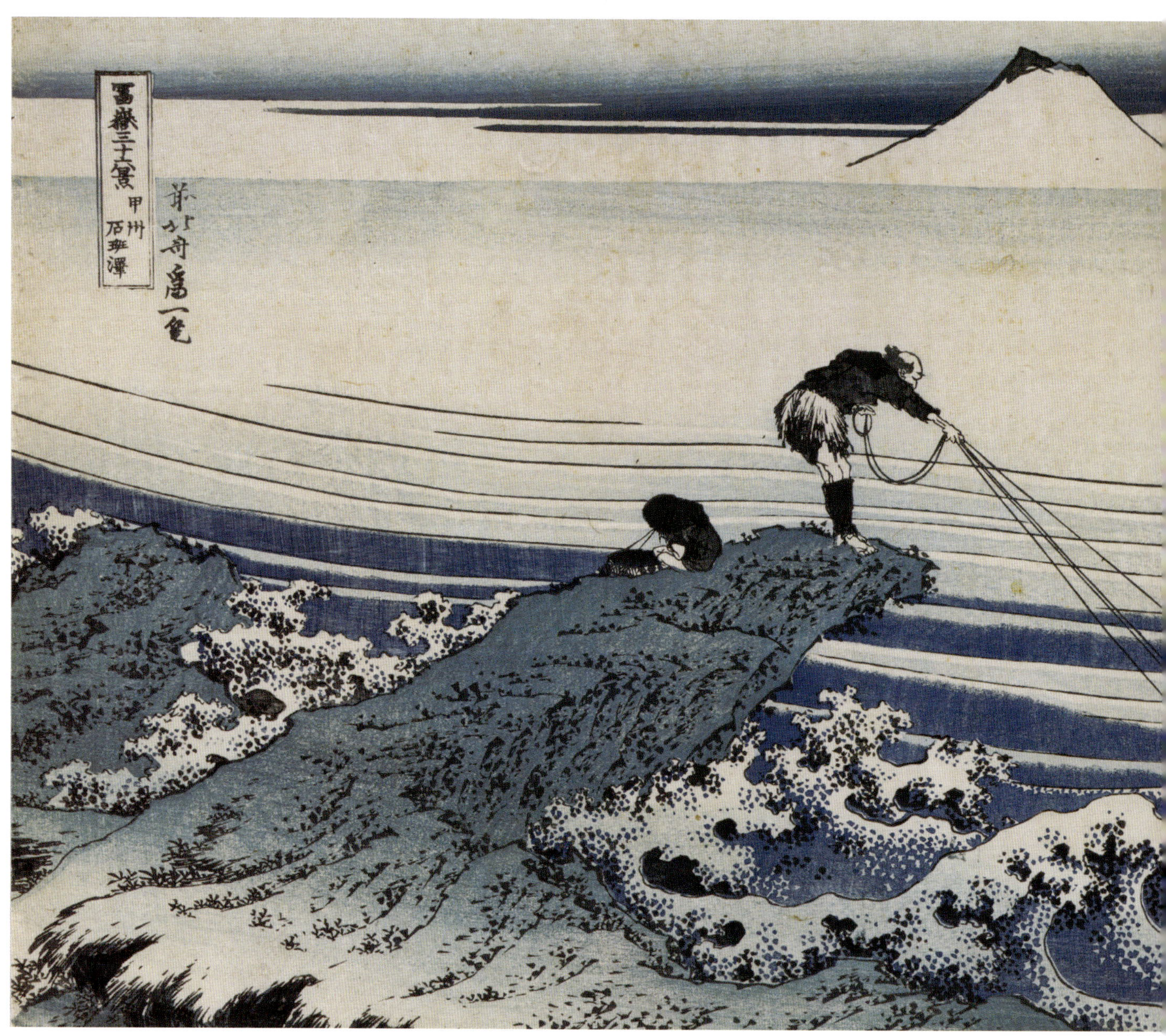

"Kajikazawa in Kai Province" from the series *Thirty-six Views of Mount Fuji* by Katsushika Hokusai.
Edo period, 19th century. Tokyo National Museum. Source: ColBase at https://colbase.nich.go.jp

The Blues in Hokusai, Hiroshige and Eishō
Ukiyo-e and Woodblock Prints

Ukiyo-e refers to woodblock prints primarily created during the Edo period, depicting the customs and scenes of that era. The subjects often included famous landscapes, Yoshiwara (the red-light district), courtesans, Kabuki actors, and sumo wrestlers. Beginning with Hishikawa Moronobu, the early works were monochromatic, featuring black and white, but later, they incorporated colored pigments, particularly red, and flourished with the emergence of polychrome woodblock printing techniques. Prior to this, the commonly used indigo dye was seen as having subdued color and lacking durability. During the Bunka and Bunsei periods, a synthetic pigment called "Berlin

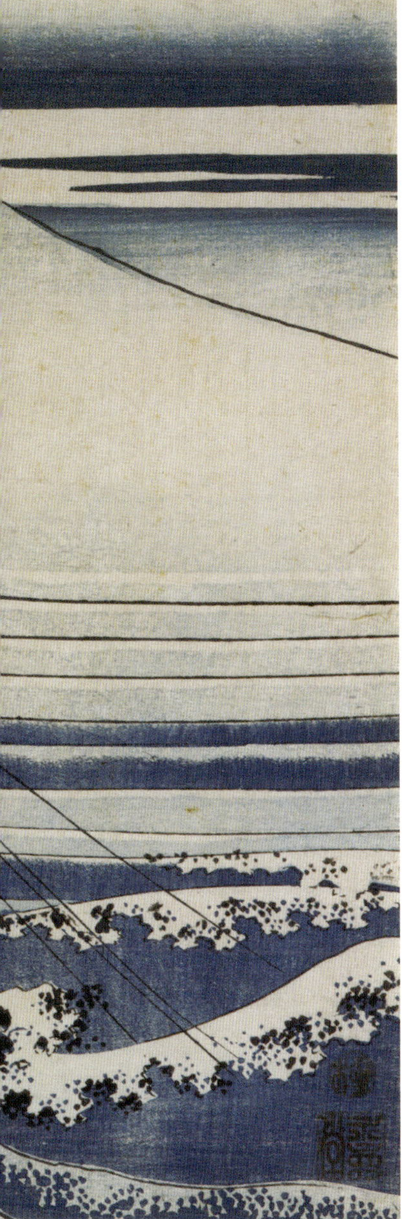

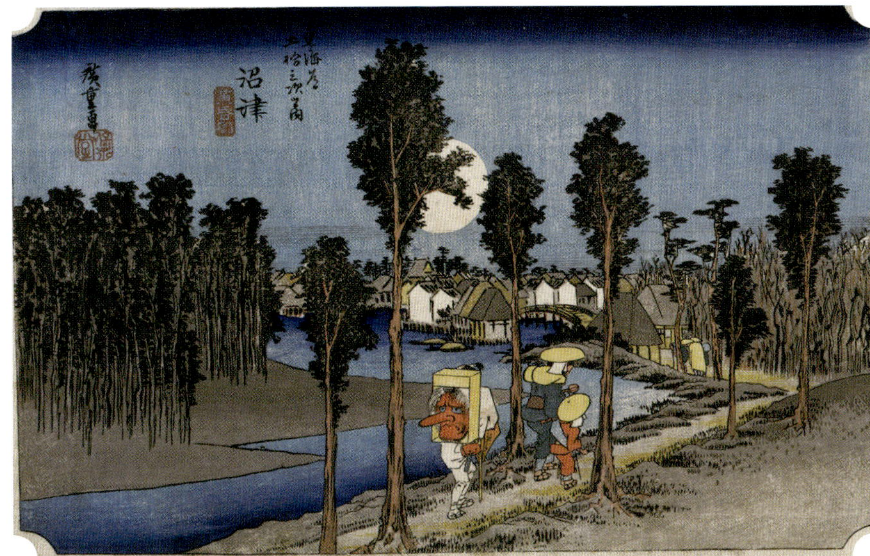

"Numazu, Twilight Scene" from the series *The Fifty-Three Stations of the Tōkaidō* by Utagawa Hiroshige. **Edo Period, 19th century** Tokyo National Museum. Source: ColBase at https://colbase.nich.go.jp

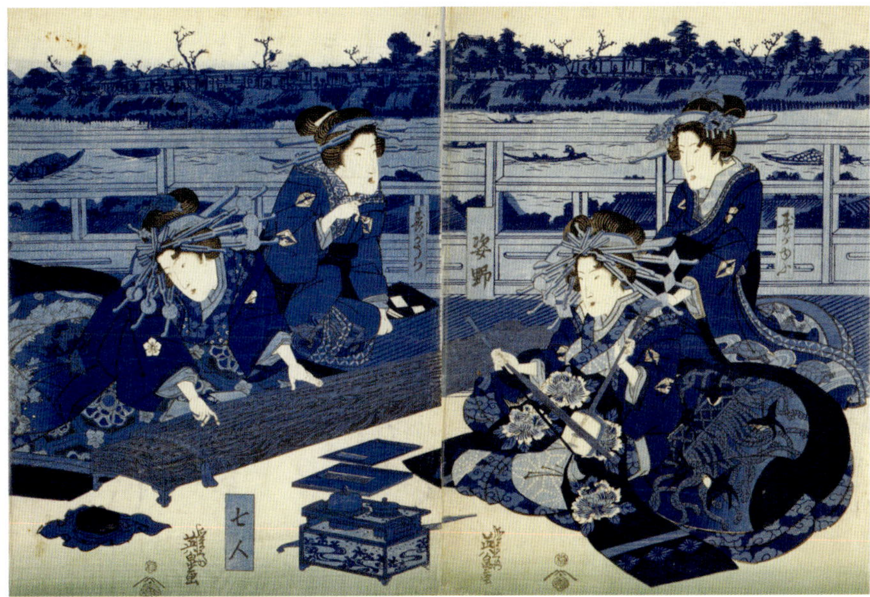

Detail from "Keisai Blue Printed Nishiki-e" by Keisai Eisen. Edo period 19th century
National Diet Library Digital Collection

Blue" was introduced from Europe due to its vibrant and durable hues. This blue pigment rapidly gained popularity among artists as it offered vivid and lasting colors.

As a result, this new blue expanded the creative possibilities in ukiyo-e, particularly in the genre of landscape painting, which later became a significant part of ukiyo-e. This new blue, with its brilliant hues and ease of shading, enabled artists to portray essential elements of nature such as the sky and water convincingly. Works created using Berlin Blue by artists like Katsushika Hokusai, Utagawa Hiroshige, and Keisai Eisen gained international attention, and it's said that Western artists admired this blue pigment, referring to it as "Hokusai Blue" or "Hiroshige Blue," among other names.

Indigo prints (or "ai-zuri-e") were monochromatic or primarily used variations of indigo in ukiyo-e prints. They are believed to have been created in response to the luxury regulations that prohibited the depiction of beauties, including kabuki actors, courtesans, and geisha, in full color woodblock prints during the Bunsei period as a countermeasure.

The Color Green in Japanese Culture

From ancient times, green has been a color symbolizing the revival of life and deeply associated with vitality, growth, and prosperity. In Japanese, the word "midori" does not merely represent a color but rather expresses a fresh and youthful state. Additionally, infants are referred to as "midoriko," and wet, glossy hair is described as "midori no kurokami." These terms depict nature's hues and the vitality of life. Green is universally perceived as a calming and soothing color, offering tranquility to the eyes and emotions across cultures worldwide.

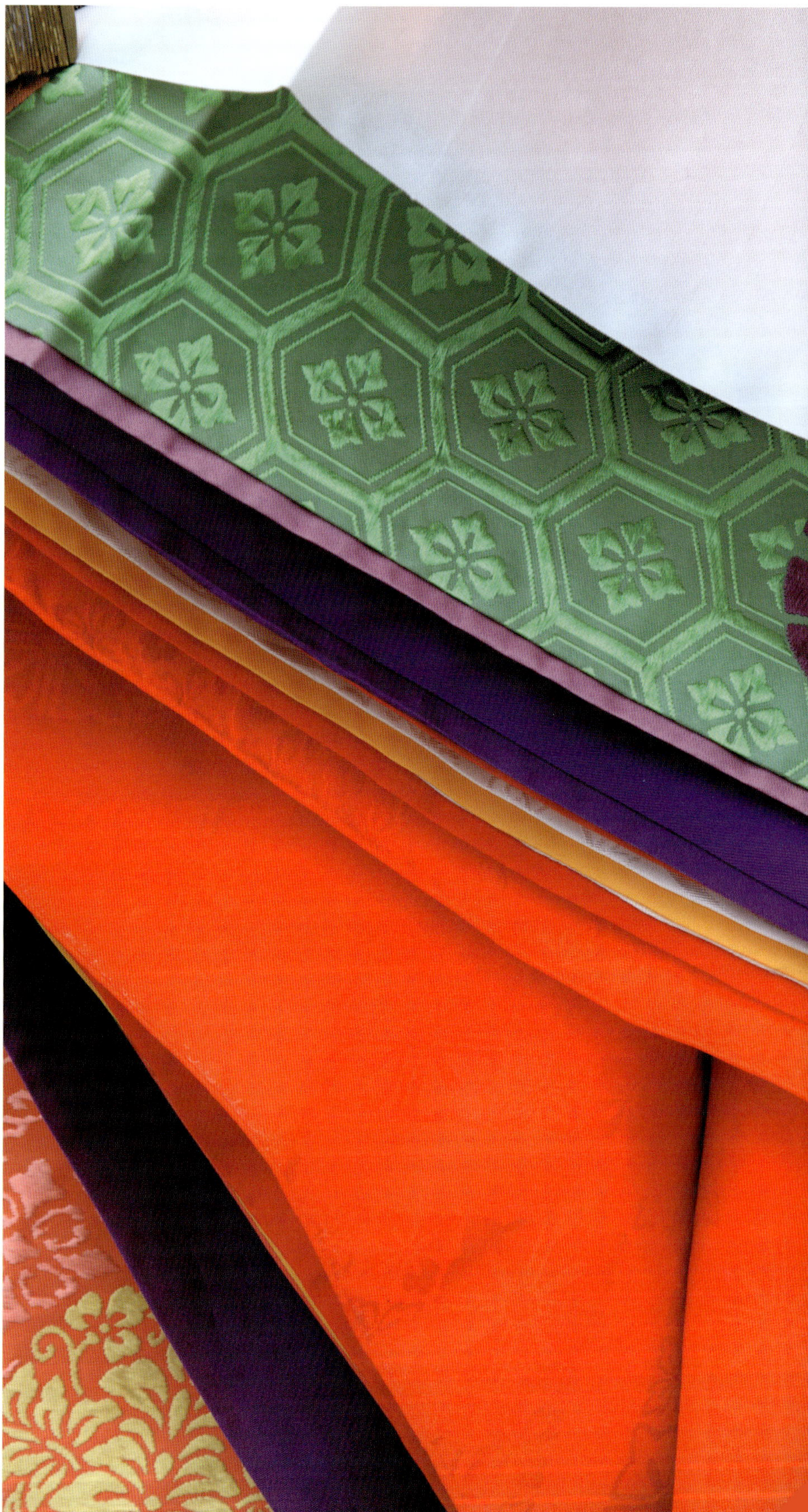

Right Misogi (Purification) Ritual at Shimogamo Shrine, Kyoto.
Top far right Kōtoku-in Temple, Kyoto.
Bottom far right Gio-ji Temple, Kyoto.

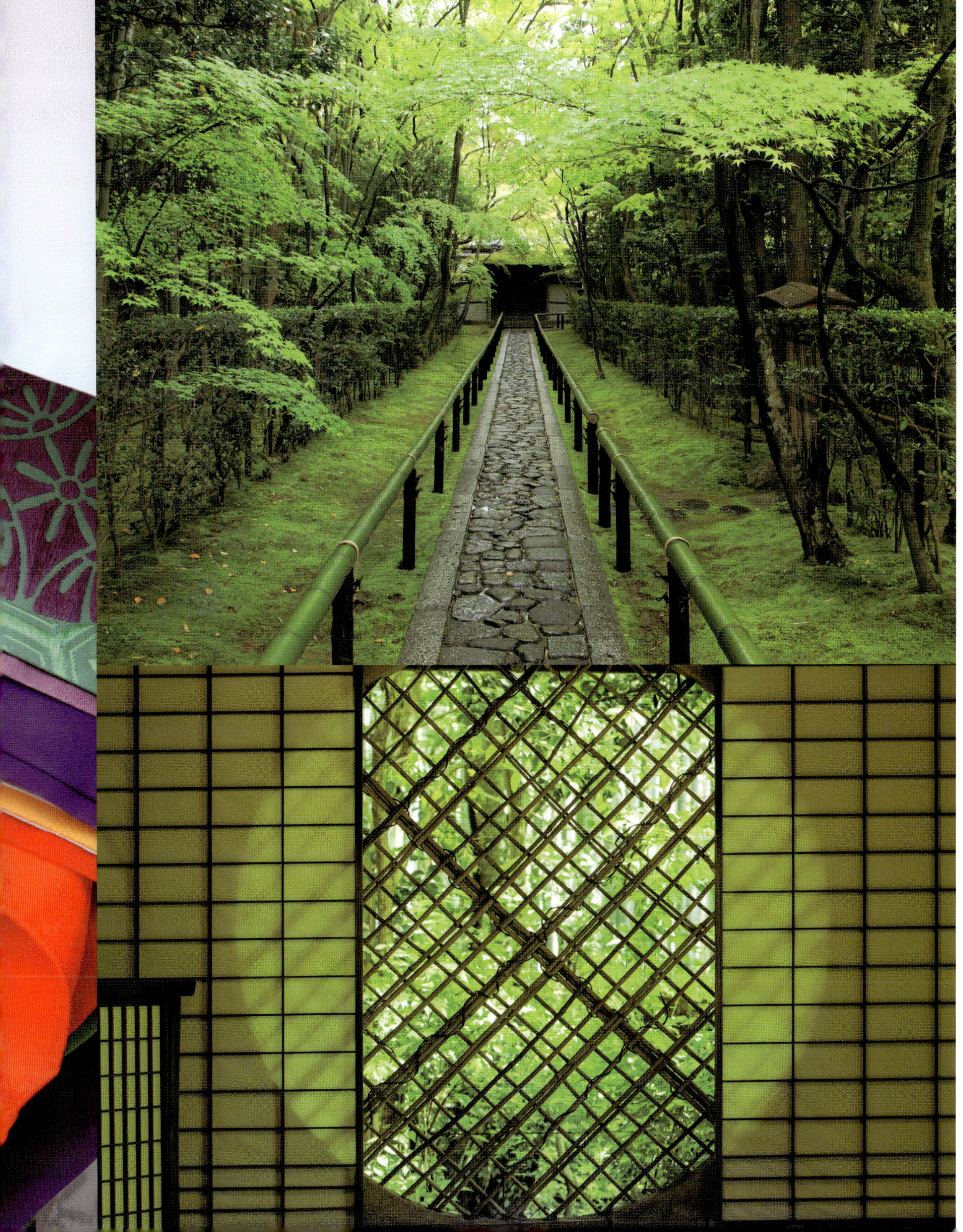

Japanese Color Schemes Based on Green

Green is a color created by layering blue and yellow, but its image is uncertain across time and cultures, often encompassing various shades ranging from blue to yellow and frequently being confused with both blue and yellow. This is mainly because green is primarily represented in nature by the leaves of plants, which display a variety of colors ranging from blue to yellow. Green, symbolizing nature, serves as a color representing vegetation. Trees and plants sprout in spring, emitting fresh greenery, thereby creating an environment conducive to sustaining life on Earth. Incorporating such green (nature) into one's life is desired by everyone, but chlorophyll, the pigment present in plant leaves, is fragile and weak, dispersing when exposed to water and gradually discoloring to a dirty brown with time. It serves no purpose as a dye or pigment.

Therefore, the green used in Japanese painting is a pigment primarily composed of copper, including "rokushō" made by grinding malachite, also known as "malachite green," and "Rokushō" produced artificially by oxidizing copper. Additionally, in the colors used in decorative ancient tombs from the Kofun period, green earth such as serpentine was sometimes utilized.

White or black is generally safe to pair with green, while coordinating with other colors can be challenging. In similar color combinations, bright yellow-green or dark blue-green achieve desirable natural effects. Japanese people have a preference for combining green with its complementary color, red, and have excelled in using sophisticated complementary colors in various aspects of life, clothing, and art.

In terms of color psychology, shades of green evoke a sense of tranquility, providing rest and reassurance. When one's mental balance is disrupted or emotions become turbulent, green has the effect of calming the mind and guiding it towards a brighter disposition.

Color Scheme Based on Pale Colors

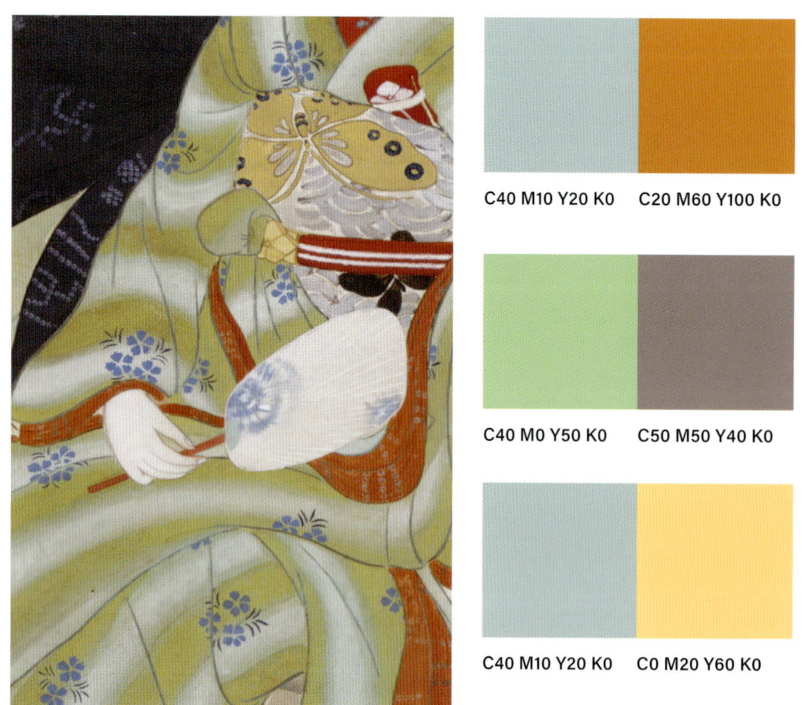

C40 M10 Y20 K0   C20 M60 Y100 K0   C40 M10 Y20 K0   C40 M0 Y0 K0

C40 M0 Y50 K0   C50 M50 Y40 K0   C40 M0 Y50 K0   C20 M30 Y0 K0

C40 M10 Y20 K0   C0 M20 Y60 K0   C40 M10 Y20 K0   C20 M60 Y80 K0

Detail from "Hanabi Incense" by Itakura Seikō, 1917.
Kyoto City University of Arts Art Research Center.

Color Scheme Based on Vibrant Colors

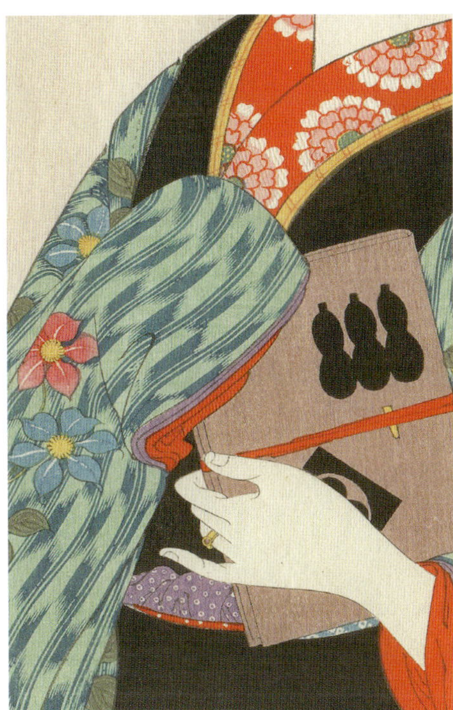

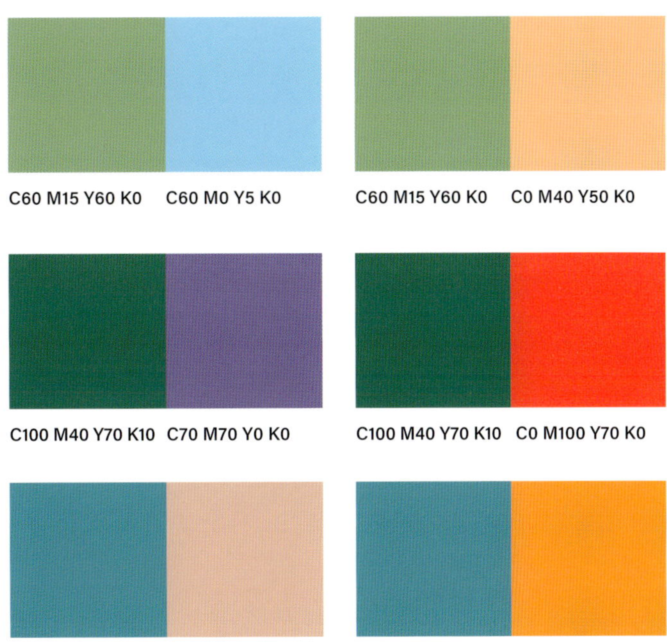

C60 M15 Y60 K0 C60 M0 Y5 K0

C60 M15 Y60 K0 C0 M40 Y50 K0

C100 M40 Y70 K10 C70 M70 Y0 K0

C100 M40 Y70 K10 C0 M100 Y70 K0

C90 M20 Y30 K0 C10 M40 Y30 K0

C90 M20 Y30 K0 C0 M60 Y100 K0

Detail from "True Beauty: Kaeshi" by Toyohara Chikanobu, 1897. Yamaguchi Prefectural Hagi Art Museum and Uragami Memorial Museum.

Color Scheme Based on Deep Colors

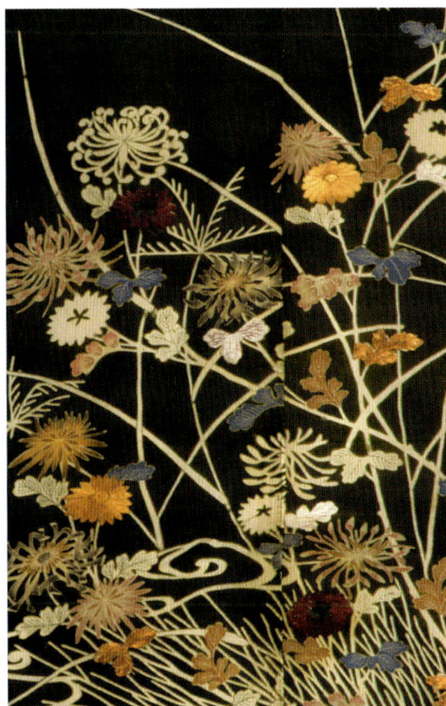

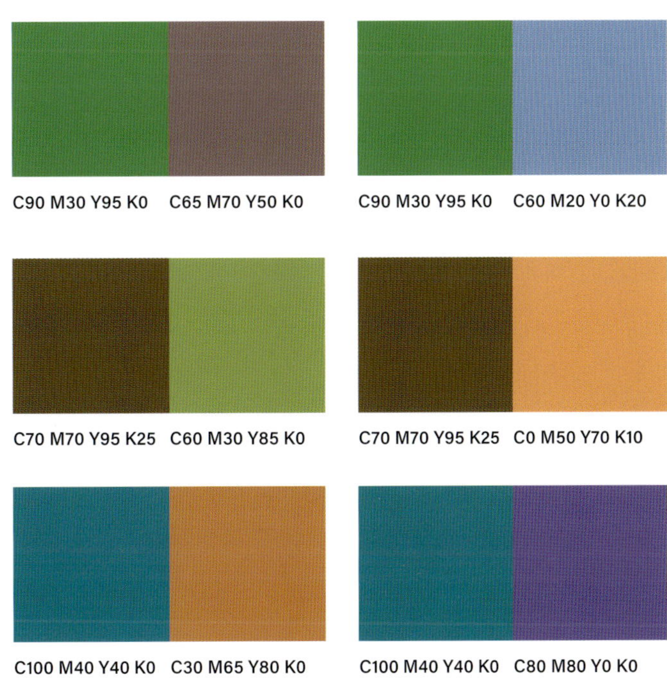

C90 M30 Y95 K0 C65 M70 Y50 K0

C90 M30 Y95 K0 C60 M20 Y0 K20

C70 M70 Y95 K25 C60 M30 Y85 K0

C70 M70 Y95 K25 C0 M50 Y70 K10

C100 M40 Y40 K0 C30 M65 Y80 K0

C100 M40 Y40 K0 C80 M80 Y0 K0

**Detail from "Light Green Crepe Silk Kimono with Chrysanthemum and Bamboo Fence Water Pattern".
Edo period, 18th century**. Tokyo National Museum.
Source: ColBase at https://colbase.nich.go.jp

Three *maiko* (apprentice geisha) are depicted enjoying incense fireworks on a low table. One is lying down with her elbows propped up, another is seated sideways, and the third is shown from behind, holding a folding fan. The design of the maiko's kimono is traditional, but the painter's originality is evident in the coordination with the *obi* (sash) and the color combinations of layered garments. The gentle contours of the girls, captured with soft lines, convey a sense of purity and freshness, radiating elegance.

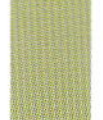

Kikujin/Aoshirotsurubami
Pale Greenish Gray

It is named after the color of fermented *koji* mold, referring to a dull bluish-green color. Although koji dust and bluish-white oak are thought to be different color names, in the *Sai Gu Ki*, a manual of court ceremonies, there is a mention of "koji dust and bluish-white oak being one thing," suggesting they represent the same color. According to the *Enshiki* (a book of regulations and customs), the actual dyeing process produces a dull yellowish-green color due to the interaction of harvested Japanese indigo and madder root. This color was used for everyday garments, contrasting with the color of the ceremonial robes worn by the emperor, which were dyed with Japanese wax tree, indicating it was a restricted color.

Kokikuchinashi/Fukakikuchinashi
Deep Orange

In the *Engishiki*, "Kuchinashi" refers to a color dyed only with yellow safflower madder flowers, while "Kokikuchinashi" represents a deeper orange color achieved by combining flowers and seeds, producing a deeper color. Despite the small amount of madder flowers used, there were times when its usage was prohibited due to its resemblance to the color of the Crown Prince's robe, described as "yellow ootan."

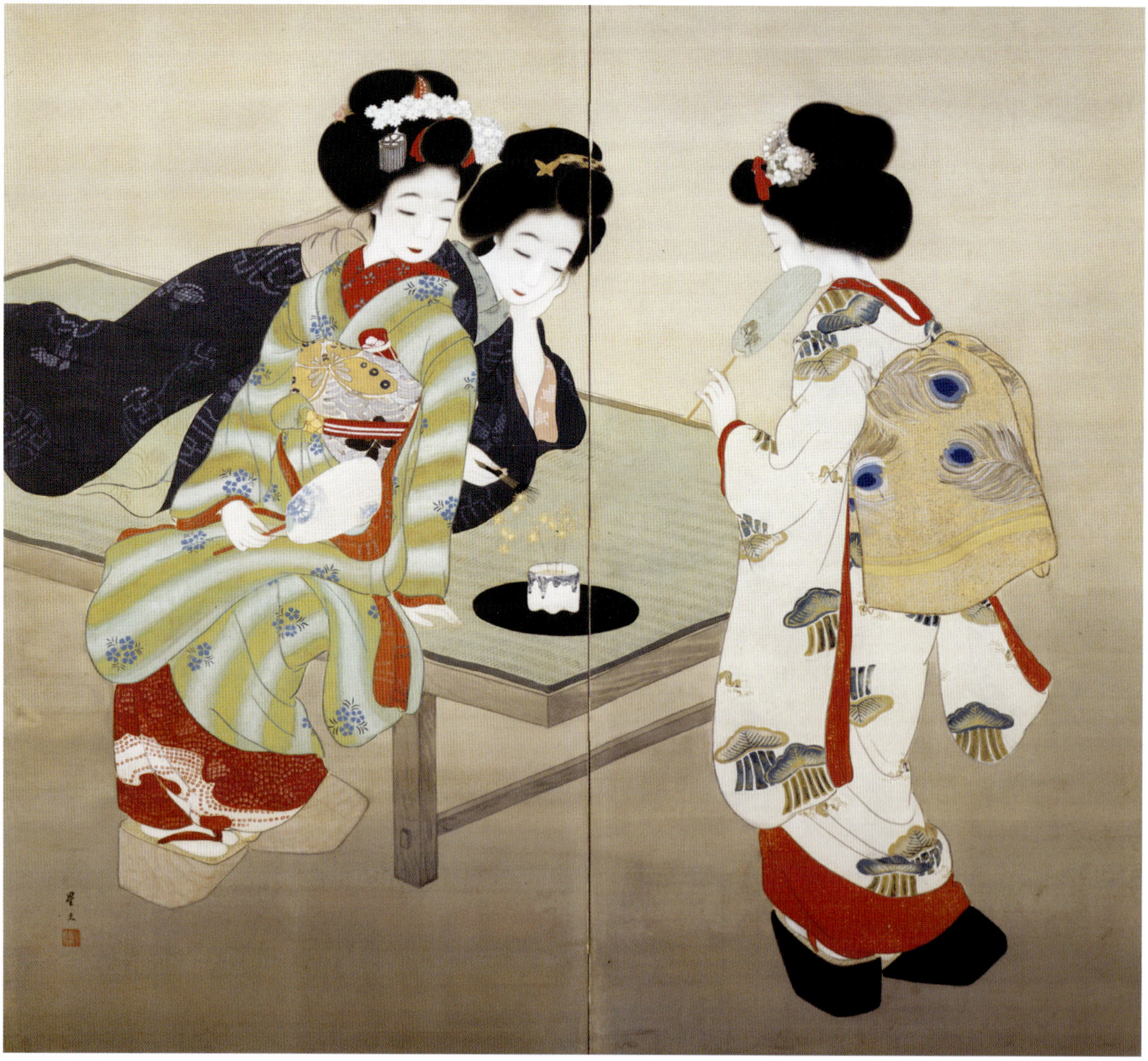

132 Kikujin/Aoshirotsurubami
42 Kokikuchinashi/
Fukakikuchinashi
102 Wasurenagusairo

"Incense Fireworks" by Hoshiko Itakura 1917.
Kyoto City University of Arts Art Research Center.

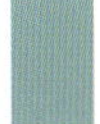

Wasurenagusairo
Forget-me-not Blue

This color describes a bright blue resembling the bright blue perennial plants in the borage family, originally native to Europe and cultivated for ornamental purposes. Toshi Ueda translated the English "Forget-me-not" as "Wasurenagusa" and in his work *Umi Shion* (1905), he wrote a poem whose title translated "by the shore of the flowing water, the color of the sky reflected in the water is shallow blue" where "the color of the sky" refers to the color of the Virgin Mary's robe.

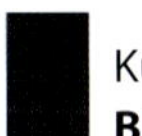

Seijiiro/Hisoku
Celadon Green

Celadon refers to a type of porcelain coated with a blue-green glaze. Due to the iron content in the glaze, it takes on a unique bluish-green color tinged with gray. In *The Tale of Genji*, it was called "aoji." It began to be referred to as "seiji" (celadon) from the Meiji period onwards. Its mysterious beauty also earned it the name "secret color." The English term "celadon" also refers to this bluish-green porcelain, and it has become a color name in its own right.

Kuroiro
Black

Kuroiro is one of the achromatic primary color names and the darkest color. It is used to describe the range of shades from glossy lacquer black to dense ink black. It is also used as a general term for colors close to black, including various shades of darkness. Black is often perceived as somber and heavy, as it has the lowest brightness among colors.

The figures of the two women bathing in a slightly green-tinted bath appear as if they could disappear at any moment into the steam filling the bathroom. Capturing and portraying that swaying, ephemeral atmosphere, this work is reminiscent of the brushwork of the ancient paths. This piece, inspired by the hot springs of a villa by Lake Ashinoko in Hakone, originally under the patronage of Mikage, is now considered a masterpiece.

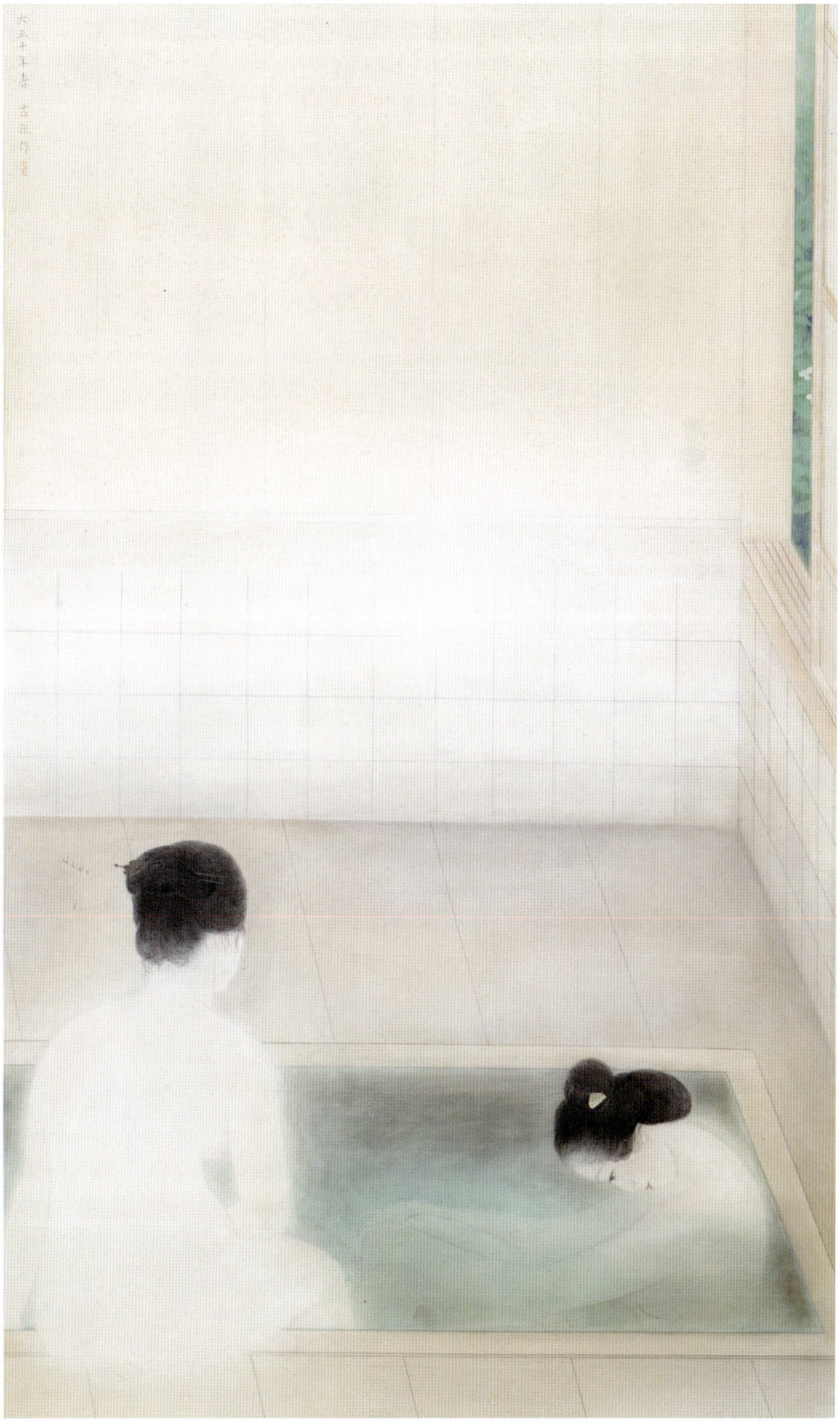

"Leaving the Bath" by Kobayashi Kokei, 1921.
Tokyo National Museum.
Source: ColBase at https://colbase.nich.go.jp

151 Seijiiro/Hisoku   **280 Kuroiro**

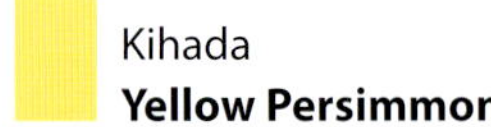

Moegi
Fresh Yellow Green

This is a bright yellow-green color resembling fresh green onion leaves. There is a lighter variation of this color called "Usu-moegi." These color names have been widely used since the Heian period. Moegi was considered a youthful color, and it is mentioned in *The Tale of the Heike* when describing the appearance of young samurai.

Kihada
Yellow Persimmon

Used to describe a slightly greenish yellow color obtained from dyeing with the bark of the Japanese Judas tree (Cercidiphyllum japonicum). To create the yellow dye, the bark is crushed to make an infusion, and it is then mordanted with ash or alum. Together with Japanese pagoda tree (kariyasu), gardenia (kuchinashi) and turmeric (ukon), it is one of the representative traditional dyes in Japan. The decoction also has insect-repellent effects, and in ancient times, paper dyed with this decoction was used for sutras and family registers.

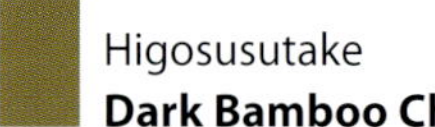

Higosusutake
Dark Bamboo Charcoal

A color derived from "Susutake" which is a dark brownish-green color resembling bamboo charred by soot. Higosusutake has a stronger orange undertone compared to "Susutakeiro," which is closer to the original color of charred bamboo. The "higo" in the color name is believed to refer to a place or a person's name, although this is not certain. Various colors with "susutake" in their names are seen in the period following the Genroku era (late 17th century) and later.

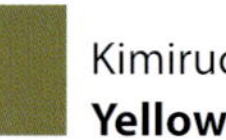

Kimirucha
Yellowish Olive Brown

A dark yellowish-green color, similar to today's olive green. It was favored during the Edo period and can be found in various dyeing materials from the mid to late Edo period. "Umimatsu" refers to an olive-like color; "So-umimatsu" indicates a color closer to the original Umimatsu, and "Kimirucha," a similar shade, describes a dull olive color with a yellowish tint.

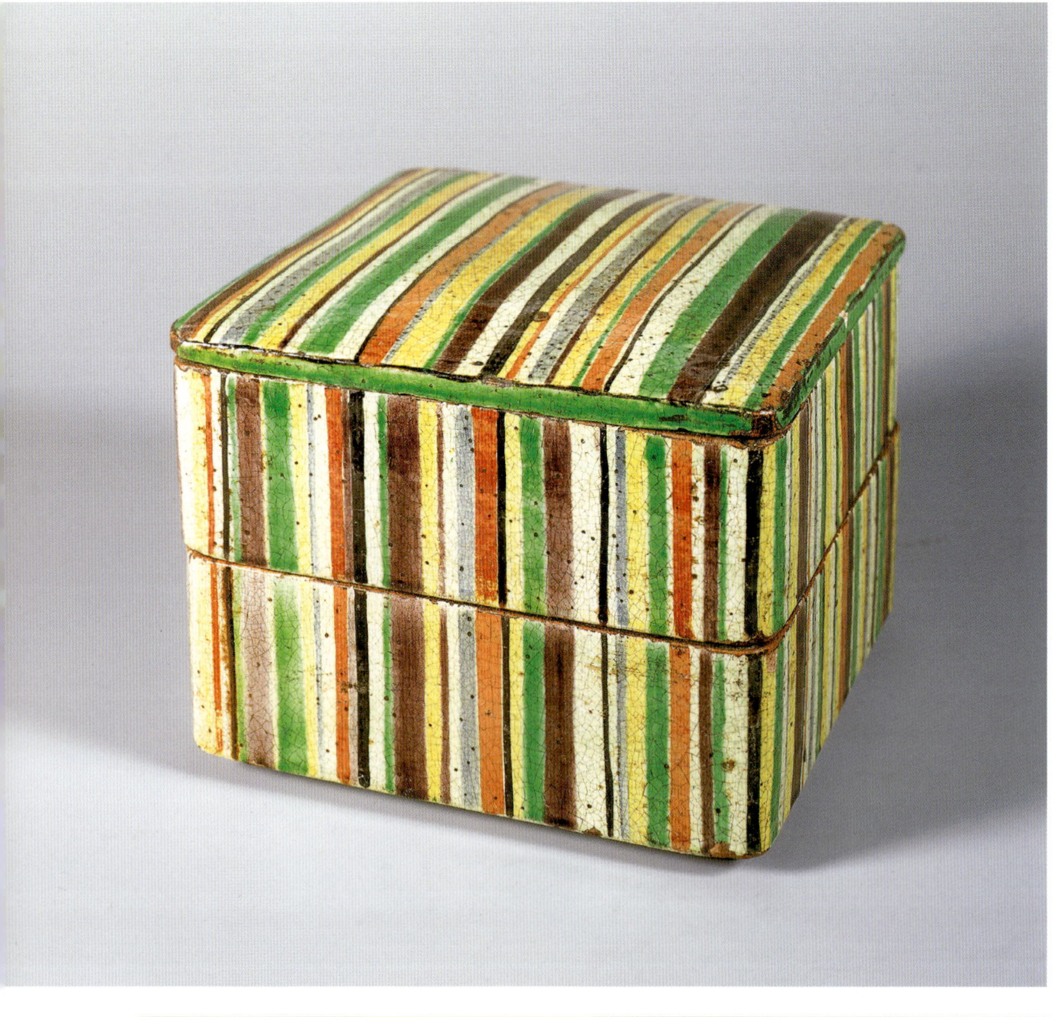

This is a rectangular two-tiered container. The ceramic base is made of light brown earthenware, and it is coated with white slip and soft glaze. It features a vertical stripe pattern with variations in width, using five-color pigments along with other shades of brown and the base's white color to create a modern and colorful appearance. The inside of the lid and the interior of the container are colored in green, and the bottom of each tier reveals the white clay beneath the slip glaze.

"Colored Porcelain Striped Two-Tiered Stacking Containers" by Awaiya Genemon. Edo period, 19th century.
Ishikawa Prefectural Museum of Art.

| 141 Moegi | 179 Kihada | 222 Higosusutake | 208 Kimirucha |

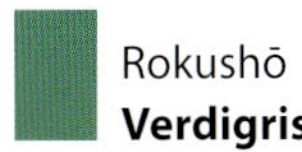

Rokushō
Verdigris

Refers to a subdued bluish-green color. Rokusho is a natural pigment created by grinding malachite (peacock stone) into a deep green pigment. In contrast to the red-based pigment cinnabar, verdigris is widely used in the coloring of architectural structures and sculptures in shrines and temples as a representative green-based pigment.

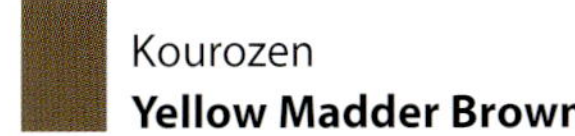

Kourozen
Yellow Madder Brown

This name refers to the wood of the hawthorn tree, and the combination of the yellow heartwood of the tree with the red of sumac, vinegar, and lye creates a yellow-red color when dyed. Since the Heian period, it has been designated as the color of ceremonial robes worn by the emperor. Although it is considered an absolute taboo color, it has persisted to this day due to its complex hue, which is said to vary subtly depending on the era. Due to the beautiful autumn leaves of the hawthorn tree, the color yellow is also named "Mijiba," which combines the yellow of hawthorn with the red of autumn leaves.

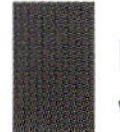

Fujisusutake
Wisteria Bamboo Charcoal

It refers to a dark grayish-purple color with a hint of wisteria, leaning towards a dark reddish-grayish-purple shade. The color tone is noted in the color chart *Tekagami Moyō Setsuyō* as "Fujisusutake," meaning "the color dyed by applying red-brushed mouse fur to plum." There are around twenty color names derived from bamboo dyes, including "Higo-botchiku" and "Shara-otomebotchiku," many of which can be found in color sample books and pattern books from the Genroku to Hoei periods.

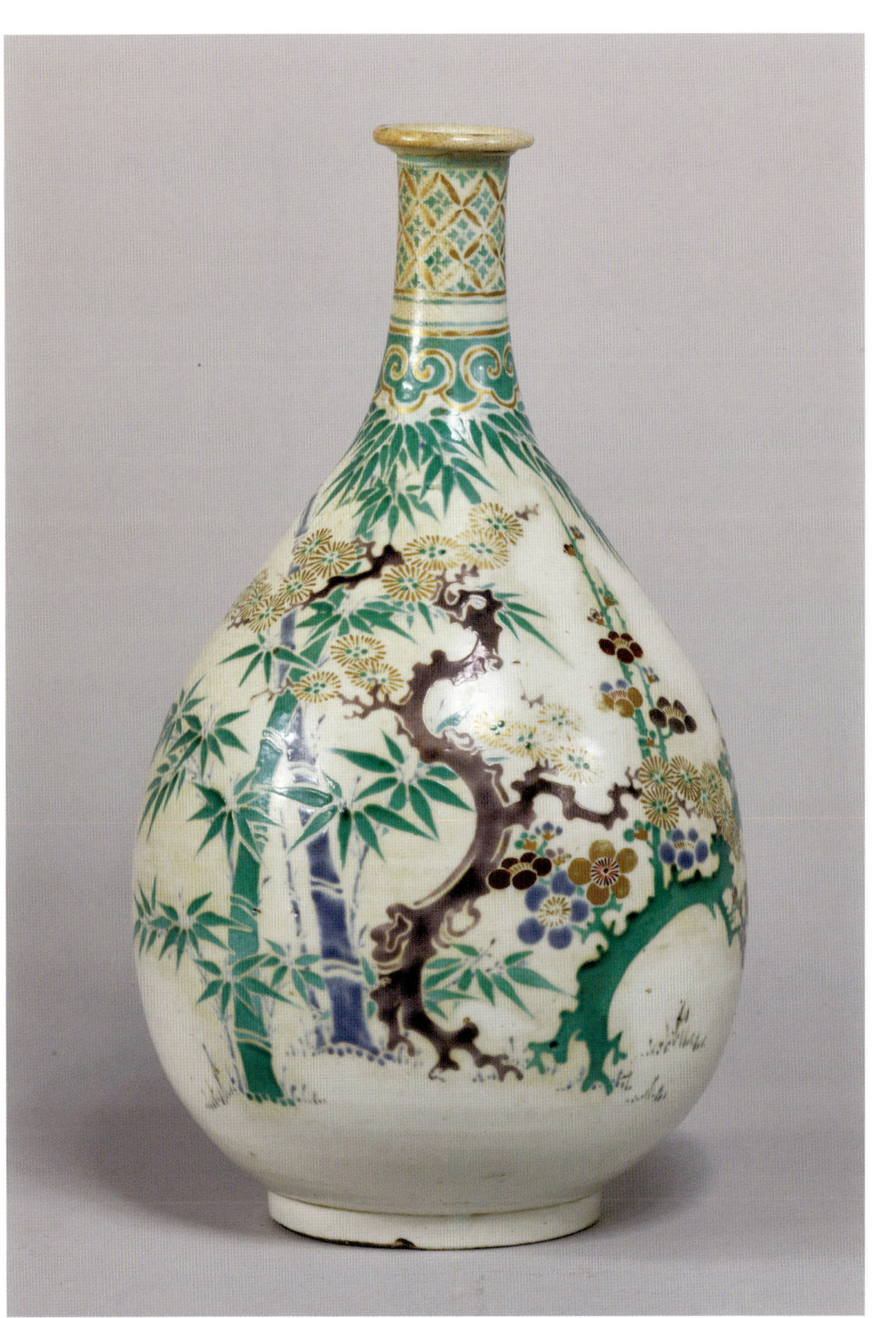

This vase features lucky motifs of bamboo and plum trees, colored in green, and pine trees and plum blossoms depicted in varying shades of ink. It was formerly referred to as "Daiseiji Ninsen" and was considered one of the variants of Old Kutani ware. These auspicious designs were popular at the time, and it is evident that they were imitated beyond their place of origin.

"Colored Porcelain Bottle with Pine, Bamboo, and Plum Design". Imari Ware. Edo period, 17th century. Tokyo National Museum.
Source: ColBase at https://colbase.nich.go.jp

153 Rokushō   **61 Kourozen**   **85 Fujisusutake**

This large plate features a central design of a phoenix with its wings spread wide, surrounded by lotus petals as decorative elements. The plate is divided by lotus petal patterns and features designs in *nanako* (cloisonné) style and *saaya* (fine silk fabric) patterns. The bold composition and rich color palette create a powerful and unique style. This porcelain was fired to meet the demands of domestic daimyo families and others.

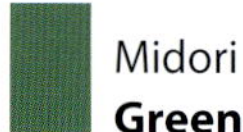

Midori
Green

Refers to the deep green color of plant leaves and is used as a general term for green colors. In the *Engishiki*, deep green dye was made using indigo and cutweed, while medium and light greens were made using indigo and *kihada* (a tree indigenous to Japan). In the past, there were no natural dyes that could produce a green color, so it was necessary to create it by mixing blue and yellow. In Japan, when plants turn green, they are often described as "blue." For example, phrases like "blue mountains" and "blue fields" refer to green rather than the actual color blue.

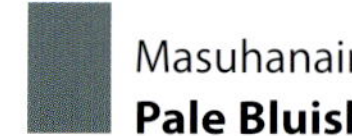

Masuhanairo
Pale Bluish

A pale bluish color with a touch of "astringency," it refers to a light blue-gray color. During the An'ei and Tenmei eras (1772–1789) in Edo, the popular actor of the time, Ichikawa Danjuro V (pseudonym: Shirasaru), introduced this light blue-gray as a sort of dynastic color of the Ichikawa family. This color came to be known as "Masuhanairo." The "masu" in Masuhanairo refers to the three *masu* shapes of the Ichikawa family crest, which are combined in a square pattern, and "Hanairo" refers to the color of *sukui* (a type of cloth).

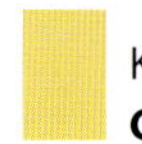

Kariyasuiro
Greenish Yellow

It refers to a yellow color with a greenish tint dyed using a broth made from cutweed and ash. Yellow dyeing with cutweed has been practiced since ancient times because the results are more durable than from dye sources such as safflower, yellow buckthorn, or gardenia. Additionally, it is noted in the *Engishiki* that not only yellow but also greenish colors were made using a combination of indigo and cutweed broth. The cutweed obtained from Mt. Ibuki in Shiga Prefecture was considered the best for this purpose. The name "cutweed" originated from the minimal effort required to harvest the plant.

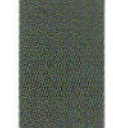

Tonocha
Bluish Green

This is a bluish-green color with a touch of gray, also known as "Reki cha." In the color chart of *Tekagami Moyō Setsuyō* (a guidebook for dyeing techniques), it is written that the light color of "Omeshi-Onando" is called "Reki tea," and its dyeing exhibits a grayish-green color. Agarwood refers to fragrant wood from tropical rainforests, used as material for incense and joss sticks. Tonocha is believed to be named after the color of the wood of black agarwood.

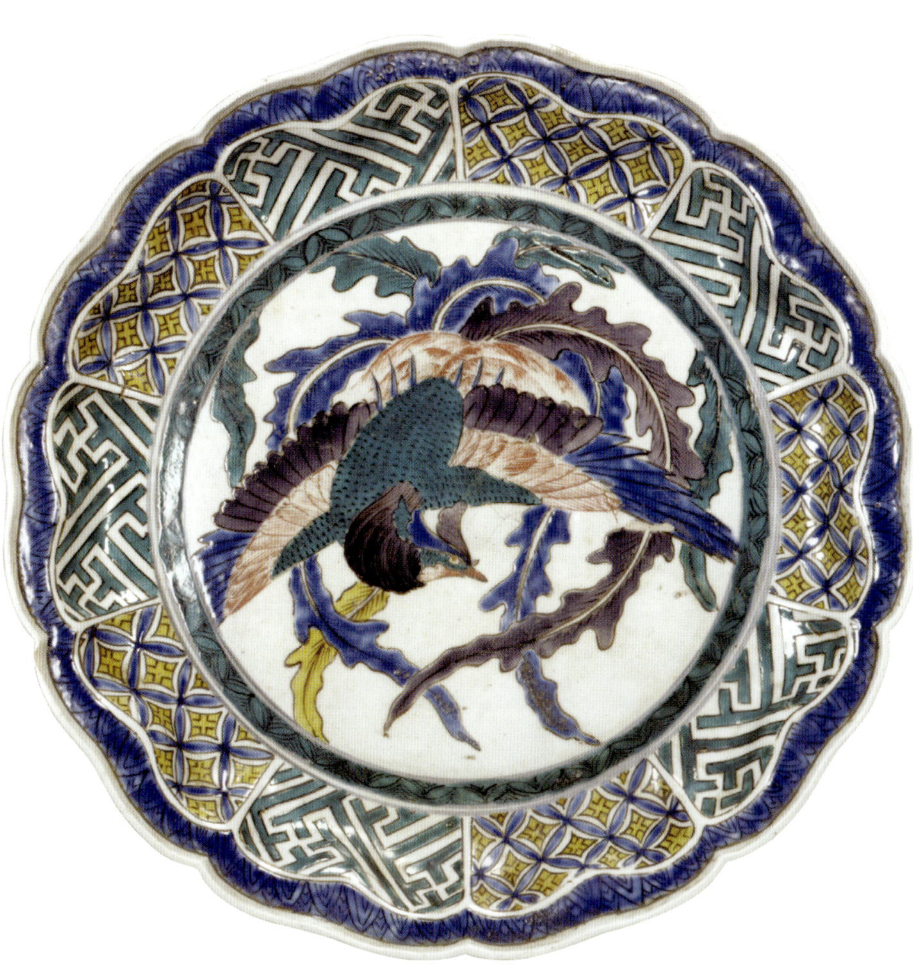

"Colored Porcelain Plate with Flying Phoenix Design".
Imari ware. Edo period, 17th century.
Tokyo National Museum. Source: ColBase https://colbase.nich.go.jp

154 Midori   **120 Masuhanairo**   **183 Kariyasuiro**

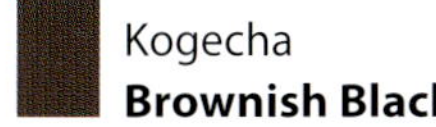

Tetsuiro
Muted Bluish Green

The faded bluish-green color reminiscent of the burnt skin of iron is often referred to as "kusu". Iron, known as "Kurogane," signifies not the color black but rather a dark shade of bluish-green. Some color names associated with iron include "Tetsunando," "Tetsukon," "Tetsunezumi," and "Tetsufukawa," all of which represent various shades of faded bluish-green. This color became popular during the Meiji and Taisho periods and was commonly used for the aprons of foremen and assistants.

Kogecha
Brownish Black

A color with a brownish-black hue, resembling the color of something burnt or scorched. It is essentially a rich, dark brown with a blackish undertone. In dyeing terminology, the names of colors are often related to the depth and intensity of the color, such as *kon* (dark) or *kuro* (black). However, when it comes to brown, only "Kogecha" is used to describe this specific shade. Various materials are used to create this shade, including Japanese sumac, Japanese pagoda tree, and Japanese oak, among others.

This flat plate is divided into paving-stone pattern with each square section containing various small patterns such as *shihoudai* (four-directional crest), *nanako* (cloisonné), *seigaiha* (wave patterns), *marubon* (circle patterns), and curly stripes. The plate is beautifully balanced with vibrant colors of green, dark blue, yellow, and purple. Additionally, within the square sections featuring shihoudai patterns drawn in red, there are intricately designed *mokume* (wood-grain) patterns with facing phoenixes in yellow and dark blue, creating a very intricate and tasteful design, resulting in a charming piece.

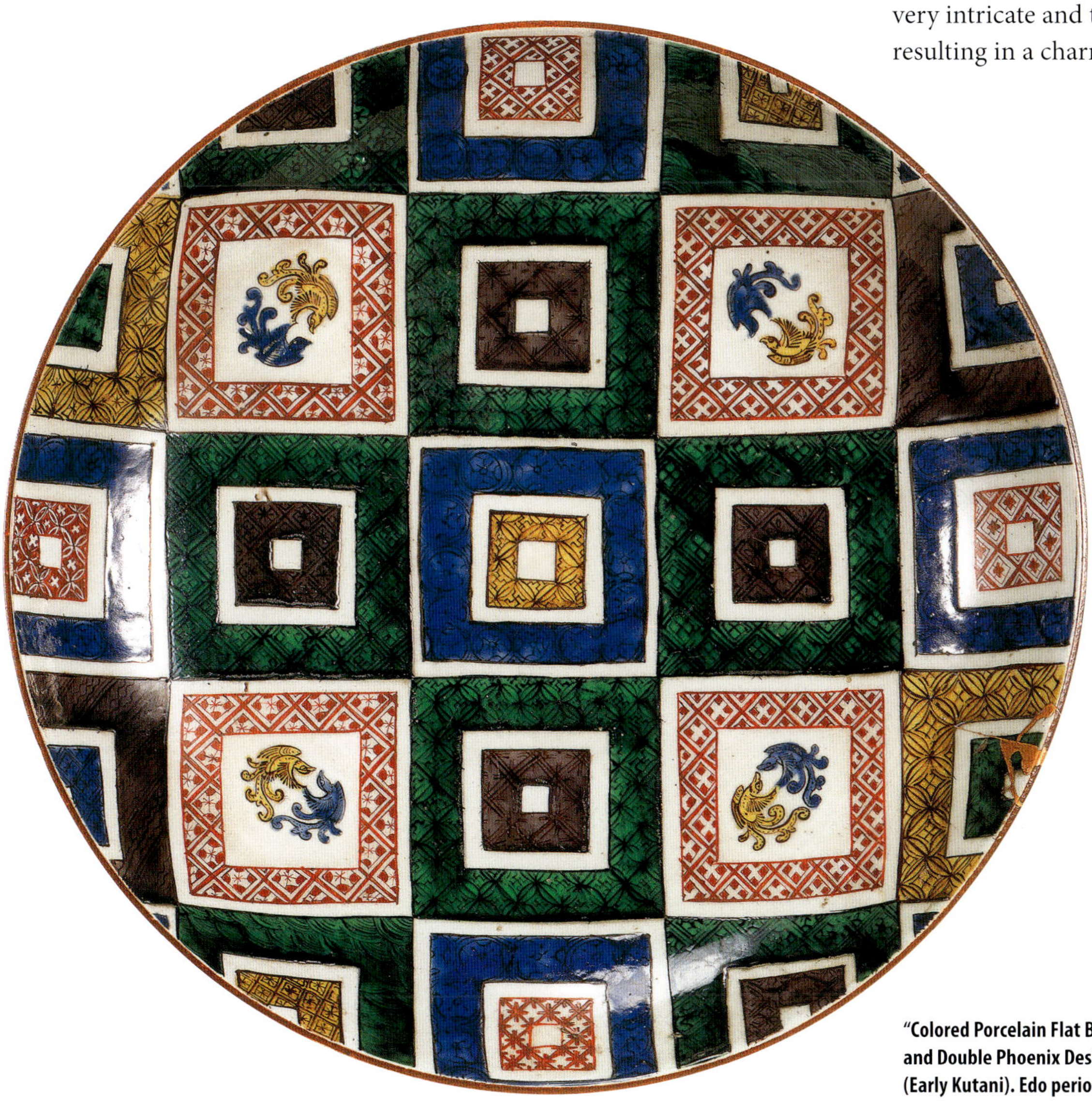

"Colored Porcelain Flat Bowl with Stone Pavement and Double Phoenix Design". Ko-Kutani (Early Kutani). Edo period, 17th century.
Ishikawa Prefectural Museum of Art.

160 Tonocha	122 Tetsuiro	249 Kogecha

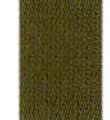

Noshime Hanairo
Dark Bluish Gray

This is a darker blue color with a stronger grayish tone compared to "Noshime-ro." In the *Tekagami Moyō Setsuyō* it is described as "Masuhanairo," a favored color of Ichikawa Danjūrō V, who preferred lighter flower-like colors. Noshime is a plain weave fabric woven with raw silk for the warp and half-processed silk for the weft, used as an undergarment beneath hemp robes.

Uguisuiro
Dark Greenish Yellow

Derived from the color of the nightingale's feathers, it is a darker shade with a greenish tint compared to "Hiwairo" (color of a species of warbling bird). For dyeing, a combination of indigo and soybean broth is used as the base color, while dyestuffs like Japanese wax tree or alum are applied for the top dyeing. This color name emerged during the Edo period along with the trend of brown colors. Within this color scheme, there is a deeper brown shade known as "Uguisucha."

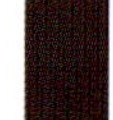

Nisemurasaki
Purple-like

Nisemurasaki is a term used for colors that resemble purple but are not dyed using the traditional *murasaki* (purple) plant. Instead, nisemurasaki is created by under-dyeing with indigo and then overlaying it with colors like madder or sappanwood. Similar substitute colors like "Nisemomoiro" and "Nisebeni" were also dyed using this method.

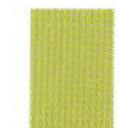

Hiwairo
Yellowish Green

HIwairo is a yellowish green color, while "Hiwa- moege" is used for a greener shade of yellow-green. This color name has been used since the Muromachi period and eventually became a representative color name for greenish yellow shades. When this color takes on a brownish tone, it is known as "Uguisucha," which became popular during the Edo period.

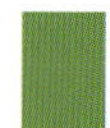

Moegi
Fresh Yellowish Green

Moegiiro is a color name that describes the fresh, yellowish green color seen in the budding leaves of plants. It is sometimes written as "moegi" to emphasize the impression of new growth in tree leaves or the fresh green shoots of scallions. It is considered a springtime color and is often paired with colors like red and red plum.

Aka-shiro Tsurubami
Pale Reddish Orange

This is a pale orange color with a reddish tone, resembling the color of acorns with a light reddish overlay. "Tsurubami" refers to oak trees, and their acorns have been used for dyeing. The right to wear this color was reserved for high-ranking officials such as the Emperor, Crown Prince, and those with the title of Sangi or higher.

Usukō
Pale Incense

Usukō refers to a pale incense color, which is a light yellow-brown. Extracting dyes from aromatic woods such as agarwood and orchids is called "kōzome," and the resulting color is referred to as "Kōiro." Since the dye is extracted from aromatic woods, it is believed that the scent of agarwood remained for some time after dyeing. Therefore, during the Heian period, this color was often associated with the aroma of cloves.

"Eitai (Famous Places of the Eastern Capital)" by Utagawa Toyokuni.
National Diet Library Digital Collection.

131 Noshime Hanairo   **135 Uguisuiro**   **95 Nisemurasaki**   **186 Hiwairo**

The vibrant moegi (fresh yellowish green) figured silk fabric is adorned with a design of willows and flower sprays covering the entire surface. Various techniques such as *yūzen* dyeing, *shibori*, and embroidery were employed. Shibori is a dyeing technique that involves intricate patterns resembling fawn spots, created as a result of the luxury ban during the early Edo period, which prohibited the opulent hand-shibori dyeing technique known as *kanoko* shibori. Shibori includes techniques like paste-resist shibori (*koshizome*), brush-drawn shibori (*egakibata*), and the stencil-based shibori used in this kimono. This kimono dates back to the late Genroku period to the early Kyōhō period (around 1700–1720).

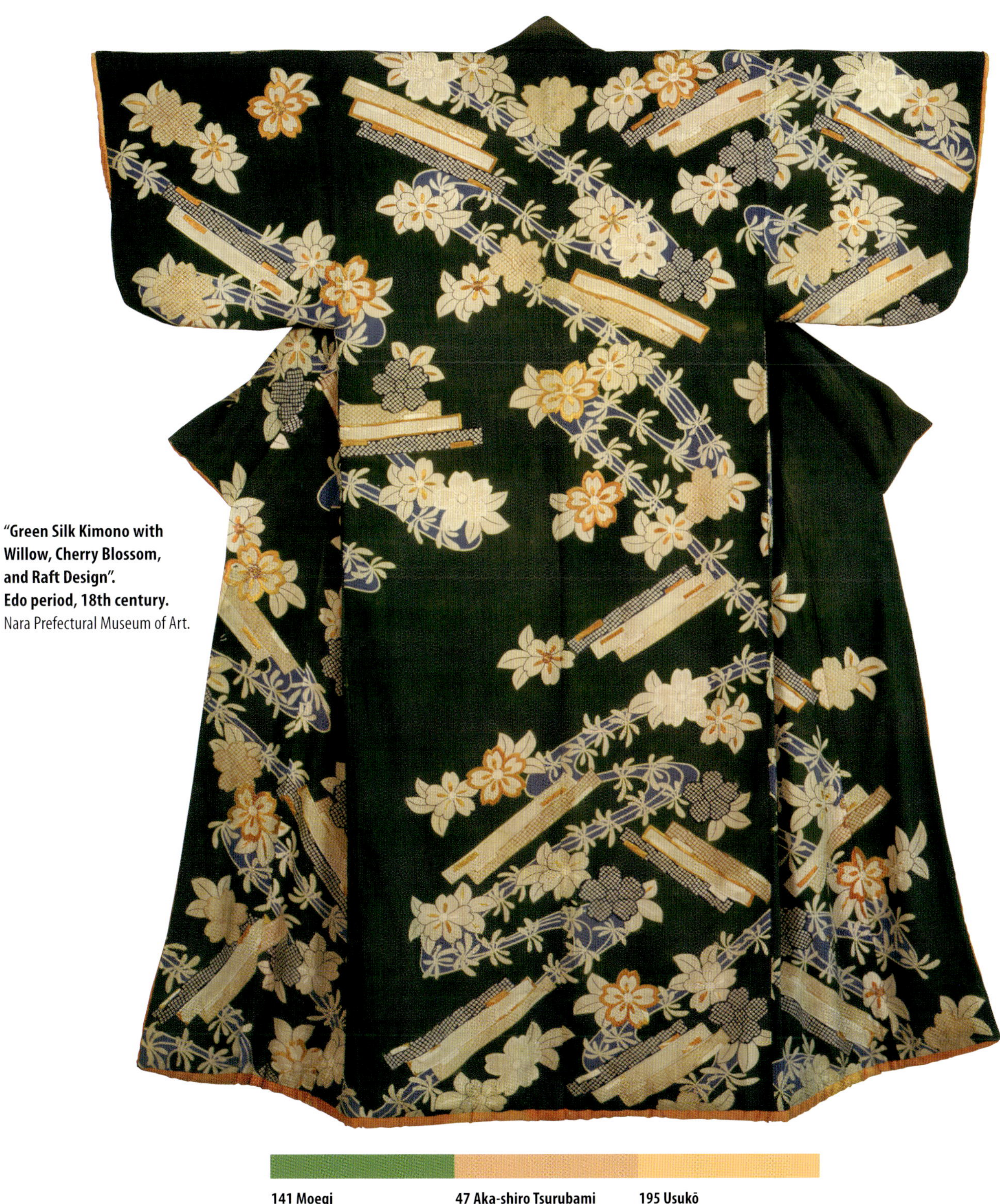

"Green Silk Kimono with Willow, Cherry Blossom, and Raft Design".
Edo period, 18th century.
Nara Prefectural Museum of Art.

141 Moegi   **47 Aka-shiro Tsurubami**   **195 Usukō**

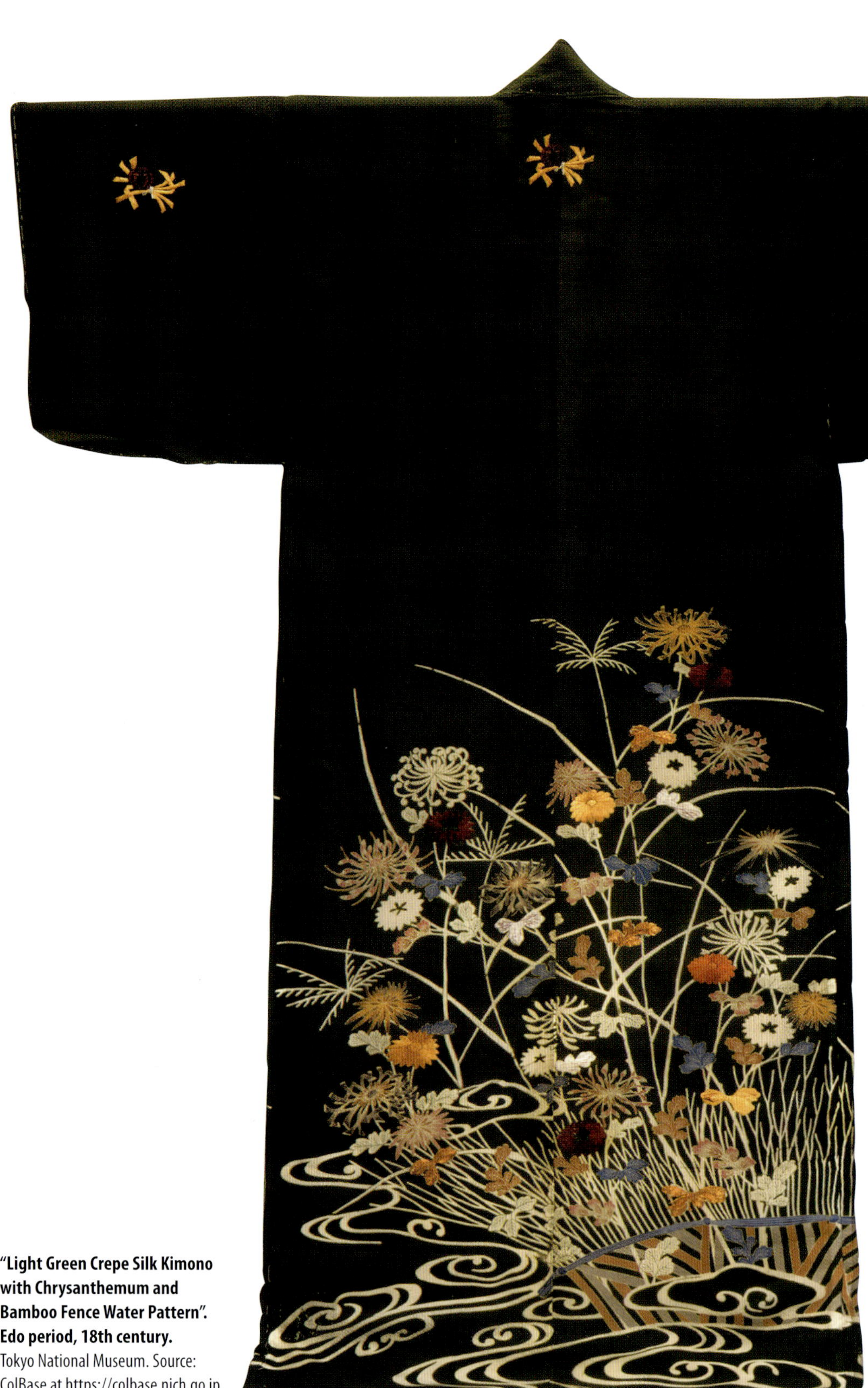

"Light Green Crepe Silk Kimono with Chrysanthemum and Bamboo Fence Water Pattern".
Edo period, 18th century.
Tokyo National Museum. Source:
ColBase at https://colbase.nich.go.jp

At the hem of this moegi-colored silk kimono multiple layers of flowing water, drawing curved lines, intertwine, forming swirling vortexes here and there. This flowing water pattern, called "rinzu mizu," retains traces of the Rinpa style. Additionally, grass patterns imbued with a sense of the autumn season are depicted from the waist down using *yūzen* dyeing and embroidery, creating a chic and luxurious kimono. Embroidered on the back are combinations of the Hōtō crest and the Noshi crest. The Idate crest, different from family crests, became fashionable around the Genroku period (1688–1704).

163 Mushiaoi　　　49 Usugaki　　　166 Kuchibairo

 Mushiaoi
Insect Blue

Refers to a dark greenish-blue color resembling the wings of jewel beetles, also known as "summer insect color." The wings of jewel beetles exhibit a beautiful green or purple color with a glossy sheen depending on the angle of light, and this color has been used in traditional crafts for a long time. To express the jewel beetle color in textiles, it is said that using green for the warp threads and a reddish-purple for the weft threads creates a similar effect.

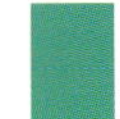 Usugaki
Pale Persimmon

A light color resembling that of persimmons. Usugaki can refer to a range of light persimmon colors, and can also indicate a shade lighter than "Sharegaki" (a deeper persimmon color). In the Edo period (late 18th century), Usugaki and Sharegaki became popular especially in kimono and accessories.

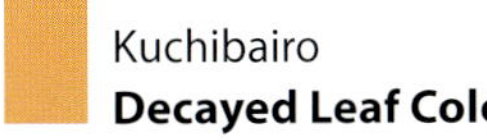 Kuchibairo
Decayed Leaf Color

Describes a color that resembles the brownish-orange hue of decaying fallen leaves from deciduous trees. This traditional color name has been used since the Heian period and encompasses various shades, such as "red kuchibairo," "yellow kuchibairo," and "blue kuchibairo." It is often worn as a seasonal color during autumn.

Aomidori
Blue Green

Refers to a green color with a slight bluish tint, distinct from pure green. It's a basic color term used to describe colors that fall between blue and green. Although the color is in the green family, it has a unique hue with a hint of blue.

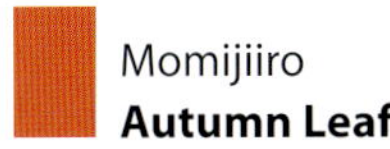 Momijiiro
Autumn Leaf

Represents the brilliant red color seen in autumn foliage. Momijiiro is a vivid shade of red, and during the Heian period, it was a designated color for the outer layer of a garment (usually red) with the inner layer being "suou" (dark purplish-red). This color term originates from the Japanese word "momiji," which means "color emerging from rubbing" and was initially used to describe the changing colors of leaves. Among these, the maple tree is particularly famous for its vibrant autumn colors, leading to the association of "momiji" with maple leaves.

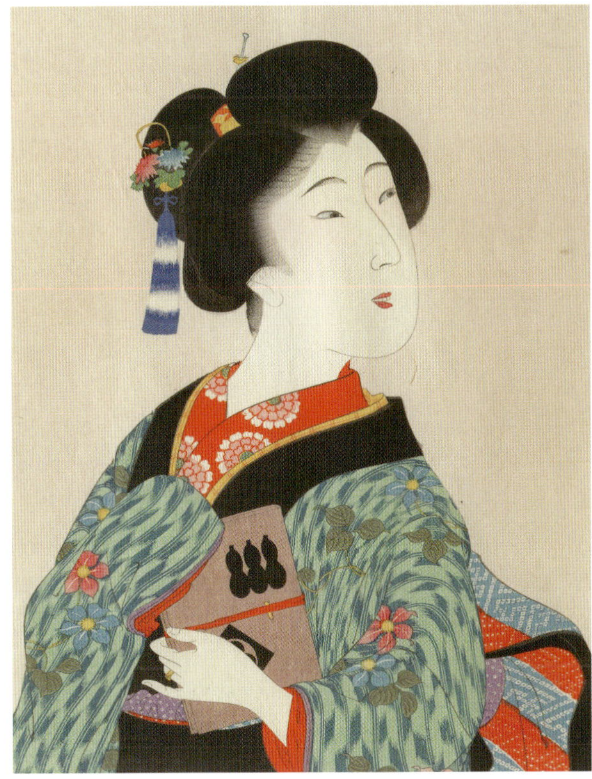

"True Beauty: Kaeshi" by Toyohara Chikanobu, 1897.
Yamaguchi Prefectural Hagi Art Museum and Uragami Memorial Museum.

150 Aomidori   **17 Momijiiro**

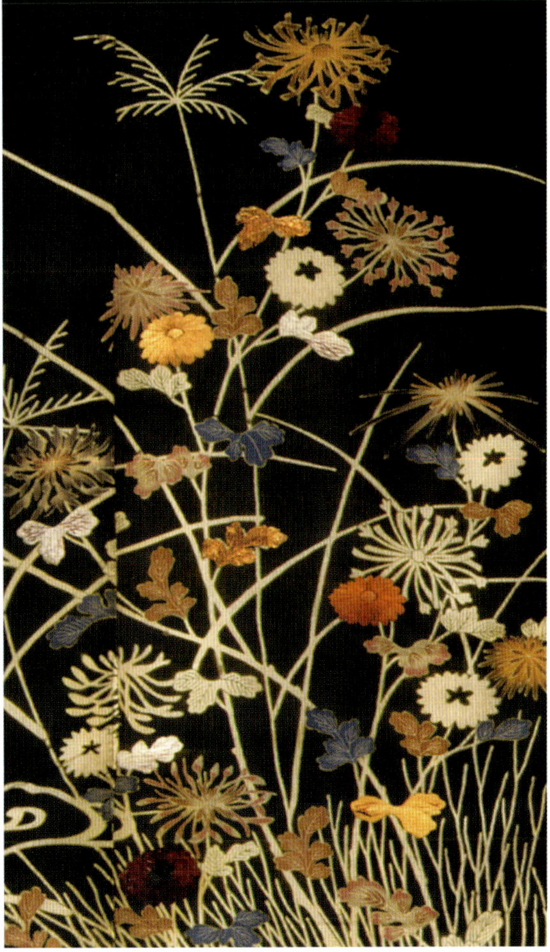

Detail from "Light Green Crepe Silk Kimono with Chrysanthemum and Bamboo Fence Water Pattern". Edo period, 18th century.
Tokyo National Museum. Source: ColBase at https://colbase.nich.go.jp

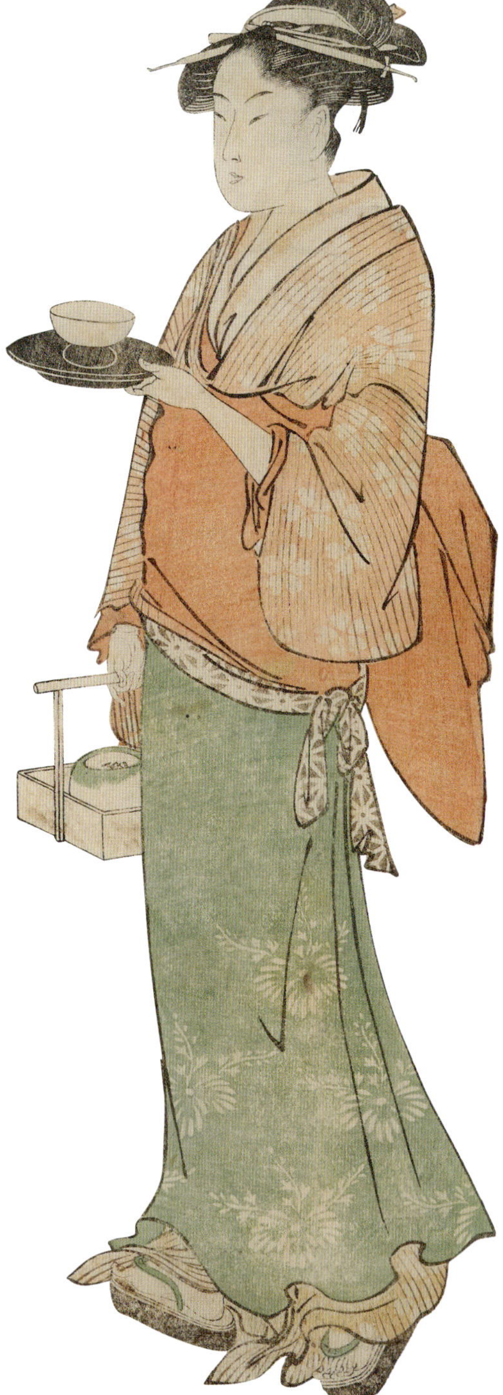

A detail of "Okita of the Naniwaya Teahouse" by Kitagawa Utamaro. Edo period, 18th century.
Tokyo National Museum.
Source: ColBase at https://colbase.nich.go.jp

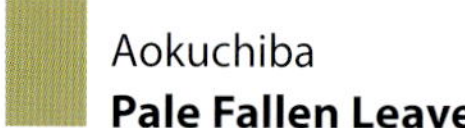

Aokuchiba
Pale Fallen Leaves

Unlike the vibrant fallen leaves that color in autumn, "Aokuchiba" refers to the color of leaves decaying amidst still green foliage. While "Akakuchiba" and "Kikuchiba" refer to leaves with a reddish or yellowish hue respectively, the name "Aokuchiba" expresses those with a greenish tinge. This color name dates back to the Heian period. Regarding garment color combinations, it's described as "moenegi weave on the outside, blue on the inside," with a tone more yellow than blue.

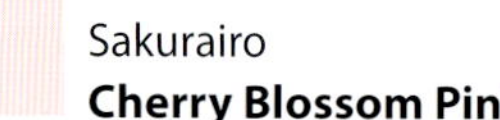

Sakurairo
Cherry Blossom Pink

A faint pink color with a slight crimson hue, reminiscent of cherry blossoms, and the lightest pink shade in the spectrum of cherry blossom dyes. While nowadays "sakura" primarily refers to the Yoshino cherry tree (*Prunus x yedoensis*), which produces large, single-petaled flowers, the ancient "sakura" referred to mountain cherries with small, elegant flowers and single petals. These mountain cherry blossoms were cherished for their unique beauty and symbolism.

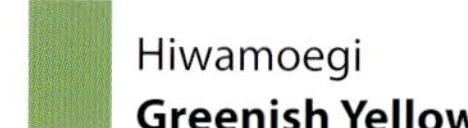

Hiwamoegi
Greenish Yellow

Refers to a vivid yellow-green color with a strong yellowish tint, similar to the color of a "hiwa"—a species of Japanese warbler. The dye-making method is historically described as "compounding hiwamoegi by combining it with kaya wood, adjusting the intensity of the color by increasing the amount of mordant and reducing the indigo, to achieve a green with a strong yellowish tone." However, the name "hiwamoegi" is not found in pattern books.

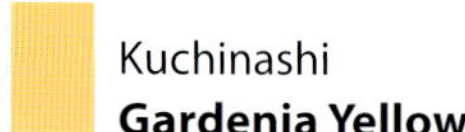

Kuchinashi
Gardenia Yellow

Refers to a color created using the fruits of the evergreen shrub Cape Jasmine, or "Kuchinashi" (*Gardenia jasminoides*), which produces a slightly reddish yellow color. The fruits of the Cape Jasmine have been used as a yellow dye since ancient times. The *Engishiki* (an ancient Japanese book of laws and customs) mentions three types of this dye for various uses: deep, light, and yellow. The deep and light shades were created by combining the jasmine and safflower dyes to achieve colors resembling the kuchinashi fruit. The color was prohibited due to its similarity to the color work by the Crown Prince. Additionally, "kuchinashi" can also mean "mute" or "silent," and so was used to refer things that were forbidden to speak of.

Here, the famous beauty Okita, waitress at the Nanwaya teahouse, gracefully carries a tea bowl on a saucer in one and a tobacco tray in the other. Among the Three Beauties of Kansai, Okita was the most popular, and Utamaro seemed to have favored her as well. He created more than fifteen works featuring her. Her appearance, depicted with subdued colors, exudes a sense freshness and modesty. This version of "Okita of the Naniwaya Teahouse" is a rare ukiyo-e print that can be viewed from both sides, printed on thin Japanese paper with woodblocks, showing both the "front" and "back."

133 Aokuchiba   **1 Sakurairo**

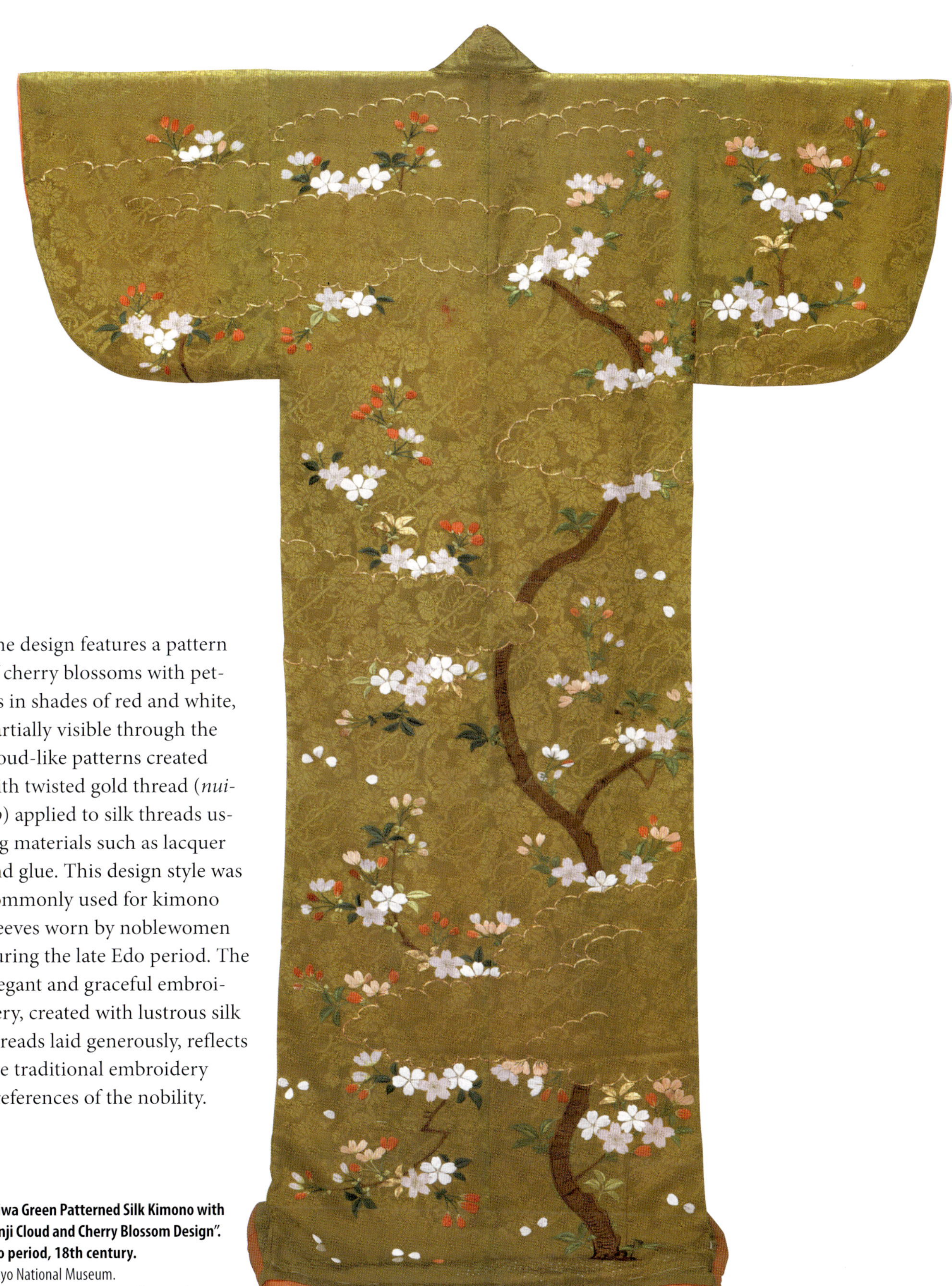

The design features a pattern of cherry blossoms with petals in shades of red and white, partially visible through the cloud-like patterns created with twisted gold thread (*nui-do*) applied to silk threads using materials such as lacquer and glue. This design style was commonly used for kimono sleeves worn by noblewomen during the late Edo period. The elegant and graceful embroidery, created with lustrous silk threads laid generously, reflects the traditional embroidery preferences of the nobility.

**"Hiwa Green Patterned Silk Kimono with Genji Cloud and Cherry Blossom Design".
Edo period, 18th century.**
Tokyo National Museum.
Source: ColBase at https://colbase.nich.go.jp

142 Hiwamoegi   169 Kuchinashi

The Colors Used in Japanese Gardens

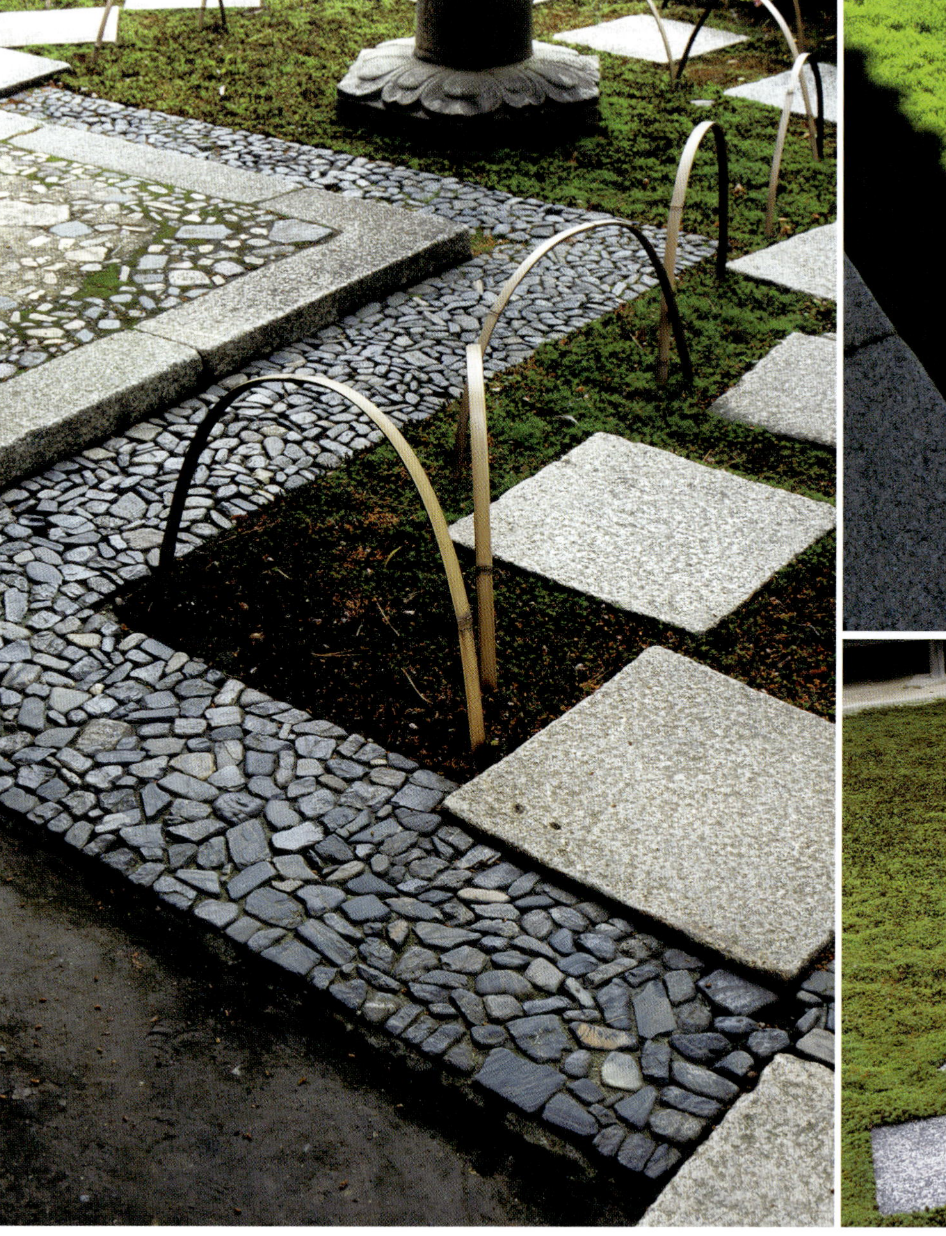

Katsura Rikyū is a villa built in the early Edo period by Prince Toshihito and Prince Tadatomo of the Hachijo-no-miya family on the land that is now in Nishikyo Ward, Kyoto City. It consists of three buildings: the Furishoin, the Nakashoin, and the Shingoten. Within the stroll-style garden, there are tea rooms such as Gekkaro, Shokeitei, and Shoikken, all preserved in their original forms. The design sensibility of Katsura Rikyū is a culmination of various architectural styles, incorporating a free selection of natural materials and a sharp sense of composition. The "True Stepping Stones" in front of the Mikoshi Yori are a stone-paved area with cut stones extending diagonally in a straight line from the Chumon gate to the Mikoshi Yori. It creates a tense atmosphere in the front garden of the Mikoshi Yori. The naturally arranged stepping stones, partially covered with moss, help soften this tension.

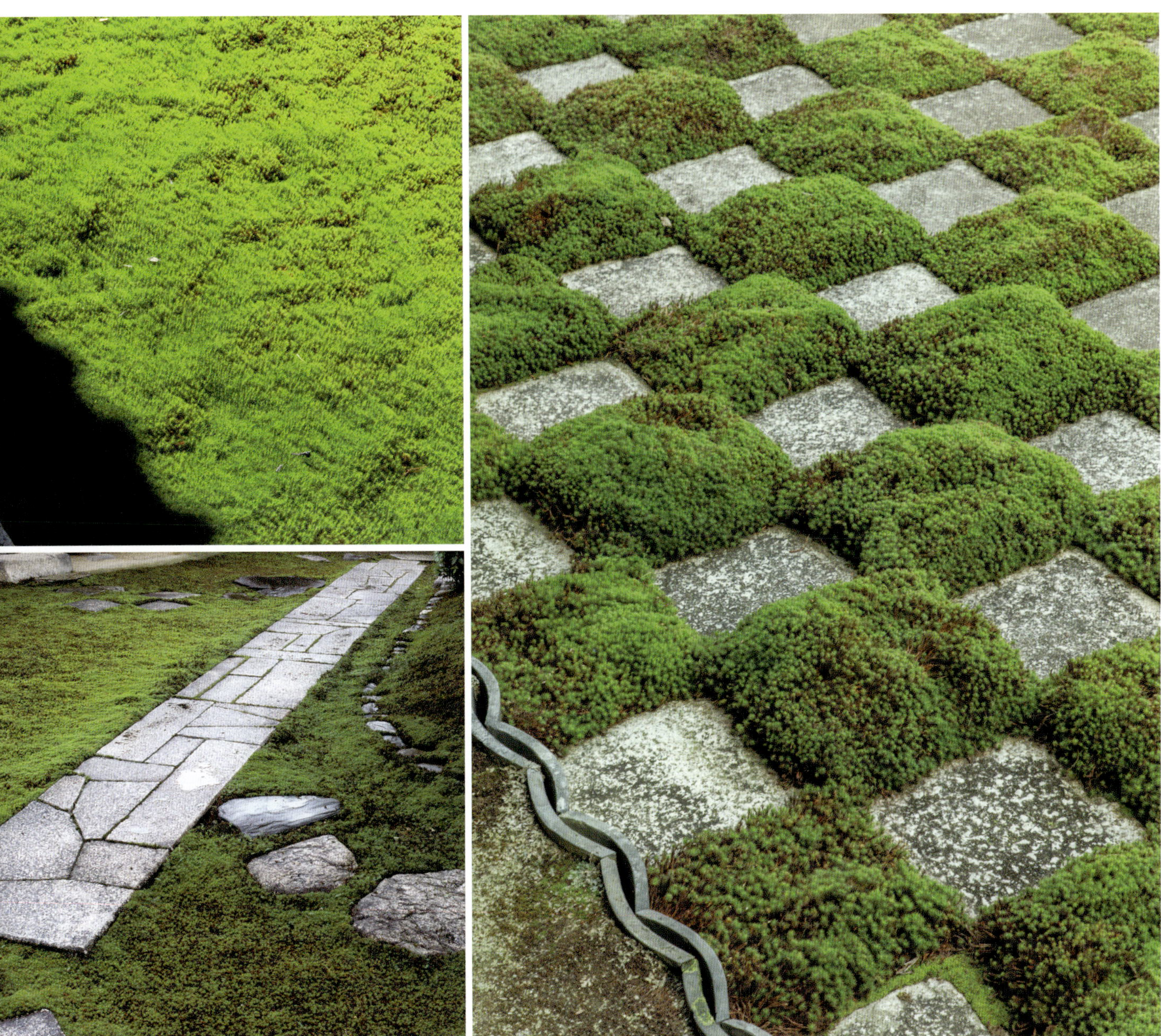

In the year 1939 (Showa 14), the "Eight-phase Garden" at Tofuku-ji's Hojo was created as a masterpiece garden by Mirei Shigemori. Among them, the checkered-pattern garden stands out, with a beautiful balance of lush green moss on the cedar ground and the geometric shapes of the stone paving. The stone paving was originally laid from the Imperial Envoys' Gate to the front of the Hojo's South Garden, and it was repurposed for this garden as per the temple's proposal. Isamu Noguchi, a sculptor from America who later studied gardening and pottery in China and Japan, referred to this garden with innovative design as a "Mondrian-style garden from a new perspective.

Japanese Color Names Drawn from Nature

Choshun Color

It refers to a dull pink color with a hint of red. It is named for the "Changchunhua", a rose species native to China. The rose's color is associated with it. Roses were introduced from China and other places, and in the Heian period, they were called

Color names inspired by the beauty of nature have been used by the Japanese people since time immemorial. Colors like "coral vermilion," "Korean red flower," "crimson hanging flower," "lapis lazuli blue," and "turmeric yellow" are just of few of myriad examples. These color names have reflected the Japanese people's sensibilities throughout the ages. By creating words to describe subtle differences in colors, they have refined their sense of beauty. Traditional colors derived from the changing seasons and the colors found in nature often incorporate names of natural elements such as flowers and birds.

In contrast, Western color names often revolve around mineral-based pigments. This difference can be attributed to the rich natural environment of Asia, including Japan, where people have a history of extracting dyes from local plants, trees, roots, fruits, flowers, and bark. Knowing the many color names that have been created by the Japanese reminds us of the unique culture that appreciates the changing seasons. Understanding these traditional color names can help rekindle our sensitivity to nature, as well as our memory of traditional color sensibilities, which we may be losing over time.

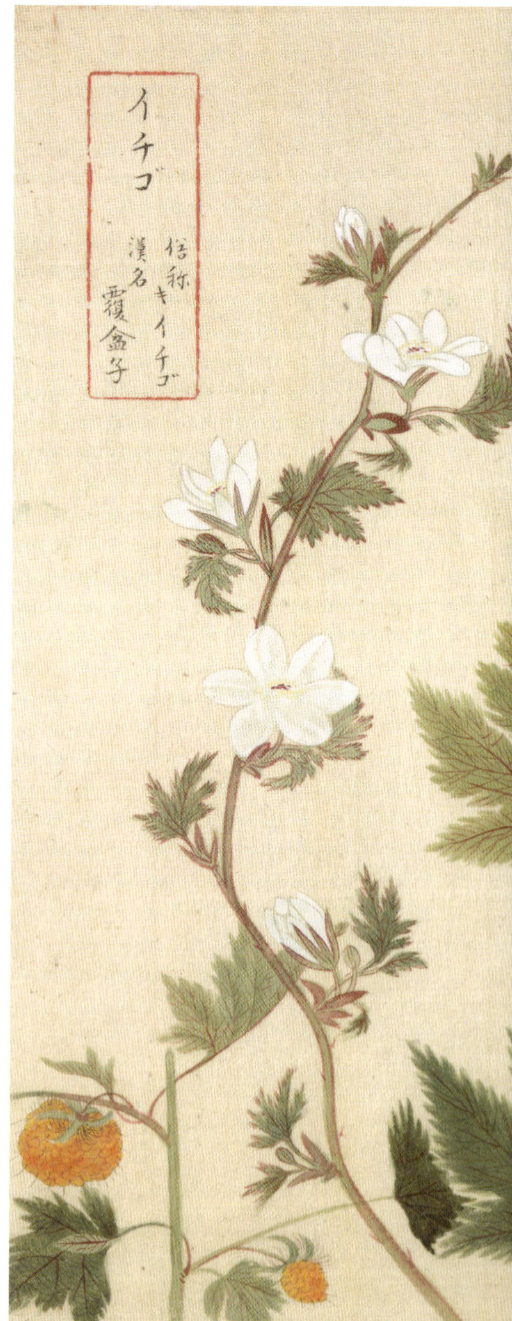

From "Botanical Illustration—Volume 1". National Diet Library Digital Collection.

"sōbi" and were admired by nobles for ornamental purposes. The color name originated from the faded roses that became popular in Europe in the late 19th century and resembles the color of the flowers of the changchunhua, which is purplish-red, hence it is also known as "Old Rose." This color became popular around the early Taisho period for its subdued tone, attracting popularity among women.

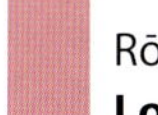

Rōtasu Pinku
Lotus Pink

It is a pink color reminiscent of lotus flowers. In Buddhism, the lotus is considered a sacred flower, and in Indian Buddhism, it is said that the lotus bloomed to announce the birth of Buddha. Additionally, because it blooms pure and untouched amidst the mud, it is likened to the Pure Land Paradise and strongly associated with Buddhism. In the center of the Pure Land is a lotus pond where four types of lotus flowers emit blue, yellow, red, and white light, and the lotus pedestal where Amitabha stands is well known. In China, it is referred to as the "gentleman among flowers."

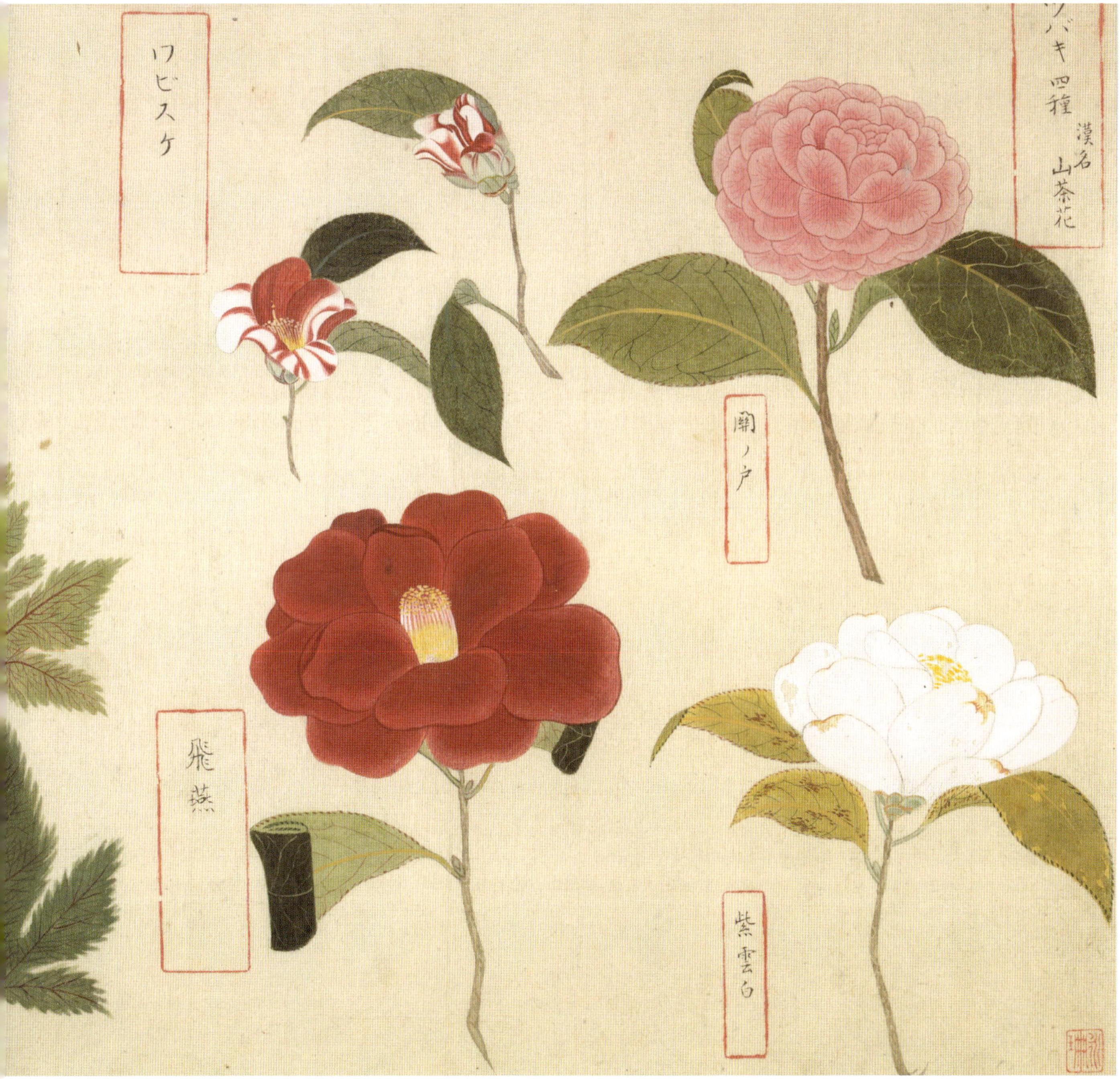

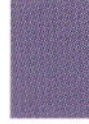

Shioniro
Hydrangea

A light purple color with a slight bluish tinge, representing the color of the Japanese hydrangea flower. It is made by steeping purple roots and using the ash water of camellia. This color was greatly favored by the aristocracy, for whom purple was the ideal color. In works such as *The Tale of Genji*, the color appears in fabrics and fingerstalls during the autumn season. The color combinations for the lining of a garment include "outer: light color, inner: blue" and "outer: purple, inner: fuchsia," among others.

Rindōiro
Gentian

It refers to a slightly dusky bluish-purple color resembling the flowers of the gentian. Like bellflower, gentians adorn the autumn season with their bluish-purple blooms, each having its own distinct color name despite slightness in the color differences. In terms of the lining color, gentians are described as "outer: light fuchsia, inner: blue," while bellflowers are described as "outer: indigo or light purple, inner: pale blue." Gentians are dried and used in traditional Chinese medicine as a digestive aid. They are extremely bitter, and have been used to stimulate bile production. A common name for "gentian" is "dragon's bile."

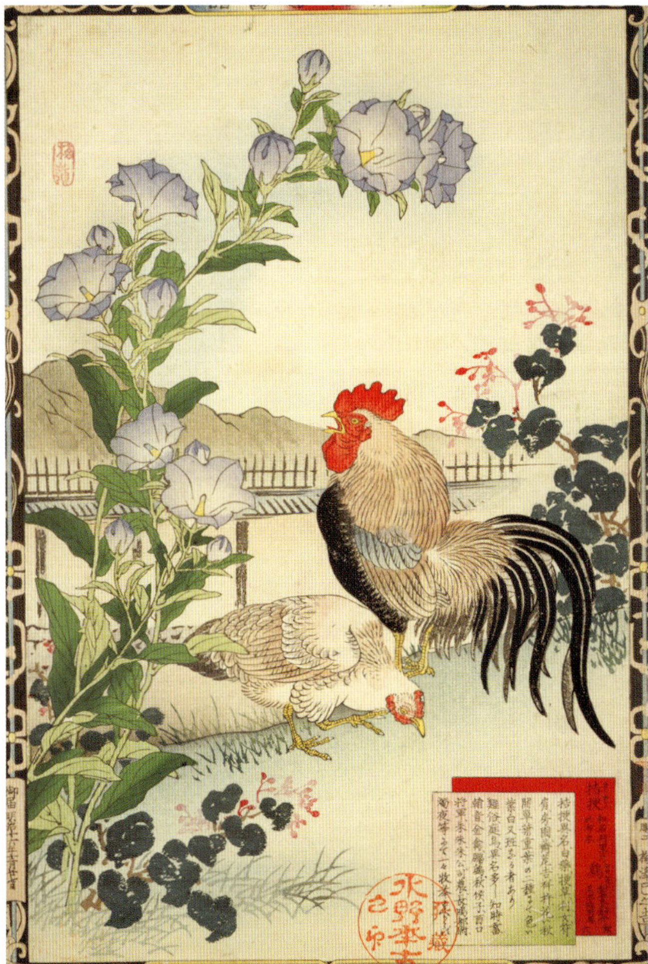

"**Bellflower and Rooster**" from *Album of Flowers and Birds* by Kōno Bairei, 1883. National Diet Library Digital Collection.

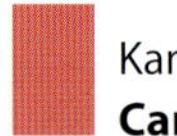

Kameria Tsubaki
Camellia

It is a vivid dark pink color with a reddish hue, representing the color of the winter camellia flower. Camellias originated in the East, and in the 17th century, they were brought to Europe by the Czechoslovakian missionary G.J. Camellus, and were named for him. In France, they gained popularity through the play "La Dame aux Camélias" by playwright Alexandre Dumas fils, and in the 19th century, red and white camellias were highly esteemed as corsages. Camellia flowers come in various colors, including red, light pink, dark pink-purple, and white, and because of their charm and ability to thrive in the flower-scarce season, they have been widely admired.

Fujibakamairo
Fujibakama Flower

This is a grayish shade of wisteria color, representing the color of the flowers of the *fuji-bakama* plant, which bears white and slightly purplish-pink flowers in early autumn. *Fuji-bakama* is a perennial plant in the *Asteraceae* family. It has a pleasant fragrance, even when dried. In autumn, it produces small, tubular flowers in a pale reddish-purple color that bloom densely. It is one of the seven flowers of autumn, and is an ornamental garden favorite.

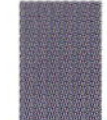

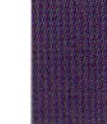

Sumireiro
Violet

It refers to a slightly bluish dark purple color reminiscent of the flowers of the *sumire* (violet) Sumire has been cherished by the Japanese since the Manyoshu period (8th century) and even appears as a color name in the Heian period, although it is not found in Heian literature as a dyeing color. In the *Kosōshō* there is reference to a lining color scheme of "outer: purple, inner: light purple," but in the *Shōzoku Shō* from the Muromachi period, it is mentioned as a garment color. This shows that the hue has changed over time.

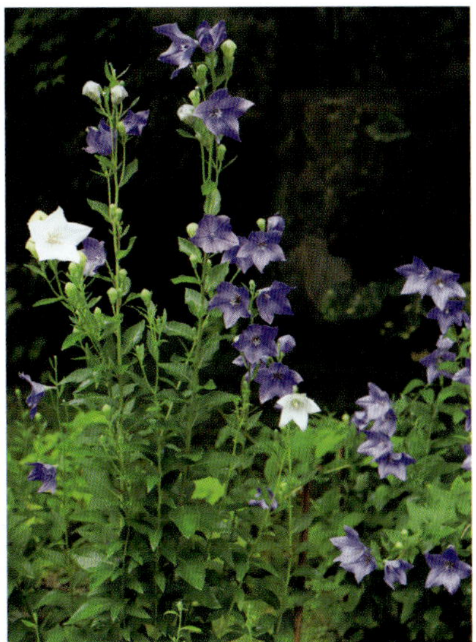

Kikyō, Tenju-an, Kyoto.

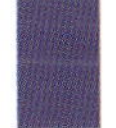

Kikyōiro
Bellflower

It refers to a bright bluish-purple color resembling the flowers of the *kikyo* plant, also known as the bellflower. It is one of the representative traditional color names for shades of blue-purple. The color scheme for clothing includes combinations such as "surface: niai (deep indigo), reverse: dark navy blue" and "surface: light purple, reverse: blue," commonly worn in the autumn. According to the book *Some Monogatari* (a book of dyeing secrets) the dyeing process involves underdyeing with indigo and overdyeing with crimson or sumac for color mixing. However, in *Toyosei Somemono no Kagami* (a book of modern dyeing techniques) a similarly-made color is referred to as "Nise-ni-se Kikyō" (imitation bellflower), suggesting that originally purple roots rather than indigo were used.

Ominaeshiiro
Japanese Globeflower

It refers to a bright yellow with a greenish tint similar to the color of the daffodil flower. The color scheme for clothing evokes the combination of the pale yellow flowers of the daffodil and the green leaves, with the surface being yellow, the warp threads being green, the weft threads being yellow, and the lining being blue, representing the colors of early autumn. In the Kamakura period, the monk Sojo Echin in *Moso* tells the legend of a woman who, upon hearing that her beloved married another woman, threw herself into a river in despair. It is said that from the clothes she left behind, including a mountain anemone robe, daffodils began to bloom. The Noh play *Narukikyo* is based on this legend.

Himawariiro
Sunflower

This is a vivid yellow color with a touch of red, similar to the color of sunflowers. It is slightly redder than dandelion yellow, giving it the appearance of having fully absorbed the sun's warmth. Sunflowers are annual plants in the aster family, native to North America, and are widely cultivated for ornamental purposes. They come in many varieties and are a much-loved sight in summer and autumn. Their name comes from their tendency to turn in the direction of the sun.

Yamabukiiro
Kerria

It refers to a strongly yellow color reminiscent of the flowers of the *yamabuki* plant, also known as the Japanese rose. Its branches are slender and sway easily in the wind. Yamabukiiro has been considered one of the representative traditional colors in the yellow range since the Heian period. It is frequently used in Heian literature, such as *The Tale of Genji* and *Eiga Monogatari*, often representing the colors of spring. The dyeing process typically involved using *shikon* (purple gromwell) and *beni* (red safflower) or other dyes. Yamabuki is a deciduous shrub in the rose family (Rosaceae) and is native to various mountainous regions in Japan. It is also cultivated for ornamental purposes.

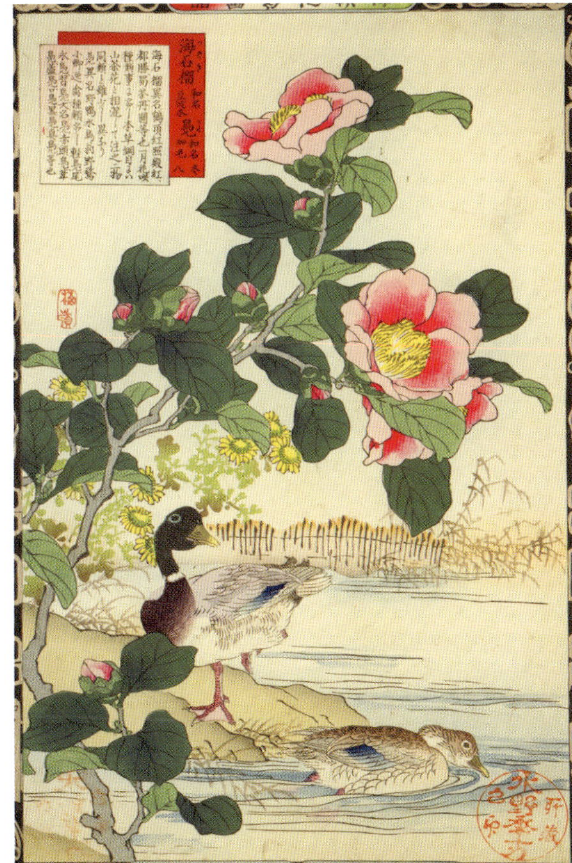

"Sea Hibiscus and Duck" from *Album of Flowers and Birds* by Kōno Bairei, 1883. National Diet Library Digital Collection.

The Color Yellow in Japanese Culture

Yellow is a color with complex meanings and symbolism. In China, it has long been associated with the color of the earth and symbolized the center of the world. It was also the color representing the emperor and symbolized authority. This perception of color has also influenced Japan and contributed to its unique beliefs. On the other hand, in Western culture, yellow was associated with Judas Iscariot, who betrayed Jesus, causing it to be associated by extension with cowardice and deceitfulness. A yellow cast to the skin was associated with illness, as in conditions such as jaundice or infections such as cholera. However, it is also seen as a symbol of intellect and the color of life, representing the sacred as well as the profane.

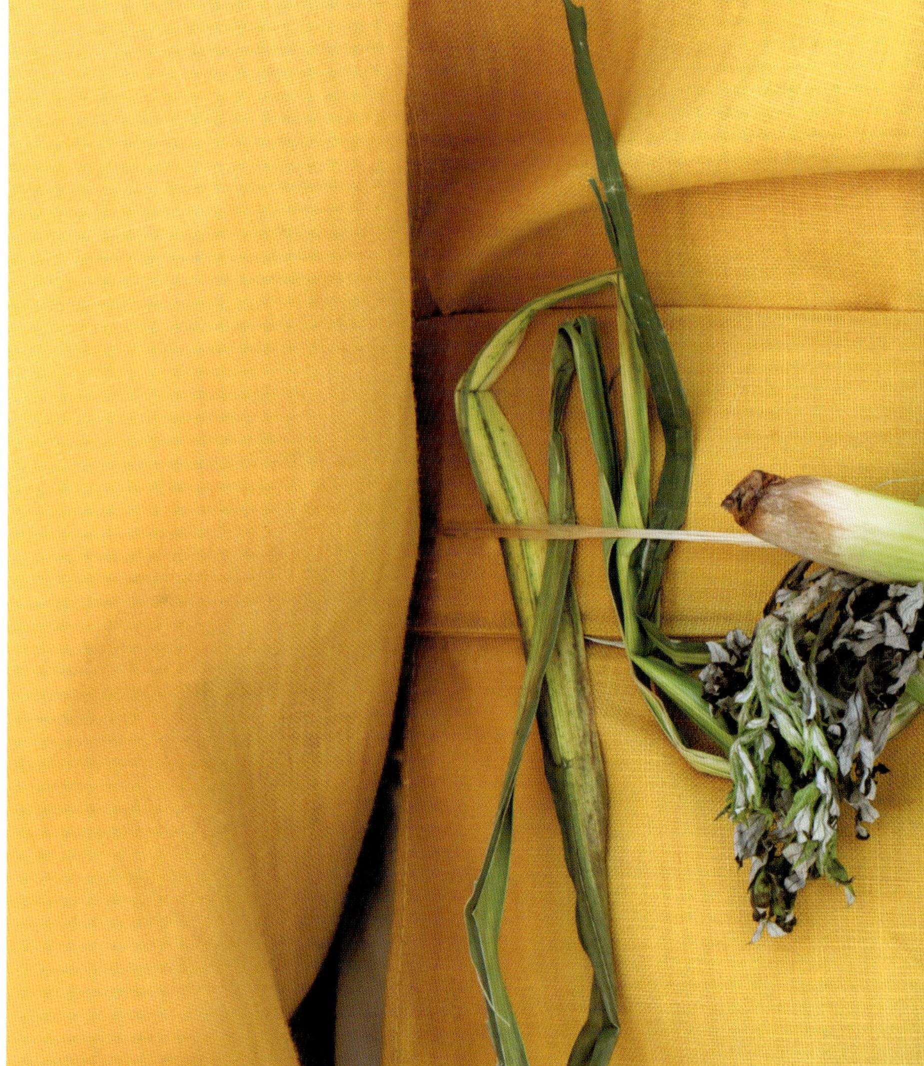

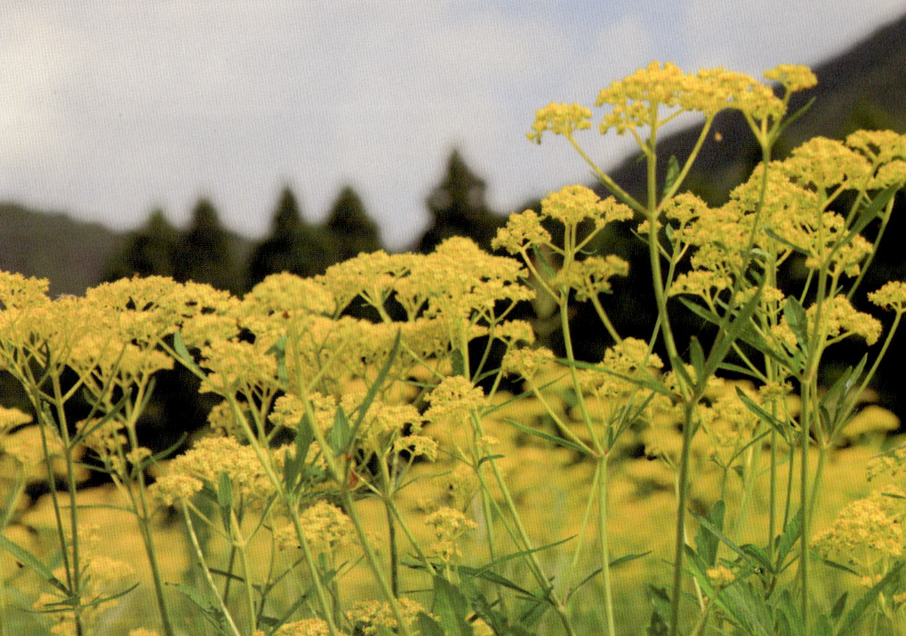

Top Horse Racing Ritual at Kamigamo Shrine, Kyoto.
Bottom right Autumn Foliage at Jōjakkō-ji Temple, Kyoto.
Bottom far right Ominaeshi Flowers in Koshikibata, Kyoto.

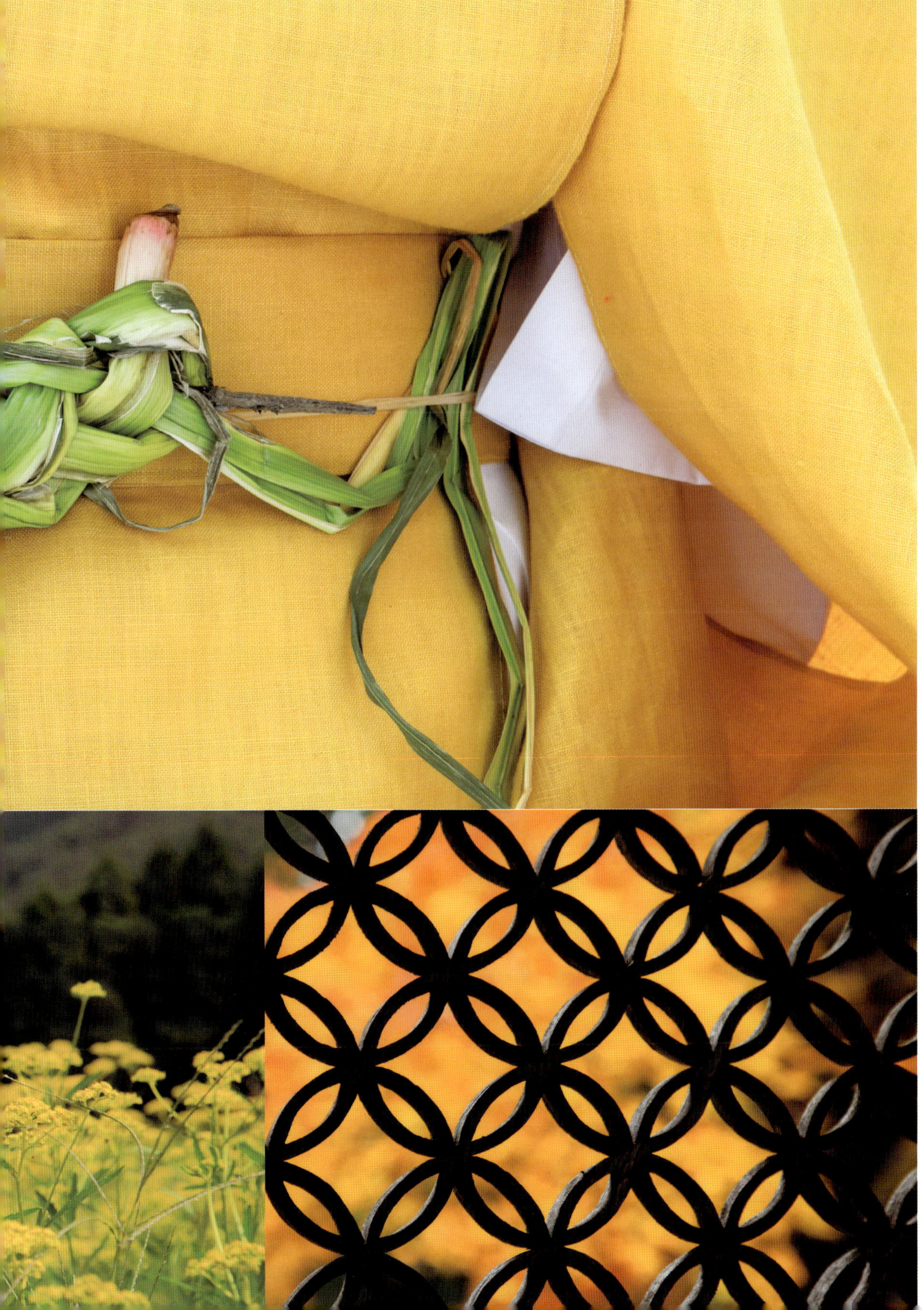

Japanese Color Schemes Based on Yellow

Yellow is a color that evokes feelings and things that are flashy, warm, bright, strong, cheerful, clear, and somewhat exciting. Some of the things that yellow symbolizes include brightness, liveliness, activity, and attentiveness. Therefore, the imagery associated with yellow includes softness, brightness, joyfulness, happiness, cheerfulness, and pleasant texture. Like red, yellow is seen as dispersing outward, but compared to orange, its intensity is slightly weaker, with a softening effect.

In ancient Chinese Yin-Yang and Five Elements theory, yellow was placed in the center of the five elements and represented the emperor, hence the association of yellow with imperial authority. In Japan, Prince Shotoku, who established the Twelve Grades of Cap and Rank system, incorporated the Chinese Five Elements theory of "blue, red, yellow, white, black" into six stages, adding purple at the top, and created twelve grades with variations in intensity. Dark yellow and light yellow corresponded to the seventh and eighth grades, respectively. The Chinese concept of granting the highest authority to yellow spread to Okinawa, as seen in the dyeing and weaving techniques of the Ryukyu Kingdom's royal family, such as the "beni-gara" patterns.

In human vision, yellow appears brighter because it is perceived more sensitively than other colors under the same light intensity. Therefore, combinations of yellow and black are often used to create high visibility from a distance, exploiting the contrast effect.

In terms of color coordination, white and black, vermilion, dark brown or green, deep red-purple opposite colors, purple, complementary blue-purple, are compatible with yellow, as seen in the Noh costumes of the Muromachi period, the wall paintings of the Momoyama period, and the palette of ukiyo-e prints. Yellow harmonizes with most other colors and serves as a complementary color that enhances other colors. Combining yellow with similar colors such as orange or yellow-green creates a natural autumnal atmosphere.

Color Scheme Based on Pale Colors

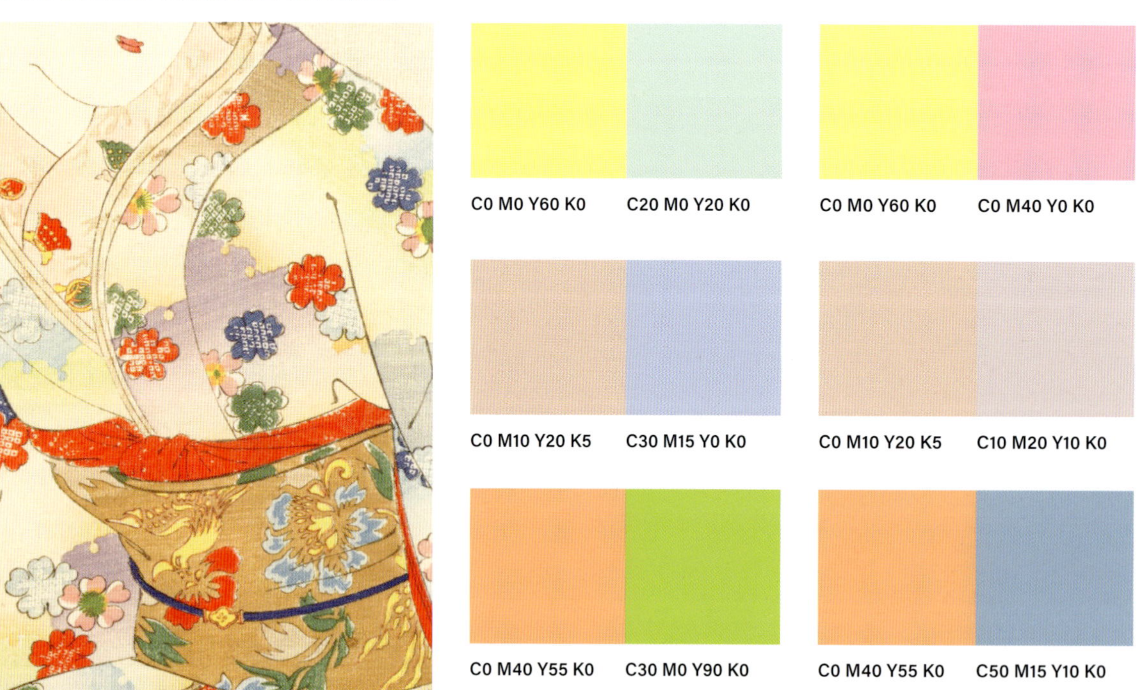

C0 M0 Y60 K0	C20 M0 Y20 K0	C0 M0 Y60 K0	C0 M40 Y0 K0
C0 M10 Y20 K5	C30 M15 Y0 K0	C0 M10 Y20 K5	C10 M20 Y10 K0
C0 M40 Y55 K0	C30 M0 Y90 K0	C0 M40 Y55 K0	C50 M15 Y10 K0

Detail from "Lady Playing the Koto" by Toyohara Chikanobu, 1897. National Diet Library Digital Collection.

Color Scheme Based on Vivid Colors

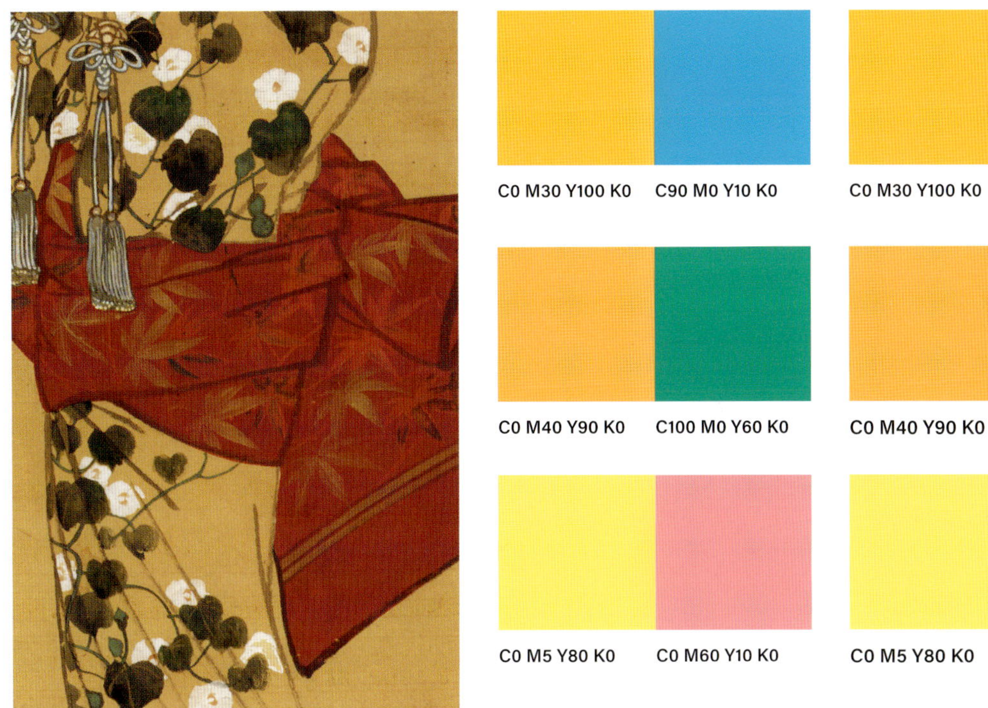

C0 M30 Y100 K0   C90 M0 Y10 K0

C0 M30 Y100 K0   C0 M100 Y100 K0

C0 M40 Y90 K0   C100 M0 Y60 K0

C0 M40 Y90 K0   C0 M70 Y100 K0

C0 M5 Y80 K0   C0 M60 Y10 K0

C0 M5 Y80 K0   C30 M0 Y90 K0

**Detail from "Beauty with Lantern" by Mihata Joryū.
Early 19th century.**
Kyoto Prefecture collection (Managed by Kyoto Cultural Museum).

Color Scheme Based on Dark Colors

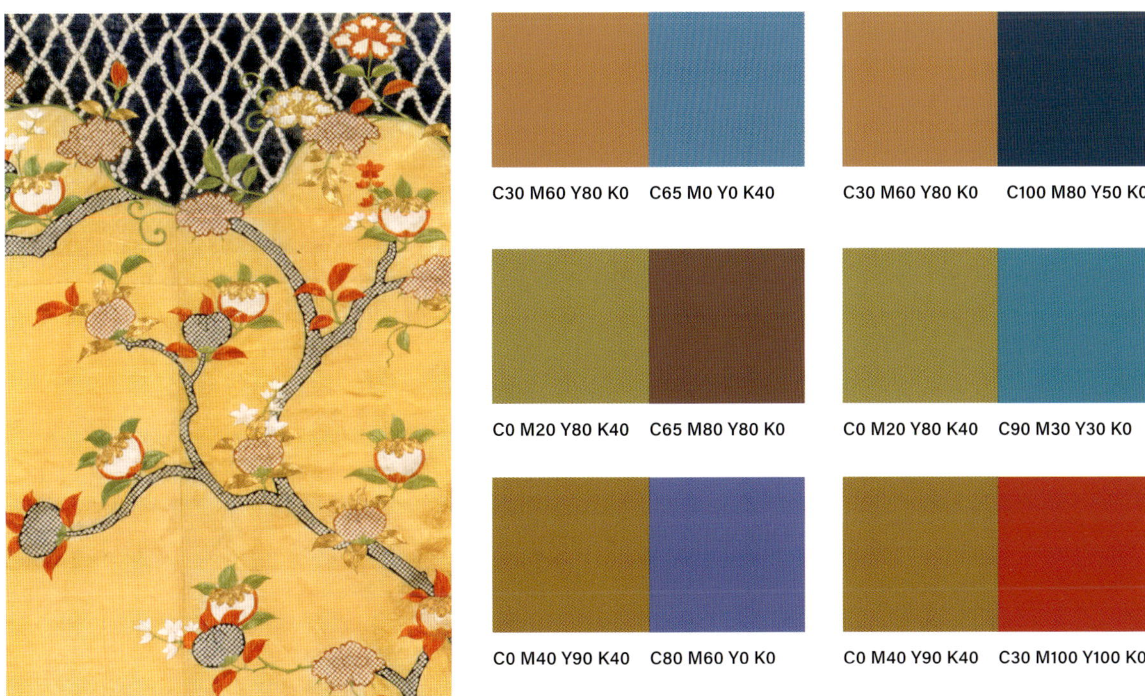

C30 M60 Y80 K0   C65 M0 Y0 K40

C30 M60 Y80 K0   C100 M80 Y50 K0

C0 M20 Y80 K40   C65 M80 Y80 K0

C0 M20 Y80 K40   C90 M30 Y30 K0

C0 M40 Y90 K40   C80 M60 Y0 K0

C0 M40 Y90 K40   C30 M100 Y100 K0

**Detail from "Gold Brocade Kimono with Peony,
Tangerine, and Net Design". Edo period, 18th century.**
Tokyo National Museum. Source: ColBase at https://colbase.nich.go.jp

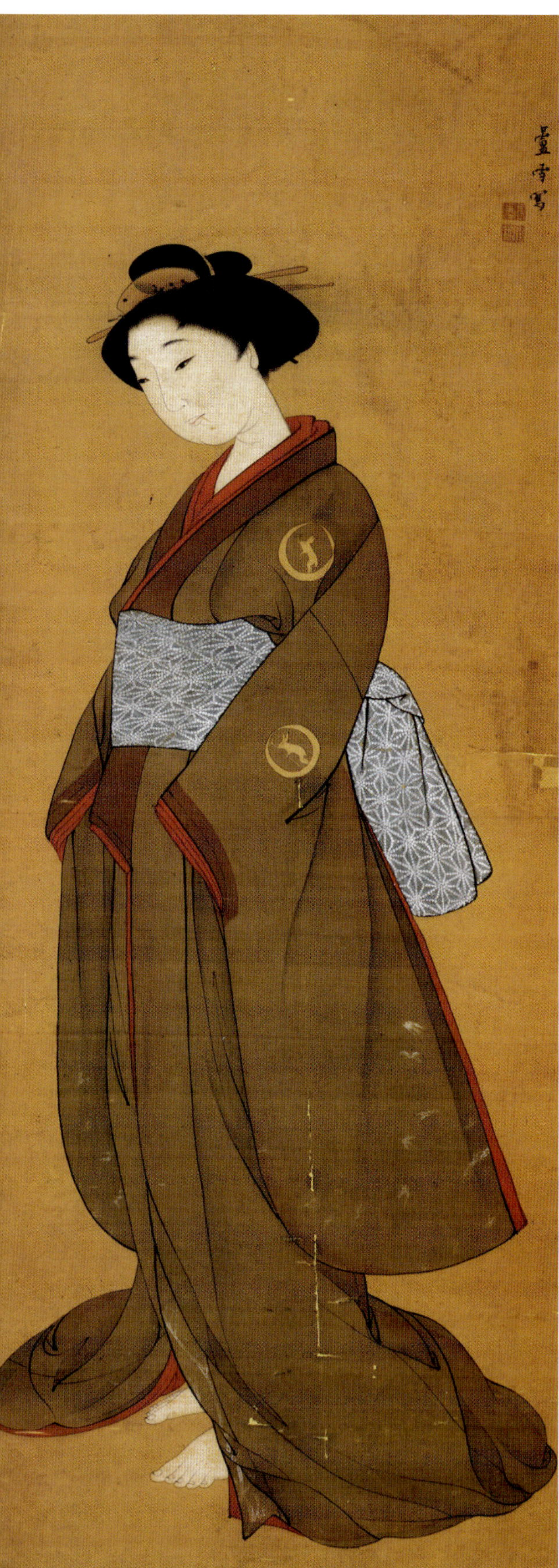
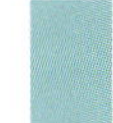

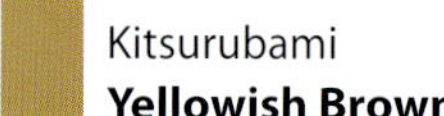

Kitsurubami
Yellowish Brown

A subdued yellow-red color with a hint of black. "Tsurubami" was made using a mixture of acorn dye, madder, and camellia ash. While there is also a dark black iron-dyed tsurubami color, the *Ifukurei* (the Taihō Code's clothing regulations) simply refers to this color as "tsurubami" and calls the camellia ash-dyed tsurubami "Kitsurubami" (yellow tsurubami). Additionally, there is mention in the *Soni Ryo* (monastic regulations) of a color referred to as "Mokuren," which was considered to be the same color as kitsurubami.

Byakugun
Pale Green

This is a pale blue color created by grinding the blue mineral azurite. Depending on the grain size and color intensity, it is called *gunjō* (ultramarine blue), *konjō* (deep blue), or *shiraguni*. In nature, azurite is often found together with malachite, a green mineral that is also ground to create pigment.

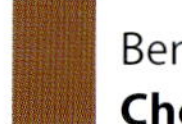

Bengarairo
Chestnut Husk

Bengarairo is a reddish-brown color similar to the pigment *bengala*. This strong reddish-brown pigment is created by roasting iron-rich soil to oxidize it into red rust, which is then used as a pigment. Paint made by adding persimmon tannin to bengala was used on the walls and lattice doors of *machiya* (townhouses) and was known as "bengala koushi" or "bengala lattice." The name "bengala" is derived from Bengal, now Sri Lanka, where high-quality reddish-brown iron oxide was produced. The Japanese language does not include the "L" sound, hence the variation resulting in "Bengara."

The thin kimono in a nightingale color allows the light crimson base to lightly show through, creating a feeling of freshness. Although the "fabric" of the kimono is considerably faded, we can still see the pattern willows and a flock of swallows, drawn with white lead powder, evoking a sense of early summer. While the head indicates of the round-face style of the Otsujo school, the upward slant of the eyes and the graceful tilt of the neck exhibit the charming irregular beauty characteristic of Rosetsu. Additionally, the delicate lines of the garment pattern twist intricately around the hem, lending it a unique expression.

Nagasawa Rosetsu (1754–1799) was a painter from the mid to late Edo period who studied under Maruyama Ōkyo. He developed his own unique decorative painting style characterized by bold compositions and free brushwork, leaving a legacy of many splendid wall paintings.

"Portrait of a Beautiful Woman" by Nagasawa Rosetsu.
Edo period, late 18th century.
Kyoto Prefecture (Managed by Kyoto Museum of Culture).

172 Kitsurubami   **101 Byakugun**   **57 Bengarairo**

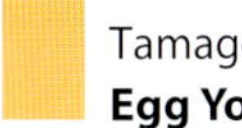

Tamagoiro
Egg Yolk

Derived from the yolk of a chicken egg, it refers to a bright yellow with a hint of red. It seems that tamagoiro was commonly used as the base color for kosode fabrics during the Edo period. A slightly lighter dyed konjū (dark yellow) is generally considered the typical tamagoiro. Later, in modern times, a darker yellow came to be referred to as tamago-ran'ōiro. A pale yellow resembling the color of eggshells is called "Torinokoiro." This color has been used since the Heian period and is reminiscent of the color of bird feathers.

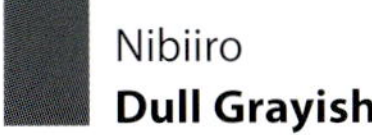

Sango-shuiro
Coral Vermilion

This is a vivid reddish-orange color resembling polished red coral. Coral has long been incorporated into jewelry and decorative items, with red coral being particularly prized. Coral comes in three main shades: white, peach-colored, and red. The deep red coral is particularly prized. The color contrasts beautifully with the black hair of Japanese women, making it a popular choice for hair accessories and *kanzashi* (hairpins).

Nibiiro
Dull Grayish

Nibiiro, like Tsurubami, is a dull grayish color in the monochrome spectrum. Later, it came to denote a bluish-gray shade achieved by adding a touch of indigo, resulting in a color resembling that of rusty iron. It was a color worn in mourning attire. The intensity of the dull color varied based on the wearer's relationship with the deceased. The emperor's attire in this dull shade, worn during mourning for a relative, was specifically termed "Shakujō."

This painting depicts a beautiful woman lighting a lantern that hangs on a *sudare* (bamboo blind) at around twilight on a summer evening. The pattern on her kimono features gourds blooming white flowers, appropriate for this season, along with vines wrapping around the twisted lower half of the kimono. A prominent feature is the large crimson obi, which complements the thick garment lines of the kimono. The cuffs are secured with clasps adorned with tassels, likely to prevent the sleeves from opening when the hands are raised. Sanpakujo Ryū was a painter from the late Edo period and a disciple of Okamoto Toyohiko. Around the Tenpō era (1830–1844), he painted *bijin-ga* (beautiful women) in a ukiyo-e style in the Kansai region. One of his disciples was Yoshiwara Shinryū.

"Beauty with Lantern" by Mihata Joryū.
Early 19th century.
Kyoto Prefecture (Managed by Kyoto Museum of Culture).

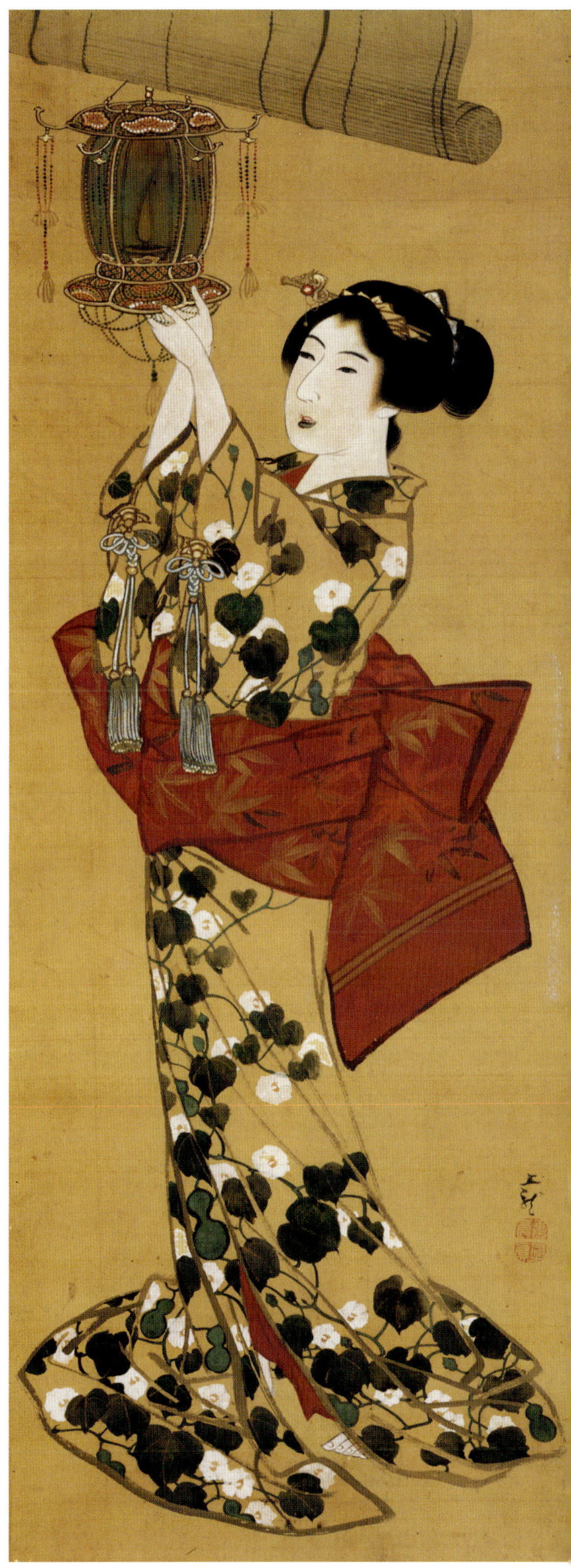

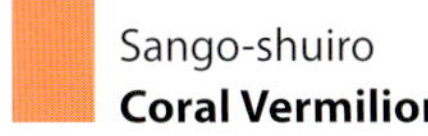

168 Tamagoiro   37 Sango-shuiro   275 Nibiiro

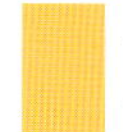

Hanabairo
Color of Flower Leaves

It's a hue of yellow with a hint of red, leaning more towards yellow compared to Yamabuki (Japanese rose) color. The term for the color of flower petals originally referred to a type of woven fabric. In *Kasumegaseki Shou* (written around1235), it's referred to as "Hanabairo". According to this text, the vertical threads (*kyou*) are yellow, while the horizontal threads (*tawara*) are yamabuki-colored. Is it not essentially the same as Hanakasaneiro? The lining (*ura*) is blue. This woven fabric color is one of the hues used for *kasane* (layered) garments, woven with yellow for the vertical threads and yamabuki for the horizontal threads. It's a garment color typically worn from March to April.

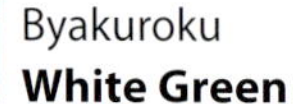

Byakuroku
White Green

This refers to a finer and paler shade of green compared to "Ryokusho" (green-blue). The Qing Dynasty's painting manual *Jieziyuan Huazhuan* explains how to make *ryokush* by grinding malachite into water. Because the particle sizes vary, it's divided into "head green, second green, third green." Although there is no specific name for "Byakuroku," "head green" corresponds to this color.

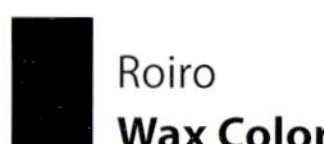

Roiro
Wax Color

This refers to the color used in *roiro* lacquerware techniques. Roiro is achieved by applying refined raw lacquer without adding oils, resulting in a color that is close to black. After the topcoat, it is polished with rapeseed oil and diatomaceous earth to create a glossy finish.

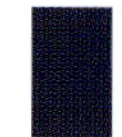

Touou
Yellow Wisteria

Touou is a warm, vivid yellow pigment used in Japanese painting and yuzen dyeing. It is derived from the resin of the gamboge tree, a member of the *Clusiaceae* family that grows in India and Thailand. This resin is collected, solidified, and used as a plant-based pigment. Its chemical composition contains arsenic sulfide, making it poisonous. There are also mineral-based yellow pigments containing arsenic sulfide, known as orpiment or arsenic sulfide yellow.

Tetsukoniro
Dark Navy Blue

This hue is a mixture of dark green iron color and intermediate navy blue. Dyeing involves pre-dyeing with indigo, then layering with persimmon tannin, and finally achieving coloration with iron gall ink to add a blackish tone.

The entire surface of this plate is densely adorned with chrysanthemum flowers, painted in yellow hues. The oak tree is depicted with undulating lines, its leaves colored in green, while the trunk and branches are depicted in blue. Such plates, painted lavishly throughout the entire piece, fall into the category of "blue-handed" among early Imari ware's colored paintings. Both in design and coloration, the boldness typical of this style is splendidly displayed in this fine example.

Tendrils of ivy twist like vines along the edge of a black lacquered comb. The leaves are in shades of blue and yellow, and the fruits are a soft red. The design stands out beautifully against the black background. The material known as *bekkō* is made by layering the shells of a species of sea turtle called hawksbill turtle, compressing them with water and heat. It was highly favored as a material for hair ornaments. Preferences varied depending on era and region, with some favoring translucent amber-colored bekkō, others opting for bekkō with black markings, and still others preferring bekkō decorated with makie.

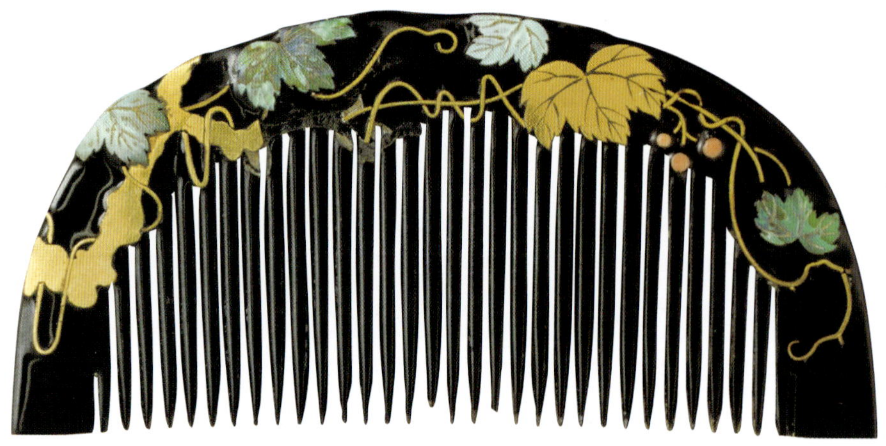

"Tortoiseshell Comb with Ivy and Mother of Pearl Inlay". Taisho Period. Tortoiseshell with Black Lacquer Finish.
National Museum of Japanese History.

177 Hanabairo	**145 Byakuroku**	**277 Roiro**

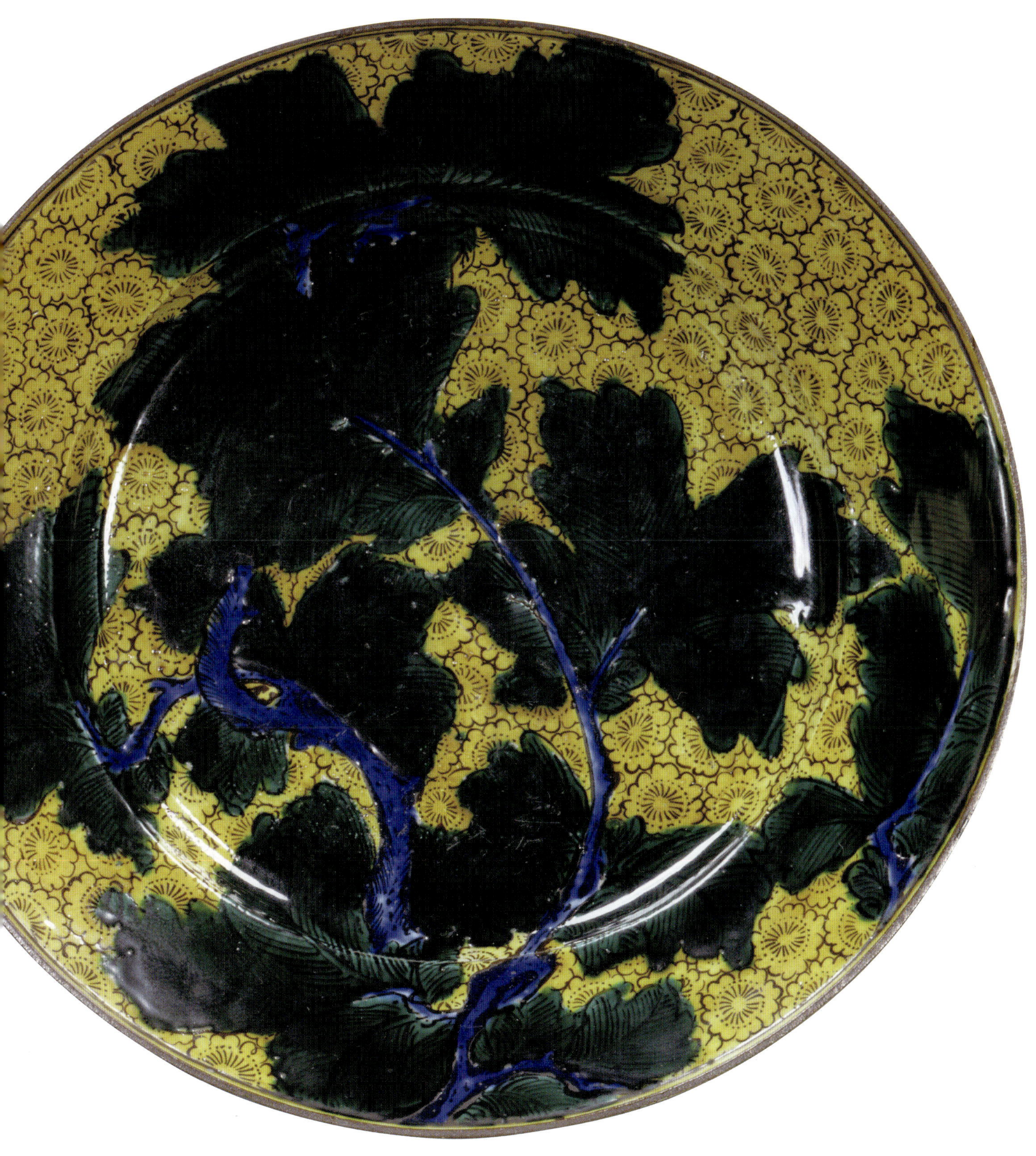

"Polychrome Painted Bowl with Pine Tree Design".
Imari Ware. Edo period, 17th century.
Tokyo National Museum. Source: ColBase at https://colbase.nich.go.jp

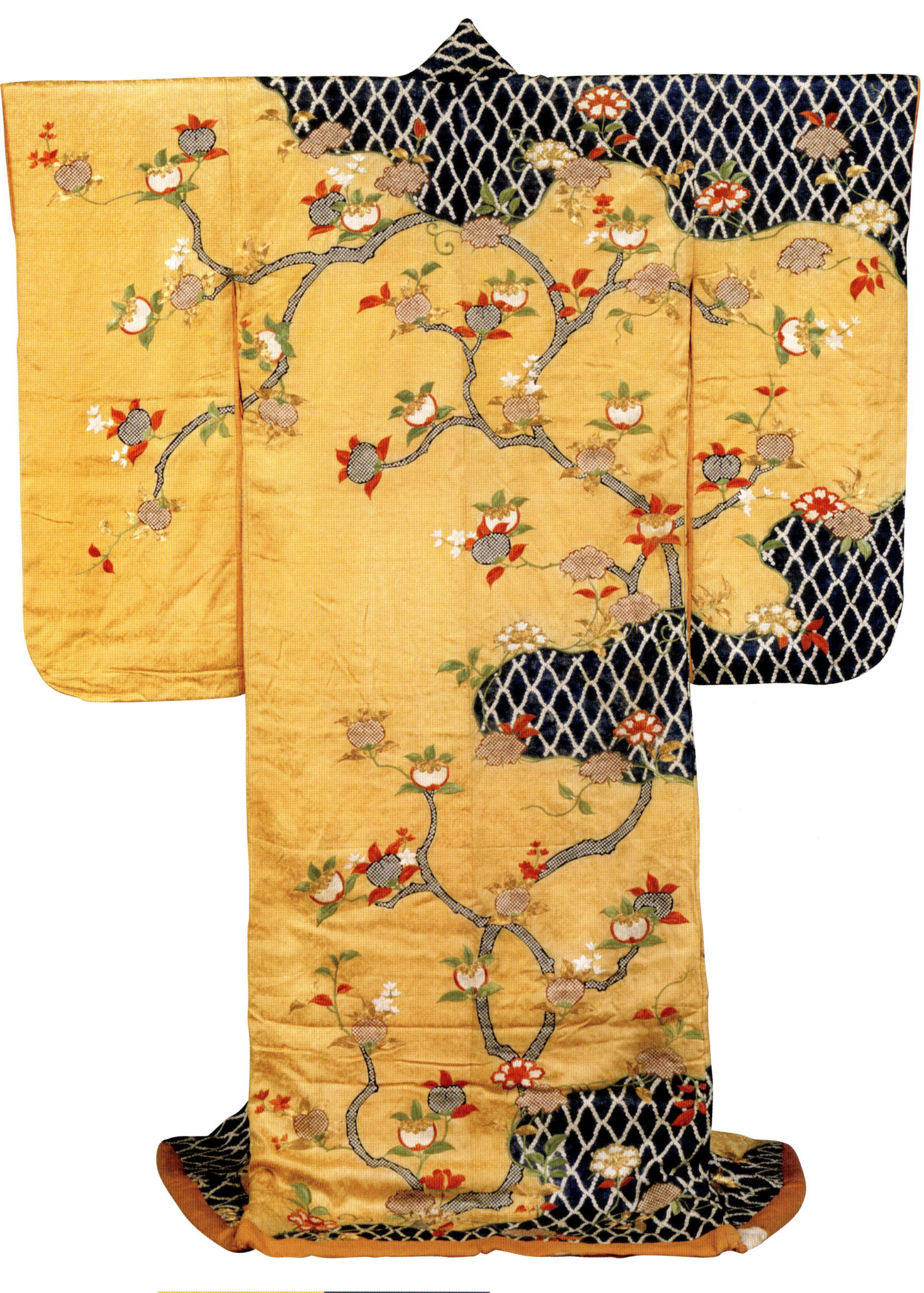

<table>
<tr><td>170 Ukoniro</td><td>124 Sabitsuchi Onando</td></tr>
</table>

"Gold Brocade Kimono with Peony, Tangerine, and Net Design". Edo period, 18th century.
Tokyo National Museum. Source: ColBase at https://colbase.nich.go.jp

Dyed in a deep turmeric color, from the hem to the shoulders, tangerine trees extend with gracefully undulating fruits. Lattice patterns are beautifully arranged from shoulder to waist and along the hem. This furisode (long-sleeved kimono) combines techniques such as embroidery, *shibori* (tie-dyeing), and *surihitta* (discharge dyeing), and was typical of samurai women's attire. The pattern of the trees is said to have its origins in the Tree of Life in Western Asia. In this furisode, the design incorporates peony flowers representing wealth and the tangerine fruit symbolizing eternal youth.

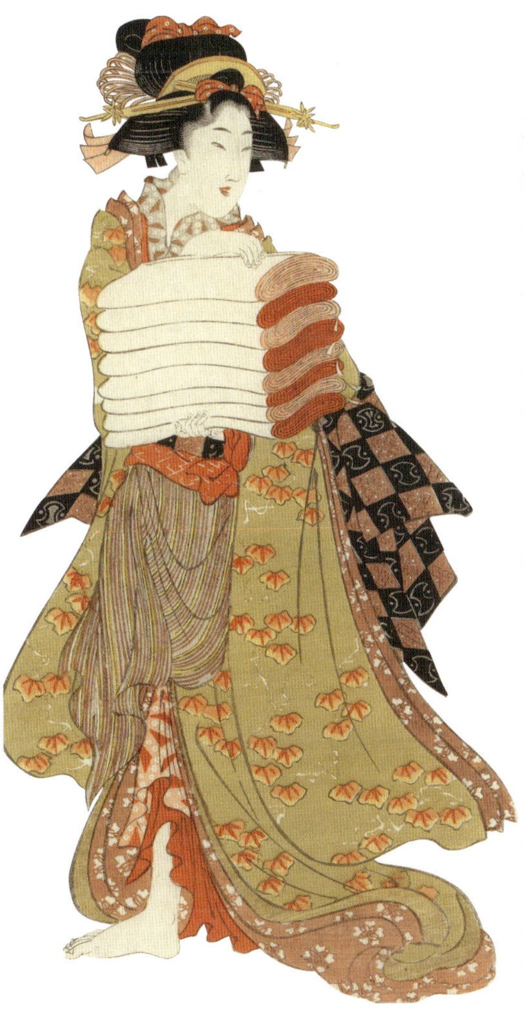

A young girl is depicted holding bolts of red and light pink fabric in both hands, possibly as an offering to Ebisu, the god of commerce. This portrays a figure busy working while wearing an apron, in the style of Kikugawa Eishan's depiction of a beautiful woman. The Ebisu Festival is a year-round event mainly held in commercial households on the 20th day of the tenth month of the lunar calendar, celebrating prosperity in business. Relatives and acquaintances are invited, and a feast is held. Additionally, when accepting faith, commercial establishments often form associations with fellow traders to establish an Ebisu Association.

Detail from "Part of a Picture of a Large Cup for the Ebisu Festival, the Clear Brightness from Dawn North and South" by Katsukawa Shunsen (Second Generation Haruyoshi). Around the Bunka era (1804–1817). Yamaguchi Prefectural Hagi Art Museum and Uragami Memorial Museum.

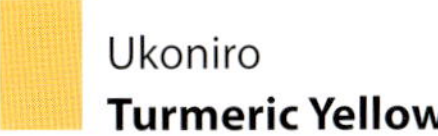
Ukoniro
Turmeric Yellow

Turmeric is a perennial herb from the ginger family, and its root is used to create a bright yellow dye. Turmeric dyeing has insect-repelling and antibacterial properties, so cotton dyed with turmeric was used for antique fabrics and baby clothes. The root contains the yellow pigment curcumin which, when powdered, becomes the spice known as turmeric and is used as a coloring agent in dishes like curry powder and butter.

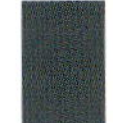
Sabitsuchi Onando
Rusty Iron Imperial Blue

This is a dark, slightly muted greenish-blue color. "Sabitsuchi" refers to rusted iron, but in this context, it conveys a sense of wabi-sabi, the beauty of imperfection and simplicity.

"Onando" is a slightly darker shade of blue. Therefore, "Sabitsuchi Onando" is a muted, slightly dark, greenish-blue color. Such complex and nuanced color names became more common in the late Edo period.

Toumorokoshiiro
Corn Color

This refers to a warm, shallow yellow color reminiscent of the color of corn kernels. It is also known as "Shokumaiiro." The exact dyeing method is not well-known, but the dye can be made using yangmei bark and alum. Surprisingly, this color has a relatively long history, as it became popular during the late An'ei and Tenmei periods (1772–1789), along with colors like "Tobiiro" and "Hiwacha."

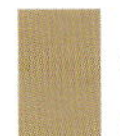
Odoiro
Ocher

A deep yellow-brown color made from a mixture of powdered iron oxide and clay. It has a slightly reddish hue. Like other red-based pigments such as *taisha* and *bengara*, it is also a compound of iron oxide. Fine particles of this color were used as an upper coat paint for walls, including on the surfaces of the Takamatsu Kozuka Kofun (a burial mound). This pigment has been known since ancient times, as it can be found in the *Manyoshu* (a collection of Japanese poems from the Nara period) and has been used as a painting pigment in Japanese art.

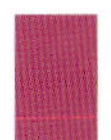
Botan
Peony

Botan is a vibrant reddish-purple color, dyed using indigo and safflower. Peonies are highly regarded in China for their ornamental and medicinal purposes, often described as the "flower of wealth and honor." This color name associated with peonies appeared in Japan during the Muromachi period and was used for Noh costumes, among other things. As a color for garments, it was described as "white on the outside and red plum on the inside," while for female courtier attire in April, it was "pale suō and white."

178 Toumorokoshiiro	**173 Odoiro**	**12 Botan**

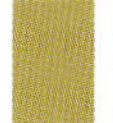

Kihada
Yellow Persimmon

Kihada is a deciduous tall tree of the citrus family that grows in mountainous areas. It is said to be named for its yellowish inner bark, which resembles yellow skin. The dyeing method involves crushing the bark of the tree to create a decoction and then using lye or alum as a mordant. Since the decoction is already a bright yellow, it was often used without additional mordants in the past.

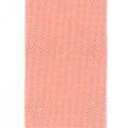

Karashiiro
Mustard Color

Karashiiro is a somewhat muted yellow color, like that of Japanese mustard seeds. Both Japanese and Western mustard are named after colors in the yellow spectrum. The mustard plant (*karashi-na*) is a perennial herb believed to originate from Central Asia and is cultivated in Hokkaido and the Tohoku region. The powdered seeds of its flowers are used to make wasabi, widely used in cooking. Mustard has been cultivated in China for over two thousand years and was introduced to Japan in ancient times.

Momoiro
Peach Color

Momoiro is a soft shade made with safflower, resembling the color of peach blossoms. In ancient color names, peaches were called "tsuki." In Japan, this color is commonly

referred to as "pink" in everyday usage, while in the West "pink" is more closely associated with the color of carnations. In Tang Dynasty poems, peach blossoms were celebrated as the most favored flowers, but in Japan, the color peach is often associated with a somewhat less refined, sensual image.

Tamagoiro
Egg Yolk

"Tamagoiro" refers to a bright yellow color with a hint of red, similar to the color of a boiled egg yolk. The dyeing process is a slightly lighter version of turmeric dyeing and has been practiced since the early Edo period. Illustrations featuring tamagoiro as the background color can be found in pattern books for kimono sleeves.

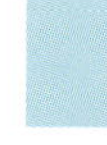

Kamenozoki/Nozokiiro
Pale Indigo

Kamenozoki is the lightest shade of indigo dye. It can be interpreted as meaning "just dipped in an indigo jar" or "peeking into a jar." It may also refer to the color seen when looking into a jar of water. This is a unique and descriptive color name for the lightest shade of indigo.

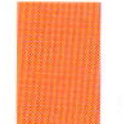

Benihi
Vivid Vermilion

While "Hon-hi" (true vermilion) is a color made using madder with a lye mordant, "Beni-hi" is a slightly yellowish, vivid red color created by overlaying yellow dyed with turmeric, kihada, or osmanthus with safflower dye.

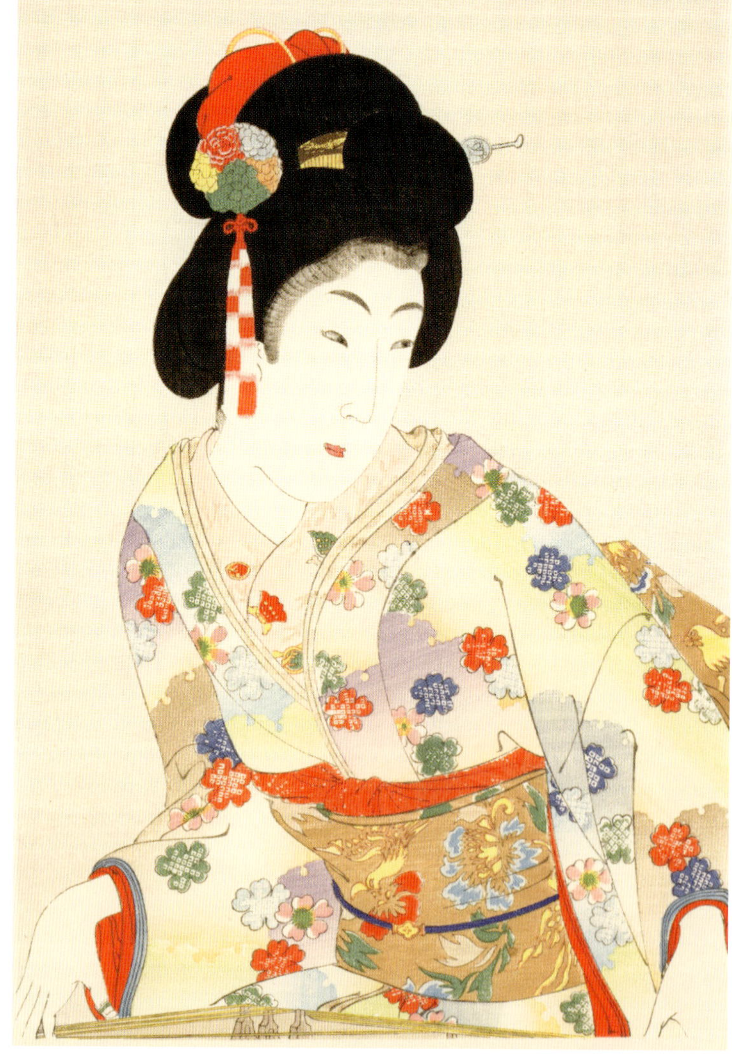

Dyed in tamagoiro, from the waist to the hem of the kimono, ivy leaves are colored in various shades and hang rhythmically. On the other hand, the colorful leaves on the shoulders and sleeves are creatively transformed into birds in flight, which is quite unique. This technique of transformation, known as "mitate," was a trend during the Edo period and became popular among commoners, including in playful works and ukiyo-e prints. Mitate patterns can also be frequently seen in kimono sleeve designs from the same period.

Detail from "A Woman Playing the Koto" by Toyohara Chikanobu, 1897.
National Diet Library Digital Collection.

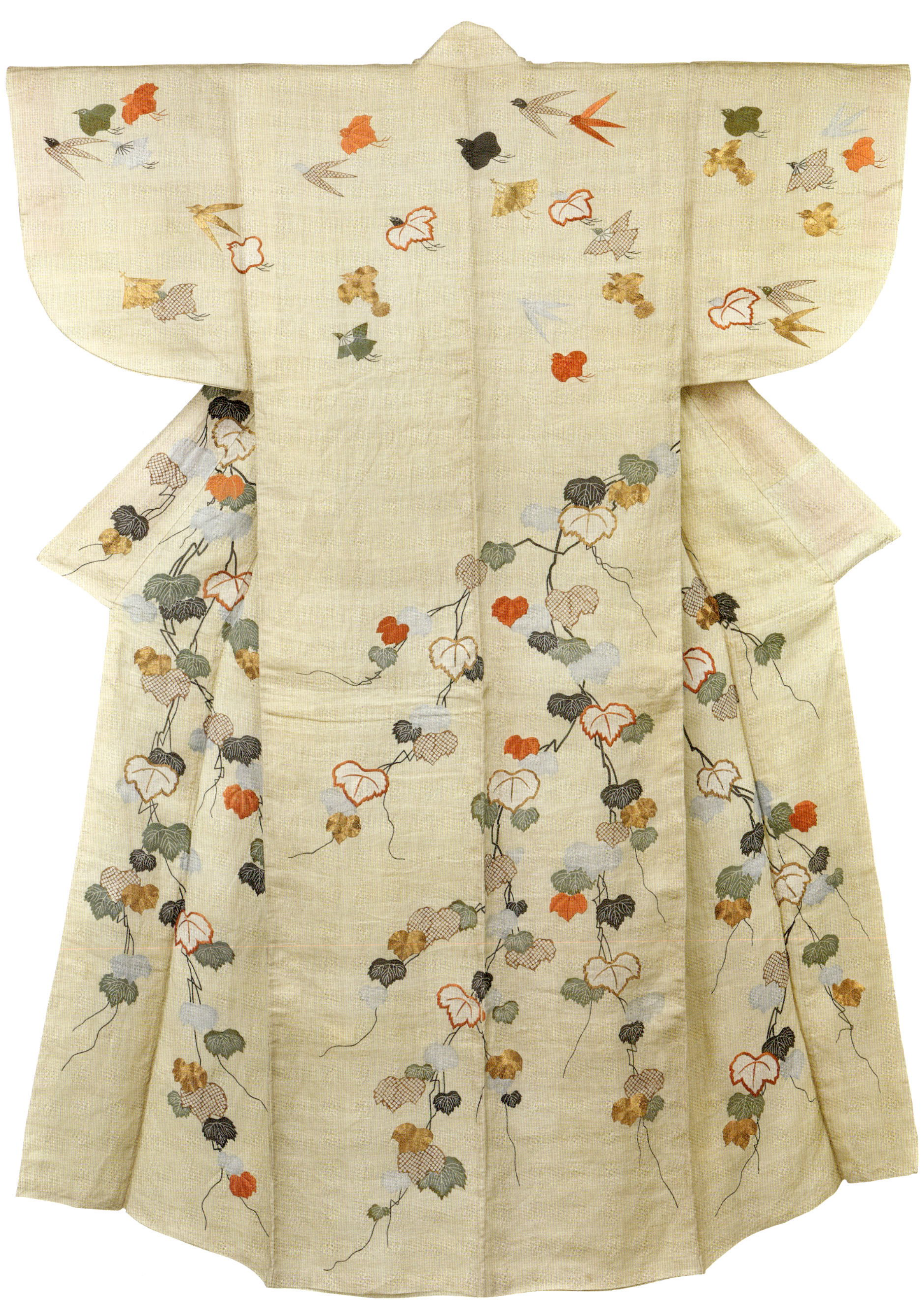

"Eggshell-colored Linen Kimono with Bird and Ivy Pattern". Edo period, 18th century.
Tokyo National Museum. Source: ColBase at https://colbase.nich.go.jp

Bird Color Names

Birds are a delightful part of daily life, and many colors bear their names. Most of these color names are derived from the colors of the birds' plumage. Using the birds' vibrant feather hues to describe colors gives one a feeling of admiration, affection, and respect for nature. It also provides an opportunity to understand how much our culture of colors has been influenced by nature.

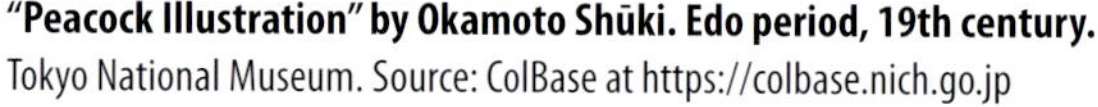

"Peacock Illustration" by Okamoto Shūki. Edo period, 19th century. Tokyo National Museum. Source: ColBase at https://colbase.nich.go.jp

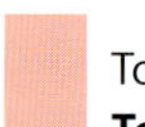

Tokihairo/Tokiiro
Toki Color, Rosy Color

Refers to the pale pinkish hue seen on the wings or tail feathers of the Toki bird, or crested Ibis. Historically, a similar color was achieved using peach dye, and even today, it remains an indispensable color for youth-oriented traditional Japanese attire. Until the Edo period, the Toki lived throughout Japan and was a familiar color name known to many. The practice of naming colors after familiar fauna and flora like Toki, and Uguisu (Bush Warbler) started during the Edo period.

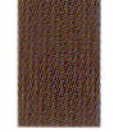

Tobiiro
Black Kite Color

A color name derived from the hue of the Tobi bird's feathers. While this bird's English name is "Black kite," its color is a dark reddish-brown. The dyeing process, according to the *Some Monogatari* involved an under-dye of willow or plum bark followed by layering with sumac and then dyeing with iron or alum mordant. From the early Edo period, this color appeared frequently in kimono design templates and miscellaneous notes, becoming a representative of the brown color palette. During the Tenmei era, it became a popular color for men's fabric, leading to variations like black Tobi and red Tobi.

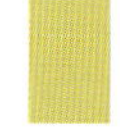

Kanariairo
Canary Color

Refers to a slightly muted yellow resembling the color of wild canaries. Since the 16th century, canaries, which underwent selective breeding primarily in Europe, became popular pets. In Japan, they were introduced and became popular for breeding during the Tenmei period (1781–1789) after arriving in Nagasaki. Originally native to the Canary Islands in Northwest Africa, the wild species has a dull yellowish-brown plumage, but selective breeding led to the vibrant yellow variation.

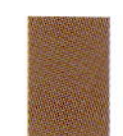

Suzumeiro
Sparrow Color

Used to describe a dark brown with a reddish tint, similar to the color of a sparrow's head. There are cases where "Suzumecha" (sparrow tea color) is considered identical to suzumeiro, and cases where it is seen as a slightly grayish-brown color resembling a sparrow's feather, but they are not strictly distinguished. Dyeing is done using sumac and willow or plum bark.

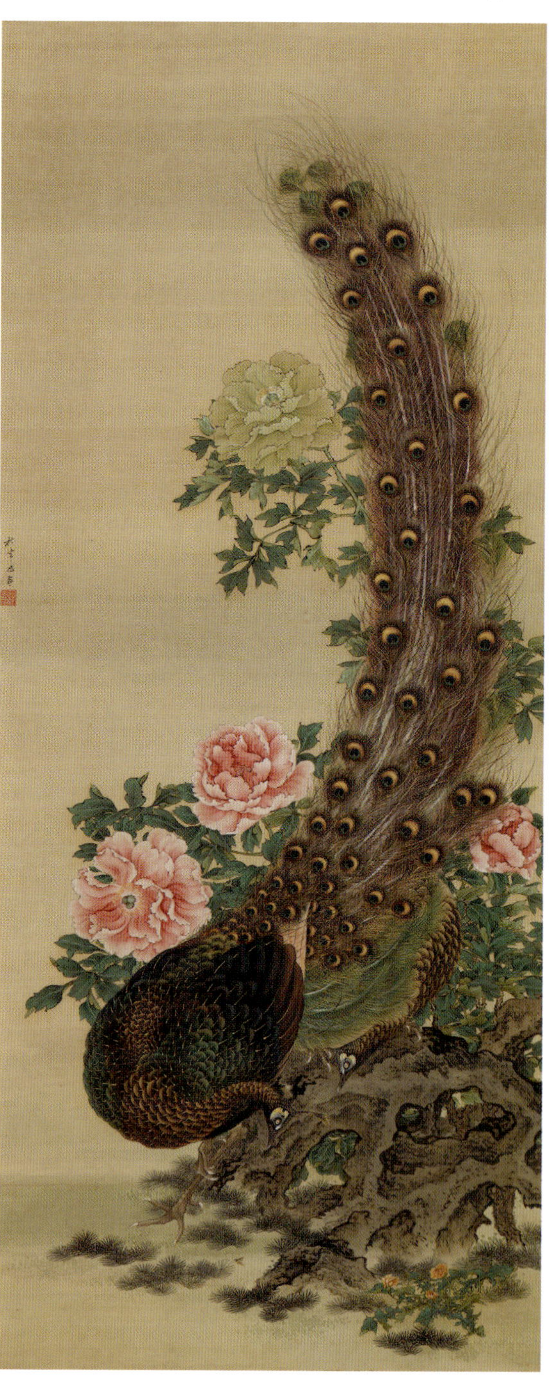

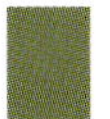

Yamabatoiro
Mountain Pigeon

A color resembling the feathers of a mountain dove, it is a subdued bluish-green hue achieved through dyeing processes similar to blue-white sumac or *kikujin* (mold used in fermentation), using *kariyasu* (a type of sumac) dyeing and *murasaki* (purple) root dyeing. While the feathers from the neck to the back of wild doves appear gray at first glance, depending on the light, this color may reveal reddish-purple or greenish hues within the gray. Although not commonly found in the attire of nobles or warriors, this color appears in such works as the *Heike Monogatari* and others.

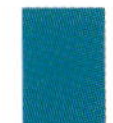

Kujakuao
Peacock Blue

This name refers to the glossy blue-green color of the feathers of male peacocks and can be described as either blue or green. It has long been popular in textiles, glazes, painting and many other arts.

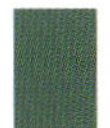

Kamo no hairo
Duck Feather

Refers to a strong greenish-blue hue similar to the feathers on the head and neck of ducks. The plumage colors of male and female ducks vary with the seasons, encompassing shades like green, bluish-green, and greenish-blue. English color names such as "teal blue" or "teal green" specify more particular shades. Although the *Manyōshū* contains a verse by Ōtomo no Yakamochi stating, "The feathers of waterfowl, as well as the hairs of the bear, / Show a limitless variety of blue, it is said," the specific color remains unknown.

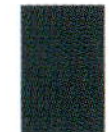

Tamamushiiro
Tamamushi Beetle

Tamamushiiro refers to a dark greenish-blue color, similar to the color of a tamamushi beetle's wings. It is believed that the color name came from a phrase in *Gan'i Shō*, a book on court customs of aristocrats, which gave the term a specific meaning. Tamamushi beetles have wings that appear as beautiful shades of green and purple when viewed from different angles, which is why they have been used in art and crafts throughout the ages. The Tamamushi Shrine at Hōryū-ji Temple is famous for its use of tamamushi.

Rakudairo
Camel Color

Rakudairo, a color resembling the grayish brown of a camel's fur, became known in Japan after two Bactrian camels were presented to the Tokugawa shogunate by the captain of a Dutch merchant ship in the third year of the Shōhō era (1646). However, the use of camel hair fabrics and color names became more common in modern times.

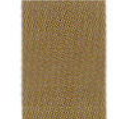

Kitsuneiro
Fox Color

Refers to a light brown color resembling the fur on the back of a fox. This color name is rarely used to describe the beauty of a color. Instead, it is commonly used to describe the appearance of food, such as bread or rice cakes, when they are deliciously browned, as in "the surface has turned a nice fox color."

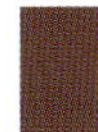

Ebicha
Shrimp Tea/Grape Tea

Used to describe a reddish-brown or dark reddish-purple color. The term "ebi" (shrimp) in "ebitacha" may have originated from the similarity to the color of crustaceans, although currently, it is also written as "ebicha" meaning shrimp tea. From the mid to late Meiji period, it was favored as the color of *hakama* (a type of traditional Japanese clothing) for female students and teachers. They often chose this color to emulate the renowned Heian-era female writer Murasaki Shikibu, resulting in terms like "Budōcha Shikibu" (Grape Tea Shikibu).

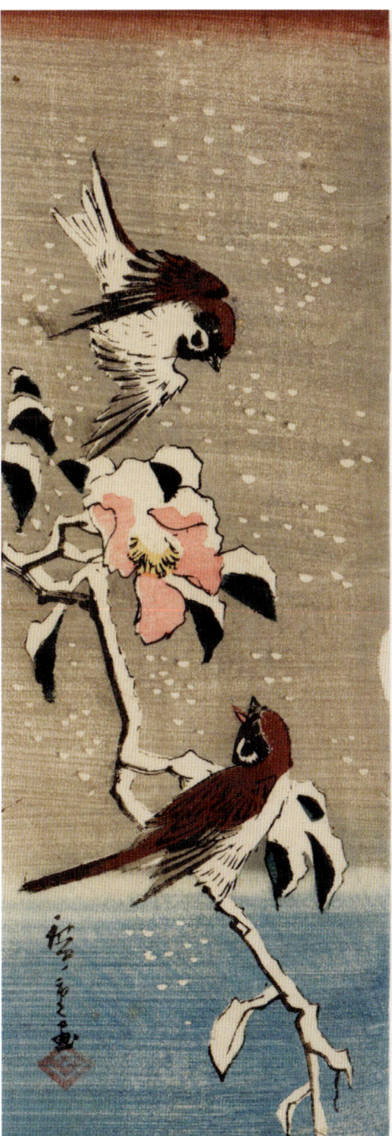

"Sparrows and Camellias in the Snow"
by Utagawa Hiroshige. Edo period, 19th century.
Tokyo National Museum.
Source: ColBase at https://colbase.nich.go.jp

The Color Brown in Japanese Culture

Brown is a natural color that resonates with the daily senses of Japanese people, as it is constantly seen in the color of tree trunks, soil, and rocks. It also refers to the color of skin, hair, and eyes, as well as the feathers of animals and birds. The color name "Chairo" became established after the habit of drinking tea spread, and during the Edo period, shades of brown favored by Kabuki actors like Danjūrō and Shibikan also gained popularity. Various color names, along with "Nezumiiro" (grayish brown), became trendy among common people, to the extent that the fashion of the time was said to be "forty-eight shades of brown and one hundred shades of gray."

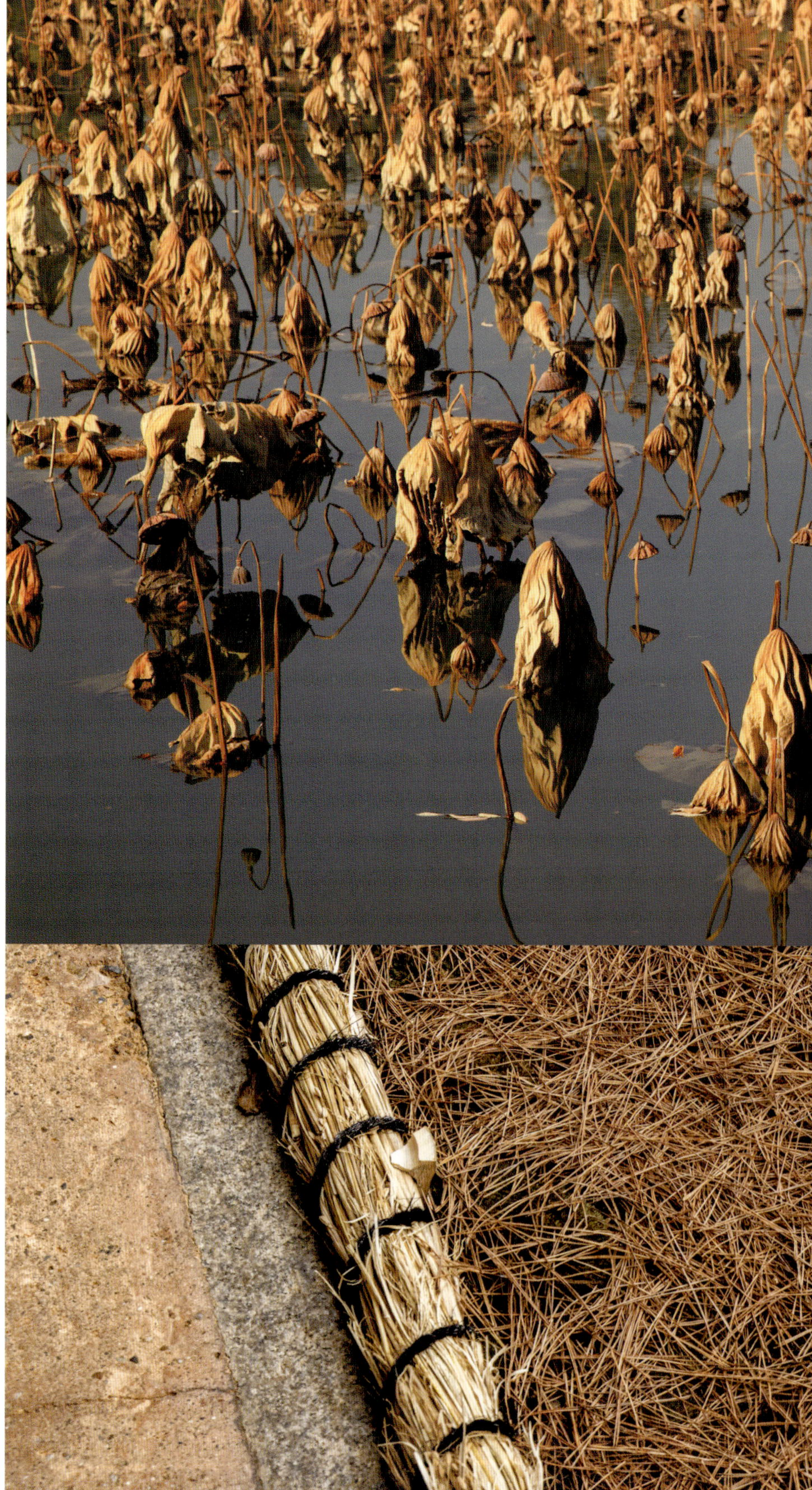

Top Ōsawa Pond, Daikaku-ji Temple, Kyoto.
Bottom right Pine Needles on the Ground at Hōsendō Garden, Kyoto.
Bottom far right Scattered Autumn Leaves, Ōsawa Pond, Kyoto.

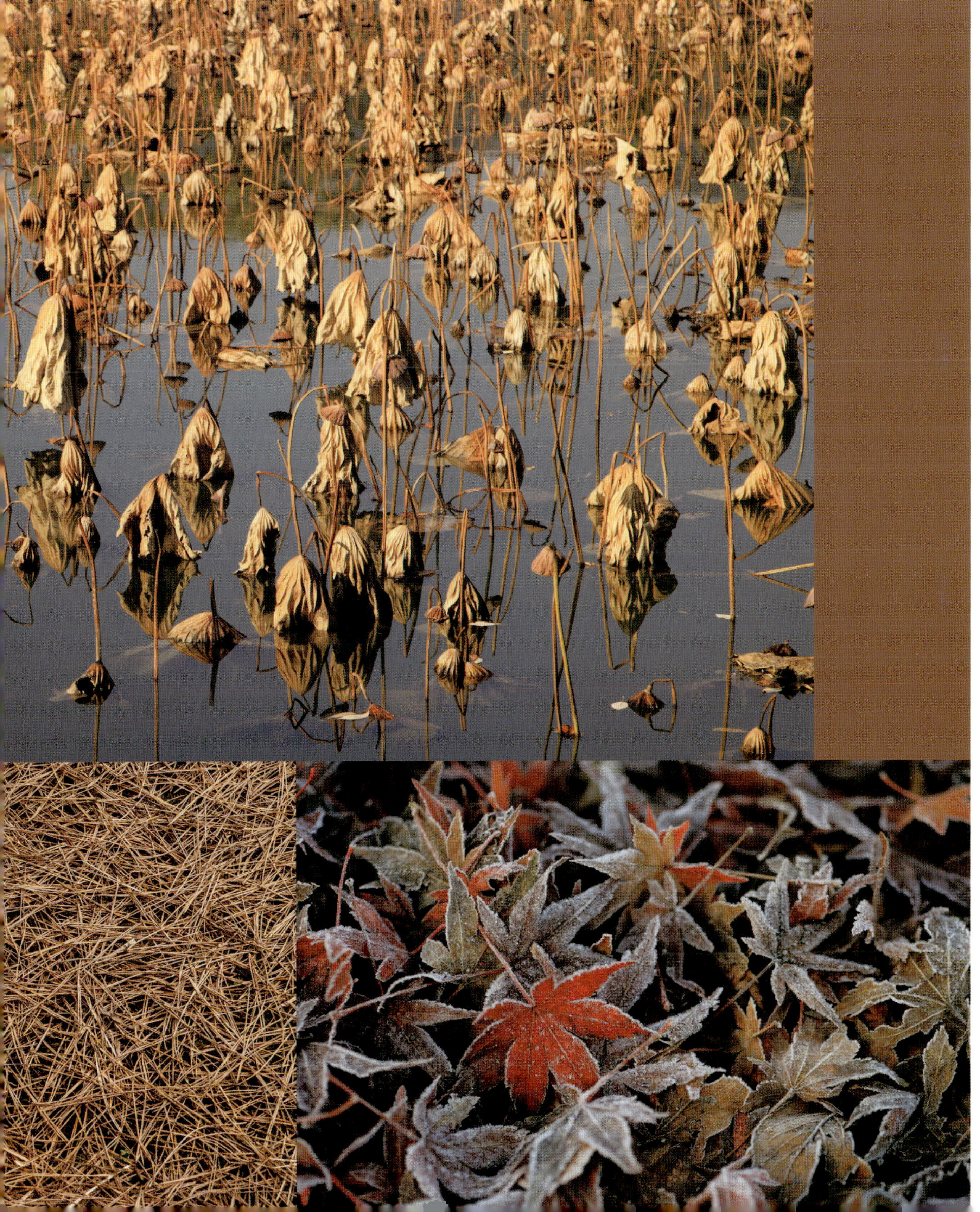

Japanese Color Schemes Based on Brown

Brown is a graceful color reflecting the hues of nature. We see it all over the natural world and in day-to-day human life—the wood and clay used to build our structures, the ceramics we use, the tea and coffee we enjoy. In fact the word "chairo," meaning brown, originated from the color of tea, which became a daily pleasure. The practice of brewing and drinking tea as a medicinal herb was introduced from China by the monk Eisai, who traveled there to study in the third year of the Kenkyū era (1192). The cultivation of tea in Japan began in earnest after this, starting with the establishment of tea cultivation at Kozan-ji Temple in Togao, Kyoto.

During the Muromachi period, along with the rise of the tea ceremony (*chanoyu*), brown became synonymous with Japanese tea and deeply permeated various aspects of culture related to elegance, tranquility, and rustic simplicity. In the Edo period, a dedicated system of tea masters serving the imperial court, shogunate, daimyos, and others was established, leading to the spread of tea-drinking habits among farmers and common people. This eventually gave rise to the kinds of tea we consume today, such as sencha, hojicha, and bancha, contributing to the widespread use of the term "chairo."

As a dye, brown was traditionally obtained by immersing threads or fabrics in concoctions made from the bark, fruits, or shells of trees like oak, oak gall, chestnut, and Japanese sumac, often combined with the dual mordanting process using iron and lime or alkaline water. Brown is not as frequently used in color names as red or blue, but it covers a wide range of hues, from a reddish-brown to a deep blackish-brown. It is always fashionable in both in our home decor and the clothes we wear.

Color combinations featuring brown often incorporate traditional analogous or complementary colors. Inspiration can be drawn from colors found in nature, such as the foliage that adorns hills and fields, the hues of withered leaves, and the golden tones of the autumn season.

Color Scheme Based on Light Colors

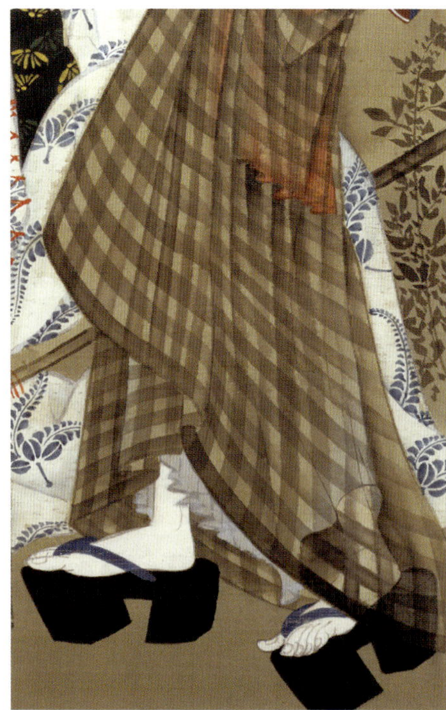

**Detail from "Two Beauties Catching Fireflies"
by Hōtei Gosei, 1820.**
Collection of Itabashi Art Museum, Itabashi City.

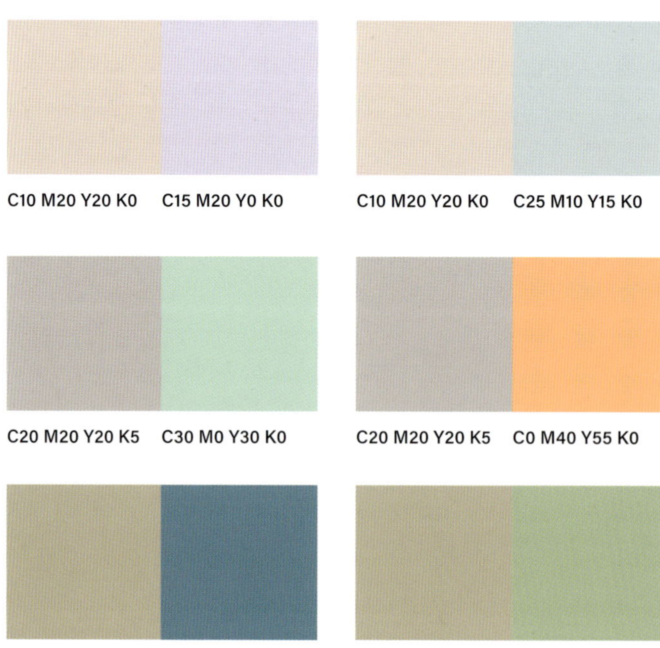

C10 M20 Y20 K0	C15 M20 Y0 K0	C10 M20 Y20 K0	C25 M10 Y15 K0
C20 M20 Y20 K5	C30 M0 Y30 K0	C20 M20 Y20 K5	C0 M40 Y55 K0
C20 M20 Y40 K10	C70 M30 Y30 K5	C20 M20 Y40 K10	C20 M0 Y45 K20

Color Scheme Based on Vivid Colors

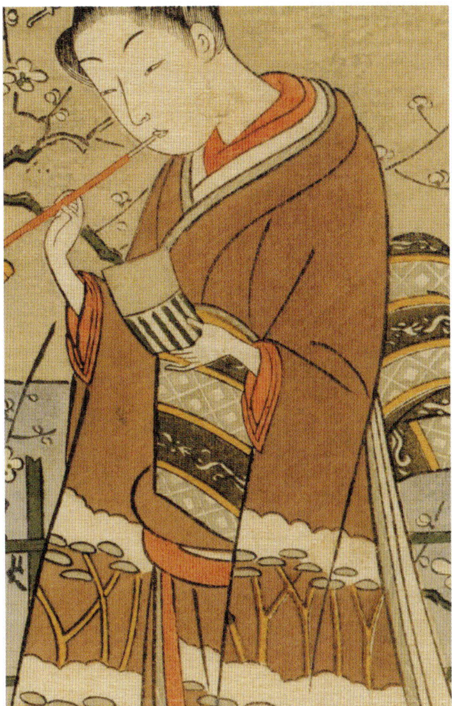

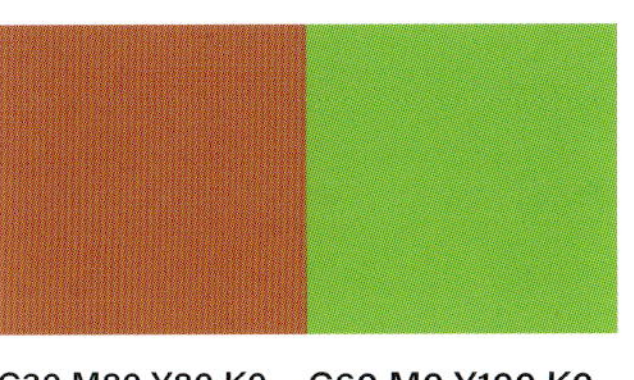

C20 M60 Y100 K0 C0 M45 Y100 K0

C20 M60 Y100 K0 C70 M60 Y0 K0

C40 M60 Y80 K0 C100 M0 Y80 K0

C40 M60 Y80 K0 C25 M40 Y70 K0

C30 M80 Y80 K0 C75 M0 Y30 K0

C30 M80 Y80 K0 C60 M0 Y100 K0

**Detail from "Sleeping Dragon and Winter Plum"
by Suzuki Harunobu. Edo period, 18th century.**
Collection of Tokyo National Museum.
ColBase at https://colbase.nich.go.jp

Color Scheme Based on Dark Colors

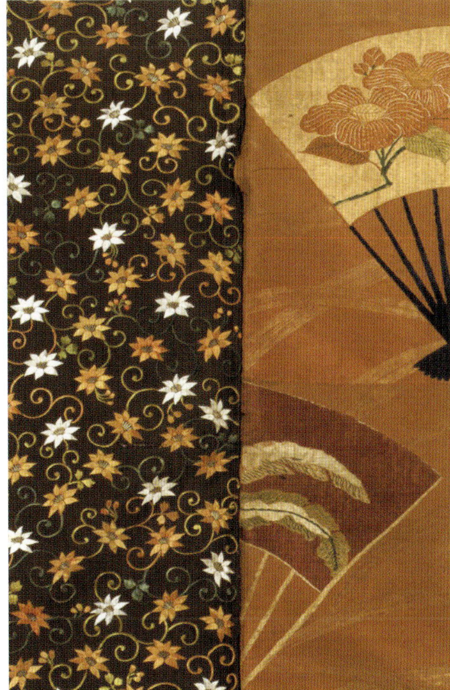

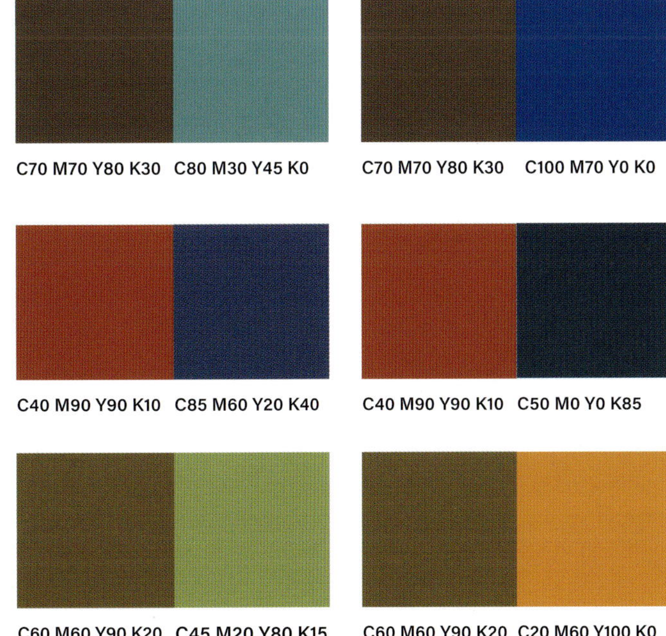

C70 M70 Y80 K30 C80 M30 Y45 K0

C70 M70 Y80 K30 C100 M70 Y0 K0

C40 M90 Y90 K10 C85 M60 Y20 K40

C40 M90 Y90 K10 C50 M0 Y0 K85

C60 M60 Y90 K20 C45 M20 Y80 K15

C60 M60 Y90 K20 C20 M60 Y100 K0

**Detail from "Black Tea Kosode with Scattered Fans
and Grass Embroidered with Fine Wire Thread".
Azuchi-Momoyama to Edo period, 17th century.**
Tokyo National Museum.
Source: ColBase at https://colbase.nich.go.jp

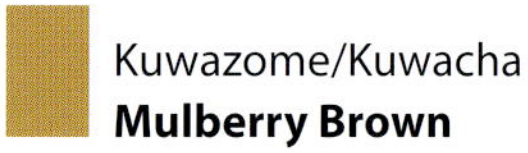

Kuwazome/Kuwacha
Mulberry Brown

Kuwazome is a color made using the decoction of mulberry tree bark and root bark, mordanted with ash or alkali, and it is a light brown color with golden tones. Some use this color name for fabrics dyed using mulberry fruits, but the fruits produce a darker reddish-purple color. Within the Kuwazome hue, there is a slightly yellowish light brown called "Kuwairo shiracha," which became popular for women's kimono linings in the later Edo period.

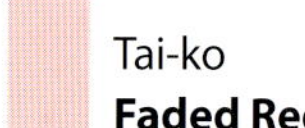

Tai-ko
Faded Red

Tai-ko represents an extremely pale shade of red obtained from faded red dye. It was associated with lower-ranking officials and servants' clothing. It is mentioned in the *Teijō Zōki* that this color was achieved not with costly safflower but by using crushed plum tree bark as a dye.

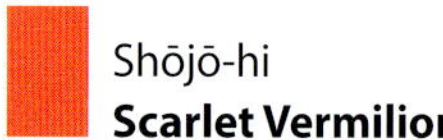

Shōjō-hi
Scarlet Vermilion

Shōjō-hi is a highly vibrant and clear vermilion color. It was commonly found in silk gauze textiles, particularly those imported through Nanban trade that began in the mid-16th century. This color has a long history of use and was often seen in luxurious textiles like *ro-asa* (a type of silk gauze) and velvet, which samurai wore as *jinbaori* (sleeveless battle surcoats) with elaborate designs to compete in elegance on the battlefield.

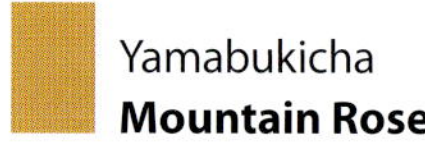

Yamabukicha
Mountain Rose

"Yamabukiiro" refers to a yellow color with a brownish hue derived from the color of the mountain spray. It is also referred to as "Dark yamabuki" or "Kincha" when it leans towards a golden brown. According to the dyeing method described in *Toyo Seiso Momosuku*i (1696), after dyeing with bayberry and drying it, alum is added to the bayberry juice for a second time to add a darker shade.

A woman leans close to a peony blooming in a pale pink hue. She seems drawn into the imposing presence of the flower, larger than her own face. Clad in a kimono adorned with delicate strokes of white and navy-blue hydrangea flowers, she kneels gracefully, a black obi featuring butterfly motifs tightly fastened around her waist. Her slender, dignified figure exudes an air of melancholy. Perhaps she is captivated by the flower's spirit. Kotai Murase (1887–1940) was a Japanese painter active during the early Showa and Taisho periods.

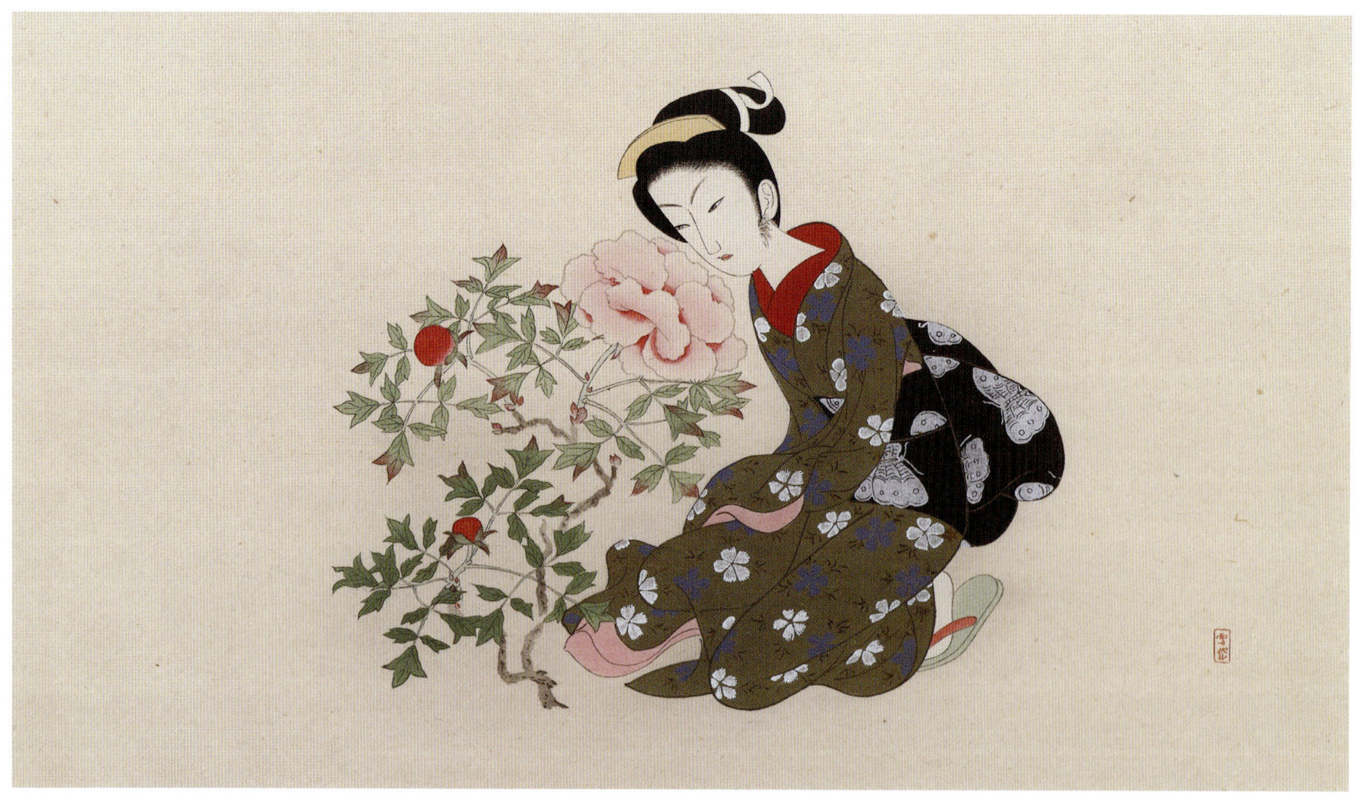

200 Kuwazome/Kuwacha **2 Tai-ko** **16 Shōjō-hi**

"Peony Viewing" by Komura Setsudai, 1942.
Saitama Prefectural Museum of Modern Art.

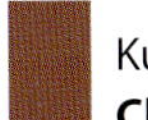

Benihiwada
Red Cypress Bark

This is a reddish brown color derived from the bark of the cypress tree (*benihi*). It shares similarities with vermilion, but has a slightly deeper brownish hue due to a more pronounced red tint. This color is believed to have been used from the late Edo period onwards, as indicated in the *Konya Jinzaburō Kakisho* (1784).

Kurumegaki
Chestnut Plum

This color name refers to a dark brownish-red with hints of chestnut brown. The "kuri" in "Kurumegaki" originates from the reddish hue of plum blossoms, and similar colors such as "Umecha" or "Umegara" also refer to shades of red derived from the plum blossom. This color is obtained by using crushed plum tree bark as a dye, followed by enhancing the color with alum. In the later Edo period, a reddish version of this color known as "Shibakincha" became fashionable.

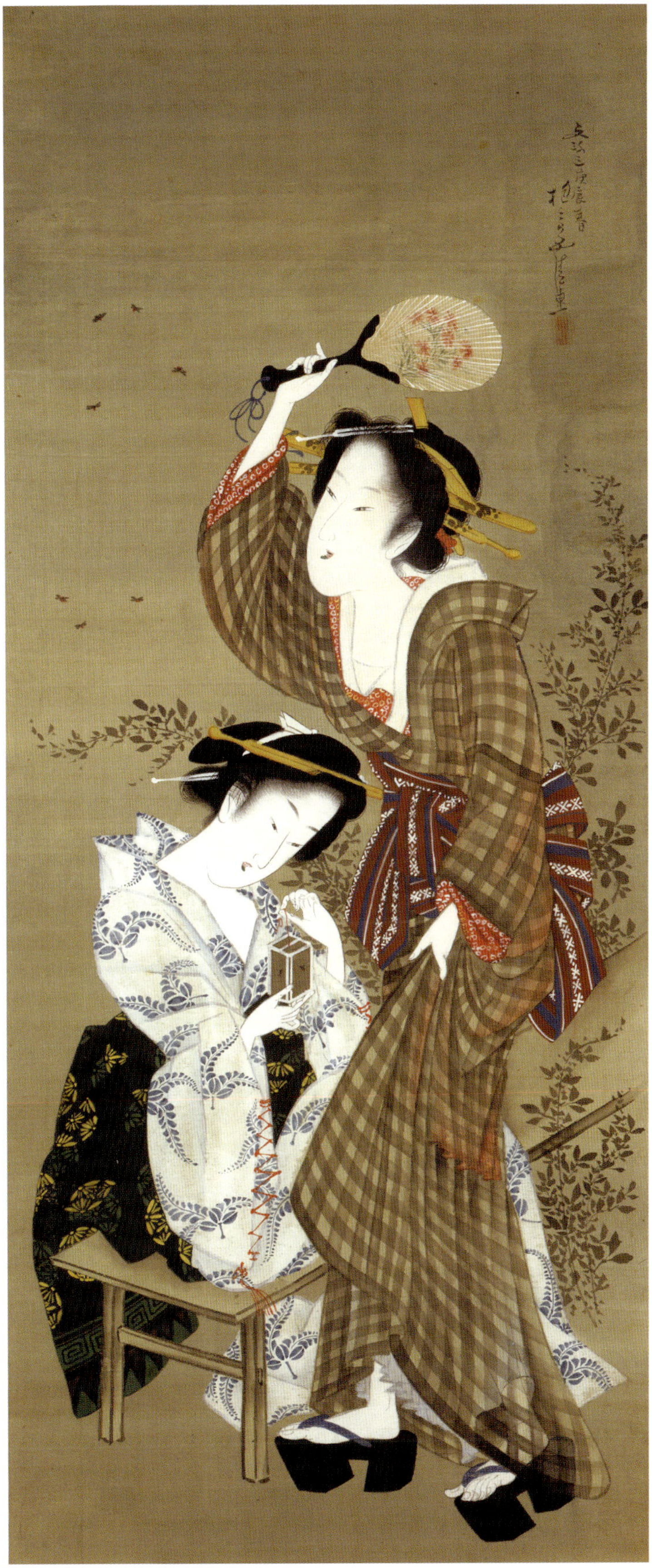

In the dim light, figures wielding fans chase after fireflies, evoking a sense of allure amidst the coolness of a summer evening. On the right, a woman in light attire reveals white feet peeking out from beneath a red tie-dyed *juban*. On the left, a woman in a blue-patterned yukata has decorative red thread embellishments on her sleeves, her expression holding a youthful charm as she holds a cage for insects. Their delicate facial features, with small, slightly upturned eyes and lips, vividly embody the characteristic beauty depicted in Gosei's portraits of beautiful women. His excellent sense of color coordination in his subjects' attire is apparent here. Hōtotei Gosei was an Ukiyo-e artist from the later Edo period, said to have studied under Katsushika Hokusai but reportedly was expelled. He was known for his illustrations in Kyōka books such as *Kyōka Hyōbanki* and *Kyōka Nenchū Gyōji*, and he excelled in portraying beautiful women both in prints and paintings.

"Two Beauties Catching Fireflies" by Hōtei Gosei, 1820.
Itabashi Art Museum.

198 Yamabukicha	242 Benihiwada	245 Kurumegaki

The painting depicts a young woman from a merchant family having her hair styled by an older hairdresser. The hairdresser asks the girl if she's pleased with the finished style, and the girl responds with a satisfied expression reflected in the mirror, her hand resting on the back of her hair. Such everyday scenes are still part of daily life, but in this artwork, one can fully appreciate Utamaro's skillful observation of a woman's world. "Mi no koku" in the banner says that the time is around ten o'clock in the morning.

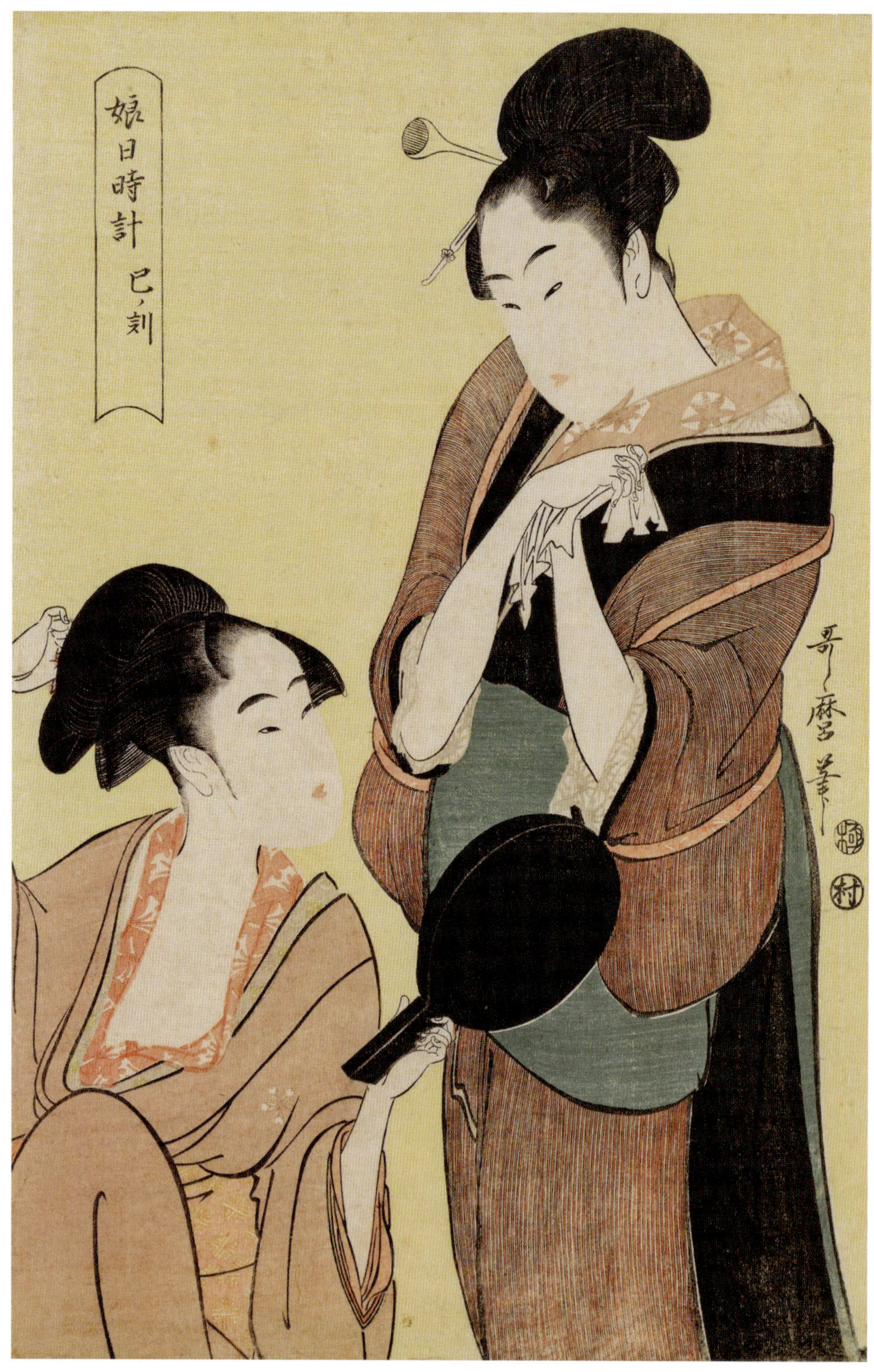

"Daughter with a Sundial—Hour of the Snake" (Important Cultural Property) by Kitagawa Utamaro Edo period, 18th century. Tokyo National Museum. Source: ColBase at https://colbase.nich.go.jp

236 Edocha	146 Usuao	191 Torinokoiro

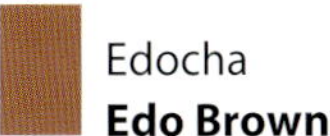

Edocha
Edo Brown

A muted yellowish-brown color with reddish undertones. It was a popular color during the early Edo period and was referred to as "Edocha" meaning the preferred color of the Edo period. Later, it was also called "Tosecha," meaning the best brown of the time. This shade is achieved by dyeing with bayberry and then adding vermilion.

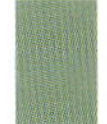

Usuao
Pale Blue

A pale, yellowish-green color. While today this is considered a green color, in the past, it was considered part of the blue spectrum and was described with the color name "Moegi."

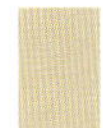

Torinokoiro
Eggshell

A very pale yellow-brown color resembling the color of chicken eggshells. A thick paper made from the bark of mulberry, which is the raw material for Japanese paper, is called "torinoko-gami" and refers to a yellow color close to cream. It was color name favored during the Heian period, and the color itself was considered elegant and refined.

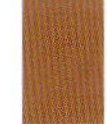

Kabacha
Birch Tea Brown

A deeper version of the color "Kabairo." The term "kaba" typically refers to the bark of white birch trees today, but in the past, it was also used to refer to certain varieties of cherry trees. According to the *Konyacha Zome Kuchishoden* (published 1666), it involves layering a dark reddish-brown color dyed with *ume* (plum) skins with a red color from vermilion or similar. It was yet another favorite during the Edo period.

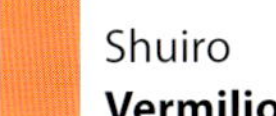

Shuiro
Vermilion

A bright red color from the pigment *shu* (vermilion). It has a slightly yellowish hue. "Shu" refers to cinnabar, a mercury sulfide pigment. Natural vermilion was called "shu-sa" or "shu-sha." As vermilion from Chenxiu in China was particularly prized, it was often referred to as "Chensha." Synthetic vermilion, called "ginsyu" (silver vermilion), was also created as a more affordable alternative.

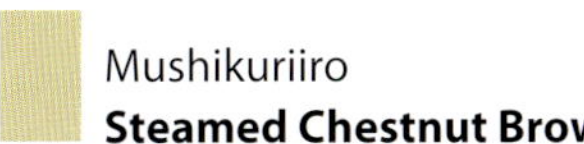

Mushikuriiro
Steamed Chestnut Brown

A light, soft yellow color reminiscent of steamed chestnuts. It differs from "Kuriiro" or "Ochiguri," both of which refer to the reddish-brown color of chestnut skins. Other chestnut-related color names include "Kurikawairo" (chestnut bark color), "Urikoiro" (chestnut shell color), and "Kuriume" (slightly brighter chestnut color).

Near the famous plum trees of Kameido known as "Goryu Ume" (the "Resting Dragon Plum") in Tokyo, a close-knit group of young people is gathered. Here a young man helps to light a girl's pipe. Harunobu often portrayed scenes of pure love between men and women, the warm affection of parents and children, and the everyday life of the common people. He was skilled at creating a romantic and elegant world of painting, establishing a refined and charming artistic style.

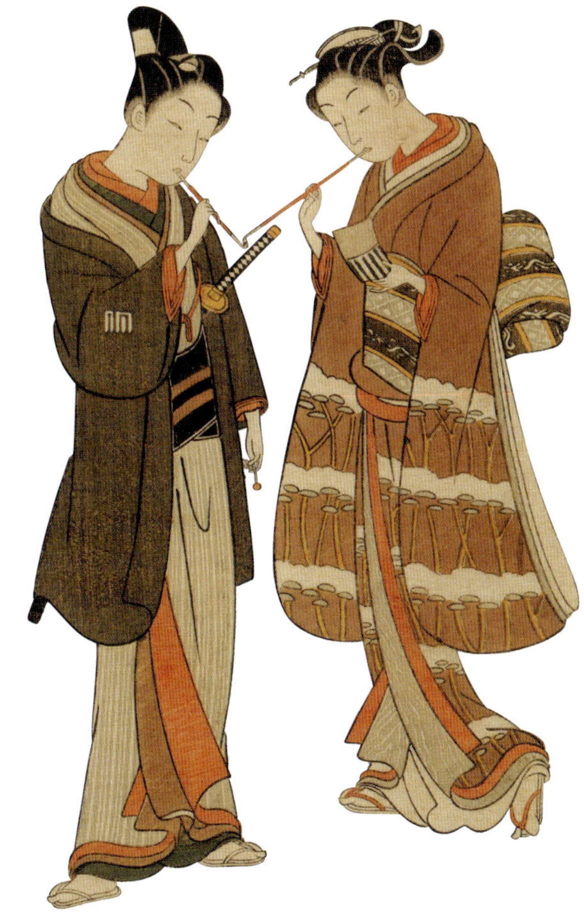

Detail from "Sleeping Dragon and Winter Plum" by Suzuki Harunobu. Edo period, 18th century.
Tokyo National Museum.
Source: ColBase at https://colbase.nich.go.jp

237 Kabacha   35 Shuiro   182 Mushikuriiro

The painting on this square-shaped dish depicts the Chinese Song Dynasty poet Huang Tingjian (Huang T'ing-chien) and is believed to represent a scene of two seagulls playing by the water's edge. The dish is designed to resemble a frame, with cloud scroll patterns adorning the raised outer edge and peony motifs surrounded by cloud scroll patterns on the inner edge. The surface of the dish is coated with white slip, over which Kōrin applied a graceful underglaze decoration using iron red, while on the reverse side, Kōrin's younger brother Shinshō (Gansan) inscribed a firm inscription in a well-defined style. This piece is a collaborative work by the two brothers.

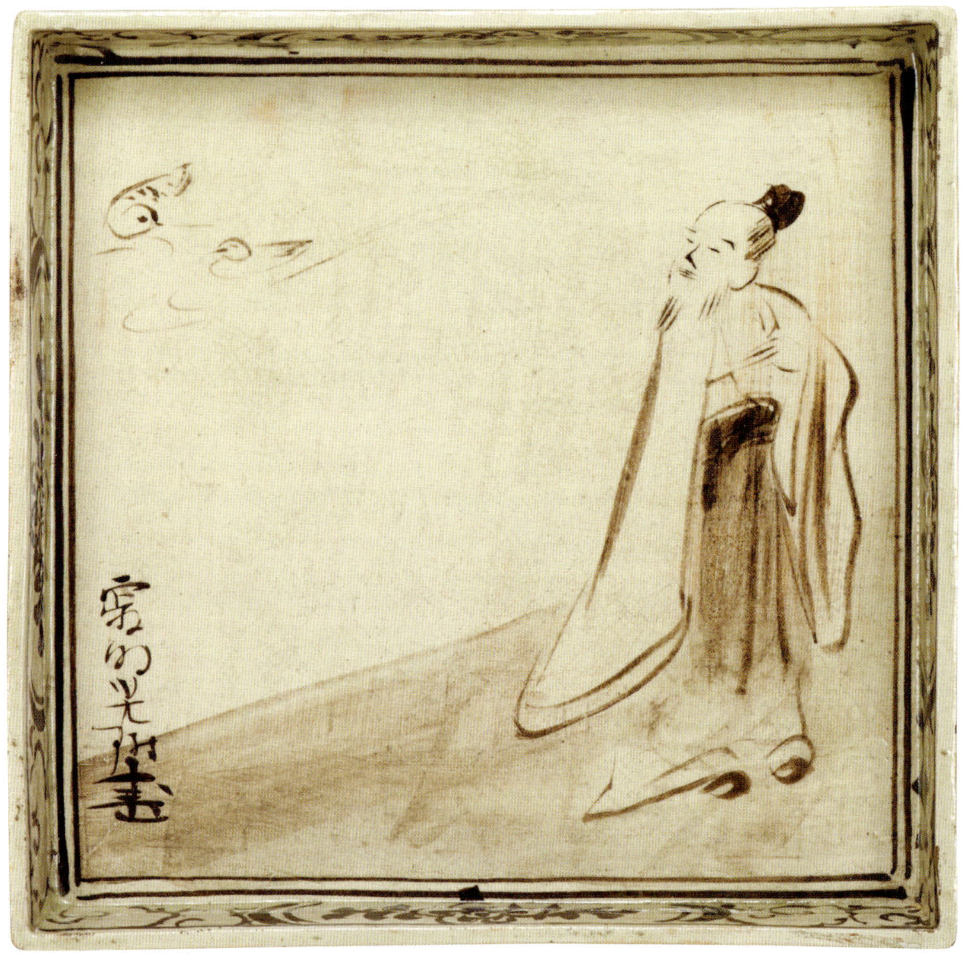

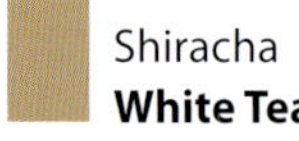

193 Shiracha   218 Susutakeiro

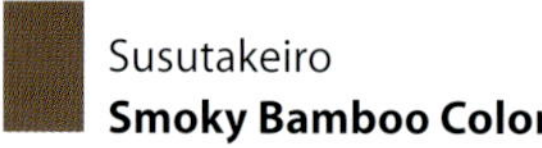

"Rust-painted Plate with a View of Seagulls"
(Important Cultural Property). Collaborative work
by Ogata Kōrin and Shinshō. Edo period, 18th century.
Tokyo National Museum. Source: ColBase at https://colbase.nich.go.jp

Shiracha
White Tea

Shiracha is a light shade of brown with a hint of white, similar to beige. The term "chamimosa" is used for a white cloth used to wipe tea bowls during tea ceremonies. When this cloth becomes stained with tea residue, it is called "shirocha," which refers to the same color. During the middle of the Genroku period (1688–1704), relatively dark shades of brown were in fashion. However, as indicated in the words of Eisei Shunsui in *Doubousu Geien/ Idoukenai* from the Bunka-Bunsei period, a lighter brown color began to regain popularity among tea enthusiasts and the general public.

Susutakeiro
Smoky Bamboo Color

Susutakeiro is a dark brown resembling the color of soot-covered bamboo, evoking the serene look of aged bamboo. This subtle variation in bamboo color appealed to the refined tastes of the Edo era. It gained widespread popularity, especially during the Ho'ō period (1751–1764), and was used extensively for *kosode* (short-sleeved kimono), *haori* (jacket), and *obi* (sash) colors. While a dark charred brown is typical, lighter shades also fell under this color name. Additionally, there is a color name "Susutakecha," which was likely created to suit the tea culture preferences of the Edo period.

This is a Shino ware tea bowl, characterized by its large, robust cylindrical shape and freely expressive brushwork. It features a depiction of a bridge and a thatched roof hut, earning it the name "Hashihime" (Bridge Princess). When viewed from the side, it has a squat shape with a widened bottom, while from the top, the mouth is an uneven ellipse, showcasing the gravitas of Shino ware. In Mino kilns, tea ceramics in Momoyama style such as Ki-Seto, Seto black, Shino, and Oribe were fired from the Tenshō to Keichō periods, and this tea bowl was produced from the late Azuchi-Momoyama period when the tea ceremony flourished among the warrior class, continuing into the early Edo period.

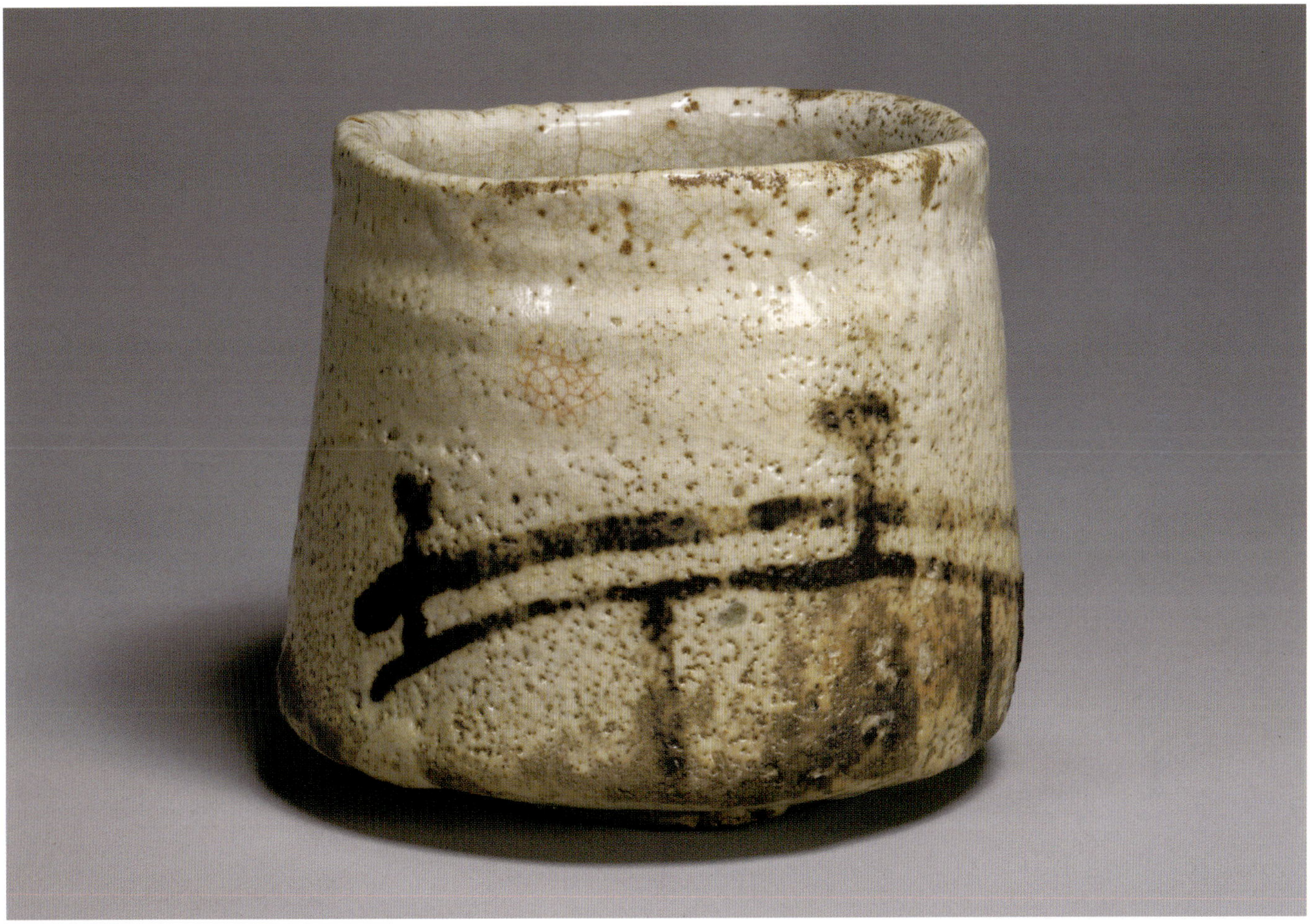

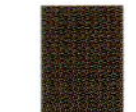

254 Shironeri	250 Kurotobi

"Shino Ware Tea Bowl" with the inscription "Hashihime".
Mino Province. Azuchi-Momoyama to Edo period, 16th to 17th century.
Tokyo National Museum. Source: ColBase at https://colbase.nich.go.jp

Shironeri
White Slip

Shironeri refers to a pure white color reminiscent of untwisted raw silk. The term "shironeri" describes the technique of eliminating the yellowish tint from raw silk to achieve this glossy, pure white silk color. It has been used traditionally as a symbol of sacredness and, in recent years, has been appreciated as a color denoting cleanliness and nobility.

Kurotobi
Black Kite

Kurotobi is a dark reddish-brown color, somewhat darker than the typical reddish-brown of "Tobiiro." According to Ochiai Tamehisa's essay "Hokosome" (1753–1789), this color, along with black, became fashionable as a base color for *kosode* during the Kyōhō period (1716–1735), and it was popular as an obi color during the An'ei period (1772–1780).

In the center, a straight bamboo shoot is boldly depicted, with two bamboo shoots drawn with red soil on either side. The rhythmic strokes of dark green glaze create a flowing effect, enhancing the coloration. This type of Oribe ware, delicately glazed with green, is called "Yashichita Oribe" as it was fired in the Yashichita kiln in Kani City, Gifu Prefecture. The Yashichita Oribe represents the culmination of Oribe ware with its bold and vivid impression.

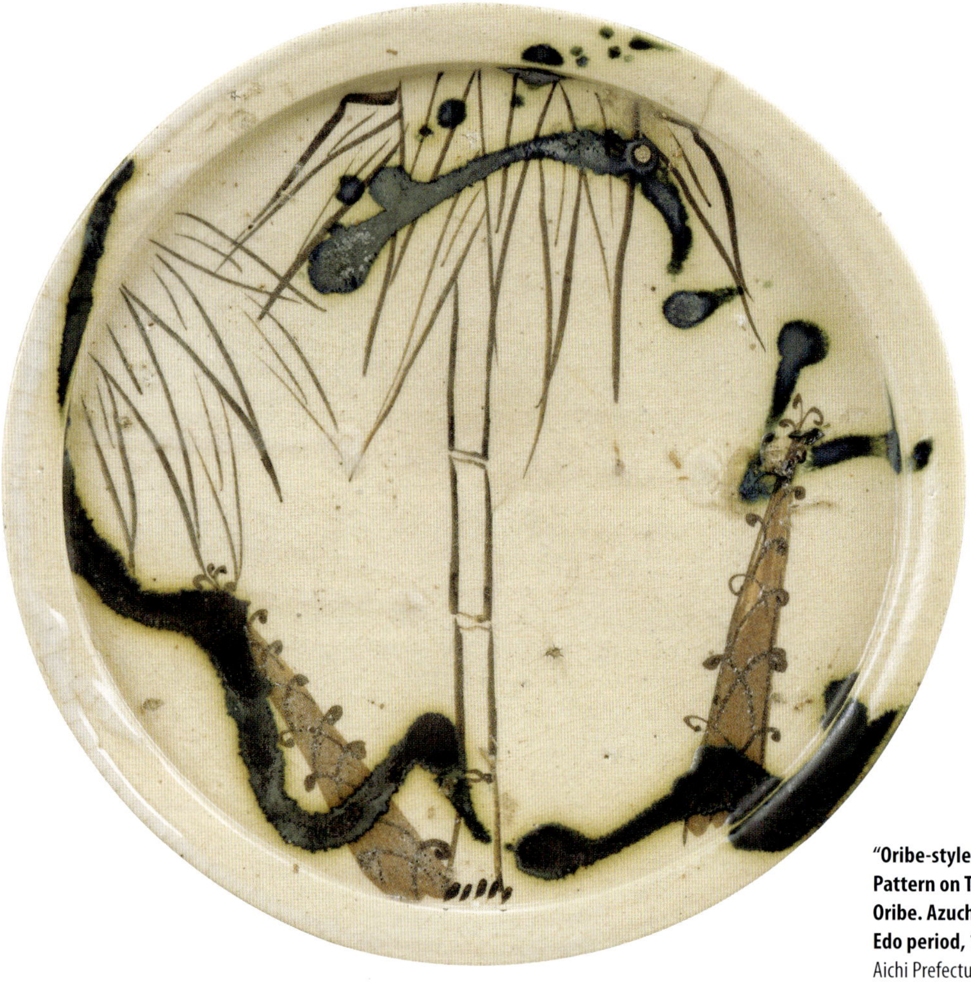

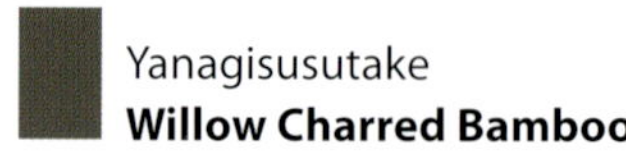

"Oribe-style Plate with Bamboo Pattern on Three Feet". Yashichida Oribe. Azuchi-Momoyama to early Edo period, 17th century.
Aichi Prefectural Ceramic Art Museum.

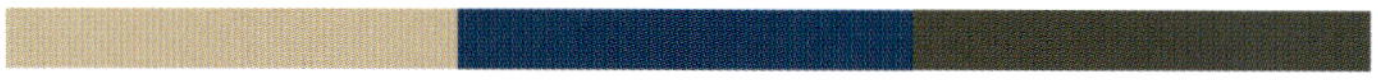

| 192 Tonokoiro | 113 Gosuiro | 213 Yanagisusutake |

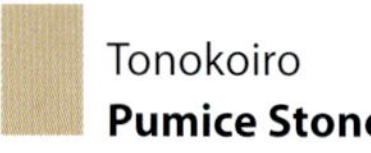

Tonokoiro
Pumice Stone

A light beige color resembling the color of whetstone powder. Whetstone powder is the fine powder that emerges when sharpening blades on a whetstone, and it is used for preparing the base of lacquerware and woodwork. It was also used as an undercoat for heavy makeup to smooth out the wrinkles on the faces of actors and performers.

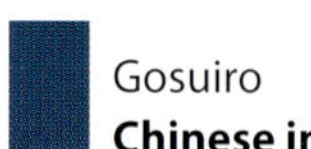

Gosuiro
Chinese ink

An indigo colorant used for the blue pigment in underglaze ceramics. Gosu is a clay-like raw material containing cobalt, manganese, iron, and other elements. When used to paint patterns on ceramics and then fired, it can produce various shades of blue depending on its concentration. This color is popular in porcelain production in places like Arita, Seto, and Shimizu-yaki. In China, it has been used since the Yuan Dynasty and was initially imported from the western regions under the name "Su Ma Li Qing."

Yanagisusutake
Willow Charred Bamboo

Refers to a dark yellow-green color with a grayish tint. It is derived from the popular color "susutake" (bamboo charcoal) during the Genroku period. "Yanagi" means having a greenish hue. The *Some Monogatar* (a book of

In the margins of the large plate, there is a lyric "Every tree is in autumn colors," while the painting depicts a pictur-esque landscape painted by a Southern-style artist. Trees are arranged on the slope, and the colors and contours of the mountains, imbued with autumn scenery, evoke a sense of the deepening season. This is the largest among Seto ware plates, and on the reverse, concentric circles and interlocking vine patterns are drawn around the periphery. During the Edo period in Seto, a technique called "Oniita" was prevalent, which involved underpainting using ceramic pigments high in iron oxide.

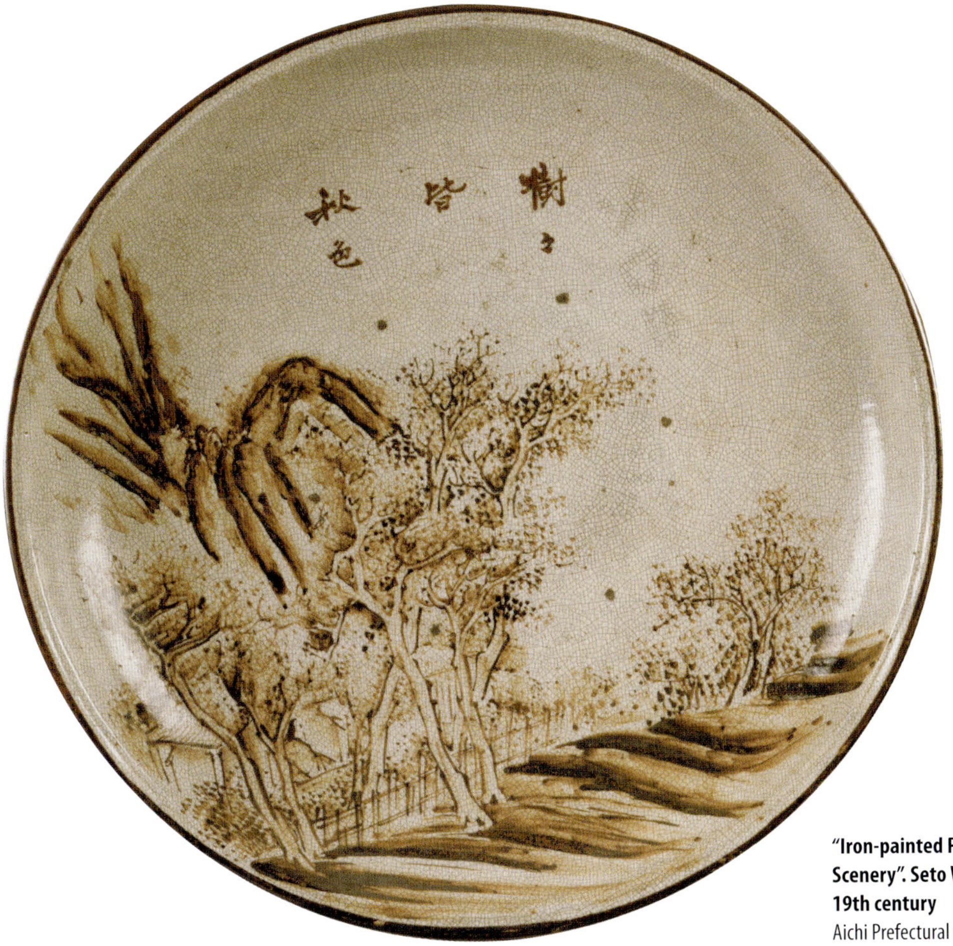

"Iron-painted Plate with Autumn Scenery". Seto Ware. Late Edo period, 19th century
Aichi Prefectural Ceramic Museum.

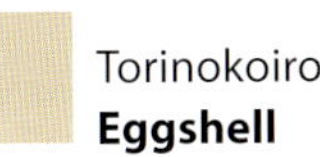

191 Torinokoiro

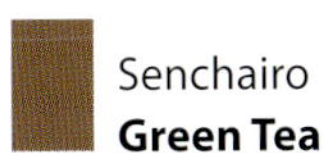

228 Senchairo

dyeing secrets from1696) mentions various dyed colors, including "Susutake," suggesting that this shade emerged as a variation of susutake during that time. The dyeing process involves first under-dyeing with a solution made from willow bark and then developing the color with iron gall ink or alum mordant.

Torinokoiro
Eggshell

Refers to a very pale yellow-brown color. "Torinoko" means or "chick," and it represents the color of eggshells. This color name is associated with the elegant and subtle colors favored in the Heian period.

Senchairo
Green Tea

A dark brown color resembling the color of strong green tea when it is brewed. While tea leaves are green, the hot water poured over them doesn't turn green as cha does, but in-stead takes on a yellowish-brown shade. This color is sometimes referred to as "Senjicha-zome" because it is dyed by the brew of sen-cha (steeped green tea).

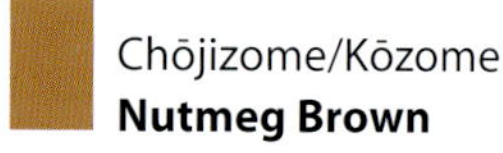

Chōjizome/Kōzome
Nutmeg Brown

Refers to a yellow-brown color produced by dyeing with cloves. Similar colors were often achieved using other materials like myrobalan plum. According to *Shoshoku Teshibana* (published in 1772), there were two methods: one using cloves and the other using substitute dyes. Cloves, a fragrant spice, were used to dye materials a beige-like shade. When dyed without a mordant, it results in a light beige, while with a mordant, it achieves a deep yellow-brown.

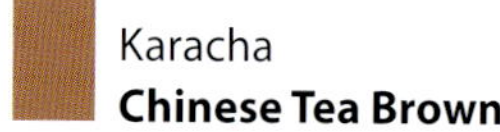

Karacha
Chinese Tea Brown

Used to describe a light brown color with a slight grayish-red tint. It is believed to refer to the color of Chinese tea which became popular from the Momoyama period to the Edo period. During the Edo period, the custom of tea drinking spread to the common people. As a result, the color of tea was commonly used in dyeing clothing and textiles.

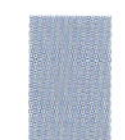

Asakihanada/Asahanada
Light Blue

This color name is used to describe the palest shade of indigo dye. During the Heian period, it was one of the colors for the day wear for lower-ranking officials. In later periods, it was sometimes referred to as "Usuhana," but generally, the brighter shades of indigo dye were called "Asagiiro."

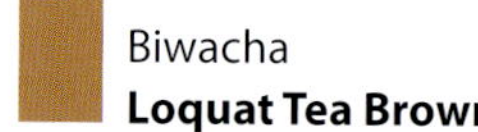

Biwacha
Loquat Tea Brown

Describes the muted yellow-brown color resembling ripe loquat fruit. In the *Tekagami Moyō Setsuyō* (a compendium of patterns and designs) is a note, "Biwacha, commonly referred to as Kawarakeiro." Kawarake is an earthenware that is fired without being glazed, resulting in this loquat fruit color. Both are light yellow-brown shades.

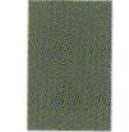

Oitakeiro
Old Bamboo Color

"Take" is a color of aged bamboo, mellow green with a tinge of gray. Unlike the vibrant shade of "Wakatakeiro" (fresh bamboo color), this is a subdued tone. As young bamboo, bright green with vitality, matures into a robust greenish-blue bamboo, its hue fades further as it becomes aged. The color name derives from this transition as the bamboo ages and loses its vibrancy. The stronger the grayish tinge, the more pronounced the impression of aging becomes.

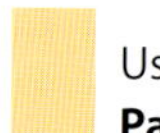

Usuki
Pale Yellow

This color name generally refers to a very light shade in indigo dyeing, representing a bright blue-green hue. During the mid-Heian period, there was confusion between this pale yellow color and the very light blue-green shade called "Asagi." This confusion is evident in texts like the *Imakagami*, where it mentions the difficulty in distinguishing between "Awakiiro" (pale yellow) and "Kinaruiro" (golden yellow). To differentiate, during the Edo period, the term "Usutamago" was used to distinguish the very pale yellow shade.

Detail from "Modern Beauty from Thirty-Six Flower Selections: Plum" by Utagawa Toyokuni.
National Diet Library Digital Collection.

203 Chōjizome/Kōzome   **235 Karacha**   **117 Asakihanada/Asahanada**

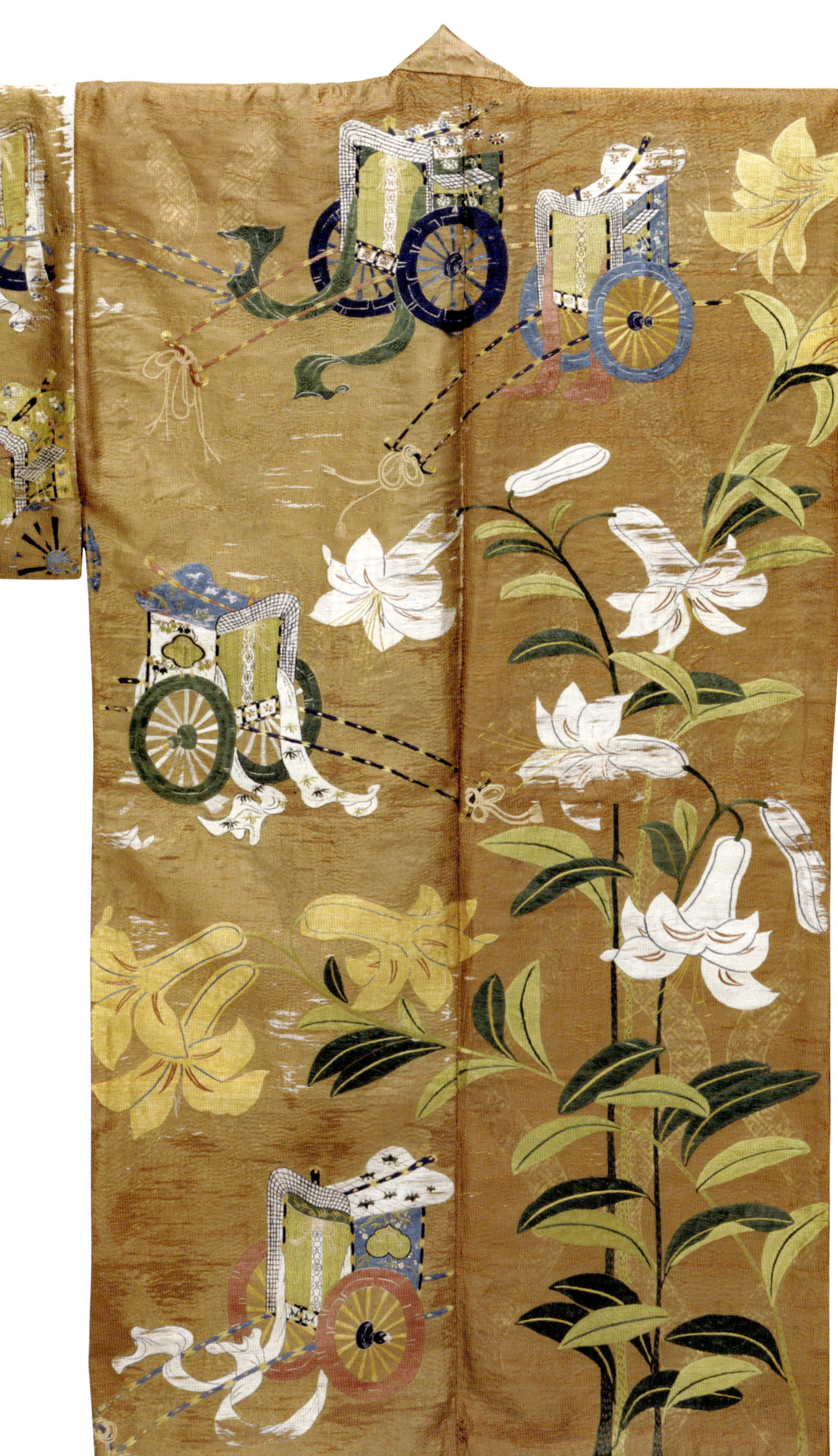

On a brown background, large white and yellow lilies are embroidered, along with a small Imperial carriage patterns. The lilies in the foreground are boldly arranged from the hem to the shoulder. In contrast, the smaller carriages are arranged less prominently, becoming a distant landscape, creating a sense of scale reversal that enhances this intriguing design. Though considerably faded, parts of the gold leaf patterns remain visible. In areas where there is no embroidery on the brown background, vertical wavy lines resembling rippling water are depicted in gold leaf. This pattern, called "Tachiyuku," often used in court attire designs along with the motif of imperial carriages, reflects an aspiration towards courtly culture and dynasty.

"Tea-colored Lily and Imperial Cart Pattern Embroidered Brocade". Azuchi-Momoyama period, 16th century.
Tokyo National Museum.
Source: ColBase at https://colbase.nich.go.jp

204 Biwacha 159 Oitakeiro 176 Usuki

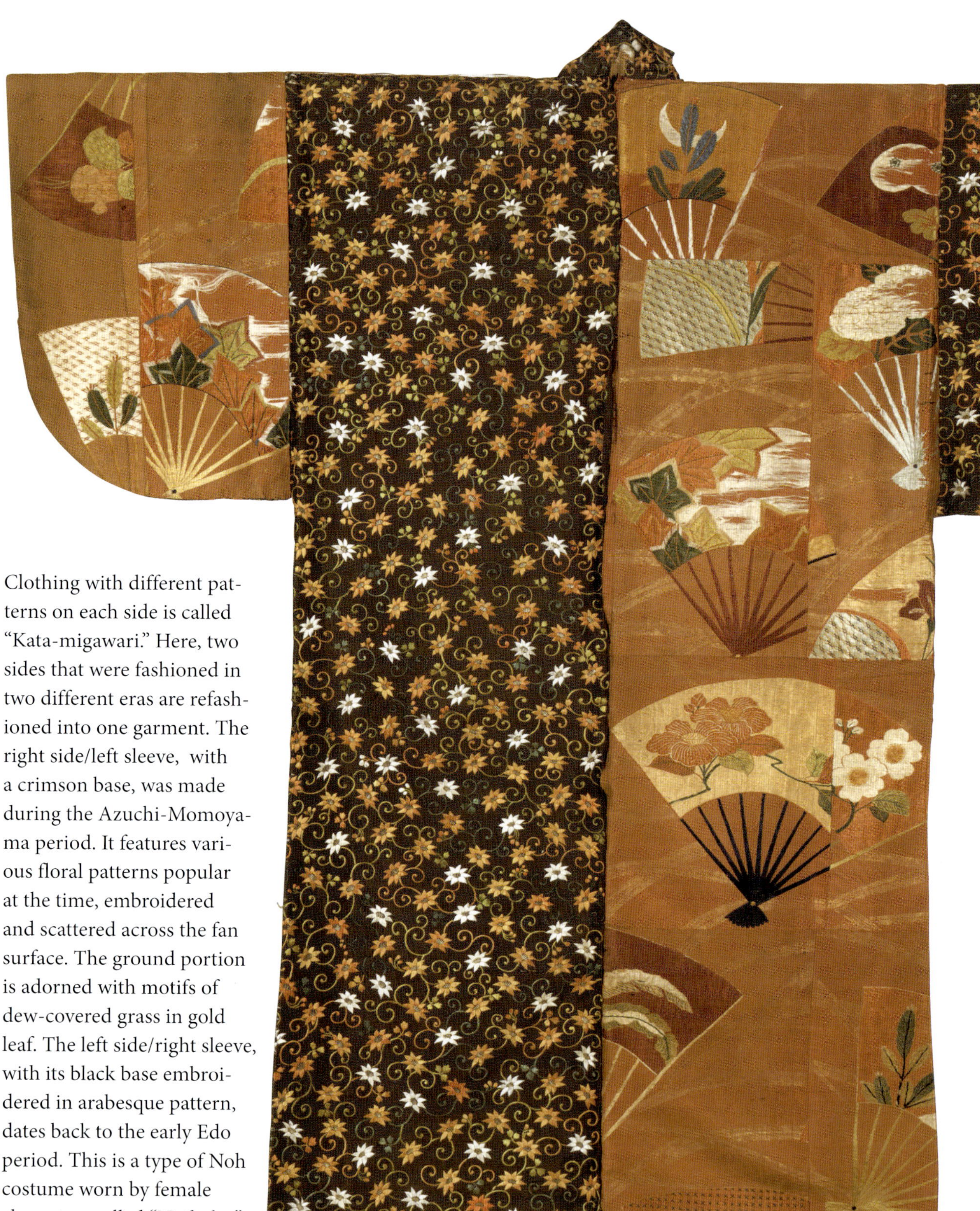

Clothing with different patterns on each side is called "Kata-migawari." Here, two sides that were fashioned in two different eras are refashioned into one garment. The right side/left sleeve, with a crimson base, was made during the Azuchi-Momoyama period. It features various floral patterns popular at the time, embroidered and scattered across the fan surface. The ground portion is adorned with motifs of dew-covered grass in gold leaf. The left side/right sleeve, with its black base embroidered in arabesque pattern, dates back to the early Edo period. This is a type of Noh costume worn by female characters called "Nuihaku."

"Black Tea Kosode with Scattered Fans and Grass Embroidered with Fine Wire Thread". Azuchi-Momoyama to Edo period, 17th century. Tokyo National Museum. Source: ColBase at https://colbase.nich.go.jp

247 Kuwa no miiro/ Kuwa-zome

205 Kohakuiro

196 Umezome

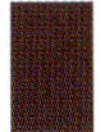

Kuwa no miiro/Kuwa-zome
Mulberry Fruit Color

This color name refers to the deep color of ripe mulberry fruit. In ancient times, "Kuwa-zome" was the name given to this dark reddish-purple color. The dyeing process involves first lightly dyeing with yangmei bark and then overdyeing with a concentrated mulberry tree extract.

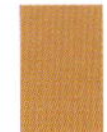

Kohakuiro
Amber Color

A color resembling the translucent yellowish-orange of amber. Amber is fossilized resin from geological eras, often found with insects and other inclusions. It has been cherished under names like "Kohaku" or "Akadama" (red ball) since ancient times and used in jewelry and ornaments. Today, it is often used to describe the color of clear, beautiful liquids, such as cognac and whiskey, by writers like Ryunosuke Akutagawa, Natsume Soseki, and Tatsuo Hori, who referred to whiskey as "liquid amber."

Umezome
Plum Dyed

A lightly dyed reddish pale brown color achieved by using *ume-ya shibu*, the liquid extracted from boiling plum wood with hazelnut bark extract added to it. During the Edo period, there were specialized plum juice artisans called "umeshibu-umeya nakama" in Osaka. The term "umezome" refers to colors lightly dyed two or three times with a reddish-brown hue. Colors that have been repeatedly dyed to become darker are called "akabume" (red plum), and those that have darkened considerably due to repeated dyeing are called "kurobume" (black plum). The dyeing process was straightforward and became popular in many households.

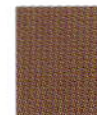

Hiwadairo
Cypress Bark Color

A dark brownish color with a reddish tint, named after the color of tree bark, particularly cypress bark. This traditional color name appears in Heian literature and can be traced back nearly to ancient times. The color originally referred to as "Mokuraniro" or "Jubarairo" (both meaning "wood color" or "bark color") was later referred to as "Hiwadairo."

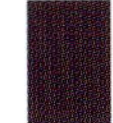

Nasu-kon
Eggplant Navy

A deep blue-purple color reminiscent of the color of eggplants. Achieved by overdyeing a dark indigo dye with *suō* (a red dye extracted from gardenia fruits). "Kon" (dark blue) is a slightly purplish dark blue, and "Nasu-kon" and "Shikon" are variations with added red tones. Eggplants are mentioned in documents like the *Shōsōin Monjo* from the 8th century in Japan, and the *Engishiki* from the 10th century describes their cultivation and use.

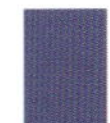

Benikakehanairo
Gentian

A bright and elegant purplish-blue color. This color is created by adding red dye (*beni*) over the base color (*kake*) of a flower color (*hanairo*). The color name reflects the dyeing technique itself. While similar to "Benikake-sorairo," it has a richer purple tone. Other colors with the "benikake" prefix include "Benikake-nando" (a reddish-blue color) and "Beni-kake-kūshoku."

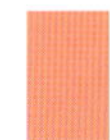

Jinzanmomi
Medium Yellowish Red

A substitute for *beni* (red) dye using *suō* (a red dye extracted from gardenia fruits), resulting in a moderately deep reddish-red color with a faint yellowish tint. According to *Honchō Seji Tan'ki* written by Kikuoka Sensui in 1734, there is a mention of "Kyoto's Choja-machi, a man named Kikyōya Jinzaburō, who dyes a color similar to akan [madder], called nakabeni," indicating that Jinzaburō created a dye resembling *akane* without using *beni*, and this color was called "Jinzanmomi."

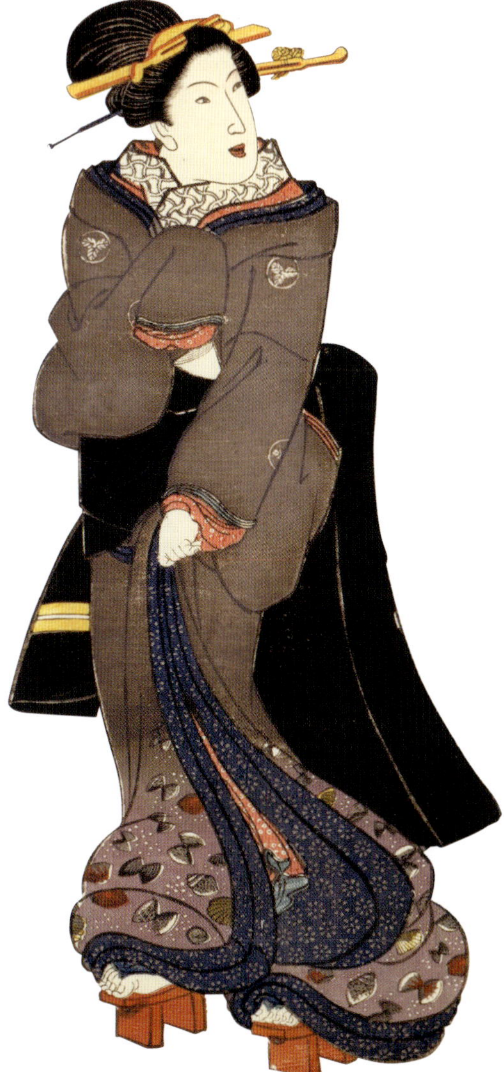

Detail from "Sakura Viewing Along Sumida Riverbank" by Keisai Eisen.
National Diet Library Digital Collection.

241 Hiwadairo	90 Nasu-kon	81 Benikakehanairo	38 Jinzanmomi

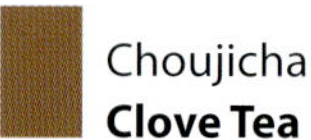

Choujicha
Clove Tea

A brownish color with a slight hint of black, derived from the process of dyeing with cloves since the Heian period. In *Moroiro Tezome Kusa* (1772), it is mentioned that there are two types: one dyed with the fragrance of cloves and another with a substitute dye. This name refers to the brown color obtained from clove dyeing, but substances such A willow or peach were often used to achieve the same shade. This brown shade was a popular color for garments like *kosode* (short-sleeved kimono) and *haori*, as seen in pattern books from the early Edo period.

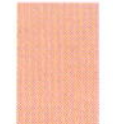

Tokihairo/Tokiiro
Toki Color

A light pink color, similar to the hue seen on the underside of a *toki* (Japanese crested Ibis) bird's wings, its feathers, and its tail. It's believed that dyeing fabrics in this color began during the Edo period. A similar color in ancient times was achieved using peach-derived dyes. Even today, this beautiful shade is an indispensable color for youthful kimono.

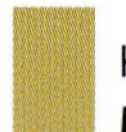

Karashiiro
Mustard

A slightly dull yellow, inspired by the color of the mustard spice made from ground mustard seeds. The mustard plant is a perennial plant of the Brassicaceae family. It blooms small yellow flowers in the spring, producing tiny seeds. The spicy condiment made from these ground seeds, known as Japanese mustard, is widely used in cooking. Western mustard is made from white or black mustard seeds.

Kigaracha
Yellow Sparrow Tea

This is a deep yellow orange shade, sometimes also called wood-dried tea. The dyeing method involves an under-dye using peach or willow, followed by applying plum to bring out a slight hint of red on the surface. It became popular during the early to middle Edo period and was favored both in the pleasure quarters and in the towns.

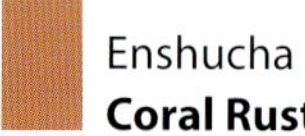

Enshucha
Coral Rust

A bright brown with a hint of red, named after the tea master of the early Edo period, Kobori Enshu, who also excelled as an architect and landscape designer. He favored this color. It is believed that this color was popularized in the years from 1624 to 1643, the period when Enshu was active.

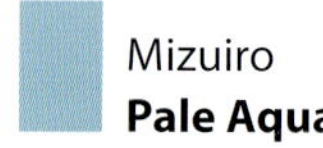

Mizuiro
Pale Aqua

A very light blue color with a hint of green, resembling clear water. In the time of the *Man'yōshū* collection, this color was called "Mizu-midori" (water green). During the Heian period, both names were used. As the medieval period approached, "Mizuiro" became more dominant, and is the name used today.

Carrying a paper lantern, in the rainy night she heads towards the shrine pilgrimage; it is Osen, the daughter of the water tea house at Kasamori Inari. The motif of a shrine pilgrimage in the midst of wind and rain is likened to the Noh play *Ariawase*, where the poet Ki no Tsurayuki, persistently passing in front of the shrine of the deity Myojin on horseback, provokes the deity's wrath, yet is forgiven due to the virtue of waka poetry. "Mitate" refers to the enjoyment of interpreting contemporary customs in the context of classical literature.

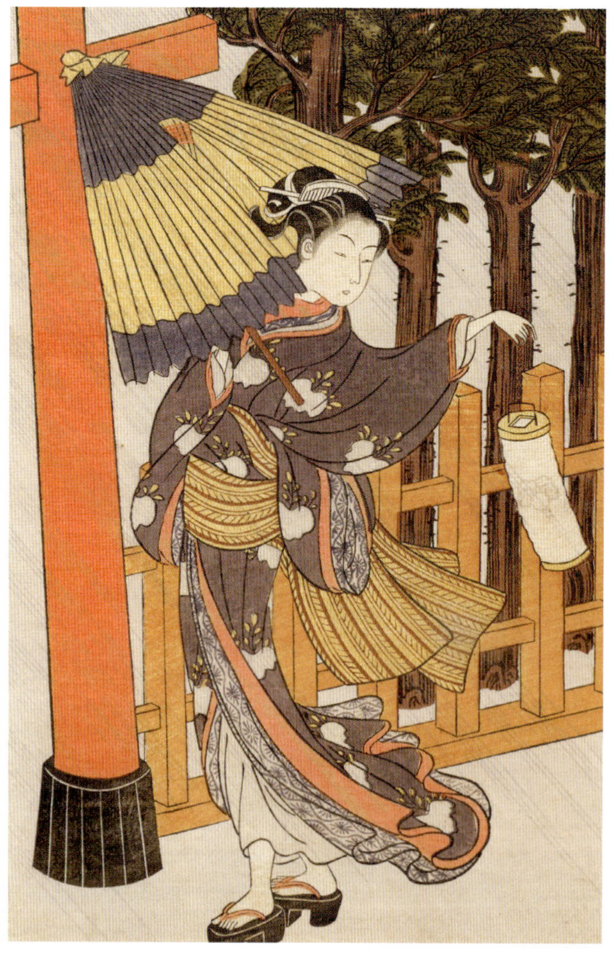

"Beauty Visiting a Shrine on a Rainy Night, Observing Ants Passing By" by Suzuki Harunobu. Edo Period, 18th century. Tokyo National Museum. Source: ColBase at https://colbase.nich.go.jp

225 Choujicha	5 Tokihairo/Tokiiro	187 Karashiiro

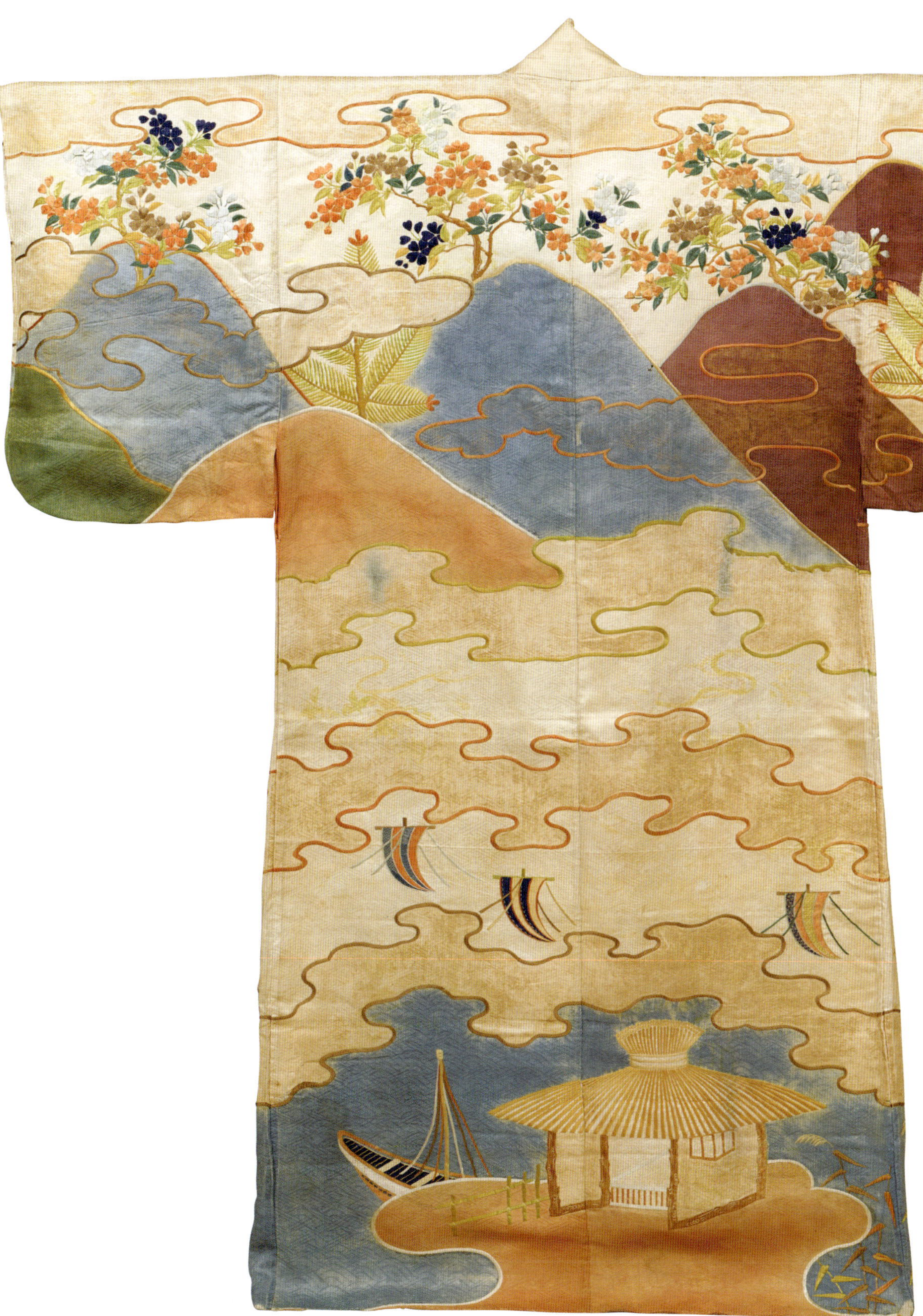

Near the hem, a boat-house is located on the shore with boats anchored nearby. Near the waistline, sails peek through the gaps of golden brocade clouds, catching the wind. Multiple mountain ranges are illustrated from the body to the sleeves, with the mountain slopes dyed in shades of red and purple. In the distant landscape, pine and cherry trees are depicted with embroidery.

"Kimono with Distant Mountains, Sailing Ship, and Pavilion Design on White Damask Fabric".
Edo period, 18th century.
Tokyo National Museum.
ColBase at https://colbase.nich.go.jp.

201 Kigaracha   239 Enshucha   97 Mizuiro

Kabuki Actor Color Names

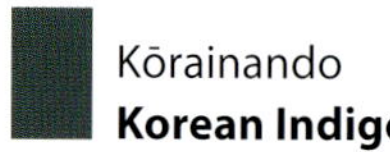

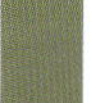

Kōrainando
Korean Indigo

During the Kansei era (1789–1801), a dark indigo color derived from the fourth-generation Matsumoto Koshiro (Takarazuka-ya), a prominent figure in the Kabuki world. The fifth-generation of Takarazuka-ya was known as Hanadaka Koshiro, named for his exceptionally high nose and a strong, intimidating style of performance with his mouth forming a straight line, which was highly acclaimed even among the people of Edo.

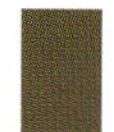

Rokōcha
Roadside Tea

In the year of Hōreki 6 (1756), the second generation Segawa Kikunojō, also known as Ōji Rokō, was highly praised as one of the most beautiful actors of the time. The color of Rokōcha can be described as a slightly reddish-brown shade added to yellow tea.

Baikoucha/Kusayanagi
Grass Tea

Originally called "Hajime Kusayanagi," this color was favored by the founder of Kabuki, Ichikawa Danjuro, thus it was named after his stage name, "Baiko." The hue is a light, pale yellow-green with a hint of astringency, reflecting the flamboyance of his acting style.

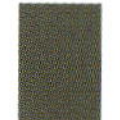

Iwaicha
Hemp Leaf Green

This color is said to have been favored by the fifth-generation Onoe Hanshirō, a renowned female impersonator, and it was named after him. It is a somewhat greenish-brown shade.

During the Edo period, there were prohibitions known as Sumptuary Laws placed restrictions on extravagant and flamboyant colors. Wealthy commoners used these laws to their advantage, favoring subdued colors such as tea, black, and gray. Kabuki actors played a significant role in promoting this trend. It was during the Bunka and Bunsei periods that various color names associated with popular costumes and actors gained popularity.

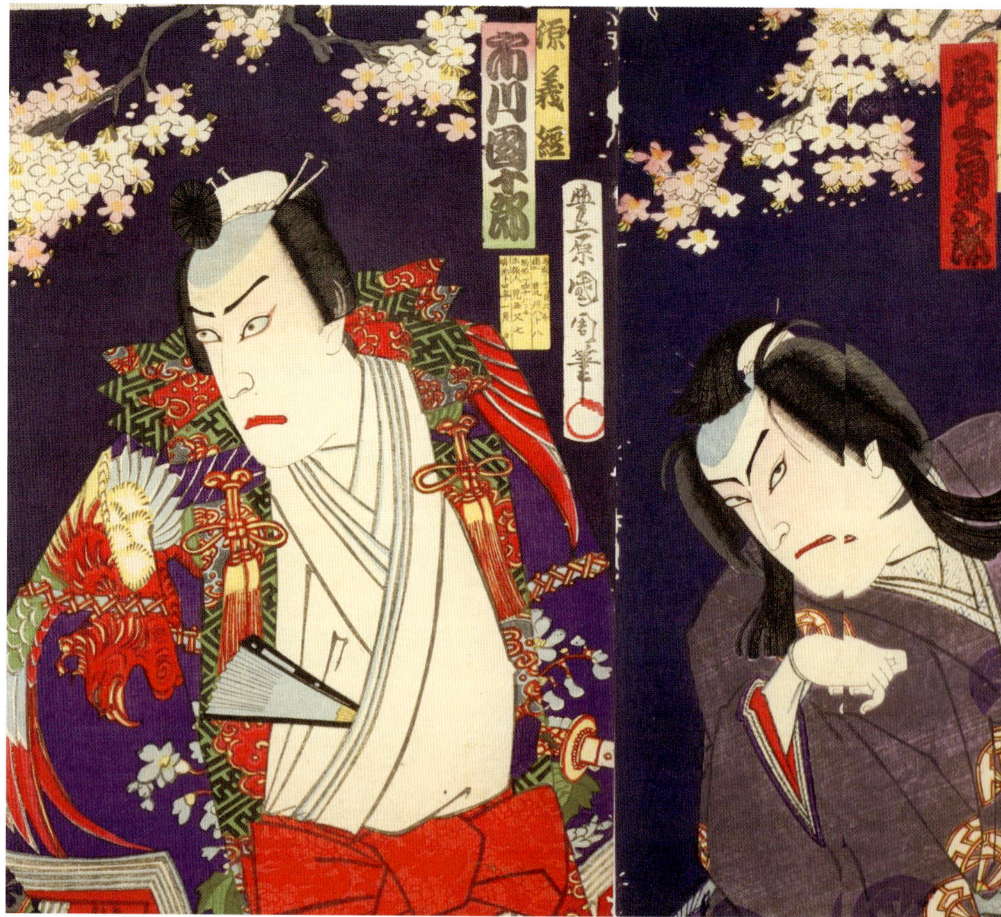

212 Rikancha   233 Danjūrōcha   238 Shikancha

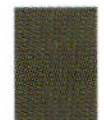

Rikancha
Green Brown

This color was named after the preferred shade of brown used by the popular Kabuki actor, the first generation Arashi Rikan (also known as the second generation Arashi Kisaburō), in Osaka during the Bunka and Bunsei periods (1804–1830). The color has a slightly greenish-dark brown hue.

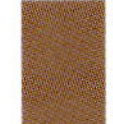

Danjūrōcha
Plum Brown Tea

The traditional curtain used in Kabuki theater is composed of three colors: *moegi* (green), *kaki* (persimmon), and black. The kaki color is almost equivalent to this Danjūrō tea. It is said to have originated from its use in the kimono for the role "Zanshi" handed down in the Ichikawa family.

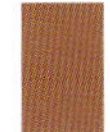

Shikancha
Reddish Brown

This color, a slightly muted reddish-brown shade, was favored by Shibikan (Nakamura Shibikan), and its popularity grew along with his. Nakamura Shibikan was a stage name used by various kabuki actors from the late Edo period onwards. The first Nakamura Shibikan was the third Nakamura Utaemon. This name was derived from his stage name, Shibikan. In a manuscript from the Bunsei era, titled *Morisada Mankou*, it is mentioned that during the Bunsei era, Shikancha, Ichikoucha, Rikancha were popular in Kyoto and Osaka, while Rokoucha and Baikoucha were popular in Edo. Trends driven by actor popularity extended to cosmetics and pharmaceuticals, with Shibikan fragrance being one example.

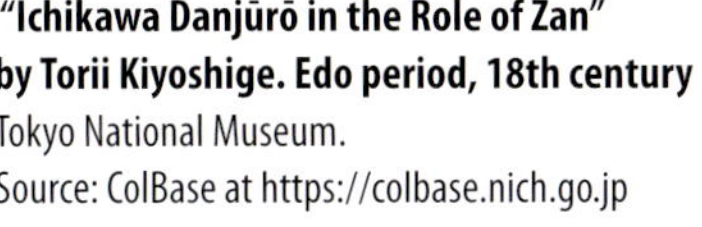

**"Ichikawa Danjūrō in the Role of Zan"
by Torii Kiyoshige. Edo period, 18th century**
Tokyo National Museum.
Source: ColBase at https://colbase.nich.go.jp

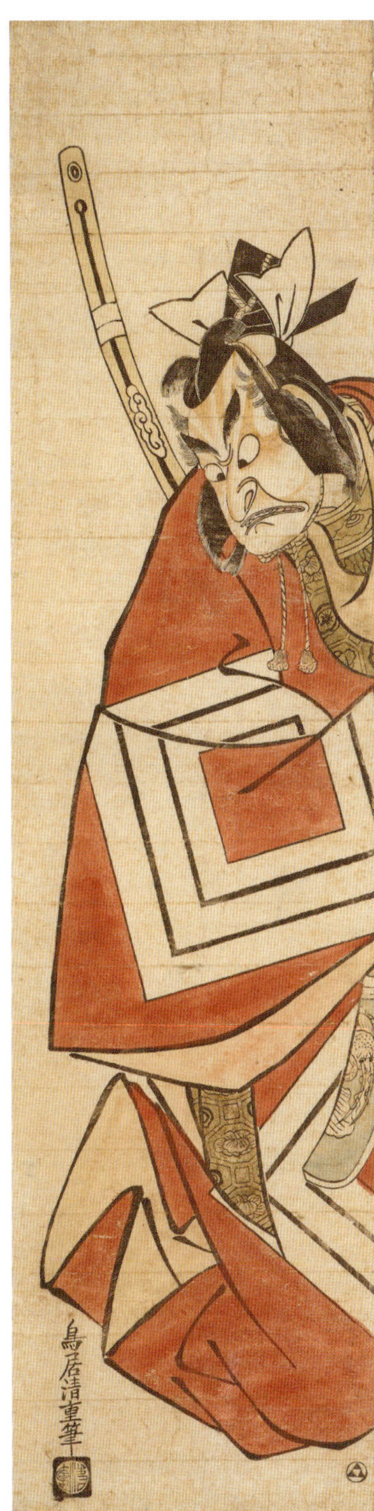

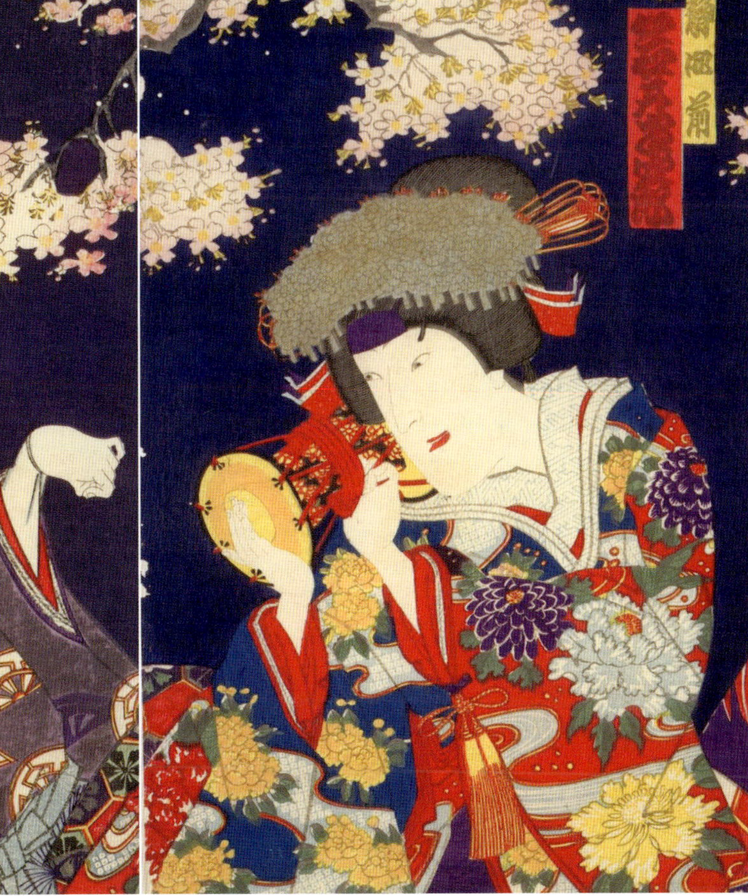

"Minamoto no Yoshitsune: Ichikawa Danjuro as Shizuka Gozen, Iwai Hanshiro as Kitsune Tadanobu, Onoe Kikugoro" by Toyohara Kunichika, 1881.
Tokyo National Museum.
Source: ColBase at https://colbase.nich.go.jp

125 Kōraionando   136 Rokōcha   138 Baikōcha/Kusayanagi   209 Iwaicha

Black and White in Japanese Culture

From the shining purity of pure white to the deep darkness of jet black, black and white are considered neutral colors. However, in reality, pure white and pure black do not exist. Even in a colorless world, there is always some hue present, exhibiting an extremely rich and complex chromaticity. These colors, which only possess a sense of light and dark, are thought to encompass all colors and can be seen as the origin of color and the starting point from which colors emerge.

Right Hanakasa (Flower Umbrella) Procession, Gion Festival, Kyoto.
Top far right New Year's Atmosphere, Yoshida Residence, Kyoto.
Bottom far right Hojo North Garden, Tōfuku-ji Temple, Kyoto.

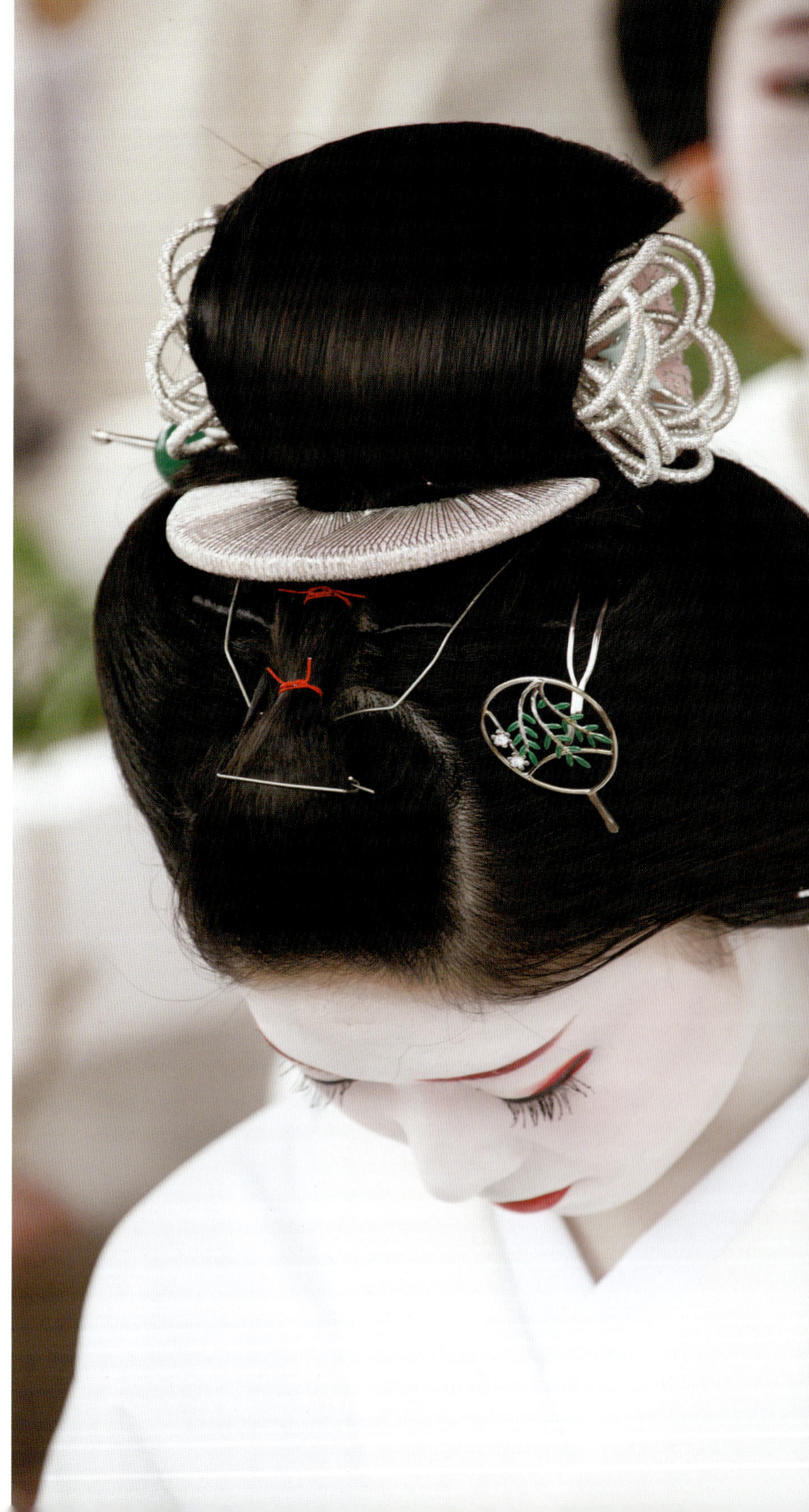

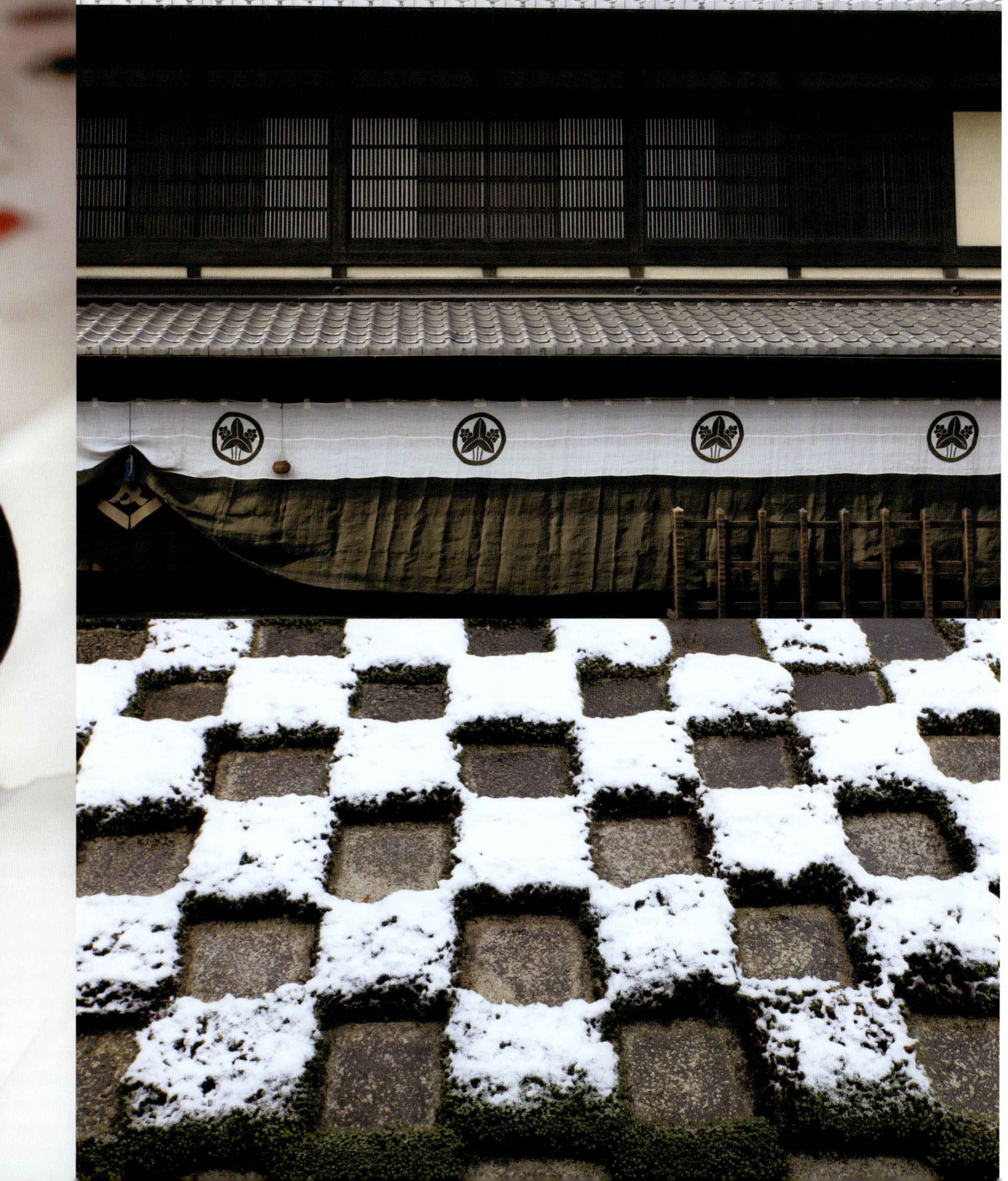

Japanese Color Schemes Based on Black and White

People have traditionally regarded black as a color opposite to red or white, often associating it with fear. The concept that all colors are contained within black comes from ancient Chinese philosophy, particularly the Five Elements, as expressed in the saying "In ink, there are five colors." This implies that black encompasses all colors within it. This concept isn't merely descriptive, but is an attempt to discern the numerous shades that stir within the depths of the spirit through the medium of ink.

In traditional color terminology, there exists a beautiful glossy black created by mixing ink with lacquer. In dyeing, there are garments dyed in sumi-zome, a black color reminiscent of charcoal, and mouse-colored mourning attire. The tradition of smoking earthenware with soot continues as a tradition of polishing black pottery.

White stands in contrast to black. White has long been considered the most sacred color in Japan, exclusively used for religious ceremonies. Due to its ability to be dyed any color, white also symbolizes purity and cleanliness, representing offerings to the gods.

In terms of achromatic color schemes, they contain all colors equally, thus harmonizing with any other color without causing discord, adapting their hues to complement those of the partner color.

When using a two-color scheme, it becomes evident that harmony is easily achieved by placing black or white between each color when the boundary between them becomes unclear. This technique is widely employed to mitigate clashes between strong colors. Pairings with a stark contrast between light and dark, such as black and white, exhibit a strong effect, evident in mediums like ink wash painting, prints, photography, and fashion.

Color Scheme Based on Pale Colors

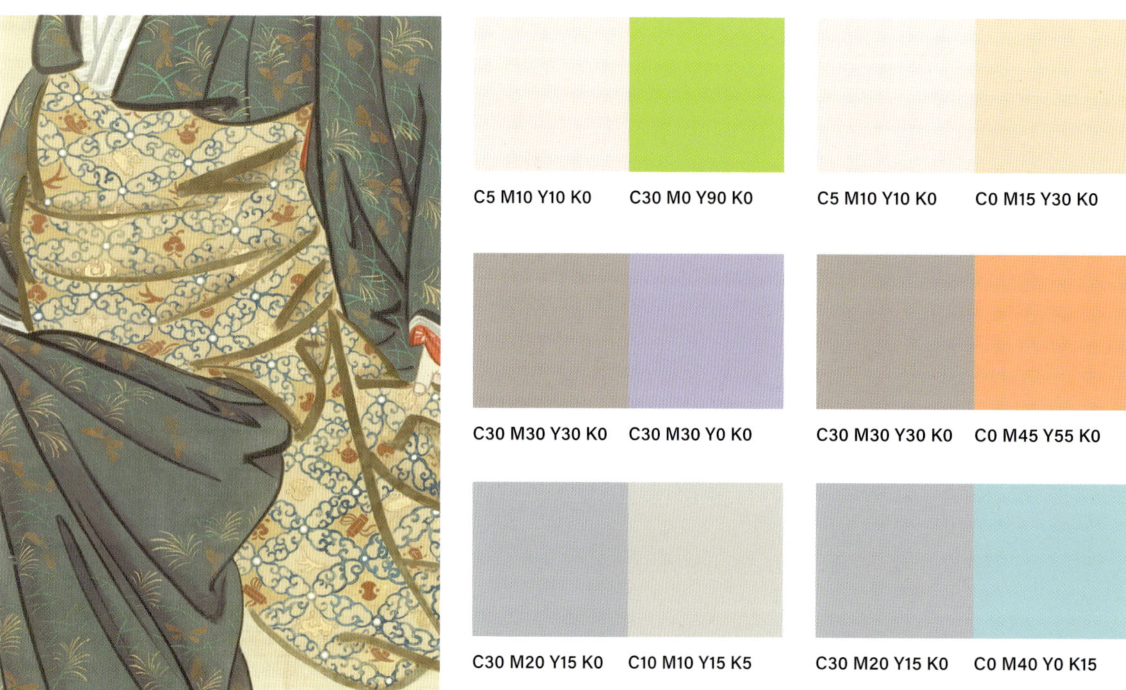

C5 M10 Y10 K0	C30 M0 Y90 K0	C5 M10 Y10 K0	C0 M15 Y30 K0
C30 M30 Y30 K0	C30 M30 Y0 K0	C30 M30 Y30 K0	C0 M45 Y55 K0
C30 M20 Y15 K0	C10 M10 Y15 K5	C30 M20 Y15 K0	C0 M40 Y0 K15

Detail from "Portrait of a Standing Beauty" by Yamaguchi Soken. Edo period, 19th century.
Tsuruga City Museum.

Color Scheme Based on Vibrant Colors

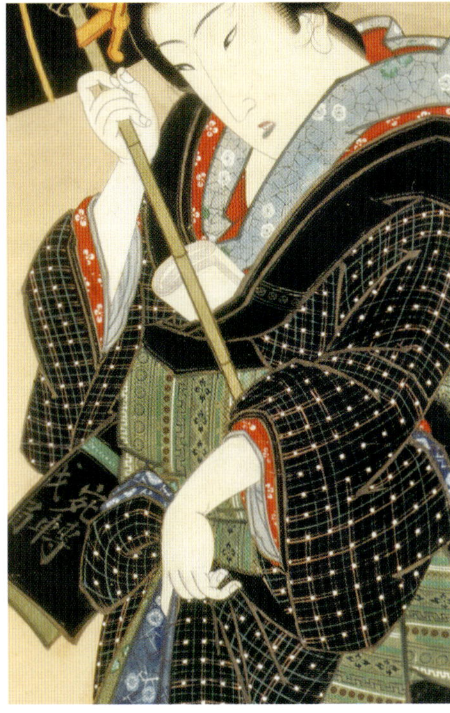

**Detail from "Portrait of a Beautiful Woman with
Snake-Eye Umbrella" by Kaseiro Jakugo.
Late Edo period, 19th century.**
Kumamoto Prefectural Museum of Art.

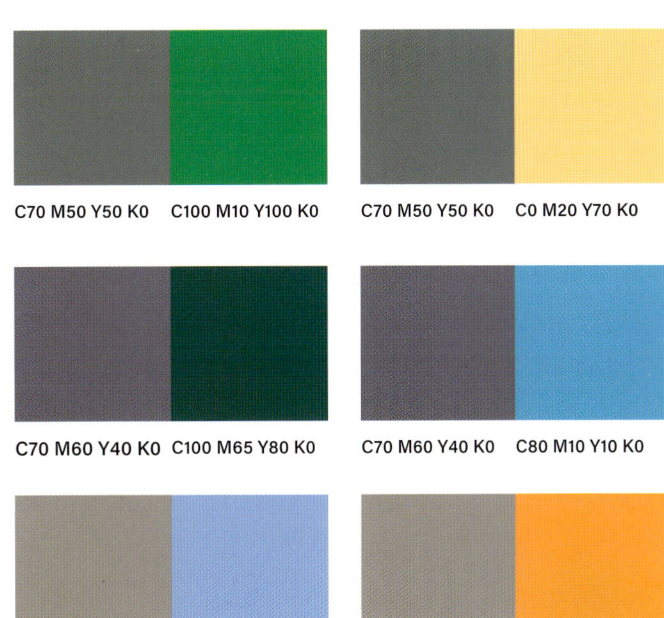

Color Scheme Based on Deep Colors

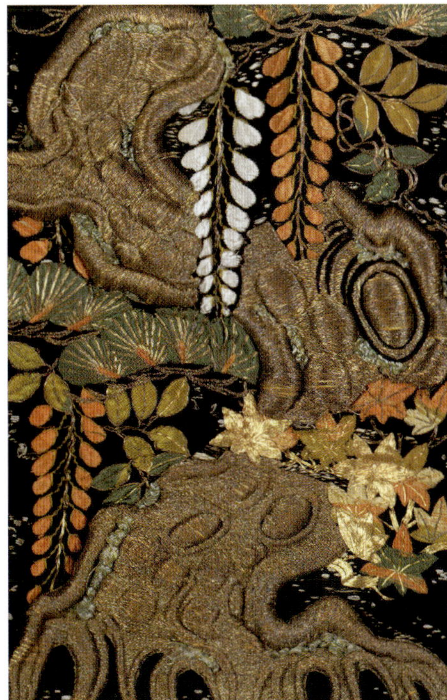

**Detail from "Black Silk Crepe Kimono with Pine, Wisteria,
and Maple Leaf Patterns". Edo period, 19th century.**
Tokyo National Museum.
Source: ColBase at https://colbase.nich.go.jp

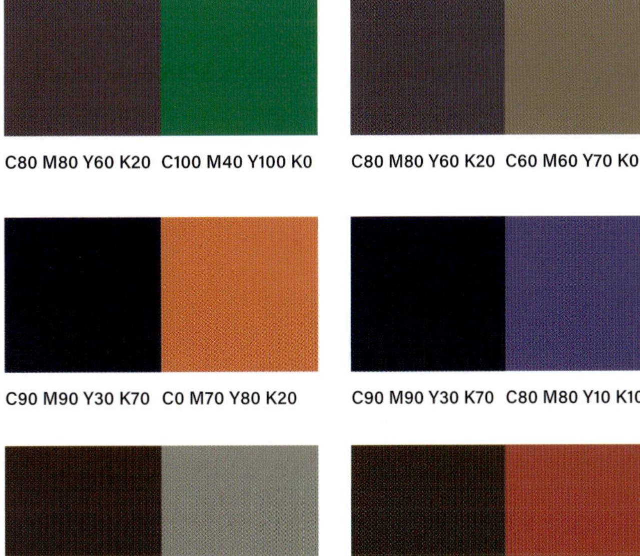

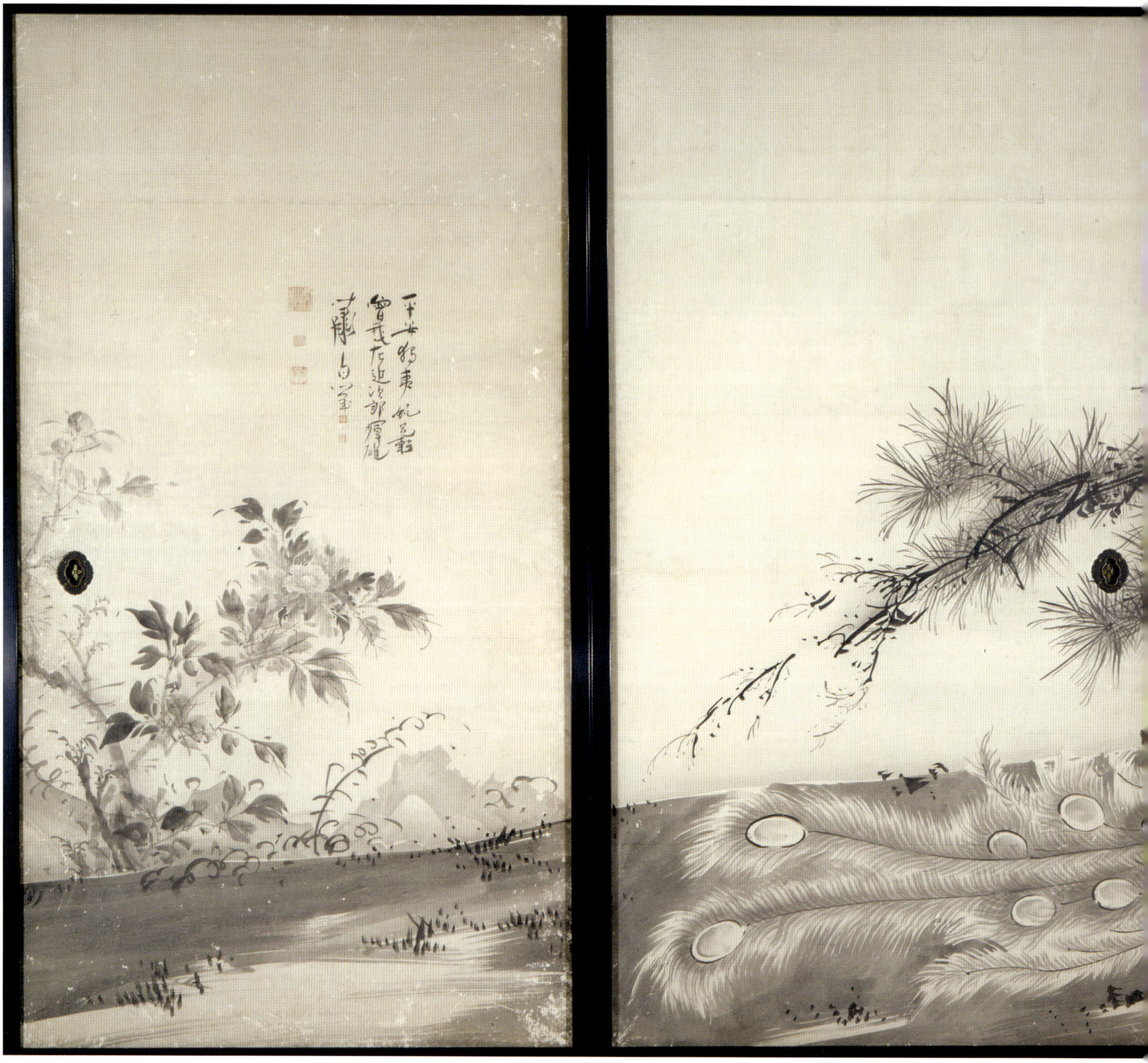

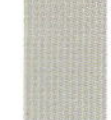

"Peacocks and Pine Trees" by Soga Shohaku, c. 1767.
Mie Prefectural Art Museum.

This is a masterpiece by Shohaku Soga, painted on all four panels of a sliding door (*fusuma*) using masterful gradations in ink. The aged pine trees, with their twisting branches reaching out, are captured with energetic brushwork, and life seems to flow to the tips of the branches. The sloping ground, depicted with flowing ink, is expressed with a subtle shade of ink that makes a pair of peacocks almost disappear into it. Shohaku's unique skill is truly unmatched.

Sumiiro/Sumizome
Ink Black/Ink Dye

Sumiiro is a color that resembles ink and is considered the closest shade to black. The ink used in calligraphy and painting is made by burning high-quality soot from pine roots or rapeseed oil, mixing it with glue, and solidifying it by adding fragrances. In ancient China, ink made from pine soot, known as Tang ink, had a bluish-black hue, while in Japan, ink made from rapeseed oil soot mixed with safflower resulted in a reddish-black shade.

Giniro/Shironezumi
Silver/Silver Gray

Giniro refers to a white color with a silvery, shimmering grayish tone. Silver undergoes a chemical reaction to turn black when it reacts with sulfur. This reaction is used artificially to create smoked silver, which develops a deep gray color. Silver has been held second only to gold in value. Gold has been likened to the sun, silver to the moon.

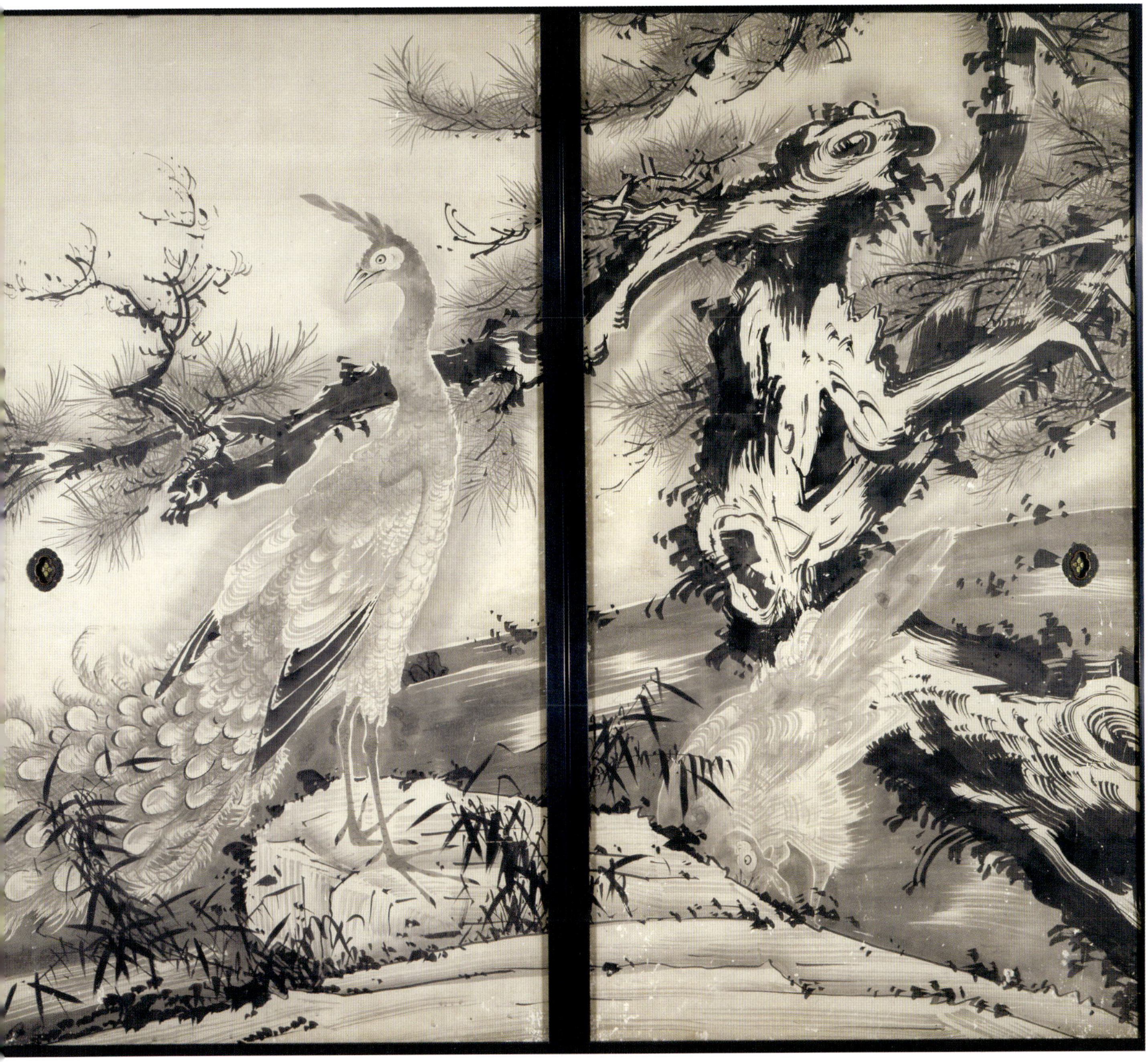

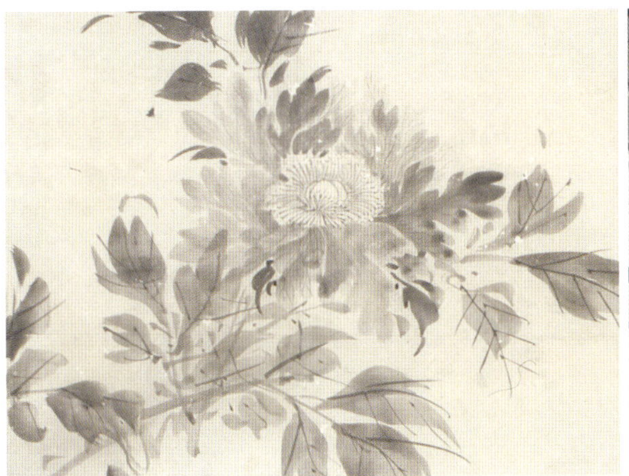
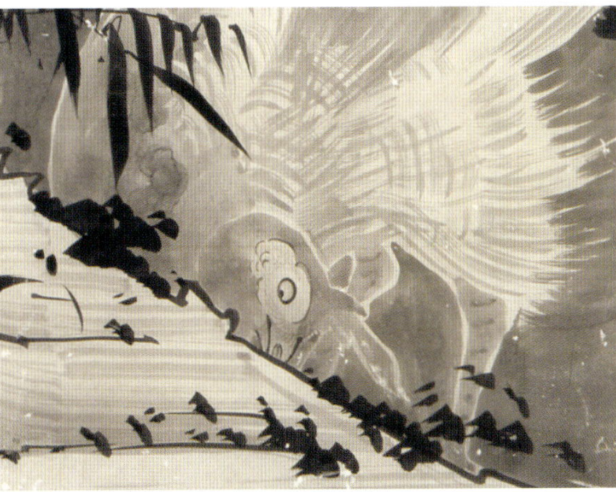

279 Sumiiro/Sumizome   **282 Giniro/Shironezumi**

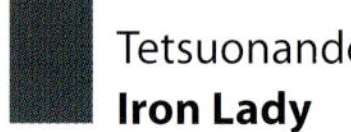

Kurotsurubami
Black Oak

This color is achieved through iron mordant dyeing with oak gall resulting in a dark gray color close to black. Oak gall, also known as *konara* or *ichiigashi*, is said to be the ancient name for the fruit of the *Quercus serrata* tree. To create Kurotsurubami, the dye is made by extracting the tannin from the crushed acorns of this tree and then mordanting it with an iron-rich solution, resulting in a deep navy-black color. Without mordanting, it would become a yellowish brown called "Kikizumi." Black, in this context, does not refer to the color of objects but is an abstract term signifying darkness. Similarly, the Edo period's trend for "toki" (mouse) color, which originated from oak gall, is considered a dark gray color close to black.

Tetsuonando
Iron Lady

Tetsuonando refers to a shade of dark greenish blue with a hint of iron gray. The dyeing process is described in the book *Some Monosahinam* (1853) as "Dye with a mixture of indigo, ash, water in equal parts, and add iron to give color, then add vinegar." It appears to have been a commonly-used color, although there is no evidence of it being a fashionable choice. In the Edo period, characterized by a preference for subdued colors, this practical color name was used in everyday life. There is also a variant called "Sabitsuchi Gonna," which is a slightly muted shade.

Akabeni
Crimson

This is a vibrant red color that was commonly found in early Edo period pattern books and dyeing literature, attesting to its popularity during that time, alongside colors like "Hishinzome" (scarlet) and "Benishikishirone" (crimson mottled with white). The book *Onna Kagami Hiden Sho* (1650) discusses the preferences of Kyoto women for their kimono, revealing that red and crimson shades were popular among the upper-class women.

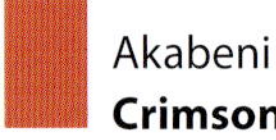

Hatobanezumi
Pigeon Feather Gray

This is a shade of grayish purple with a hint of reddish-gray, reminiscent of the color found on the back feathers of pigeons. Pigeon feathers were said to gleam with iridescent colors, and in medieval times, the color of the emperor's attire, known as "Kojiro Iro," was also referred to as "Hatobaneiro." Similar to Hatobanezumi, this color emerged in the late Edo period amid a nostalgic trend and became popular as a base color for traditional Japanese clothing, along with "Fujiiro" (wisteria purple).

Rikyū ucha
Rikyū Tea

Rikyū ucha is used to describe a greenish, pale brown color that resembles faded powdered tea (*matcha*). While Rikyū is the name of Sen no Rikyū , a renowned tea master during the Muromachi and Momoyama periods, this color name likely originated from associations with powdered tea. It seems that dyers or kimono makers borrowed the name Rikyū to label this trendy color. Other color names associated with Rikyū include "Rikyū shirocha" (Rikyū white tea), "Rikyū Nezumi" (Rikyū gray), and "Rikyū Namakabe" (Rikyū raw plaster), among others.

A woman with small, upturned eyes and full lips slightly arched upwards, walks while gracefully holding a snake-eyed umbrella, her body slightly bent. Her figure exudes allure. The coordination between her kimono and black umbrella is exquisite, while the color of the boldly tied obi adds a chic touch to the ensemble.

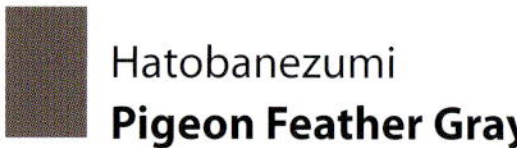

"Portrait of a Beautiful Woman with Snake-Eye Umbrella" by Kaseiro Jakugo.Late Edo period, 19th century.
Kumamoto Prefectural Museum of Art.

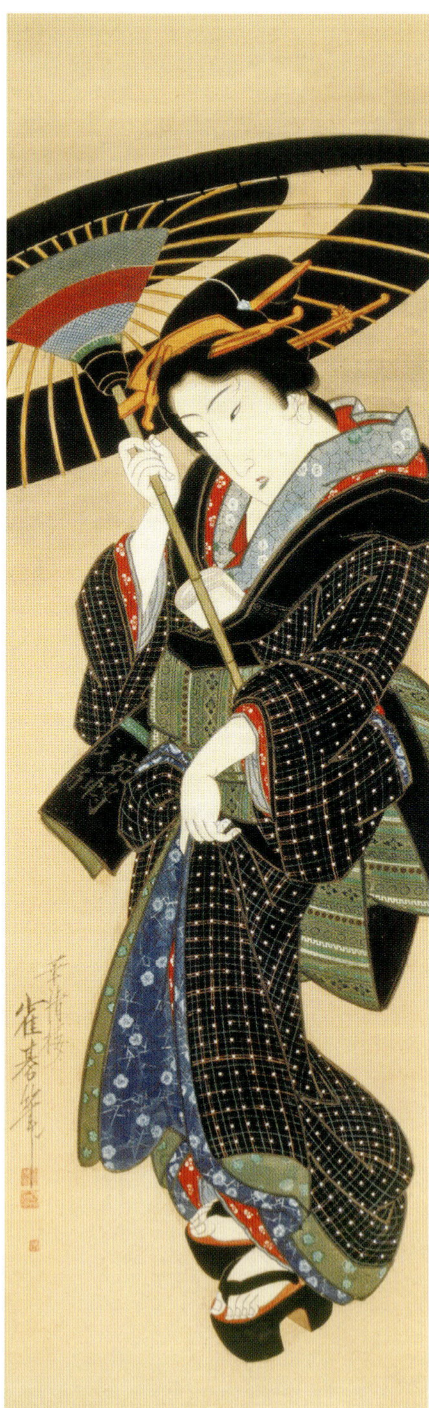

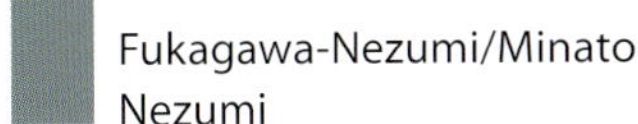

Fukagawa-Nezumi/Minato-Nezumi

Deep River Gray/Harbor Gray

These color names refer to light shades of pale blue with a slight hint of gray. Fukagawa was a prosperous district near the Tomioka Hachimangu Shrine, and the geisha from this area were known as "Tatsumi Geisha," known for their pride and noble bearing. In the late Edo period, a trend emerged among the geisha of Fukagawa for sophisticated and stylish colors, contrasting with the flashy and extravagant colors of the time. Other color names with a greenish gray hue include "Kamogawa-Nezumi," "Yodo-Nezumi,"" Minato-Nezumi," and "Senkou-Nezumi," among others.

In a large-scale brush painting, on the right side, a woman wears an ornate kimono adorned with hollyhock flowers. With her are local housewives, while on the left side, there are palace maids and more housewives, along with daughters. This is considered one of the benchmark works of Hokusai in his late thirties, along with the "Courtesan" (owned by the Freer Gallery of Art), sharing similarities in coloring and painting techniques. It is speculated to be a work from around the fourth to fifth years of Kansei (1792–1793), while Hokusai was in his early-mid-thirties. Among Hokusai's hand-painted portraits of beautiful women, it is one of his earliest and most precious works.

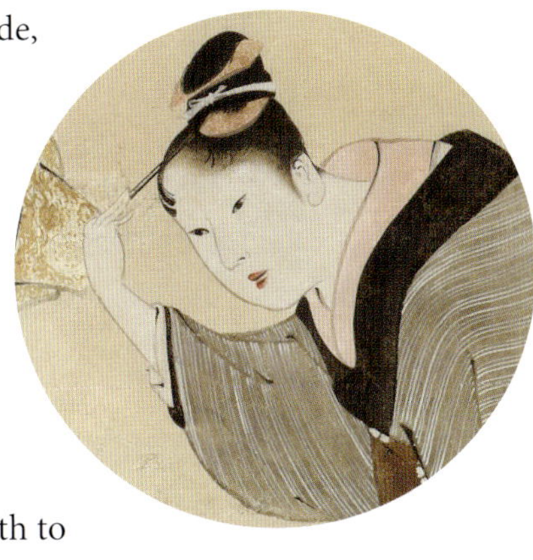

Detail from "Customs of Women" by Katsushika Hokusai.

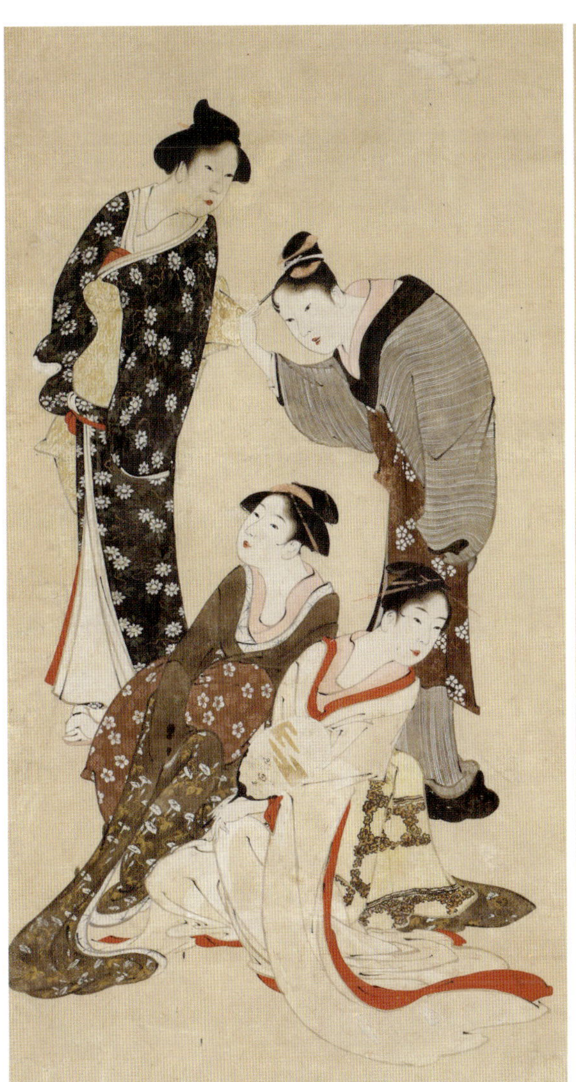

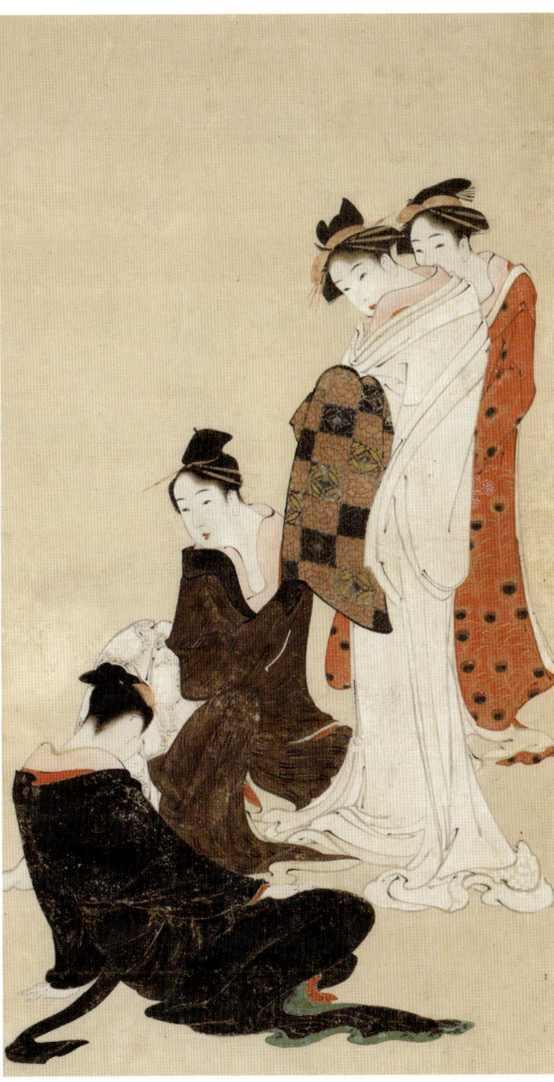

"Customs of Women" by Katsushika Hokusai, c. 1792–1794. Shimane Prefectural Museum of Art (Nagata Collection).

264 Hatobanezumi   **221 Rikyū ucha**   **257 Fukagawa-Nezumi/Minato-Nezumi**

The surface of the box is coated entirely with black lacquer, adorned with a gold *hiramaki-e* design featuring a pear motif on a *nashiji* ground, depicting patterns of cypress fence and chrysanthemum branches. While the depiction of the chrysanthemum branches is relatively orthodox, the technique of hiramaki-e represents one of the styles of *makie* (Japanese lacquer decoration) that characterizes the Momoyama period, specifically showcasing the characteristics of the Takadaiji makie style. A sunk-in box refers to a small box where noble individuals store fragrant woods such as agarwood.

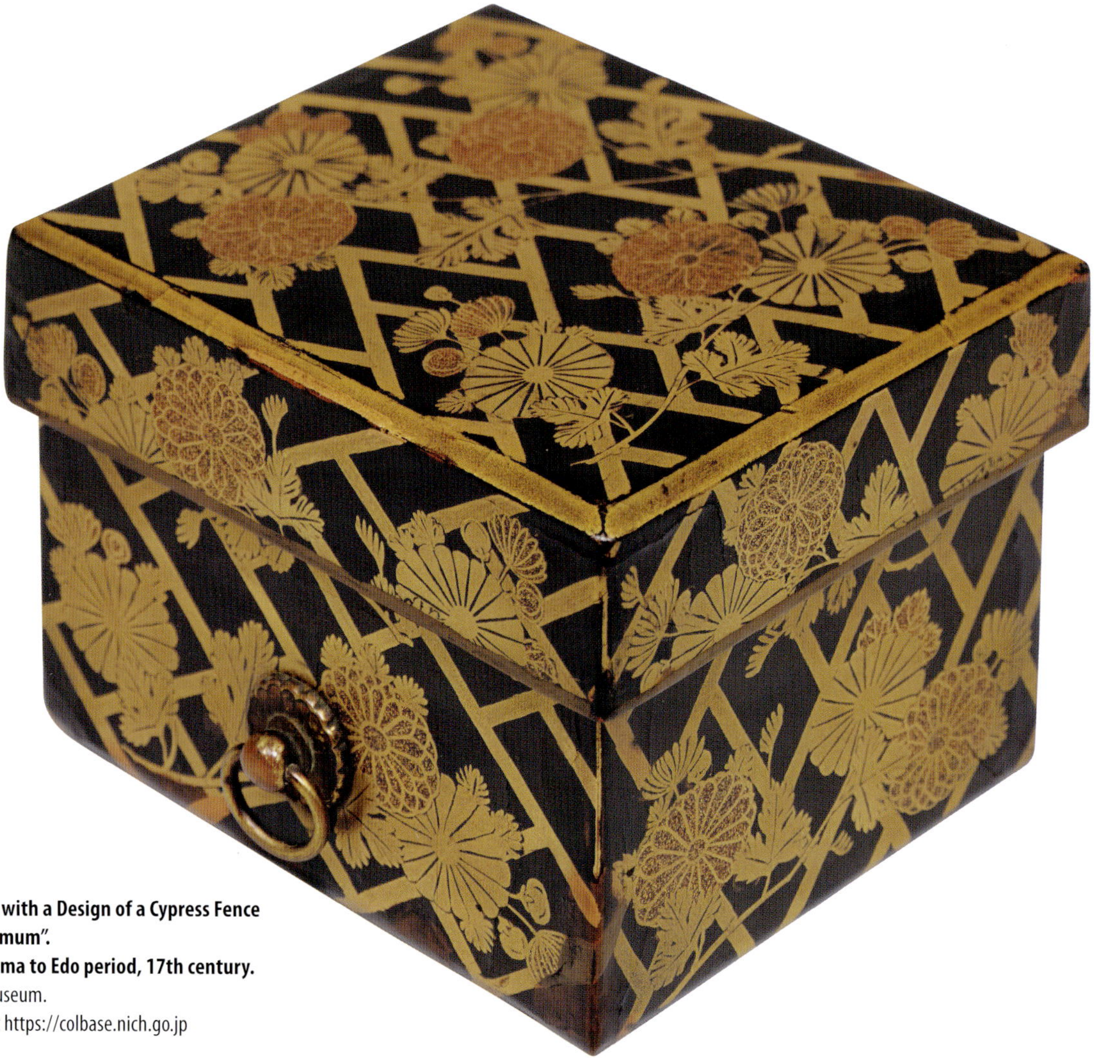

"Lacquered Box with a Design of a Cypress Fence and Chrysanthemum".
Azuchi-Momoyama to Edo period, 17th century.
Tokyo National Museum.
Source: ColBase at https://colbase.nich.go.jp

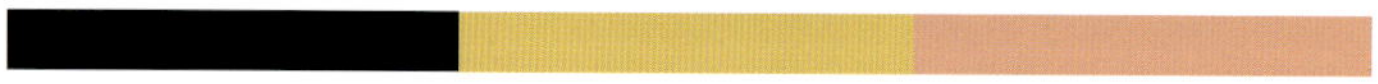

| 277 Roiro | 181 Kiniro | 240 Tokigaracha |

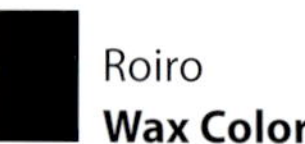

Roiro
Wax Color

Roiro refers to a deep, beautiful black color resembling wet lacquer. It is derived from the technique of *roiro-nuri,* one of the coating methods in lacquer craftsmanship. Among them, *honkataji roiro-nuri* requires an extensive process and high-level skills; specialized Roiro artisans are needed to polish the surface smoothly.

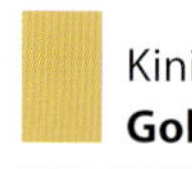

Kiniro
Gold

Kiniro represents a beautiful yellow color with a glossy shine resembling gold. The unique luster of gold is highly attractive, and pure gold is considered a symbol of eternity as it does not tarnish. This supernatural color has been used in both Japan and the Western world to express the dignity of deities and gods.

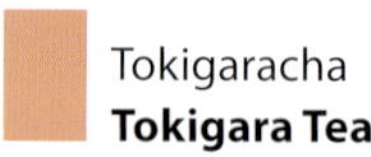

Tokigaracha
Tokigara Tea

Tokigaracha refers to a muted pale yellowish-red color, the name deriving from "toki" (a crested Ibis) and "karacha," believed to be a corrupted form of "karacha," meaning Tang tea. It is used to describe a pinkish beige color. During the Edo period, various shades of tea were created, and this color also emerged as one of the color tones of that time.

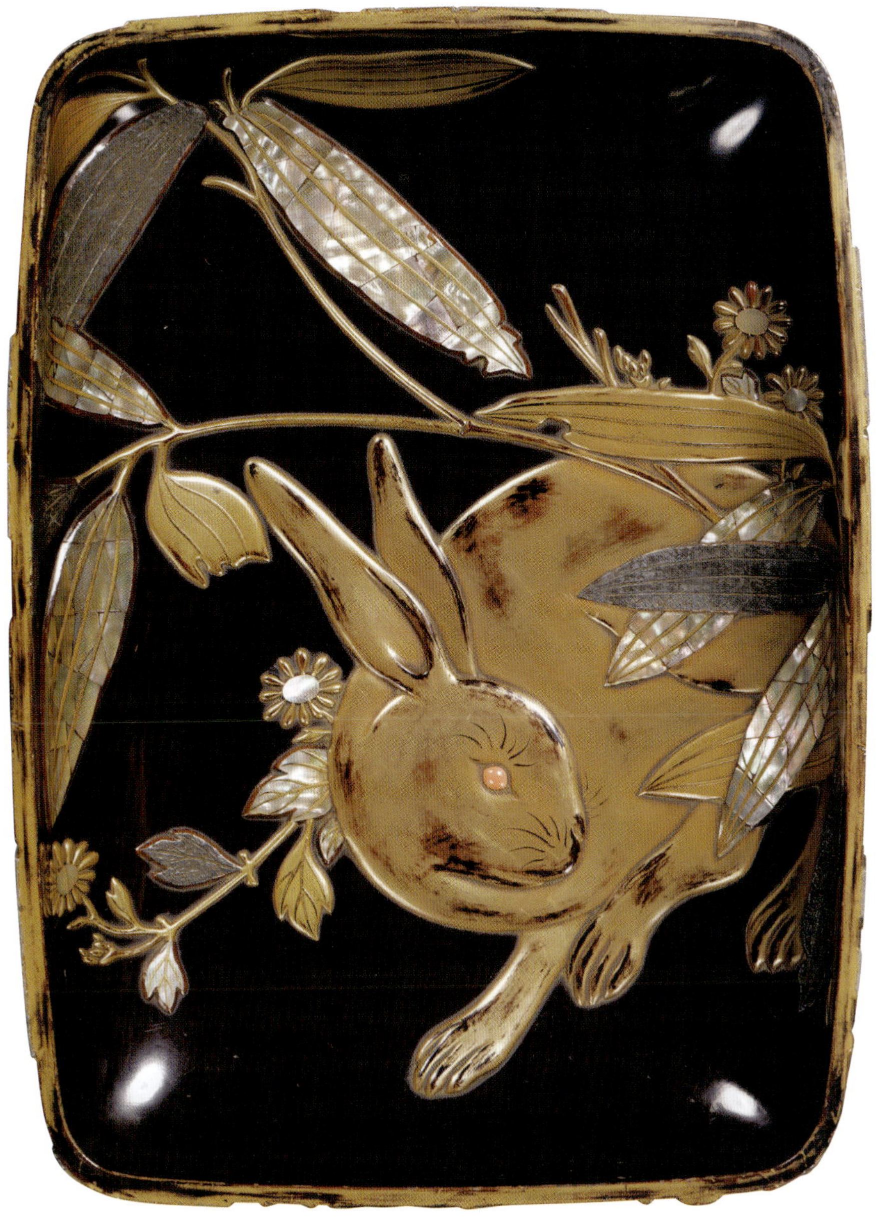

The entire surface of this inkstone box is coated with black lacquer. On the lid's surface and along the sides, there is gold *takamaki-e* (high-relief gold lacquer) depicting leaves and beans using *raden* (mother-of-pearl inlay). On the underside of the lid, bamboo curves are adorned with chrysanthemum flowers, and a large rabbit is depicted. The bold use of decorative materials and the composition of the design show the influence of Ogata Korin, whom Nagata Yuji admired. Nagata Yuji was a *maki-e* artist active in Kyoto during the mid-Edo period, around the years of Shotoku to Kyoho (1711–1736). He created maki-e works following the style of Ogata Korin and devised the technique of raising takamaki-e using tin powder.

"Lacquered Writing Box with a Design of Rabbits in Mother-of-Pearl Inlay". Attributed to Nagata Yuji. Edo period, 19th century.
Tokyo National Museum.
Source: ColBase at https://colbase.nich.go.jp

199 Bekkouiro   **282 Giniro/Shironezumi**

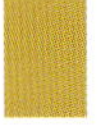
Bekkouiro
Tortoiseshell Color

Bekkouiro is a deep yellow color with a slight reddish tint, resembling the shell of a species of sea turtle called "Taimai." Taimai shells are semi-transparent with irregular black and yellow patterns. They have been used for making accessories such as combs, hairpins, and hair ornaments since ancient times.

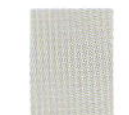
Giniro/Shironezumi
Silver/Silver Gray

Giniro refers to the bright, luminous gray color represented by the metal silver. "Shironezumi" (white mouse) represents a bright gray color. The name "Shiroganeiro" may also refer to this color. Silver, second only to gold in malleability, is processed into leaf, powder, and other forms and used similarly to gold.

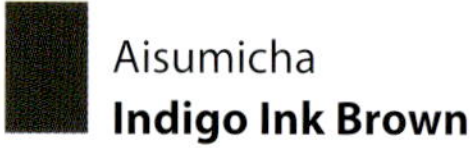

Aisumicha
Indigo Ink Brown

Aisumicha is a name used to describe a black with a hint of indigo. Despite the "cha" (tea) in the name, it falls into the black color spectrum. It was popular during the mid-Edo period.

Shironeri
White Silk

In ancient times, many fabrics were kept in their natural state, while pure white silk, which had been treated with something in order to whiten it, was considered special. White was the color of the emperor's robes and held sacred significance in rituals. Even in the early modern period, in Edo and the Kansai region, both pure white and the sense of coolness associated with it were much admired.

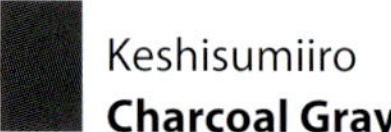

Keshisumiiro
Charcoal Gray

Keshisumiiro is used to describe a dark gray resembling the color of charcoal when the pale ashes are blown off the extinguished wood charcoal. While it is a shade close to black, it leans more towards a lighter gray, akin to "Usumosuiro" (pale gray).

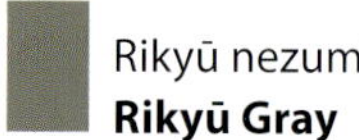

Rikyū nezumi
Rikyū Gray

This is a color in the greenish-gray range. Similar to "Rikyūyanagi" and others, it's named after the tea master Sen no Rikyū. This color name evokes the atmosphere of matcha green tea and wabi-sabi aesthetics, adding a stronger grayish tone to represent a subdued, rustic flavor. The cool and subtle shades of Rikyū nezumi were admired by the sophisticated people of Edo.

Shiro
White

This is the brightest of all colors, and its name is one of the oldest in Japanese history. Animals such as white horses, white deer, white foxes, white dogs, and white hawks, all symbolizing auspiciousness, appear in mythology. In the medieval aesthetics, it was considered a color evoking feelings of tranquility, mystery, and serenity.

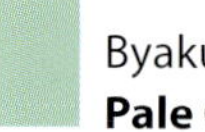

Suzumecha
Sparrow Tea

This is a deep brownish tea color with a touch of red, reminiscent of the color of a sparrow's head, although some interpretations also consider the grayish-brown color of a sparrow's feathers. The dyeing process involves using the bark of willow or the bark of the Japanese plum tree. This color name became more common during the Edo period and is relatively new among traditional color names.

Byakuroku
Pale Green

It describes a pastel green color, also known as "Byakurokusei," subsequently shortened to "Byakuroku." Byakurokusei is a light green rock pigment made by grinding malachite (a copper carbonate hydroxide mineral) with water. While it is chemically similar to verdigris, its particles are much finer.

Kuroiro
Black

The origin of "black" is thought to relate to darkness ("kura"), contrasting with light ("aka"). Black often expresses the opposite meaning to white or red, symbolizing various aspects of life. Therefore, it is commonly used in the colors of Buddhist monks' robes and mourning attire.

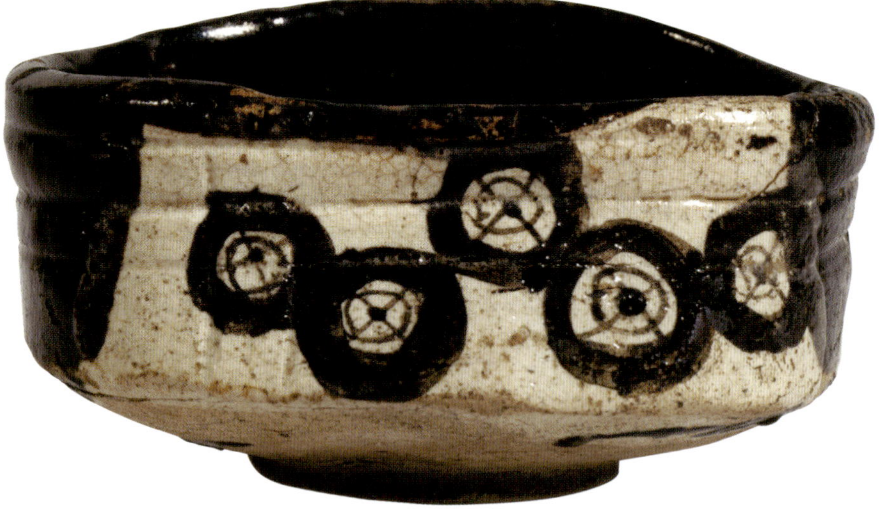

This is a black Oribe tea bowl decorated with a connected circular pattern of five. According to the inscription on the box, this work is named "Satsukiame" (May Rain) by the painter Kumagai Morikazu, who likened the connected circular pattern to the ripples created by raindrops falling into a puddle. Black Oribe refers to pottery where black glaze is applied overall, and patterns are drawn with the same black glaze. Pieces with only black glaze are called "Iribe Kuro," while those with patterns are referred to as "Kuro Oribe."

271 Aisumicha   **254 Shironeri**

"Black Oribe Ring-Connected Motif Teacup" inscribed "Samidare (May Rain)" by Shinhozaemon. Momoyama era, early 17th century. Aichi Prefectural Museum of Art (Kimura Jōzō Collection).

Oribe ware, characterized by its style and design influenced by Furuta Oribe, a prominent figure in the tea ceremony world during the late Momoyama period and early Keicho era (1596–1615), was first created during this time. The name "Oribe" is used to describe pottery with these distinctive features. The distorted oblong shape known as "kutsugata" is commonly seen in Oribe ware tea bowls.

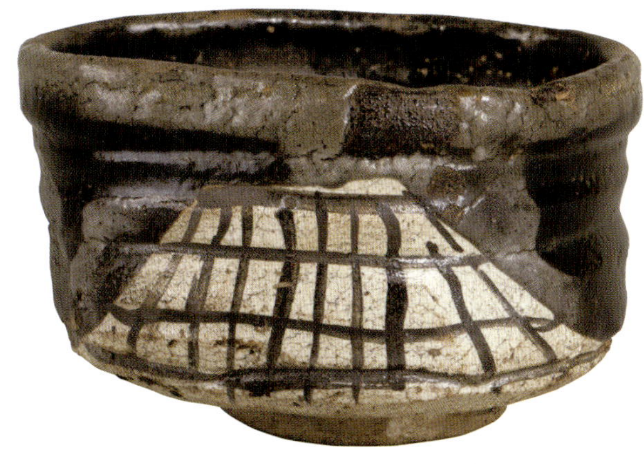

"Black Oribe Kutsugata Tea Bowl". Inscribed "Kakutaro" Mino Ware. Edo period, 17th century. Tokyo National Museum. Source: ColBase at https://colbase.nich.go.jp

276 Keshisumiiro   **259 Rikyū nezumi**

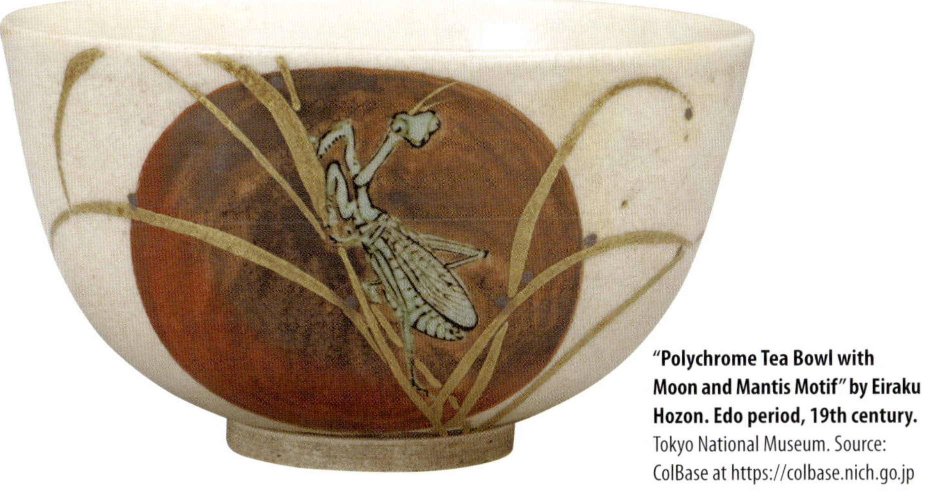

"Polychrome Tea Bowl with Moon and Mantis Motif" by Eiraku Hozon. Edo period, 19th century. Tokyo National Museum. Source: ColBase at https://colbase.nich.go.jp

251 Shiro   **232 Suzumecha**   **145 Byakuroku**

On a background resembling the color of the moon is a round, brown circle. Emerging from the grass, a mantis seems to be staring at the viewer. Eiraku Hozon (1795–1854) was a late Edo period potter who originally hailed from the Nishimura family of Kyoto's Dofuku Kiln. He later transitioned to glazed ceramics, adopted the name Eiraku, and became a renowned artisan representing the late Edo period in Kyoto pottery.

On a black background, a white crane is depicted on the outer side, while inside the bowl, there is a raised image of a turtle. This design symbolizes good fortune, as cranes and turtles are both associated with longevity. Niōya Dōhachi (1783–1855) was a late Edo period potter and the second son of the first generation Takahashi Dōhachi, a potter from Kyoto's Awataguchi ware. While he learned pottery under the tutelage of the literati potter Okuda Keigawa, his works exhibit a style influenced by the Rinpa school, resembling artists such as Nishikawa Sukenobu and Kanō Sanraku.

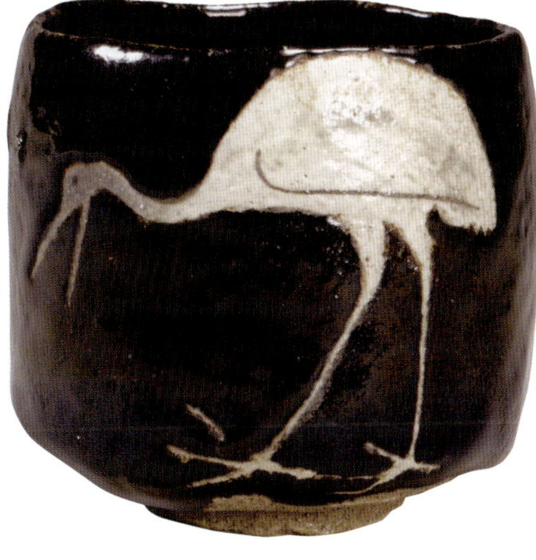

"Black Raku Crane and Turtle Design Tea Bowl" by Ninnami Dōhachi. Edo period, 19th century. Tokyo National Museum. Source: ColBase at https://colbase.nich.go.jp

280 Kuroiro   **251 Shiro**

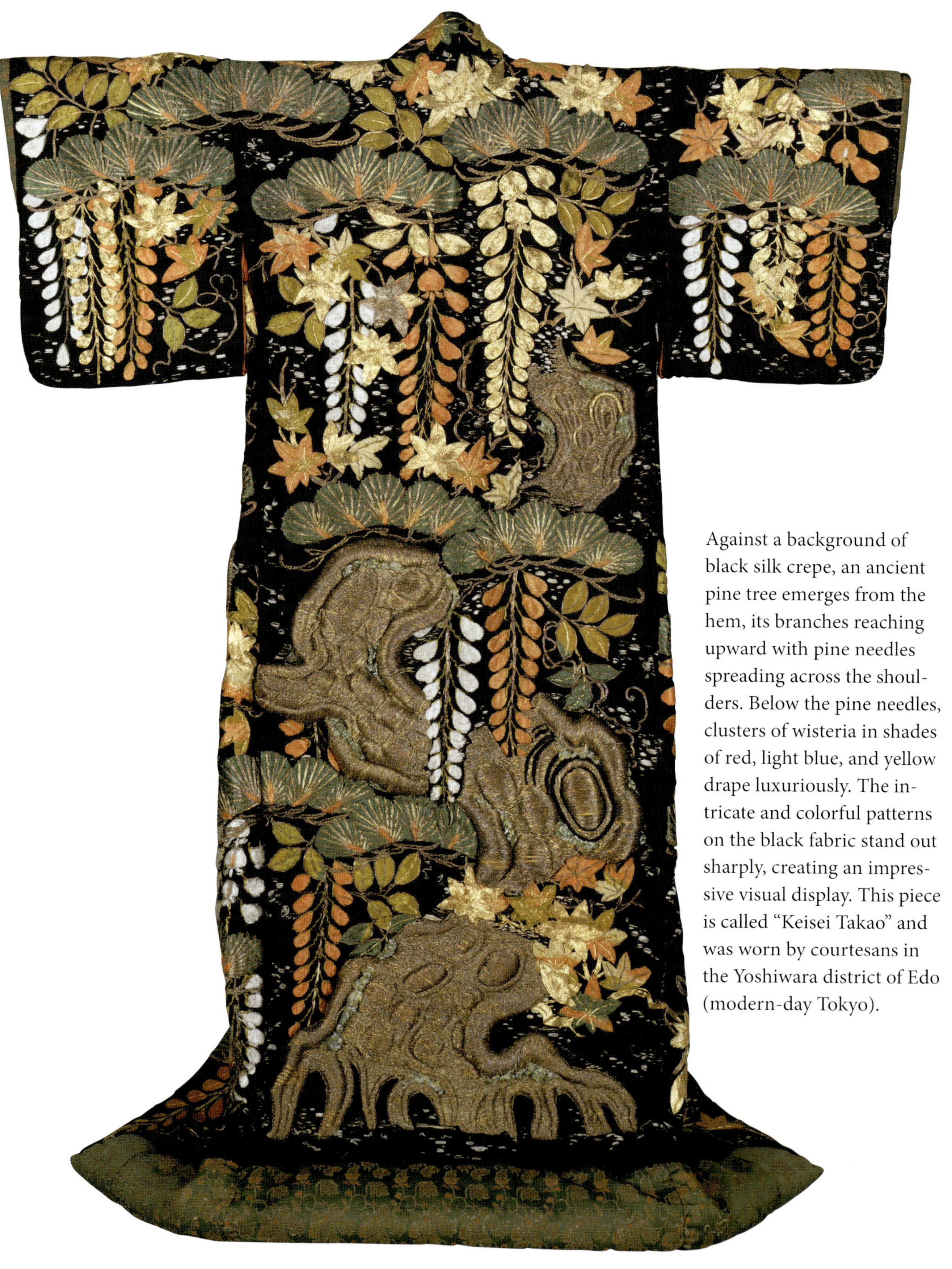

Against a background of black silk crepe, an ancient pine tree emerges from the hem, its branches reaching upward with pine needles spreading across the shoulders. Below the pine needles, clusters of wisteria in shades of red, light blue, and yellow drape luxuriously. The intricate and colorful patterns on the black fabric stand out sharply, creating an impressive visual display. This piece is called "Keisei Takao" and was worn by courtesans in the Yoshiwara district of Edo (modern-day Tokyo).

268 Kenpōzome/
Yoshiokazome

43 Araigaki

181 Tanpopoiro

"Black Silk Crepe Kimono with Pine, Wisteria, and Maple Leaf Patterns". Edo period, 19th century.
Tokyo National Museum. Source: ColBase at https://colbase.nich.go.jp

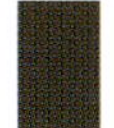

Kenpōzome/Yoshiokazome
Black Tea Dye

Refers to a black-brown dye technique believed to have been passed down by Yoshiohka Kenpō, the founder of the Yoshiohka-ryū martial art in the early Edo period. Initially, it involved dyeing with betel nuts using an iron-rich liquid for coloration. Some sources mention that they were skilled in sharkskin pattern (same-komon) dyeing using stencil techniques. During the Edo period, black dyeing was also called "kenpō."

Araigaki
Washed Persimmon

Araigaki refers to a light orange color that results from washing and sun-drying persimmons, which reduces their color intensity. Persimmon color is named after the color of persimmon fruit, and within the persimmon color range, there are variations like Honda persimmon, Yamato persimmon, lighter Usugaki persimmon, and chic Shudaki persimmon. In the Tenwa era (1681–1683) of the Edo period, washed persimmon dyeing became widespread, and during the An'ei and Tenmei eras (1772–1788), lighter persimmon colors became fashionable.

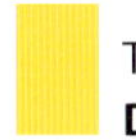

Tanpopoiro
Dandelion Yellow

This term describes a bright yellow color resembling the petals of a dandelion flower. In English, it is referred to as "dandelion," likening the color to the teeth of a lion, as the name suggests. The name "dandelion" itself can be traced to the resemblance of the cut ends of the stems, which curl up into a round shape like a drum. "Dandelion" color was used as a description for shades of yellow with a hint of green.

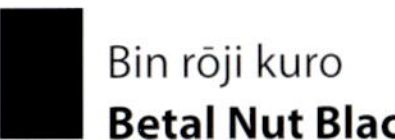

Bin rōji kuro
Betal Nut Black

A dignified black color with a hint of blue. Betel nuts (*Areca catechu*) were used as a dye material for silk fabric. The betel nuts were used to create a black dye by repeatedly applying iron solution to the fabric. Additionally, applying indigo dye as an underlayer could produce a beautiful black color. This technique was sometimes referred to as "ai-shitakō" due to the use of indigo.

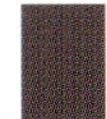

Murasaki-tobi
Purple Black

A dark, grayish purple color created using sumac as the main dye and a darkened red-purple color. According to "Hankosomi" (a historical source), this color became popular for women's kimono linings and undergarments during the An'ei and Tenmei eras (1772–1788) in the Edo period.

Gofun
Powdered Shell

A white pigment used in Japanese painting that has a slight yellowish tint. It is made by grinding seashells, then washing and drying the powder. Its primary component is calcium carbonate. Gofun has been used since the Muromachi period (14th to 16th centuries) and is utilized as a paint material to enhance the coloration of base layers and to create various color tones when mixed with other pigments.

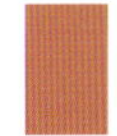

Akani
Red Earth

A type of red pigment with a slightly yellowish hue. The term "tan" means "red soil," and various red pigments, including lead oxide, iron oxide, and mercury sulfide, were referred to as "tan."

"Inari Pilgrimage" by Utagawa Toyoharu, 1795.
Tokyo National Museum.
Source: ColBase at https://colbase.nich.go.jp

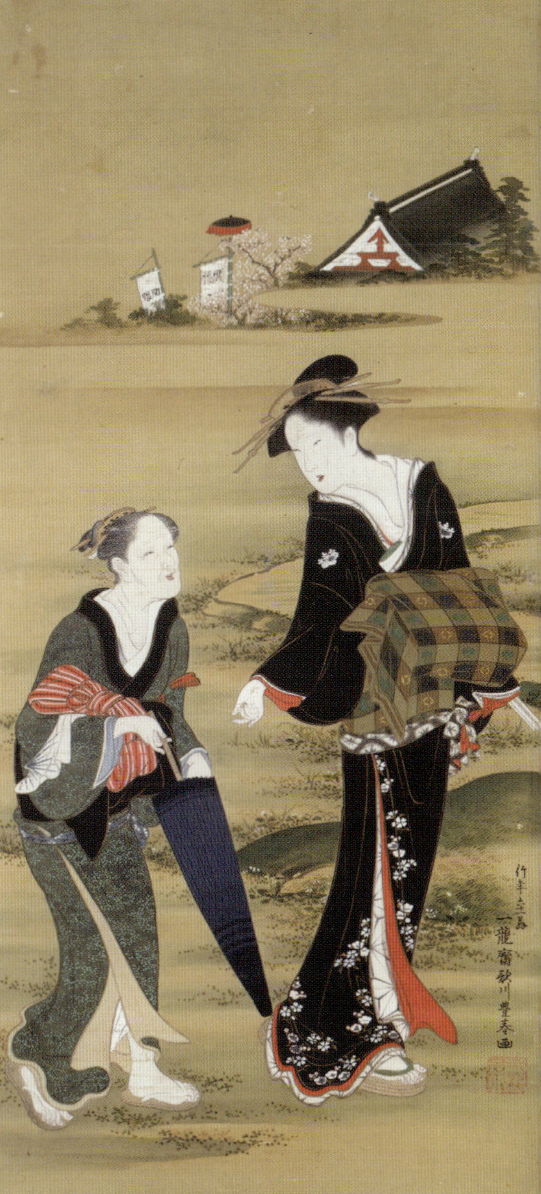

274 Bin rōji kuro	91 Murasaki-tobi	252 Gofun	22 Akani

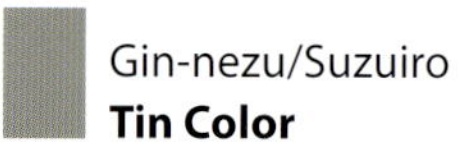
Gin-nezu/Suzuiro
Tin Color

"Nezumi" refers to a color resembling the tone of silver, with a touch of coolness reminiscent of metal. It corresponds to a light shade among the colors of ink, resembling the color of tin." Silver, traditionally referred to as "Shirogane," falls into the white spectrum. Both "Gin-nezumi" and "Shiroganeiro" are terms of aesthetic appreciation, conveying a sense of sophistication with their bright gray hues.

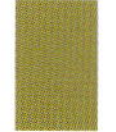
Nataneaburairo/Nataneyuiro
Rapeseed Oil

This color is a greenish yellow-brown, resembling the color of the oil extracted from rapeseed seeds. "Nataneaburairo" is used to describe this hue, distinguishing it from "Nanohanairo" which refers to the color derived from rapeseed flowers. Dyeing with rapeseed became popular during the Edo period when the oil was widely used as lamp oil. It gained popularity during the Genbun era (1736–1741) for hemp garments and later during the Tenmei era (1781–1789) as an undergarment color.

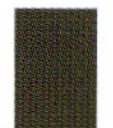
Dobunezumi/Mizonezumi
Slightly Darker Gray

This term is used to describe a slightly darker shade of gray compared to "Su-Nezumi" (simple gray). The color name "Dobunezumi" can be found in dye sample books from the mid-Edo period, indicating its common use during that time. It may not be the most beautiful color, but it was symbolically used for Japanese men's suits.

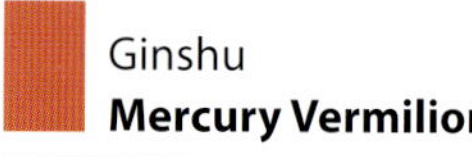
Ginshu
Mercury Vermilion

"Ginshu" refers to a synthetic vermilion pigment made by roasting mercury with sulfur, resulting in a vivid red with a yellowish undertone, brighter than natural vermilion. Historically, cinnabar was obtained from natural cinnabar ore, and by roasting it with sulfur, ginshu was produced. Ginshu was commonly used as a vermilion ink pigment.

An elegant, slender lady wearing an indigo-colored *kosode* and a wide *obi*. Her posture is modest and her steps are small and quiet. Her hairstyle features a *sensu-kazashi* topknot with *maruyama bin* sideburns, adorned with hairpins and a comb. Sugimura Souken (1759–1818) was a painter of the mid to late Edo period, who studied under Maruyama Oukyo and was counted among the Ten Elders of the Maruyama School. He excelled in depicting beautiful women displaying Japanese customs.

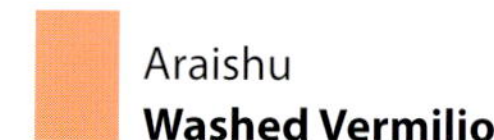
Araishu
Washed Vermilion

This color is similar to vermilion but washed out and diluted, resulting in a pale reddish-orange shade. Similarly, there is a color called "Araigaki," observed from the Tenwa to Genroku eras, which shares this washed-out quality. It is commonly used in contemporary kimono colors. Just as vermilion comes in various shades, ranging from dull reddish to vibrant red, this paler version is utilized in a wide range of hues, from muted yellowish red to vivid red.

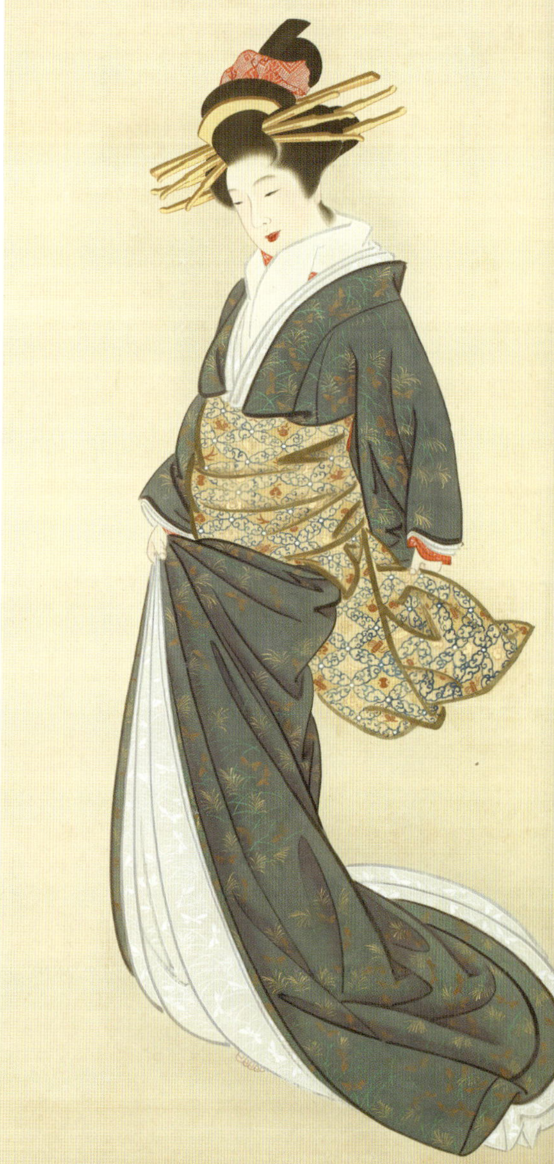

"Portrait of a Standing Beauty" by Yamaguchi Soken. Edo period, 19th century.
Tsuruga City Museum.

256 Gin-nezu/Suzuiro   **190 Nataneaburairo/ Nataneyuiro**

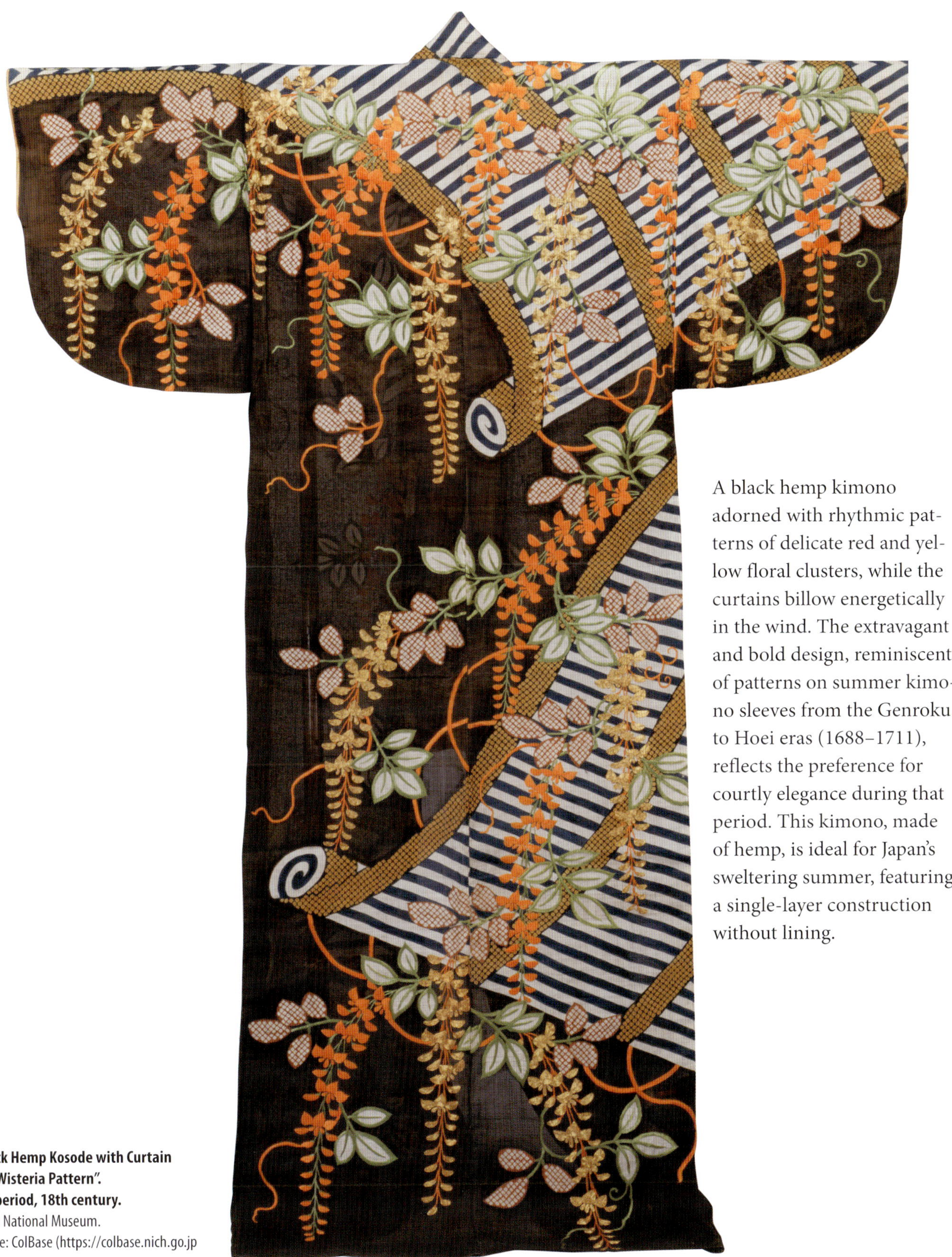

A black hemp kimono adorned with rhythmic patterns of delicate red and yellow floral clusters, while the curtains billow energetically in the wind. The extravagant and bold design, reminiscent of patterns on summer kimono sleeves from the Genroku to Hoei eras (1688–1711), reflects the preference for courtly elegance during that period. This kimono, made of hemp, is ideal for Japan's sweltering summer, featuring a single-layer construction without lining.

"Black Hemp Kosode with Curtain and Wisteria Pattern".
Edo period, 18th century.
Tokyo National Museum.
Source: ColBase (https://colbase.nich.go.jp

267 Dobunezumi/Mizonezumi 21 Ginshu　　**40 Araishu**

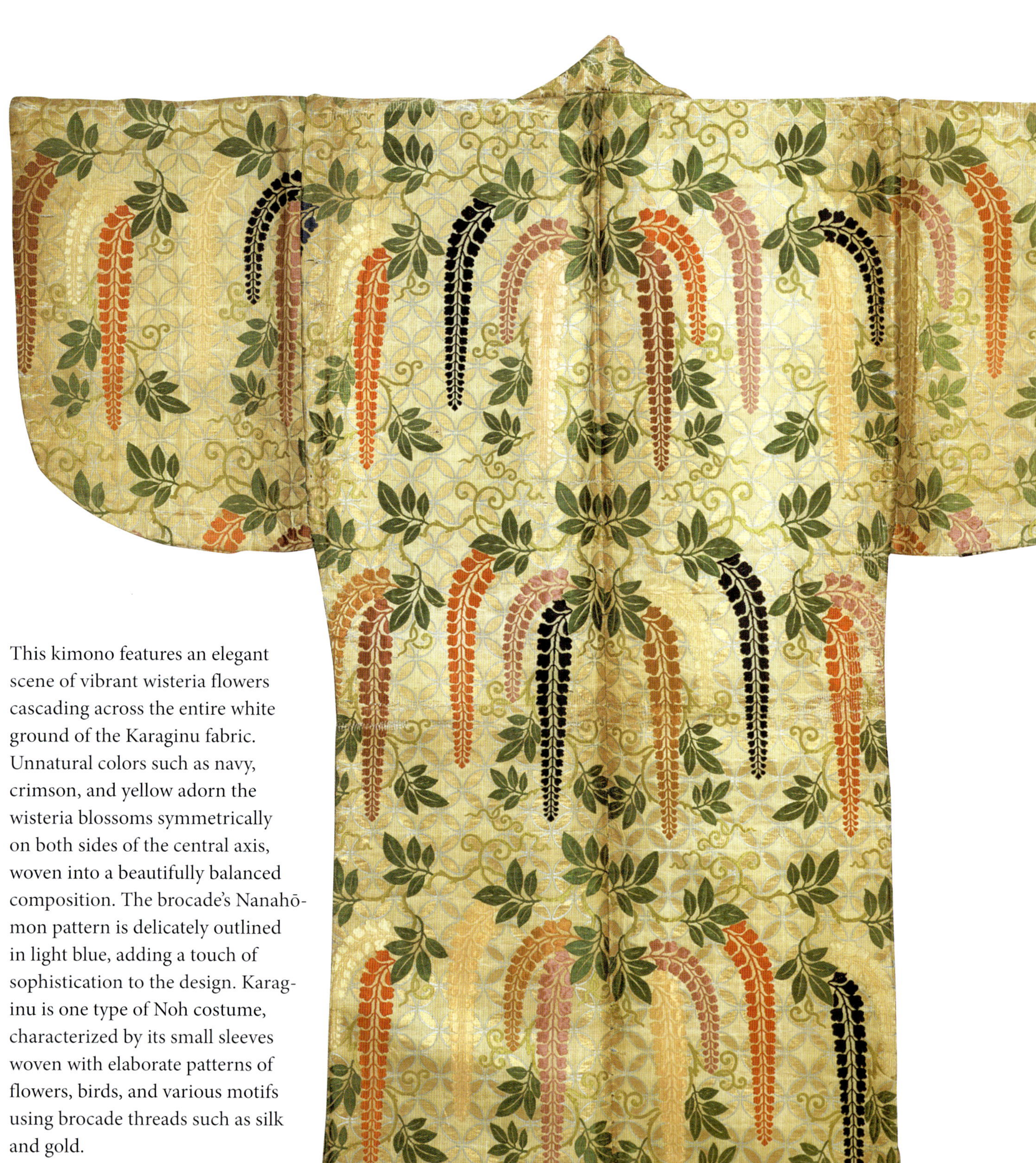

This kimono features an elegant scene of vibrant wisteria flowers cascading across the entire white ground of the Karaginu fabric. Unnatural colors such as navy, crimson, and yellow adorn the wisteria blossoms symmetrically on both sides of the central axis, woven into a beautifully balanced composition. The brocade's Nanahō-mon pattern is delicately outlined in light blue, adding a touch of sophistication to the design. Karaginu is one type of Noh costume, characterized by its small sleeves woven with elaborate patterns of flowers, birds, and various motifs using brocade threads such as silk and gold.

"White Fabric with Linked Seven Treasures and Wisteria Pattern". Edo period, 17th–19th centuries.
Tokyo National Museum.
Source: ColBase at https://colbase.nich.go.jp

<table>
<tr><td>188 Mokuraniro</td><td>215 Sensaicha</td><td>48 Anzuiro</td></tr>
</table>

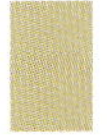

Mokuraniro
Magnolia Color

Refers to a color that is a reddish ash-yellow. Mentioned in the *Soini-rei*, which states, "Monks and nuns are allowed to wear clothes of colors such as mokuran, seiboku, seki, yellow, and faded colors," and the *Reigi-gi-kai* commentary notes that this color and yellow oak are one and the same. According to *Anzai-zuihitsu*, which records terminology related to etiquette, the dye was made with plum or astringent persimmon, resulting in a dark reddish-brown color. Plums were called "mokuran" because they have a pleasant fragrance similar to orchids.

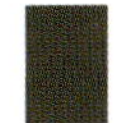

Sensaicha
Chitose Tea

Refers to a dark greenish-brown color created by adding brown to chitose green, or a dark, subdued olive color. During the Edo period, various intermediate colors, including olive-based subdued intermediate colors like Sensaicha, were called "tea" colors, as mentioned in *Shuzan Mankō*. It was used for women's patterned *tsumugi* silk and also for men's cotton fabrics during the Bunsei era (1818–1830).

Anzuiro
Apricot

Named after the color of ripe apricots, it is a pale golden orange. Apricots, originally from China, were introduced during the Nara period, as recorded in the herbal book *Yamato Honzo*. They were enjoyed for their fruit, and their kernels were used for medicinal purposes.

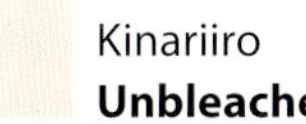

Kinariiro
Unbleached

Refers to the color of yarn or fabric that is not dyed or bleached, showing a slight off-white with a tinge of yellow. This color name emerged during the Showa era, reflecting the strong natural and earthy colors that became popular during that time. Kinariiro is one of the colors that made its way into the Japanese color palette of the 1970s.

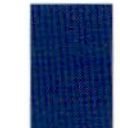

Konjiiro
Navy Blue

It is a blue pigment that originated from China along with azurite, a blue copper mineral. Among them, the particularly bright purplish-blue color is called "Konjō" or navy blue. Due to its high cost, it was synthesized during the Meiji period, and synthetic dyes such as Berlin blue or Prussian blue were used, with "beroai" being used as a shorthand in ukiyo-e prints.

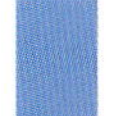

Gunjōiro
Ultramarine Blue

Refers to a deep blue color. Lapis lazuli, known as "blue stone," was imported from the south and highly valued as a raw material for gunjouiro. The color of mineral pigments becomes lighter as the particles become finer. "Konjōiro" (navy blue) has coarser particles than "Gunjōiro," and even finer particles produce "Shiro-gun" (white gunjou). This blue color, made from ground minerals, is indispensable for depicting seas and flowing water in Japanese painting.

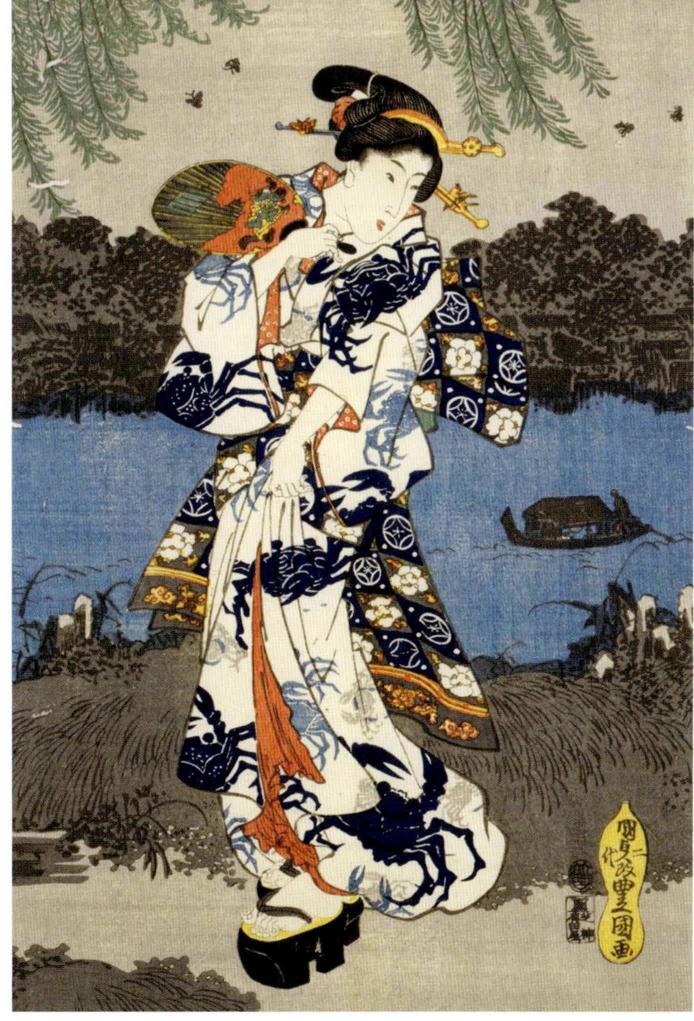

Detail from "Inside the Sun, Moon, and Stars" by Utagawa Toyokuni.
National Diet Library's Digital Collection.

253 Kinariiro   82 Konjiiro   104 Gunjōiro

The Bold Color Schemes of the Kanbun Kosode

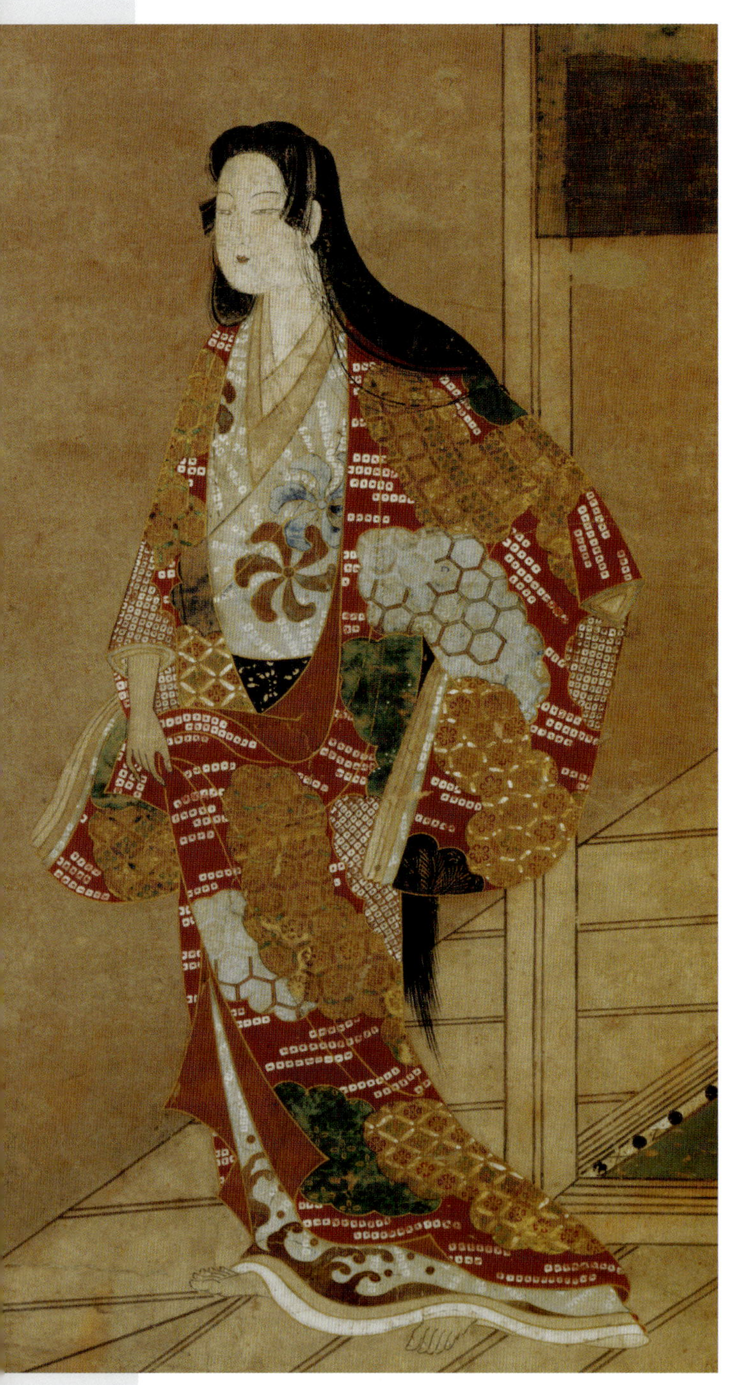

The "Kanbun kosode" is a style of kosode (a type of kimono) that became popular during the early Edo period, specifically during the Kanbun era (1661–1673). It features a distinctive and bold composition, characterized by large patterns on the right side of the back and shoulder area, while the left side remains a wide, blank white space. This design was quite daring and unexpected for its time. The use of asymmetrical motifs covering the entire kosode stands in stark contrast to the kosode style of the Momoyama period, which reserved specific spaces for patterns.

The Kanbun kosode is created using the shibori dyeing technique, with a particular emphasis on *koshizori shibori* (deer's head shibori) and combining it with embroidery. Notably, gold threads started to be favored over the gold-leaf stamping technique that was characteristic of the predecessor called "Keicho kosode."

After the Kanbun era, fashion books known as "hinagata-bon" were published, which documented patterns, techniques, and color schemes for kosode. These books served as references, especially for those from the expanding middle class who had become economically prosperous and wanted to order customized clothing. In addition to traditional motifs such as flowers and birds, these hinagata-bon included innovative and avant-garde designs like document boxes, drum bodies, booklets, frames, brushes, and ink. All the patterns found in the oldest surviving hinagata-bon, *Shinsen O-hiinakata* (1666) feature this Kanbun kosode style.

This artwork depicts a woman wearing a luxurious kimono adorned with gold leaf, standing at the edge and gazing anxiously into the distance. It is believed to represent the scene from the *Ise Monogatari* called "Kawachi-goe," where a woman sends off her husband, who is about to cross the mountains in the middle of the night to visit another woman, and expresses her turmoil by composing a waka poem on the veranda.

26 Shakudouiro	117 Asahanada	171 Kikuchiba

"Portrait of a Beautiful Woman on a Veranda"
Artist Unknown. Edo period, 17th century.
Tokyo National Museum. Source: ColBase at https://colbase.nich.go.jp

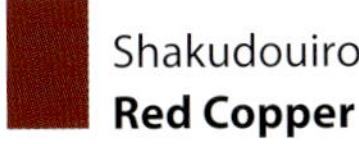

Shakudouiro
Red Copper

Shakudouiro is a dark red color with a glossy finish, resembling the color of red copper. Red copper is a unique copper alloy in Japan, consisting of around three to five percent gold and a small amount of silver. It has been used for various crafts and copper statues since the Nara period. The name often refers to a color with a shiny, almost black luster and is frequently used to describe the color of sun-tanned skin. It is a distinct color from regular copper.

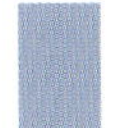

Asahanada
Light Blue

Asahanada is a color lighter than indigo but deeper than light blue. In ancient times, it seems to have been used as a general term for single-dyed colors produced with indigo. In an imperial decree from the fourth year of Emperor Monmu's reign in the *Nihon Shoki* (Chronicles of Japan), it is mentioned that "his morning clothes were…asahanada." During the Heian period, it was considered a color for the day wear of the lower ranks.

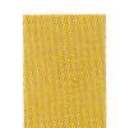

Kikuchiba
Yellowed Autumn Leaves

A color name dating back to the Heian period, used as a collective term for the brownish-yellow-orange hues seen when fallen leaves start to decay. It is a broad term encompassing various shades, including yellow red, and blue, depending on the color tone. In terms of clothing, it is described as "front: dark red, back: dark yellow," and it is worn during the autumn season. It's said that this color has as many as forty-eight different shades. During the Edo period, the color name shifted to refer to tea-related colors.

"White Silk Crepe Kosode with Bamboo and Fishing Net Design". Edo period, 17th century.
Tokyo National Museum.
Source: ColBase at https://colbase.nich.go.jp

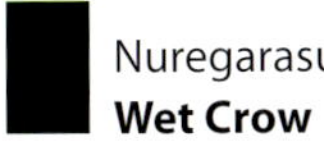

Nuregarasu
Wet Crow

A term used to describe the glossy appearance of a crow's feathers when they are wet from rain. It is also known as "Ukuro," "Karasu no Nurehaneiro," or simply "Nurehaneiro." This color has been used since the time of the *Manyoshu* (*Ten Thousand Leaves*) to describe the hair of Japanese women, and has long been as a term of endearment for glossy black hair.

Shironeri
White Silk

In addition to serving as a color name, "Shironeri" refers to a type of small-sleeved garment made from white neri silk, used for Noh costumes. It is typically worn by male actors of high rank, but occasionally, it may also be used for female characters' outerwear.

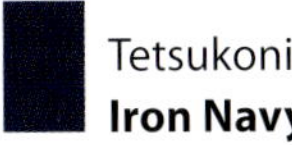

Tetsukoniro
Iron Navy Blue

A dark blue color with a touch of iron, leaning towards a slightly greenish hue. The name is derived from the color of iron rust or the iron content in the pigment used for pottery painting, called *gusu* or *go-su*. Indigo dyeing can sometimes develop a slight purplish hue over time, and intensely purple-toned dark blue colors were referred to as "shikon" or "nasukon." The dyeing process involves under-dyeing with indigo, followed by over-dyeing with oak gall ink (a liquid once used for blackening teeth) to enhance the blackish tones.

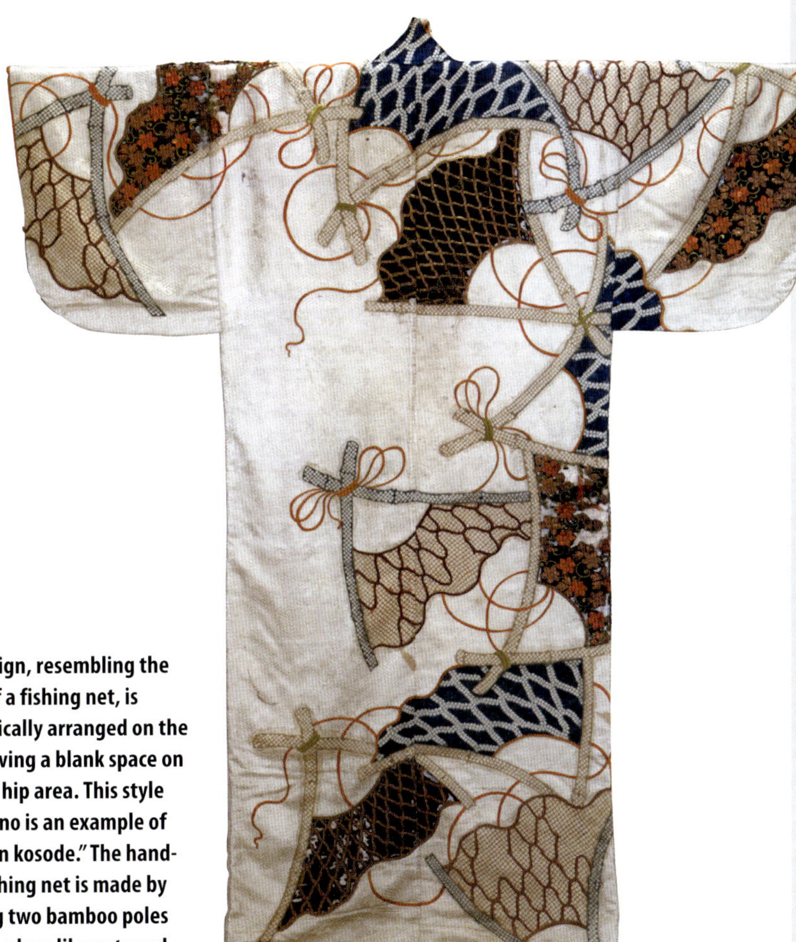

The design, resembling the mesh of a fishing net, is rhythmically arranged on the fan, leaving a blank space on the left hip area. This style of kimono is an example of "Kanbun kosode." The hand-held fishing net is made by crossing two bamboo poles to form a bag-like net used for scooping fish.

272 Nuregarasu   233 Shironeri   115 Tetsukoniro

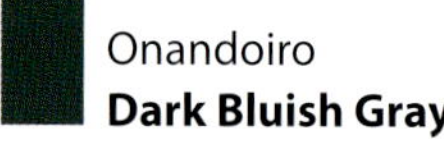

Onandoiro
Dark Bluish Gray

Onandoiro is a general term for dark bluish-gray or dark bluish-gray. "Onando" originally referred to a room for storing clothing and furnishings. This color became popular as a representative of blue shades, and during the Hōreki era (1751–1764), it was favored as the lining color for men's garments.

Fukamurasaki
Deep Purple

Fukamurasaki is a deep purple color achieved by dyeing with purple gromwell (*Lithospermum erythrorhizon*) root using a mixture of lye and vinegar. In the 11th year of Empress Suiko's reign (603 CE), the highest-ranking color for ceremonial robes was purple. In ancient times, one's rank and status were distinguished by clothing colors, and it was established that a darker shade within the same hue indicated a higher rank.

Kiniro
Gold

Kiniro is a color that resembles a gold metallic luster with a shade leaning towards orange. It is used for coins, jewelry, and is often applied thinly as gold leaf for decorative purposes. In the art of lacquerware, gold powder is scattered to create a glistening effect.

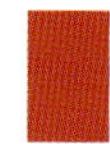

Zakuroiro
Pomegranate Red

Zakuroiro refers to the deep red color of ripe pomegranate fruit or a vibrant orange color reminiscent of its flowers. In Japan, the preference has historically leaned towards the color of pomegranate flowers rather than the fruit itself, so the color name originally corresponded to a more orange hue. According to the *Honzo Wamyo* (a dictionary of plant names), pomegranates were cultivated in the Heian period, and various colors such as dark purple, deep black, brown, yellow-brown, golden, and dark brown could be obtained by changing the mordant from the bark and fruit peel.

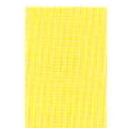

Kihada
Yellow Persimmon

Kihada is a deciduous tall tree belonging to the citrus family that grows in mountainous areas. The yellow dye is obtained from the boiled juice of its yellow bark. The color is similar to "Kariyasu" but has a more vibrant yellow-green hue. Paper dyed with the liquid extract is called "kihada paper," and it has been used for sutra copying since the Asuka period due to its insect-repelling properties. The colored papers found in the Shosoin Repository, such as yellow paper, yellow-dyed paper, and light yellow paper, are believed to have been dyed using kihada.

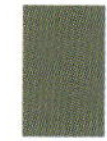

Yanaginezumi/Mamegaracha
Willow Gray/Muted Gray

While "Yanaginezumi" refers to a color that combines the greenish-gray shade of willow leaves with a grayish color, "Mamegaracha" is a general term for a light grayish color with a hint of green. In the *Tekagami Moyō Setsuyō* the two names seem to be alternates for each other. During the Edo period, colors were often categorized with two different names, such as the Forty-eight Colors and Hundred Grays, to distinguish colors with low saturation. Generally, colors that conveyed warmth and subtlety were referred to as "cha" (tea), while softer, cooler colors were called "nezu" (gray).

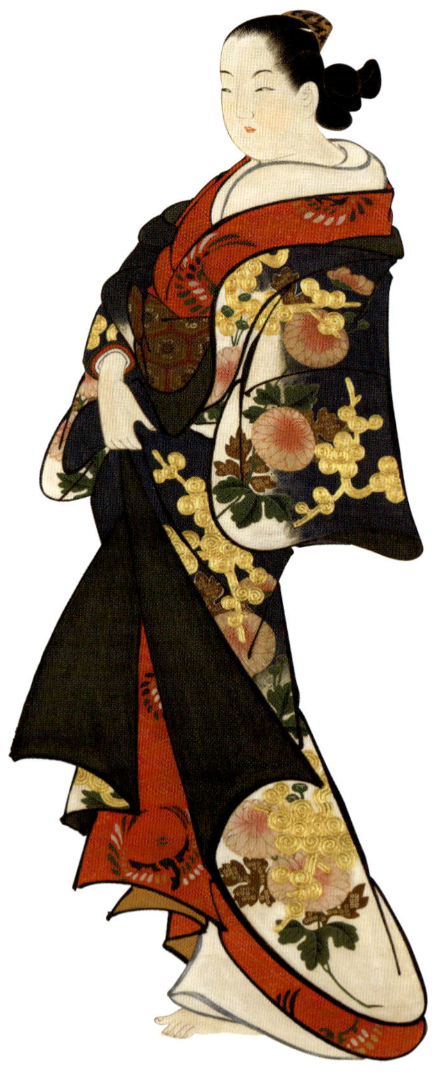

Detail from "Portrait of a Courtesan" by Kaigetsudō Ando. Copied by Kobori Tomo.
Tokyo National Museum.
Source: ColBase at https://colbase.nich.go.jp

128 Onandoiro   94 Fukamurasaki   281 Kiniro   23 Zakuroiro

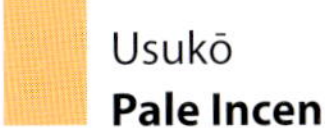

Usukō
Pale Incense

Usukō is a light yellow-brown. For "kōiro" (incense colors), there are "Chojiiro" dyed with cloves and "Karacha" dyed with garro wood. Unlike the darker incense colors that are made using cloves and iron with a lye solution, Usukō is dyed solely with the boiled extract of fragrant wood, without the use of mordants.

This furisode features a bold design with large chrysanthemums prominently displayed on the shoulders. The petals on the shoulders are alternately formed using embroidery and shibori (tie-dyeing), while the black background is adorned with small red and white flowers as well as radiating designs created through embroidery. This pattern represents the needles of the Karimatsu pine tree. The radiating lines resemble the needles spreading outwards while the three central circles resemble stamens. This dynamic design, which depicts a graceful curve on the right half of the garment, effectively embodies the distinctive characteristics of Kanbun kosode. It was traditionally worn by unmarried women as formal attire.

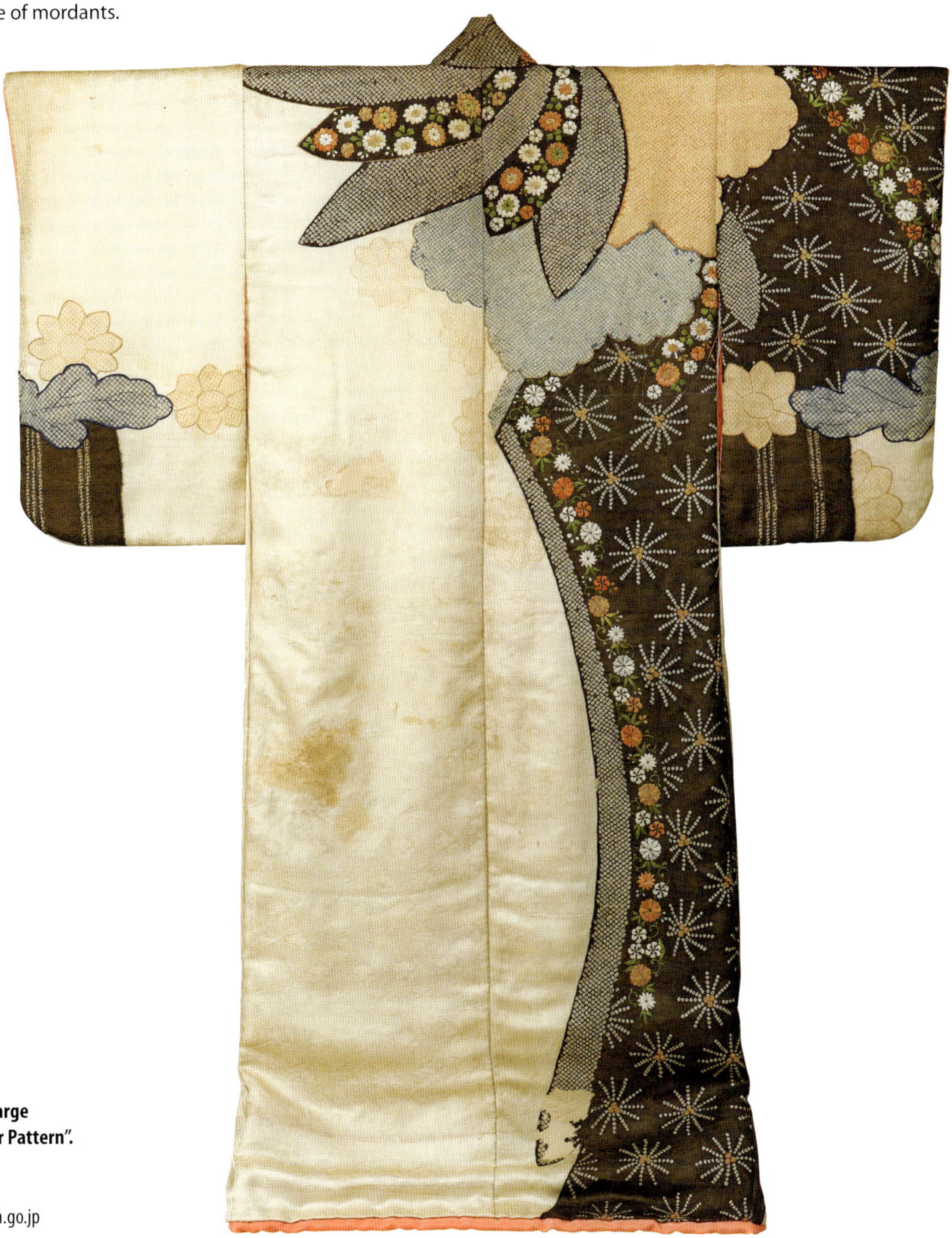

**"White Silk Crepe Furisode with Large Chrysanthemum and Small Flower Pattern".
Edo period, 17th century.**
Tokyo National Museum.
Source: ColBase at https://colbase.nich.go.jp

179 Kihada	258 Yanaginezumi/ Mamegaracha	195 Usukō

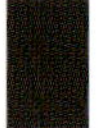

Aisumicha
Indigo Ink Brown

A color name used in the Edo period, referring to a strong grayish shade created by mixing indigo with dark tea. According to *Tekagami Moyō Setsuyō* it this color signified the resolution of disputes among men who, as a sign of reconciliation after a fight, dyed their clothing in the same color and wore it together.

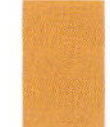

Kuchibairo
Decayed Leaf Color

A slightly brownish-yellow-orange color resembling the color of decaying leaves. It's dyed using Japanese pagoda tree, dyer's sumac, sometimes supplemented with safflower, madder, indigo, and other dyes. There are numerous variations, known as the "Forty-eight shades of Kuchiba." During the Edo period, this name was used to describe brownish shades. The *Rakukubo Monogatari* from the Heian period mentions garments like "Kuchiba karakoromo" and "Kuchiba no usumono no tsutsumi," indicating its popularity as a clothing color during that era.

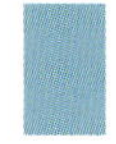

Mizuiro
Pale Aqua

This color is named for water which, though colorless, reflects the blue of the sky in seas, lakes, and rivers. It is a light shade of blue with a hint of indigo. Throughout the Edo period, this was favored as a color for summer kimonos and became trendy as the background color for curtains.

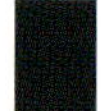

Binrojizome
African Brown

A blackish-brown dye made from the fruit of the betel nut. The betel is an evergreen tree of the palm family native to Malaysia. Juices extracted from the betel nut and the bark of the yangmei tree are used to dye silk, further treated with iron or alum, and this process is repeated to achieve a deep black color Additionally, dyes made from the bark of the yangmei tree, pomegranate, and gallnuts were commonly used.

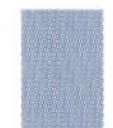

Asahanada
Light Blue

This color is achieved by lightly dyeing with indigo. According to *Engishiki*, indigo is the sole ingredient for creating this blue shade. In later periods, "Asagi" became the more frequently used name for this color. As indigo dye tends to turn yellowish when lightened, a pale green variation of this color called "Mizu Hanada" was recognized.

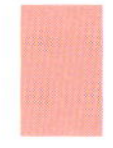

Ikkonzome
Baby Pink

This color is a slightly purplish-pink shade achieved by dyeing silk with approximately one kilogram of dried safflower blossoms, which produces a flower cake called "ikko." One ikko of safflower was used to dye one bolt of silk. While the use of safflower was heavily restricted, the use of a small amount to achieve a light pink color was permitted, leading to the origin of this particular color name.

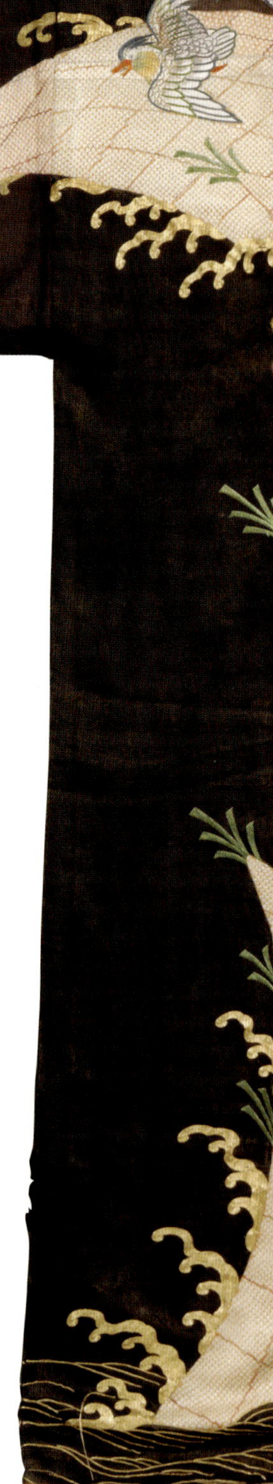

"Black Silk Crepe Furisode with Wave and Ducks Design" (Important Cultural Property). Edo period, 17th century.
Tokyo National Museum.
Source: ColBase at https://colbase.nich.go.jp

271 Aisumicha   166 Kuchibairo   97 Mizuiro

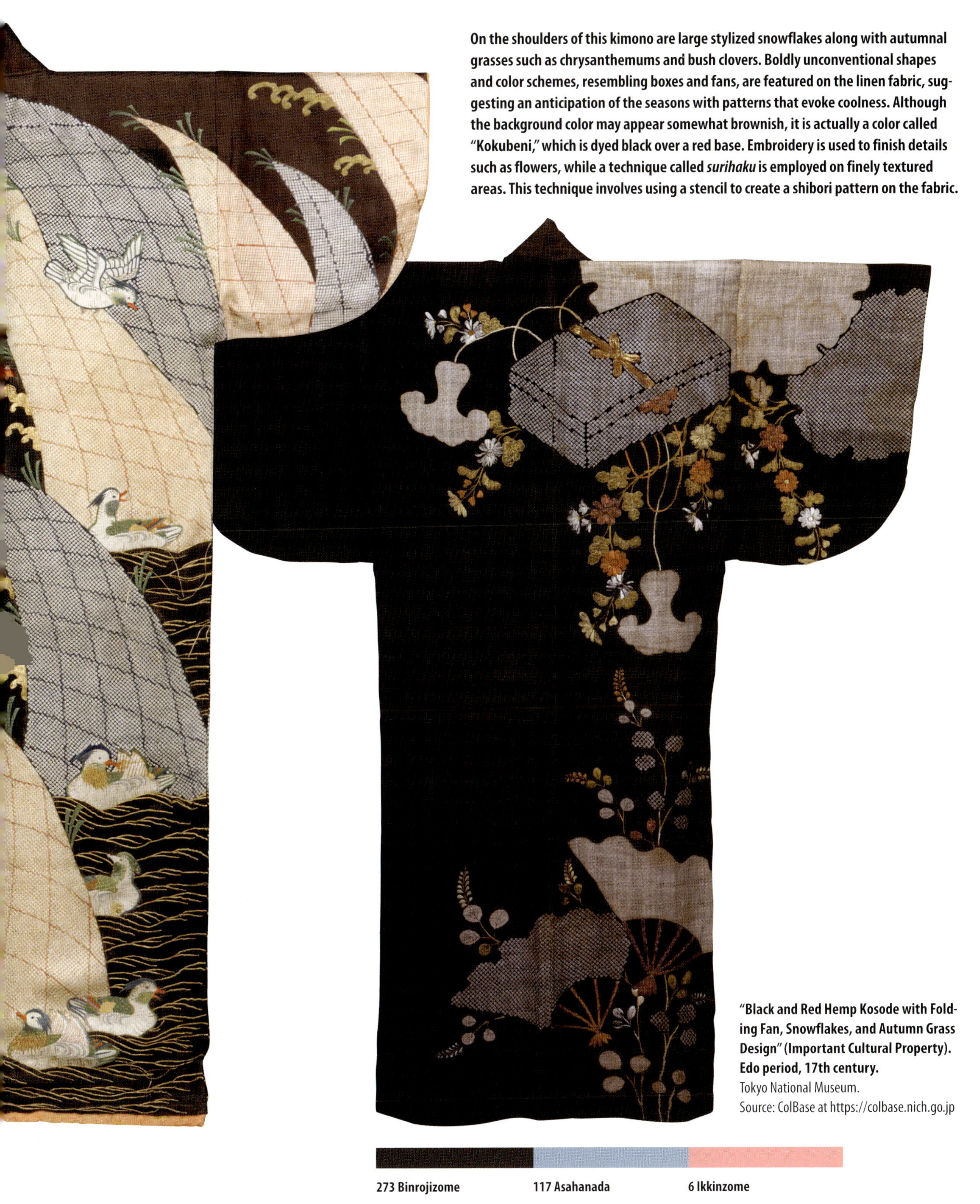

On the shoulders of this kimono are large stylized snowflakes along with autumnal grasses such as chrysanthemums and bush clovers. Boldly unconventional shapes and color schemes, resembling boxes and fans, are featured on the linen fabric, suggesting an anticipation of the seasons with patterns that evoke coolness. Although the background color may appear somewhat brownish, it is actually a color called "Kokubeni," which is dyed black over a red base. Embroidery is used to finish details such as flowers, while a technique called *surihaku* is employed on finely textured areas. This technique involves using a stencil to create a shibori pattern on the fabric.

"Black and Red Hemp Kosode with Folding Fan, Snowflakes, and Autumn Grass Design" (Important Cultural Property). Edo period, 17th century.
Tokyo National Museum.
Source: ColBase at https://colbase.nich.go.jp

273 Binrojizome   117 Asahanada   6 Ikkinzome

Gold and Silver in Japanese Culture

Gold has symbolized eternity and immutability in Buddhism since ancient times, and it has also been a symbol of the highest spiritual realm. During the Fujiwara period, which created Japan's indigenous culture such as Yamato-e painting and Shinden-zukuri architecture, people dreamed of the Pure Land and created a golden world akin to the Golden Hall of Chuson-ji Temple. Against the backdrop of such Buddhist culture, golden ornaments and temples were created. Silver, following gold, has been highly valued as a precious metal since ancient times. Gold and silver are likened to the sun and moon, respectively, and are often mentioned together.

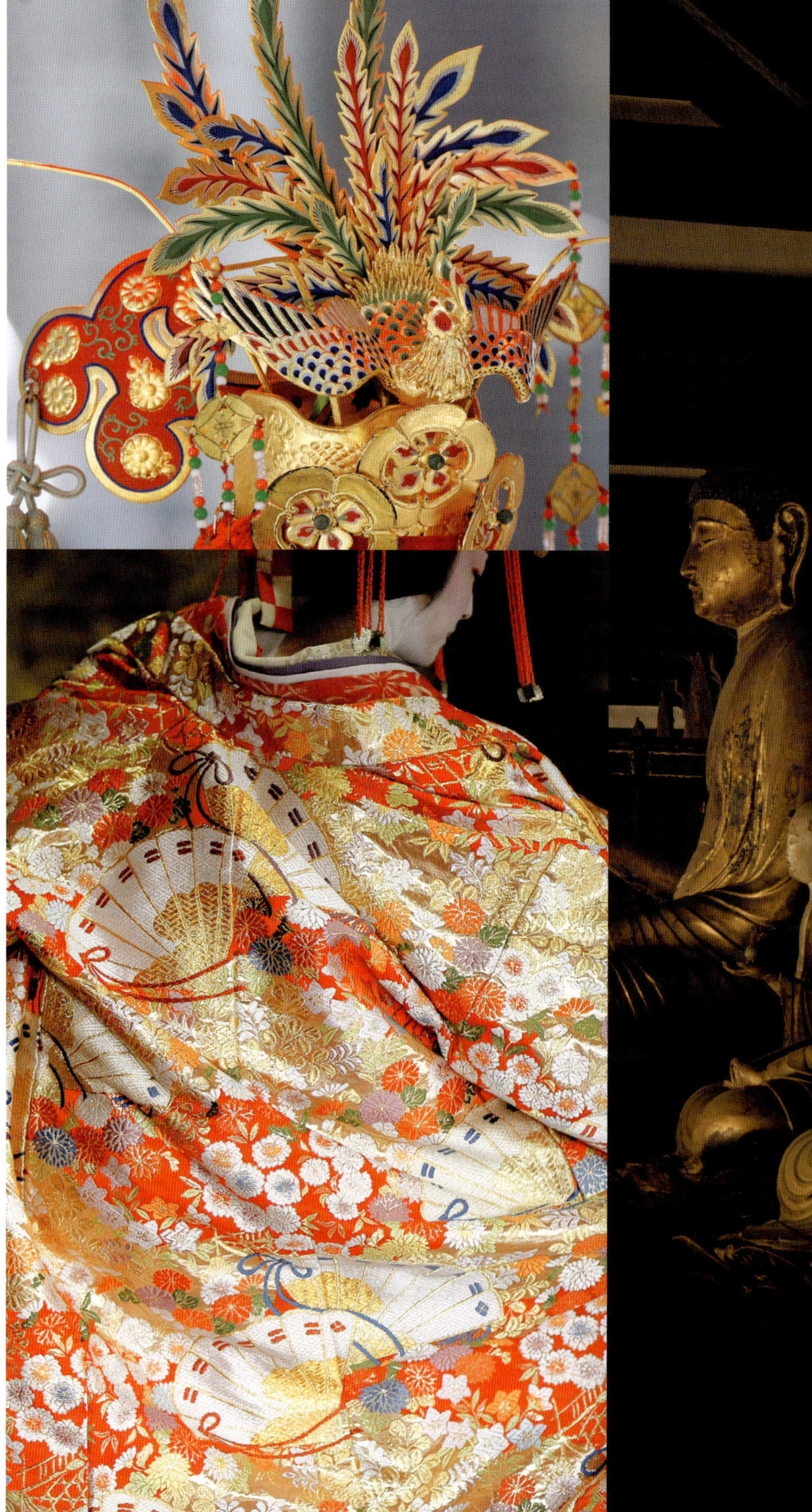

Top right Naginata Hoko Child Attendants at Gion Festival, Kyoto.
Bottom right Doll Offering at Hōkyō-ji Temple, Kyoto.
Far right Nine statues of Amida Buddha (National Treasure) at Jōruri-ji Temple, Kyoto.

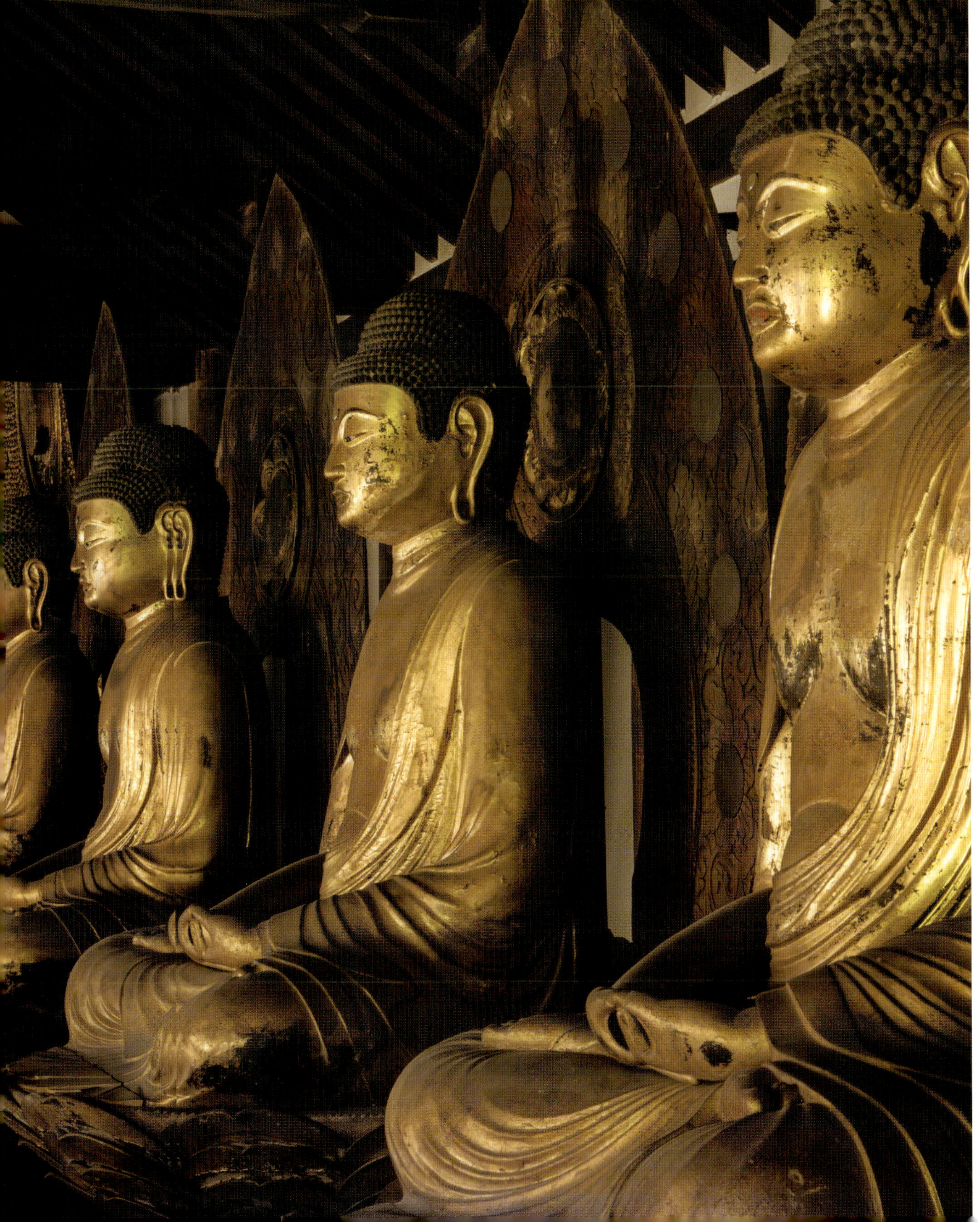

Japanese Color Schemes Based on Gold and Silver

In the year 1298, *The Travels of Marco Polo*—Polo's recounting of his travels in which he introduced the rich cultures and treasures of Asia—states that Japan boasted such a plentiful production of gold that it was called the "Land of Zipangu" or "Golden Land."

The book states that "The palace of this king is made of gold. The roofs are all covered with pure gold. The floors are also entirely covered with pure gold, two fingers thick." As discoveries of gold mines continued to increase, Toyotomi Hideyoshi, who was particularly obsessed with gold, created a "golden tearoom."

During the Warring States period, military commanders adorned their armor and helmets with gold to demonstrate their power. Inside their castles, walls were adorned with splendid gold leaf paintings, shining brightly with gold foil and colored sands scattered throughout. Gold and silver were also used in clothing, with gold and silver threads and foil generously used in the small sleeves of military commanders and their wives, as well as in Noh costumes.

Gold became an essential color during the Azuchi-Momoyama period. It was during this time that the technique of applying gold and silver decorations to lacquerware, known as *makie-e*, became popular and captured the eyes of the Portuguese traders who arrived from distant Europe.

This legacy was passed down to the artists of the Kan'ei era, who used gold and silver in folding screens and fan paintings. Influenced by the introduction of gold brocade and gold seals from China, gold and silver were also used in costumes. Gold and silver threads and foil were generously used in the small sleeves of military commanders and their wives, as well as in Noh costumes.

Among the many metals contained in the earth, gold (yellow gold), silver (white gold), copper (red gold), iron (black gold), and lead (blue gold) are singled out and comprise the "five metals."

Color Scheme Based on Gold

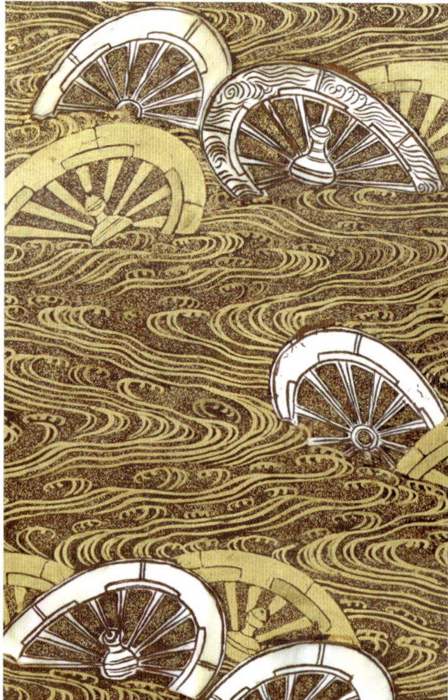

Detail from "Single-wheeled Cart Design Lacquerware Box with Mother-of-Pearl Inlay". National Treasure. Heian Period, 12th century. Tokyo National Museum. Source: ColBase at https://colbase.nich.go.jp

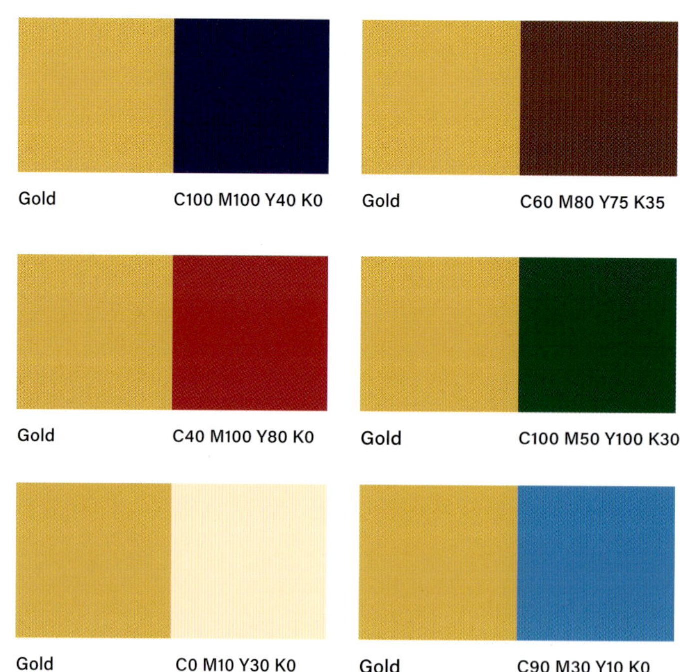

Gold	C100 M100 Y40 K0	Gold	C60 M80 Y75 K35
Gold	C40 M100 Y80 K0	Gold	C100 M50 Y100 K30
Gold	C0 M10 Y30 K0	Gold	C90 M30 Y10 K0

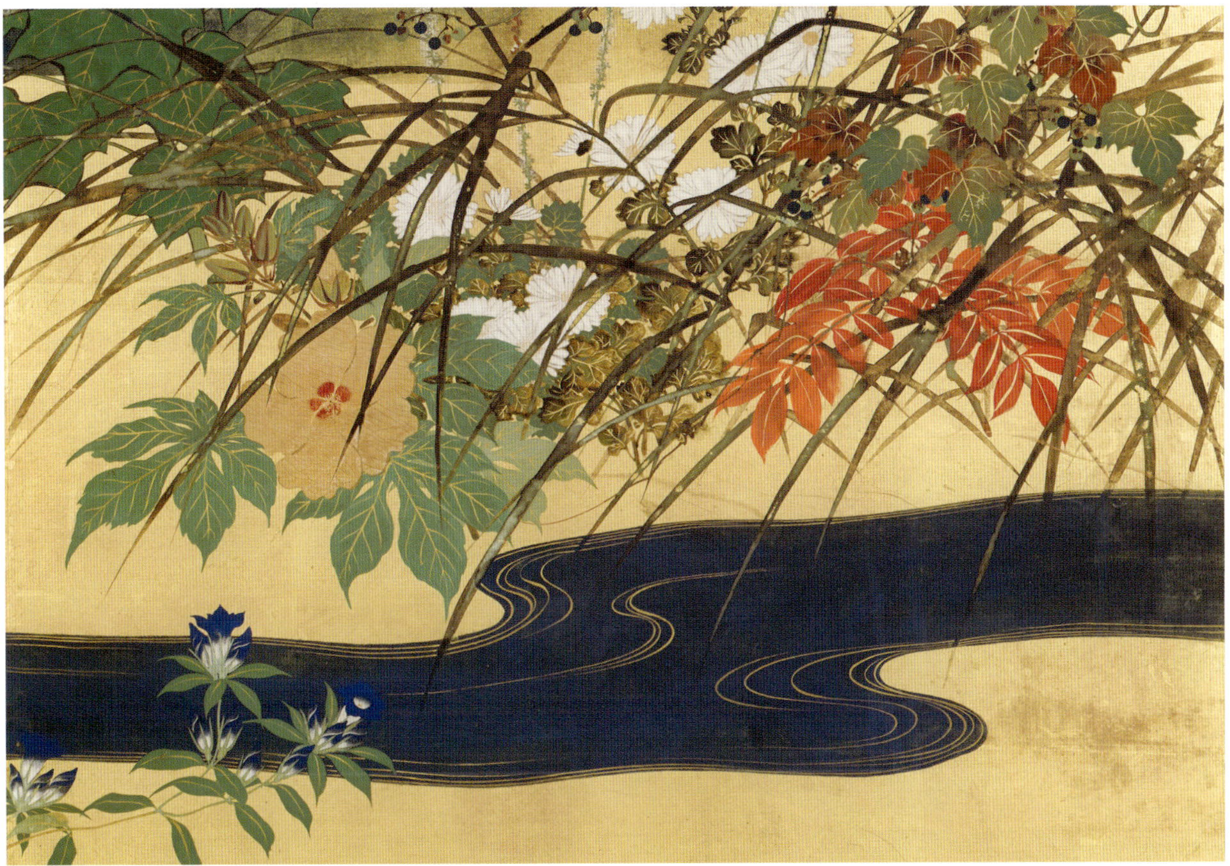

Detail from "Folding Screen with Flowing Water and Four Seasons Plants and Flowers" by Sakai Hōitsu. Edo period, 19th century.
Tokyo National Museum. Source: ColBase at https://colbase.nich.go.jp

Color Scheme Based on Silver

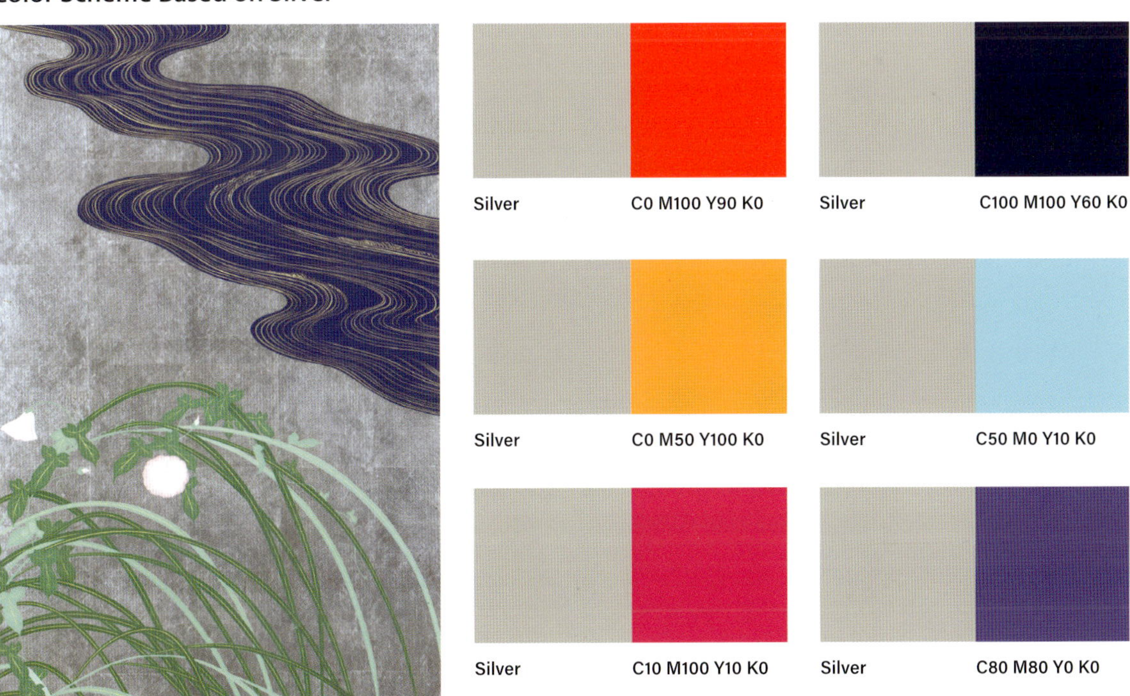

Silver	C0 M100 Y90 K0	Silver	C100 M100 Y60 K0
Silver	C0 M50 Y100 K0	Silver	C50 M0 Y10 K0
Silver	C10 M100 Y10 K0	Silver	C80 M80 Y0 K0

Detail from "Folding Screen with Summer Grasses"
by Sakai Dōitsui, 1893. Tokyo National Museum. Source:
ColBase at https://colbase.nich.go.jp

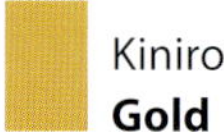

Kiniro
Gold

Gold color has been used to symbolize power and, since the Azuchi-Momoyama period, it became one of the dominant colors in paintings, bringing strong radiance to the overall composition along with the prosperity of golden and jewel-encrusted screens decorating the interiors of samurai castles.

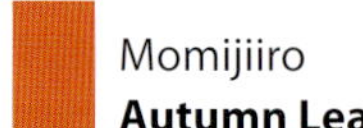

Momijiiro
Autumn Leaf

This deep orange red is often likened to the color of autumn foliage. The term "momiji" comes from the idea of "rubbing out color," referring to the way leaves change color from early autumn until they dry up fully in winter. In a costume book called *Gan'ishō* published at the end of the Kamakura period, a garment of this color is described as "front: red, back: deep red," reflecting the overlapping layers of intensely red maple leaves.

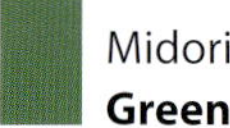

Midori
Green

Refers to the deep green color of leaves. While it's possible to make green dye using plant materials, the pigments are fragile and tend to change to brown. The only pigment that can naturally produce a green color is verdigris, a copper compound. Therefore, to dye in green tones, a method involving overlapping blue and yellow dyes has traditionally been used.

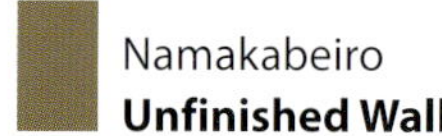

Namakabeiro
Unfinished Wall

Used to describe the ashy reddish-brown color of walls that have not fully dried. This color, part of the low-saturation mouse color spectrum, became popular during the mid to late Edo period. Variations of this unfinished wall color include "Aoisunewall" with a hint of blue, "Fujisunewall" with a hint of purple, "Edosunewall" which adds a touch of red to the blue wall, and "Rikyūsunewall" with a dark green tint, among others.

The large screens of "Sumiyoshi Matsuri-zu" depict the lively scenes of the Sumiyoshi Shrine festival, with the left panel illustrating the departure of the Sumiyoshi Shrine's portable shrine from the temple grounds, and the right panel showing the shrine's arrival at the Suzaku Shrine in Sakai. The procession features townspeople participating in a festive parade, dressed in various costumes and heading from Sakai's beach avenue toward the Suzaku Shrine. At the Suzaku Shrine, various ceremonies, including ritual sumo wrestling, are taking place. At the entrance to the street that corresponds to the modern Daidosuji (Kishu Highway), a moat and wooden gates, characteristic of Sakai since medieval times, are visible.

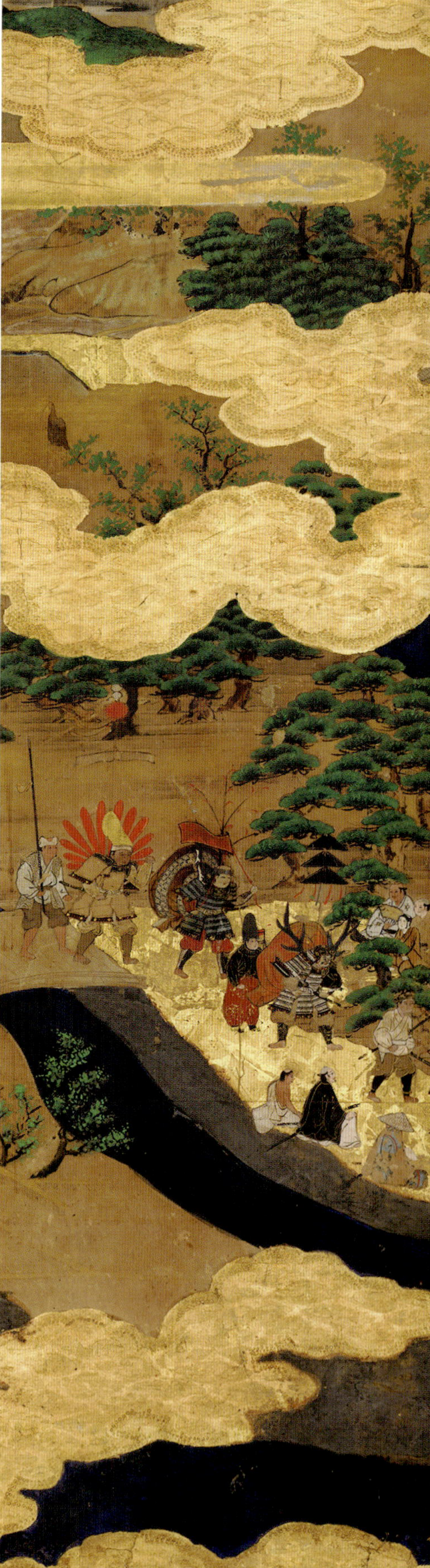

**Detail from "Folding Screen with Sumiyoshi Festival Scene".
Right Panel. Early Edo period, 17th century.**
Sakai City Museum Collection.

281 Kiniro	17 Momijiiro	154 Midori	219 Namakabeiro

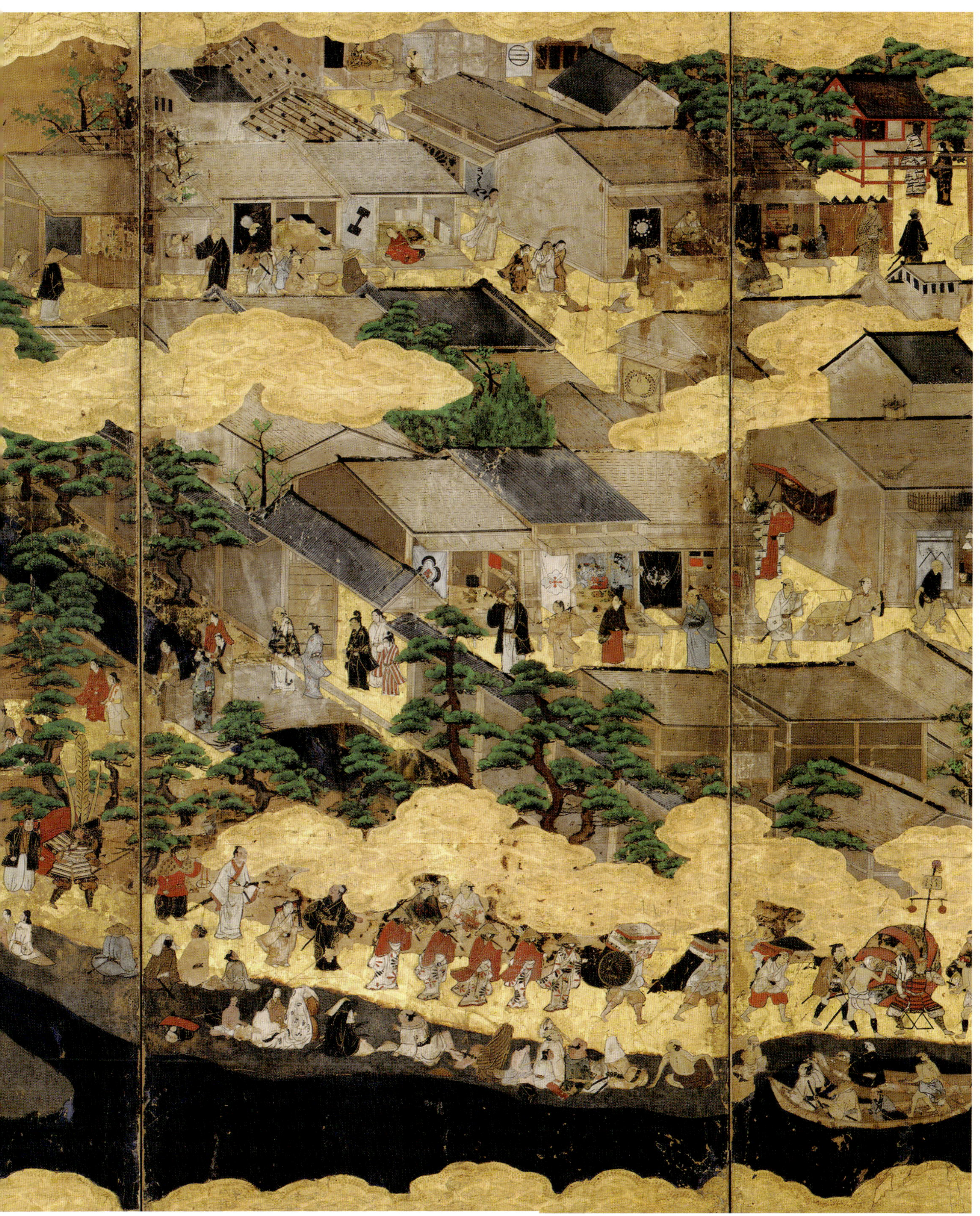

This is lacquerware piece is a *chiribako* with a design of waves and plovers drawn in gold lacquer with lead plates. The gold parts are created using the *maki-e* technique, in which a pattern is drawn with lacquer and then fine gold powder is sprinkled over it to create the design. The use of lead plates between the maki-e waves creates a bold and distinctive accent design. A *jūbako* is a set consisting of an outer box with a handle and inner boxes and was used for activities like flower viewing and autumn leaf viewing.

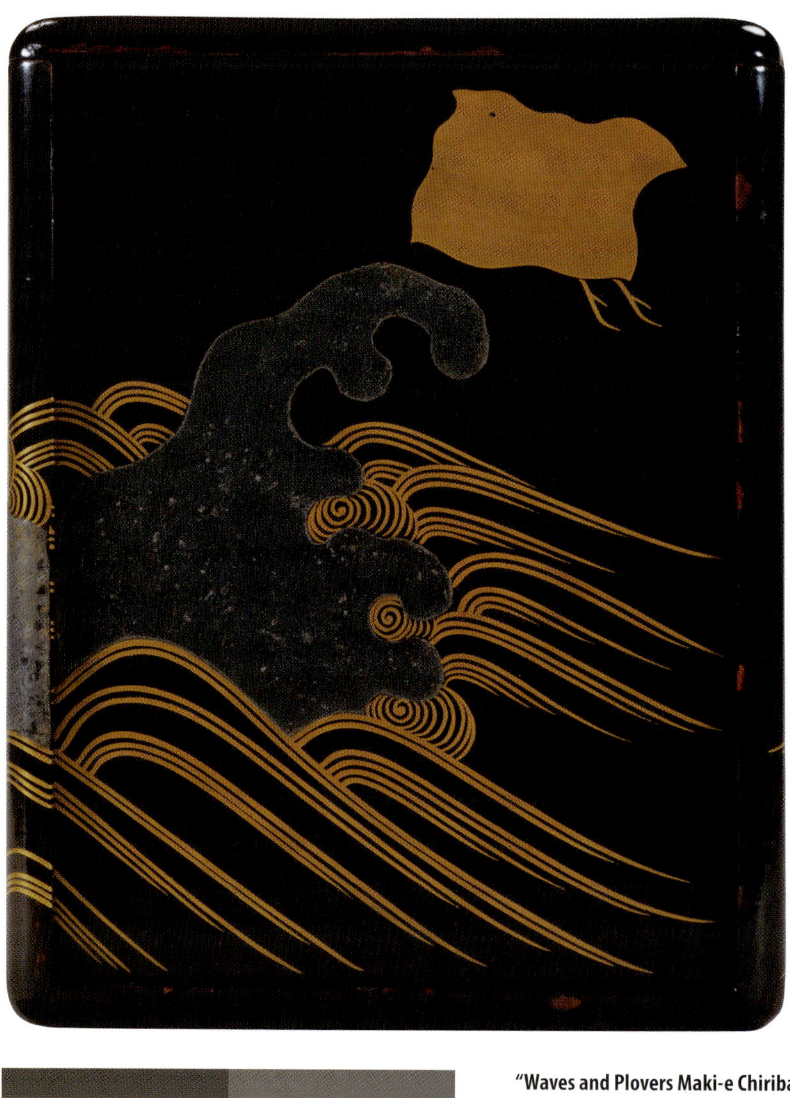

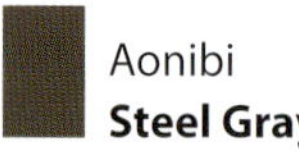
266 Aonibi

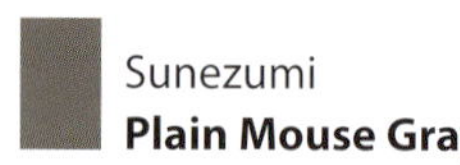
260 Sunezumi

"Waves and Plovers Maki-e Chiribako"
by Nagata Yūji. Edo period, 18th century.
Tokyo National Museum. Source: ColBase: https://colbase.nich.go.jp

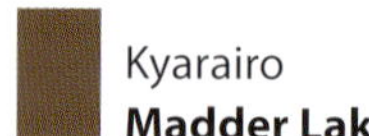

Aonibi
Steel Gray

Sunezumi
Plain Mouse Gray

Kyarairo
Madder Lake

It is used for dark colors. It is created by applying betel nut dye over a base of safflower dye, resulting in a deep gray hue. However, it is often dyed with a base coat using soot and alum mordant, a technique known as "suo hoso" dyeing. This dyeing method was favored for the ground color of luxurious *kosode* from the early Edo period, particularly for Noh costumes.

While "nezumi" generally refers to the color of a mouse's fur, "Sunezumi" is a neutral gray without any particular hue. There are various color names with "nezumi" in them that indicate muted or grayish shades. During the Edo period, many colors with "nezumi" in their names emerged, and the prefix "so" was added to distinguish colors like this one.

A dark yellow-brown color associated with the color of agarwood. The term "kyarairo" comes from the abbreviation of the Sanskrit word "kiyaraagru," where "kiyara" means black and "aagru" refers to agarwood. Agarwood is a highly regarded aromatic wood, especially among those who practice the Way of Incense (Kodo). In the mid-Edo period, this color was also referred to as "Garacha," and there

The design features delicate ripples filling the entire space, and white and gold-painted wagon wheels used on carts are placed here and there, appearing as if they are floating. Wooden wagon wheels were soaked in water to prevent them from drying out and cracking, and this view of the wheels became a motif known as "Kataguruma" (wagon wheels). This box employs two techniques: *maki-e*, in which the motif is painted with lacquer and then gold powder is sprinkled on while still wet, and *raden*, in which the processed insides of shells are flattened and affixed. These techniques rhythmically depict wagon wheel pattern.

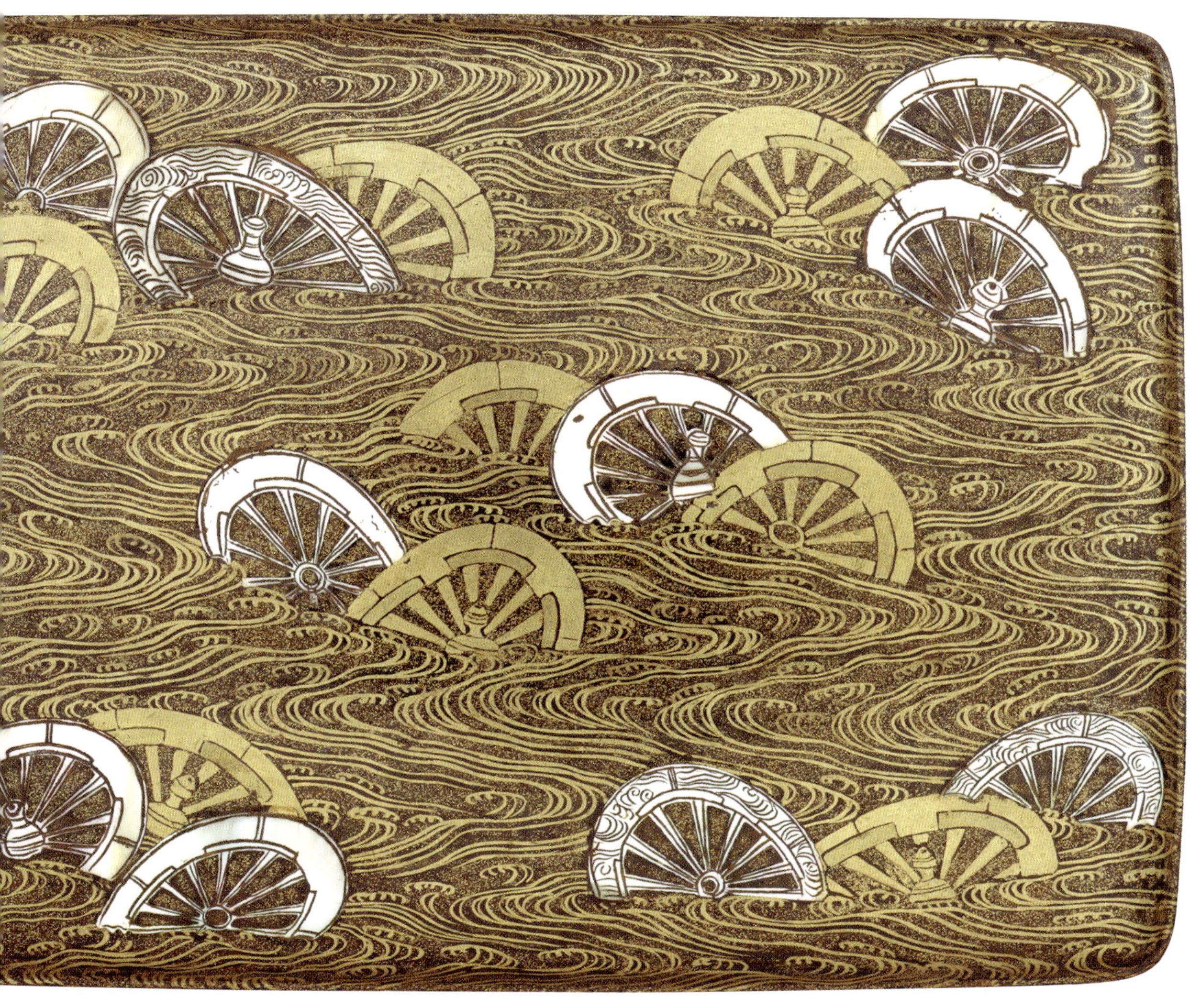

224 Kyarairo	281 Kiniro	283 Hakkin

"Single-wheeled Cart Design Lacquerware Box with Mother-of-Pearl Inlay". National Treasure. Heian period, 12th century.
Tokyo National Museum. Source: ColBase: https://colbase.nich.go.jp

were other color names like "Garasusumi-take" associated with agarwood.

Kiniro
Gold

Gold has been revered in China since the Yin Dynasty and is called "Huangjin," particularly for its reflective shine, representing all metals. Among the five metals, gold represents actual gold, while silver represents white gold, copper represents red gold, iron represents black gold, and lead represents blue gold.

Hakkin
Platinum

It refers to a lustrous silver-white color tinged with gray. Platinum, also known as "Plachina," is a metal harder than silver and possesses excellent ductility and malleability. It is chemically very stable except when exposed to aqua regia, molten alkalies, or cyanide solutions. The origin of the word "platinum" dates back to 1735 when a Spanish naval officer discovered a white metal resembling silver on the banks of the Pinto River in Colombia. It comes from the Spanish "Platina del Pinto," meaning "little silver of the Pinto River."

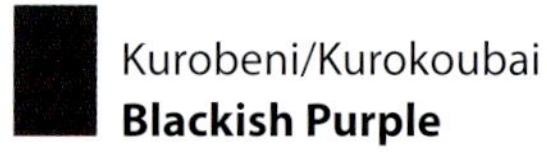

Kurobeni/Kurokoubai
Blackish Purple

A reddish purple-black color or a deep blackish-purple color. It is often used as a base color with red dye underneath, and then a blackish hue is applied using betel nut dye. However, it is frequently created as an under-dye with the use of alum mordant and the dyeing technique called "sufanzome." This dyeing technique was popular for luxurious kimono fabric during the early Edo period and was especially used for Noh costumes.

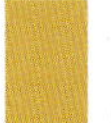

Kiniro
Gold

Refers to a color with the pure luster and brilliance of pure gold. During the Fujiwara period, a temple was built in the first year of the Tenji era (1124) to enshrine three statues of the Fujiwara clan: Kiyohira, Motohira, and Hidehira. The temple's walls were painted with gold leaf, hence it was called the "Kiniro-dō" or "Golden Hall."

Kurenai
Crimson Red

The dye to create this vibrant red color was made with carmine extracted from safflowers. Safflowers, similar to thistles. Originally from Egypt, they were introduced to China around the 4th to 5th century and were said to have been brought to Japan from the southern Wu region.

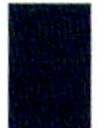

Kon
Dark Blue

This is a deep shade achieved though intensive use of indigo dye. The more intensely dyed a fabric was, the more time and expense it required, and therefore, it was reserved for higher-ranking individuals. The meticulously dyed deep kon was called "superior kon" or "true kon."

A ship with colorful sails, unfurling layer upon layer, sails on the sea with the wind, on a golden ground threaded with gold. This is a Nishiki-ori fabric, combining the auspicious pine motif with the symbol of a ship, created by weaving together patterns of sails. Nishiki-ori originally referred to woven fabrics imported from China, but in Japan, it came to include textiles woven to resemble those, using gold threads, brocades, damasks, and other intricate weaves.

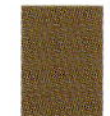

Gofun
Shell White

A white pigment used in Japanese painting that has a slight yellowish tint. It is made by grinding and drying oyster shells. It came into use during the Muromachi period. Before that time white lead was used.

Ginsusutake
Silver Soot Bamboo

Ginsusutake refers to a slightly lighter yellowish-brown color than "Susutake" (soot bamboo) color. The term "ginsu" (silver) is used to indicate a slightly whitish tone, while "kin" (gold) is used to indicate a slightly yellowish tone. Although this color has been noted since the early Edo period, various bamboo soot shades started to appear around the Genroku era, and it is likely that this shade was among them. It is said to have been favored by the Lord of Kii Province, hence it's also called "Kishu tea," and it is said that Sen no So'oku, the founder of the Urasenke school of tea ceremony, also favored this color.

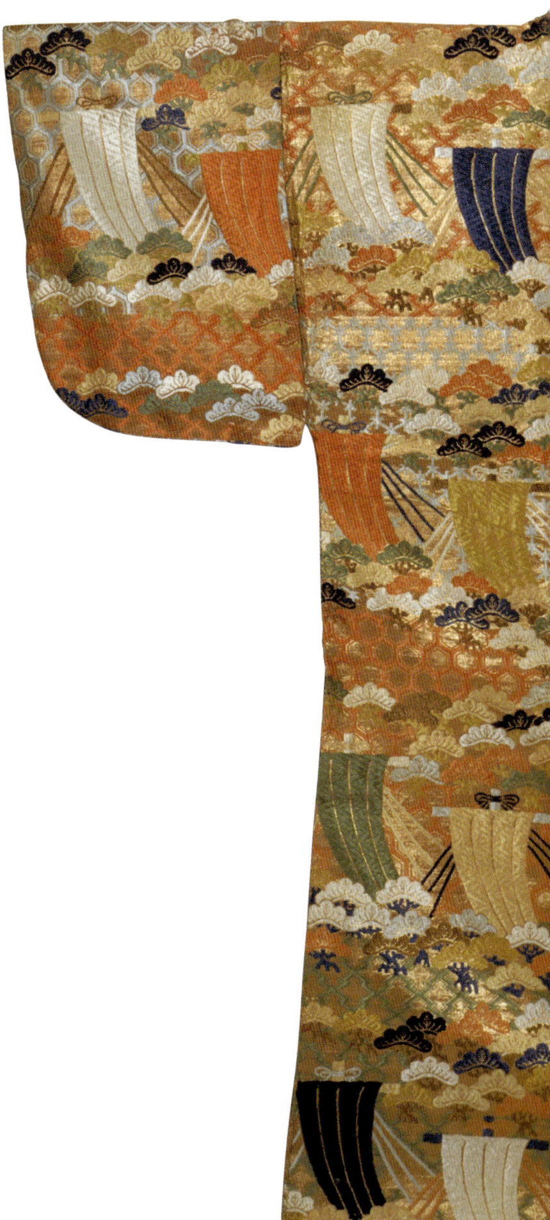

Gold Background with Pine and Sail Pattern in Karafuto Weave". Edo period, 18th century.
Tokyo National Museum.
Source: ColBase at https://colbase.nich.go.jp

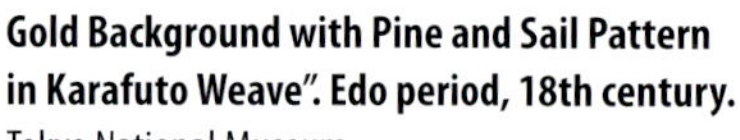

114 Kon　　　　**252 Gofun**　　　　**223 Ginsusutake**

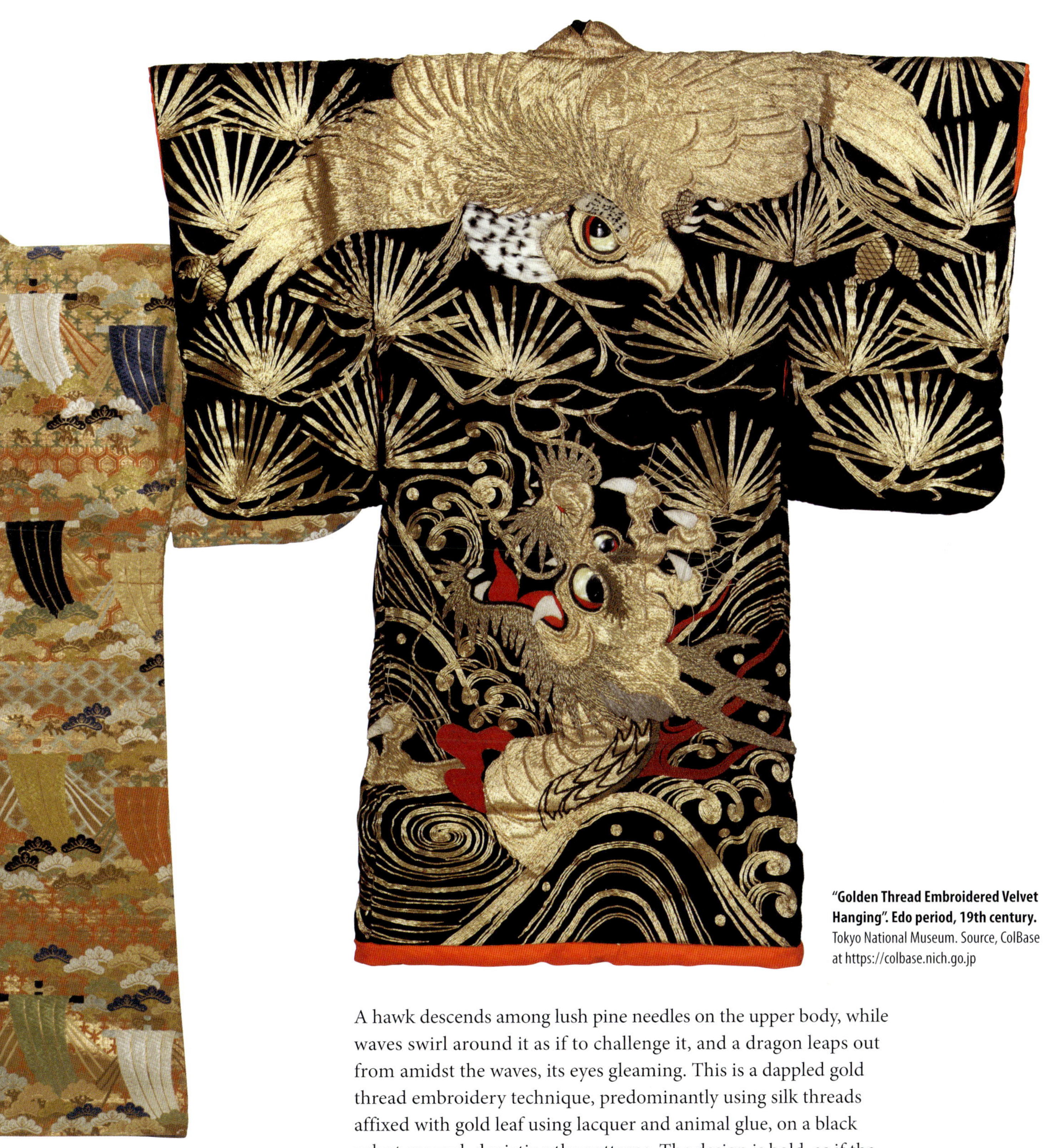

"Golden Thread Embroidered Velvet Hanging". Edo period, 19th century.
Tokyo National Museum. Source, ColBase at https://colbase.nich.go.jp

A hawk descends among lush pine needles on the upper body, while waves swirl around it as if to challenge it, and a dragon leaps out from amidst the waves, its eyes gleaming. This is a dappled gold thread embroidery technique, predominantly using silk threads affixed with gold leaf using lacquer and animal glue, on a black velvet ground, depicting the patterns. The design is bold, as if the two entities are about to spring into action. This is said to be a *dōfurisode* worn by the fashionable women of the late Edo period.

270 Kurobeni/Kurokoubai   281 Kiniro   18 Kurenai

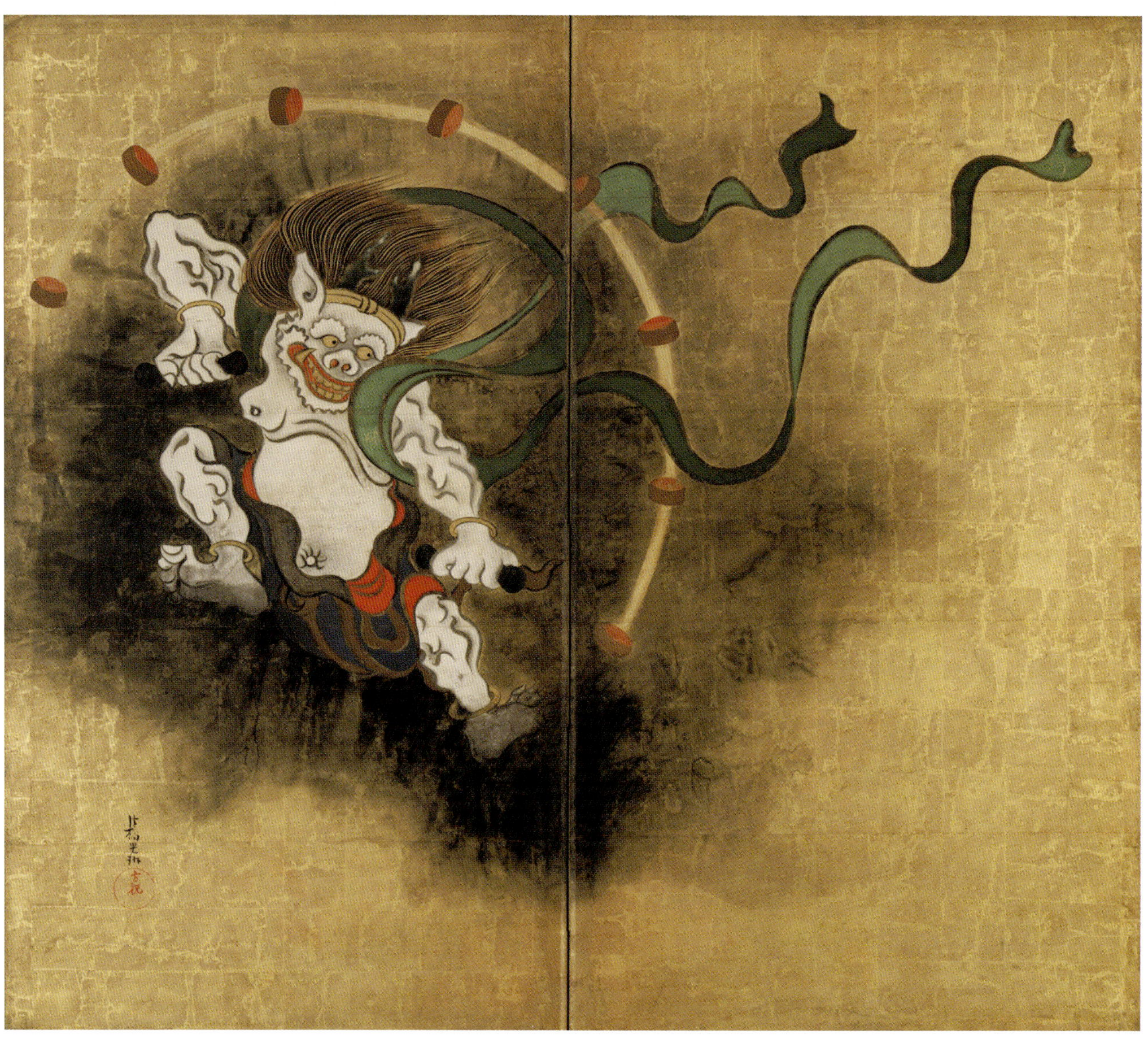

"Wind God and Thunder God Folding Screen" (Important Cultural Property) by Ōgata Kōrin. Edo period, 18th century. Tokyo National Museum.

The Elegant Colors of the Rinpa School

The Rinpa school is represented by the painter Ogata Kōrin, with "rin" coming from Kōrin. Previously, it had been referred to as the Sōtatsu-Kōrin school or the Kōrin school, but after the late 1940s, Rinpa became the more common term.

Established by Tawaraya Sōtatsu and Hon'ami Kōetsu in the early Edo period, developed by the brothers Ogata Kōrin and Ogata Kenzan in the mid-period, and established in Edo by Sakai Hōitsu and Suzuki Kiitsu.

Its characteristics are based on the tradition of Yamato-e, seeking decoration and design beauty using brilliant colors, gold and silver leaf, and skilfully incorporating silver leaf. Its art was embraced and developed by nobles, lords, and commoners alike, exerting a significant influence on the world of modern Japanese painting and craft design.

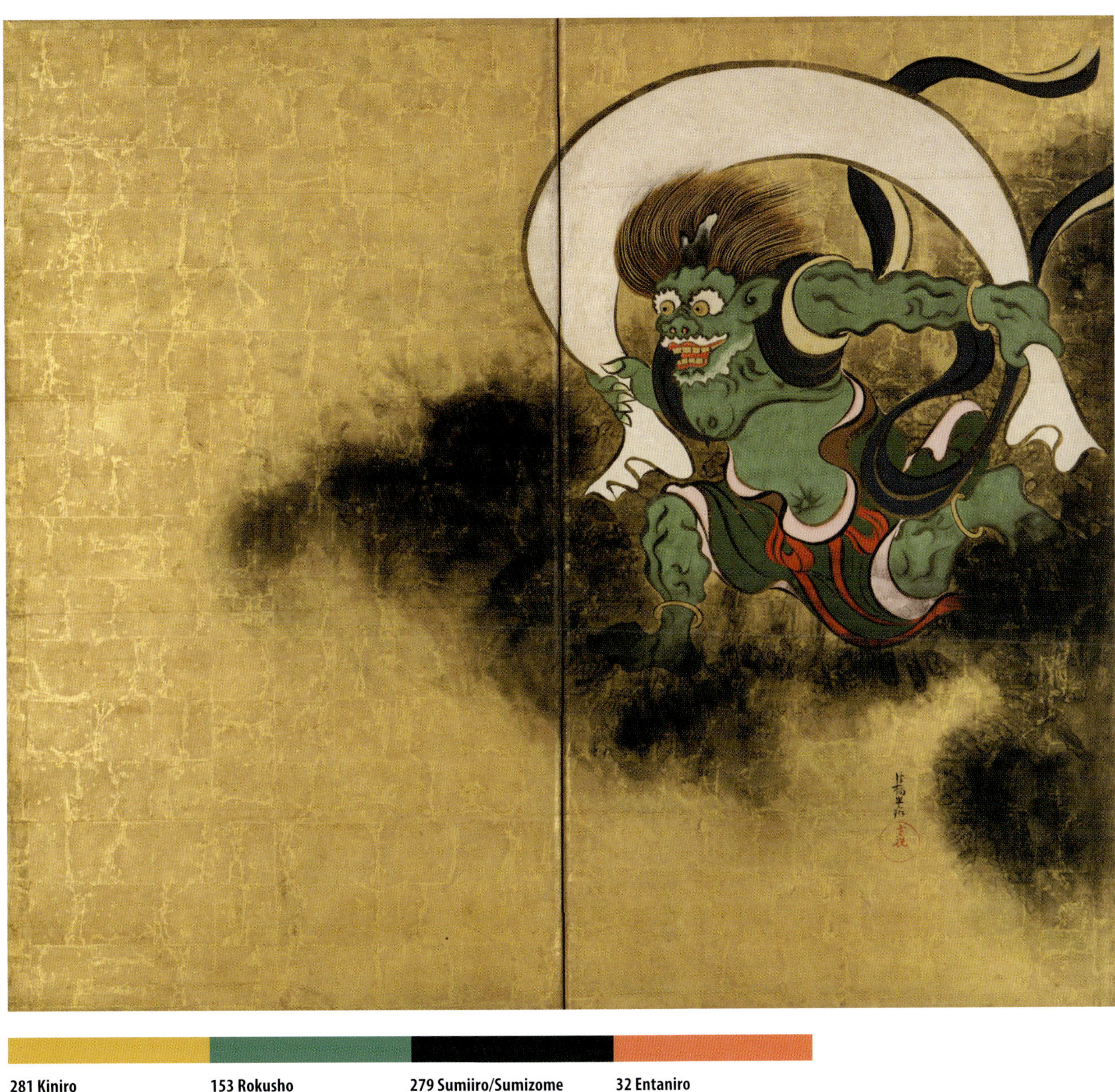

281 Kiniro   153 Rokusho   279 Sumiiro/Sumizome   32 Entaniro

One of the differences from other schools is that Rinpa artists were not official painters of the shogunate or the imperial court, such as those of the Kano and Tosa schools. Furthermore, they did not have a hereditary system, and their connections were based solely on personal relationships over time.

In a pair of folding screens with a golden background, the Wind God and Thunder God fly together among the clouds. The Wind God is depicted on the right, and the Thunder God on the left. Ink-smeared rain clouds are arranged to create a sense of depth in space, while also highlighting the distinct figures of the Wind God and Thunder God.

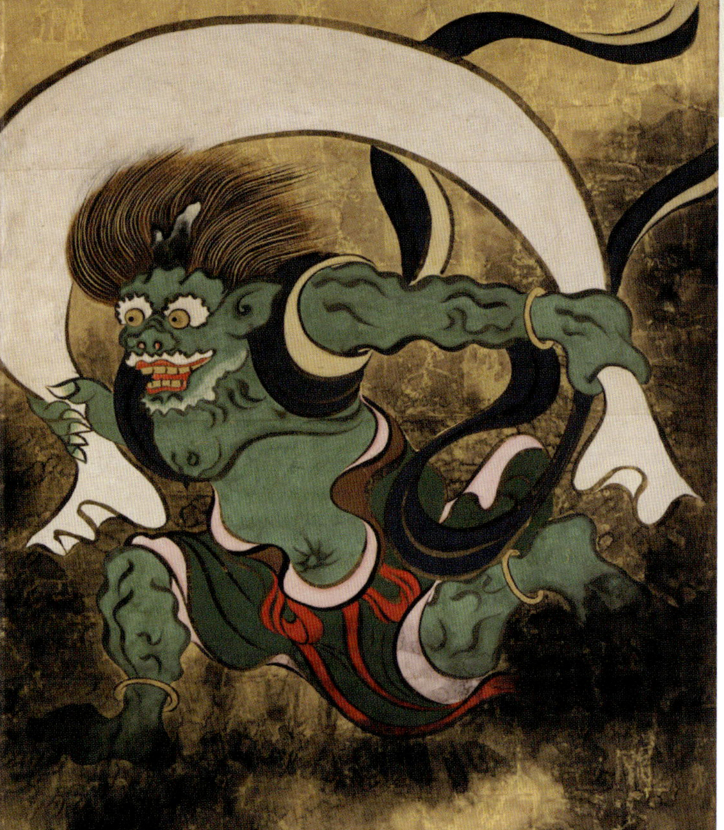

Detail from "Wind God and Thunder God Screen Folding Screen" by Ōgata Kōrin.
Tokyo National Museum. Source: ColBase at https://colbase.nich.go.jp

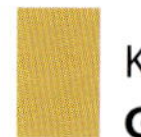

Kiniro
Gold

Gold has symbolized eternity and an unparalleled spiritual world in the realm of Buddhism since ancient times. Marco Polo praised Japan as the "Golden Country," and during the Azuchi-Momoyama period, figures like Toyotomi Hideyoshi created tea rooms adorned with gold leaf, making gold an indispensable color of that era.

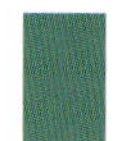

Rokusho
Malachite Green

A slightly bluish, subdued green color. Malachite is one of the green pigments used in Japanese painting, specifically known as "Iwa-ryokusho" or malachite green. Natural malachite, primarily composed of copper carbonate and copper hydroxide, is crushed into a powder, mixed with water, vigorously ground, and the dark green sediment at the bottom is called "ryokusho." The fine particles that float to the top are called "byakuroku," and the coarse particles that accumulate in the middle are called "nakagreen."

Sumiiro/Sumizome
Ink Black

Sumiiro, generally referred to as "ink black," represents the blackest shade among the five gradations of ink intensity: *koge* (burnt), *koi* (thick), *omo* (heavy), *awa* (light), and *sei* (clear). It is said to have been introduced to Japan during the reign of Empress Suiko in the 7th century when a Korean monk named Doncho brought paper and ink to the country. It is believed that the technique was transmitted even earlier.

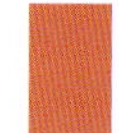

Entaniro
Vermilion Red

A bright orange color made from lead oxide. In ancient times, vermilion was highly favored, second only to red. It is a pigment made by adding sulfur and saltpeter to lead and then roasting it. Vermilion was used as an undercoat for various structures, including temples and shrines, due to its rust-preventing properties and the reverence for the color red.

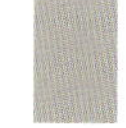

Giniro
Silver

Used for a bright gray color resembling silver. Gold and silver can produce a wide range of subtle shades through alloying. While in the Western tradition, silver objects are polished to maintain their shine, in Japan, a subdued, tarnished silver color was preferred, reflecting a unique sense of aesthetics.

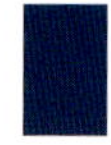

Rurikon
Lapis Lazuli Blue

A deep blue color with a hint of lapis lazuli. This traditional color name is found in scriptures, representing various elements, including the hair of deities and the land of the Buddha. It is said that Rurikon became popular in Edo for both men's and women's kimono during the Enpo-Tenna (1673–84) and Meiwa (1764–72) periods.

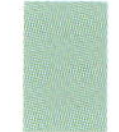

Byakuroku
Pale Green

A light green color with a hint of white. In Japanese painting, it refers to "Iwa-ryokusho" (malachite green), a green pigment made by grinding malachite, a mineral, into a powder and mixing it with water. The term "haku" means pale or light.

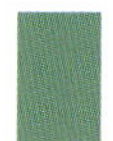

Wakatakeiro
Fresh Bamboo Green

Refers to a fresh, vibrant green color resembling the young shoots of bamboo. It is considered the opposite of "Rochikuiro" (elder bamboo color). As the color deepens, it becomes "Aotakeiro" (blue bamboo color), and when it takes on a dull greenish tone, it becomes "Rochikuiro." Bamboo, which thrives throughout the four seasons in China and grows straight and upright, has been regarded as a plant representing an unworldly and virtuous gentleman.

On the right panel, the Wind God, holding a windbag, is depicted in malachite green, while on the left panel, the Thunder God, descending energetically, is captured in shell white. This artwork faithfully traces the National Treasure "Wind God and Thunder God Screen" painted by Tawaraya Sotatsu. The Wind God governs the wind and was known as the "Feng Bo" in ancient China, while the Thunder God, deifying thunder and lightning, is the deity responsible for creating thunderstorms It's worth noting that on the reverse side of this artwork, Sakuai Hotokei added the "Summer and Autumn Grasses Screen." To preserve the artwork, the front and back were separated, and they are now displayed as separate screens.

This artwork is a reproduction of Sakai Hōitsu's "Summer and Autumn Grasses" screen, which was painted as part of the interior decoration for the Phoenix Hall erected at the 1893 Chicago World's Columbian Exposition. Doi Ichii (1846–1913) was a Japanese painter of the Meiji era and the second son of Yamamoto Sodō. He studied the Rinpa painting style under Suzuki Kiitsu and was deeply influenced by Hōitsu's artistic style, eventually becoming the adopted son of Sakai Uguisu. The "Summer and Autumn Grasses" screen was later added by Hōitsu to the reverse side of Kōrin's "Wind God and Thunder God" screen. It depicts various summer and autumn flowers and grasses on a silvery ground, reminiscent of moonlight, rendered in refreshing colors.

"Folding Screen with Summer Grasses" by Sakai Dōitsui, 1893. Tokyo National Museum. Source: ColBase at https://colbase.nich.go.jp

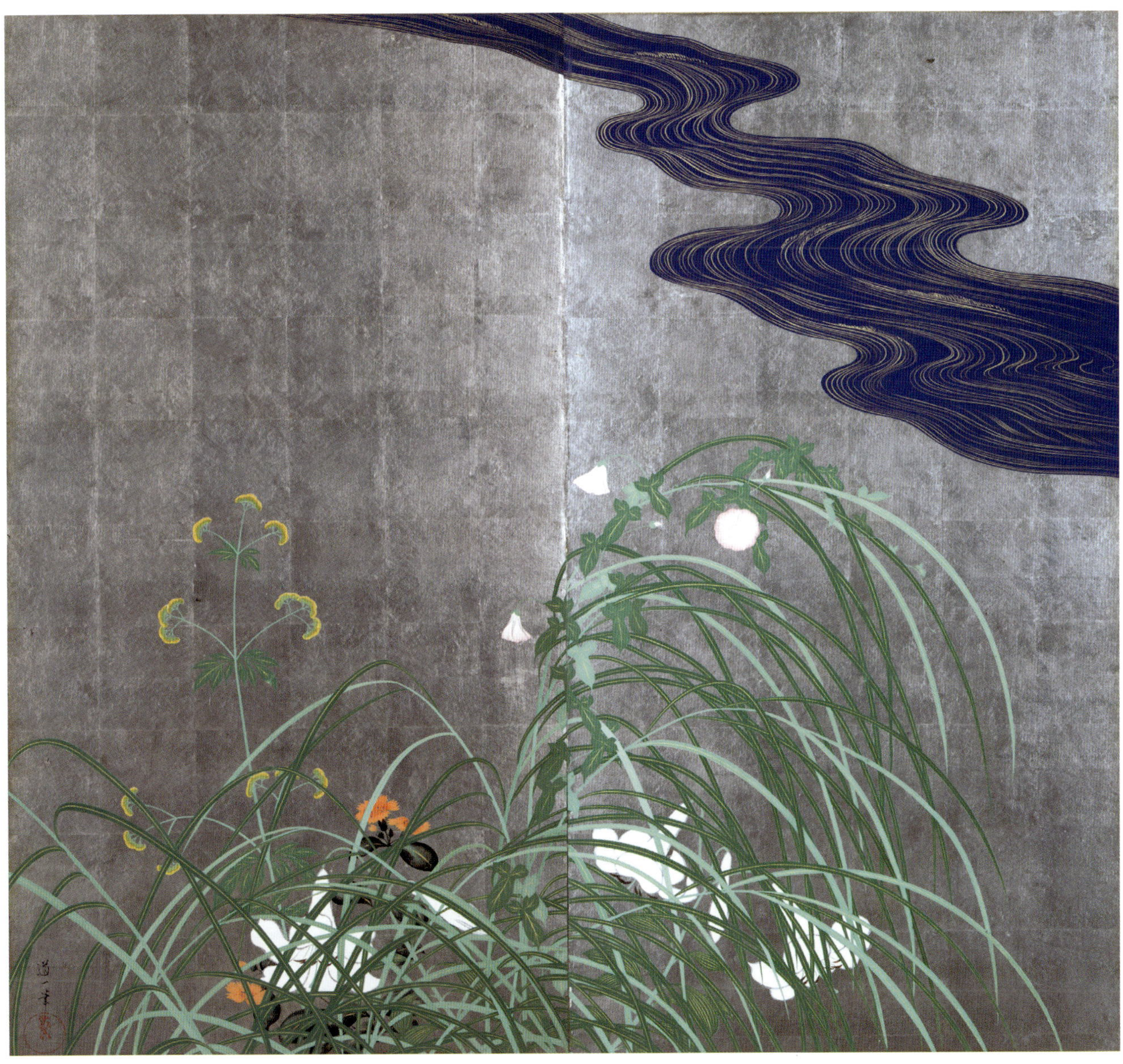

| 282 Giniro | 112 Rurikon | 145 Byakuroku | 147 Wakatakeiro |

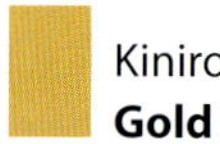 Kiniro
Gold

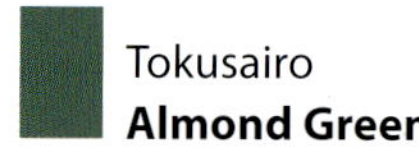 Ruriiro
Bright Lapis Lazuli Blue

Tokusairo
Almond Green

Gold, which reflects even the slightest light and catches the human eye, is sometimes referred to as "yamabuki" (a type of yellow flower). Additionally, brownish hues with a golden tint are called "kinaka" or "kincha." Gold, with its everlasting brilliance similar to the sunlight, was desired by those in power for the aspiration of attaining Buddhahood in the Pure Land in the afterlife. They built temples and lavishly adorned them with gold leaf.

This is a vivid blue color achieved by grinding the laps lazuli stone itself or by adding a small amount of cobalt oxide to a feldspar glaze, which has been said to have medicinal properties even though it contains indigo dye. Lapis lazuli was primarily sourced from Persia. In Europe, it was transported by sea from Afghanistan, so blue pigments made from lapis lazuli were called "ultramarine," which means "beyond the sea."

A dark green color reminiscent of the stems of horsetail plants. It is also known as "Kagemoe-gi." Horsetail is a perennial evergreen fern, and its stems are hard and rough due to the presence of silica, making them suitable for polishing surfaces like wood. As a color for garments, it is associated with combinations such as "front: black-blue, back: white" and "front: fresh yellow-green, back: white."

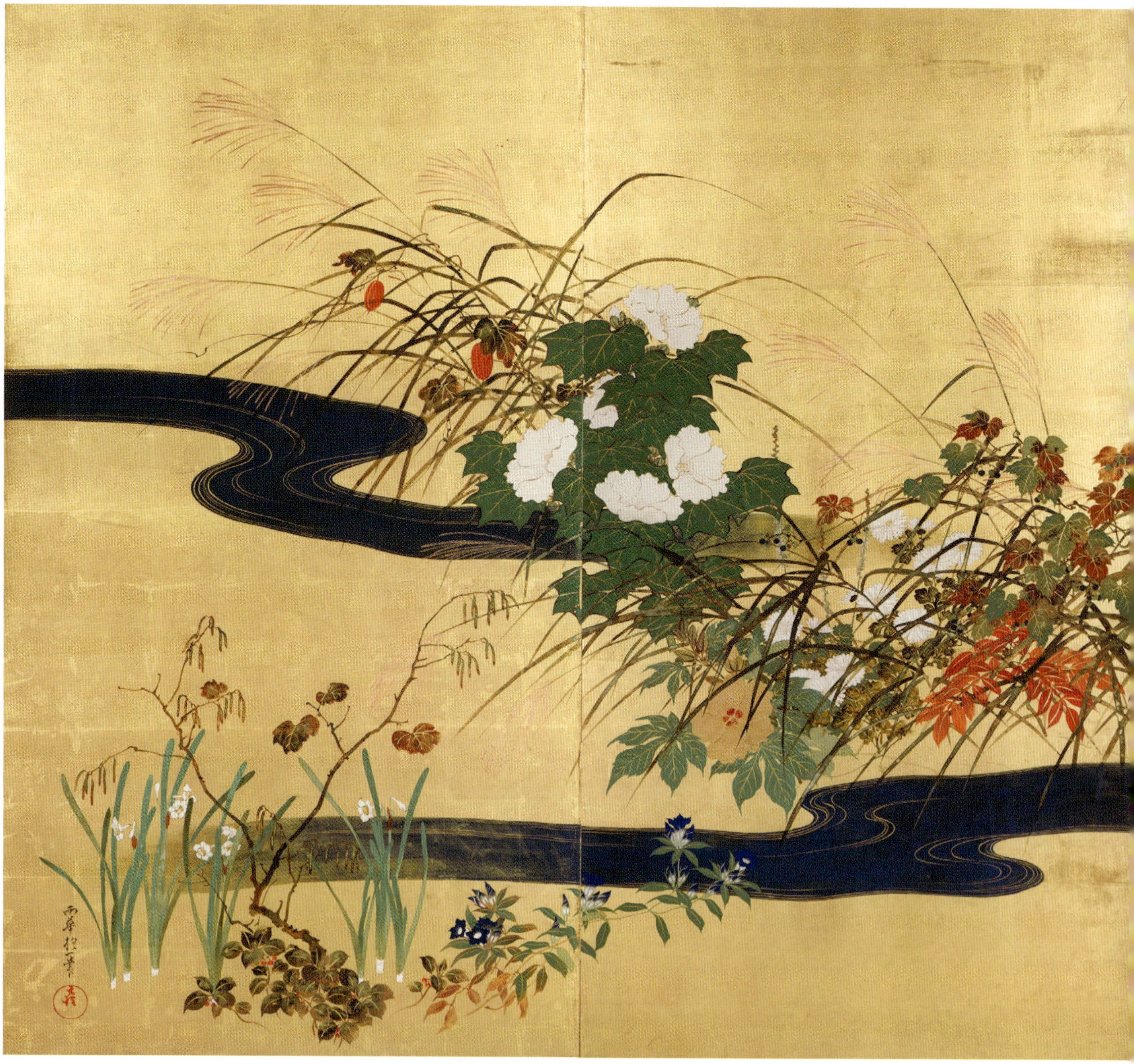

| 281 Kiniro | 111 Ruriiro | 155 Tokusairo | 11 Tsutsujiiro |

This color name is derived from the color of azalea flowers and represents the bright red hue with a hint of purple found in their petals. It is one of the traditional colors in the red-purple category, along with peony color. This color name has been in use since the Heian period, and it is associated with seasonal use, particularly from spring to early summer, with combinations such as "front: red plum, back: blue" and "front: red plum blossom, back: blue."

On the right side of the gold-leafed folding screen, a deep navy blue stream flow leisurely from right to left. Seasonal flowers and grasses generously showcase their splendor. White peonies and white lilies bloom at the base, along with scarlet hollyhocks with their blue petals. The ivy leaves entwining around the pampas grass are adorned with colorful autumn foliage, swaying gracefully in the breeze. In the lower left corner, a modest bellflower with its bluish-purple blossoms quietly awaits attention. This folding screen provides a delightful visual experience of the serene beauty of each season.

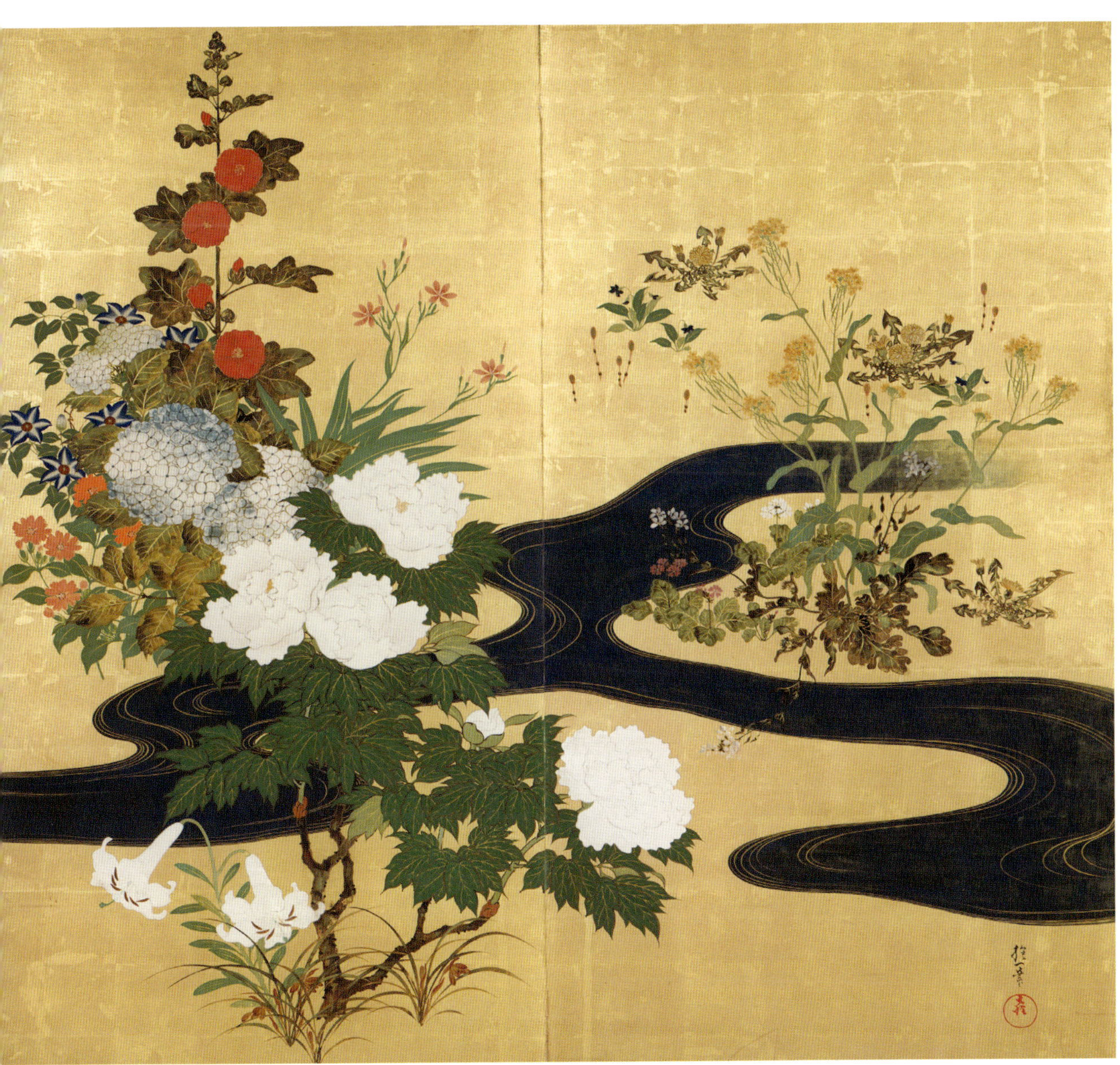

"Folding Screen with Flowing Water and Four Seasons Plants and Flowers" by Sakai Hōitsu. Edo period, 19th century. Tokyo National Museum. Source: ColBase at https://colbase.nich.go.jp

The Mystical Colors in Sumi-e Ink Painting

Sumi-e, or ink wash painting, is a unique form of Eastern painting born in China during the Tang Dynasty (9th century). It was introduced to Japan along with Zen Buddhist philosophy around the late Kamakura period (13th to 14th centuries), with influences on our country's spiritual culture and art world that are immeasurable, shaping significant developments in painting history since the Middle Ages.

Sumi-e is not just a realistic technique; it arrived as a fully developed painting form encompassing subjects, compositions, and techniques. Its expressive style, capturing the forms of objects through the gradation and blending of ink without the use of color, revolutionized the traditional line drawing methods, creating a different realm of sculptural expression.

During the tumultuous Warring States period, ink wash painting, previously confined to Zen temples, spread throughout Japan thanks to disciples of Sesshu and warrior-painters. This era marked a transition from Zen-inspired themes to more colorful subjects like landscapes and birds-and-flowers paintings, seamlessly integrating sumi-e into Japanese culture.

Representative works of sumi-e from this period include Tōhaku Hasegawa's "Pine Forest Folding Screen," symbolizing the emergence of genuine sumi-e capable of rivaling Chinese art in both subject matter and skill.

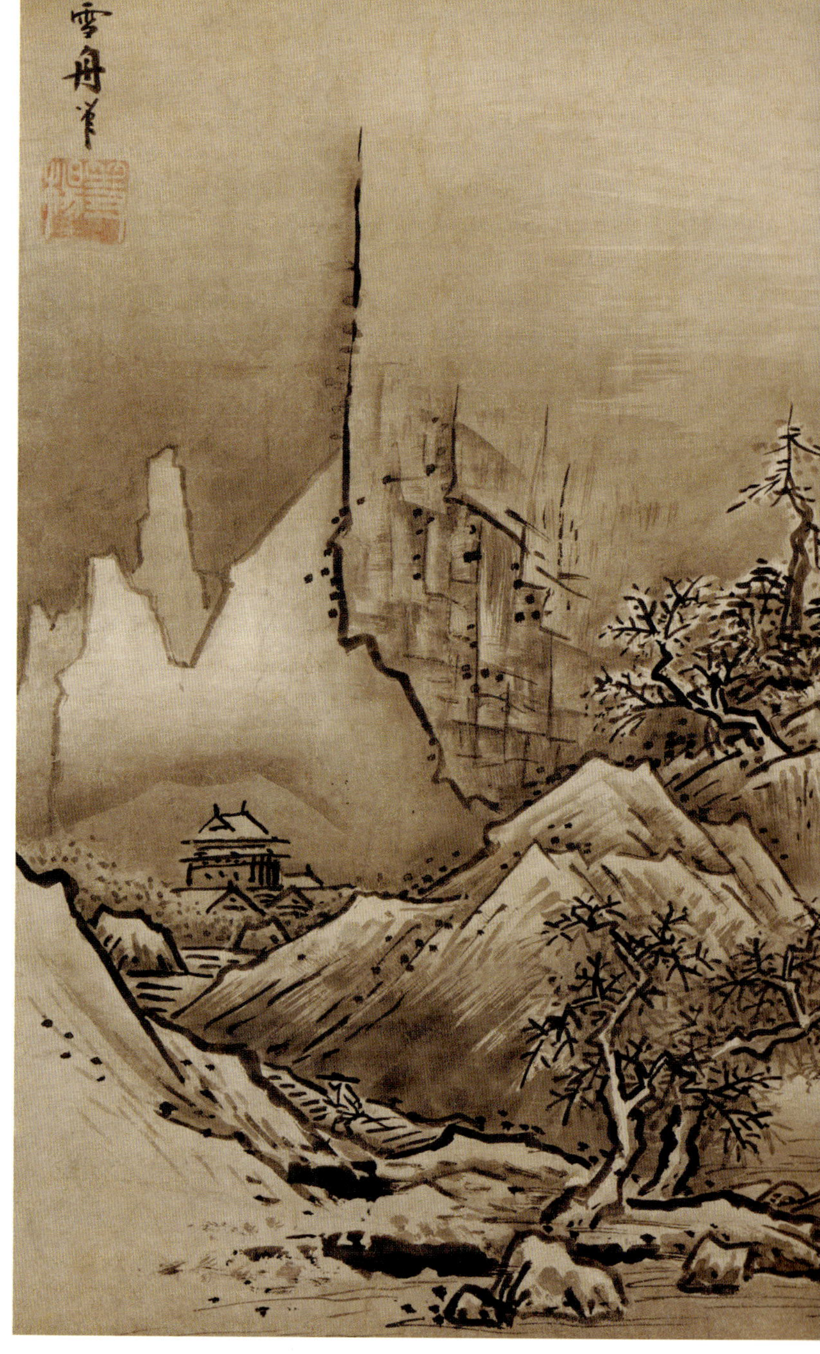

| 220 Kobicha | 262 Namariiro | 265 Umenezu/Umenezumi |

The dynamic and powerful brushwork in the landscape on the right-side panel is refreshingly light yet profound. The supple yet powerful brushwork seems effortlessly executed. The horizon of the pavilions merges with the surroundings without any conflict with nature. The vertical cliff on the left panel displays a confident brushwork, as if representing the will of heaven to find a pure world here. The figure walking on the snowy path toward the pavilion appears to depict Sesshū himself in the pursuit of enlightenment.

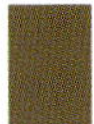

Kobicha
Flattering Brown

Kobicha is a rich brown color with a slight yellowish tint. The traditional dyeing method involves using a solution made from the bark of bayberry trees and dyeing the fabric with iron mordant. It became one of the prevalent colors in the Edo period, resulting from the creation of various intermediate shades between brown and grayish hues, and it is said to have gained popularity throughout Edo around the Tenpō era (1830–1844).

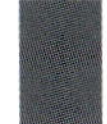

Namariiro
Lead Gray

This is a grayish color with a bluish tint, similar to the color of lead metal. While the color name originally referred to a bright gray color with metallic luster, it came to denote a rusted or tarnished shade. This color is used to depict overcast skies, heavy and somber atmospheres, such as impending rain or gloomy sea conditions, due to its dark and weighty impression.

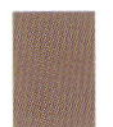

Umenezu/Umenezumi
Plum Mouse Gray

A gray color with a reddish tint, reminiscent of the color of red plum blossoms, it gets its name from the combination of "ume" (plum) and "nezumi" (mouse). It's color born from plum dyeing. It is one of the Forty-eight Tea Hundred Mouse shades of the Edo period, representing a slightly darker reddish-gray compared to "Sakuranezumi" (cherry blossom gray). "Mousy" shades were fashionable, emphasizing various combinations of soft grays and pinks.

Mirucha
Sea Pine Tea

A dark olive color created by adding brown to the original color of "Mirucha" (seaweed green). It was widely used for dyeing during the Edo period. Variations include "Sumirucha" (plain seaweed tea) for colors closer to the original "Umimatsu," and "Kimirucha" (yellow seaweed tea) for those with a slightly yellowish hue. The dyeing process involves using bayberry bark with alum and iron mordant, as mentioned in the *Kon'ya Chazome Kuchiden-sho*.

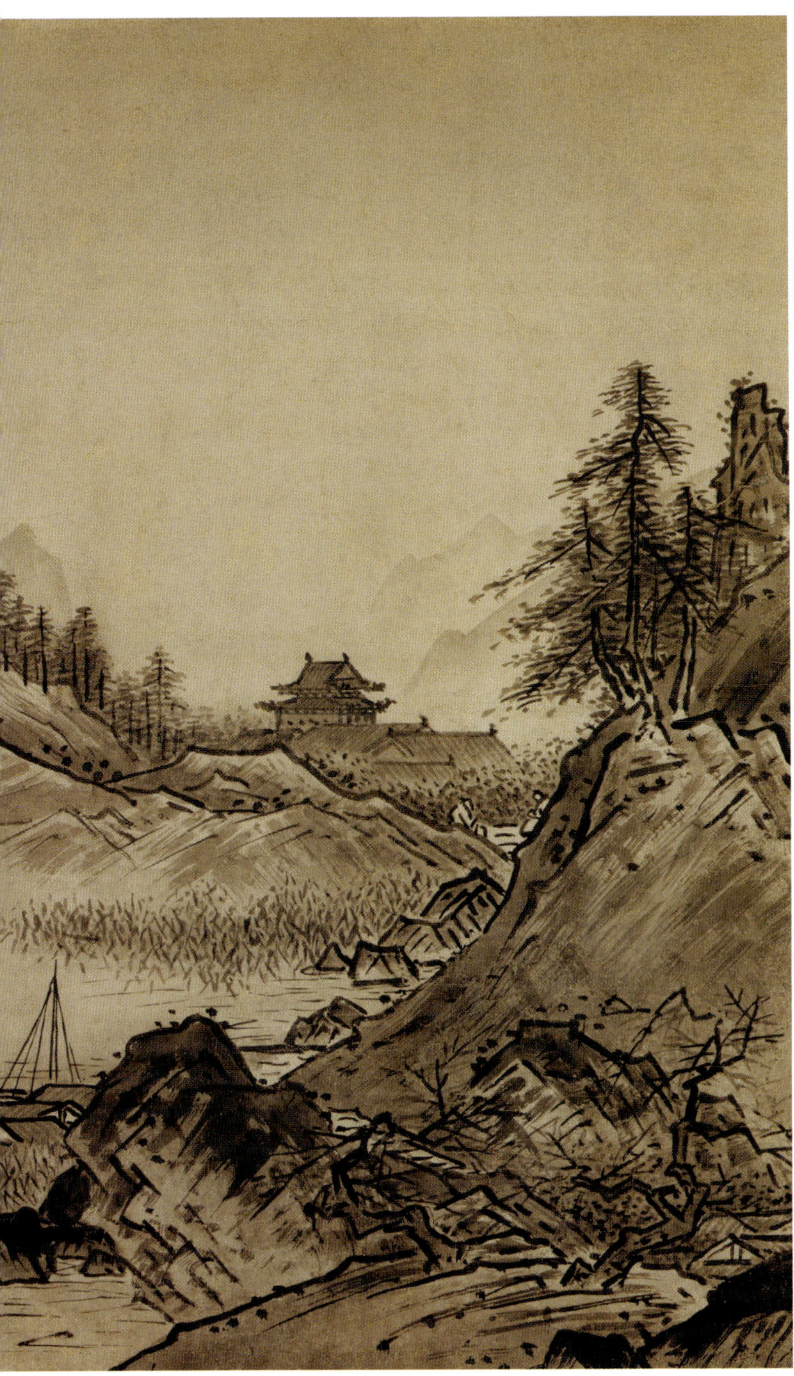

211 Mirucha

"Autumn and Winter Landscape" by Sesshū Tōyō. Muromachi period, late 15th to early 16th century. Tokyo National Museum.
Source: ColBase at https://colbase.nich.go.jp

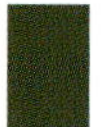

Matsubairo
Pine Needle Green

A deep yellow-green color resembling pine needles. This color, along with "Aotake" (blue bamboo), is commonly associated with green. Pine trees have long been regarded as sacred due to their evergreen beauty, symbolizing the divine and eternal. The name "Matsuba-nezumi" is used to describe a greenish-gray color, comparing it to the color of pine needles. "Tokiwairo" (eternal green) has also been a traditional color name associated with pine trees since the Heian period.

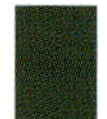

Chitose-midori
Millennial Green

A dark, intense green color reminiscent of pine, which bears green leaves that never change amidst the changing seasons, symbolizes longevity and constancy. "Chitose-midori" symbolizes an unchanging green even after a thousand years, conveying auspiciousness. It is thought to be dyed by combining the colors of *tade-ai* (madder and indigo). It is a derivative color of "Senzai-midori," and there are variations like "Satocha" and "Sensaicha."

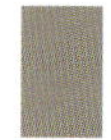

Nezumiiro
Mouse Gray

Refers to a pale blackish-gray color with a bluish tint, resembling the color of mouse fur. This gray is often considered a neutral color, During the Edo period, many color names emerged in association with gray, which led to the term "Suzunezumi" (plain gray) to distinguish it from other shades of gray.

Akuiro
Lye Gray

Lye gray has a light yellowish undertone, resembling the color of lye soap. Lye has been traditionally used for mordant dyeing, fabric bleaching, and washing. Lye is created by soaking ash, obtained from burning straw or wood, in water. While clear lye is achieved through multiple filtrations, lye gray is the term for the initially refined cloudy color. Although similar to "Haiiro" (gray), the latter refers to a slightly brighter tone resulting from the complete combustion of straw or wood.

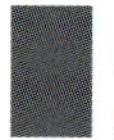

Haiiro
Gray

Gray is a neutral color that falls between white and black, belonging to the category of achromatic colors. It resembles the light black color left behind after the complete combustion of wood or straw.

This scene of a pine forest enveloped in morning mist is vividly depicted with energetic brushstrokes and varying shades of ink, creating a richly poetic atmosphere. While the composition presents a horizontal arrangement of pines, each meticulously portrayed, the pines in the foreground stand majestically while those depicted more faintly in the background create a sense of depth within the mist. The faintly visible snow-capped mountain in the upper center of the left and right folding screens enhances the sense of boundless depth in the space. Departing from the conceptual ink painting techniques of Zen forests and avoiding strict adherence to Chinese painting conventions, the artist portrays familiar subjects with a fresh perspective, evoking a simple yet profound resonance. The clusters of pine needles are depicted with coarse brushstrokes of a straw brush, while the bold strokes of dense ink lifting up the foreground pines convey a sense of dynamism amidst the overall serene imagery.

"Pine Forest Folding Screen" (National Treasure) by Hasegawa Tōhaku.
Azuchi-Momoyama period, 16th century.
Tokyo National Museum. Source: ColBase at https://colbase.nich.go.jp

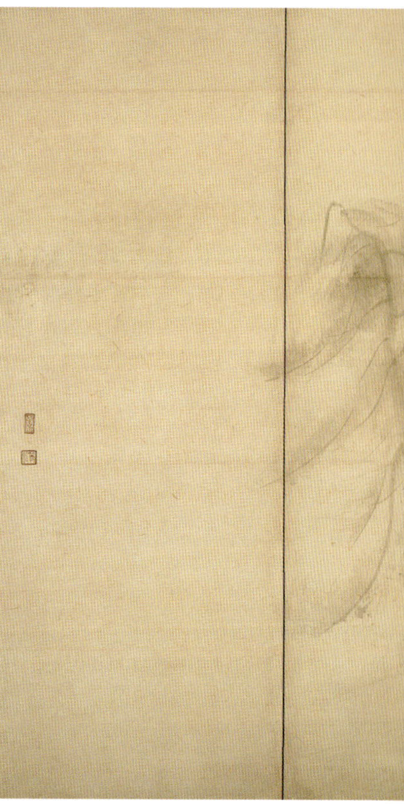

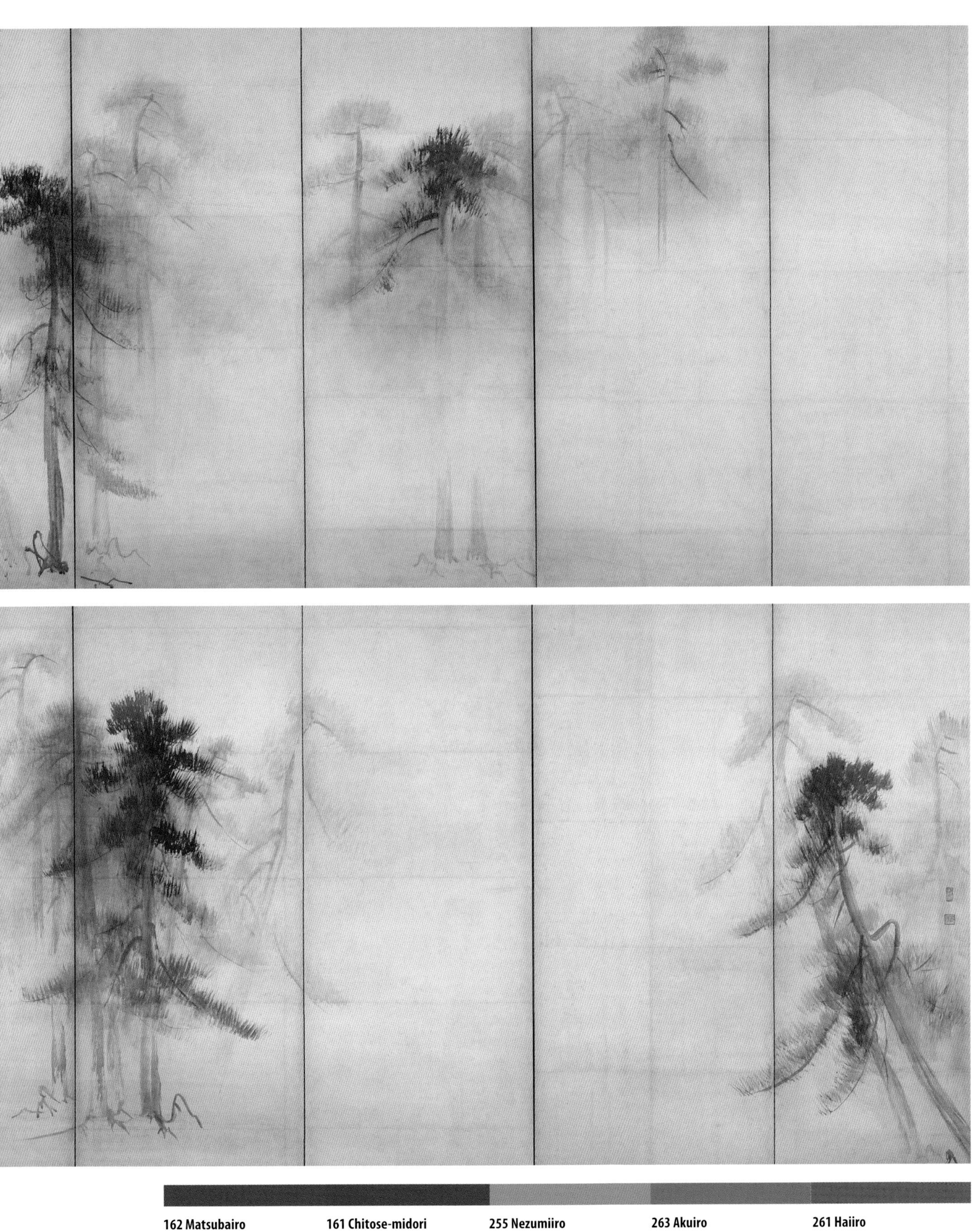

162 Matsubairo
161 Chitose-midori
255 Nezumiiro
263 Akuiro
261 Haiiro

Colors in the
Red Spectrum

This color charter utilizes Western nomenclature. The color sample numerical data is listed in the order; of Munsell values, CMYK values, RGB values, and HEX values (web color values).

1. Cherry Blossom
10RP 9 / 2
C0 M17 Y6 K0
R254 G223 B225
#FEDFE1

2. Old Rose
10RP 8.5 / 4
C0 M31 Y9 K0
R248 G195 B205
#F8C3CD

3. Silver Pink
5R 7.5 / 2
C2 M12 Y12 K10
R215 G196 B187
#D7C4BB

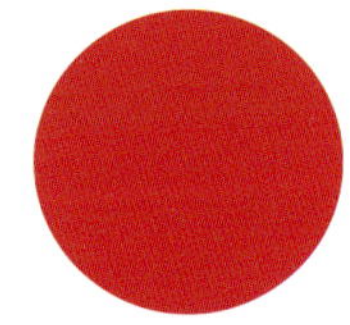

4. Silver Pink
2.5R 6.5 / 2
C34 M46 Y39 K0
R177 G150 B147
#B19693

5. Pink
2.5R 7.5 / 6
C2 M45 Y27 K0
R238 G169 B169
#EEA9A9

6. Baby Pink
7.5RP 7.5 / 6
C0 M48 Y15 K0
R244 G167 B185
#F4A7B9

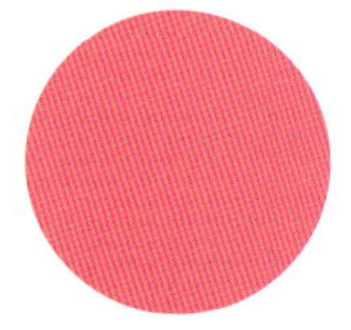

7. Fuchsia Pink
7.5RP 7 / 8.5
C0 M55 Y19 K0
R245 G150 B170
#F596A

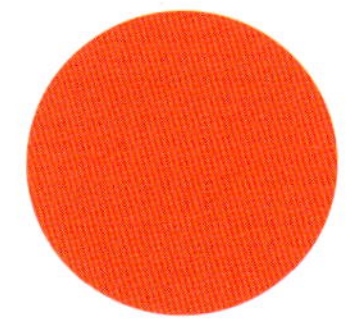

8. Pink
5.5RP 7 / 6
C2 M43 Y3 K0
R220 G159 B180
#DC9FB4

9. Lotus Pink
10RP 8 / 4
C10 M60 Y10 K0
R222 G130 B167
#DE82A7

10. Camellia
10RP 5 / 12
C10 M80 Y40 K0
R218 G83 B110
#DA536E

11. Azalea Pink
7RP 5 / 13
C0 M80 Y3 K0
R224 G60 B138
#E03C8A

12. Peony Purple
3.5RP 4.5 / 11
C25 M91 Y8 K0
R193 G50 B142
#C1328E

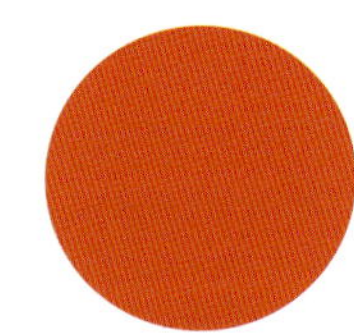

13. Rose Pink
10RP 6.5 / 10
C0 M64 Y26 K0
R232 G122 B144
#E87A90

14. Orchid Pink
7.5RP 6 / 10
C0 M73 Y24 K0
R225 G107 B140
#E16B8C

15. Cherry Pink
7.5RP 5 / 12
C5 M83 Y40 K0
R219 G77 B109
#DB4D6D

16. Poppy Red
7.5R 5 / 14
C0 M89 Y79 K0
R232 G48 B21
#E83015

17. Bright Red
4.6R 2.8 / 4.3
C0 M86 Y90 K5
R226 G66 B31
#E2421F

18. Carmine
3R 4 / 14
C0 M100 Y65 K10
R203 G27 B69
#CB1B45

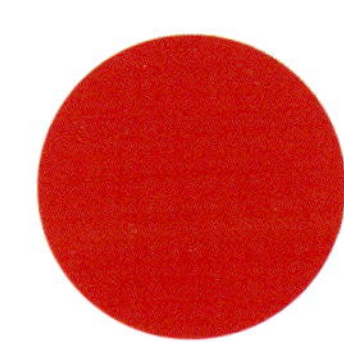

19. Geranium
5R 4.5 / 13
C15 M85 Y68 K0
R203 G64 B66
#CB4042

20. Rose Red
2.5R 4.5 / 14
C15 M98 Y61 K0
R208 G16 B76
#D0104C

21. Yellowish Red
7.5R 5 / 12
6R 4.5 / 12
C16 M86 Y70 K0
R199 G62 B58
#C73E3A

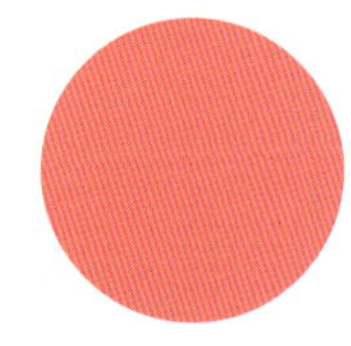

22. Yellowish Red
7.5R 5 / 12
C23 M81 Y74 K0
R206 G82 B66
#CE5242

23. Garnet
2.5R 4 / 12
C0 M90 Y68 K20
R201 G046 B054
#C92E36

24. Amber Red
7.5R 4 / 10
C35 M87 Y79 K1
R181 G68 B52
#B54434

25. Crimson
2.5R 4 / 10
C42 M93 Y68 K6
R159 G53 B58
#9F353A

30. Old Rose
2.5R 5.5 / 7
C25 M70 Y53 K0
R191 G103 B102
#BF6766

35. Scarlet
7.5R 6 / 16
C0 M65 Y75 K0
R255 G88 B65
#FF5841

40. Indian Pink
10R 7 / 9
C0 M54 Y56 K0
R251 G150 B110
#FB966E

45. Majolica Orange
5YR 7 / 10
C0 M52 Y80 K0
R233 G139 B42
#E98B2A

26. Copper Color
10R 2 / 8
C0 M90 Y79 K60
R126 G15 B9
#7E0F09

31. Scarlet
8.5R 5 / 12
C17 M79 Y74 K0
R204 G84 B58
#CC543A

36. Flamingo
10R 6 / 10
C0 M65 Y73 K0
R237 G120 B74
#ED784A

41. Cork
10R 7 / 7
C5 M55 Y60 K0
R227 G145 B110
#E3916E

46. Flesh
10R 7.5 / 6
C0 M47 Y50 K0
R240 G169 B134
#F0A986

27. Cardinal
5R 3.5 / 10
C35 M85 Y70 K2
R171 G59 B58
#AB3B3A

32. Red Lead
7.5R 5 / 12
C0 M72 Y63 K7
R215 G84 B85
#D75455

37. Coral Pink
7.5R 6.5 / 10
C0 M65 Y58 K0
R241 G124 B103
#F17C67

42. Apricot Buff
2.5YR 7 / 8
C0 M53 Y65 K0
R251 G153 B102
#FB9966

47. Peach Beige
3.5YR 7.5 / 5
C6 M42 Y55 K0
R225 G166 B121
#E1A679

28. Signal Red
10RP 5 / 10
C0 M75 Y38 K20
R208 G90 B110
#D05A6E

33. Tomato Red
8.5R 6 / 12
C0 M75 Y74 K0
R247 G92 B47
#F75C2F

38. French Rose
5R 6.5 / 10
C0 M65 Y46 K0
R235 G122 B119
#EB7A77

43. Salmon Buff
3YR 7 / 7
C0 M53 Y67 K0
R231 G148 B96
#E79460

48. Apricot
6YR 7 / 6
C0 M35 Y55 K0
R247 G185 B119
#F7B977

29. Strawberry
10RP 4 / 10
C2 M70 Y38 K30
R181 G73 B91
#B5495B

34. Orange Vermilion
10R 6 / 14
C0 M72 Y90 K0
R240 G94 B28
#F05E1C

39. Salmon Pink
7.5R 7 / 8
C0 M57 Y47 K0
R241 G148 B131
#F19483

44. Saffron Yellow
5YR 7.5 / 11
C0 M49 Y72 K0
R252 G159 B77
#FC9F4D

49. Vanilla
5YR 8 / 5
C0 M34 Y52 K0
R236 G184 B138
#ECB88A

50. Light Apricot
5YR 8 / 6
C0 M36 Y53 K0
R255 G186 B132
#FFBA84

51. Red Fallow
5YR 6 / 6.5
C5 M52 Y70 K14
R199 G133 B80
#C78550

52. Terracotta
3YR 5 / 6
C38 M67 Y82 K3
R163 G99 B54
#A36336

53. Yellowish Pink
7.5R 3 / 8
C0 M67 Y78 K30
R178 G59 B39
#B23B27

54. Burnt Sienna
1.5YR 5 / 9
C26 M70 Y78 K0
R193 G105 B60
#C1693C

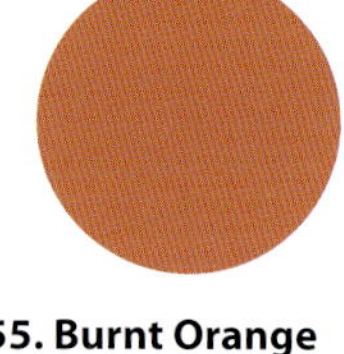

55. Burnt Orange
8.5R 5.5 / 10
C24 M72 Y72 K0
R196 G98 B67
#C46243

56. Brick Dust
7.5R 4.5 / 6
C43 M72 Y71 K4
R163 G94 B71
#A35E47

57. Copper Brown
8.5R 4 / 8
C44 M74 Y75 K12
R154 G80 B52
#9A5034

58. Pompeian Red
7.5R 4 / 8
C45 M82 Y72 K11
R153 G70 B57
#994639

59. Russet Brown
5R 3 / 6
C48 M78 Y66 K10
R149 G74 B69
#954A45

60. Raspberry Red
7.5RP 3.5 / 8
C51 M93 Y58 K10
R142 G53 B74
#8E354A

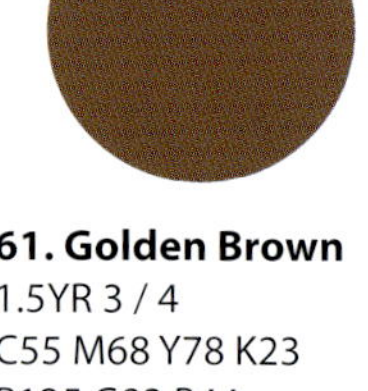

61. Golden Brown
1.5YR 3 / 4
C55 M68 Y78 K23
R125 G83 B44
#7D532C

62. Deep Scarlet
2.5R 4 / 5
C54 M75 Y65 K14
R134 G71 B63
#86473F

63. Cinnabar red
5R 5 / 6
C42 M70 Y58 K1
R169 G99 B96
#A96360

64. Ash Rose
5R 6 / 4.5
C30 M54 Y46 K0
R185 G136 B125
#B9887D

Colors in the
Purple Spectrum

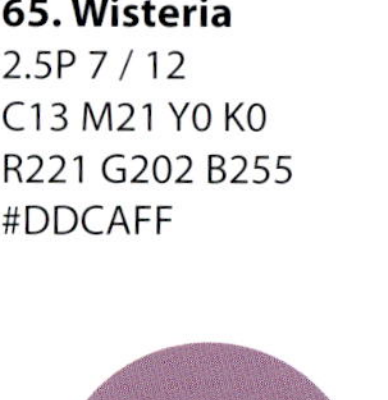

65. Wisteria
2.5P 7 / 12
C13 M21 Y0 K0
R221 G202 B255
#DDCAFF

66. Lilac
7.5P 6.5 / 7
C38 M60 Y0 K0
R180 G129 B187
#B481BB

67. Pale Lilac
3.5P 6.5 / 7
C43 M51 Y0 K0
R178 G143 B206
#B28FCE

68. Crocus
3.5P 5.5 / 8
C55 M63 Y0 K0
R152 G109 B178
#986DB2

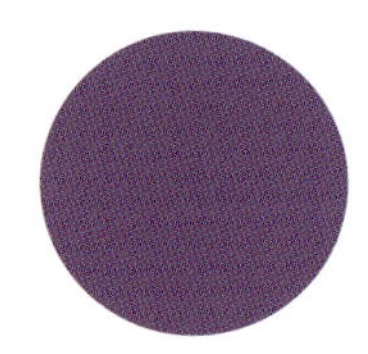

69. Royal Purple
3P 3.5 / 7
C60 M74 Y0 K14
R119 G66 B141
#77428D

70. Iris
6.5P 4 / 10
C71 M87 Y14 K0
R111 G51 B129
#6F3381

71. Gentian
10PM 5 / 12
C38 M40 Y0 K36
R102 G98 B164
#6662A4

72. Heliotrope
1P 6 / 7
C42 M42 Y0 K0
R155 G144 B194
#9B90C2

73. Wisteria
10PB 6 / 8
C58 M52 Y0 K0
R139 G129 B195
#8B81C3

74. Aster
10PB 4.5 / 6
C72 M67 Y21 K0
R112 G100 B154
#70649A

75. Salvia Blue
7PB 6 / 7
C64 M44 Y0 K0
R123 G144 B210
#7B90D2

76. Lavender Gray
8.5PB 5.5 / 5
C69 M56 Y17 K0
R110 G117 B164
#6E75A4

77. Heliotrope
2.5P 6 / 8
C55 M58 Y1 K0
R143 G119 B181
#8F77B5

78. Bellflower
1.5P 4 / 8
C75 M75 Y10 K0
R106 G76 B156
#6A4C9C

79. Violet
5P 3.5 / 7
C74 M83 Y22 K0
R102 G50 B124
#66327C

80. Mauve
1.5P 5.5 / 10
C58 M60 Y0 K0
R138 G107 B190
#8A6BBE

81. Gentian
8.5PB 4.5 / 7
C82 M70 Y14 K0
R78 G79 B151
#4E4F97

82. Prussian Blue
6PB 3 / 12
C100 M85 Y15 K0
R17 G50 B133
#113285

83. Victoria Violet
7PB 2 / 8
C100 M90 Y42 K12
R33 G30 B85
#211E55

84. Purple
5P 3 / 7
C81 M87 Y40 K7
R89 G44 B99
#592C63

85. Prune
10P 3.5 / 1
C75 M70 Y57 K25
R87 G76 B87
#574C57

86. Amaranth Purple
4RP 4.5 / 7
C45 M80 Y37 K0
R168 G73 B122
#A8497A

87. Pansy
2.5P 2 / 8
C0 M80 Y3 K73
R70 G14 B68
#460E44

88. Amethyst
8P 2.5 / 7
C77 M92 Y48 K21
R98 G41 B84
#622954

89. Amethyst Mauve
10P 3.5 / 8
C71 M89 Y48 K12
R109 G46 B91
#6D2E5B

90. Eggplant
7.5P 2.5 / 2.5
C40 M73 Y10 K73
R87 G42 B63
#572A3F

91. Indian Purple
6.5RP 3 / 3
C70 M78 Y61 K30
R96 G55 B62
#60373E

92. Plum Purple
10P 4 / 3
C73 M77 Y54 K17
R94 G61 B80
#5E3D50

93. Shark
2.5P 3 / 2
C82 M80 Y48 K15
R83 G61 B91
#533D5B

94. Deep Royal Purple
3P 2.5 / 5
C90 M93 Y43 K16
R74 G34 B93
#4A225D

95. Plum
5RP 2.5 / 3
C75 M84 Y62 K42
R86 G46 B55
#562E37

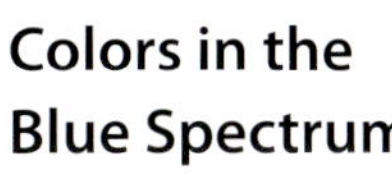

Colors in the Blue Spectrum

96. Horizon Blue
5B 8.5 / 2
C42 M0 Y11 K0
R165 G222 B228
#A5DEE4

97. Pale Aqua
3.5B 7.5 / 4
C55 M6 Y17 K0
R129 G199 B212
#81C7D4

98. Turquoise Blue
5B 6.5 / 6.5
C82 M18 Y27 K0
R51 G166 B184
#33A6B8

103. Sky Blue
10B 6.5 / 8
C72 M13 Y7 K0
R88 G178 B220
#58B2DC

108. Saxe Blue
6.5B 5 / 7
C90 M32 Y23 K0
R30 G136 B168
#1E88A8

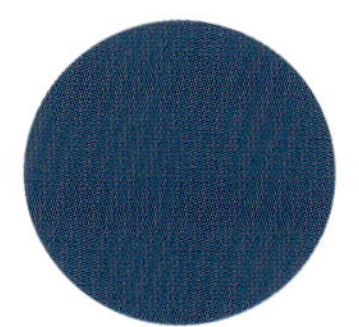

113. Deep Dark Blue
2.5PB 3 / 4
C80 M20 Y0 K60
R0 G73 B109
#00496D

118. Light Saxe Blue
3.5B 6 / 3
C66 M30 Y34 K0
R102 G153 B161
#6699A1

99. Peacock Blue
7.5B 4 / 6
C100 M0 Y25 K25
R69 G70 B155
#00708E

104. Ultramarine
2PB 6.5 / 8
C67 M21 Y0 K0
R81 G168 B221
#51A8DD

109. Sapphire Blue
8.5B 4 / 7
C100 M60 Y41 K2
R0 G98 B132
#006284

114. Navy Blue
5.5PB 2 / 5
C100 M85 Y50 K24
R15 G37 B64
#0F2540

119. Venet
7.5BG 5 / 4.5
C85 M35 Y50 K0
R38 G135 B133
#268785

100. Aqua Green
7BG 7 / 4
C68 M10 Y33 K0
R102 G186 B183
#66BAB7

105. Cobalt Blue
3PB 5 / 11
C73 M20 Y0 K0
R46 G169 B223
#2EA9DF

110. Blue
5PB 4 / 10
C96 M48 Y0 K0
R0 G103 B192
#0067C0

115. Steel Gray
7.5PB 1.5 / 2
C80 M65 Y0 K77
R38 G30 B71
#261E47

120. Smoke Blue
8.5B 5 / 4
C78 M48 Y42 K0
R87 G124 B138
#577C8A

101. Pale Ultrama-rine
3B 7 / 4.5
C52 M0 Y20 K0
R120 G194 B196
#78C2C4

106. Azure Blue
7.5B 5.5 / 7
C83 M31 Y17 K0
R58 G143 B183
#3A8FB7

111. Lapis Lazuli
6PB 4 / 12
C97 M65 Y0 K0
R0 G92 B175
#005CAF

116. Indigo
5.5PB 1.5 / 3
C100 M86 Y60 K45
R8 G25 B45
#08192D

121. Smoke Blue
5B 4.5 / 0.5
C78 M57 Y52 K7
R86 G108 B115
#566C73

102. Forget-me-not-blue
3PB 7 / 6
C52 M10 Y0 K0
R125 G185 B222
#7DB9DE

107. Cerulean Blue
5B 5 / 8
C95 M31 Y30 K0
R0 G137 B167
#0089A7

112. Royal Blue
6PB 2.5 / 7
C100 M85 Y39 K4
R11 G52 B110
#0B346E

117. Oriental Light Blue
2.5PB 6 / 6
C35 M9 Y0 K20
R132 G185 B203
#84B9CB

122. Fir Green
8BG 3 / 2
C90 M63 Y66 K30
R38 G69 B61
#26453D

123. Marine Blue
5B 3.5 / 3.5
C95 M63 Y56 K17
R13 G86 B97
#0D5661

124. Blue Conifer
8BG 3.5 / 1.5
C83 M59 Y60 K13
R64 G91 B85
#405B55

125. Canton Blue
10BG 3 / 3
C88 M58 Y61 K15
R48 G90 B86
#305A56

126. Electric Blue
2.5B 3 / 2
C90 M63 Y59 K21
R37 G83 B89
#255359

127. Iridescent Green
7.5G 3 / 4
C90 M63 Y66 K30
R38 G69 B061
#20604F

128. Tapestry Blue
5B 3.5 / 2
C92 M65 Y62 K25
R12 G72 B66
#0C4842

129. Goblin Blue
5B 4.5 / 3
C87 M56 Y52 K6
R51 G103 B116
#336774

130. Slate Blue
8.5B 4 / 3
C90 M63 Y51 K7
R46 G92 B110
#2E5C6E

131. Oriental Blue
8.5B 4 / 4
C92 M60 Y47 K4
R43 G95 B117
#2B5F75

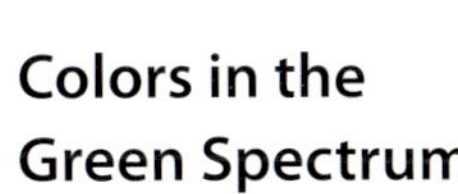

Colors in the
Green Spectrum

132. Elm Green
1.5GY 7.5 / 3
C37 M23 Y63 K0
R177 G180 B121
#B1B479

133. Olive Yellow
7.5Y 6.5 / 6
C38 M31 Y76 K0
R173 G161 B66
#ADA142

134. Green Pigeon
5GY 5 / 4
C16 M0 Y64 K55
R97 G115 B41
#617329

135. Sage Green
10Y 4.5 / 3
C67 M54 Y84 K14
R108 G106 B45
#6C6A2D

136. Beech
2.5Y 4.5 / 1
C64 M57 Y73 K10
R116 G103 B62
#74673E

137. Citron Green
1.5GY 6.5 / 4
C52 M37 Y73 K0
R147 G150 B80
#939650

138. Silver Sage
5GY 6 / 2.5
C57 M38 Y63 K0
R137 G145 B107
#89916B

139. Moss Green
2GY 6 / 5
C62 M41 Y83 K2
R131 G138 B45
#838A2D

140. Willow Green
8.5GY 7 / 5
C56 M24 Y65 K0
R145 G173 B112
#91AD70

141. Spring Green
8.5GY 6 / 8.5
C70 M23 Y86 K0
R123 G162 B63
#7BA23F

142. Fresh Green
6.5GY 6.5 / 8.5
C56 M13 Y77 K0
R144 G180 B75
#90B44B

143. Apple Green
8.5GY 7.5 / 7.5
C57 M1 Y72 K0
R134 G193 B102
#86C166

144. Mist Green
8.5GY 8 / 2
C36 M10 Y45 K0
R181 G202 B160
#B5CAA0

145. Opal Green
5G 8 / 3
C44 M0 Y37 K0
R168 G216 B185
#A8D8B9

146. Light Green
2.5G 7 / 3
C57 M19 Y52 K0
R145 G180 B147
#91B493

147. Porcelain Green
2.5G 6.5 / 5
C68 M13 Y59 K0
R93 G172 B129
#5DAC81

152. Ripple Green
5G 6.5 / 1.5
C58 M30 Y45 K0
R134 G166 B151
#86A697

157. Cactus
8.5GY 4.5 / 3
C76 M51 Y75 K12
R81 G110 B65
#516E41

162. Jade Green
8.5GY 4 / 3
C80 M55 Y79 K20
R66 G96 B45
#42602D

166. Fallow
7.5YR 6.5 / 8
C7 M49 Y80 K0
R226 G148 B59
#E2943B

148. Evergreen
3G 4.5 / 7
C82 M0 Y78 K40
R27 G129 B62
#1B813E

153. Verdigris
5G 5.5 / 6
C83 M23 Y63 K0
R36 G147 B110
#24936E

158. Sea Moss
2.5GY 4 / 3
C72 M56 Y78 K20
R91 G98 B46
#5B622E

163. Green Duck
10G 3.5 / 3
C89 M55 Y67 K17
R32 G96 B79
#20604F

167. Yellow Gold
1.5Y 7 / 10
C8 M40 Y83 K0
R221 G165 B45
#DDA52D

149. Jewel Green
8G 4.5 / 8
C92 M28 Y67 K0
R0 G137 B108
#00896C

**154. Malachite
Green**
3.5G 5 / 6
C86 M36 Y70 K0
R34 G125 B81
#227D51

159. Antique Green
2.5G 5 / 2
C71 M46 Y60 K2
R106 G131 B114
#6A8372

164. Lincoln Green
9G 3.5 / 4
C93 M54 Y71 K20
R9 G97 B72
#096148

168. Yolk Yellow
1.5Y 8 / 10
C0 M29 Y74 K0
R249 G191 B69
#F9BF45

150. Sea Green
7.5BG 5 / 12
C88 M0 Y53 K0
R0 G170 B144
#00AA90

155. Almond Green
5G 4.5 / 4
C86 M46 Y70 K8
R45 G109 B75
#2D6D4B

160. Chinese Green
2.5BG 5 / 2
C77 M50 Y57 K4
R79 G114 B108
#4F726C

165. Forest Green
5G 3.5 / 1.5
C81 M60 Y68 K22
R70 G93 B76
#465D4C

169. Naples Yellow
2Y 8.5 / 7
C0 M25 Y70 K0
R246 G197 B85
#F6C555

151. Celadon
7BG 7 / 3
C61 M14 Y34 K0
R105 G176 B172
#69B0AC

156. Teal
2.5GB 4 / 4
C80 M36 Y64 K13
R49 G107 B98
#316B62

161. Bottle Green
2.5G 3.5 / 2.5
C83 M55 Y69 K22
R54 G86 B60
#36563C

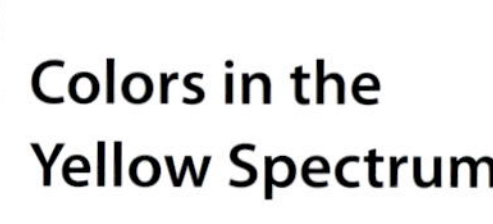

Colors in the Yellow Spectrum

170. Golden Yellow
2.5Y 7.5 / 8
C3 M29 Y88 K0
R239 G187 B36
#EFBB24

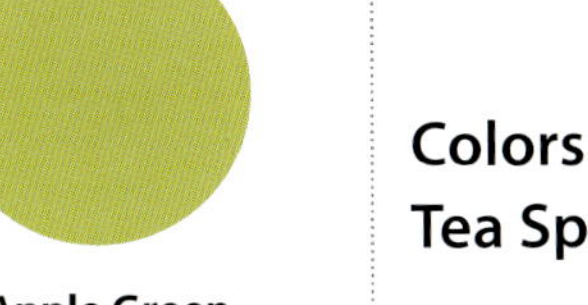

Colors in the Tea Spectrum

171. Honeysweet
2.5Y 7.5 / 7
C14 M33 Y75 K0
R217 G171 B66
#D9AB42

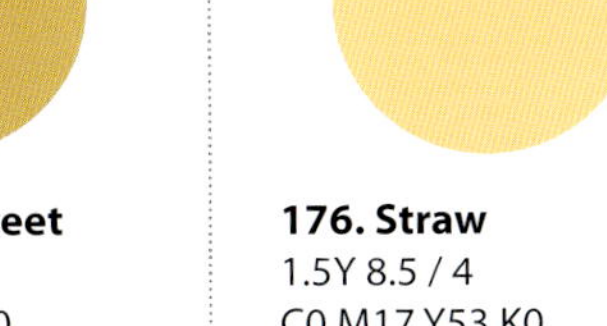

176. Straw
1.5Y 8.5 / 4
C0 M17 Y53 K0
R250 G214 B137
#FAD689

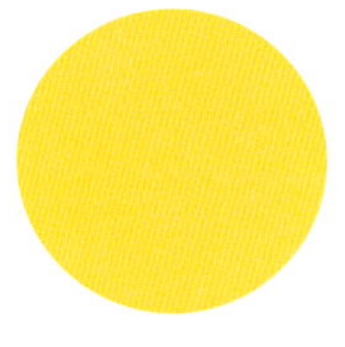

181. Dandelion Yellow
5Y 9 / 12
C0 M10 Y95 K0
R255 G226 B0
#FFE200

186. Apple Green
1.5GY 7.5 / 9
C32 M15 Y85 K0
R190 G194 B63
#BEC23F

172. Curry Yellow
2Y 6.5 / 5.5
C31 M44 Y77 K0
R186 G145 B50
#BA9132

177. Sun Gold
2.5Y 8.5 / 8
C0 M25 Y72 K0
R247 G194 B66
#F7C242

182. Chartreuse Yellow
7.5Y 8 / 2.5
C16 M15 Y52 K0
R217 G205 B144
#D9CD90

187. Mustard
3Y 7 / 6
C0 M16 Y70 K27
R202 G173 B95
#CAAD5F

191. Cream
2.5Y 8.5 / 1
C14 M20 Y39 K0
R218 G201 B166
#DAC9A6

173. Yellow Ocher
8.5YR 6.5 / 4.5
C31 M45 Y66 K0
R182 G142 B85
#B68E55

178. Maize
2Y 8 / 8
C4 M29 Y71 K0
R232 G182 B71
#E8B647

183. Chrome Lemon
7Y 8 / 8
C7 M15 Y74 K0
R233 G205 B76
#E9CD4C

188. Reddish Yellow
5Y 7 / 4
C0 M10 Y44 K22
R199 G179 B112
#C7B370

192. Peach
9YR 7.5 / 4
C5 M20 Y38 K15
R215 G185 B142
#D7B98E

174. Sunflower
2.5Y 8.5 / 12
C0 M25 Y86 K0
R255 G196 B8
#FFC408

179. Lemon Yellow
7.5Y 8.5 / 9
C0 M5 Y73 K0
R251 G226 B81
#FBE251

184. Citron Yellow
10Y 8 / 11
C16 M9 Y82 K0
R221 G210 B59
#DDD23B

189. Citron Gray
2.5Y 7 / 1
C36 M33 Y54 K0
R180 G165 B130
#B4A582

193. Ecru
8.5YR 7 / 3
C32 M40 Y57 K0
R188 G159 B119
#BC9F77

175. Sunflower
2.5Y 8 / 12
C5 M27 Y90 K0
R252 G200 B0
#FCC800

180. Canary
7Y 8 / 9
C2 M11 Y75 K0
R247 G217 B76
#F7D94C

185. Canary Yellow
7.5Y 9 / 8
C19 M16 Y83 K0
R236 G224 B052
#ECE038

190. Oil Yellow
6.5Y 6 / 8
C46 M42 Y84 K0
R162 G140 B55
#A28C37

194. Flax
2Y 7.5 / 3
C16 M30 Y60 K0
R220 G184 B121
#DCB879

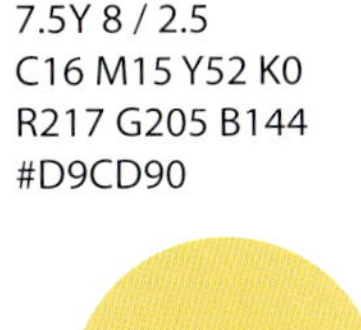

195. Champagne
7.5YR 8 / 6
C0 M34 Y60 K0
R235 G180 B113
#EBB471

200. Buff
1.5Y 6.5 / 7.5
C25 M44 Y83 K0
R201 G152 B51
#C99833

205. Amber
7.5YR 6 / 9
C20 M58 Y85 K0
R202 G122 B44
#CA7A2C

210. Seaweed
6.5Y 4 / 3
C64 M56 Y78 K16
R108 G96 B36
#6C6024

215. Bronze Green
2.5GY 3 / 1
C77 M61 Y70 K30
R77 G81 B57
#4D5139

196. Peach Buff
1.5Y 6.5 / 9
C17 M44 Y89 K0
R209 G152 B38
#D19826

201. Yellow Sparrow Tea
10YR 6 / 7
C28 M48 Y83 K0
R193 G138 B38
#C18A26

206. Brown Gold
7.5YR 6 / 8.5
C20 M56 Y89 K0
R199 G128 B45
#C7802D

211. Seaweed Brown
3.5Y 3.5 / 1
C68 M59 Y75 K22
R98 G89 B44
#62592C

216. Olive Drab
10G 3 / 2
C89 M60 Y67 K30
R15 G76 B58
#0F4C3A

197. Marigold
1.5Y 8 / 13
C0 M37 Y87 K0
R255 G177 B27
#FFB11B

202. Camel
2.5YR 5 / 14
C0 M37 Y59 K25
R191 G121 B78
#BF794E

207. Light Olive Yellow
9Y 6 / 5
C45 M33 Y76 K0
R165 G160 B81
#A5A051

212. Drab
1.5GY 4 / 2
C72 M58 Y73 K19
R97 G97 B56
#616138

217. Dun
10BG 4 / 3
C87 M54 Y54 K5
R55 G107 B109
#376B6D

198. Gold
1.5Y 6.5 / 9
C17 M44 Y89 K0
R209 G152 B38
#D19826

203. Buff
7.5YR 5.5 / 6
C36 M57 Y79 K0
R176 G119 B54
#B07736

208. Seaweed Yellow
6.5Y 5.5 / 4
C57 M48 Y78 K6
R134 G120 B53
#867835

213. Deep Sea Moss
7.5GY 4 / 1.5
C76 M57 Y70 K17
R74 G89 B61
#4A593D

218. Sepia
8YR 3.5 / 2.5
C62 M63 Y73 K21
R110 G85 B47
#6E552F

199. Tortoiseshell
10YR 6 / 10
C0 M30 Y92 K22
R198 G138 B16
#C68A10

204. Ocher Beige
6.5YR 5.5 / 6
C35 M58 Y75 K0
R177 G120 B68
#B17844

209. Slate Olive
5GY 4.5 / 1
C69 M52 Y63 K7
R100 G106 B88
#646A58

214. Dark Olive
1.5GY 3.5 / 1.5
C76 M61 Y74 K30
R75 G78 B42
#4B4E2A

219. Tawny Olive
1.5Y 5 / 1.5
C58 M56 Y70 K8
R125 G108 B70
#7D6C46

220. Dark Brown
10YR 4 / 4
C58 M59 Y78 K14
R135 G102 B51
#876633

225. Fawn
5YR 5 / 4
C50 M61 Y76 K9
R150 G99 B46
#96632E

230. Bronze
3.5YR 5 / 5
C48 M66 Y79 K7
R152 G95 B42
#985F2A

235. Cinnamon
10R 5.5 / 6
C38 M64 Y65 K0
R180 G113 B87
#B47157

240. Melo Pink
10R 7 / 6
C10 M55 Y57 K0
R219 G142 B113
#DB8E71

221. Dusty Olive
2.5Y 5.5 / 1
C57 M50 Y70 K3
R137 G125 B85
#897D55

226. Drab
7.5YR 5 / 4
C50 M56 Y71 K5
R150 G114 B73
#967249

231. Etruscan Rose
10R 5 / 5
C48 M66 Y70 K6
R160 G103 B75
#A0674B

236. Garnet Brown
8.5R 4.5 / 8
C38 M70 Y71 K3
R175 G95 B60
#AF5F3C

241. Mahogany
9R 3.5 / 6
C49 M73 Y70 K18
R133 G72 B54
#854836

222. Oriental Gold
2.5Y 5 / 3
C55 M53 Y82 K7
R141 G116 B42
#8D742A

227. Nut Brown
1.5YR 6 / 2
C51 M56 Y57 K1
R148 G122 B109
#947A6D

232. Brick Red
10R 4.5 / 5
C52 M69 Y73 K15
R143 G90 B60
#8F5A3C

237. Etruscan Orange
10R 5 / 8
C36 M72 Y76 K2
R179 G92 B55
#B35C37

242. Oxblood Red
7.5R 3.5 / 5
C52 M74 Y70 K18
R136 G76 B58
#884C3A

223. Maple Sugar
8.5YR 4.5 / 4
C54 M58 Y76 K10
R130 G102 B58
#82663A

228. Tobacco Brown
3.5YR 4.5 / 4
C55 M66 Y75 K14
R133 G91 B50
#855B32

233. Shrimp Brown
5YR 5/5
C0 M50 Y60 K45
R162 G101 B64
#A26540

238. Copper Rose
7.5R 5 / 7
C37 M72 Y68 K0
R181 G93 B76
#B55D4C

243. Chestnut
10R 3 / 5
C58 M74 Y72 K30
R106 G64 B40
#6A4028

224. Dark Brown
10G 3 / 2
C89 M60 Y67 K30
R15 G76 B58
#0F4C3A

229. Raw Sienna
7.5YR 5 / 6
C46 M57 Y80 K4
R155 G110 B35
#9B6E23

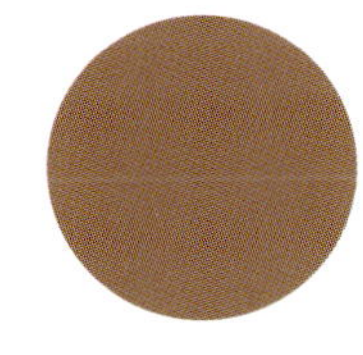

234. Sparrow
7.5R 3 / 4
C0 M50 Y59 K47
R134 G67 B55
#864337

239. Coral Rust
10R 6 / 7
C21 M64 Y67 K0
R202 G120 B83
#CA7853

244. Auburn Brown
10R 2.5 / 4
C58 M73 Y70 K26
R114 G72 B50
#724832

245. Dark Cardinal
6.5R 4 / 7
C50 M78 Y69 K13
R144 G72 B64
#904840

246. Garnet
6R 3 / 4.5
C55 M77 Y68 K27
R115 G67 B56
#734338

247. Mulberry
10RP 3 / 4
C69 M86 Y65 K35
R100 G54 B60
#64363C

248. Arabian Red
10R 3 / 3
C61 M70 Y68 K25
R114 G73 B56
#724938

249. Burnt Umber
1.5YR 2 / 2
C68 M73 Y71 K40
R86 G63 B46
#563F2E

250. Woodland Brown
7.5R 2 / 2
C71 M74 Y69 K41
R85 G66 B54
#554236

Monochromatic Colors

251. White
N10
C0 M0 Y0 K0
R255 G255 B255
#FFFFFF

252. Chalk
2.5Y 9.2 / 0.5
C0 M0 Y2 K0
R255 G255 B251
#FFFFFB

253. Generated Color
10YR 9 / 2
C0 M5 Y10 K5
R247 G239 B227
#F7EFE3

254. Snow White
N9.5
C0 M3 Y11 K0
R252 G250 B242
#FCFAF2

255. Mouse Gray
7.5P 6 / 1
C48 M40 Y37 K0
R148 G148 B149
#949495

256. Silver Gray
2.5PB 6.5 / 0.5
C52 M39 Y36 K0
R145 G152 B159
#91989F

257. Aqua Gray
2.5B 6 / 2
C63 M38 Y40 K0
R119 G150 B154
#77969A

258. Eggshell Green
2.5G 6 / 1
C61 M41 Y53 K0
R128 G143 B124
#808F7C

259. Celadon Gray
8.5G 5 / 1
C66 M50 Y54 K1
R112 G124 B116
#707C74

260. Mouse Gray
N5
C65 M53 Y53 K0
R120 G125 B123
#787D7B

261. Ash Gray
N5
C0 M0 Y0 K70
R130 G130 B130
#828282

262. Lead Gray
2.5PB 5 / 1
C8 M0 Y0 K73
R120 G120 B120
#787878

263. Covert Gray
2.5Y 5.5 / 0.5
C58 M51 Y60 K1
R135 G127 B108
#877F6C

264. Lilac Hazy
10P 5 / 1.5
C68 M64 Y51 K6
R114 G99 B110
#72636E

265. Rose Gray
5R 5.5 / 3
C48 M59 Y49 K0
R158 G122 B122
#9E7A7A

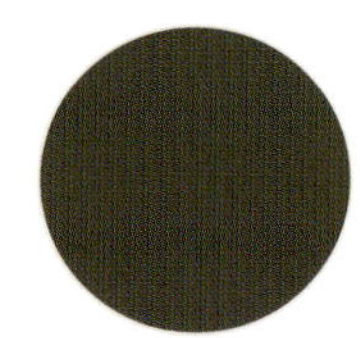

266. Steel Gray
2.5B 4 / 0.5
C78 M63 Y62 K20
R83 G89 B83
#535953

267. Dove Gray
5RP 3.5 / 0.5
C78 M65 Y65 K30
R79 G79 B72
#4F4F48

268. Russet Gold
5YR 2 / 1
C76 M71 Y73 K47
R67 G52 B27
#43341B

269. Black Berry
10RP 3 / 1
C73 M69 Y63 K30
R82 G67 B61
#52433D

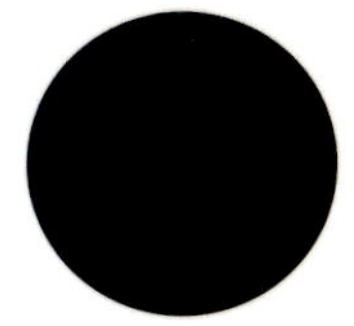

274. Bluish Black
7.5BG 1 / 2
C50 M13 Y0 K100
R0 G8 B26
#00081A

279. Charcoal Gray
N2
C92 M78 Y73 K66
R28 G28 B28
#1C1C1C

283. Platinum
7.5P 8 / 1
C22 M16 Y17 K0
R192 G192 B192
#C0C0C0

270. Dusky Purple
5P 1.5 / 1.5
C86 M85 Y64 K50
R63 G43 B54
#3F2B36

275. Olive Gray
N4
C5 M0 Y0 K80
R101 G103 B101
#656765

280. Lamp Black
N1
C91 M84 Y74 K71
R8 G8 B8
#080808

271. Dark Slate
2.5PB 3 / 0.5
C86 M72 Y68 K47
R55 G60 B56
#373C38

276. Charcoal Gray
N2.5
C0 M0 Y0 K88
R67 G67 B67
#434343

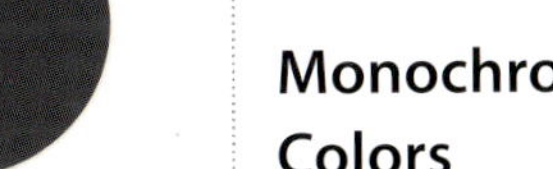

Monochromatic Colors

272. Moist Crow
10GY 2 / 8
C100 M0 Y100 K96
R0 G11 B0
#000B00

277. Ivory Black
N1.5
C0 M0 Y0 K100
R12 G12 B12
#0C0C0C

281. Gold
10YR 8 / 12
C15 M34 Y89 K0
R230 G180 B34
#E6B422

273. African Brown
10R 2.5 / 0.5
C79 M72 Y72 K50
R58 G50 B38
#3A3226

278. Midnight Blue
10B 2 / 0.5
C92 M78 Y64 K48
R11 G16 B19
#0B1013

282. Silver
N7.5
C31 M23 Y28 K0
R189 G192 B186
#BDC0BA

Index of Color Names

Master List of Illustrations

For data on paintings and crafts, the order is: Title of the artwork, cultural property designation, artist, era (century), place of creation, number of pieces, quality and shape, dimensions, and owner. For photographs, the order is: Title, shooting location, and photographer. Dimensions are given in centimeters.

6 / Rainfall from the Eaves, Enko-ji Temple, Kyoto. Photography by Akira Nakata.

6 / Aoi Festival—Ritual at the Shrine, Kamigamo Shrine, Kyoto. Photography by Akira Nakata.

6 / Morning Glow at Mt. Hiei, Kyoto. Photography by Akira Nakata.

7 / Misogi Ritual, Kamigamo Shrine, Kyoto. Photography by Akira Nakata.

7 /Five-color Curtain, Myoshin-ji Temple, Kyoto. Photography by Akira Nakata.

6–7 / Yusei Garden, Sanzen-in Temple, Kyoto. Photography by Akira Nakata.

8 / Peach Blossom Festival, Iwashimizu Hachimangu Shrine, Kyoto. Photography by Akira Nakata.

8 / Kurama Fire Festival, Yuki Shrine, Kyoto. Photography by Akira Nakata.

8 / Thousand Torii Gates, Fushimi Inari Taisha, Kyoto. Photography by Akira Nakata.

10 / "Dyed Asa Aya Kosode with Snow Circle and Kerria Pattern" Edo period, 18th century. Asa Aya (silk). Tokyo National Museum.

11 / "Red Crepe Kosode with Bamboo Sparrow and Chrysanthemum Pattern" Edo period, 19th century. Tokyo National Museum.

11 / "Red Damask Ground with Plum Grove Pattern in Yuzen Dyeing and Shibori Stitching Kosode" Edo period, 19th century. Silk. Dimensions: 155 × 63 cm. National Museum of Japanese History.

12–13 / "Screen Depicting Leisure Under the Blossoms" (National Treasure) by Kano Nagamasa, Edo period, 17th century. Six panels, One pair, Color on paper. Dimensions (each): 148.6 × 355.8 cm. Tokyo National Museum.

15 / "Various Dance Forms" by unknown artist, Edo period. Color on paper. Dimensions: 38.9 × 25.5 cm. Itabashi Art Museum Collection.

16 / "Beauty by Autumn Hedge" by Nishikawa Sukenobu, Edo period, early 18th century. One scroll, Color on paper. Dimensions: 90.8 × 37.7 cm. Aichi Prefectural Museum of Art Collection (Kimura Teizo Collection).

17 / "Woman Resting in Grass" Takehisa Yumeji, Early Taisho period, 20th century. Color on silk. Dimensions: 88.6 × 32 cm. Shizuoka City Museum of Art Collection.

19 / "Brooch" by Katsutani Takijirō, 1892. One piece. Tokyo National Museum.

19 / "Melon Design Maki-e Square Red Box" Edo period, 17th century. One set, Lacquered wood. Tokyo National Museum.

20 / "Polychrome Porcelain Teapot" by Ninami Michihachi and Sahira. Edo period, 19th century. One pot, Ceramic. Dimensions: Height 11.8 × Top diameter 5.8 × Base diameter 5.3 × Body diameter 9.3 cm. Tokyo National Museum.

21 / "Jar for Tea Leaves with the Moon and Plum Blossoms" (Important Cultural Property) by Nonomura Ninsei, Edo period, 17th century. One jar. Tokyo National Museum.

22 / "Enamel Peony Design Covered Jar" Imari Ware (Kakiemon Style), Edo period, 17th century. One set, Ceramic. Dimensions: Height 26.4 × Top diameter 24.8 × Base diameter 12.1 cm. Tokyo National Museum.

23 / "Enamel Flower and Bird Design Large Deep Bowl" (Important Cultural Property), Imari Ware (Kakiemon Style), Edo period, 17th century. One pot, Ceramic. Dimensions: Height 21.4 × Top diameter 30.3 × Foot diameter 16.5 cm. Tokyo National Museum.

24 / "Polychrome Chicken and Textile Patterned Flat Dish" Imari Ware, Edo period, 18th century. One pot, Ceramic. Dimensions: Height 5.5 × Top diameter 25.2 × Foot diameter 9.1 cm. Tokyo National Museum.

25 / "Polychrome Porcelain Gourd-shaped Water Pourer with Grape and Squirrel Pattern" Imari Ware (Kakiemon Style). Edo period, 17th century. One pot, Ceramic. Dimensions: Height 15 × Length 17.5 × Width 9.5 cm. Tokyo National Museum.

26–27 / "Red Silk Kosode with Triangular and Bamboo Design Shibori and Embroidery" Late Edo period, 19th century. One piece, Silk. Dimensions: 163.5 × 65 cm. National Museum of Japanese History.

27 / "Dawn Pilgrimage in Spring" by Utagawa Toyokun. Set of three, Large-format woodblock print. Ivy House Yoshizo Edition. National Diet Library Digital Collection.

28 / "Red Crepe Furisode with Curtain and Cypresses Fan Pattern in Shibori Stitching" Edo period, 19th century. One piece, Silk. Dimensions: 172 × 61.5 cm. National Museum of Japanese History.

28 / "Snow Viewing" by Utagawa Toyokuni. Edo period, 18th century. Set of three, Large-format woodblock print. Dimensions: 37.2 × 24.6 cm. Tokyo National Museum.

30 / "Beauty with Pillar Clock" by Nishikawa Sukenobu, Edo period, 18th century. One scroll, Color on silk. Dimensions: 88.3 × 31.4 cm. Tokyo National Museum.

30–31 / "White Damask Furisode with Chrysanthemum, Cloud, Bird, and Butterfly Patterns" Edo to Meiji period, 19th century. One piece, Embroidered on damask, stitched and tie-dyed. Dimensions: 172.5 × 64 cm. Tokyo National Museum.

32 / "Red Crepe Kosode with Bamboo, Sparrow, and Chrysanthemum Pattern" Edo period, 19th century. One piece. Tokyo National Museum.

33 / "Portrait of a Courtesan Looking Over Her Shoulder" Edo period, 17th century. One scroll, Color on silk. Dimensions: 63 × 31.2 cm. Tokyo National Museum.

34 / "Mist, Spring Plum Viewing" by Utagawa Toyokuni, 1858. Set of three, Large-format woodblock print. Hayashi So Version. National Diet Library Digital Collection.

35 / "Red Damask Kosode with Plum Grove Pattern in Yuzen Dyeing and Shibori Stitching" Edo period, 19th century, One piece, Silk. Dimensions: 155 × 63 cm. National Museum of Japanese History.

36 / "Crimson and Fresh Green Segment with Japanese Iris Pattern Tang Weave" Edo period, 18th century. One piece. Dimensions: 148.5 × 69.5 cm. Tokyo National Museum.

37 / "Collection of Beautiful Women" by Utagawa Toyokuni. One print, Large-ormat ukiyo-e. Published by Kawaguchiya Ubei. Digital Collection of the National Diet Library

38–38 / "Kabuki Theater Folding Screen" by Hishikawa Moronobu, Edo period, 17th century. Six-panel folding screen. Dimensions (each) 170 × 397.6 cm. Tokyo National Museum.

40 / "Shirabyoshi Hanako, Ichikawa Danjuro" by Toyohara Kunichika, 1890, Set of three, Large-format ukiyo-e. Published by Fukuda Kumajiro. Digital Collection of the National Diet Library.

41 / "Scarlet Vermilion Jinbaori with Embroidered Dragon, Phoenix, and Wave Patterns" Edo period, 19th century.One piece. Dimensions: 103 × 130 cm. Tokyo National Museum.

42 / "Light Blue Velvet Child's Kosode with Chrysanthemum and Water Pattern" Edo period, 19th century. One piece, Velvet with cut-out embroidery. Dimensions: 156.5 × 63.6 cm. Tokyo National Museum.

43 / "Lobster and Shimenawa with Young Pine Pattern Hakama" Late Edo period, 19th century. One piece. Tokyo National Museum.

44 / Kushi Matsuri (Comb Festival), Yasaka Jinja Shrine, Kyoto" Photography by Nakata Akira.

44–45 / "Dawn at Mt. Hiei, Kyoto" Photography

whitening process. Dimensions: 113 × 50.5 cm. Tokyo National Museum.

95 / "Leaving the Bath" by Kobayashi Kokei, 1921. One piece, Paint on silk. Dimensions: 185.4 × 99.9 cmm. Tokyo National Museum.

96 / "Colored Porcelain Striped Two-Tiered Stacking Containers" by Awaiya Genemon. Edo period, 19th century. Dimensions: Width 19.4 × Depth 18.5 × Height 15.3 cm. Ishikawa Prefectural Museum of Art.

97 / "Colored Porcelain Bottle with Pine, Bamboo, and Plum Design" Imari Ware, Edo period, 17th century. Made of porcelain. Tokyo National Museum.

98 / "Colored Porcelain Plate with Flying Phoenix Design" Imari Ware, Edo period, 17th century. Dimensions: Height 4.3 × Diameter 31.7 × Base diameter 18.4. Tokyo National Museum.

99 / "Colored Porcelain Flat Bowl with Stone Pavement and Double Phoenix Design," Early Kutani, Edo period, 17th century. Dimensions: Diameter 34.7 × Base diameter 20.4 × Height 7.5 cm. Ishikawa Prefectural Museum of Art.

100 / "Eitai (Famous Places of the Eastern Capital)" by Utagawa Toyokuni. Large ukiyo-e Print. Published by Sano Ki. Digital Collection of the National Diet Library.

101 / "Green Silk Kimono with Willow, Cherry Blossom, and Raft Design" Edo period, 18th century. Dimensions: 145 × 61.5 cm. Nara Prefectural Museum of Art.

104 / "Okita of the Naniwaya Teahouse" by Kitagawa Utamaro. Edo period, 18th century. Fine Woodblock Print. Tokyo National Museum.

105 / "Hiwa Green Patterned Silk Kimono with Genji Cloud and Cherry Blossom Design" Edo period, 18th century. Patterned Silk (Kinu) Embroidery. Tokyo National Museum.

106 / "Rainfall in Enrindou" at Katsura Imperial Villa, Kyoto. Photographed by Nakata Akira, managed by the Imperial Household Agency Kyoto Office.

106–107/ Hojo North Garden at Tofukuji Temple, Kyoto. Photographed by Nakata Akira.

107 / Garden at Tofukuji Temple's Kaizan Hall, Kyoto. Photographed by Nakata Akira.

107 / "True Stepping Stone" in front of the portable shrine at Katsura Imperial Villa, Kyoto. Photographed by Nakata Akira, managed by the Imperial Household Agency Kyoto Office.

108 / "Botanical Illustration Book, Volume 1" National Diet Library Digital Collection.

110 / "Bellflower and Rooster" from Album of Flowers and Birds by Kōno Bairei, 1883. National Diet Library Digital Collection.

111/ "Sea Hibiscus and Duck" from Album of Flowers and Birds by Kōno Bairei, 1883. National Diet Library Digital Collection.

111p / Kikyō, Tenju-an, Kyoto. Photographed by Nakata Akira.

112–113 / Horse Racing Ritual at Kamigamo Shrine, Kyoto. Photographed by Nakata Akira.

112p / Ominaeshi at Koshihata, Kyoto. Photographed by Nakata Akira.

113p / Autumn Foliage at Jōjakkō-ji Temple, Kyoto. Photographed by Nakata Akira.

114 • 122 / "Woman Playing the Koto" by Toyohara Chikanobu, 1897. Large ukiyo-e print. Published by Akiyama Buemon. National Diet Library Digital Collection.

115 • 117/ "Beauty with Lantern" by Mihata Joryu, early 19th century. One scroll, Paint on silk. Dimensions: 103.6 × 37 cm. Kyoto Prefecture (managed by Kyoto Culture Museum).

115 • 120 / "Gold Brocade Kimono with Peony, Tangerine, and Net Design" Edo period, 18th century. Brocade (Kinu) embroidery. Dimensions: 161 × 60 cm. Tokyo National Museum.

116 / "Portrait of a Beautiful Woman" by Nagasawa Rosetsu, Late 18th century. One scroll, Paint on silk. Dimensions: 100.8 × 37.9 cm. Kyoto Prefecture (managed by Kyoto Culture Museum).

118 / "Tortoiseshell Comb with Ivy and Mother of Pearl Inlay" Taisho Period. Tortoiseshell with black lacquer finish. Dimensions: 9.5 × 4.5 cm. National Museum of Japanese History.

119 / "Polychrome Painted Bowl with Pine Tree Design" Imari Ware, Edo period, 17th century. One piece, Ceramic. Dimensions: Height 7.3 cm x Diameter 35 cm x Base diameter 16.3 cm. Tokyo National Museum.

121/ "Part of a Picture of a Large Cup for the Ebisu Festival, the Clear Brightness from Dawn North and South" by Katsukawa Shunsen (Second Generation Haruyoshi). Around the Bunka era (1804–1817). One piece. Large-format woodblock print. Yamaguchi Prefectural Hagi Art Museum and Uragami Memorial Museum.

123 / "Eggshell-colored Linen Kimono with Bird and Ivy Pattern" Edo period, 18th century. One garment. Tokyo National Museum.

124 / "Peacock Illustration" by Okamoto Shūki. Edo period, 19th century. One scroll, Color on silk. Dimensions: 120.5 × 50.4 cm. Tokyo National Museum.

125 / "Sparrows and Camellias in the Snow" by Utagawa Hiroshige. Edo period, 19th century. One short brochure-type ukiyo-e print. Tokyo National Museum.

126–127/ Ōsawa Pond, Daikaku-ji, Kyoto. Photography by Nakata Akira.

126 / Scattered Autumn Leaves, Ōsawa Pond, Kyoto. Photography by Nakata Akira.

127 / Pine Needles on the Ground at Hōsendō Garden, Kyoto. Photography by Nakata Akira.

128 • 131 / "Two Beauties Catching Fireflies" by Hōtei Gosei, from 1820 (Bunsei 3). Paint on silk. Dimensions: 95.7 × 37.5 cm. Itabashi Art Museum.

128 • 133 / "Sleeping Dragon and Winter Plum" by Suzuki Harunobu. Edo period, 18th century. Medium-sized ukiyo-e print. Tokyo National Museum.

129 • 140/ "Black Tea Kosode with Scattered Fans and Grass Embroiered with Fine Wire Thread" Azuchi-Momoyama to Edo period, 17th century. One garment. Tokyo National Museum.

130 / "Peony Viewing" by Komura Settai, 1942. Woodblock print on paper. Dimensions: 25.5 × 39 cm. Saitama Prefectural Museum of Modern Art.

132/ "Daughter with a Sundial—Hour of the Snake" (Important Cultural Property) by Kitagawa Utamaro. Edo period, 18th century. Large ukiyo-e print. Tokyo National Museum.

134 / "Rust-painted Plate with a View of Seagulls" (Important Cultural Property) collaborative work by Ogata Kōrin and Shinsei. Edo period, 18th century. One ceramic plate. Dimensions: 2.9 × 22.2 cm. Tokyo National Museum.

135 / "Shino Ware Tea Bowl" with the inscription "Hashihime" Mino Province, Azuchi-Momoyama to Edo period, 16th to 17th century. One ceramic bowl, Dimensions: Height 11.5 cm, Opening diameter 12.6 cm, Base diameter 7.6 cm. Tokyo National Museum.

136 / "Oribe-style Plate with Bamboo Pattern on Three Feet" (Yashichida Oribe) from the Momoyama to Edo period, early 17th century. One ceramic plate. Dimensions: 4.6 × 24.2 cm. Aichi Prefectural Ceramic Museum.

137 / "Iron-painted Plate with Autumn Scenery" from the Seto during the late Edo period, 19th century. One piece. Dimensions: 9.1 × 47.3 cm. Aichi Prefectural Ceramic Museum.

138 / "Modern Beauty from Thirty-Six Flower Selections: Plum" by Utagawa Toyokuni. Large format ukiyo-e print, published by Sano Ki. National Diet Library Digital Collection.

139 / "Tea-colored Lily and Imperial Cart Pattern Embroidered Brocade" from the Azuchi-Momoyama period, 16th century. One garment. Tokyo National Museum.

141 / "Sakura Viewing Along Sumida Riverbank" by Keisai Eisen. Triptych, large format ukiyo-e print, published by Ei-tatsu. National Diet Library Digital Collection.

142 / "Beauty Visiting a Shrine on a Rainy Night, Comparison with Ari-toshi Myojin" by Suzuki Harunobu. Edo period, 18th century. Medium-sized ukiyo-e print. Tokyo National Museum.

143 / "Kimono with Distant Mountains, Sailing Ship, and Pavilion Design on White

Damask Fabric" Edo period, 18th century. One garment, Dimensions: Length 153 cm, Sleeve drop 75 cm, Sleeve length 56 cm, Sleeve width 35 cm. Tokyo National Museum.

144–145 / "Minamoto no Yoshitsune: Ichikawa Danjuro as Shizuka Gozen, Iwai Hanshiro as Kitsune Tadanobu, Onoe Kikugoro" by Toyohara Kunichika, 1881. Triptych, large format ukiyo-e print, published by Kodama Matsushichi. National Diet Library Digital Collection.

145 / "Ichikawa Danjūrō in the role of Zan" by Torii Kiyoshige. Edo period, 18th century. Wide pillar format ukiyo-e print. Tokyo National Museum.

146 / Hanakasa (Flower Umbrella) Procession, Gion Festival, Kyoto. Photography by Nakata Akira.

147 / New Year's Atmosphere, Yoshida Residence, Kyoto. Photography by Nakata Akira.

147 / Hojo North Garden, Tofuku-ji Temple, Kyoto. Photography by Nakata Akira.

148 • 160 / "Portrait of a Standing Beauty" by Yamaguchi Soken. Edo period, 19th century. One scroll, color on silk. Dimensions: 130.5 × 60.5 cm. Tsuruga City Museum.

149 • 152 / "Portrait of a Beautiful Woman with a Snake-eye Umbrella" by Kaseiro Jakugo, late Edo period, 19th century. One scroll, color on paper. Dimensions: 92.6 × 29.4 cm. Kumamoto Prefectural Museum of Art.

149 • 158p / "Black Silk Crepe Kimono with Pine, Wisteria, and Maple Leaf Patterns" Edo period, 19th century. One garment. Tokyo National Museum.

150–151 / "Peacocks and Pine Trees" by Soga Shohaku, c. 1767. Four-panel folding screen, Ink painting on paper. Dimensions: 172 × 86 cm. Mie Prefectural Art Museum.

153 / "Customs of Women" by Katsushika Hokusai, c. 1792–1794. Dual scroll, Color on paper. Shimane Prefectural Museum of Art (Nagata Collection).

154 / "Lacquered Box with a Design of a Cypress Fence and Chrysanthemum" from the Azuchi-Momoyama to Edo period, 17th century. Single wooden lacquered box. Dimensions: 10.1 × 8.8 × 7.2 cm. Tokyo National Museum.

155 / "Lacquered Writing Box with a Design of Rabbits in Mother-of-Pearl Inlay" attributed to Nagata Yuji, Edo period, 19th century. Single wooden lacquered box. Tokyo National Museum.

156/ "Black Oribe Ring-Connected Motif Tea-cup" inscribed "Samidare (May Rain)" by Shinhozaemon, Momoyama era, early 17th century. One piece. Dimensions: Height 7.1 × Diameter 10.1 to 13.3 cm × Base diameter 6 cm. Collection of Aichi Prefectural Museum of Art (Kimura Teizo Collection).

157 / "Black Oribe Kutsugata Tea Bowl" inscribed "Kakutaro". Mino Ware, Edo period, 17th century. One piece. Dimensions: Height 8.9 cm × Diameter 14.5 × 11.6 cm, Foot diameter 6.4 cm. Tokyo National Museum.

157 / "Polychrome Tea Bowl with Moon and Mantis Motif" by Eiraku Hozon, Edo period, 19th century. One piece, Ceramic. Dimensions: Height 7.1 × Diameter 12.2 × Foot Diameter 4.7 cm. Tokyo National Museum.

155p / "Black Raku Crane and Turtle Design Tea Bowl" by Ninnami Dōhachi, Edo period, 19th century. One piece. Ceramic. Dimensions: Height 9.5 × Diameter 9.7 × Base diameter 5.4 cm. Tokyo National Museum.

157p / "Inari Pilgrimage" by Utagawa Toyoharu, 1795. One piece, Color on silk. Dimensions: 61 × 28 cm. Tokyo National Museum.

159p / "Black Hemp Kosode with Curtain and Wisteria Pattern" Edo period, 18th century. One piece. Embroidered and dyed on linen (plain weave). Dimensions: 155.5 × 57.5 cm. Tokyo National Museum.

160p / "White Fabric with Linked Seven Treasures and Wisteria Pattern" Edo period, 18th century. One piece. Tokyo National Museum.

163 / "Inside the Sun, Moon, and Stars" by Utagawa Toyokuni. Series of three large-format woodblock prints. Published by Aritaya. National Diet Library Digital Collection.

164 / "Portrait of a Beautiful Woman on a Veranda" by unknown artist, Edo period, 17th century. One scroll, Paint on paper. Dimensions: 41.8 × 19.4 cm (after restoration). Tokyo National Museum.

165/ "White Silk Crepe Kosode with Bamboo and Fishing Net Design" Edo period, 17th century. One piece, Crepe silk, Shibori tie-dye, and Embroidery. Tokyo National Museum.

166 / "Portrait of a Courtesan" by Kaigetsudō Ando, copied by Kobori Tomo. One scroll. Tokyo National Museum.

167 / "White Silk Crepe Kimono with Large Chrysanthemum and Small Flower Pattern" Edo period, 17th century. One piece, Crepe silk, Embroidery, and Shibori tie-dye. Tokyo National Museum.

168 / "Black Silk Crepe Furisode with Wave and Ducks Design" (Important Cultural Property). Edo period, 17th century. One piece. Tokyo National Museum.

169 / "Black and Red Hemp Kosode with Folding Fan, Snowflakes, and Autumn Grass Design" Edo period, 17th century. One piece. Tokyo National Museum.

170 / Naginata Hoko Child Attendants at Gion Festival, Kyoto. Photography by Nakata Akira.

170 / Doll Offering at Hōkyō-ji Temple, Kyoto. Photography by Nakata Akira.

171/ Nine Statues of Amida Buddha (National Treasure) at Joruri-ji Temple, Kyoto. Photography by Nakata Akira.

172 • 177 / "Single-wheeled Cart Design Lacquerware Box with Mother-of-Pearl Inlay" (National Treasure) Heian Period, 12th century. One set, Lacquered wood. Dimensions: Length 22.4 × Width 30.6 × Height 13.5 cm. Tokyo National Museum.

173 • 184–185 / "Folding Screen with Flowing Water and Four Seasons Plants and Flowers" by Sakai Hoitsu. Edo period, 19th century. Two panels, one pair, Color on gold leaf paper. Dimensions (each): 162 × 172 cm. Tokyo National Museum.

173 • 183 / "Folding Screen with Summer Grass" by Sakai Dōitsu, 1893. Two panels, One piece, Color on silver leaf paper. Dimensions: 120.7 × 129.4 cm. Tokyo National Museum.

174–175 / "Folding Screen with Sumiyoshi Festival Scene". Early Edo period, 17th century. Six panels (One pair). Color on gold leaf paper. Dimensions (each): 107.6 × 236 cm. Sakai City Museum.

176 / "Wave and Plover Design Lacquerware Box" by Nagata Yūji, Edo period, 18th century. One set, Lacquered wood. Tokyo National Museum.

178 / "Gold Background with Pine and Sail Pattern in Karafuto Weave" Edo period, 18th century. One piece. Tokyo National Museum.

179 / "Golden Thread Embroidered Velvet Hanging" Edo period, 19th century. One piece. Tokyo National Museum.

180–182 / "Wind God and Thunder God Folding Screen" (Important Cultural Property) by Ōgata Kōrin, Edo period, 18th century. Two panels, One pair, Color on gold leaf paper. Dimensions (each) 164.5 × 182.4 cm. Tokyo National Museum.

186–187p / "Autumn and Winter Landscape" by Sesshū Tōyō, Muromachi period, late 15th to early 16th century. Two scrolls, Ink on paper. Dimensions (each): 47.7 × 30.2 cm. Tokyo National Museum.

188–189p / "Pine Forest Folding Screen" (National Treasure) by Hasegawa Tōhaku, Azuchi-Momoyama period, 16th century. Six panels, One pair, Ink on paper. Dimensions (each): 156.8 × 356 cm. Tokyo National Museum.

Published by Tuttle Publishing, an imprint of Periplus Editions (HK) Ltd.

www.tuttlepublishing.com

ISBN 978-4-8053-1818-8

NIPPON DENTO NO HAISHOKU JITEN
Copyright 2023 Nobuyoshi Hamada
English translation rights arranged with GENKOSHA CO., Ltd.
through Japan UNI Agency, Inc., Tokyo
English translation © 2024 Periplus Editions (HK) Ltd

Images contributed by:
Aichi Prefectural Ceramic Museum
Aichi Prefectural Museum of Art
Ishikawa Prefectural Museum of Art
Ishikawa Prefectural Museum of History
Itabashi Ward Museum of Art
Osaka Castle Tower (Tenshukaku)
Kyoto City University of Arts Art Resource Centre
Kyoto Museum of Culture
Imperial Household Agency Kyoto Office
Kumamoto Prefectural Museum of Art
National Diet Library
National Museum of Japanese History
Saitama Prefectural Museum of Modern Art
Sakai City Museum
Shizuoka City Museum of Art
Shimane Prefectural Museum of Art
Joruri-ji Temple
Tsuruga City Museum
Tokyo National Museum
Nara Prefectural Museum of Art
Mie Prefectural Museum of Art
Yamaguchi Prefectural Hagi Museum & Urakami Memorial Hall

North America, Latin America & Europe
Tuttle Publishing
364 Innovation Drive
North Clarendon
VT 05759-9436 U.S.A.
Tel: (802) 773-8930
Fax: (802) 773-6993
info@tuttlepublishing.com
www.tuttlepublishing.com

Japan
Tuttle Publishing
Yaekari Building 3rd Floor
5-4-12 Osaki Shinagawa-ku
Tokyo 141 0032
Tel: (81) 3 5437-0171
Fax: (81) 3 5437-0755
sales@tuttle.co.jp
www.tuttle.co.jp

Asia Pacific
Berkeley Books Pte. Ltd.
3 Kallang Sector, #04-01
Singapore 349278
Tel: (65) 6741-2178
Fax: (65) 6741-2179
inquiries@periplus.com.sg
www.tuttlepublishing.com

28 27 26 25 24   10 9 8 7 6 5 4 3 2 1
Printed in China   2408EP

TUTTLE PUBLISHING® is a registered trademark of Tuttle Publishing, a division of Periplus Editions (HK) Ltd.

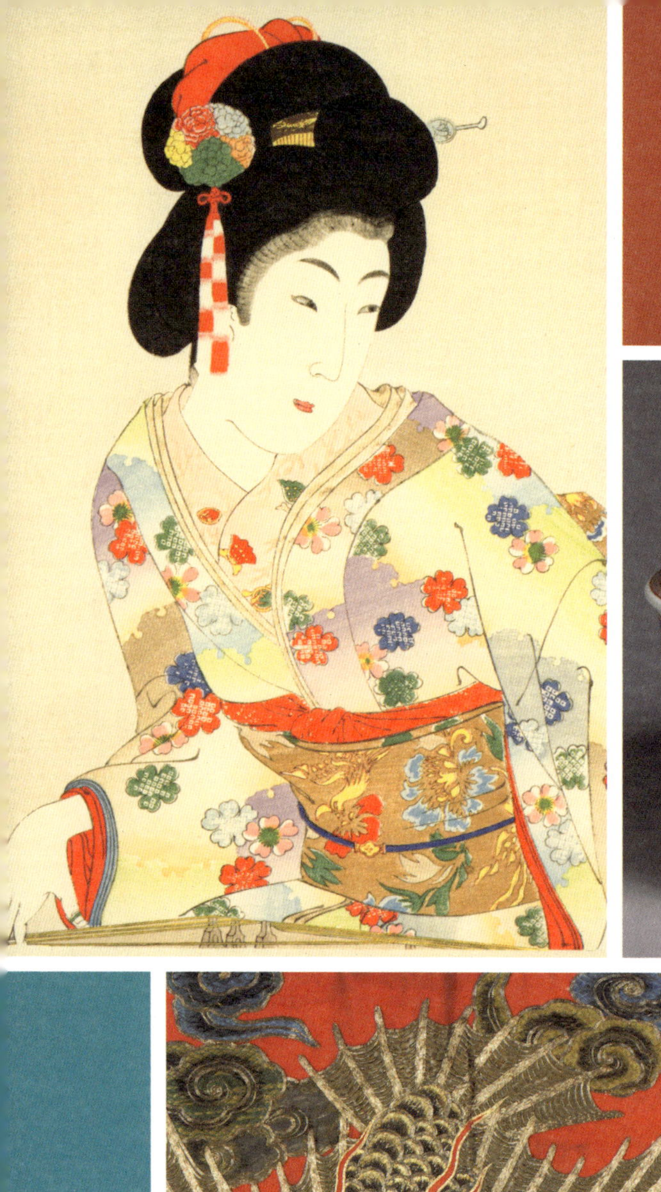
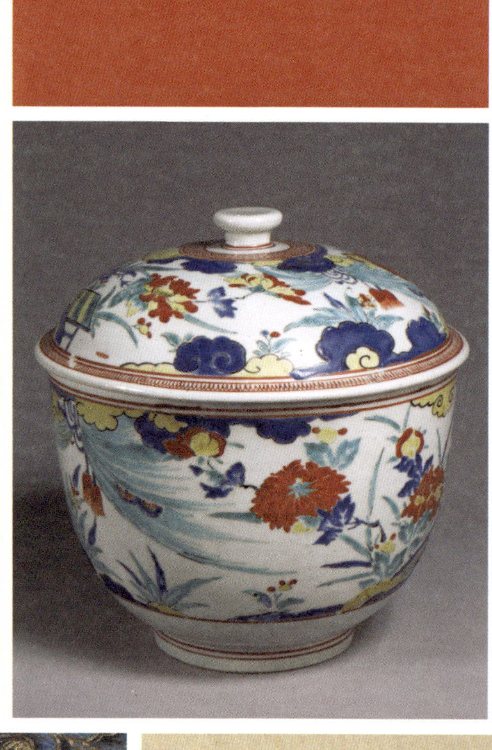
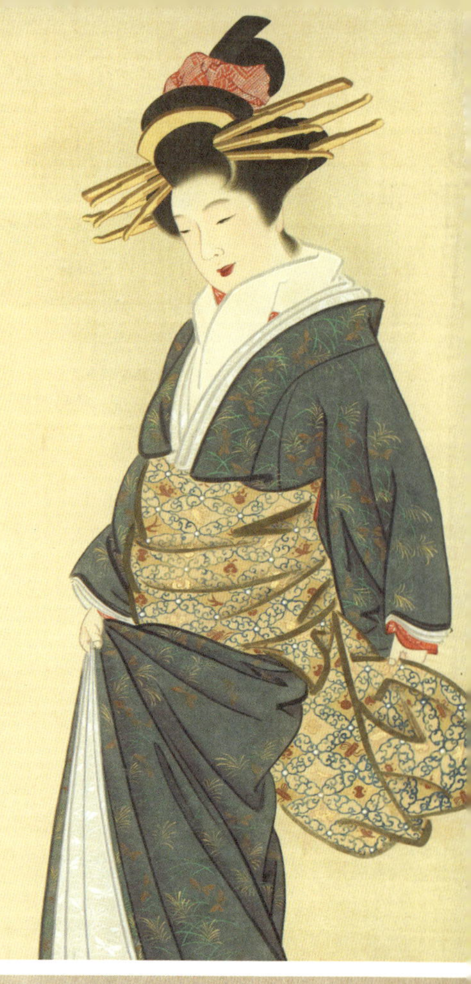
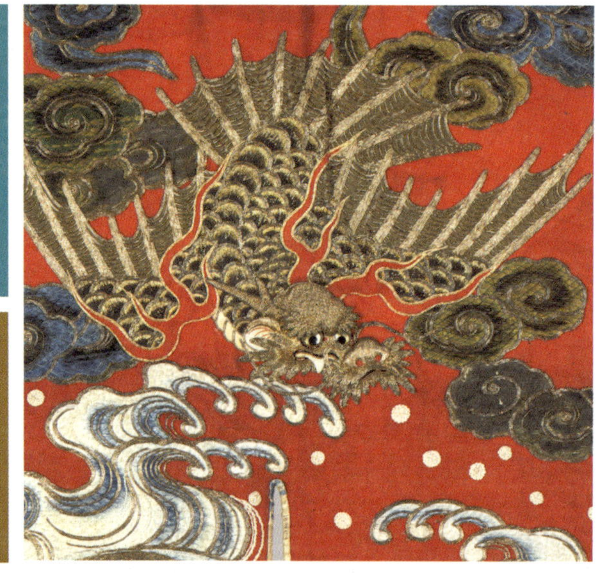
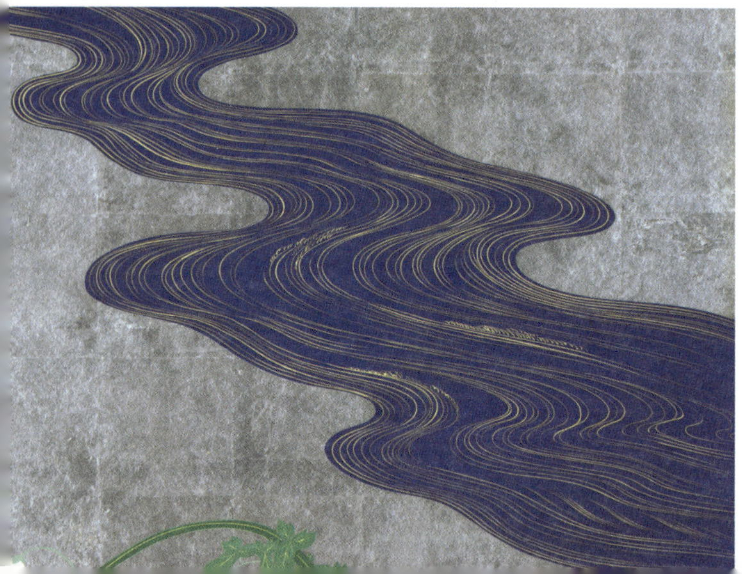
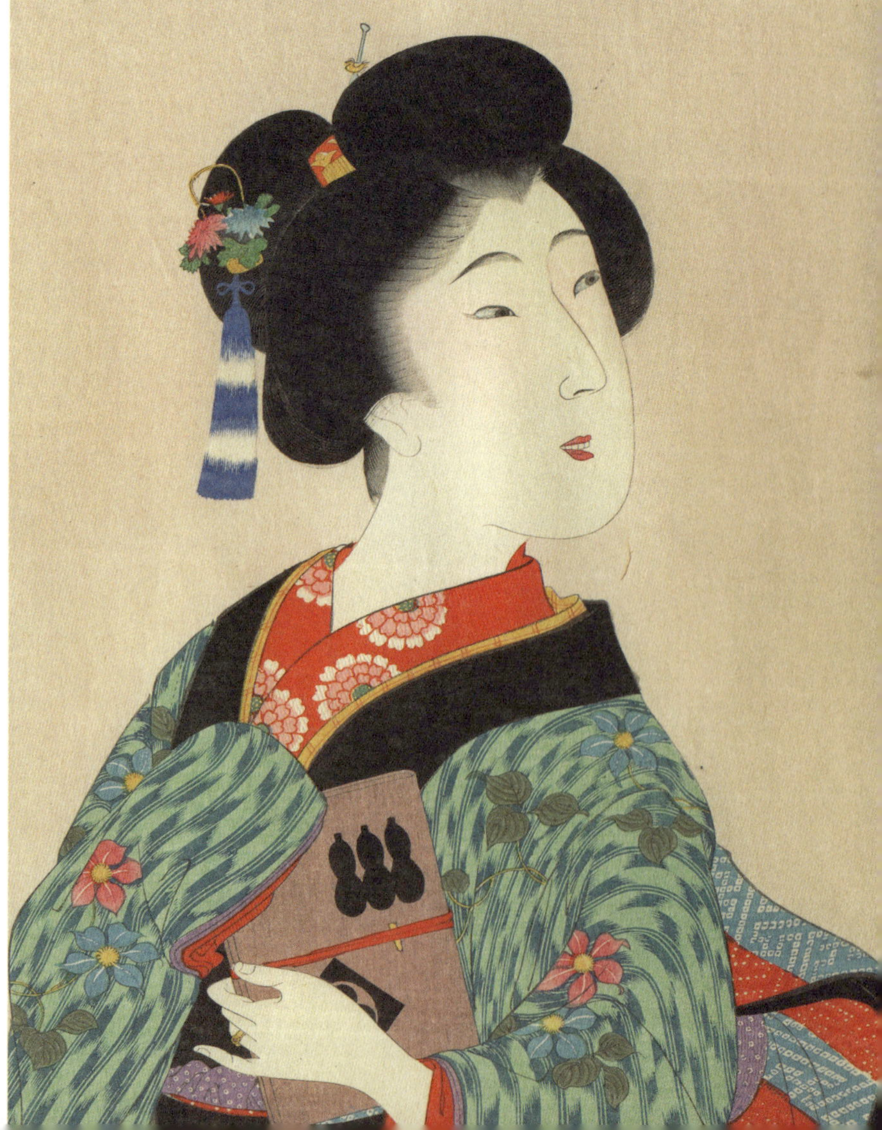